American Politics

American Politics
The Enduring Constitution

SECOND EDITION

William Lasser
Clemson University

Houghton Mifflin Company Boston New York

Sponsoring Editor: Melissa Mashburn
Assistant Editor: Lily Eng
Editorial Assistant: Vikram Mukhija
Project Editor: Elena Di Cesare Montillo
Editorial Assistant: Chrissy Lee
Production/Design Coordinator: Jennifer Meyer Dare
Senior Manufacturing Coordinator: Marie Barnes
Marketing Manager: Sandra McGuire
Associate Marketing Manager: Beth Foohey

Cover Design: Len Massiglia
Cover Image: Everett C. Johnson, Folio, Inc.

Illustration Credits

Chapter 1: p. 3, Women's Liberation: Archive Photos; p. 9, Prop. 209: Associated Press/Wide World Photos; p. 14, FDR Poster: David J. and Janice L. Frent Collection; p. 16, cartoon "Do you promise": © 1995 Jack Zeigler from The Cartoon Bank, Inc.; p. 17, Gore on Letterman: CBS/Photo by Alan Singer.

Credits continue on page C-1.

Printed in the U.S.A.

Library of Congress Catalog Card Number: 98-72057

ISBN: 0-395-90207-X

123456789-QH-02 01 00 99 98

For Max Hoffman Lasser, with love

Contents

⭐ PART TWO
The People and Their Government

8 Interest Groups 198

9 Political Parties 228

10 Campaigns and Elections 258

Preface

American politics has changed greatly over the past decade, as it has countless times over the two centuries since the creation of the Republic. In 1989, American foreign policy was still defined by the Cold War conflict with the Soviet Union. As late as 1991, the conventional wisdom held that the Republican Party had a stranglehold on the presidency. Before 1994, the same pundits and analysts believed that a Republican takeover of the Congress was as likely as the early arrival of Haley's Comet. Even three years ago, when the first edition of *American Politics* was published, economists, political scientists, and politicians all agreed that the United States government was destined to run multibillion dollar budget deficits as far into the future as anyone could imagine.

All of this, of course, is history: today, the Cold War is over; the Republicans control Congress while a Democrat sits in the White House; and politicians argue not about how to reduce the deficit but how to spend the surplus. Yet even as we adjust to these new realities, more change is on the way. In the next decade alone, citizens and public officials alike will have to come to grips with new technologies, an aging population base, an increasingly global economy, and a great deal more—including much that we can barely see on the horizon, much less predict with confidence and accuracy.

Change, of course, is nothing new. Prior generations of Americans watched, coped, and flourished as the national economy grew from its agricultural origins into an industrial powerhouse; as the nation evolved from a minor player in world affairs into a global superpower; as a weak national government took on an increasingly significant role in economic and social regulation; and as women, blacks, and other minorities struggled to assert their civil and political rights. The pace of change may be faster than ever before, but change itself has been an American fact of life for over two hundred years.

In the ever-changing environment of American politics—through economic depressions, a civil war, two world wars, the struggles for equal rights and for the protection of civil liberties—the Constitution of the United States has endured. Although changed twenty-seven times by formal amendment and many more times by judicial interpretation, the basic governmental structures set up by the Constitution of 1787 and the fundamental principles embodied in its seven articles remain constant. If the Framers of the Constitution could come back today, they would be surprised by the broad extension of freedom to all citizens, regardless of race, color, or gender; by the growth of America's influence and involvement in world affairs and the parallel growth in presidential power; by the expansion of federal protection for rights and liberties; and by the enormous increase in the federal government's role in regulating and managing the national economy. But they would surely recognize the separation of powers among the legislative, executive, and judicial branches, the division of power between the national government and the states, the essential principles of freedom of speech, press, and religion, and, above all, the nation's continuing commitment to the ideal and reality of government by the people.

To allow students to understand the dynamic realities of present-day American politics against the ever-present backdrop of the enduring Constitution is the purpose of *American Politics*. Throughout the text, students are presented first with the theoretical foundations of the American constitutional system, and then with descriptions and analyses of American politics as it now exists.

Armed with these two perspectives, students can then draw their own conclusions about what works and what does not in today's political environment, and why.

"If you don't like the weather in New England," Mark Twain once said, "just wait a few minutes." When it comes to politics, however, we are not so lucky. Change, though inevitable, need not progress in the direction we might hope for. Only by understanding past and present, theory and practice, and ideal and reality will students of American politics be equipped to participate intelligently and thoughtfully in the debates that will shape the future.

Second Edition Updates

The second edition of *American Politics* is fully revised and updated, with information on the most current issues and themes in American politics. Features favored by users of the first edition—for example, the "Debating the Constitution" boxes—have been expanded and tied more closely to the theme of the book. Other features have been streamlined or eliminated in order to focus students' attention on the most important themes and issues. The "Enduring Constitution" theme has been strengthened and clarified, and given more prominence throughout. Taken together, these changes and improvements build on and enhance the first edition while retaining its strengths.

Key updates in the second edition include:

- *The 1996 election.* Coverage includes a reassessment of the so-called "realignment of the 1990s"(Chapter 9); an analysis of campaign finance uses and abuses (Chapter 10); and updates on the political behavior of the American electorate (Chapter 7).
- *President Clinton's second term.* The second edition covers the legal and political troubles of the Clinton presidency—examining, for example, the role of the "new media" in the Monica Lewinsky affair (Chapter 11) and the continued decline of the moral authority of the presidency (Chapter 13).
- *The politics of the "disappearing budget deficit."* The rapid disappearance of the federal budget deficit has created a new era of fiscal politics, with implications for many aspects of American government. From a revised discussion of congressional budget politics in the chapter on Congress (Chapter 12) to a new chapter opener in the domestic policy chapter (Chapter 16)), the second edition fully addresses these changing realities.
- *Critical Supreme Court decisions.* Updates include coverage of the Court's recent decisions on affirmative action and sexual harassment (Chapter 5), free speech on the Internet (Chapter 4), federalism (Chapter 3), and presidential immunity (Chapter 13).

Features of the Second Edition

American Politics: The Enduring Constitution contains a number of features that make the text more interesting for the student, easier to teach with for the instructor, and richer and more rewarding for both. Among the features designed to enhance the text are these:

Innovative and consistent chapter structure. The chapters all follow a consistent format. Such consistency makes it easier for students to approach the text and simplifies the professor's task of choosing which material to emphasize most specifically. This structure is also designed to make it easier for students to recognize the key themes of each chapter, and to provide students with necessary background material before introducing them to more complex and difficult issues. The pattern of the chapters is as follows:

I. *A brief, captivating introduction* designed to grab the students attention and provide a focal point for the introduction of the major themes of the chapter. These teasers remind students of the "Enduring Constitution" theme by raising key constitutional questions, often in a very contemporary framework. Each introductory vignette is followed by a statement of the key themes of the chapter.

II. *Questions to keep in mind,* making the themes and goals of the chapter explicit, making review easier, and fostering students' critical thinking skills.

III. *Basic Concepts,* a sort of "core text within a text" that provides the student with the essential background needed to understand the thematic sections that follow. The "Basic Concepts" section typically includes a discussion of the Constitutional context of the material covered in the chapter, including coverage of the Framers' political philosophy.

IV. *Chapter summary, review questions, Internet resources, and suggestions for further reading* giving students the opportunity to consolidate what they have learned and explore further material.

Additional features include:

· *"Debating the Constitution" boxes.* Contemporary controversial issues, linked directly or indirectly to constitutional themes, are presented in debate boxes, which provide arguments on both sides of the question and encourage students to challenge their existing viewpoints. Debate boxes are particularly suited for stimulating formal or informal class discussions. Topics examined in these boxes include congressional term limits (Chapter 12), free press vs. fair trial (Chapter 11), and the president's authority to make war without congressional approval (Chapter 17).

· *"Global Perspectives" boxes.* Boxed material providing comparisons between the United States and other cultures and countries encourages students to think globally and to see American politics from new perspectives and with new insight. Box topics include presidential vs. parliamentary systems of government (Chapter 13) and elections in other democracies (Chapter 10).

· *"Economics and Politics" boxes.* The relationship between economics and politics is highlighted in these boxed features, which include such topics as an examination of the economic origins of the Constitution (Chapter 2) and a discussion of the racial income gap (Chapter 5).

· *Humor and human interest.* Boxes, quotes, sidebars, and photographs capture the many faces of American politics, from the humorous to the poignant. "Politics Light" boxes are aimed at entertaining students as well as giving them a new point of view.

Ancillary Package

A comprehensive supplements package accompanies this text:

· **Instructor's Resource Manual with Test Items.** Written by Laura Olson of Clemson University, this manual includes suggested lecture and discussion topics; in-class activities; and lists of supplementary readings, films, videos, and other multimedia resources, including chapter-relevant World Wide Web sites. The Test Items portion of this manual includes over 1,000 multiple-choice, True/False, and essay questions.

- **Computerized Test Bank.** A computerized version of the test items is available in a Windows format.
- **Transparencies.** The transparencies package for *American Politics,* Second Edition, contains approximately 30 transparencies drawn from the text's illustration program.
- **Study Guide.** This guide, written and completely updated by award-winning teachers Peter Galdarisi and Michael Lyons of Utah State University, provides the students with chapter summaries, learning objectives, and multiple-choice and True/False questions to help students in reviewing key points and themes of the book. Included in the Study Guide to accompany the Second Edition is a new section discussing how students can explore and use the Internet for political science research.
- **Lasser American Politics Web Site.** Accessible through the Houghton Mifflin home page (www.hmco.com/college), this web site provides free, text-specific resources to both instructors and students, including chapter overviews, student self-tests, and updates written by the author.
- **American Government Web Site.** Accessible through the Houghton Mifflin home page (www.hmco.com/college), the Houghton Mifflin American Government Web Site features a Documents Collection of primary source materials relevant to American Government. Exercises keyed to major topics in American Government ask students to explore and critically evaluate primary documents as well as political web sites. Answers to the exercises can be submitted to instructors via e-mail or printed out. Links to key political web sites are also included.

Acknowledgments

It is a cliché to suggest that a book could not have been completed without the help and support of one's editors, colleagues, students, friends, and family. But some clichés are true, and none more so than this one.

Melissa Mashburn, my editor at Houghton Mifflin, has believed in this book from her first involvement. She has guided this project with a steady hand, and I am very thankful for her guidance and advice. Lily Eng put an extraordinary amount of time, energy, and talent into this project, and—despite deadlines and the other inevitable pressures of completing a large project—remained calm, happy, and personable throughout. I have also appreciated the support and insights of Houghton Mifflin's editor-in-chief for political science and history, Jean Woy.

Several individuals who contributed to the completion of the first edition deserve repeated mention, including Paul Smith, Valerie Aubrey, and Karen Wise. I am also grateful to all of those at Houghton Mifflin who helped edit and produce this second edition, including Elena Di Cesare Montillo, Jennifer Meyer Dare, and Chrissy Lee.

I am grateful to my colleagues at Clemson University, especially Chuck Dunn, Marty Slann, and Dave Woodard, who were always willing to lend an ear or a book, and who supported me with many kind remarks about both the first edition and the revision. I am especially indebted to my colleague Laura Olson, who has been a source of much insight and who patiently and cheerfully helped me resolve many difficult questions. I am also thankful to the many professors, journalists, and government officials who graciously answered my many questions about the intricacies of the political process; to my research assistant, Candice Christman; and to the countless authors of books, journal articles, and magazine and newspaper pieces whose insights and ideas have contributed to my understanding of American politics.

Thanks are also due to the many scholars who reviewed the manuscript in whole or in part and who worked on the various supplementary materials that accompany the text. These include:

Paul B. Davis, Truckee Meadows Community College
Larry Elowitz, Georgia College and State University
Harvey C. Foyle, Emporia State University
Richard Greenwald, State University of New York, Morrisville
Don Laws, Southern Oregon University
Mark Leeper, Wayne State College
Stacy McMillen, Wayne State College
Iraj Paydar, Bellevue Community College
Timothy J. Schorn, University of South Dakota, Vermillion
Mark Shroder, Department of Housing and Urban Development
Shari Sowards, Salt Lake City Community College
M.T. Waddell, Galveston College
Timothy Wilkinson, Boise State University

Finally, I thank my wife, Susan J.S. Lasser, whose love is an unending source of joy and comfort; our son, Max, who has watched with enthusiasm as "Daddy's book" has grown up with him; and our new daughter, Adina Rose, who helped, though she did not know it, simply by being here. As with the first edition, this remains Max's book.

W. L.

PHOTO CREDIT: Eliska Morsel Greenspoon

About the Author

William Lasser is Professor of Political Science at Clemson University. A gifted teacher, he was recognized with Clemson University's Alumni Master Teacher Award in 1993. Professor Lasser is the author of *The Limits of Judicial Power: The Supreme Court and American Politics* (University of North Carolina Press, 1988); *Perspectives on American Government: A Comprehensive Reader,* Second Edition (D. C. Heath, 1996); and *Benjamin V. Cohen and the Spirit of the New Deal* (The Twentieth Century Fund, in progress).

American Politics

★ 1 ★ Introduction

When representatives of the original thirteen states met in 1787 to draft the Constitution of the United States, they faced a daunting set of questions. Were human beings even capable of governing themselves? Could the Constitutional Convention devise a system of government that would serve the interests of the public, protect and promote the rights of the people, and ensure the nation's prosperity and well-being? Above all, could the founding generation devise a constitutional system that would endure throughout the ages, serving not only its own needs but those of countless generations to come?

The answers to these questions did not come easily. The Constitution was the nation's second attempt to form a government; the first one, known as the Articles of Confederation, was widely regarded as a failure. Moreover, the founding generation was deeply divided over even the most basic issues that lay before them. Some delegates opposed the very idea of a Constitution, preferring instead to make only minor changes to the Articles of Confederation. Others viewed the effort to create a new government as a thinly disguised program to benefit a wealthy and elite minority at the expense of the public. Still others—though very few—challenged any effort to go forward with a national experiment in democracy as long as the United States continued to permit the existence of a brutal system of slavery, in which human beings were treated as moveable property, to be bought and sold at will.

That the United States still exists and is still operating under the basic outline of the Constitution of 1787 might seem to suggest that the Framers were successful in meeting the challenges they faced. American democracy has survived a vicious civil war, numerous economic depressions, and two world wars. The United States has endured staggering changes in size

An early advocate of women's rights urges women to take advantage of their right to vote, newly acquired in 1920 with the passage of the Nineteenth Amendment.

and population and dramatic revolutions in industry and technology. In recent decades, America has successfully exported democracy across the world and stands as a living symbol of what human beings can achieve when left to govern themselves.

Yet American democracy remains an unfinished experiment. The Declaration of Independence and the Constitution promised more than they were willing or able to deliver. Although it was grounded on principles of equality and justice, the Constitution sanctioned

★ ★

slavery, ignored women, and failed to defend Native Americans from oppression. The Constitution was later amended to outlaw slavery and guarantee the equal protection of the laws to all the people, but discrimination against African Americans, Latinos, Asian Americans, and other minority groups continues to this day. Women were not guaranteed the right to vote until 1920, and were not granted protection under the laws until the 1960s. Even in the late 1990s, they still face social, political, and economic obstacles to real equality.

Even as progress is made toward solving old problems, new problems and challenges continually emerge. The industrial revolution of the nineteenth century forced the American system to cope with economic arrangements unheard of when the Constitution was written. Only in the late 1800s did the national government begin to limit the power of large corporations, and only after the catastrophic depression of the 1930s did the government finally take steps to protect ordinary Americans from the ups and downs of the business cycle. In our own time, the American political system must cope with even newer challenges: how to provide health care to all citizens, how to promote prosperity in a competitive global economy, and how to rebuild America's ravaged inner cities.

Ultimately, as American history teaches, every generation must decide for itself whether effective self-government is possible. The success of one generation, or even ten, says nothing about the possibility of self-government in the future. Like the generations that fought the Civil War or survived the Great Depression, each new generation of Americans must show for itself that it is possible for men and women to prove that they are not, as Alexander Hamilton put it, "forever dependent for their political constitutions on accident and force."[1] And any such proof can be short-lived at best, valid only until history and adversity once more put the principle of self-government to the test.

Questions to Keep in Mind

✔ *What are the characteristics of a democratic form of government? What are the advantages and disadvantages of direct democracy? representative democracy? pluralist democracy?*

✔ *What is the "public interest"? What is the relationship between democracy and the public interest?*

✔ *What challenges has American democracy faced in its 200-year history? What challenges does American democracy face today?*

Politics Then and Now

The hope, confidence, and unabashed patriotism of those who created the Republic two hundred years ago seems far removed from the cynicism and scorn that mark contemporary American politics. The vast majority of Americans hold politicians and officeholders in low esteem, and assume as a matter of course that political promises are made to be broken. The nightly news shows carry intimate accounts of our politicians' personal lives, even including graphic descriptions of their real or alleged sexual exploits; meanwhile, a seemingly steady parade of political figures make their way in and out of courtrooms, or even, at times, in and out of jail. Little wonder that Americans lack heroes, especially of the political variety.

Americans of past generations, by contrast, actually liked politics and esteemed politicians. Famous orators attracted listeners by the thousands, endearing themselves to the crowds with their passionate eloquence—not to mention free food and drinks. In bars and taverns, across dinner tables and on cross-country train trips, Americans took politics seriously; talking and arguing endlessly about the issues, and personalities, of the day.

In part, of course, our ancestors were obsessed with politics because there was so little else to do for relaxation and recreation. Until this century, there was no television or radio, no movies, not even recorded music. There were plays and concerts, ball games and prize fights, but mostly Americans found amusement in books and newspapers, and with each other. Politics and current events became the topic of choice almost by default.

The American love affair with politics, however, came about by choice, not necessity. Americans (or at least those allowed to participate in politics) took the idea of democracy seriously, and regarded their participation in self-government as both a right and a duty. More than that, many actually found enjoyment in politics. Everyone likes a good fight, and politics is essentially a contest—a war with words instead of bullets. Whether participating in the battle or merely cheering the troops, Americans found politics a healthy way to vent their aggressions and emotions.

Besides, politics could be fun, and politicians could be funny. Even today, everyone can appreciate a good political joke, usually told at the politicians' expense, or a clever political quip. Political poetry and song writing have been around since before the American Revolution, and lawyer jokes are as old as the law itself. Some politicians were actually famous for their humor, none more so than Abraham Lincoln. During his first congressional race, for instance, Lincoln was repeatedly accused of lacking religious faith. At one meeting, Lincoln's opponent asked everyone in the crowd who didn't want to go to hell to stand up. Everyone did but Lincoln. "May I inquire of you, Mr. Lincoln, where are you going?" the candidate asked. Lincoln replied, "I am going to Congress."

Politics, however, is not so much comedy as drama on the grand scale. The decisions of citizens and politicians can mean the difference between war and peace, prosperity or depression, hope or despair. The lighter side of politics only serves to underscore, and perhaps help us to cope with, what is at stake. Students of American politics might well agree with the sentiments expressed by Adlai Stevenson, when he lost the presidency to Dwight D. Eisenhower for the second time. "It hurts too much to laugh," Stevenson said, "but I'm too old to cry."

Understanding American Democracy

The major theme of this book is to explain and analyze the nature of American democracy. Throughout, the central questions are these: Does the modern American political system live up to the Framers' belief in the grand possibilities of self-government? If not, why not, and what must change?

Defining Politics

It is useful to begin with a definition of **politics.** Politics is the process by which societies are governed. Except where there is a complete breakdown of authority, all human societies are ruled by some form of **government.** For our purposes we can define the government as a group of individuals who are authorized to make and enforce decisions regarding the protection and regulation of a community. The government is distinguished from other decision-making bodies in two ways. First, it has overall responsibility for the entire society. Second, it has a monopoly on the use of force.

Governments exercise so powerful an influence over private economic affairs that politics can fairly be described as the "science of how who gets what, when, and why."[2] Politics in this sense is seen as a battlefield on which various interests compete for the distribution and redistribution of scarce resources. Will the nation decide to use more of its wealth to protect the environment? Will it sacrifice some economic growth for greater job security for its citizens? Frequently, however, politics involves competition over matters in which economics plays at most an indirect part, such as free speech, human rights, and the quality of community life.

Historically, political scientists have asked two kinds of questions about government and politics. First, they have tried to classify the government by type, or form. Is it chosen by election or through hereditary succession? Is it characterized by a unified legislative and executive branch (parliamentary system), or by a separation of legislative and executive authority (presidential system)? Second, they have asked whether the government operates on behalf of all the citizens under its charge or merely serves the interests of a chosen few. The ancients distinguished between monarchies, for example, in which a king ruled on behalf of the people, and tyrannies, in which the leader ruled for his own benefit. The first set of questions asks "what kind of government?"; the second, "for whose benefit?"

Defining Democracy

No discussion of American politics can get far without mention of the word **democracy.** As soon as American children are old enough to understand the concept of politics, they are introduced to the idea of democracy, and to the idea that democracy is a good thing. Most Americans know democracy when they see it, but coming up with a viable definition is surprisingly difficult.

Under the circumstances it is tempting to provide a textbook definition (this, after all, is a textbook) and be done with it. *Democracy* comes from Greek, meaning "rule of the common people"; it was applied to a political system in which power was widely shared among those considered citizens. The Greeks specifically distinguished between democracy and **aristocracy,** or rule of the best, in which power was held by a narrow ruling class.

In this sense, democracy means simply that the people govern. Typically, popular government involves some form of elections, in which the right to vote is granted to all or at least most adult citizens, and in which the decisions of the majority prevail. The idea of **majority rule** stems from the simple proposition that all persons are equal in terms of their political rights. Since all citizens have an equal right to participate in politics, and since the political choices of each citizen have equal weight, it follows that the views of the many should outweigh those of the few. Although the people do not need to be given a vote on every issue, some form of free, fair, and open elections is essential to any functioning democracy.

> *"In a democracy the highest office is the office of the citizen."*
>
> —Supreme Court Justice Felix Frankfurter

Such a definition, although perfectly reasonable, hardly provides a full sense of what most Americans, or most political scientists, mean by democracy. The modern notion of democracy also includes respect for **individual rights** and **minority rights,** a sense of fair play, and a strong tradition of law and justice. A political system in which 51 percent of the people are allowed to terrorize and abuse the remaining 49 percent is simply not a democracy in form or substance. No democratic government would be justified in suspending the right to trial in criminal cases, or in forbidding free speech or the free exercise of religion.

No government is perfect, of course, but a democracy should at least try to live up to these standards and be willing to acknowledge its shortcomings.

One problem with this more complex sense of democracy is that its various components are often at war with one another. Majority rule and minority rights are not necessarily at odds, but they do point in opposite directions, and trying to balance the two often creates serious political tensions. The American political system has been trying to resolve such tensions since before the adoption of the Constitution.

Democracy and the Public Interest

Asking "for whose benefit" the people govern might seem redundant. It would appear obvious, after all, that the people would govern in their own interest. The interest of the people as a whole is known as the **public interest.**

The concept of the public interest, however, is more complicated than it might initially appear. First, is the public interest merely the will of the majority, or must it take into account the interests of everyone? Second, can the people be mistaken about their own interests? Should the public interest be defined not by what the people think is in their interest but by objective standards, such as peace and prosperity? In either case, the public interest would not be identical to the will of the majority at a given point in time.

The Framers of the American Constitution, in fact, believed that the majority of the people was unlikely to pursue the public interest. They based their opinion on three factors. First, many public decisions are clouded by emotion and passion. Second, many citizens lack the training and discipline necessary to enable them to judge the wisest course of action in public affairs. Third, many citizens find it difficult to take a long-term view of a political problem, or to consider the interests of all the people rather than the interests of only those like themselves.

Some political theorists, as we will see, simply assume that the decisions produced by the democratic process reflect the public interest. For others, ensuring that the democratic process produces results consistent with the public interest is a most difficult challenge. Any attempt to define the public interest as something other than the will of the people at a given point in time is fraught with difficulties, not the least of which is that theorists and analysts often disagree among themselves as to how to define and measure the public interest.

Four Models of Democracy

One way to proceed is to examine a series of models of democratic government. Two warnings are in order, however. First, all such models reflect a mixture of description and theory—how things are, and how they ought to be. Second, although an individual scholar, politician, or citizen may lean toward one model or another as a theoretical or descriptive ideal, it is probably safe to say that each model captures some essential truth about American political life.

The models can be thought of as occupying a continuum. At one extreme the primary concern is to protect the power of the majority; at the other, the concern is to check that power in order to protect minority rights.

Protesters demonstrate in opposition to California's Proposition 209, a ballot initiative designed to eliminate affirmative action in all state programs. Despite such protests, California voters approved the measure in 1996; a year later, the Supreme Court let stand a lower court ruling that the law was not unconstitutional.

The Pure (or Direct) Democracy Model

In a **pure (or direct) democracy,** all power is exercised by the people, who "assemble and administer the government in person."[3] In effect, advocates of pure democracy assume that the public interest is identical to the will of the majority, or at least that the people themselves have the best sense of what the public interest is. Pure democracy is impossible except in very small societies, since the direct involvement of all citizens would be impractical on even a modestly big scale. Although best known in the ancient world, pure democracy survives in such institutions as the New England town meeting.

On any larger scale, pure democracy can at best be approximated. Ideally, the government would be administered by a chosen group of representatives who would resemble a cross section of the population and whose decisions would closely reflect the views of the general population. When possible, important questions could be referred to the people at large, for a direct vote; in any event, citizens would be expected to remain deeply involved in politics, and would be given frequent opportunities to make their views known and to affirm or withdraw their support for their political representatives.

Pure democracy has a certain theoretical appeal. It emphasizes the democratic assumption that all citizens are politically equal. It encourages the entire citizenry

Figure 1.1 **Model of Direct Democracy**

In the model of direct democracy, public decisions are made directly by the people, who assemble and administer the government in person.

The people

to become involved in political life, to think through difficult decisions for themselves, and to take responsibility for their actions.

Many aspects of American politics take their inspiration from the pure democracy model. In many states, although not on the national level, citizens can take direct responsibility for important legislative decisions. The freewheeling exchanges on many talk radio shows are an echo of pure democracy's faith in the ability of ordinary citizens to discuss and resolve public issues among themselves. The modern emphasis on public opinion polls rests on the unstated assumption that the views of the people should be accorded great respect by those who actually govern.[4]

The Representative Democracy Model

Pure democracy is not for everyone. The Framers of the Constitution regarded pure democracies as unstable and dangerous. The problem, in their view, was twofold:

- *The absolute power of the majority.* In a pure democracy, there is no check on the power of the majority. Naturally enough, the majority will tend to favor its own interests over those in the minority, ignoring the rights of individuals who disagree with it.
- *The triumph of passion over reason.* Large legislative assemblies provide a perfect opportunity for emotion to win out over reasoned argument. Thus pure democracies will consistently favor the quick fix over the long-term solution and the emotionally satisfying answer over the thoughtful judgment.

Figure 1.2 **Model of Representative Democracy**

In the model of representative democracy, public decisions are made by a limited group of individuals who represent the people. The representatives are selected by the people in regular, competitive elections and are answerable to them.

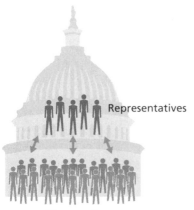

Representatives

The people

The solution to these problems, according to the Framers, was **representative democracy.** In a representative democracy, public decisions are made by a small number of individuals selected by, and ultimately answerable to, the larger body of citizens. The job of the representative is not simply to reflect the will of the people, but to improve on it. In general, representative democracies aim to make it possible for politicians to make difficult or unpopular decisions.

Thus it is essential to representative democracy to maintain some distance between the people and their representatives. Elections should be held infrequently, allowing time for the people to judge their representatives fairly and calmly. Moreover, each representative should answer to a large number of constituents, to ensure that he or she reflects the broadest possible set of viewpoints and interests.

The relationship between the people and certain government decision makers should be even more remote. In the American constitutional system, for example, senators are elected every six years; originally, they were elected indirectly, by the state legislatures. Federal judges are even more distant from the people, serving in their offices for life.

Many aspects of the American system of government find their origin in the idea of representative democracy. Ultimate power rests with the people, but the daily exercise of power is delegated to elected representatives whose job is to make the best possible decisions, regardless of the emotions of the moment or the narrow interests of the majority.

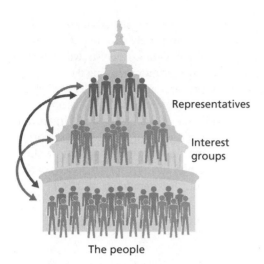

Representatives

Interest groups

The people

Figure 1.3 **Model of Pluralist Democracy**

In the model of pluralist democracy, interest groups can act as intermediaries between the people and their representatives. Interest groups may try to influence all branches of government as long as they do so openly and in direct competition with other groups. Interest groups may also appeal directly to the people in order to influence government.

The problem with representative democracy is its inherent contradiction: all power flows from the people, yet it seems that the people themselves cannot be trusted with that power. In effect, advocates of representative democracy argue that the public is not the best judge of the public interest. Instead, representative democracy sets up a system that forces citizens to vote for a government that, by design, will frequently fail to reflect their own views.[5]

The Pluralist Model

Another model of democracy emphasizes the importance of various groups as intermediaries between the people and their government. According to this theory, the public interest is best served by encouraging citizens to form organized interest groups, which then compete with one another in the public policy arena. The **pluralist model** sees government as a neutral playing field on which interest groups can struggle or cooperate, as they see fit. Thus it is essential that the government be open and accessible to all groups of citizens. Groups can work their influence on legislators, executive officials, even judges; what is crucial is that they do so openly, and in direct competition with others.

By stressing the importance of interest groups, advocates of the pluralist model strike a kind of balance between pure democracy and representative democracy. Like pure democracy, pluralism seeks to avoid the idea that government officials should substitute their own judgment for that of the people. Like representative democracy, pluralism recognizes that the mass of citizens are busy with their own lives, are often poorly informed about political issues, and are prone to emphasize their own short-term interests over the long-term public good.

The pluralist solution is to dilute the conflict between majority and minority by encouraging the formation of countless interest groups. Some interest groups might draw their strength from sheer numbers, others from economic strength, still others from a mass of dedicated workers. Moreover, the same citizen might belong to several organized interest groups, not all of which will agree on any particular issue. Some interests may win frequently, others may lose consistently. Often, the existence of a mass of conflicting interests will promote compromise and help prevent the division of society into two or more warring parts.

According to its supporters, the pluralist approach provides an opportunity to alleviate the worst aspects of direct democracy without having to elevate political leaders above the people who elected them. While recognizing the legitimacy of the citizen's self-interest, it makes it clear that politics requires compromise, cooperation, and broad-based support. It also encourages individual citizens to combine their efforts in order to compete more effectively in the political marketplace. However, critics of pluralism argue that the government's playing field is hardly level and that some groups can compete far more effectively than others.[6]

The Elite Model

A final model stands as a direct challenge to the promises and pretensions of democratic government. The **elite model** suggests that real political power in most democracies rests with a small group of powerful individuals and groups. To advocates of the elite model, democracy represents the worst of all possible worlds: having duped the people into participating in a phony democracy, those with real political power are free to ignore the public interest and concentrate on their own.

There are many versions of the elite model, depending on the group, or groups, identified as constituting the elite. Most commonly, the elite group is identified as having economic power—bankers, capitalists, or the rich in general. A more recent version suggests that real power rests with a *meritocracy*—those educated at the best schools and occupying key positions in business, law, the media, government, and academia. Some theorists recognize that control of society can shift from one elite group to another, whereas others maintain that a single group is permanently in control. Although most elite theorists implicitly or explicitly suggest that it is wrong for elite groups to wield as much power as they do, some argue that it is good for the wisest, most informed, or most successful citizens to wield the most influence.

Elite theory provides an easy way to explain why many political decisions made in the United States are contrary to the interests of the majority or go directly against the clear views of the people. It also explains why many laws that seem to favor the common people have little effect in real life. Tax laws that appear to impose high taxes on the rich, for example, are filled with loopholes that allow the wealthiest citizens to pay less than their apparent share.

Elite theory is less successful in explaining the many government policies that go against the interests of the elites who supposedly control the government. Generous programs for the poor and middle-class entitlements, for example, hardly seem designed to promote the interests of the

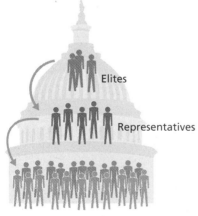

Figure 1.4 The Elite Model of Democracy

In the elite model of democracy, public decisions are made by a small number of powerful individuals and groups who dominate government representatives behind the scenes. Elite groups can get government to act in their own self-interest, often at the expense of the people.

Elites

Representatives

The people

wealthy. Advocates of elite theory have answers to these objections, of course, but their theory seems better at explaining certain aspects of democratic politics than in providing an all-encompassing model.[7]

The Challenges of American Politics

These four models of democracy provide more questions than answers. Each model describes some aspect of American democracy but falls short in its description of other areas. A complete explanation of American democracy must draw on, or be informed by, all four models.

The questions raised by these four models of democracy represent the core issues of this book. They were central questions when the Republic was created, and they remain key questions today.

Winning the Right to Govern

To the generation that fought in the American Revolution, the great problem of politics was to ensure that the government acted on behalf of the people, rather than against them. The great danger in any political system, they believed, was that the government would be seized by an aristocratic elite, who would use their power to exploit the people. The history of England, from the revolutionaries' point of view, had been one continuous struggle between the people and their rulers—first to take power from the king and place it in the hands of Parliament, then to take power from an aristocratic Parliament and put it back in the hands of the common people. That is why the colonists were so insistent that there should be no "taxation without representation": otherwise, the British government would simply use the people of America to enrich itself.

Much of the force behind the pure democracy model comes from the revolutionary experience. Government by the people cannot be taken for granted; it was established only after a costly war with Great Britain and has been maintained over two centuries in even bloodier wars. Moreover, government by the people is constantly threatened by powerful interest groups and, arguably, by the government itself. Ensuring that the people do govern remains a vital challenge of American democracy.

Harnessing the Power of Government

After establishing the people as the source of all legitimate political power, the next problem was to create a government strong enough to advance the public interest. The Framers recognized that a government that was too weak was just as dangerous as one that was too strong. During the Revolutionary War, for example, the weak coalition of state governments that formed the United States was often incapable even of supplying the troops with food, clothing, and ammunition.

The idea of a strong national government was bitterly opposed by critics of the Constitution, who feared a return to the kind of tyranny they had just escaped. And while the

Constitution did create a strong national government, for more than a century its powers were more potential than real. Opponents of national power fought federal programs to advance the national economy and resisted efforts to discourage slavery. After the Civil War, opponents of national power frustrated national programs to protect the rights of the newly freed slaves.

The need for a strong and involved national government became especially clear in the late nineteenth century, as private corporations gained enormous economic power over both workers and consumers. In the 1880s the national government began the long and difficult process of regulating private industry, especially railroads and large industrial trusts, or combinations of businesses. At the same time, big business learned to use government to advance its own interests—for example, using the courts and antitrust laws to break the power of labor unions.

The real test, however, would not come until the 1930s, when the administration of President Franklin D. Roosevelt confronted the Great Depression. This enormous economic calamity brought industry and finance to a standstill, left millions unemployed, wiped out lifelong savings, and forced massive bankruptcies and foreclosures of businesses, homes, and farms. To Roosevelt and his advisers, the challenge was to harness the power of government to help the people survive.

Roosevelt's policies involved a massive expansion of the national government into every area of economic life. In a few short years, Congress passed laws strengthening national control over the banking system, the financial markets, and industry. For the first time Washington became responsive to groups of citizens who had previously been ignored by government or trampled underfoot. These included farmers, the elderly, and workers, and in later years, blacks, women, and the poor. For the first time the national government became a major counterweight to the influence of powerful economic and social elites.

The successes of the New Deal and post–New Deal programs are easy to take for granted, but they are real, and together they have ensured that the national government would remain a strong and active force in American life. In other respects, however, the government was less successful. Its failure to solve many economic and social problems (and, according to some, its tendency to make some things worse) has given rise to serious questions about the proper exercise of national power. Would the nation be better off with less government or more? Should economic and social programs be focused at the state and local level or in Washington?

Government regulation of business was a major thrust of Franklin D. Roosevelt's "New Deal," earning Roosevelt the strong support of workers and labor unions.

Controlling the Majority and the Government

A strong government in the hands of the majority creates its own problems. Above all, as the Framers recognized, it is necessary to prevent the majority from abusing its power and threatening the rights and interest of those in the minority.

For the Framers, this problem was apparent in the way the state governments acted, or were threatening to act, in redressing the problems of indebted farmers. Of particular importance was Shays's Rebellion, in which a group of indebted farmers stormed the Massachusetts State House demanding debt relief—infringing the legal rights of those to whom they owed the money. Although the government of Massachusetts resisted their demands and quickly put down the rebellion, the incident sent shivers down the spines of many Americans. Perhaps, they argued, the Revolution had given the people too much power: a democratic majority, it was now clear, could abuse the rights of the minority just as easily as an aristocratic minority had abused the rights of the majority. The Framers set out to redress this problem by creating a constitutional system that would follow the will of the many while respecting the rights of the few.

Any attempt to separate the majority from the direct control of their government raised again the original problem of how to keep the government from deviating from the interests of the people. The Framers sought to solve this problem with an elaborate set of devices that separated power among different levels and branches of government. Ideally, the Framers believed, the government would resist short-lived whims of popular opinion that could threaten the rights of the minority, but would ultimately be responsive to the long-term, carefully considered opinions of the people.

It is easy to see the origins of the representative democracy model in the Framers' approach. As we will see in later chapters, in fact, the plan of the Constitution embodies the concept of representative democracy, which the Framers knew as republicanism.

The Fragmentation of Popular Authority

Whether the Framers succeeded in striking the proper balance between popular government and minority rights is an open question, and one that requires constant reassessment. The problem is complicated in modern times by the changing nature of the government's role.

Over the last century, the national government has increasingly found itself in the business of serving not only society at large but also particular interests and groups. As society has grown more complex and as government has expanded its reach, this balancing act has become more difficult. Government agriculture programs, for example, often aim to protect both the public in general and farmers in particular. Thus the government protects dairy farmers by artificially raising the cost of milk, and passes the cost along to all consumers. At the same time this program aims to provide the public with a constant supply of high-quality milk. The danger in all such cases is that the particular interest will gain at the expense of the people. Instead of helping its citizens, in other words, the government helps its clients.

Government itself has adapted to this changing role. As the number and complexity of government programs have grown, government agencies and officials have become more and more specialized, and increasingly responsive to the interests of very narrow segments of American society. Thus the Department of Agriculture deals mostly with farmers, and need not worry as much about consumers. Congress too has become increasingly specialized and decentralized, so that law and policy are made by committees and subcommittees that take on a similar focus and bias. At the same time the political parties—which used to play the key role in representing the unorganized majority—have lost much of their clout and influence. Arguably, at least, the government has become extremely responsive to small pressure groups but mainly unresponsive to the people at large.

The pluralist model, in large part, arose as a way of justifying and legitimating the active, modern state. Central to pluralism are two assumptions, neither of which is self-evident. First, pluralism assumes that the competition of groups on a level playing field will result in the victory of the public interest. Second, it assumes that the playing field is in fact level. In any event, finding the appropriate level of governmental responsiveness to group interests remains a central challenge to modern American democracy.

The Challenges of Modern Democracy

These, then, are the challenges of modern democracy. First, the people must create a government that is responsive and responsible to the majority. Second, the government must be given sufficient powers to advance the interests of the public. Third, the system must somehow make it difficult for the majority to abuse its power and trample on the rights of the minority. Finally, the government must be able to respond to the interests of particular segments of society without losing the capacity to govern the whole society.

Creating and maintaining democratic government is no easy task. For better or worse, American democracy has been under construction for some two centuries. How well American government succeeds in achieving its difficult and conflicting goals, and how it might do so more effectively, are central themes of this book.

Studying American Politics

Studying American politics may seem a daunting prospect. The subject matter is vast and the issues complex, ranging from the political philosophy of the Framers of the Constitution to the intricacies of the federal budget process. Nevertheless, this book assumes no prior knowledge of American history or politics. Each theme or concept is laid out in clear terms, and is presented in a readable, accessible, and—I hope—entertaining way. Throughout, the text will guide you through the various parts of the system and help you to keep your eye focused on the broader themes and issues.

Each chapter begins with an introductory essay designed to stimulate thought and preliminary discussion of a central issue, and a list of thematic questions, which will quickly orient you toward the key themes of the chapter. This introductory material is followed by a section called "Basic Concepts," which presents the necessary background information needed to understand and evaluate the issues discussed later in the chapter. Typically, the Basic Concepts sections cover the views of the Framers of the Constitution, essential definitions, and other nuts-and-bolts points.

"Do you promise to fool all of the people some of the time and some of the people all of the time, but never to fool all of the people all of the time?"

The Basic Concepts sections are followed by a series of thematic sections designed to enhance your understanding of the American political system. These thematic sections often present American government "the way it is," challenging you to weigh the pros and cons of the current system, and to evaluate modern practices in light of the assumptions, concerns, and arguments of those who wrote the Constitution. Each chapter is followed by a summary, a list of key terms, a set of review questions, and references to recommended readings and internet sites.

You will also find a small amount of boxed material in each chapter. These boxes include a feature called "Debating the Constitution," each of which highlights a particular constitutional controversy related to the themes of the chapter. Your instructor may assign these as readings, or may use them as the basis for class discussions, formal debates, or writing assignments. Many chapters also contain boxed features on "Global Perspectives," which compare the American political system with those of other democracies, and on "Economics and Politics," which underscore the close connections between these two critical fields. Again, these boxed features can be used in a number of ways, depending on your instructor's teaching style and approach.

A Final Word

Politics is not all serious business. Politics, and politicians, are funny. Pick up the cartoon page of your local paper, and notice how many strips deal with politics. Watch a few late-night television monologues, and count the number of political jokes (all right, don't count). Read Dave Barry, or listen to the music of the Capitol Steps. This book contains

Appearing on the David Letterman show, Vice President Al Gore smashes an "ash receiver, tobacco (desk type)" to symbolize his effort to break the government's wasteful habits. Despite a reputation for stuffiness, Gore came equipped with his own Top 10 list of "good things about being vice president" (No. 4: You don't have to be funny to get invited on the Letterman show).

much of great importance and gravity. But it also includes the humorous, the unusual, and the strange. You will find political cartoons, anecdotes, satires, and quips—even a few jokes. Don't be afraid to smile or laugh. I won't tell.

Summary

Politics is the process by which societies are governed. Each society is ruled by a government, which has overall responsibility for the entire society and a monopoly on the use of force. Historically, political scientists have asked two kinds of questions about government and politics: who governs, and for whose benefit?

The American political system can be described as a democracy—a form of government in which the people govern. The modern notion of democracy includes the ideas of broad participation and majority rule and also of respect for individual rights, a sense of fair play, and a commitment to law and justice. These goals are not always easy to reconcile with one another.

Theoretically, at least, the government should serve the public interest. Scholars disagree as to whether the public interest is simply the will of the people, or whether it can be determined objectively and outside of the political process. Different models of democracy can be traced to differing conceptions of the public interest.

The pure democracy model emphasizes the direct rule of the people. Its advocates assume, in effect, that the public interest is equal to the will of the people or best determined by the people at large. The representative democracy model emphasizes the process of representation, in order to filter the views of the people. Supporters of this model thus assume the possibility that representatives might see the public interest more clearly than the public itself does. The pluralist model stresses the need for individuals to form organized groups in order to pursue their self-interest; its advocates assume the result of the clashes of private interests is the public interest. The elite model questions whether any democratic system pursues the public interest at all, suggesting that the system actually serves the interests of only the wealthiest or most powerful citizens.

These four theoretical models provide a backdrop for understanding four key problems facing any democracy. First, the people must create a government that is responsive and responsible to the majority. Second, the government must be given sufficient powers to advance the interests of the public. Third, the system must somehow make it difficult for the majority to abuse its power and trample on the rights of the minority. Finally, the government must be able to respond to the interests of particular segments of society without losing the capacity to govern the whole society.

This book approaches these problems by emphasizing the relationship between how American government was designed to work and how it really works at the turn of the twenty-first century.

Key Terms

Politics
Government
Democracy
Aristocracy
Majority rule
Individual rights
Minority rights
Public interest
Pure (or direct) democracy
Representative democracy
Pluralist model
Elite model

Review Questions

1. Define politics. Try to identify political decisions that have affected you and your community. Do you have any initial thoughts on whether these decisions have made life better or worse for you or others?

2. What are five important characteristics of modern democracy?

3. Identify the four models of democracy described in this chapter. What are the strengths and weaknesses of each type of democracy?

4. What challenges face the United States or any nation in establishing or maintaining a stable, democratic system of government?

Suggested Readings

Ackerman, Bruce. *We the People*. Cambridge, Mass.: Belknap Press of Harvard University Press, 1991.

Dahl, Robert A. *A Preface to Democratic Theory*. Chicago: University of Chicago Press, 1956.

Miller, Nicholas R., "Pluralism and Social Choice," *American Political Science Review* 77 (1983), pp. 734–747.

Mills, C. Wright. *The Power Elite*. New York: Oxford University Press, 1956.

Sartori, Giovanni. *The Theory of Democracy Revisited.* Chatham, N.J.: Chatham House Publishers, 1987.

Wolff, Robert P. *In Defense of Anarchism.* New York: Harper & Row, 1970.

Internet Resources

Library of Congress-based site with links to a wide variety of web resources, including links to U.S. and foreign government agencies, at:

http://lcweb.loc.gov/global/explore.html

Political science megasite with links to a large number of sites with relevance to politics and political science, at:

http://www.lib.umich.edu/libhome/Documents.center/frames/polscifr.html

2 ★ The Constitution

★★★★★★★★★★★★★★★★★★★★★★★★★★★★★★★★

July 24, 1974, marked the beginning of the end of Richard Nixon's presidency. That morning the United States Supreme Court had unanimously ordered Nixon to release tape recordings of key White House conversations. In the afternoon the House Judiciary Committee came to order to consider approving articles of impeachment. Although the country did not know it yet, one of the tapes contained a "smoking gun"—clear evidence that the president had ordered the Central Intelligence Agency to block an FBI investigation of the White House–inspired break-in at Democratic national headquarters in the Watergate Hotel.

At 4:00 P.M. Pacific time, as the reporter Theodore White described it, presidential attorney James St. Clair "stood before the cameras at the Surf-and-Sand Hotel" near the president's California retreat "and stated that the President would turn over all subpoenaed tapes to Judge [John] Sirica as soon as they could be made ready; he would, said St. Clair, 'Comply with [the Court's] decision.'" A television cameraman back in Washington muttered, "That's news?"

But it was news. Here on live television was the embodiment of the American commitment to "a government of laws, and not of men." Here was the most powerful man in the world, the president of the United States, being called to answer for his conduct to the courts, to Congress, and, ultimately, to the American people. As the people closest to Nixon already knew, the tapes would show that

the president had lied to the people, abused his powers, and committed an obstruction of justice. Within three weeks, after the House Judiciary Committee had recommended articles of impeachment and the leaders of Nixon's own party had withdrawn their support, the president was standing on the White House lawn saying good-bye to his staff and to his presidency.

Watergate was a complicated affair, filled with criminality, dirty tricks, and abuses of power. In later years, Nixon would be rehabilitated as an elder statesman, and some would suggest that the only difference between his presidency and a dozen others was that Nixon simply got caught. Still, Watergate remains a

THE WHITE HOUSE
WASHINGTON

August 9, 1974

Dear Mr. Secretary:

I hereby resign the Office of President of the United States.

Sincerely,

Richard Nixon

The Honorable Henry A. Kissinger
The Secretary of State
Washington, D.C. 20520

Saluting victory in the face of defeat, Richard Nixon bids farewell to the White House for the last time on August 9, 1974.

particularly egregious example of presidential power run amok, of an administration so committed to maintaining its own power that it was willing to put its own interest over that of the nation.

Yet Watergate also shows the American system of checks and balances at its best. Although it took nearly two years, Nixon's wrongdoing was ultimately exposed. The investigation of the Nixon White House was led by a special Senate committee, the House Judiciary Committee, and two "special prosecutors," who, though they worked for the Justice Department (and hence the president), pursued the case with vigilance. This triumph of constitutional law over personal politics was accomplished by the combined efforts of all three branches and is symbolized for the ages by the Supreme Court's decision to require the release of the White House tapes. And although Nixon's first vice president also had been forced to resign for criminal conduct, the transition of power to Vice President Gerald R. Ford was smooth and orderly.

Ironically, the president who was most contemptuous of the American constitutional system provided the most stunning proof of the system's vitality and resiliency. For the American system of government, Watergate was truly the best and worst of times.

The Framers of the Constitution of the United States were determined to create a system of government that would work despite the evils that all too often pervade human affairs. Having lived through the colonies' fight with Great Britain, the Framers knew that political power was naturally subject to abuse and that even the best political institutions could become warped and degraded. For the Framers, designing the Constitution involved the solution of a difficult paradox: the government needed to be strong enough to control the governed, yet capable at the same time of controlling itself.

If the success of a political system is measured by longevity, then the Framers succeeded brilliantly. After two hundred years, the structure of the American constitutional system has hardly changed. Yet as the Watergate case illustrates, the Constitution has had its trying moments. Time and time again the system has been tested—by economic depression and civil war, by foreign crisis and domestic upheaval, by timid or overzealous leadership. Although the record has been far from perfect, the Constitution has weathered all of its storms, arguably emerging stronger for the tests.

Today, as in 1787, the United States faces difficult challenges. The government must still work to achieve the appropriate balances between efficiency and liberty, between majority rule and minority rights, and between the rule of law and the need for flexibility. Because the nation is constantly growing and evolving, no solution to these problems is ever complete or permanent. The Constitution, like the nation itself, must continually be redefined and rediscovered.

Questions to Keep in Mind

Does the American constitutional system more closely resemble the pure democracy model or the representative democracy model? Why?

How does the Constitution attempt to create efficiency in government without jeopardizing the liberty of the people?

What distinguished the Federalist supporters of the Constitution from its Antifederalist critics? What were the key disagreements between the two groups? What echoes of those disagreements can be found in modern American politics?

Basic Concepts ★ ★ ★ ★ ★ ★ ★ ★ ★ ★ ★ ★ ★

The foundation of the American political system remains the **United States Constitution**, written in 1787. Although the meaning of the Constitution has evolved over the course of two centuries, the themes and principles of the original document remain the starting point for any discussion of American government and politics.

Origins of the Constitution

Many thinkers and much history contributed to the United States Constitution. The Constitution drew its inspiration from sources as diverse as the Bible, the ancient Greek philosophers, the English legal system, and the events of the American Revolution and the 1780s. No quick or easy summary of the origins of the Constitution can do the subject justice, but a brief overview can suggest some of the ideas and experiences behind the events of 1787.

Philosophical Origins   The political philosophy of the Constitution owes much to the English philosopher **John Locke** (1632–1704). Locke was the author of several significant books and pamphlets, most importantly the *Second Treatise on Civil Government*. The *Second Treatise* argues that government draws its legitimacy only from the consent of the governed, and that government exists only to protect the lives, liberty, and property of the people. Moreover, the consent of the governed is an ongoing process, and the people have a permanent right to bring down their government when they think it necessary, and to establish a new one in its place. Locke's views were echoed in the Declaration of Independence and embodied in the preamble of the Constitution.

Locke's writings contain other key principles that the colonists accepted almost as a matter of course. Among them are these:

- *Equality*. Locke argued that all men were created equal and thus shared the same fundamental rights. Although he and his American followers did not extend this logic to women, Native Americans, or other racial minorities, their emphasis on equality was

"An assembly of demigods" was how Thomas Jefferson described the Constitutional Convention of 1787. In this nineteenth-century reconstruction, George Washington addresses his fellow delegates.

nonetheless revolutionary. It represented a direct challenge to the medieval emphasis on fixed—and politically unequal—social classes, making democracy possible. Moreover, Locke and his followers expressed themselves in broad terms, easing the way for the extension of equality centuries later.

- *Reason.* Locke's emphasis on reason opened up a new world by undermining long-held beliefs based on tradition and emotion. The idea of creating governments based on rational analysis was revolutionary in itself, as was Locke's demand that unequal social and political arrangements be justified by argument instead of simply accepted on faith.
- *Natural law and natural rights.* Locke argued that governments and societies should operate in a manner consistent with the laws of nature. Human behavior could thus be measured against an absolute standard that included the concept of natural rights for all people. Some natural rights were given up in order to form a society, but others—life, liberty, and property—could not be sacrificed.
- *Social contract.* The social contract provided a method by which the inhabitants of a country could join together for the mutual protection of their rights. Locke's emphasis on the social contract underscores the key principles of his philosophical viewpoint. It is an agreement among equals, based on reason and choice, and made according to the dictates of the natural law. It is designed to protect natural rights, and forms the only legitimate foundation for the subsequent exercise of political power. To Americans in 1787, the drafting and ratification of the Constitution seemed to be a virtual reenactment of the social contract.

The central ideas in Locke's *Second Treatise* were not completely new, and in many cases were more fully developed by other writers. Some of his ideas, such as his view that the legislative branch should be supreme, were rejected outright by most Americans. But Locke was widely quoted and much admired by the colonists. He was a major source of inspiration for both the American Revolution and the Constitution.

The Framers of the Constitution took for granted that government should be divided into legislative, executive, and judicial branches, although there was little agreement on exactly what this separation of powers meant. The popularity of the separation of powers as a governing principle can be traced to the writings of Charles Secondat, Baron de **Montesquieu,** a French writer of the mid-1700s.

Montesquieu did not invent the separation of powers, but he was the first to connect the separation of powers with the preservation of liberty. The genius of the separation of powers, he wrote, is that it prevents tyranny by ensuring that no one person or institution can command the full powers of government.

The Colonial Experience
Magna Carta, the Mayflower Compact, Colonial Charters. The Americans of 1787 were long accustomed to the idea of written expressions of basic law. English history had provided the **Magna Carta**, an agreement in 1215 between King John and his barons, as well as the English Bill of Rights of 1689. Although neither Magna Carta nor the English Bill of Rights guaranteed equal rights to all citizens, the Americans viewed these and similar documents with great reverence.

The idea of written charters of law was also embedded in the American consciousness from firsthand experience. Before landing at Plymouth, for example, the Pilgrims signed their names to the **Mayflower Compact,** a written agreement that established a system of government for the new colony. In other colonies the basic laws were set out in royal charters, written documents issued by the king and authorizing settlement under English law.

Colonial Governments. The British government had ultimate authority over the colonies, but many decisions were left to colonial governors and legislatures. Although the governors were appointed from London, the legislatures were elected by the colonists themselves. Thus from early on the colonists had experience with self-government and practice in the art of democratic politics. Much of the conflict between the colonies and the British government in the years before the Revolution centered on Great Britain's efforts to frustrate self-rule and reassert its control over the colonial governments.

The Revolution. Much of the Constitution's emphasis on limiting the power of government and protecting the rights of the people can be traced to specific events and experiences of the American Revolution. Many Americans saw the Revolution as a justifiable reaction to England's systematic effort to deprive the colonists of their fundamental rights. Above all, the colonists objected to taxation without representation and to the occupation of Boston by British troops.

The Constitution also drew heavily from the state constitutions adopted after the colonists broke with Great Britain. The purpose of a written constitution, wrote the people of the town of Concord, Massachusetts, was to secure the people "in the possession and enjoyment of their rights and privileges" against "any encroachment of the governing part."[1] Written constitutions—like written contracts in everyday life—provided some protection against government abuse of power and the destruction of the people's rights.

The Declaration of Independence The colonies formally broke with Great Britain in July of 1776, with the adoption of the **Declaration of Independence.** The Declaration, approved unanimously by the representatives of the thirteen colonies, declared the colonies to be "free and independent states."

The Declaration of Independence is not a part of the Constitution (it was adopted more than thirteen years earlier). However, its broad statements of principle have become an essential part of the American political tradition and are reflected in the Constitution. These principles include equality, natural rights, limited government, and the consent of the governed. All of these principles and more are contained in two famous sentences, written by Thomas Jefferson: "We hold these truths to be self-evident, that all men are created equal, that they are endowed by their Creator with certain unalienable rights, that among these are Life, Liberty, and the pursuit of Happiness. That to secure these rights, Governments are instituted among Men, deriving their just powers from the consent of the governed."

Following Locke, the Declaration of Independence also justifies the right of the people to rebel against their existing government and to create new governments as they think appropriate. Whenever any government becomes destructive of the ends for which it was created, Jefferson wrote, "it is the Right of the People to alter or abolish it, and to institute new Government, laying its foundation on such principles and organizing its powers in such form, as to them shall seem most likely to effect their Safety and Happiness." At the time, this statement provided a justification for the separation from Great Britain and the creation of the first state governments. Later, it would provide a clear rationale for the adoption of the United States Constitution.

The Articles of Confederation During the Revolutionary War, the former colonies co-ordinated their actions through the Continental Congress, which consisted of representatives from each state. It quickly became apparent that a more formal organization was necessary, and in November 1777 Congress adopted the **Articles of Confederation.** The Articles went into effect in March 1781, upon ratification by the states.

The Articles of Confederation laid out the relationship between the states and the new national government. The Articles made it clear that the states were independent, and that the national government was merely a convenient forum through which the states could act collectively.

All national power under the Articles was exercised by Congress, which remained a body of "ambassadors" from the states. There was no president (only an ineffective Committee of the States), and no national judiciary, which meant that Congress had to rely on the state governors and the state courts for the interpretation and enforcement of its laws. Moreover, Congress was denied certain powers altogether, the most important being the power to impose taxes directly on the people (instead, Congress had to request money from the states) and the power to regulate commerce. Defects in the Articles were almost impossible to correct, since amendments required the unanimous consent of all thirteen states.

During the war, with the need for national unity and efficiency at its peak, the Articles worked just well enough. As soon as the war ended, however, their shortcomings became all too clear, triggering a movement to reform or replace them with a new constitution.

The Crisis of the 1780s The reform movement gained momentum with the growing political and economic crisis of the 1780s. The postwar American economy was in disarray, suffering from widespread bankruptcies and large-scale unemployment. American traders

The View from 1787

Americans found much to lament and criticize in the state of their country in the mid-1780s. Many of their comments sound equally plausible in today's political environment. Here are two examples:

Our citizens seem to be seized with a general emulation to surpass each other in every article of expence [sic]. Those who possess affluent fortunes lead the way, and set the example. Others, whose estates are not sufficient to bear them out, madly adopt the same expensive system, and in order to support it, contract debts which they have no rational prospect of discharging. All they seem to wish, is to obtain credit, to figure away, and to make a brilliant appearance at the expence of others.

—Thomas Reese of South Carolina, 1788

[Instead of choosing a man for his abilities, integrity, and patriotism, the people] choose a man, because he will vote for a new town, or a new county, or in favour of a memorial; because he is noisy in blaming those who are in office, has confidence enough to suppose that he could do better, and impudence enough to tell the people so, or because he possesses in a supereminent degree, the all-prevailing popular talent of coaxing and flattering.

—James Monroe of Virginia, 1787

were barred from the West Indies, and the British army continued to pose a direct threat from military posts in the Northwest. Even worse, the spirit of self-sacrifice and devotion to duty that had won the Revolutionary War seemed to have evaporated into an atmosphere of greed and self-indulgence.

To a growing number of political leaders, the problems of the 1780s could be traced directly to the shortcomings of the Articles of Confederation, and particularly to the inherent inability of the national government to impose order on the several states. Operating under a heavy war debt and facing difficult economic circumstances, the states fell into petty quarrels, and the people dissolved into warring parts. The general feeling, as James Madison described it, was "that our governments are too unstable, that the public good is disregarded in the conflicts of rival parties, and that measures are too often decided, not according to the rules of justice and the rights of the minor party, but by the superior force of an interested and overbearing majority."[2] To Madison and others, the solution was to create a new national government that would have the strength and will to refocus and reenergize the American experiment.

From Annapolis to Philadelphia   The initial leadership came from Virginia, which invited the other states to send delegates to a convention in September 1786 in Annapolis, Maryland. Only five states responded, but among the delegates were James Madison and Alexander Hamilton, who would play key roles in writing and drafting the 1787 Constitution. The **Annapolis Convention** called for a second convention to determine precisely what changes were necessary in the structure of the national government, and sent its recommendation to Congress.

Shays's Rebellion   While Congress hesitated over whether to agree to a new convention, the nation's attention was drawn to a dramatic incident in Massachusetts, known as **Shays's Rebellion.** Daniel Shays was the leader of a group of indebted and impoverished farmers who tried to convince the Massachusetts government to grant them relief from their crushing burden of debt. When the legislature refused, Shays's group attacked the federal arsenal at Springfield, apparently the first stage in what was to be the attempted overthrow of the state government. The "rebellion" was a fiasco, and was easily defeated, but the incident touched off a nationwide wave of fear and resentment. Congress was finally inspired to act, calling for a constitutional convention to meet in Philadelphia in the summer of 1787.

James Madison in 1788. Madison's skill at both political theory and practical politics earned him the title "Father of the Constitution." Madison prepared for the debate over the Constitution by undertaking a systematic study of political history and theory, with particular emphasis on the ancient city-states, such as Athens and Sparta.

The convention met from May to September. Its meetings, held in Constitution Hall, were closed to the press and public, in order to allow full and uninhibited debate. Its members included such leading national figures as Benjamin Franklin and George Washington, who gave the convention an air of prestige and respectability. Although Washington was unanimously elected president of the convention, real leadership came from a small group of committed nationalists, including Alexander Hamilton of New York, James Madison of Virginia, and James Wilson of Pennsylvania. An official secretary kept records, but they were not released until 1819. More revealing journals were kept by James Madison and other delegates.

The Virginia Plan   The proposal that guided the convention's deliberations for the first several weeks came from the Virginia delegation. Although offered officially by Edmund Randolph, the so-called **Virginia Plan** embodied above all the political philosophy of James Madison. It envisioned the creation of what Randolph called "a strong *consolidated* union, in which the idea of states should be nearly annihilated."[3] Thus the plan proposed to allocate the seats in both houses of Congress on the basis of population, overturning the one state–one vote rule that had been the basis of the Articles of Confederation. Moreover, Congress would be granted a veto over all state legislation.

The Virginia Plan's strong tilt away from the states and toward the national government caused great controversy. Most aggrieved were the representatives of the small states, who feared that their interests would be swallowed up by those of the larger states. Also opposed were those who feared it would allow an unwise concentration of power in the national government. In other respects, however, the plan won widespread approval. It called for a two-house legislature and a national executive and judiciary, which were quickly adopted and formed the basic structure of the new government.

The New Jersey Plan and the Great Compromise   Meanwhile, opponents of the Virginia Plan proposed an alternative designed to preserve the strong role of the states in the national government. **The New Jersey Plan,** introduced by William Paterson of New Jersey, called for the equal representation of every state in a one-house legislature. Paterson defended his plan by noting that any other arrangement would subvert the sovereignty of the states that made up the federal Union. The New Jersey Plan pleased the small states, but was easily blocked by a coalition of large states, which correctly saw it as nothing but a slight modification of the Articles of Confederation.

In the end the convention settled on what came to be known as the **Great Compromise.** Under this arrangement the House of Representatives would be apportioned by population and the Senate would preserve equal representation for each state.

Slavery   The convention also compromised on another troubling question—slavery. Although there was considerable opposition to slavery by 1787, the delegates to the Philadelphia convention made no effort to abolish it. Instead, they argued over less central issues, such as how the slaves in the South were to be counted for the purposes of taxation and representation. Eventually they agreed to count slaves at a ratio of three-fifths of free citizens—giving the South several extra representatives, but obliging them to pay proportionally more in taxes as well. The delegates also agreed to compromise on whether to ban the importation of slaves, agreeing to allow Congress to do so only after 1808, and gave in to southern demands that the states be required to return escaped slaves to their owners.

Later generations would look back on the founding generation's compromise on slavery with a mixture of disgust and indignation. To modern Americans, the very idea that the Constitution could sanction slavery is reprehensible. Indeed, there is evidence to suggest that the Framers of the Constitution recognized the fundamental contradiction between the Constitution's emphasis on liberty and its compromise on slavery; although slavery is discussed in the document three times (the three-fifths, the fugitive slave, and the slave trade clauses), the words *slave* and *slavery* are conspicuously absent. James Madison, likewise, defended the three-fifths compromise in the *Federalist Papers* not in his own words but by quoting the hypothetical argument of "one of our Southern brethren."[4]

Despite growing opposition to slavery in the North, the delegates to the Constitutional Convention agreed to accept its existence in the southern states in order to reach agreement on the Constitution.

Although the Framers' actions are impossible to justify in moral or theoretical terms, finding some sort of compromise on slavery was probably the only way to ensure that the five southern states would support the Constitution. In the end, of course, the Framers' decision only postponed the crisis over slavery, which eventually erupted in a full-fledged civil war that nearly destroyed what they had built.

The Ratification Debate   Many more conflicts would occur, and many more compromises would be made before the proposed Constitution was published in September 1787. The new charter required approval by special state ratifying conventions—and was to go into effect when ratified by only nine states. Since the Articles of Confederation required all thirteen states to agree to any amendments, this procedure made it crystal clear that the Constitution was meant to supplant, and not merely amend, the Articles of Confederation. Delaware ratified first, in December 1787. The ninth state, New Hampshire, ratified in June 1788. Technically, the Constitution went into effect at that point, although the assent of New York and Virginia, which came later, was critical to the creation of a permanent union.

The ratification fight was not easy. In several states the supporters of the Constitution had to resort to what is known today as hardball politics. In Pennsylvania, for example, opponents of the Constitution tried to slow down the ratification process by boycotting the state legislative session—thus depriving the legislature of the minimum number of members needed to do business. In response, pro-Constitution legislators physically captured two members of the opposition, hauled them into the legislative chamber, and proceeded to a vote.[5] In the end, the backers of the Constitution succeeded only by making key concessions to their opponents, especially by agreeing to support a Bill of Rights to protect the people from the national government.

Key Principles and Provisions of the Constitution

The Constitution consists of seven articles followed by twenty-seven amendments. The very structure of the Constitution testifies to the importance of the separation of powers principle: Article I deals primarily with congressional powers, Article II with the powers of the presidency, and Article III with the powers of the courts. Articles IV–VII deal with more specialized provisions, such as the relationship of the states to each other and the process of constitutional amendment.

The organization of the Constitution is not rigid or mechanistic. Given the relationships it creates among the various parts of the system, it is not surprising that the various articles are linked and overlap. While the judicial branch is discussed in Article III, for example, the appointment and removal of judges is treated in Article II. Likewise, restrictions on the powers of the states can be found in both Articles I and IV.

Amendments to the Constitution are presented at the end of the document, in order of adoption. The first ten amendments—adopted by Congress in 1789 and approved by the states in 1791—are known as the Bill of Rights.

Various important aspects of the Constitution are discussed in the following sections. The first three topics deal with general principles embodied in the Constitution. The last four are concerned with specific clauses or provisions of the Constitution.

Federalism   The Constitution divides power between the national government and the state governments, an arrangement known as **federalism.** In theory, at least, the national government is a government of delegated powers, meaning that it can exercise only those powers specifically granted to it by the Constitution. The states, by contrast, retain all powers not specifically granted to the national government or retained by the people.

The national government is often referred to as the government of the United States, or the federal government.

Federalism is discussed in detail in Chapter 3.

Figure 2.1   Sources of Power Under the Articles of Confederation and the Constitution

The Articles of Confederation—which begin "We, the States"—were created by the state governments. The Constitution, by contrast, begins "We, the People." It was created by the people and gives certain powers to the United States government while reserving others to the states.

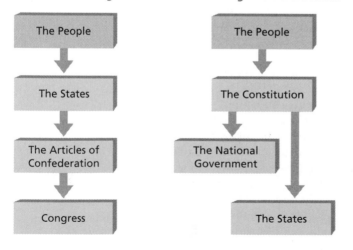

Separation of Powers and the System of Checks and Balances   The Constitution creates three separate branches of the federal government—legislative, executive, and judicial.
Under this **separation of powers,** the legislative branch is responsible for passing laws, the
executive branch for carrying them out, and the judicial branch for interpreting them,
punishing offenders, and resolving disputes. In the national government under the Constitution, these branches correspond to Congress (legislative), the presidency (executive), and
the courts (judicial). The Constitution further divides the legislative power into two houses
of Congress, the Senate and the House of Representatives.

Figure 2.2   **Checks and Balances**

*Madison's theory of checks and balances works because each branch has "the constitutional means
and personal motives to resist encroachments of the others." Below are depicted some of the constitutional means available to each branch to police the other two.*

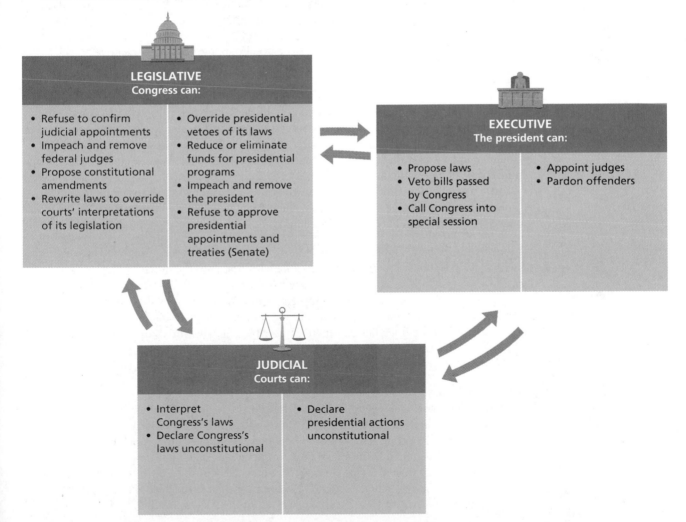

The Constitution does not call for a rigid separation of powers among the three branches. Instead it requires each branch to share key parts of the others' powers, making it easier for each branch to check the other two. This design is known as the system of **checks and balances.** For example, Congress must submit laws to the president for approval. The president can veto (reject) the laws, but Congress can override the president's veto by a two-thirds vote of each house. Executive officials and judges are appointed by the president but must be confirmed by the Senate. Laws passed by Congress can be struck down as unconstitutional by the Supreme Court, but Congress can initiate the process of constitutional amendment to override the Court. Overall, the system of checks and balances is designed to promote compromise among the three branches and to prevent the domination of the government by any one branch.

The separation of powers in the United States stands in sharp contrast to the constitutional arrangements in most modern democracies. Instead of separating powers, most modern democracies fuse legislative, executive, and judicial powers into the legislature, or parliament. The leader of the executive branch, or prime minister, is drawn from and elected by parliament, and also serves as its leader. The leaders of the various executive departments are also drawn from the parliament. The judges are usually appointed by the executive branch.

Efficiency   Although the separation of powers suggests a concern with controlling and limiting the powers of government, the Constitution also aims at an efficient administration of government. Thus the Constitution establishes an executive branch and puts a single individual (the president) at the top. Similarly, the Constitution grants broad powers to Congress. Unlike the Articles of Confederation, for example, the Constitution authorizes Congress to levy taxes directly on individuals, eliminating the need for Congress to request funds from the several state governments.

In effect, the Constitution aims both to create a strong national government and to limit its ability to infringe on the rights of the people. Maintaining the uneasy relationship between efficiency and liberty remains an ongoing challenge.

Commerce Clause   The Constitution grants Congress the power to regulate commerce "with foreign Nations, and among the several States, and with the Indian Tribes." By implication, the regulation of commerce entirely within a single state is left to that state. Over the years, however, Congress and the Supreme Court have interpreted commerce "among the several States" (interstate commerce) broadly, to include even local commerce that has a *substantial effect* on interstate commerce. In the twentieth century, Congress has used the Commerce Clause to protect civil rights and to regulate everything from illegal drugs and prostitution to environmental pollution, workplace safety, and minimum wages.

Supremacy Clause   The Constitution declares itself—along with all laws and treaties made under it—to be the "supreme Law of the Land." The judges in every state are bound to obey it, regardless of any state law or state constitutional provision. The **Supremacy Clause** is enforced most directly by the United States Supreme Court, which has the power to declare state laws unconstitutional if they conflict with valid federal laws.

The Supremacy Clause underscores the Framers' view of the Constitution as superior to the laws of the several states. As such, it has been considered the linchpin of the constitutional system—that is, the piece that holds the rest of the system together.

The Bill of Rights   The first ten amendments to the Constitution, known as the **Bill of Rights,** were proposed by Congress as a package in 1789 and ratified two years later (see Table 2.1). The absence of a Bill of Rights in the original document provoked tremendous criticism from the opponents of the Constitution. After first arguing that a Bill of Rights was unnecessary, Madison and other supporters of the Constitution agreed to the addition. Madison himself, by then a member of the House of Representatives, guided the Bill of Rights through the first Congress.

Table 2.1
Constitutional Amendments

Number	Ratified	Summary	Time for Ratification
1*	1791	Freedom of religion, speech, press, assembly	2 years, 3 months
2*		Right to bear arms	
3*		Guarantee against quartering of soldiers	
4*		Protection against unreasonable searches and seizures	
5*		Right to due process of law; rights of criminal defendants; prohibition against use of private property for public use without just compensation	
6*		Right to jury trial, right to counsel in criminal cases	
7*		Right to jury trial in civil cases	
8*		Prohibition against cruel and unusual punishments, excessive bail	
9*		Unenumerated rights reserved to the people	
10*		Preservation of state powers	
11	1795	Restriction on judicial power in suits against states	11 months
12	1804	Changes in manner of choosing president and vice president	6 months
13	1865	Abolition of slavery	10 months
14	1868	Rights of citizens, guarantee of due process, equal protection of the laws	2 years, 1 month
15	1870	No racial discrimination in voting	11 months
16	1913	Authorization of federal income tax	3 years, 7 months
17	1913	Election of U.S. senators by popular vote	1 year, 1 month
18	1919	Prohibition of alcoholic beverages	1 year, 1 month
19	1920	Guarantee of women's right to vote	1 year, 3 months
20	1933	Change of presidential inauguration from March to January	11 months
21	1933	Repeal of Eighteenth Amendment	9 months
22	1951	Limitation of president to two terms in office	3 years, 11 months
23	1961	Provision of the District of Columbia with a role in presidential elections	9 months
24	1964	Ban on poll tax in federal elections	1 year, 4 months
25	1967	Presidential disability and succession	1 year, 10 months
26	1971	Guarantee of eighteen-year-olds' right to vote	3 months
27	1992	Ban on congressional pay raise until after the next election	202 years, 7 months

*Denotes amendments that make up the Bill of Rights.

Elastic (or Necessary and Proper) Clause   Another key power of Congress is found in the **Elastic Clause,** also known as the Necessary and Proper Clause. This provision gives Congress the power to enact "all Laws which shall be necessary and proper for the carrying into Execution" of its other powers. For example, since Congress is authorized to collect taxes, it can also punish those who refuse to pay taxes. In effect, the Necessary and Proper Clause guarantees that Congress is able to exercise its legitimate powers through whatever means it thinks appropriate—subject only to the specific restrictions of the Bill of Rights and other limitations of the Constitution.

This principle is so vital to the constitutional plan that it is easy to take it for granted, but critics of national power opposed it for decades after 1787. Thomas Jefferson, for example, argued against Hamilton that the Necessary and Proper Clause was actually a *limitation* on congressional power, meant to ensure that Congress restricted itself only to those means "absolutely necessary" for the execution of its delegated powers. The Supreme Court formally rejected Jefferson's view of federal power in 1819, in the case of *McCulloch* v. *Maryland*.[6] A complete discussion of *McCulloch* appears in the next chapter.

Amending the Constitution

The Framers, expecting that "useful alterations" to the Constitution would "be suggested by experience," provided several mechanisms for amending the Constitution. They made the process difficult, however, fearing that otherwise the Constitution would be changed too frequently and for insufficient reasons.[7]

After fourteen years of prohibition, Americans tired of the constitutional ban on "intoxicating liquors" and demanded repeal of the Eighteenth Amendment. Liquor consumption did drop sharply during prohibition, but the ban was difficult to enforce and led to a booming illegal trade. Thoroughly discredited, prohibition was repealed by the Twenty-First Amendment in 1933.

To become a part of the Constitution, amendments must be proposed and then ratified. Each step can be achieved in two ways. The usual method involves approval by two-thirds of each house of Congress and ratification by three-fourths of the state legislatures. Only once was another path followed: the Twenty-first Amendment, which repealed the Eighteenth Amendment's prohibition on alcoholic beverages, was ratified not by the state legislatures but by special conventions called in each state. Constitutional amendments can also be proposed by a convention called by Congress on the demand of two-thirds of the states.

Many constitutional amendments have been proposed, but few have survived the ratification process to become a part of the Constitution. Since 1789, in fact, more than ten thousand amendments have been proposed in Congress, of which only thirty-three were approved by Congress and sent to the states, and only twenty-seven were actually adopted.[8] Considering that the first ten amendments were added to the Constitution practically as part of the original ratification process, it can be said that the Constitution has been formally amended only seventeen times in more than two hundred years.

Six amendments have been approved by Congress but rejected by the states. Among the most important are the Child Labor Amendment, proposed in 1924, and the Equal Rights Amendment, proposed in 1972. Both amendments were defeated by a coalition of conservative and religious groups after a long and difficult political struggle. Ironically, the objectives of both proposals have been largely achieved anyway by a combination of congressional and judicial action.

The states have tried several times in recent years to make Congress call a constitutional convention to deal with such issues as school prayer and a balanced budget. None of these attempts has yet achieved the support of the necessary two-thirds margin, or thirty-four states.

Change through Interpretation   Far more common than constitutional change by amendment have been changes brought about by *interpretation.* Certainly the most obvious and important role in constitutional interpretation is played by the Supreme Court, which over the years has adjusted its views on the Constitution to take account of changes in technology, social science, or public opinion. But Congress and various presidents have also taken it upon themselves to keep the Constitution up-to-date by their own interpretations of the document.

The Supreme Court is able to play its role in constitutional interpretation because of its power of **judicial review.** Judicial review is the Court's power to declare acts of Congress (as well as state laws and other government actions) unconstitutional. Judicial review also provides the Court with the power to uphold federal laws, thus granting them increased legitimacy, and indeed from early on the Court has interpreted federal power under the Constitution in generous terms. As Chief Justice John Marshall wrote in 1819, the Constitution requires "that only its great outlines should be marked, its important objects designated, and the minor ingredients which compose these objects be deduced from the nature of the objects themselves." The Constitution is "intended to endure for ages to come," Marshall proclaimed, and "must be adapted to the various crises of human affairs."[9]

Over the years the Supreme Court has frequently displayed great flexibility in interpreting the Constitution. While conceding, for example, that the Fourteenth Amendment's guarantee of "equal protection of the laws" was designed primarily to protect Americans from discrimination based on race, the Court has extended the amendment's reach to include discrimination based on sex as well. Similarly, the Court has extended the meaning of "free speech" to include not only spoken words but also symbolic speech—for example, burning an American flag as a gesture of protest. It has also found a right to privacy in the various provisions of the Bill of Rights and interpreted it to include a woman's right to choose an abortion. Critics charge that the Court has overstepped the proper bounds of its own authority by departing too much from the constitutional text, but almost everyone agrees that some flexibility is essential.

Both the executive and the legislative branches have also developed new constitutional interpretations to cope with changing circumstances. Although the Constitution requires that treaties be ratified by the Senate, for example, presidents have long entered into so-called executive agreements with foreign nations, which do not require Senate approval.

The Story of the Twenty-seventh Amendment

It took 203 years, but in 1992 the Twenty-seventh Amendment officially became a part of the Constitution.

The amendment, which bans any changes in the pay of senators and representatives until "an election of Representatives shall take effect," was proposed in 1789 by James Madison. Along with the congressional pay amendment, Madison also proposed eleven others—ten of which were ratified and became the Bill of Rights. The other two—the pay amendment and one dealing with the apportionment of representatives among the states—failed to achieve the approval of three-fourths of the states.

The congressional pay amendment, in fact, was ratified by only six states between 1789 and 1791.

One more state ratified in 1873, but for all intents and purposes the amendment was dead, and forgotten—or so it seemed. Unlike the usual practice today, the First Congress put no time limit on ratification of the amendment, and it was recalled to life in the 1970s and 1980s, a symbol of the public's growing dissatisfaction with Congress. Finally, on May 7, 1992, Michigan became the thirty-eighth state to ratify—thus achieving the necessary three-fourths requirement.

Still, whether the amendment had become a part of the Constitution was unclear. Traditionally, the Supreme Court has held that ratification of constitutional amendments must be roughly contemporaneous. In 1921, in fact, the Court observed that the two unratified amendments from 1789 were probably dead. But the Court has also made it clear that the final decision in such cases is up to Congress.

In the case of the Twenty-seventh Amendment, Congress made noises about blocking the amendment. Within weeks, however, the congressional leadership bowed to public pressure, and Madison's amendment officially became a part of the Constitution.

The Supreme Court accepted the validity of such agreements in 1937, although the precise limit of the president's power to act without the "advice and consent" of the Senate is still not clear.[10] In similar fashion, Congress has evolved various mechanisms to insulate the federal bureaucracy from presidential control. For example, it has established independent agencies, whose heads cannot be dismissed by the president except in circumstances specifically laid out by Congress. These limitations were first applied to such agencies as the Interstate Commerce Commission and the Federal Communications Commission, and were accepted as valid by the Supreme Court in 1935. More recently, Congress has established independent counsels, or special prosecutors, to investigate wrongdoing in the executive branch without interference from the White House.

Much informal constitutional change took place in the 1930s and 1940s. The Great Depression of the 1930s led to Franklin Roosevelt's New Deal, which greatly expanded federal power in the domestic arena. America's involvement in World War II, and the nation's international dominance in the postwar order, made new arrangements in the international arena necessary as well. These developments have not always been smooth, and the Supreme Court has not always gone along, at least not immediately. Over time, however, the three branches reached a common agreement on the broad contours of the new interpretation of the Constitution.

The Framers and Their Ideas

Despite many changes by amendment and interpretation, the core of the Constitution today is essentially as the Framers envisioned it two hundred years ago. Thus their ideas—and those of their opponents—remain extremely relevant.

Federalists and Antifederalists

The debate over the new Constitution divided Americans into two camps. Supporters of the Constitution called themselves **Federalists,** a name as confusing now as it was then. They viewed the Articles of Confederation as fundamentally flawed and called for a complete restructuring of the relationship between the states and the national government. Their opponents were stuck with the rather unfortunate name **Antifederalists,** which was even less informative than Federalists and carried a negative connotation besides.

> *"Though written constitutions may be violated in moments of passion or delusion, yet they furnish a text to which those who are watchful may again rally and recall the people; they fix too for the people the principles of their political creed."*
>
> —Thomas Jefferson, letter to Joseph Priestly, June 19, 1802

The substance of the disagreement between the Federalists and the Antifederalists boiled down to a contest over who would have the ultimate political power in the new Republic. The Antifederalists conceded that the national government should be granted modest additional powers, but argued that the states should retain a large degree of independence. The Federalists, by contrast, argued that power should be shared between the states and the national government. At bottom, however, it was clear that the Federalists favored a considerable shift of power from the states to the national government.

Who Was Who in 1787 It is difficult to draw a neat line dividing the men who became Federalists from those who became Antifederalists, although many have tried. Careful examination of the evidence has undercut the once popular theory that the Federalists were rich and the Antifederalists poor. Although the Federalists tended to be younger than their opponents, there were no clear differences between the two groups based on religion or profession.

Where the Federalists and Antifederalists did differ was in social status and social outlook: the Federalists were social aristocrats, the Antifederalists social democrats. The Federalists were better educated, better mannered, more widely traveled. The Federalists, as their own John Jay declared, were "the better sort of people, . . . who are orderly and industrious, who are content with their situations and not uneasy in their circumstances." The Antifederalists, by contrast, were simpler, down-home people who read newspapers instead of philosophical treatises and who identified more with hard work than with high society: "nothing but the horse-jockey, the mushroom merchant, the running and dishonest speculator," as the Federalists put it.[11] The Federalists were concentrated along the eastern seaboard, the Antifederalists in the upcountry regions.

There were differences of opinion within both the Federalist and Antifederalist camps. These differences were apparent even at the Constitutional Convention in Philadelphia. On some issues, the convention split between the small and the large states. On others, especially those dealing with slavery, the dominant split was between North and South.

An Economic Interpretation of the Constitution

Writing in 1913, the historian Charles Beard put forward a startling argument: the Framers of the Constitution, he wrote, were "a small and active group of men immediately interested through their personal possessions in the outcome of their labors." In other words, the men who drafted the Constitution "were, with a few exceptions, immediately, directly, and personally interested in, and derived economic advantages from, the establishment of the new document."*

The Constitution, in Beard's view, was precisely designed to benefit four groups of Americans: those who had money; holders of public securities; manufacturers; and traders. All four groups had done poorly under the Articles of Confederation, Beard argued, and all four did well under the Constitution. Farmers, by contrast, were hurt by economic policies embodied in the Constitution. Poor farmers, who owned no land, were "excluded at the outset from participation . . . in the work of framing the Constitution." Landowners, both small and large, were allowed to participate in the process but lost out nonetheless. Beard attempted to prove his thesis by showing that the division over the Constitution generally pitted the poor and those who owned land against those who owned personal wealth.

Modern historians have categorically rejected the Beard thesis. His methodology was flawed, his data incomplete and often erroneous. The line of cleavage between supporters and opponents of the Constitution was far more complex than Beard admitted. There were farmers, and merchants, on both sides of the question. As the historian Forrest McDonald concluded in the 1950s, "on all counts . . . Beard's thesis is entirely incompatible with the facts."†

Despite its rejection by modern historians, the Beard thesis does contain a germ of truth. The division between the Federalists and the Antifederalists is best expressed as a matter not of economic class but of social class. As a group the Federalists were better educated, more cosmopolitan, and more sophisticated than their opponents. Whatever their economic status (Madison in particular was in tough shape financially), they considered themselves to be the nation's natural aristocracy.‡

Despite its evident weaknesses, the Beard thesis stood at the center of the historical debate on the Constitution for nearly half a century. The reason has more to do with the twentieth century than the eighteenth. Beard's book provided strong ammunition for the Progressive movement, which sought to reform American politics to make it more responsive to the poor and the middle class. On several occasions, progressive legislation—a federal income tax, laws protecting labor unions, and minimum wage and maximum hours laws—was declared unconstitutional by the Supreme Court. One way around that problem was to follow Beard and make a frontal attack on the Constitution itself.

Arguments over the economic origins of the Constitution have not disappeared entirely. Ironically, the Framers' interest in protecting private property has become a rallying cry of modern conservative legal scholars, who argue that the Supreme Court should take a more active role in protecting private property interests.

* Charles A. Beard, *An Economic Interpretation of the Constitution* (New York: Macmillan, 1913), p. 324.
† Forrest McDonald, *We the People: The Economic Origins of the Constitution* (Chicago: University of Chicago Press, 1958), p. 357.
‡ See Gordon S. Wood, *The Creation of the American Republic, 1776–1787* (New York: W. W. Norton, 1972).

The Federalists, for example, were divided on the makeup and purpose of the Senate. Some saw the Senate as representing the states and thus advocated giving each state the same number of senators; others argued that the Senate should represent the people, and called for proportional representation based on population. Still others viewed the Senate as the "aristocratic" house; Alexander Hamilton, for example, proposed at the convention that senators be given lifetime appointments.

The Antifederalists, likewise, were divided on many questions. The most important was whether to go along with the Constitution at all. To some Antifederalists, the Constitution was wholly illegitimate; others worked instead to correct what they saw as its most serious defects, especially the absence of a Bill of Rights. And while most of the Antifederalists were committed to a version of pure democracy, others expressed concerns about "the excess of democracy" in the states.[12]

It is also worth noting who was not represented in either the Federalist or the Antifederalist camps. Women were left out completely, although even at that time some, such as Abigail Adams, argued for a more equal role. African American slaves, of course, were almost wholly excluded from politics, although free blacks in some northern states were accorded full citizenship rights.[13] Native Americans too were left out of the process of writing and ratifying the Constitution, because the Indian tribes were regarded as foreign nations.

The fight between the Federalists and the Antifederalists was hardly a fair one. With their superior political skills and greater talents, the Federalists were able to set the agenda and dominate the debate. This point was not lost on the Antifederalists, who complained bitterly that they had been "browbeaten by many of those . . . [who] think themselves . . . of Superior rank."[14] The Federalists caught their opponents off guard and kept them on the defensive throughout the battle.

The Federalists' Vision

The Federalists set out their political philosophy most clearly in a series of newspaper articles written during the debate over the ratification of the Constitution in New York. Together they are known as the *Federalist Papers,* and they remain one of the most innovative and important works in American political theory. They were written by Alexander Hamilton, James Madison, and John Jay. Following the custom of the day, they were published under a pseudonym, "Publius"—derived from the Latin for "the people."

The American Experiment   To the Federalists, the Constitution was an extraordinary experiment in self-government. Whether or not their experiment would succeed was very much an open question—largely because the idea of self-government itself was a novelty in the modern world. That the people of a nation could choose their form of government had until then been more a matter of theory than practice.

 The Federalists did not simply want human beings to govern themselves—they wanted them to do so intelligently and justly. The problem, as John Jay put it, is that human beings are "ambitious, vindictive, and rapacious." Popular assemblies would almost always succumb to the power of passion. "Pure democracies," wrote Madison, "have ever been spectacles of turbulence and commotion; have ever been found incompatible with personal security or the rights of property; and have in general been as short in their lives as they have been violent in their deaths."[15]

Successful self-government thus required that the people govern *indirectly,* by electing officials to represent them. But it was dangerous and foolhardy to assume that those in charge of the government would be immune to human frailties and weaknesses. They too would be self-interested, power hungry, and ambitious. Thus the Federalists were left with the age-old problem of how to control the government. Making the government weak was no answer, since the weakness of the national government was the fatal flaw of the Articles of Confederation.

Curing the Mischiefs of Faction   The most difficult challenge facing the Federalists was to devise what Madison called "a republican remedy for the diseases most incident to republican government."[16] The most serious disease was the existence of factions, and Madison devoted the whole of *Federalist No. 10* to discussing its causes and cures.

A **faction,** according to Madison, is a group of individuals motivated by "some common interest or passion" that is harmful to the rights of others or to the long-term interests of the community. Factions could be large or small, but their existence was unavoidable. The "causes of faction," Madison wrote, are "sown in the nature of man"; give people the freedom to think and to act, and they will naturally come together with others and seek to advance their mutual interests. Only the truly extraordinary would take the long-term view or bother to balance their own interests against the public interest or the demands of justice.

It was impossible to eliminate factions without destroying liberty, so it was essential to find a way to control them. Small factions could be controlled easily by democracy itself. If a small group had an interest at odds with that of the majority, it would simply be outvoted. The problem was large factions, especially majority factions, because they could use the democratic process to take control of the government. As experience showed, they often did.

Since pure democracies could not control factions, the solution was to create a republic, or representative democracy, instead. In a republic, the people would govern only indirectly, through their elected representatives. Furthermore, a republic could be larger than a democracy. Together these two differences would weaken the effectiveness of majority factions and dilute their influence.

Representation. Madison's argument was based on a radically new interpretation of the very idea of representation. The purpose of representation was not to "re-present" the views of the whole population, but instead to pass them through a filter composed of the wisest and most responsible citizens. The representatives of the people were expected to decide public issues as they—not their constituents—thought best. Furthermore, Madison reasoned that a small representative assembly would create an atmosphere more conducive to deliberation and discussion than the rough-and-tumble atmosphere of large assemblies. "Had every Athenian been a Socrates," he wrote, "every Athenian assembly would still have been a mob." In the relatively small houses of Congress (originally sixty-five representatives and twenty-six senators), Madison hoped, reason would have a chance to prevail.

Expanding the Republic. The influence of factions would be further weakened by creating one large republic instead of many small ones. Traditionally, popular governments were confined to small geographic areas, like the Athenian city-state. By contrast, Madison argued that bigger was better.

Large republics were superior to small democracies for three reasons. First, in a large republic with large representative districts, each member of the legislature would represent a more diverse mix of people. A small district might be dominated by a single ethnic, religious, or economic interest group, allowing its members to act as a majority faction and elect one of their own to represent them. In a large district, however, no one interest group would prevail. Second, while a particular group might constitute a majority at the state or local level, it would be reduced to one minority among many when forced to operate at the national level. Finally, a large republic would make factions less likely to form in the first place. If a common impulse of passion did exist among a majority, it would "be more difficult for all who feel it to discover their own strength, and to act in unison with each other." Remember that in 1787, news could take days or even weeks to travel from Philadelphia to Charleston. By then, the passions of the Philadelphians might have cooled considerably. In addition, Madison argued, citizens in faraway places would be less likely to trust each other and thus less likely to act in concert.

"Founding Fathers! How come no Founding Mothers?"

Human Nature and the Separation of Powers   As we have seen, the Federalists gave the national government tremendous powers. Having created a government that was strong enough to control the governed and carry out its due responsibilities, they then had to ensure that the government would be "obliged to control itself." The Federalists found the solution to this problem in the doctrine of the separation of powers.

Federalists and Antifederalists alike took it as a fundamental principle of government that "the legislative, executive, and judicial departments should be separate and distinct, in all free governments."[17] Furthermore, as in Great Britain, every state in the Union had established particular institutions corresponding to each of these powers. The problem was that neither the British Constitution nor that of any American state "separated" powers in any strict sense. In every case the executive branch could be found to possess *some* legislative and judicial powers, the legislative branch *some* judicial and executive power, and the judicial branch *some* legislative and executive power. Even constitutions that declared the three branches to be completely distinct from one another allowed some degree of mixing and blending.

For the Antifederalists, this mixing and blending merely underscored the imperfections inherent in any actual system of government. For the Federalists, however, and especially for Madison, the overlap of powers among the three branches was not a flaw at all, but the very basis of the system. By making the three branches compete directly with each other, Madison hoped to force them to control each other. The key was Madison's insight into human nature.

Politicians, Madison realized, were by nature ambitious. Given the opportunity, they would resist any threats to their own power. The members of one branch of government thus had a personal incentive to resist the members of the other branches. All that was necessary was that the members of each branch be given the constitutional means to resist the others, and the rest would take care of itself. Is Congress overstepping the bounds of its authority? The president, concerned for his own power, will exercise a veto. Is the president interfering with the administration of justice? The courts, in self-defense, will declare such

Is the Constitution Democratic?

The Constitution has been attacked as antidemocratic since it was first proposed for adoption in 1787. To the Antifederalists, as the historian Gordon S. Wood has written, "the constitution was 'so essentially differing from the principles of the revolution and from freedom' that it was unbelievable that it could have even been proposed." Time and time again the opponents of the Constitution decried it as part of a grand scheme "by a few *tyrants* . . . to lord it over the rest of their fellow citizens, to trample the poorer part of the people under their feet, that they may be rendered their servants and slaves."*

It is easy to take it for granted that the Constitution is designed to promote and protect democracy. But critics have continued to echo the Antifederalists' chief complaint for over two hundred years. "Is the Constitution democratic?" is as relevant a question today as it was in 1787.

The Constitution is not democratic

The case against the Constitution can be briefly stated:

- *The American constitutional system is designed to frustrate and override the views of the majority.* The Framers' feared majority factions, and equated democracy with mob rule. Pure democracies, Madison wrote, "have ever been spectacles of turbulence and contention; have ever been found incompatible with personal security or the rights of property; and have in general been as short in their lives as they have been violent in their deaths."† Thus they built into their system of government innumerable barriers to government by the people. The people were represented directly only in the House of Representatives, and even that body was designed with safeguards to allow its members to resist the day-to-day whims and passions of the people.

- *The Constitution protected slavery, ignored women, and provided no protections for Native Americans.* The modern complaint that the American political system sanctions discrimination against racial minorities and women is nothing new. Even in the 1780s, opponents of slavery balked at the Framers' refusal to take a stand against slavery, and Abigail Adams—whose husband John was a leading advocate of the Constitution—was not alone in opposing the legal subjection of women. ("I desire you would Remember the ladies," she had written John in 1776. "Do not put such unlimited power in the hands of the Husbands.") Nor did the Constitution make any serious effort to protect the rights of Native Americans.

- *The Constitution enshrines an economic system which favors the wealthy and guarantees inequality.* Although historians have debunked the idea that all the supporters of the Constitution were wealthy (see the box, An Economic Interpretation of the Constitution, on page 38), the constitutional system nonetheless made every effort to protect the well-off and said nothing about aiding the rest. The Federalists made no secret of their views; the proposed constitutional system, wrote

actions unconstitutional. Without the friction caused by the three branches fighting over the same turf, ambition could not counteract ambition.[18]

The great side effect of this system of checks and balances is the protection of liberty. Congress may check the president only because its ambitious members fear for the loss of their own power, but so what? The important thing is that the president is checked by someone, for whatever reason, and that the rights of the people are preserved. Madison's theory borrows heavily from the philosophy of Adam Smith, the Scottish advocate of mod-

Madison, was designed to frustrate "[a] rage for paper money, for an abolition of debts, for an equal division of property, or for any other improper or wicked project."‡

Arguments against affirmative action

Supporters of the Constitution answer its critics point-by-point:

- *The Framers opposed direct democracy, but ensured that all power flowed from the people.* The authors of the *Federalist Papers,* for example, were explicit about their support for the republican form of government, which they defined as "a government which derives all its powers directly or indirectly from the great body of the people, and is administered by persons holding their offices during pleasure for a limited period, or during good behavior." James Madison added: "It is *essential* to such a government that it be derived from the great body of society, not from an inconsiderable proportion or a favored class of it." The Framers' goal was to create a government that would advance the interests of all the people; the problem with direct democracy was that a majority faction could seize power and use it to override the rights of the minority or the long-term interests of the people.§
- *The original Constitution did permit slavery and discrimination, but a series of constitutional amendments and strong action by the national government have dramatically changed the character of the American political system.* Even the strongest supporter of the Constitution would admit that the original Constitution allowed the continued existence of slavery and did nothing to protect the rights of

women or other minorities. But the Constitution did provide a mechanism for constitutional amendments, and over the years its protections have been continually extended. In 1868, for example, the Constitution was amended to guarantee the "equal protection of the Laws"; in 1919 it was changed to ensure that women were not denied the right to vote. Moreover, Congress and the Courts have acted on numerous occasions to implement and expand these basic constitutional protections for women and minorities.

- *The Constitution "enshrines no particular economic philosophy" and allows the government to protect the economically disadvantaged.* Although the Constitution protects private property from arbitrary seizure by the government, it gives the national government broad discretion to implement social and economic policies deemed just and appropriate. Over the course of two centuries, Congress has moved frequently to regulate private economic activity in order to secure the public interest, and authorizes the government to implement such programs as social security and welfare to protect those at the bottom of the socioeconomic ladder. The Constitution's broad grants of power to the national government ensure that economic policies reflect changing circumstances and evolving ideas about economic efficiency and justice.

*Gordon S. Wood, *The Creation of the American Republic* (New York: W. W. Norton, 1969), pp. 499, 488.
†Federalist No. 10.
‡Ibid.
§Federalist No. 39

ern capitalism. The baker wakes up early in the morning, Smith wrote, not because he cares whether his fellow citizens starve to death (he might care, but why chance it?), but because he gets paid to do so. Just as the public benefits from the baker's private motive of greed, so too does it benefit from the politician's private motive of ambition.[19]

By transforming the separation of powers from an unworkable ideal into a practical system of checks and balances, Madison managed to overcome the most serious obstacle to legitimate government: human nature itself. "It may be a reflection on human nature," he wrote in a famous passage, "that such devices should be necessary to control the abuses of government. But what is government itself, but the greatest reflection on human nature? If men were angels, government would not be necessary. If angels were to govern men, neither external nor internal controls would be necessary."[20]

The Antifederalists: Defeat But Not Oblivion

The American constitutional plan, of course, was largely the work of the Federalists. The Antifederalists lost on almost every key issue except the Bill of Rights, and failed even to leave behind a great work, comparable to the *Federalist Papers,* to record their objections. The writings they did produce, like the views they expressed in the debate over the Constitution, were unsystematic and fragmented, and lacked the intellectual depth and vision of their opponents. Because they lost, moreover, history has treated them unkindly, neglecting their insights and contributions.

However, the Antifederalists deserve consideration. They insisted on adding a Bill of Rights to the Constitution. They correctly predicted that the balance between the states and the national government would, over time, tilt increasingly in the direction of the central government. They warned of the powers of the federal judiciary, of what was later called the imperial presidency, and of the dangers of a distant and unresponsive Congress.

The Antifederalists' influence persists in more subtle ways as well. Their essential views

Antifederalists in Modern Life?

The Antifederalists lost the struggle over the Constitution, but echoes of their views can still be heard in the American political debate. Ironically, both liberals and conservatives have picked up on key Antifederalist themes. For example:

- Vice President Dan Quayle caused controversy in 1992 by denouncing the cultural elite in America, echoing the rhetoric of Antifederalist critics of those who supported the Constitution in 1787. Elite bashing was also a favorite sport of Nixon's first vice president, Spiro Agnew, who attacked intellectuals and the press with zeal in the 1970s.

George Bush—although a graduate of Yale—tried to cultivate an antielitist image by stressing his passion for country music, pork rinds, and beer over Beethoven, caviar, and Chablis.

- Democratic attacks on big business and on corporate elites reflect Antifederalist concerns over the mercantile interests. In the 1993–1994 health care debate, for example, both Bill and Hillary Clinton made villains out of insurance companies—all the while lobbying for business support for their proposals.

- Like the Antifederalists, many modern conservatives look to religion and moral education for a solution to society's problems. Hence the importance of family values and prayer in modern political rhetoric. The Federalists, by contrast—like modern-day liberals—doubted the effectiveness of such an approach.

on politics have not disappeared and continue to appeal to a large percentage of the American electorate today. Consider the highlights:

- *Democracy.* The Antifederalists shared a deep belief in the basic instincts and sensibilities of the common people, and distrusted highly educated and wealthy elites. They resisted the Federalists' notion that the views of the people need to be refined and filtered before being enacted into public policy. To refine or filter the public's views, they argued, meant in reality to ignore them completely.

  The Antifederalists were aware of the dangers of majority factions. But they did not see majority factions as the most dangerous problem facing democratic government, fearing instead the tyranny of a rich and powerful minority.

- *Virtue.* The Antifederalists, like their opponents, admitted that the people suffered a constant temptation to act in their narrow self-interest, forgetting or trampling on the rights of others and the needs of the nation at large. In their view, however, the way to correct this situation was to attack it directly, by educating the people in their responsibilities to others and to the community. The goal was to instill what the Antifederalists called "republican virtue," "civic virtue," or simply "virtue." Virtue could be preserved, in their view, only by forging close attachments to a small community. The keys to creating a virtuous citizenry was the education of children and the influence of family and religion. Thus children would learn—and adults would be reminded of—their duties as citizens.

  Perhaps the central feature of republican virtue was the quality of self-sacrifice— the ability, or even the desire, to overcome self-interest and act for the benefit of others, especially the whole community. The continuing importance of sacrifice is evident especially in times of war, when millions of citizens act in ways that are difficult to explain using Federalist psychology or political science.

- *Community.* The idea of virtue hints at the idea of community, a key concept in the Antifederalist scheme. The Federalists sought to dilute the importance of local majorities, preferring to shift decision-making power to the more diverse arena of national politics. For the Antifederalists, however, the ability of local communities to control their own destinies was paramount. From the Pilgrims forward, Americans had followed a strong tradition of *separatism*—a doctrine with religious roots that encouraged like-minded citizens to create their own communities and run them their own way. The separatist tradition was closely linked to a deep religious and social conservatism that favored small communities strictly isolated from the "contaminating" influences and ideas of big cities. The desire to escape the corrupting influence of liberal Holland, after all, was a key motivating factor in the Pilgrims' move to America in the first place.

The differences between Federalists and Antifederalists were profound and fundamental, but one should not lose sight of the essential principles on which the two groups could agree. Madison himself agreed that "to suppose that any form of government will secure liberty or happiness without any virtue in the people is a chimerical [or illusory] idea"; at a minimum, the people had to have sufficient "virtue and intelligence to select men of virtue and wisdom" to lead them.[21] The Antifederalists, for their part, recognized the dangers of unchecked majority rule and insisted on some degree of checks and balances. Both believed the purpose of legitimate government to be the protection of the lives, safety, and liberties of the people, and both believed in the rule of law.

The foundations of American government were laid by the Federalists. But, as the political scientist Herbert J. Storing wrote, "the Anti-Federalist reservations echo through American history; and it is in the dialogue, not merely in the Federalist victory, that the country's principles are to be discovered."[22]

Summary

The United States Constitution was approved by the Constitutional Convention of 1787 and went into effect upon ratification by nine states in 1788. It replaced the Articles of Confederation, which was widely regarded as deeply flawed.

The Constitution was a fundamentally new charter of government. It greatly strengthened the power of the national government over commerce and in many other areas. It established an independent executive branch, headed by the president, and an independent judiciary, headed by the Supreme Court. Although it added significantly to the powers of Congress, it divided the legislative power into two branches—the House of Representatives, which was elected by the people, and the Senate, which represented the states. Above all, it rejected the idea that the states were sovereign and declared instead the sovereignty of the people and the supremacy of the Constitution over state laws.

The Framers of the Constitution, who called themselves Federalists, included such key figures as James Madison of Virginia and Alexander Hamilton of New York. Their opponents, including Thomas Jefferson, called themselves Antifederalists and favored only modest changes in the Articles of Confederation. The Framers sought to create a system of government that would be powerful and efficient, yet would control itself and not infringe on the liberties of the people. Thus even as they strengthened the powers of the national government, the Framers built in key checks and balances. These included the separation of powers, which allowed each branch of the government to check the others, and federalism, which allowed the states and the national government to check each other. At the urging of the Antifederalists, the Framers added to the Constitution the Bill of Rights, which explicitly protected certain rights from infringement by the national government.

The Federalists and Antifederalists differed in many ways. In general the Federalists were better educated and more cosmopolitan than their rivals. Their social outlook was aristocratic. Although they were not wholly pessimistic about human nature, the Federalists sought to create a system of government that would work even though neither the people nor their rulers were always virtuous. They were distrustful of the masses and feared above all the unchecked power of the majority. Thus they preferred to put power in the hands of those who, in their view, could best discern the public interest. Yet they were wholly committed to placing the ultimate political power in the hands of the people.

The Antifederalists, by contrast, identified far more closely than their rivals with the common people. They feared a strong and distant national government, especially one led by men who viewed themselves as the upper crust of society. They were opposed to many aspects of the new Constitution. They objected to the Federalists' decision to scrap the Articles of Confederation and begin over again; to the Federalists' loose interpretation of the separation of powers; to the absence of a Bill of Rights; and, above all, to the displacement of the states by the people as a whole as the building blocks of the Union.

Key Terms

United States Constitution

John Locke

Montesquieu

Magna Carta

Mayflower Compact

Declaration of Independence

Articles of Confederation

Annapolis Convention

Shays's Rebellion

Virginia Plan

New Jersey Plan

Great Compromise

Federalism

Separation of powers

Checks and balances

Elastic Clause

Supremacy Clause

Bill of Rights

Judicial review

Federalists

Antifederalists

Faction

Review Questions

1. What were the main features and defects of the Articles of Confederation? How did the Constitution seek to remedy the defects?

2. How did the Constitution compromise between the interests of large states and small states? Between slave states and free states?

3. What did James Madison mean by a "faction," and why did he especially fear majority factions? How does the Constitution seek to dilute the influence of majority factions?

4. Why is it more accurate to describe the Constitution as establishing not the separation of powers but rather a system of checks and balances?

5. What were the key differences between the Federalists and Antifederalists? Over what aspects of the Constitution did they disagree most vehemently?

Suggested Readings

Bowen, Catherine Drinker. *Miracle at Philadelphia: The Story of the Constitutional Convention, May to September 1787.* Boston: Little, Brown, 1966.

Congressional Research Service, Library of Congress. *The Constitution of the United States of America: Analysis and Interpretation.* Senate Document 99-16. 1990 Supplement, Senate Document 100-9. Washington, D.C.: United States Government Printing Office, 1991.

Farrand, Max. *The Framing of the Constitution of the United States.* New Haven: Yale University Press, 1934.

Gillespie, Michael Allen, and Michael Lienesch, eds. *Ratifying the Constitution.* Lawrence: University Press of Kansas, 1989.

Hamilton, Alexander, John Jay, and James Madison. *The Federalist Papers.*

Kammen, Michael. *A Machine That Would Go of Itself.* New York: Vintage Books, 1987.

Marshall, Burke, ed. *A Workable Government? The Constitution After 200 Years.* New York: W. W. Norton, 1987.

Storing, Herbert J. *What the Antifederalists Were For.* Chicago: University of Chicago Press, 1981.

Wood, Gordon S. *The Creation of the American Republic, 1776–1787.* New York: W. W. Norton, 1972.

Internet Resources

Annotated text of U.S. Constitution, with links to key cases at:

http://www.findlaw.com/casecode/constitution/

Full text of the Federalist Papers, available for download at:

http://www.mcs.net/~knautzr/fed/fedpaper.html

Non-partisan, non-profit organization "created to engage all Americans in our Constitution, its history, and its relevance to our daily lives" at:

http://www. constitutioncenter.org/8A1.html

Constitutional text, with links to biographies of the signers of the Constitution of 1787, at:

http://www.nara.gov/exhall/charter/constitution/ constitution.html

★ 3 ★

Federalism

Can Congress force state and local officials to carry out the programs and policies of the national government? That was the question presented by two county sheriffs who challenged the Brady Handgun Violence Prevention Act, which required them (and other state and local law enforcement officials) to conduct routine "background checks" on would-be handgun purchasers. The sheriffs conceded that Congress could regulate the sale of handguns, but argued that the Constitution barred the national government from using state and local officials, without compensation, to achieve its objectives.

In the 1997 case of *Printz* v. *United States,* the Supreme Court agreed. Writing for a narrowly divided Court, Justice Antonin Scalia laid down the law in no uncertain terms. "The Federal Government may neither issue directives requiring the States to address particular problems, nor command the States' officers, or those of their political subdivisions, to administer or enforce a federal regulatory program," he wrote. If the national government wants criminal background checks on prospective gun purchasers, Scalia concluded, it can do them itself; ask the states to cooperate voluntarily; or purchase compliance by paying the states for their services.

For Scalia and his colleagues in the majority, the national government's attempt to "commandeer" state and local officials into its service struck at the heart of the American principle of federalism, which divides power between the states and the national government. "Although the States surrendered many of their powers to the new Federal Government," Scalia concluded, they did not give up their independent existence or the ultimate power to control their own affairs.

The Court's opinion called forth a blistering dissent from Justice John Paul Stevens. "There is not a clause, sentence, or paragraph in the entire text of the Constitution of the United States that supports the proposition that a local police officer can ignore a command contained" in a valid congressional enactment, he wrote; for nearly two hundred years, the Constitution has been interpreted as allowing Congress the widest possible choice of means to achieve its legitimate ends. For Stevens, the bottom line was clear: "If Congress believes that such a statute will benefit

James Brady, wounded in a 1981 assassination attempt against President Ronald Reagan, inspired the passage of the "Brady bill," which imposed federal controls on handguns—including the mandatory background check at issue in Printz v. United States.

the people of the Nation," the Court has no choice but to accept its judgment.[1]

The sharply contrasting opinions in the *Printz* case rekindled a long-standing debate on the appropriate relationship between the national government and the states. Finding the right balance between national and state power was the critical issue facing the Framers of the Constitution in 1787. The struggle over slavery, which led to the Civil War, was in large part a contest between the states and the national government. In this century, Washington has fought with the states over economic regulation, civil liberties, and civil rights.

Over the course of two hundred years, the national government has won most of its fights with the states. The course of American history reveals a clear shift of power from the states to the national government, especially in this century. Today the federal government exercises its influence in such diverse areas as labor relations, food and drug safety, environmental protection, money and banking, stock market regulation, and health policy—all areas that at one time were primarily the responsibility of the state governments. In other areas Washington plays an indirect role, by imposing conditions on grants of aid to the states.

The history of national-state relations in the United States is not simply about conflict, however. From the beginning, the states have cooperated with the national government and with each other in a wide variety of policy areas. Moreover, various aspects of the national system, especially the representation of states in the Senate, have reinforced the close connections between the two levels of government. State and local governments still maintain primary or shared responsibility in areas such as education, law enforcement, licensing (of drivers, motor vehicles, doctors, and hair stylists, for example), and property law. In other areas the state and national governments share responsibility, with neither dominant.

This chapter explores three themes. First, it traces the distribution of power between the states and the federal government from the founding period until the present. Second, it discusses the relationship between the national and state governments today, revealing a complex picture of conflict, cooperation, and competition. Finally, it examines the advantages and disadvantages for self-government of dividing power between the states and the national government.

Questions to Keep in Mind

✔ *What was the Federalists' view of the proper balance between state and national power? How and why did they seek to achieve that balance? What was the Antifederalist view of the relationship between the states and the national government?*

✔ *How has the relationship between the states and the national government changed over the course of American history? What factors have influenced the growth of national power over time?*

✔ *What are the advantages and disadvantages of federalism? Of state-centered federalism versus nation-centered federalism?*

Basic Concepts ★ ★ ★ ★ ★ ★ ★ ★ ★ ★ ★ ★ ★

The Meanings of Federalism

Few aspects of American government have been as controversial or as easily misunderstood as **federalism**. Confusion over the meaning of federalism and disagreement over its implications arose during the debate over the Constitution and have never ceased. To add to the problem, federalism in practice has never conformed precisely to any theoretical ideal.

Federalism and Its Alternatives

Federalism refers to a political system in which power is divided between the central government and its component parts—in the United States, between the national government and the states. Exactly how power should be divided, and how to resolve disputes over the distribution of power, are difficult questions. Because the answers to these questions vary, there are many different forms of federalism.

An alternative to federalism is a **unitary system,** in which all power is held by the central government. The opposite alternative is a **confederation,** in which the national government has no independent power and the subunits are in effect independent countries. In practice, even unitary governments can and do delegate power to local subunits. Likewise, the nations of a confederacy can and do work together in various cooperative arrangements. However, in both cases it is clear who has the final say about any question.

Federalists and Antifederalists

The Articles of Confederation, as the name implies, created a confederation, in which the thirteen states remained independent. Major decisions of the central government could be made only by a unanimous vote of all the states, meaning that each state retained almost complete control of its own destiny. Significantly, it was the states, and not the people, who were represented in Congress, and the national government could act on the people of a state only with that state's cooperation.

The advocates of the Constitution of 1787 sought to create a fundamentally new form of government. The old way of thinking held that there could be one, and only one, sovereign (or ultimate authority) in each political system. Either the states were sovereign, and linked in a confederation, or the national government was sovereign, and the states were merely convenient political subdivisions without independent political authority. The Federalists rejected this way of thinking, arguing instead that the true sovereign in America was the people. Under the Constitution, the people divided up their sovereign power, giving some to the national government and some to the states.

Figure 3.1
Systems of Government

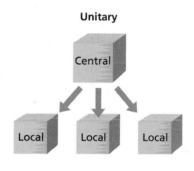

Unitary

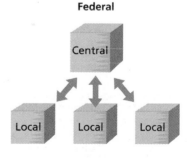

Federal

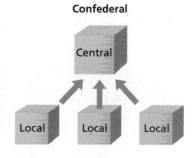

Confederal

The practical effect of the Federalists' theory was to enhance the power and influence of the national government.[2]

Oddly, the term *federalism* has come to mean the exact opposite of this usage. By modern standards, an advocate of federalism is one who believes in giving power to the states. Calls for a New Federalism, from Nixon to Reagan to the present day, have been attempts to turn back the tide of nationalism and return power to the states. The Federalist Society, to take another example, is a group of conservative lawyers and judges who generally oppose the expansion of national power.

The idea that the national government should play the predominant role in a federal system is known as *nation-centered federalism.* Its alternative, in which the states play the dominant role, is known as *state-centered federalism.*

Models of Federalism

By itself, the definition of federalism does not specify the exact relationship between the national government and the states. Not surprisingly, there have been many attempts over the years to create a more specific blueprint for the federal system. Several important models of federalism have evolved over the years. All of these models describe both how American federalism works (or worked) in practice and how it ought to work in theory.[3]

Dual or "Layer Cake" Federalism　　The constitutional theory favored by the Supreme Court in the nineteenth century was **dual federalism,** which recognized that both the states and the national government were supreme within their respective spheres of power. Dual federalism is also called **"layer cake" federalism.** Issues that required national uniformity or the combined resources of the nation—such as foreign policy or the control of navigation—were entrusted to the national government. Problems that could best be solved with reference to special local conditions or customs were left to the states.[4]

Dual federalism had the advantage of theoretical neatness, but in practice it was far less tidy. Drawing the line between state and national power was difficult, and often arbitrary. For example, the Court banned the states from most forms of railroad regulation, but permitted the states broad authority to regulate roads and highways.[5] In addition, even in the 1800s many powers were shared between the two levels of government, meaning that the two layers of the "layer cake" often blended into one another.

Cooperative or "Marble Cake" Federalism　　The weaknesses of the layer-cake model gave rise to a new metaphor. The model of **cooperative (or "marble cake") federalism** underscores the importance of cooperation between the two levels of government. It became especially popular after the 1930s, when the degree of cooperation between the states and national government became too apparent to ignore.

Advocates of cooperative federalism argue that society's problems are too difficult and complex to be

Figure 3.2 **Models of Federalism**

"Layer cake" or dual federalism emphasizes the independence of the federal government and the states, with each supreme in its own sphere. The federal government, however, is clearly the top layer: any valid federal action takes precedence over conflicting state actions. "Marble cake" or cooperative federalism emphasizes the importance of the federal and state governments working together to solve the complex problems facing the nation.

Dual federalism

Cooperative federalism

Federal and state law enforcement officials escort Timothy James McVeigh, charged in the April 1995 bombing of the Alfred Murrah federal building in Oklahoma City, from the Noble County Courthouse in Perry, Oklahoma. Federal and state officials cooperated in capturing McVeigh, who was later convicted and sentenced to death.

dealt with solely by the national or state governments alone. To achieve the best results, the two levels of government must work together. An obvious example is law enforcement. In solving a particular crime, state and local police officers can contribute a detailed knowledge of the local area and extensive contacts among the local population. The Federal Bureau of Investigation, by contrast, can provide technical expertise such as DNA fingerprinting analysis, coordination with local police in other parts of the country, and the enormous financial and manpower resources of the national government. Working together, local and national officials can often solve crimes that neither could solve alone.

Creative Federalism   An approach that gained acceptance in the 1950s and 1960s was **creative federalism,** which called for cooperation between state and national governments, along with the private sector, to solve problems like poverty and urban decay. Creative federalism stressed the need for new and innovative solutions that could be developed in one area of the country and then exported elsewhere. The federal government's role was to provide funding, coordination, and technical expertise. The creative federalism model was really an extension of cooperative federalism, although in general it envisioned a larger federal role than had previously been called for.

New Federalism   In the early 1970s, President Richard M. Nixon moved to shift creative federalism in the direction of state-centered federalism, calling this new approach the **New Federalism.** Acting on the view that the federal government had grown too strong and too intrusive into the affairs of the states, Nixon pushed the national government to return power to the states without reducing federal funding for various programs. Although Nixon made some headway in this area, his policies managed only to slow, rather than reverse, the flow of power to the national government.

Nixon's efforts were redoubled under President Ronald Reagan. Reagan's New Federalism (we might call it the *New* New Federalism) emphasized a smaller role for the national government in general, including reduced financial support for the states. Like Nixon, Reagan was only partially successful in his efforts. Advocates of the Nixon-Reagan approach to federalism got a major boost in 1994, with the election of a Republican Congress strongly committed to returning power to the states. The Republican Congress, with the approval of President Clinton, returned power to the states in several policy areas, including welfare and health care.

Table 3.1
Number of Governmental Units in the United States, 1992

United States	1
States	50
Counties	3,043
Municipalities / Cities	19,296
Towns / Townships	16,666
School districts	14,556
Special districts	33,131
Total	**86,743**

Federalism Under the Constitution

The original Federalists made sure that the Constitution created a strong national government. They not only expanded the powers of the national government but also specifically reduced state power in key areas. Moreover, they made sure that disputes over the appropriate boundaries of state and national power would be decided by the Supreme Court—a tribunal that is itself a part of the national government.

Increased Powers of the National Government   As Chapter 2 made clear, the Constitution greatly increased the powers of the national government. First, it expanded the scope of national authority in many areas, especially the regulation of commerce. Second, it gave the national government independent executive and judicial branches, allowing it to carry out and enforce its own laws. Third, it expressly declared the Constitution and laws of the United States to be supreme over state laws and state constitutions.

In addition, the Necessary and Proper Clause gave the federal government ample means to carry out its legitimate responsibilities, and the Supremacy Clause ensured that valid federal laws would take precedence over any state laws or constitutions. Thus no state can interfere with the legitimate exercise of federal authority.

Restrictions on State Power   The Constitution also boosted national power by banning all state involvement in certain policy areas. For example, the states were prohibited from making treaties with foreign countries and were denied the power to coin money or levy taxes on imports or exports. Other restrictions, although not set out explicitly in the Constitution, were added later through judicial interpretation. The federal government's power over interstate commerce, for example, was held in many cases to prohibit state regulation even when Congress had chosen not to exercise its power.

Shared and Reserved Powers   In many cases constitutional power is shared between the state and national governments. Either government can exercise such **shared powers,** or both can do so, even at the same time. Examples of shared powers include tax collection and law enforcement. In addition, many areas of state and national responsibility necessarily overlap. National regulation of commerce, for example, may overlap with state regulation of health and safety. The large number of shared and overlapping powers makes cooperation between the national and state governments a high priority.

A few powers are specifically retained by the states and denied to the national government. These are known as **reserved powers.** For example, no new states can be formed by the carving up or combining of existing states without the consent of the affected state legislatures, nor can any state be deprived of its equal representation in the Senate. Under the Twenty-first Amendment, states are given complete control over intoxicating liquors. The Tenth Amendment serves as a reminder that powers "not delegated to the United States by the Constitution, nor prohibited by it to the States, are reserved to the States respectively, or to the people." Finally, the Supreme Court has recognized that the states possess a "residual sovereignty"—powers left to them by the Constitution and upon which Congress may not impose. The states' residual sovereignty includes the right to say no to federal demands for assistance in implementing or enforcing national programs.

Some powers are denied to both the states and the national government. These include the prohibitions of the Bill of Rights. Also included are a ban on *ex post facto laws,* which retroactively make it illegal to do something that was legal when it actually occurred, and on *bills of attainder,* which are laws that convict a person of a crime without benefit of trial.

The Supreme Court as Umpire of the Federal System The Framers made sure that disputes over the meaning of the Constitution and over the appropriate boundaries of state and national power would be resolved by the federal government itself, through the agency of the United States Supreme Court. Because Supreme Court justices are nominated by the president and confirmed by the United States Senate, they have been generally sympathetic to the idea of a strong national government. Although there have been dramatic exceptions—including a few in recent years—over the long haul the Court has generally sided with the national government in its disputes with the states.

A History of Federalism Under the Constitution

The long-term history of federalism under the Constitution shows a dominant trend toward nation-centered federalism. Movement in this direction has been neither steady nor consistent, however, and until well into the twentieth century the national government played a relatively minor role in the lives of ordinary people.

The road to nation-centered federalism was paved early on by the Supreme Court, which from the beginning has generally advocated an expansive definition of national power under the Constitution. But the motivating force behind nation-centered federalism has come from the presidency and Congress, which have acted at key moments to expand national power in many areas. The most dramatic expansion of national authority came during and after the Great Depression of the 1930s.

Chief Justice John Marshall, upon taking office in 1801. An ardent nationalist, Marshall had been wounded at Valley Forge and well knew the dangers of a weak and ineffective government. Over the course of his thirty-four-year career on the Court, Marshall's decisions strengthened the national government at the expense of the states.

The Marshall Era and the Foundations of National Power

Both Federalists and Antifederalists agreed that the national government had more power under the Constitution of 1787 than under the Articles of Confederation, but how much more became a matter of great debate.

The groundwork for a broad interpretation of national power under the Constitution was laid by Chief Justice **John Marshall,** himself a Federalist, whose Court career stretched from 1801 to 1835. Strongly supported by most of his fellow justices, Marshall first established the Court's power to decide key constitutional questions, then used that power both to restrict the states and to expand the powers of the Union.

Three early decisions established the Court's right to decide constitutional questions. In the 1803 case of *Marbury* v. *Madison,*[6] the Court claimed the power to judge the constitutionality of laws passed by Congress. Seven years later, in *Fletcher* v. *Peck,*[7] the Court expanded its authority to include review of state laws that might conflict with the Constitution. Finally, in the 1816 case of *Martin* v. *Hunter's Lessee,*[8] Marshall's colleague Joseph Story declared that the Supreme Court—and not the highest state courts—would have the final say over questions of federal law, including the meaning of the Constitution.

The Marshall Court now had two ways to enhance the power of the national government. First, it could strike down state laws that interfered with the authority of the federal government. Second, it could use its power of judicial review to *uphold* acts of Congress, thereby helping to erase any doubts about their legitimacy. In his thirty-four years on the Court, Marshall led his colleagues in using both techniques. The Court struck down a number of state laws that conflicted with his nationalistic vision of the Constitution, and upheld every act of Congress that came before him except one—the minor provision of the Judiciary Act of 1789 at stake in *Marbury* itself.

In the 1819 case of **McCulloch** v. **Maryland,** Marshall used both powers. First, he upheld the constitutionality of the Bank of the United States, even though the Constitution nowhere gave Congress the power to charter a bank or even to establish a corporation. Marshall grounded his decision on the Necessary and Proper Clause, which gives Congress the power to enact all laws "necessary and proper for carrying into Execution" its other powers under the Constitution. Rejecting arguments that this provision was intended as a limitation on congressional power, Marshall ruled that the clause allows Congress wide latitude in choosing the means for carrying out its delegated powers. "Let the end be legitimate," he wrote, "let it be within the scope of the Constitution, and all means which are appropriate, which are plainly adapted to that end, which are not prohibited; but consist [sic] with the letter and spirit of the Constitution, are constitutional."[9]

> *I do not think the United States would come to an end if we lost our power to declare an Act of Congress void. I do think the Union would be imperiled if we could not make that declaration as to the laws of the several states.*
>
> —Supreme Court justice Oliver Wendell Holmes, Jr., "Law and the Court" (1913)

In the same case, Marshall also struck down a Maryland law that interfered with the operations of the national bank. Maryland had imposed a tax on securities issued by any bank within the state. Although the tax amounted to only $15,000 (not an enormous sum even by nineteenth-century standards), Chief Justice Marshall rejected it as unconstitutional. Declaring that "the power to tax involves the power to destroy," Marshall ruled that states could not tax the operations of the federal government. The bank tax was unconstitutional, Marshall ruled, because "the Constitution, and the laws made in pursuance thereof, shall be the supreme law of the land."[10]

The Supreme Court advanced the cause of nationalism in another important case in 1824. In **Gibbons** v. **Ogden,**[11] Marshall took a sweeping view of the Commerce Clause, which gives Congress control over "commerce among the states." The Constitution did not define commerce, nor did it provide a rule for deciding where local commerce ended and national commerce began. Also unclear was whether the states could make regulations that had a direct or even incidental impact on interstate commerce.

Marshall had few doubts. He interpreted commerce broadly, to include navigation as well as commercial activities, and ruled that the federal government could regulate any commerce "which concerns more states than one." Only those activities that were "completely within a state," did not affect another state, and did not concern the interests of the national government were immune from federal regulation.

Political Developments   Although the Marshall Court gave the national government broad constitutional authority, the national government's role remained relatively small. In general the national government focused on foreign affairs, economic matters, and "internal improvements"—building roads, buildings, canals, and the like. The national bureaucracy started off small but grew steadily, from approximately one thousand civilian employees in the 1790s to more than eleven thousand by the 1830s. Still, federal programs remained modest and were easily financed by customs duties, proceeds from western land sales, and taxes on liquor and other commodities.

Because the national government's programs were so limited, interactions between the state and national governments were relatively minor. In general, the two spheres of government remained clearly distinct, closely following the dual federalism model. Opportunities for both conflict and cooperation between the states and the national government were equally limited.[12]

The Challenge to National Power

Many of the decisions of the Marshall Court were highly controversial. Although Marshall faced little opposition within the Supreme Court, he was bitterly opposed by those who feared the kind of powerful national government he sought to create. Among Marshall's fiercest critics were President Thomas Jefferson and Virginia Supreme Court Justice Spencer Roane.

The Theory of States' Rights   In the seventy years between the adoption of the Constitution and the outbreak of the Civil War, these and other critics of national power presented a continual challenge to the developing theory of national supremacy. Along the way, they developed several theories designed to block the growth of the national government. Collectively, these doctrines constituted the theory of **states' rights**.

The two most important states' rights doctrines in the pre-Civil War era were **nullification** and **interposition.** Advocates of nullification—including John C. Calhoun of South Carolina—argued that each state had the right to nullify the actions of the federal government by acting in a special convention called for the purpose. Supporters of interposition claimed that the states could take direct action to prevent enforcement of unconstitutional national policies, thus "interposing" the state between the people and the national government. For example, Calhoun argued that the southern states should prevent the national government from delivering abolitionist propaganda in the mails.

The Civil War Crisis   These early skirmishes over national supremacy were only preludes to the main event. Building on Calhoun's theory, Southern leaders determined to maintain the institution of slavery eventually mounted the ultimate challenge to national supremacy, defending the states' right to secede from the Union altogether.

The legal case for secession rested on the argument that the states were supreme over, and indeed had created, the national government. Abraham Lincoln's unyielding opposition to the rebellion was in large part an expression of his belief that the states had no legal existence outside the Union and retained only those powers reserved to them by the national Constitution. In Lincoln's view, the national government could exercise power over any matter that concerned the whole nation, while the states could act only in matters of purely local concern.

The Union's victory on the battlefield dealt a severe blow to the doctrine of states' rights. After the war, the Thirteenth, Fourteenth, and Fifteenth Amendments created a constitutional basis for national intervention in what had been the internal affairs of the states—especially to protect the rights of the freed slaves and other minorities. It would be more than a century, however, before the national government put these powers into full operation.

The Struggle for National Supremacy

In the meantime, the battle for national supremacy shifted to the economic arena. Rapid economic, social, and technological change between 1870 and 1930 created serious problems for the nation and led to new opportunities for the exercise of national power. Throughout this period, Congress continually experimented with innovative applications of its constitutional powers.

There are countless examples of the national government's growing role in this period, especially in the area of economic regulation. Early on, Congress asserted control over the railroads, regulating rates and setting safety standards. The development of radio led to the creation of the Federal Communications Commission, with responsibility for licensing and monitoring broadcast stations. New federal laws regulated stockyards, the food and drug industries, and large corporate trusts. The banking system was overhauled and placed under the control of the Federal Reserve System, and the federal government's role in law enforcement was expanded, especially with the creation of a national investigation agency (later the Federal Bureau of Investigation) in 1908. In addition, the national government for the first time began to provide cash grants to the states, for purposes ranging from highway construction to agricultural extension services. All of these activities required money, leading to the amendment of the Constitution in 1913 to allow the creation of a national income tax.[13]

Despite its new roles and increased powers, the national government did not supplant the states as the primary locus of government power. In fact, the growth of the state governments kept pace with that of the national government. Areas of primary state responsibility included elementary and secondary education, public higher education, welfare, police and fire protection, and sanitation.[14] The states also expanded their roles in health and safety regulation and consumer protection.

For the most part, the Supreme Court accepted the growth of both state and national power. In certain areas, however, the Court was less accommodating. In particular, it was hostile to legislation designed to improve the wages and working conditions of laborers. For example, the Court struck down federal laws banning child labor, guaranteeing a minimum wage to women, and prohibiting "yellow dog" contracts, in which workers gave up their right to join a union. The Court also invalidated a number of similar state laws.[15]

The onset of the Great Depression brought the question of Congress's regulatory power to a head. When President Franklin D. Roosevelt took office in March 1933, the nation was mired in an economic crisis of epic proportions. Nearly one of every four Americans was unemployed; the stock market had lost 75 percent of its value; millions had lost their homes, farms, and life savings.[16] Roosevelt led Congress in passing a wide array of new federal initiatives, including laws regulating agriculture, the stock market, and various industries. Roosevelt's **New Deal** also reenacted many of the progressive labor reforms that had previously been rejected by the Supreme Court, including minimum wage and collective bargaining laws. The economic crisis prompted the states to expand their role in economic regulation as well, supplementing and augmenting the national government's response.

The employment of children—even in dangerous occupations such as coal mining, as in this 1903 photograph—was a common practice in the United States until well into the twentieth century.

At first the Supreme Court tried to block the New Deal, striking down a dozen important new programs in 1935 and 1936 alone. In 1937, however, the Court changed its mind, holding that both the state and national governments had broad powers to cope with changing economic circumstances. Accordingly, the Court upheld both state and federal laws governing a wide variety of economic issues, including minimum wages, the right to unionize, and the prohibition of child labor and substandard labor conditions.[17]

Federalism Since the New Deal

For decades after the New Deal, the Supreme Court backed away from any attempt to block state or national regulation on constitutional grounds. Although both levels of government were now free to expand their economic regulation, the national government benefited most. The nature of the federal system allowed the national government to override state laws that conflicted with its own policies, while forcing the states to accept whatever economic regulations Congress handed down.

Trends in Constitutional Federalism From 1937 until 1995, the Supreme Court did not find a single federal law to be in violation of the Commerce Clause. During this period, the Court consistently upheld Congress's authority to regulate even the most localized activities as long as they exerted a substantial effect on interstate commerce, however indirect. In 1948, for example, the Court upheld the conviction of a retail pharmacist under the federal Food, Drug, and Cosmetic Act for "misbranding" two pill boxes, containing twelve tablets, by failing to affix a required warning label. The Court adopted a similar approach to federal laws involving the environment, civil rights, and organized crime. So broad was the Court's interpretation of the Commerce Clause that many constitutional scholars concluded that there were no circumstances under which the Court would interfere with Congress's authority in this area.

In 1995, however, the Court proved the scholars wrong, ruling in *United States* v. *Lopez* that the federal Gun-Free School Zones Act of 1995 was unconstitutional. The Act made it illegal "knowingly to possess a firearm" in a school zone. Lopez, a high school senior, was convicted under the law for carrying a concealed .38 caliber handgun and five bullets on school premises.

Congress's Commerce Clause authority is broad, Chief Justice William Rehnquist admitted in his opinion for the Court, but it is not unlimited. "The possession of a gun in a local school zone is in no sense an economic activity that might . . . substantially affect any sort of interstate commerce," Rehnquist concluded. To allow Congress to punish Lopez would in effect concede that the federal government could regulate "each and every aspect of local schools." Justice Stephen Breyer, joined by three other justices, wrote a strong dissenting opinion.

Just where the *Lopez* opinion will lead is unclear. Congress's authority to regulate commerce remains broad, and the case may turn out to be a relatively inconsequential exception to the rule. If the Court builds on *Lopez* to nullify other federal laws, however, the case could mark the starting point of a new era of constitutional federalism. It may take years before the real meaning of the case is known.[18]

Two other aspects of economic regulation have caused constitutional controversy in recent years. The first involves federal efforts to regulate not activities within the states but the states themselves. In the 1976 case of *National League of Cities* v. *Usery,* the Court held that Congress could not use the commerce power to regulate traditional governmental functions, such as the wages paid to state employees. Critics of national power hoped that *National League of Cities* would usher in a new era of state autonomy, but within nine years the Court reversed itself and backed away. In *Garcia* v. *San Antonio Metropolitan Transit Authority,* the Court ruled that congressional regulation of state governments would be held to essentially the same standard as congressional regulation of the private sector, for the most part allowing Congress to regulate the states as it sees fit.[19] On the basis of *Garcia,* Congress has extended many federal regulations to cover the states as well as private individuals and corporations. For example, states must pay and withhold social security taxes on their employees, and must comply with federal laws covering pensions and benefits, the rights of the disabled, and family medical leave.

The other area of controversy involves federal efforts to require the states to enforce rules and regulations imposed by Congress. In the 1992 case of *New York* v. *United States,* the Supreme Court ruled that Congress cannot "simply commandee[r] the legislative processes of the States by directly compelling them to enact and enforce a federal regulatory program." Thus Congress could not force the State of New York to choose between taking over ownership of radioactive waste and implementing a regulatory scheme designed by Congress.[20] In 1997, the Supreme Court extended the reasoning of *New York* v. *United States,* holding in *Printz* v. *United States* that Congress could not force state and local law enforcement officials to perform background checks on prospective gun purchasers. Such a law, the Court ruled, violates the residual sovereignty left to the states under the Constitution. [21]

Federal grants provide an important mechanism by which Congress can induce the states to pursue the policies favored by the national government. Moreover, now that the states are accustomed to receiving federal money, Congress can use the threat of withholding funds as a way to pressure the states into compliance with national goals. When Congress wanted to convince the states to adopt a 21-year-old drinking age, for example, it threatened to withhold 5 percent of federal highway funds from any state that did not follow along. In 1987, the Supreme Court ruled that such a law was perfectly constitutional, at least so long as the federal policy merely offered the states a choice and did not coerce them into compliance.

The Era of Cooperative Federalism The period from 1937 to the 1960s saw the full flowering of cooperative federalism. Both the states and the national government expanded into many areas of social and economic life in a "continuous collaboration."[22] Local, state, and national officials worked together on a daily basis, sharing resources and decision-making authority. In general the national government sought to forge partnerships with the states rather than displace them altogether, a pattern that continues even today. Typically, the federal government set out broad guidelines for programs and provided much of the money. The states then were free to adapt the programs to fit local needs and would run the program on a day-to-day basis.

The national government chose the cooperative approach for several reasons:

- Including the states as partners may make social programs more acceptable to the people, many of whom remain suspicious of federal power.
- Giving the states a degree of control of social programs allows programs to be tailored to the particular conditions of states and local communities.
- Encouraging state participation permits valuable experimentation on a small scale, making it possible for the federal government to test new ideas without committing massive resources in advance.

The cooperative nature of this era should not be overstated, however. Building on the New Deal, the national government took over the major role in a number of important areas, including labor relations, the stock markets, electric power regulation, and banking. As federal grants increased, moreover, Washington's leverage over the states grew accordingly.

President Lyndon Baines Johnson's **Great Society** programs of the mid-1960s marked a period of particularly aggressive federal growth. Under Johnson, the government added new social programs to guarantee housing, food stamps, and medical care to poor and elderly citizens. Johnson also expanded the government's role in enforcing civil rights, especially in the South, and in promoting educational equality and opportunity.

President Lyndon Johnson holds out the newly signed bill establishing Medicare, one of the "Great Society" programs of the 1960s. Most of these programs were funded by Washington and administered jointly with the states.

Federal Grant Programs and the New Federalism The primary tools of cooperative federalism were federal grants, which involved a transfer of funds from the national to the state governments. Al-

Figure 3.3 **Federal Grants to the States**

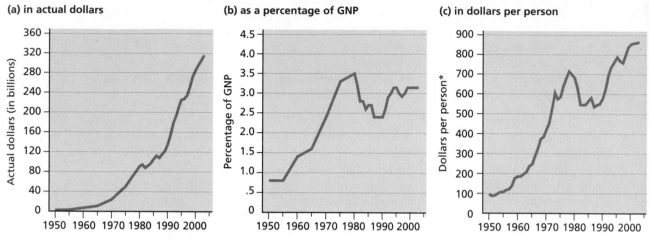

(a) in actual dollars

(b) as a percentage of GNP

(c) in dollars per person

SOURCE: FY 1999 Budget, Historical Tables, Table 12.1; 1997 Statistical Abstract, Tables 2, 3.

Figure 3.4 **Federal Grants by Function, 1940 and 1997**

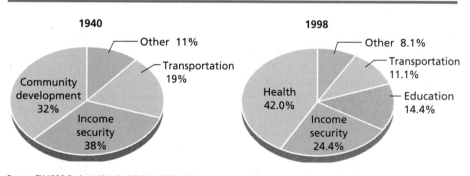

SOURCE: FY 1999 Budget, Historical Tables, Table 12.2

though the first federal grant programs date to the last century, the explosive growth of such programs dates only from the 1960s. Grant programs serve several purposes. They put federal money behind the goals set by Congress, establish minimum standards for state programs, allow for flexibility and innovation in implementation, and offer states a choice as to whether or not to participate.

Federal grants come in a variety of shapes and sizes. **Categorical grants** provide federal money for narrow and specific purposes, such as building new schools or new prisons. **Block grants** provide money for broad purposes, such as education or law enforcement, with relatively few strings attached. **Revenue sharing** simply transfers money from the federal government to the states, for use as the states see fit. In general, categorical grants allow the national government to fine-tune the details of social programs, whereas revenue sharing does not; block grants fall somewhere in the middle. Thus conservative opponents of large national programs have typically favored block grants or revenue sharing.

Figure 3.5 **State and Local Government Spending as a Percentage of Total Government Spending**

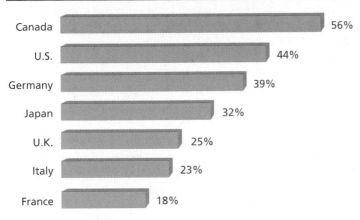

Canada	56%
U.S.	44%
Germany	39%
Japan	32%
U.K.	25%
Italy	23%
France	18%

NOTE: Percentages from 1989–1995

Grants can also be distinguished by the way they are allocated among different states and localities. *Formula grants* provide a set amount of money to each jurisdiction, according to specific rules, such as the size of a city or the number of citizens under the poverty line. *Project grants* provide money on a project-by-project basis, usually after an elaborate application procedure. Whatever their form, federal grants remain an important component of state and local finance.

In recent years the national government not only has given money to the states, but has taken it away—at least indirectly. Faced with a budget crisis of its own, Congress has increasingly implemented its programs through so-called unfunded mandates, which impose requirements on the states without paying for them. Unfunded mandates are partly responsible for the trend depicted in Figures 3.3 and 3.5: state expenditures are going up, while federal grants to the states are going down, at least on a per capita basis. In 1995, Congress approved legislation limiting the use of unfunded mandates in the future, and the impact of the *Printz* decision may make it more difficult for Congress to pass enforcement responsibilities onto the states.

Federalism Today: Cooperation and Conflict

From a theoretical point of view, Congress could take over most of all the programs currently run by the states. Congress could create a national drivers' license, take over many local police functions, license dentists and physicians, and even set up a national education system.

In practice, however, the states retain much of their power and independence. Congress *could* take over various state police functions, but it has not. It *could* set forth a comprehensive national education policy, but it has chosen to leave such decisions largely in the hands of state governments and local school boards. It *could* also enact rules to expand its influence over the nation's medical system, but instead it has left a great deal of room for the states, which still control the licensing of physicians and medical workers, make key public health decisions, and have primary responsibility for monitoring medical procedures and punishing malpractice.

Many aspects of modern federalism draw from the various models of federalism that dominated past eras in American history. As under dual federalism, policy areas remain in which the national and state governments operate independently of one another. As in the periods of cooperative and creative federalism, the two levels of government work closely together, with national grants still playing a major role in many programs. And, as always, the states and the national governments continue to fight with one another over what should be done, who should do it, and how it should be done.

Sorting out the state and federal roles in any given policy area is a complex and difficult task. This section aims at providing a broad overview of the federal-state relationship—one that is sometimes strained but often friendly, sometimes adversarial but often cooperative, sometimes inefficient and awkward but often smooth and productive.

It should be noted that the federal constitution makes no mention of local governments. For the purposes of federal constitutional law, local governments are treated as part and parcel of the state governments.

Primarily Local Functions

By tradition and practice, the states and local communities retain enormous power over a range of day-to-day activities. These include the following:

Public Education   From universities to kindergartens, public education in America is largely determined by state governments and local school boards. Washington's role is mainly to provide funds and give advice. The federal government funds a variety of specialized programs, including college loan and grant programs, school lunch programs, and special programs for the educationally disadvantaged. Even in these programs, much of the day-to-day administration is left to local schools and agencies.

Police and Fire Protection   Despite the rapid growth in federal criminal law, most law enforcement is still carried out by state, county, and local police agencies. Fire, ambulance, and other public safety activities are also matters of primarily local concern. Federal agencies (the Federal Bureau of Investigation, the Drug Enforcement Agency, and the Secret Service) work closely with local authorities, and provide special services such as advanced laboratory work. Many criminal activities, such as drug trafficking, involve both state and federal offenses. Only a few types of crime are handled exclusively by the federal government.

An important, if indirect, role in law enforcement is played by the federal courts, through the enforcement of such constitutional guarantees as due process of law and freedom from unreasonable searches and seizures. The Court's 1966 ruling in *Miranda* v. *Arizona,* for example, forced state and local police to warn suspects of their constitutional rights before questioning on alleged criminal activity.[23]

Basic Legal Codes and Procedures   Although the Constitution provided a federal court system to interpret and apply federal law, most basic legal problems and procedures are handled by the individual states. The states set their own rules concerning property owner-ship, marriages, divorce, enforcement of contracts, and ordinary civil lawsuits. States must follow the fundamental principles of the Constitution, and often choose to create uniform and consistent legal codes, but still the laws in one state may vary greatly from those in an-other. The Constitution's Full Faith and Credit Clause requires each state to respect legal proceedings—such as marriages and divorces—that occur in the other states.

Routine Services   Any local phone book reveals the range of basic services provided by state and local governments. They include the licensing of motor vehicles, drivers, and vari-ous professionals and businesses (from doctors and lawyers to hairdressers and restaurants); water and sanitation; building permits and inspections; and animal control. Various federal agencies provide funding and support services in connection with some of these functions.

Shared Functions

Many aspects of public policy are handled by a combination of local, state, and federal agencies. In many cases the federal government provides funding and sets out general rules, but the states actually administer the programs and can extend or limit services. Ex-amples include the following:

Public Health   Every level of government is involved in making and administering health policy. The federal government funds the lion's share of medical research, through the Na-tional Institutes of Health and various grant programs. It also funds the Medicare and Medicaid programs, which provide health care to the elderly and the poor. The Center for Disease Control coordinates national public health programs and policy and provides ex-pertise to state and local agencies. The Department of Veterans' Affairs provides a network of hospitals for the care of those who served in the armed forces.

The massive amount of federal money in the health system gives Washington extraor-dinary leverage and influence in health policy decisions. But the state and local govern-ments also play a key role, taking primary responsibility for community planning for health care; licensing and supervision of doctors, hospitals, and other providers; and mon-itoring the public health, including maintaining birth and death records, monitoring dis-ease outbreaks, and providing health education.

Public Works and Highways   Federal funding for public buildings, roads, airports, and other facilities gives Washington considerable influence over what is built, where, and how. Such spending is determined by Congress and various federal agencies, in cooperation with local officials and agencies. Federal grants typically require some amount of state matching funds; for example, states must match every nine dollars in interstate highway funds with one dollar of their own. Local authorities maintain and police federal highways, including interstates, but because of federal funding Washington exercises considerable influence over speed limits and other traffic rules.

Economic and Environmental Regulation   Despite the expansion of the federal gov-ernment's role in economic regulation after 1936, state laws continue to govern a wide array of economic activities. Anyone who travels from state to state will quickly recognize the impact of local differences.

New York State, for example, prohibits rental car companies from charging an optional collision insurance fee. California's standards for automobile emissions are far stricter than those imposed by the federal government. The legal relationship between workers and employers, although covered by an extensive network of federal laws, still varies from state to state.

Virtually every industry is regulated by both the federal and the state and local governments. Insurance companies must comply with federal rules concerning the soundness of their financial practices, but must follow state laws on rates and coverage. Drugstores must follow both state and federal regulations on controlled substances, and businesses in general must obey both state and federal environmental rules.

Primarily Federal Functions

The exclusive—or nearly exclusive—powers of the federal government are too numerous to list here. What follows is just a brief sampling.

Defense and Foreign Policy   The Constitution leaves defense and foreign policy almost entirely in the hands of the national government. The national government is responsible for recognizing foreign governments; sending and receiving ambassadors; declaring and waging war; making treaties and alliances; and raising and supporting an army and navy. The national government also regulates the importation of goods into the United States and controls the immigration and naturalization of noncitizens. The Constitution bars the states from entering into treaties or alliances, and prohibits them from engaging in war without the consent of Congress, "unless actually invaded." States are permitted to maintain National Guard units to deal with local emergencies. Guard units can be called into the service of the national government by order of the president.

Air Transportation, Radio, and Television   The federal government is chiefly responsible for the regulation of industries that are national in scope or whose efficiency requires uniform standards and regulation. These include air transportation, industries depending on the airwaves (such as radio and television), and railroads. Even in these industries, however, Congress has allowed room for state regulation when only local matters are involved. Thus local governments continue to provide airport police services, but security inspections of baggage and passengers are under federal control. Congress can always flex its muscles when it feels the need, of course. In 1991, for example, it extended federal regulation to basic cable television rates, which had previously been regulated only by state and local governments.

Dormant Commerce Power   In many cases the federal courts have prohibited state efforts to regulate commerce even in areas where Congress has chosen not to regulate. In such areas the courts presume that Congress's inaction constitutes a deliberate decision to avoid all regulation, state or federal.

States remain free to make local regulations that are essential to the public health or safety, but such rules must be specifically and carefully justified in every instance. Thus a state can prevent diseased meat from entering its boundaries, but it cannot prohibit the flow of out-of-state waste to its landfills. In drawing this distinction, the Supreme Court reasoned that the diseased meat created the specific danger of contagion to local herds, whereas the out-of-state waste products were no more dangerous than those produced within the state.[24]

Does Federalism Matter?

Is there, in practice, any real difference between a federal system and one in which the state governments are merely subdivisions of the central authority?

The short answer is yes: federalism does matter. In some ways federalism improves the efficiency of government. In other ways it creates confusion, duplication, and inefficiency. The following discussion focuses not on the theory of federalism, but on an analysis of how federalism really works in the United States.

Advantages of Federalism

The main advantages of federalism lie in its ability to provide uniformity when a national standard is necessary or desirable, while still allowing for flexibility and a concern for local conditions and customs when appropriate. The balance between state and national functions is hardly perfect, of course. But the federal system still goes a long way toward accommodating the conflicting needs of uniformity and diversity.

Flexibility   What works for Mississippi may not work for Massachusetts; what is good for Arkansas may not be good for Alaska. A federal system allows different states and communities to adapt to varying conditions and traditions. At the same time, the strong central government can move in to solve common problems or enforce common standards of justice. For the New York police to follow the same rules and procedures as a rural sheriff's office in the Southwest, for example, would be disastrous. However, the federal courts can help ensure that both police forces follow the basic rules of criminal procedure laid out in the Constitution, and that all those accused of a crime are afforded due process and equal protection under the law.

Experimentation   A new idea can be developed and tested at the local level. If it works, it can be adopted by other states or even by the federal government. Years ago the state of Wisconsin experimented with a progressive income tax; it worked, and the idea soon spread to other states and to the federal government. Currently, different states are experimenting with innovative solutions to the national health care problem. When President Bill Clinton proposed a national system of free vaccinations for needy children in 1993, for instance, he could draw on the experience of similar programs in several states.

A bad idea, of course, can be quietly laid to rest without its negative effects spreading beyond the local or state level.

Competition   Just as the capitalist economic system encourages efficiency through competition of private individuals and corporations, so too the federal system encourages efficiency through competition of different states. When a foreign corporation is choosing an American site for a new manufacturing plant, for example, it can enjoy the benefits of several states competing to attract its attention. Much of this competition consists simply of tax giveaways and other financial incentives, but it may also stimulate the states to improve education, job training, and infrastructure.

Should Welfare Be Controlled by the States?

A long-standing debate over federalism came to a head with the election of a Republican-controlled Congress in 1994. With the cooperation of President Bill Clinton, the new Congress dramatically overhauled federal welfare policy, shifting major responsibilities from the national government to the states.

The new welfare law replaced the Aid to Families with Dependent Children (AFDC) with a new program called Temporary Assistance to Needy Families (TANF). Unlike AFDC, which was a tightly controlled federal program, TANF gives the states money in the form of block grants, and allows the states great latitude in deciding how to spend it.

The new law is highly controversial, and remains the subject of intense debate. At stake is not only the future of welfare policy, but whether the TANF model will be applied to other areas of social policy, especially health care.

Arguments for block grants

Opportunity for experimentation. Actually, the states had been experimenting with new welfare ideas since 1992, when the Bush administration began granting state-by-state waivers, permitting departures from standard federal policies. States used waivers to try out a wide range of strategies designed to reform the nation's welfare system. For example, while the federal government talked about putting time limits on welfare and requiring that beneficiaries work, various states implemented both approaches. Among the programs tried out were "workfare" programs, fixed time limits followed by community or public work, and fixed time limits without work guarantees.

Advantages of local solutions. Supporters of block grants point out that states know best how to approach special problems within their local jurisdictions. The United States is "a large, diverse country with very different welfare needs and different communities with differing values," comments one analyst. In parts of West Virginia, for example, jobs are so scarce that talking about workfare makes no sense. Advocates of block grants argue that state-run programs are likely to be leaner, more efficient, and better managed than the federally managed program. Finally, supporters of block grants make a philosophical defense of giving power to the states. "People want

Competition may also generate demands for change through comparisons with other states ("Why can't we do this as well as Illinois?"), or through comparisons between levels of government ("The federal government manages to do this; why can't we?").

National Strength without National Uniformity Advocates of dividing power between the state and national levels stress that the benefits outlined above are achieved without sacrificing the strength of the nation as a whole. Military and foreign policy is handled by the national government, eliminating the weakness and inconvenience of government by committee in these critical areas. National economic power is strengthened by the federal government's ability to regulate interstate commerce. National standards of rights and justice can be imposed without sacrificing local power and control.

Controlling Abuses of Power An original argument in favor of federalism, advanced by James Madison, was that the two governments would keep each other in check, providing a further safeguard against abuse of power. The national government no doubt provides an effective check on state power—especially through the federal courts—but the opposite is more decisions being made in their own hometown and in their state capital than in Washington," says the governor of Utah. "And they want less government, and this is the way to get it."

Arguments against block grants

The need for federal standards. Topping the list of arguments against block grants is the fear that some states will fail to meet their obligation to provide for the truly needy. Rather than seeking innovative ways to stretch federal dollars, critics argue, some states might simply cut benefits for the poor. Likewise, advocates of tough welfare policies (such as workfare) argue that block grants have let states adopt a lax approach to welfare policy. "Historically, governors have loved to delude voters by pretending to have much tougher work requirements than they really have," one critic argues, "and that tendency is very much alive today." Critics of block grants argue that both fairness and the need for accountability require the existence of national standards. Any need for flexibility can easily be met by allowing for state-by-state waivers of federal rules, when appropriate.

The difficulty of state-based redistribution programs. Some economists and policy analysts point out that the states are ill equipped to manage programs that redistribute income from the "haves" to the "have-nots." The problem, simply stated, is that the wealthy are free to move to low-tax states that offer low welfare benefits, while the poor can move to high-tax states with generous benefits. (Under the 1969 Supreme Court decision of *Shapiro* v. *Thompson*, states cannot deny welfare benefits to new residents or impose an unreasonable waiting period.) "Since 1970," writes Paul E. Peterson, "states have been in something of a race to lower welfare benefits for fear that high benefits could attract poor people to the state—thus raising social spending and perhaps triggering an exodus of taxpayers." When Washington gave the states the opportunity to apply for waivers from federal AFDC requirements, Peterson points out, the first three proposals all proposed new restrictions on welfare. The assumption that taxpayers and welfare recipients are sensitive to variations in state welfare policy, however, has not been proven.

Sources: A. Sidney Johnson III, "States Aren't Waiting for Federal Welfare Reform," *Public Welfare* (Winter 1995), pp. 18–20; Susan Kellam, "Welfare Experiments," *CQ Researcher* (September 16, 1994), pp. 795–811; Joe Klein, "Let the States Do It," *Newsweek* (December 5, 1994), p. 35; "Blockheads: Political Use of Federal Block Grants," *New Republic* (March 20, 1995), p. 7; David Whitman and Penny Loeb, "Let 50 Flowers Bloom," *U.S. News and World Report* (March 27, 1995), pp. 22–26; Paul E. Peterson, "Who Should Do What," *Brookings Review* 13 (Spring 1995), pp. 6–11; Mark Shroder, "Games the States Don't Play," *Review of Economics and Statistics 77* (February 1995), pp. 183–191.

rarely true. In some ways the states do provide a means through which the people can make their demands heard in Washington. The tax revolt in California in the late 1970s, for example, led to a national debate on taxes and an income tax cut under Ronald Reagan. California's approval of a strong anti-affirmative action measure in 1996 may have a similar effect. In general, however, state efforts to check the national government are haphazard and uncertain.

Few would argue that the federal system has provided an effective check on the power of the national government. In fact, as we have seen, the past century has seen a nearly continuous transfer of power from the states to the national government.

Increased Responsiveness and Opportunities for Participation The existence of local, state, and national governments greatly increases the opportunities for citizens to participate in politics and the likelihood that they will find a sympathetic and responsive ear at some level of government. A group that fails to achieve results at the national level can often seek relief in the states, and vice versa. When it appeared in the 1980s that the Supreme Court might restrict abortion rights, for example, prochoice groups turned to state legislatures to protect their interests. When state laws provided insufficient protection from antiabortion protesters who blocked access to abortion clinics, the prochoice groups turned to Congress.

The opportunity to play one government off against another is not unlimited, of course. Since valid federal laws displace valid state laws, those who can mobilize at the federal level have an obvious advantage.

The Importance of Symbolism and the Dumbo Effect   Laws passed at the national level can have an important symbolic effect on the states. A national law underscores the importance of an issue and may provide critical momentum to various state efforts. Federal grants can play a similar role. States and localities that might be reluctant to carry all of the burden of new programs may do so if the federal government picks up part of the tab. Surprisingly, such programs often continue even after federal aid has ended. This phenomenon is known as the *Dumbo effect,* after the elephant in the children's story who really could fly on his own, but thought he could do so only with the aid of a magic feather.

Disadvantages of Federalism

Federalism creates problems along with the benefits. Foremost among them are these:

Lack of Accountability   When more than one governmental unit is involved in making decisions, assigning blame or credit for what goes wrong or right can be difficult. Federalism allows politicians to blame each other instead of taking responsibility themselves.

In fact, state politics commonly turns on issues that are really the concern of the national government, and national politics often centers on matters of state concern. Candidates for national office have run successfully on a pledge to improve the nation's education system—even though the national government's role in education is extremely limited. Conversely, local candidates often rail against Supreme Court decisions that, once in office, they can do nothing about. A presidential candidate will call for curriculum reform—which must be accomplished by local school boards—and a school board candidate will promise a return to prayer in the schools—which would require a constitutional amendment or a policy shift by the Supreme Court.

Cost Shifting   Critics also argue that federalism encourages cost shifting between the state and national governments and between different parts of the country. Congress, in recent years, has made a practice of creating policies but refusing to pay for them, in many cases leaving the states to pick up the tab. Conversely, the states may neglect small problems and then call for federal assistance when they turn into big ones.

Another problem is the tendency of national officials, especially representatives and senators, to use the federal government to benefit their own states at the expense of others. Because the national legislators are elected from the states and view themselves as represen-

"Look, the American people don't want to be bossed around by federal bureaucrats. They want to be bossed around by state bureaucrats."

tatives of their local constituents, they see nothing wrong with this practice and often take credit for it. Thus rural Oklahomans pay for mass transit in New York, and Rhode Islanders pay for farm programs in Kansas. In theory, this cost shifting should balance itself out, but in practice some states play this game better than others.

Lack of Coordination   A further difficulty in fragmenting governmental power is a lack of coordination between the many agencies with responsibility for a given problem. Consider, for example, the 1993 outbreak of meat contamination in the Pacific Northwest. Was the problem caused by weak federal standards and lax enforcement at federally inspected slaughterhouses? By inadequate enforcement of health standards on the part of local restaurant inspectors? By ineffective state programs for educating consumers and business operators?

Similar problems have arisen when states are struck by natural disasters, such as hurricanes and earthquakes. It may take days—while people suffer—for the local, state, and national agencies to figure out who should do what, where, and when.

Duplication and the Burden of Diverse Regulations   In an age when businesses frequently operate across state lines, keeping up with diverse local regulations may be expensive and difficult. Businesses must comply with relevant federal laws as well. These problems can be lessened by cooperation and coordination between the various states and between the states and the federal government. Many states, for example, have adopted uniform codes of law in areas such as general business law (a recent, more controversial proposal aims at uniform state procedures for the adoption of children). State laws remain diverse in many areas, however, and keeping up with varying rules and procedures can be a major headache for those who do business in many states.

Interstate Competition   Although competition among states can encourage change and social progress, it can also lead to waste and inefficiency. The Commerce Clause prohibits a state from directly discriminating against out-of-state businesses, but states are permitted to compete against each other for new businesses. In recent years, competition among states has reached a fever pitch. One bidding war among three states to attract a Canadian steel plant employing four hundred people, for example, cost the winning state's taxpayers an estimated $350,000 per new employee in tax credits, low-interest loans, and new road building projects!

"It would be hard to invent a worse way of spending money than on business incentive schemes," wrote one commentator. "States have little idea how much a job is worth, or whether they are getting value for money from their investments." One state official put it this way: "Right now, all we are doing is eating each other's lunch," he said. "At some stage we have to start thinking about dinner."[25]

The Wrong Level of Government?   Ideally, policies that require national uniformity are handled in Washington, and those that lend themselves to local solutions are left to the states. In practice, there is no guarantee that a given policy will be dealt with at the optimal level of government.

Since at least the New Deal, critics argue, the national government has tended to take over programs that might better be left to the states. For example, critics cite federal programs in housing and education as examples of policies that would be better left to the states or left unregulated. Much of the current debate over health care concerns whether the national government or the states should play the predominant role.

The problem is just as serious in the opposite direction. In many cases the states lack the resources, political will, or leverage to carry out important policies. Rich states would be able to afford more generous social programs than poor states; but once enacted, such programs would attract citizens from other states in search of higher benefits. Similarly, research has shown that it is counterproductive for states to increase the taxes of the rich, since wealthy citizens are free to move to states with lower tax rates.[26]

Too Much Politics?   Federalism certainly increases the burdens on the citizen who wishes to keep up with and participate in politics. In a single year, a citizen might be expected to vote in city, county, school district, statewide, and federal elections. For a citizen to be informed about the actions of the government, he or she must follow the actions of the city council, county council, school board, state legislature, and Congress. Add in the separation of powers (mayor, county administrator, school superintendent, governor, president, not to mention the courts), and the burden may be overwhelming to everyone but (or perhaps including) professional political scientists.

Summary

Federalism refers to a political system in which power is divided between the central government and its component parts—in the United States, between the national government and the states. A federal system can be distinguished from both a unitary system, in which all power is lodged in one central government, and a confederation, in which the national government has no independent power and the subunits are in effect independent countries.

The United States Constitution recognizes the sovereign powers of both the states and the national (or federal) government. In theory, the federal government exercises only those powers specifically delegated to it, and the states exercise all powers not specifically denied to them. In practice, the Supreme Court has historically interpreted the federal government's powers broadly, especially under the Necessary and Proper Clause, which gives the United States the power to make all laws necessary and proper to carrying out its delegated powers.

Given the Court's broad interpretation of national authority, serious federalism-based limits to national power are now difficult, although not impossible, to find. At the same time, the Court has increased its own efforts to limit the authority of the states—primarily through application of the Bill of Rights to state action—and has agreed to major federal efforts to limit state power, especially in the area of civil rights.

Still, although Constitution-based limits to federal power are few, the states and their subdivisions remain important players in the American political system. They are primarily responsible for public education, police and fire protection, basic legal codes, and the provision of routine government services. The states also share important powers with the federal government in areas such as public health, public works, economic and environmental regulation, and social welfare programs. Although the federal government plays an important role in setting broad rules and in providing funds, it also imposes requirements on the states through funded or unfunded mandates.

Federalism provides both advantages and disadvantages to the American political system. Its advantages include flexibility, the opportunity for increased participation and experimentation, and the ability to tailor solutions to the state or national level as appropriate. Its disadvantages include duplication, lack of coordination, and lack of accountability when something goes wrong. Federalism may also create "too much politics," making it difficult for even a dedicated citizen to follow public affairs.

Key Terms

Federalism
Unitary system
Confederation
Dual or "layer cake" federalism
Cooperative (or "marble cake") federalism
Creative federalism
New Federalism
Shared powers
Reserved powers
John Marshall
McCulloch v. *Maryland*

Gibbons v. *Ogden*
States' rights
Nullification
Interposition
New Deal
Great Society
Categorical grant
Block grants
Revenue sharing

Review Questions

1. What kind of division of power between the states and the national government did the Federalists envision? The Antifederalists?

2. What is meant by the terms *dual (or layer cake) federalism* and *cooperative (or marble cake) federalism*? In what policy areas does the national-state relationship come closest to the dual federalism model? In what areas does the cooperative federalism model seem more appropriate?

3. What key Supreme Court decisions helped expand the role of the federal government under the Constitution? What decisions helped limit the role of the states?

4. Describe the changing relationship between the states and the federal government since the New Deal. What goals characterized Johnson's Great Society? Nixon's New Federalism? Reagan's New Federalism? What models of federalism come closest to describing each of these periods?

5. What are some advantages and disadvantages of federalism? Identify specific examples of each.

Suggested Readings

Anton, Thomas J. *American Federalism and Public Policy.* Philadelphia: Temple University Press, 1989.

Conlan, Timothy. *New Federalism: Intergovernmental Reform from Nixon to Reagan.* Washington, D.C.: Brookings Institution, 1988.

Council of State Governments Staff. *The Book of the States.* Lexington, KY: Council of State Governments, 1996.

Elazar, Daniel. *American Federalism: A View from the States.* New York: Harper & Row, 1984.

———. *Exploring Federalism.* Tuscaloosa: University of Alabama Press, 1987.

Grodzins, Morton. *The American System.* Chicago: Rand McNally, 1966.

Hall, Kermit, ed. *Federalism: A Nation of States—Major Historical Interpretations.* New York: Garland, 1987.

Hyman, Harold M. *A More Perfect Union: The Impact of the Civil War and Reconstruction on the Constitution.* New York: Knopf, 1973.

Ingram, Helen, and Dean E. Mann, eds. *Why Policies Succeed or Fail.* Beverly Hills: Sage Publications, 1980.

Leuchtenburg, William E. *Franklin D. Roosevelt and the New Deal, 1932–1940.* New York: Harper & Row, 1963.

McDonald, Forrest, and Ellen Shapiro McDonald. "Federalism in America: An Obituary." In *Requiem: Variations on Eighteenth-Century Themes.* Lawrence: University Press of Kansas, 1988, pp. 195–206.

Nice, David C. *Federalism: The Politics of Intergovernmental Relations.* New York: St. Martin's Press, 1987.

Peterson, Paul. *The Price of Federalism.* Washington, D.C.; Brookings Institution, 1995.

Peterson, Paul, Barry Rabe, and Kenneth K. Wong. *When Federalism Works.* Washington, D.C.: Brookings Institution, 1986.

Schram, Sanford F., and Carol S. Weissart, "The State of American Federalism, 1996–1997." *Publius* 27 (Spring 1997), pp. 1–31.

Van Horn, Carl E. *The State of the States, 3d ed.* Washington, D.C.: CQ Press, 1996.

Internet Resources

The Center for the Study of Federalism, an interdisciplinary research and educational institute at:

http://www.temple. edu/federalism/

The National Conference of State Legislatures; site contains a great deal of information on current policy debates at the state and national levels at:

http://www.ncsl. org

The National Governor's Association: bipartisan organization of state governors at:

http://www.nga.org/

The Council of State Governments, an organization devoted to "promoting state solutions, regionally and nationally," since 1933, at:

http://www.csg.org/

★ 4 ★

Civil Liberties

★ ★

During the 1984 Republican National Convention in Dallas, Texas, Gregory Lee Johnson joined a group of demonstrators protesting the policies of the Reagan administration. The group marched through the Dallas streets, chanted political slogans, and staged "die-ins" designed to dramatize the consequences of nuclear war. At one point Johnson accepted an American flag from a fellow protester who had taken it from a flagpole outside a building along the route.

When the demonstration reached Dallas city hall, Johnson (as the Supreme Court put it) "unfurled the American flag, doused it with kerosene, and set it on fire. While the flag burned, the protesters chanted, 'America, the red, white, and blue, we spit on you.' After the demonstrators dispersed, a witness to the flag-burning collected the flag's remains and buried them in his backyard. No one was hurt or threatened with injury, though several witnesses testified [at Johnson's trial] that they had been seriously offended by the flag-burning." Johnson was arrested and charged with "desecrating a venerated object," a criminal offense under Texas law. He was sentenced to a year in prison and fined $2,000.[1]

Ordinarily the matter would have ended there, but Johnson appealed. Eventually his case reached the United States Supreme Court, which ruled in a 5–4 vote that burning an American flag as part of a political protest was protected speech under the First Amendment to the Constitution of the United States. "If there is a bedrock principle underlying the First Amendment," wrote Justice William Brennan, "it is that the Government may not prohibit the expression of an idea simply because society finds the idea itself offensive or disagreeable. . . . To conclude that the Government may permit designated symbols to be used to communicate only a limited set of messages would be to enter territory having no discernible or defensible boundaries. Could the Government, on this theory, prohibit the burning of state flags? Of copies of the Presidential seal? Of the Constitution?" As for whether the Framers would have agreed with his decision, Brennan made reference to the revolutionary origins of the American republic. "We would not be surprised to learn that the persons who framed our Constitution and wrote the Amendment that we now construe were not known for their reverence to the Union Jack [of Great Britain]."

Few would deny the importance of the fundamental freedoms outlined in the Bill of Rights. These rights—which include freedom of expression, religion, and assembly, freedom from unreasonable searches and seizures, the right to privacy, and the right to due process of law—are at the very core of our conception of human dignity.

Yet the Supreme Court's decision upholding the right to burn the American flag in protest was highly controversial. Critics argued that the many American citizens who loved the

Gregory Lee Johnson.

flag and saw it as a symbol of their patriotism had a right to protect it from damage and abuse. Johnson's action was more conduct than speech, they argued, and a decision limiting his right to burn the flag did not prevent him from expressing himself in any number of more acceptable ways.

As the *Johnson* case suggests, the problem in civil liberties cases is usually not over the rights themselves, but over how to define and apply them and how to balance them against each other and against other important interests. Even the most important civil liberties are not absolute; individual rights must yield when the safety of the public or another overriding interest is at stake.

Controversies over the meaning and application of the Bill of Rights reflect a deeper division in the American body politic—the problem of majority rule versus minority rights. Thus questions about rights strike at the nature and purpose of the political community itself. Should a political system be judged on how well it reflects the will of the majority, expressed through democratic institutions? Or should it be judged by how well it protects the fundamental rights of those in the minority? Frequently, those on both sides of this divide express their concerns in terms of rights—the right of some citizens to read controversial books in school, for example, might be viewed as conflicting with the right of parents to educate their children as they see fit. Likewise, the right of individuals to own handguns might be seen as conflicting with the community's right to protect itself from violence.

Civil liberties, however, are not simply for the minority. Certain liberties, especially freedom of speech and freedom of association, are central to the very idea of democratic government. Other freedoms, such as privacy and due process rights, protect everyone, whether in the majority or the minority, from the coercive power of the state.

This chapter examines three central themes. First, it explores the historical and theoretical underpinnings of the concept of rights in America. Second, it presents a snapshot of how rights issues interconnect with the various institutions and players in the American system. Finally, it provides a summary of several of the most important controversies in the civil liberties field. Throughout, the chapter reflects the importance of individual rights to the Framers' constitutional design and to their understanding of legitimate government.

Questions to Keep in Mind

What purposes were served by the Texas law at issue in the Johnson *case? Were any of these purposes unrelated to the content of Johnson's "speech"? Were any of them so important that they would outweigh Johnson's free speech rights?*

Why do the United States Supreme Court and the United States Constitution place so high a value on free speech? What is the relationship between free speech and the democratic process? Can one exist without the other?

Are the courts better equipped to deal with civil liberties questions than Congress or the state legislatures? What characteristics of courts and judges might make them more or less able to deal with such questions?

Basic Concepts ★ ★ ★ ★ ★ ★ ★ ★ ★ ★ ★ ★ ★

Definition of Civil Liberties

The term **civil liberties** encompasses the rights guaranteed by the Bill of Rights. In common usage, civil liberties issues include freedom of speech, press, and assembly; freedom of religion (and freedom from state-imposed religion); freedom from unreasonable searches and seizures; due process of law, especially in criminal cases, along with the other procedural guarantees spelled out in the Bill of Rights; and the right to privacy, which includes a woman's right to choose whether or not to have an abortion. All of these, except the right to privacy, are specifically stated in the Bill of Rights.

Civil rights, discussed in Chapter 5, refers generally to constitutional guarantees of equality under the law, especially with respect to group characteristics such as race, ethnicity, and gender. The distinction drawn here between civil liberties and civil rights is based not on any sort of technical distinction between rights and liberties, but simply on the way these words are used in practice. Although this practical distinction between civil liberties and civil rights is useful, it should not be taken too far. The two concepts overlap considerably, and civil rights and civil liberties issues are often found in the same case.

Moreover, individual civil liberties rarely present themselves in neat or orderly packages. Civil liberties often conflict with other important values, or with each other. In highly publicized criminal cases, for example, the constitutional guarantee of freedom of the press may collide with the defendant's constitutional right to a fair trial. Likewise, the right to be free from "unreasonable searches and seizures" may conflict with the public's interest in pursuing criminals and maintaining law and order.

> *"If there is any fixed star in our constitutional constellation, it is that no official, high or petty, can prescribe what shall be orthodox in politics, nationalism, religion, or other matters of opinion or force citizens to confess by words or act their faith therein."*
>
> —Justice Robert H. Jackson,
> *West Virginia* v. *Barnette*, 1943

The concept of civil liberties is based on the idea that human beings possess rights that government cannot take away. Although different theorists account for these rights in different ways, all agree that their recognition and protection by the government is essential to the maintenance of a free and democratic society.

The Classic Tradition: Locke and Jefferson

Perhaps the classic defense of rights appears in the writings of the seventeenth-century British philosopher **John Locke.** As we have seen, Locke's writings—especially his *Second Treatise on Civil Government*—greatly influenced the Founders of the American Republic.

Long before there were governments on earth, Locke argued, human beings lived in a state of freedom known as the state of nature.* Individuals in the state of nature already possessed their natural rights, including the right to property, defined as their "lives, liberties, and estates."[2] Moreover, individuals had the right to take whatever actions they thought necessary to secure those rights—including the punishment of others who tried to interfere with them.

---

* Reflecting the prejudices of his time, Locke casts his argument in terms of "men," excluding women. His argument, however, can easily be generalized to encompass all human beings.

The state of nature was at first a happy place, but over time it became more and more difficult for individuals to protect themselves from each other. The enjoyment of property in the state of nature, Locke wrote, "is very uncertain and constantly exposed to the invasions of others."[3] One man might work hard at planting and cultivating his crops, only to find them stolen one day. Another might be killed for his land or his acorns. To secure the natural rights of all, the inhabitants of the state of nature joined together to form a society and create a government. Each individual yielded to the government the right to do whatever he thinks best for his own preservation and the right to punish those who violate his or her rights. These rights are then enforced collectively by the government.

Even after they have established the government, of course, the people still possess their basic rights to life, liberty, and property. A hundred years after Locke, Thomas Jefferson called these rights "unalienable," meaning that they could not be alienated, or given or taken away. It would be absurd for the government to have the power to infringe the very rights it was created to protect. Closely following Locke, Jefferson wrote that among these unalienable rights were "life, liberty, and the pursuit of happiness."

The Primacy of Thought and Speech   It was the English political theorist **John Stuart Mill,** writing in the nineteenth century, who developed the classic defense of civil liberties. Liberty depends on freedom of opinion, Mill wrote in his appropriately titled essay *On Liberty,* and freedom of opinion depends on freedom of speech. When the government silences the expression of opinion, Mill wrote, it harms not only the individual but also society at large, which loses the opportunity to listen and learn. Even a seemingly absurd opinion might turn out to be true, and even the expression of falsehoods benefits society, by bringing the truth into clearer focus.

Without freedom of opinion and expression, Mill argued, individuals in society were doomed to live their lives according to the rules and principles laid down by others, whether through government, society, custom, or religion. This deprived them of their very essence as human beings—the freedom to make choices about how to live. A society that discourages freedom of thought and speech forces each individual to conform to the same rules and the same lifestyle. "Individuals are lost in the crowd," Mill wrote. No such society "ever did, or could rise above mediocrity."[4]

Freedom of thought and discussion is most necessary in a democracy, which depends on an informed and involved public. All ideas, even those deemed absurd or dangerous, must be allowed to compete in what Supreme Court justice Oliver Wendell Holmes called the marketplace of ideas. Even false speech has value, and must be allowed unless there is a "clear and present danger" to life or property. "If there be time to expose through discussion the falsehood and fallacies," wrote Justice Louis D. Brandeis, "the remedy to be applied is more speech, not enforced silence."[5]

American democracy, in the view of civil libertarians, is impossible without free speech. "Debate on public issues should be uninhibited, robust, and wide-open," wrote Justice William Brennan in 1964. "It may well include vehement, caustic, and sometimes unpleasantly sharp attacks on government and public officials."[6] How can people govern themselves unless they are free to express their opinions, debate with one another, and consider available alternatives?

Civil Liberties and the Constitution

The Framers of the original Constitution deliberately chose not to include a **Bill of Rights.** Their rationale was clear. A Bill of Rights, they believed, was both unnecessary and potentially dangerous: unnecessary because the powers of the new national government were carefully limited to those specifically listed in the Constitution; potentially dangerous because any such listing would necessarily be incomplete and would create the false impression that any rights not directly stated did not exist.

The Antifederalists, and some of the Federalists, regarded the absence of a Bill of Rights as a fundamental defect in the new Constitution. A Bill of Rights was found in virtually every state constitution, after all, and had been an important part of the English political tradition since the time of Magna Carta. Eventually the Federalists gave in, promising to adopt a Bill of Rights at the first opportunity after the ratification of the Constitution. Accordingly, the Bill of Rights was introduced in Congress by James Madison, debated at length throughout the summer of 1789, and finally sent to the states for approval. The Bill of Rights was ratified in 1791 and became the first ten amendments to the Constitution.

Civil Liberties in the Original Constitution   The Framers of the original Constitution did not completely neglect civil liberties. Above all, they believed that the rights of the people would be protected by the Constitution's structural checks and balances. Most important, of course, were the concepts of federalism and the separation of powers. It is in this sense that Alexander Hamilton declared that "the Constitution is itself, in every rational sense, and to every useful purpose, A BILL OF RIGHTS."[7]

There were also several specific clauses in the original Constitution aimed at protecting civil liberties:

- *The writ of habeas corpus.* The writ of **habeas corpus** (from the Latin meaning "you are to have the body") is a judicial order demanding that a prisoner be brought before a court or judge, providing a method by which the prisoner can be released from illegal confinement. Without the writ of habeas corpus or a similar power, prisoners could be arrested and held without cause, even without being officially charged with a crime. In modern times the writ of habeas corpus is only one of several devices by which the state and federal courts can ensure that individuals are not held illegally.

  The Constitution provides that the writ of habeas corpus "shall not be suspended, unless when in Cases of Rebellion or Invasion the public safety may require it." Since this provision appears in Article I of the Constitution, along with other limitations on the power of Congress, it might be assumed that only Congress could suspend the writ. In 1861, however, Abraham Lincoln suspended the writ in an attempt to restore order during the early stages of the Civil War. Lincoln defended his suspension of the privilege by underscoring his duty to uphold the Constitution at all costs—even at the cost of one of its provisions.[8]

- *Prohibition against ex post facto laws and writs of attainder.* The Constitution makes it illegal for the states or the national government to pass laws that criminalize behavior that was legal at the time it occurred (ex post facto laws), and laws that single out particular individuals and declare them guilty of a criminal offense without benefit of a trial (writs of attainder). Both ex post facto laws and bills of attainder violate fundamental principles of fairness and due process of law. In addition, writs of attainder violate the separation of legislative and judicial powers. Several of the leaders of the American revolution, including Thomas Jefferson and Benjamin Franklin, were actually declared guilty of treason by the British legislature in a bill of attainder.

- *Privileges and Immunities Clause.* The original Constitution also declared that "the Citizens of each State shall be entitled to all Privileges and Immunities of Citizens in the several States." Exactly what these privileges and immunities are was not spelled out, but in later years the Supreme Court ruled that they include, at a minimum, the right to buy and sell property, to bring lawsuits, and to engage in lawful work. In effect, the Privileges and Immunities Clause guarantees that states cannot discriminate against outsiders in favor of their own citizens.

The Bill of Rights and the States   Congress clearly intended the Bill of Rights as a check on the power of the national government rather than on the states. The First Amendment is addressed directly to the national government: "*Congress* shall make no law respecting an

The Supreme Court banned state-sponsored school prayer in 1962, in the landmark case of Engle v. Vitale. *Recent cases make it clear, however, that students have a First Amendment right to pray in school, whether alone or in groups, as long as school authorities do not organize, sponsor, or endorse the activity.*

establishment of religion, or abridging the free exercise thereof . . . ." The Tenth Amendment, likewise, states that "the powers not delegated to the United States by the Constitution, nor prohibited by it to the States, are reserved to the States respectively, or to the people." Other provisions of the Bill of Rights are not addressed explicitly to the federal government, but that they too were intended as a limitation on federal power is apparent from the historical context. The Supreme Court confirmed this interpretation in the 1833 case of *Barron* v. *Baltimore.*[9]

Until the current century, therefore, the Supreme Court was powerless to apply the Bill of Rights to the states. If a state passed a law that violated a citizen's right to free speech, the victim had no recourse other than the state courts and the state Bill of Rights. Since state courts typically reflected the political outlook of the state legislatures, they were rarely zealous about interfering with state laws and offered little real protection of individual rights. Around 1900, however, the Supreme Court began to apply the Bill of Rights to the states on a provision-by-provision basis (see Table 4.1). The vehicle used by the Court was the Fourteenth Amendment.

Table 4.1
Selective Incorporation of the Bill of Rights

First Amendment	*Totally incorporated*
Establishment clause	*Everson* v. *Board of Education* (1947)
Free exercise clause	*Cantwell* v. *Connecticut* (1940)
Free speech	*Gitlow* v. *New York* (1925)
Free press	*Near* v. *Minnesota* (1931)
Free assembly	*DeJonge* v. *Oregon* (1937)
Freedom of association	*NAACP* v. *Alabama* (1958)
Second Amendment	*Not yet incorporated*
Third Amendment	*Not yet incorporated*
Fourth Amendment	*Totally incorporated*
Searches and seizures	*Wolf* v. *Colorado* (1949)
Exclusionary rule	*Mapp* v. *Ohio* (1961)
Fifth Amendment	*Partly incorporated*
Grand jury indictment	Not yet incorporated
Double jeopardy	*Benton* v. *Maryland* (1969)
Self-incrimination	*Malloy* v. *Hogan* (1964)
Due process clause	Directly repealed in Fourteenth Amendment
Public use	*Missouri Pac. Rw. Co.* v. *Nebraska* (1896)
Just compensation	*Chicago, B. & Q. Rr.* v. *Chicago* (1897)
Sixth Amendment	*Totally incorporated*
Speedy trial	*Klopfer* v. *North Carolina* (1967)
Public trial	*In re Oliver* (1948)
Impartial jury	*Parker* v. *Gladden* (1966)
Confront witnesses	*Pointer* v. *Texas* (1965)
Subpoena witnesses	*Washington* v. *Texas* (1967)
Right to counsel	*Powell* v. *Alabama* (1932) (capital cases)
	Gideon v. *Wainwright* (1963) (felony cases)
	Duncan v. *Louisiana* (1968) (serious cases)
	Argersinger v. *Hamlin* (1972) (jail involved)
Seventh Amendment	*Not yet incorporated*
Eighth Amendment	*Partly incorporated*
Excessive bail	Not yet incorporated
Excessive fines	Not yet incorporated
Cruel and unusual punishments	*Robinson* v. *California* (1962)

Adapted from Craig R. Ducat and Harold W. Chase, *Constitutional Interpretation*, 1988, pp. 845–846. Reprinted by permission of Wadsworth Publishing Co.

The Fourteenth Amendment, adopted in 1868, does not specifically state that the guarantees of the Bill of Rights should apply to the states. However, it does require that the states provide **due process of law** to all persons within their jurisdiction. At a minimum, due process of law means that the state must provide a hearing, trial, or other proceeding before depriving any person of life, liberty, or property. But the Supreme Court has also held that state laws that violate the specific provisions (or clauses) of the Bill of Rights also constitute denials of due process. In other words, the Court held, the Fourteenth Amendment "incorporates" the provisions of the Bill of Rights and makes them applicable to the states.

This long line of **incorporation** cases began in 1896, when the Supreme Court ruled in *Missouri Pacific Railway Company* v. *State of Nebraska* that the Fifth Amendment's guarantee that "private property shall not be taken for public use without just compensation" applied to takings by the states as well as the federal government. Likewise, in the 1925 case of *Gitlow* v. *New York,* the Court applied the First Amendment's Free Speech Clause to the states. By the 1970s, most of the provisions of the Bill of Rights had been incorporated.[10] Still, a few significant provisions are not yet, and perhaps will never be, incorporated. These include the right to a grand jury proceeding and the requirement that jury verdicts be decided by unanimous vote.[11]

Rights Not Specifically Listed in the Bill of Rights   Does the Bill of Rights provide an exhaustive list of rights? Hamilton argued vehemently that no such list could be complete; his opposition to a national Bill of Rights was based at least partly on his fear that rights not listed would be permanently lost. In modern times this question has taken on a new importance, as the Supreme Court has struggled to define rights, especially privacy, that are not clearly stated in the Bill of Rights.

Those who defend the Court's efforts to define and enforce unenumerated rights point to the broad and open-ended language of several key provisions, especially the Due Process Clause and the Ninth Amendment. In general, they value the extra protection of rights more than they fear the increased power of the federal courts. Those on the other side point out that these unwritten rights are highly controversial, and enforcing them often means limiting other rights or overriding other important values or interests. Additionally, they are concerned about the increased power of unelected judges at the expense of democratically elected legislatures.

Liberty and Community: Two Conceptions of Rights

One reason civil liberties are so controversial is that those on opposite sides of an issue typically view political life in very different ways. Groups that defend the rights of criminal defendants, for example, focus on the awesome power of the state and the terrible fate that awaits an innocent person convicted of a crime. Their opponents see crime from the victim's perspective, fearing not the police officer but the criminal. Some look at public school prayer and see the evils of state-imposed religion; others see only the community's effort to promote religious values. Whether on abortion, gun control, pornography, or homosexuality, Americans often seem to be talking past, rather than to, one another.

The debate over civil liberties strikes deep chords in the American political psyche and reflects cultural differences that extend back more than two centuries. Depending on the issue, conflicting sides have very different views on the role of government, the relationship between the state and national governments, and the concept of rights itself.

The Civil Libertarian Perspective Following Locke and Jefferson, civil libertarians argue that the first duty of government is the protection of individual rights. And, following Mill, they assert that the government should foster an atmosphere that nurtures and encourages the development of human individuality.

The major threat to individual rights, as civil libertarians see it, is the tyranny of a majority seeking to impose its political, moral, and religious views on every citizen or minority group. Those with unpopular or unconventional views, or members of minority cultures, are made to conform to the majority's standards, by law, social pressure, or outright persecution or harassment. In the process, civil libertarians argue, the majority deprives itself of the opportunity to grow and change, and may become easy prey for dictators and demagogues.

Because majorities have the power to make the law, the threat to civil liberties comes most directly from legislatures—whether local, state, or national. Thus it is not surprising that civil libertarians have often turned to the courts for protection against the majority. The federal courts, whose judges are appointed for life and who are therefore insulated from political pressure, have been particularly important in the protection of civil liberties.

Consider, for example, the controversy over book banning in the public schools. In some communities, local majorities have tried to remove certain books from school libraries on the grounds that they contain objectionable ideas or points of view (J. D. Salinger's *Catcher in the Rye* seems to be a perennial target). Such restrictions on free speech are anathema to advocates of individual rights, who have turned to the federal courts for protection. In 1982, the Supreme Court ruled that school officials could remove such books only if their reason for doing so was unrelated to a desire to restrict access to particular ideas.[12]

Emotions run high on both sides of the gun control issue. Advocates of gun ownership often point to the people's Second Amendment right to "keep and bear arms," but many constitutional scholars argue that the amendment guarantees only the people's collective right, expressed through the states, to sponsor "well-regulated" militias.

The Communitarian Perspective Those on the other side in civil liberties cases are not opposed to freedom. However, they place great value on the idea of *community.* Since human beings do not live as isolated individuals, communitarians argue, they can find fulfillment and purpose only within the context of their relationship with others.

From a communitarian point of view, an excessive commitment to individual rights degrades the life of the community and violates the rights of the majority, which in turn violates the rights of all those in the majority. Communitarians recognize the importance of due process of law for criminal suspects, for example, but they argue that law-abiding citizens have rights too—including the right to feel safe and secure in their own neighborhoods. And although freedom of thought and speech may be praiseworthy in the abstract, communitarians believe that the community should have the right to limit speech, such as pornography or hate speech, that degrades the quality of community life.

The centrality of community life has deep roots in American history. The founders of Plymouth Colony, for example, came to America to create a community, not merely to allow each individual to exercise his or her individual rights. Even the Declaration of Independence, although remembered for its emphasis on individual rights, speaks of collective rights. Individuals are endowed by the Creator with inalienable rights, but "it is the right of the *people* to alter or abolish" governments that no longer serve their ends.

Civil libertarians are not blind to the importance of community. Nor are communitarians hostile to individual liberty. These two worldviews reflect differences in emphasis rather than a complete lack of agreement. But the cultural divide represented by these worldviews is wide and pervades every aspect of American political life.

The Politics of Civil Liberties

The Supreme Court is the focal point for any discussion of civil liberties. Virtually every important civil liberties issue seems to find its way to the Supreme Court, and for most of this century the Court has been the first and best hope of those seeking to advance the cause of civil liberties. But other institutions—including the lower courts, Congress, the executive branch, the states, and interest groups—also play important roles in the civil liberties area.

This section provides a brief overview of how these various institutions can both threaten and protect the liberties of the people.

The Supreme Court and Civil Liberties

The idea that an independent judiciary could enforce the rights of the people represented a major development in American political science. Although not new in 1789, this idea had never before been tried in practice. As recently as 1776, the American colonists had no way of protecting their rights except through the method endorsed by Locke and Jefferson: revolution. Jefferson even thought an occasional revolution was good for the body politic. "The tree of liberty must be refreshed from time to time with the blood of patriots and tyrants," he once wrote. "It is its natural manure."[13]

In the American system, by contrast, individual rights can be enforced by the courts, and particularly by the Supreme Court of the United States. The Constitution does not explicitly confer this power, but the Court claimed the power early on and has exercised it ever since. Until this century, however, the Court's ability to protect individual rights rarely carried into actual practice, and it was not until after World War II that resolving conflicts over individual rights became the Court's central political role.

That the Court was not always involved with questions dealing with individual rights is surprising only in retrospect. Until 1896, as we have seen, the Court did not even begin to apply the Bill of Rights to the states, which meant that the Court could protect the people only from the encroachments of the federal government. But the Court is itself a branch of the federal government, and has generally been reluctant to interfere with the laws and policies of its co-equal branches. Moreover, as James Madison suggested, individual rights are best protected by negating the power of majority factions to abuse them in the first place, a strategy incorporated into the design of Congress and the presidency as well as the courts. Even recently, there has been relatively little real conflict between the Court and the other branches over civil liberties issues. Most of the highly controversial Supreme Court decisions on civil liberties issues have involved state or local laws or policies.

That individuals should be protected from the government by a branch of the government itself may seem paradoxical. But the Supreme Court is not an ordinary governmental institution. The justices are insulated from political pressures by their lifetime appointments, and have historically enjoyed the respect and confidence of the American people. The Court has been careful to keep a weather eye on public opinion, however, often pulling back from its most controversial decisions when they have generated too much opposition.

The Supreme Court was most active in the civil liberties area between the mid-1950s

The liberal decisions of the Warren Court provoked a fierce reaction that in many ways continues to this day. Ironically, the smaller sign complains that the constitutional rights of those behind the "Impeach Earl Warren" movement have been violated.

and the mid-1970s, especially during the tenure of Chief Justice Earl Warren (1953–1969). The **Warren Court** was often extremely controversial, particularly when it banned organized school prayer, pushed hard for school desegregation, and enforced the rights of criminal defendants. Recently the Court has taken a more conservative approach, pulling back on some of its previous decisions and making few new advances in civil liberties.

The Lower Federal Courts

Many cases that reach the Supreme Court are first heard by the federal district courts and the federal courts of appeals. For several reasons, the decisions made by the judges of these lower courts can have a marked impact. First, many cases never reach the Supreme Court; the decisions of the lower courts are then final. Second, the way lower court judges handle the cases before them, and the way they frame their opinions, may greatly influence the issues that reach the Supreme Court and the way those issues are resolved. For example, novel legal theories may be tried out first in lower court decisions and eventually accepted by the Supreme Court. Finally, the lower courts must implement and apply the decisions of the Supreme Court in later cases; how they do so may greatly influence the practical effect of Supreme Court decisions.

Some lower court judges have become famous in their own right. Judge Frank Johnson of Alabama became known for his determination to improve conditions in mental hospitals and prisons. Judge John Sirica, who presided over the Watergate trials in 1973 and 1974, helped bring about the resignation of Richard Nixon.

Congress

All too often, Congress is thought of only in terms of the threats it poses to civil liberties. The Supreme Court's power of judicial review, after all, is important precisely because it provides a check on legislative action. But Congress represents a far lesser threat to civil liberties than the state legislatures, and often finds itself trying to protect civil liberties from a more conservative judiciary.

In 1986, for example, the Supreme Court allowed the air force to punish an orthodox Jew who, against regulations, insisted on covering his head while indoors. A year later Congress overturned the air force policy by legislation, protecting the rights of those wearing religious headgear. Similarly, Congress passed a law to override the Supreme Court's 1978 decision allowing police officers to search a newspaper office for photographs relevant to a criminal investigation.[14]

Many laws passed by Congress advance rather than restrict civil liberties. The Administrative Procedures Act, for example, requires federal agencies to provide due process of law, usually including some sort of hearing, to those affected by its actions or decisions. The Freedom of Information Act allows Americans to force government agencies to release documents and records unless the material is protected for national security or other valid reasons.

Congress and the Supreme Court are engaged in an ongoing dialogue over civil liberties issues.[15] Sometimes the Court takes the lead, at other times Congress is out in front. Sometimes the Court is protecting rights against congressional interference; at other times Congress is protecting the people from the Court. Federal policy on some civil liberties questions may emerge only after numerous fits and starts over a period of decades.

The Executive Branch

The awesome power of the executive branch makes it an obvious threat to civil liberties. The executive branch's powers to make rules and regulations, enforce the laws, and act in times of emergency all provide opportunities for the suppression of individual rights. But the executive branch also plays an important role in defining and enforcing the civil liberties of the people.

A key player is the solicitor general of the United States, who is in charge of the government's litigation in the Supreme Court. The solicitor's role is not limited to cases in which the United States is a party. His voice also carries great weight in helping the justices decide which cases to take on, and his arguments on behalf of other parties (known as "friend of the court" or *amicus curiae* briefs) may tip the balance in close cases.

The president and his subordinates can also play a direct role in the protection of civil liberties. In 1957, for example, President Dwight D. Eisenhower sent federal troops to Little Rock, Arkansas, to enforce a Supreme Court decree on school desegregation.[16] Other presidents have acted to protect civil liberties through executive orders. Immediately on taking office, for example, President Bill Clinton reversed a ban on abortion counseling by government-funded family planning clinics.

The States

The states have largely played the role of villains in the civil liberties area. Most of the Supreme Court's landmark civil liberties decisions would have been unnecessary had state or local governments not violated individual rights to begin with. The Framers fully expected that the states would be prone to infringing on fundamental rights, because states have less effective means of controlling the influence of majority factions.

Even state judges find it difficult to resist the will of the majority. Most are drawn from the ranks of state and local politicians. In most states they are popularly elected and, unlike federal judges, do not serve for life. In a few states the people have the right to recall a judge whose decisions are too unpopular. As Supreme Court justice Joseph Story put it in 1816, "The Constitution has presumed . . . that state attachments, state prejudices, state jealousies, and state interests, might sometimes obstruct, or control, or be supposed to obstruct or control, the regular administration of justice."[17]

To neglect individual states' contributions to the preservation of civil liberties in the United States, however, would be a great mistake. A reporter forced to testify in a criminal trial and asked to reveal the name of a confidential source will find no solace in the decisions of the Supreme Court, but reporters in twenty-six states can claim the protection of local "shield laws" and refuse to speak. Similarly, several states have enacted specific laws guaranteeing a woman's right to choose an abortion, no matter what the United States Supreme Court might say in the future.

In recent years, as the Supreme Court has moved toward a more conservative attitude on civil liberties questions, lawyers and legal scholars have rediscovered the importance of the states as the first line of civil liberties defense. Many state supreme courts have responded to the call by advancing civil liberties through their own state constitutions. Civil libertarians have also learned the hard way that justice is often best served by making sure that a case is properly resolved at the local level before it gets to court.

Interest Groups

The oldest and most important civil liberties interest group is the American Civil Liberties Union (ACLU), which was founded in 1920 to defend the Bill of Rights. The ACLU is at the forefront of virtually every important civil liberties issue, and appears before the Supreme Court more often than any other group or agency except the United States government itself. The ACLU is usually described as a "liberal" group, although in fact its commitment to civil liberties, even when exercised by Ku Klux Klansmen and Nazis, has at times brought it into conflict with traditional liberals.

In recent years a number of like-minded groups have joined the ACLU in its legal and legislative activities. Typically these groups are more specialized than the ACLU, often focusing on a single issue. Examples of such groups include the National Abortion Rights Action League (NARAL), the Women's Legal Defense Fund, the National Committee to Abolish the Death Penalty, and the NAACP Legal Defense Fund.

The ACLU's success in winning major court cases prompted a number of conservative organizations to adopt similar legal strategies to advance their goals. Most prominent are several antiabortion groups formed since the Supreme Court's 1973 decision in *Roe* v. *Wade* and a number of conservative religious groups, such as the Reverend Pat Robertson's Christian Coalition, that advocate prayer in the public schools and other government policies designed to advance religious values and traditions. Other conservative groups more generally involved in civil liberties cases include the National Legal Center for the Public Interest and the Center for Individual Rights.

What Rights Do I Have?
What Rights Do Others Have?

A complete review of the civil liberties decisions of the Supreme Court since the beginning of the Warren era in 1953 would (and does) fill volumes. This section aims instead at a brief survey.

It should be noted at the outset that the volumes of law and commentary on the meaning and application of the Bill of Rights stem from ten very brief and open-ended amendments to the Constitution. For many reasons, interpreting these provisions is no easy task:

- The Bill of Rights is framed in broad generalities, but in real life its provisions must be applied to very specific sets of facts. Often the words of the Constitution provide little more than general guidance as to how they should be applied in a particular case.
- The Bill of Rights was written in 1789, but must be applied today, more than two hundred years later. Should its provisions be applied as they were intended or understood at the time? Or in light of modern experience and sensibilities? Those who seek to understand how the Bill of Rights was intended or understood in 1789 must confront the extreme difficulty of determining exactly what the Bill of Rights meant in historical context.

- Is it appropriate for the justices to interpret the Bill of Rights in light of their own experiences and views on public issues?
- How should conflicts between the various provisions of the Bill of Rights be settled? Are some rights more fundamental than others?
- Are there pressing circumstances that justify limiting the application of the Bill of Rights? If so, how should such circumstances be defined? How can such exceptions be permitted while still maintaining the vitality of the Bill of Rights?

This section illustrates how the Supreme Court has dealt with these and other questions across a wide range of civil liberties issues.

Freedom of Speech

The First Amendment guarantee of freedom of speech reflects the Founders' view of the dangers of official censorship. The Supreme Court's concern over the years has been to protect speech that communicates ideas, however obnoxious or offensive. Constitutional scholars today often substitute the phrase "freedom of expression" to underscore the Court's recognition that nonspoken communications (such as placards, symbols, and gestures) are also protected under the First Amendment.

The Free Speech Clause, like the rest of the Constitution, applies only to government restrictions on expression. In general, private individuals or corporations remain free to limit free speech. Thus a newspaper might voluntarily refrain from using certain words, and might refuse to print advertisements or letters that it considers inappropriate or offensive. Likewise, many private contracts, such as those containing confidentiality agreements, expressly limit free speech.

Illegal Advocacy   The earliest free speech cases concerned whether the government could punish speech advocating or inciting violence, revolution, or other criminal activity. Even John Stuart Mill recognized that not *all* speech could be free. A speech charging that corn dealers were thieves might be permissible when delivered in the context of a political rally, but not if delivered to a hungry mob gathering in front of a corn dealer's house. In the 1918 case of *Schenck* v. *United States,* Oliver Wendell Holmes turned Mill's point into a legal rule: speech would be permitted unless it created a "clear and present danger" of serious harm. The **clear and present danger test,** Holmes wrote, allowed the government to make it illegal to falsely shout "fire" in a crowded theater.[18]

The clear and present danger test, much modified and interpreted, remains the principle behind many of the modern Court's free speech decisions. Incitement to riot or to commit some other criminal act is punishable under current law only if the speech is directed to inciting or producing "imminent lawless action" and then only if the speech is *likely* to cause such action. Moreover, as the Court decided in the 1957 case of *Yates* v. *United States,* the Constitution prohibits the government from punishing those who advocate illegal activity merely as an "abstract doctrine" divorced from advocacy of specific action.[19]

In practice, the Supreme Court has made it even more difficult for the government to stop fire-breathing orators, especially if their concerns are even remotely political in nature. In 1973, for example, a large group of anti–Vietnam War protesters moved onto a public street, interfering with traffic. The police hustled the crowd to either side. One protester, named Hess, then spoke up in a loud voice. He said either, "We'll take the f——ing street later" or "We'll take the f——ing street again," and was arrested for disorderly conduct. One might think that Hess's outburst was a call to imminent lawless action, but the justices disagreed. At worst, they concluded, Hess was calling on the crowd to disobey the police order "at some indefinite future time." At best, his statement "could be taken for present moderation," a suggestion to the crowd to take the street later, but not at the moment.[20]

Campus "speech codes" prohibiting racist and sexist speech have drawn fire from civil libertarians and conservatives alike.

"Fighting Words"   Certain broad categories of speech have always been considered outside the coverage of the First Amendment. One of these involves **fighting words**—words aimed directly at another individual and "likely to provoke the average person to retaliation, and thereby cause a breach of the peace." In the 1942 *Chaplinksy* case, for example, the Supreme Court upheld the conviction of a New Hampshire man who called the city marshal a "God damned racketeer" and "a damned Fascist."[21] The *Chaplinsky* decision has been steadily eroded over time. In subsequent cases the Supreme Court has made it clear that speech cannot be banned merely because it is "unpopular" or "invites dispute." Seven years after *Chaplinsky,* for example, the Court reversed the conviction of an abusive speaker who had condemned an angry crowd as "snakes," "slimy snakes," and "slimy scum." Although the Court's action rested on technical grounds, Justice William O. Douglas wrote a broad opinion that declared that free speech may "best serve its high purpose when it induces a condition of unrest, creates dissatisfaction with conditions as they are, or even stirs people to anger."[22]

Obscenity and Pornography   The Supreme Court has been careful to protect the communication of all ideas, however offensive or repulsive. Like fighting words, however, obscenity has never been deemed worthy of First Amendment protection. The reason, according to the Court, is that obscenity does not constitute an attempt to communicate ideas.

Under the Supreme Court's decision in *Miller* v. *California* (1973), the mere fact that a book or film is sexually explicit is not enough to make it obscene. To be judged obscene, the work as a whole must appeal to a *prurient* (improper and obsessive) interest in sex; it must depict specific sexual acts or particular body parts in a patently offensive way; and it must be without serious literary, artistic, political, or scientific value. The decision on whether or not a specific book or movie is obscene is left to local judges and juries, who are expected to apply the contemporary standards of their community.[23] Thus a movie may be judged obscene in one town but not in another.

The power of local juries to enforce community standards is limited, however. Years ago a Georgia jury declared that the movie *Carnal Knowledge,* a major studio film starring Art Garfunkel and Ann-Margret, was obscene. The Supreme Court reversed, holding that mere nudity and suggested sexual intercourse were not enough to make a film obscene, no matter how prudish a community might be. Moreover, whether or not a work has serious literary, artistic, political, or scientific value must be measured against a national standard rather than the standards of a particular community.

Drawing the line between obscene and nonobscene speech is not easy. At one point, Justice Potter Stewart stated that he could not define obscene speech, but "I do know it when I see it." In general the courts have distinguished between hard-core and soft-core pornography, and have tried to protect artistic or scientific works. It may be acceptable for the state to restrict nonobscene adult movies to particular areas of town, and it is definitely permissible to restrict child pornography.[24]

Symbolic Speech Under most circumstances, as we have seen, speech is protected under the First Amendment. Actions, in general, are not. But what about actions that are intended to communicate specific ideas?

The use of symbols as a substitute for words is clearly protected by the First Amendment. The courts have upheld the right of Ku Klux Klansmen to wear a bedsheet, of war protesters to wear a black armband, and of Nazis to wear swastikas and Nazi uniforms.[25] In such cases the Court has regarded the symbolic expression as "akin to pure speech," and thus constitutionally protected.

More problematic are cases in which actions, rather than symbols, are used to express ideas. Can a state make it illegal to burn an American flag? To burn a cross? To refuse to pledge allegiance to the flag? And even tougher are cases in which the actions involved, while ordinarily unprotected, become subject to the First Amendment only when they are used to express an idea. The state can ban public displays of nudity, for example, but can it stop nude dancers, who are arguably expressing their artistic creativity? The state can ban sleeping in a public park, but can it stop political protesters from staging a "sleep-in" to protest the plight of the homeless?

The Supreme Court's decisions in these cases follow no clear line. In general the judges have been driven by two concerns. The first is whether the state's action is directed primarily at the suppression of ideas or at the regulation of conduct. The second is whether the interests that the state is seeking to advance are important in comparison with the free speech rights at stake.

When the Court sees a deliberate attempt to interfere with free expression, it usually decides in favor of the speaker. Thus the Court has struck down laws banning flag burning and cross burning, along with laws compelling schoolchildren to salute the flag.[26] But where the state's interference with speech is judged unintentional and incidental, the state usually comes out on top. Hence the Court upheld the law against nude dancing (the state was relatively unconcerned with the message being communicated, and the dancer could express virtually the same message even though forced to wear pasties and a g-string). It also upheld the law banning sleeping in the park (the state had good reasons to stop *anyone* from sleeping in the park, and the protesters were not barred from expressing their message in other ways).[27]

Freedom of the Press Also high on the First Amendment's list of priorities is freedom of the press. The right of the press to report on and criticize the actions of the government, and to comment freely on public issues, is essential to democratic government. Protection of the press falls into two major categories.

First, the press is generally free from **prior restraints** on publication. In other words, only under the rarest circumstances can the government prevent a newspaper or magazine from publishing a story. Instead it must wait until publication actually occurs and then seek punishment. The only exceptions are for emergency conditions such as the publication of troop movements in wartime.[28] One case that qualified for a temporary prior restraint occurred in 1971, when the Nixon administration tried to stop the *New York Times* and the *Washington Post* from publishing the details of the Pentagon Papers, a top-secret report on American actions during the Vietnam War. After a full hearing, the Court lifted the ban, which had been in effect for just over two weeks. Although the case produced no clear legal rule, the six justices in the majority agreed that the papers—which dealt only with the history of the Vietnam conflict—posed no danger to American security. Another temporary stop-the-presses order was issued by a federal district court in 1979, when the *Progressive* magazine threatened to reveal how to make a hydrogen bomb. When it was revealed that all of the information in the article was available elsewhere, the government dropped the case.[29]

Second, the press is protected against libel suits—that is, lawsuits by those who feel that their reputations have been damaged in print. (Similar cases involving spoken rather than written words are known as slander cases.) Under the Supreme Court's decisions in a line of cases beginning with the 1964 case of *New York Times* v. *Sullivan*, the truth is always protected against libel actions, and even falsehood is often protected. To prevail in a libel suit, a public official or public figure (such as a politician, entertainer, or anyone else who has voluntarily put himself or herself before the public) must prove not only that the material in question is false but also that the newspaper or magazine knew it was false or acted with reckless disregard for whether it was true or not. Private individuals carry a lesser burden and must typically show only that the newspaper or magazine acted without due care in publishing the falsehood. In 1976 the Supreme Court ruled that even a prominent individual is not a public figure for libel purposes unless she has "voluntarily thrust herself to the forefront of any particular public controversy in order to influence the resolution of the issues involved in it."[30]

Television coverage of high-profile criminal cases has turned otherwise unknown judges into media figures. Here, Judge Hiller Zobel presides over the trial of Louise Woodward, the British nanny charged with murder in the death of a young child in her care.

The Constitution's protection for false speech stems from the recognition that too strict a libel code would have a chilling effect on the press, discouraging robust reporting of the news. In general the current libel law leaves the press free to investigate and print a wide variety of unflattering stories about public figures. In 1988, for example, the Supreme Court held that public figures could not sue for emotional distress over material that was clearly intended as parody.[31]

Broadcast Media Generally, broadcast media (television and radio stations) are entitled to less than complete First Amendment protection. The reason is twofold. First, the public airwaves are considered a scarce public resource. The right to broadcast on a specific frequency is granted by government license, and can be regulated in the public interest. Second, children and other unwilling listeners are more likely to be exposed to offensive or inappropriate material on the public airwaves than to material in printed form.

In a 1978 case, for example, the Court ruled that the government could restrict indecent language broadcast over the radio. The speech in question was a monologue by the comedian George Carlin, titled "Filthy Words," in which Carlin enumerated the seven dirty words you can't say on television—"the ones you definitely wouldn't say ever."

The proliferation of cable television stations and the rapid evolution of computer technology has cast both of these rationales into doubt, as the Supreme Court recognized in the landmark 1997 case of *Reno* v. *American Civil Liberties Union.* In a strongly worded opinion, the justices struck down the Communications Decency Act, a congressional statute that aimed to regulate the transmission of "patently offensive" and "indecent" material across the Internet. The statute's fatal flaw was its extraordinary breadth; the terms employed were so vague and ill-defined, wrote Justice John Paul Stevens, that they might "extend to discussions about prison rape or safe sexual practices, artistic images that include nude subjects, and arguably the card catalogue of the Carnegie Library."[32]

Freedom of Religion

The First Amendment protects religious freedom in two ways. First, it directly prohibits the government from interfering with the "free exercise" of religion. Second, it bans any laws "respecting an establishment of religion," a phrase generally taken to guarantee a degree of separation between church and state.

Other constitutional provisions also protect religious liberty. A provision in the main body of the Constitution declares that "no religious Test shall ever be required as a Qualification to any Office or public Trust under the United States." In one of the few cases arising out of this provision, the Supreme Court nullified a Tennessee law barring members of the clergy from becoming state legislators.[33] In addition, the Supreme Court has held that laws or practices that discriminate on the basis of religion may violate the Fourteenth Amendment's guarantee that the laws be applied equally.

That freedom of religion was important to the Framers is beyond dispute. Exactly what they meant by freedom of religion, however, is not clear. At a minimum, the Framers wanted to prohibit an official national church (the original Bill of Rights, remember, did not apply to the states) and to ensure that religious dissenters did not suffer any legal restrictions based solely on their religious views. At least some of the Framers would have gone further, banning government support of churches and prohibiting the government from forcing citizens to comply with laws that violated their religious beliefs.

Strangely, although the **Free Exercise Clause** and the **Establishment Clause** appear in the same amendment—indeed, in the same part of the same sentence—the Supreme Court has interpreted and applied each provision separately. The most interesting Supreme Court cases in recent years have seemed to pit the two clauses against one another.

Free Exercise Clause   The Free Exercise Clause prevents the government from interfering with the right of Americans to worship or not worship as they see fit. It was clear from the beginning that the government could not single out a particular religion for unfair treatment or discriminate against nonbelievers. More controversial was whether the government could apply its general laws in such a way as to violate a citizen's religious beliefs.

Early Supreme Court cases drew a sharp line between religious *beliefs,* which were covered by the First Amendment, and religious *actions,* which enjoyed no special constitutional protection. In a series of cases beginning in the 1960s, however, the Court held that the government must often bend its rules where strict enforcement of the law would compromise religious interests. In legal terms, the Court required the government to show that the enforcement of the law in such cases served a "compelling interest." Thus, the justices ruled in 1972 that a state could not apply a compulsory school attendance law to the Old Order Amish, whose religious beliefs required an end to conventional schooling at age fourteen.[34]

In 1990 the Supreme Court appeared to reverse itself on the question of religious exemptions to general laws. In *Employment Division* v. *Smith,* Justice Antonin Scalia returned to the belief/action distinction of *Reynolds* v. *United States,* upholding the application of a state's policy against illegal drugs to a Native American who used peyote (a hallucinogen) as part of a religious service. Scalia's opinion was based not on the compelling interest test but on the theory that religiously motivated actions were not exempt from otherwise valid laws. In effect, the Court thus abandoned the compelling interest test in such cases.[35]

In 1993, however, the Court made it clear that *Smith* does not apply to laws designed to discriminate against a particular religious group or practice. In *Church of the Lukumi Babalu Aye* v. *City of Hialeah,* the justices nullified a city ordinance banning animal sacrifices, which constitute an important part of the religious practice of the Santiera religion. The key issue for the Court was that the city of Hialeah, Florida, had enacted the ordinance because the opening of a Santiera church in the city was "distressing to many members of the Hialeah community." Because the law was aimed at a particular church, it could be justified only if it were necessary to serve "interests of the highest order."[35]

Religious exemptions to general laws are not usually required, but they are typically permitted. Paradoxically, allowing the state to make exceptions in order to foster religious freedom may raise Establishment Clause concerns.

Establishment Clause   In the modern era, the constitutional requirement prohibiting laws "respecting an establishment of religion" has become a source of considerable controversy. On the one side are those who believe in a wall of separation between church and state. On the other are those who believe in government "accommodation" of religion. Those in the first group stress government neutrality, and oppose government attempts to aid religion, even indirectly. Their opponents argue that the First Amendment does not require the government to be hostile to religion, but allows and even requires that government foster an atmosphere friendly to religion.

The Court favored the separationist approach in the 1960s and 1970s, banning, for example, organized prayer and Bible reading in the public schools. More recently, however, the separationists have lost ground, and the Court has moved toward a more accommodationist position. Although the legal standard remains in flux, of late the Court has tended to uphold state laws unless they constitute a state endorsement of religion. Under this evolving standard the Court has permitted prayer in a public high school by student groups with no official support; upheld the practice of opening state legislative sessions with a prayer; allowed the government to sponsor some holiday displays but not others;

and upheld a state scheme offering tax incentives to the parents of all students attending private schools, both religious and secular. But in 1992 the justices invalidated prayers at public high school graduations, on the grounds that the practice did represent a state endorsement of religion.[37]

A Conflict Between the Two Religion Clauses? The Supreme Court's interpretations of the two religion clauses has created a curious dilemma. Some have argued that the exceptions permitted or required under the Free Exercise Clause actually constitute state support for and recognition of religion, in violation of the Establishment Clause.

A 1971 case on taxation of church property nicely illustrates the point. The state of New York exempted from taxation all property used exclusively for religious, educational, or charitable purposes. Some argued that, by subsidizing religion, this exemption violated the Establishment Clause. Others argued that this kind of tax exemption was actually required by the Free Exercise Clause, since the taxation of religious institutions constituted government interference with religion.

The Supreme Court took a position in between, allowing—but not requiring—tax exemptions based on religion. The First Amendment must have enough "play in the joints" to allow a "benevolent neutrality," wrote Chief Justice Warren Burger. New York's law neither sponsored nor inhibited religion, he concluded, and was therefore constitutional.[38]

Freedom of Assembly

Another First Amendment right is "the right of the people peaceably to assemble, and to petition the Government for a redress of grievances." The Supreme Court has interpreted this provision not only to allow public protest gatherings but also to protect a more general right of free association.

Freedom of assembly is closely linked to freedom of speech, and the two freedoms often overlap. The difficulty is that even a peaceful protest gathering involves more than "pure speech." Those participating in even a peaceful protest may break various laws and ordinances by their *actions,* irrespective of what they say or why they have gathered. For example, they may intrude on private property; interfere with the business of the courts or other government agencies; impede traffic; violate fire codes or other safety rules; or intimidate others who are seeking to exercise their constitutional rights. The Court has tried to draw a clear line between which activities are permitted and which are not, but with limited success. It upheld a Louisiana law banning picketing "in or near" a courthouse, for example, but rejected South Carolina's attempt to break up a civil rights march on the grounds of the statehouse. More recently, the courts have allowed prosecution of abortion protesters who block access to abortion clinics or otherwise harass patients and doctors.[39]

Human Rights and American Foreign Policy

Should the United States be as aggressive in protecting civil liberties abroad as it is at home? Or is a concern for human rights incompatible with a realistic foreign policy that puts American interests first?

For most of the nation's history, presidents have proclaimed that the protection of human rights was an important part of U.S. foreign policy. George Washington cited human rights in his efforts to convince the nation to side with the French revolutionaries. Woodrow Wilson declared that the United States entered World War I "to make the world safe for democracy." Franklin Roosevelt's stated goals for World War II were the "four freedoms—freedom of speech, freedom of religion, freedom from want, and freedom from fear."*

Even more often, however, presidents have pursued American interests with little regard for human rights. Many of our allies and trading partners—Saudi Arabia, Jordan, China, the Philippines, and India, to name just a few—make little effort to protect the rights of their citizens. To ensure stability in Europe after World War II, the United States agreed to Soviet domination of Poland, East Germany, and other Eastern European states. The Korean and Vietnam Wars were fought in defense of regimes whose human rights records were far from exemplary.

In recent years virtually every president has made the protection of human rights an important part of American foreign policy. Presidents from Nixon forward put human rights high on their agenda with the Soviet Union, and a concern for human rights also affected U.S. policy toward South Africa, the Philippines, and China. Presidents who have pledged categorically to put human rights above other American concerns, however, have had a hard time following through. For example, Jimmy Carter tried to influence the Shah of Iran to give greater protection to human rights. Iran made little progress in this area, but Carter did not withdraw his support for the Shah. Likewise, Bill Clinton granted China favorable trading privileges despite its lack of progress on human rights issues.

Are American policy makers simply hypocritical, using human rights to score rhetorical points but ignoring them in practice? The issue is not so simple. Many American presidents have been concerned about human rights abroad, and would have gladly supported human rights if possible. The problem is that emphasizing human rights can make it more difficult for the United States to pursue other important policy goals. Pressing South Korea on human rights in the 1950s, for example, would have risked alienating a reliable ally in the United States' effort to contain communism. Insisting on greater protection of human rights in the Middle East, some argue, might destabilize friendly nations and make the peace process more difficult. Denying privileged trade status to China might have slowed economic progress in that country, arguably making long-term reforms less likely while causing the United States to lose major trading opportunities in a huge emerging market.

America's mixed record on supporting human rights abroad stems not so much from hypocrisy as from fundamental conflicts among our various foreign policy goals, and from an unwillingness to admit that the protection of human rights may at times be at odds with the way we define our national interest. If American foreign policy is to move in the human rights direction, policy makers and citizens alike will need to recognize the choices and tradeoffs that such a policy requires.†

---

* Wilson speech of April 2, 1917, in *The Messages and Papers of Woodrow Wilson* (New York: The Review of Reviews Corporation, 1924): I: 381; Franklin D. Roosevelt, "The Annual Message to the Congress," January 6, 1941, in *The Public Papers and Addresses of Franklin D. Roosevelt* (New York: Macmillan, 1941), XIII: pp. 663–678.

† James Schlesinger, "Quest For a Post–Cold War Foreign Policy," *Foreign Affairs* 72 (Winter 1993): 17–28; Alan Tonelson, "Jettison the Policy," *Foreign Policy* 97 (Winter 1994):121–132; Michael Posner, "Rally Round Human Rights," *Foreign Policy* 97 (Winter 1994): pp. 133–139.

Freedom of Association   **Freedom of association** cases require the Court to walk a thin line between protecting the right of individuals to gather together and recognizing the legitimate power of the government to advance the public interest. In a 1958 case, the Court unanimously blocked Alabama's attempt to force the National Association for the Advancement of Colored People (NAACP) to reveal its membership list and other records. The NAACP, the Court said, was entitled to act to defend its members' right to keep their association confidential. And in a 1995 case, the Court ruled that the private organization in charge of the South Boston St. Patrick's Day Parade could ban gay Irish groups from participating. Yet the courts have allowed the government to force private clubs to open up their memberships to women and minorities.[40]

Criminal Law

One of the hottest areas of constitutional law involves the rights of criminal suspects, defendants, and prisoners. The Supreme Court's rulings protecting those who find themselves under arrest or in prison have sparked an angry backlash, including popular demands that government "get tough on crime," protect the rights of crime victims, and reform the criminal justice system. All three branches of the federal government as well as the states have responded to these demands, and in recent years the Supreme Court has been far friendlier to law enforcement than it was just a few decades ago.

Amid all the sound and fury of the law and order debate, it is easy to lose sight of the critical principles at stake. Conservatives are fond of saying that "a conservative is a liberal who has been mugged." Liberals might respond that "a liberal is a conservative who has been arrested."

Searches and Seizures   The Fourth Amendment protects the right of the people against **unreasonable searches and seizures.** In general the police cannot conduct a search or make an arrest unless they first obtain a warrant from a magistrate—usually a justice of the peace or a similar judicial officer. Such warrants must be specific, and must be based on "probable cause" that a crime has in fact occurred.

There are exceptions to these rules, based on the realities of modern life. A police officer who witnesses a crime in progress does not need a warrant to make an arrest. Police officers can also make routine searches of a prisoner for weapons as part of the normal arrest process. And no search warrant is necessary if an individual voluntarily cooperates with the police.

Under the Supreme Court's decision in *Mapp* v. *Ohio*, evidence from an illegal search must be excluded from any subsequent criminal trial.[41] This so-called **exclusionary rule** has been the subject of great controversy, because of the possibility that a person who is clearly guilty will go free simply because the policeman erred. The Court has stuck to the exclusionary rule, however, for at least three reasons. First, the rule works directly where it needs to, compelling the police to meet the Court's standards if they want to achieve criminal convictions. Second, there is no other clearly effective way to enforce the Fourth Amendment. The most plausible alternative is to allow the victim of an illegal search to sue the police officer or department for damages, but the results of such a suit would be chancy at best, especially when brought by a convicted criminal and decided by a jury. Finally, the exclusionary rule avoids making the judiciary appear to be a partner in the illegal actions of the police department.

In recent years the Supreme Court has modified the exclusionary rule by creating a number of exceptions. Most important, the Court now allows the use of illegally seized evidence as long as the police officer acted in a "good faith" attempt to abide by the Constitution.[42]

The Fifth Amendment and the Miranda *Warnings*

The Fifth Amendment states that "No person . . . shall be compelled in any criminal case to be a witness against himself." Thus any American is entitled to "plead the Fifth," refusing to answer questions that might be self-incriminating. The protection against self-incrimination applies not only to appearances in criminal court but also to any other setting in which the government seeks to compel testimony—before Congress, in an administrative hearing, or in a police station. The Fifth Amendment does not apply when the government has granted immunity from prosecution or when it seeks nontestimonial evidence, such as blood or hair samples.

In 1965 the self-incrimination privilege led to the Supreme Court's landmark decision in *Miranda* v. *Arizona.*[43] Anyone who watches television police shows is familiar with the essence of the case. When suspects are taken into custody, they must be warned prior to questioning that they have a Fifth Amendment right to remain silent, that anything they say can be used against them in court, that they have the right to an attorney, and, in serious cases, that an attorney will be provided without charge if necessary. Collectively, this information is known as a *Miranda* warning. *If the police fail to inform a suspect of his* **Miranda *rights,*** *nothing the suspect says in response to questioning can be used in court.* There are exceptions, of course—there always are—but the general rule is clear. Moreover, once a suspect has insisted on his right to speak with a lawyer, all questioning must stop instantly. If illegal questioning leads police to find physical evidence, that evidence must generally be excluded also.

The *Miranda* warnings apply not just to formal interrogations but also to informal police questioning. As in the Fourth Amendment area, the Supreme Court has gradually weakened *Miranda* over the years, creating a variety of special exceptions. For example, a suspect can be questioned without being "Mirandized" if the public safety requires quick action. Likewise, evidence found as a result of an illegal interrogation may be admissible if it would have been found anyway. Finally, according to a 1991 Supreme Court decision, *Miranda* does not apply when there is no direct police questioning. In *Fulminante* v. *Arizona,* the Court upheld the conviction of a prisoner whose confession was obtained by trickery, using a policeman pretending to be a fellow prisoner, rather than by interrogation.[44]

Like the Court's search-and-seizure decisions, Miranda has caused great controversy. Critics charge, once again, that *Miranda* allows the guilty to go free, and that it hampers police efforts to solve crime and punish criminals. But *Miranda,* if anything, stands on firmer ground than the Fourth Amendment cases. The warning requirement protects against coerced confessions—which may be false—especially by making sure that all questioning takes place with a lawyer present. Before *Miranda,* there was a very great risk that a frightened, isolated, and intimidated suspect would confess to a crime he or she did not commit.

In practice, *Miranda* hardly hampers police work. Its strict standards have probably made police departments more careful about obtaining evidence and more professional about they way they work. In any event, many suspects voluntarily waive their *Miranda* rights. Some 90 percent of all criminal suspects plead guilty, and many others are found guilty through good detective work, without reliance on any confession at all. Undoubtedly some of the guilty do go free, although the number in absolute terms is probably small.[45]

The Death Penalty   One of the most emotional controversies in the area of criminal law is whether and how the death penalty should be applied. The United States is one of the few industrialized nations that still permits executions, and the number of executions carried out each year has been rising steadily since the 1970s. Civil libertarians and death penalty advocates have clashed on two separate issues: whether the death penalty should be allowed at all, and, if so, what safeguards should be required to prevent unjust executions.

The Supreme Court answered the first question in a series of decisions in the 1970s, ruling that the death penalty, if fairly and carefully administered, did not violate either the Due Process Clause or the Eighth Amendment prohibition on cruel and unusual punishments. The Court did bar mandatory death penalties, and required that the law set out clear guidelines for juries to follow in deciding whether to impose a death sentence.[46]

The second question has flared up more recently. Many Americans have grown impatient with the extraordinary difficulties and delays in actually executing a prisoner who has been sentenced to death. The average death row inmate spends more than eight years in prison before execution, exhausting every possible legal appeal. In the past few years the Supreme Court has greatly tightened up avenues for repeated appeals of death penalty convictions, so much so that some have accused the justices of being in an unseemly hurry to see the punishments carried out.[47]

The Court's frustration with the endless delays and legal machinations in death penalty cases is perhaps understandable, but in the process the very real possibility that an innocent person will be killed has increased greatly. In a recent case, the Court held that a prisoner's claim of innocence—by itself—does not constitute grounds for ordering a federal court review, even when the state courts refuse to hear critical new evidence. The Court has also upheld the death penalty as applied to the mentally retarded and to children as young as sixteen.[48]

A serious concern of those who oppose capital punishment is that judges and juries may not apply the death penalty fairly to blacks and other minorities. The evidence on this point is inconclusive, although studies do suggest that the death penalty is more likely to be imposed when the victim of the crime is white than when the victim is black. The Supreme Court, however, has consistently rejected arguments that the death penalty is invalid because of racial discrimination.[49]

Other Criminal Law Rights   The Constitution provides a number of other protections that apply especially in the criminal law context. The Sixth Amendment guarantees that an American is entitled to a "speedy and public trial, by an impartial jury"; "to be informed of the nature and cause of the accusation"; "to be confronted by the witnesses against him"; "to subpoena witnesses"; and "to have the Assistance of Counsel for his defense." Many of these provisions have been interpreted broadly by the Supreme Court. For example, the right to counsel has been extended to require that the state provide counsel in serious criminal cases to those who cannot afford to hire a lawyer. The right to an "impartial jury" has been interpreted to require that the jury pool be drawn from a cross-section of the community, and to ban the exclusion of potential jurors on the basis of race or sex. The Eighth Amendment bans "cruel and unusual punishments" and "excessive bail," and has been extended to prohibit inhumane prison conditions.[50]

Should Capital Punishment be Abolished?

In the 1970s, the Supreme Court ruled that the death penalty—properly administered—does not violate the Constitution of the United States. Over the past twenty years, the number of executions has increased markedly: between 1968 and 1976, for example, not a single prisoner was executed in the United States; in 1995 alone, fifty-six prisoners were put to death. This increasing use of the death penalty has fueled the centuries-long controversy over capital punishment, with proponents and opponents as passionate as ever.

No: Keep the death penalty

The death penalty is fair and just.   Supporters of capital punishment believe that it is fundamentally fair for someone who deliberately takes the life of another to be forced to give up his or her own life. The punishment for a crime should be proportionate to the offense, they argue; when the crime is first-degree murder, proportionality requires nothing less than capital punishment. To those who argue that the death penalty violates the sacredness of human life, proponents respond that the existence of the ultimate penalty actually underscores the value that society places on the lives of the victims. These arguments, supporters of capital punishment argue, are backed up by the Bible and by the practice of many centuries.

Capital punishment deters crime.   Supporters of capital punishment point out the obvious—but important—fact that each execution deters at least one potential killer from ever murdering again. They also claim that other would-be killers are deterred by the possibility of the death sentence. Numbers are hard to come by, not least because death penalty cases are, in statistical terms at least, relatively rare. It is clear that many violent criminals are repeat offenders; according to one study, some 40 percent of prisoners on death row were on probation, parole, or pretrial release when they committed murder. Less clear is whether potential first-time offenders would be deterred by the possibility of capital punishment.

Capital punishment is sanctioned by the Constitution.   The Constitution prohibits "cruel and unusual punishments," death-penalty advocates concede, but the text and history of the Constitution make it clear that the Framers did not consider capital punishment cruel or unusual. The Fifth Amendment, for example, implicitly recognizes that the state can take life (along with liberty and property) as long as it provides "due process of law." Moreover, the death penalty was recognized in 1787 in every state of the Union.

Under current law, defendants in capital cases are amply safeguarded against the unfair or erroneous imposition of the death penalty.   As the law now stands, a defendant cannot receive the death penalty unless he or she is found guilty of first-degree murder with "aggravating circumstances" by a unanimous jury. Mandatory death penalties are not permitted, and the defendant is given the opportunity to raise mitigating circumstances and to provide other evidence to argue that his or her life should be spared. Death sentences are subject to mandatory appeal, and must be confirmed not only by the trial judge, but by one or more appellate courts. Furthermore, defendants are given the opportunity to seek review all the way up to the Supreme Court of the United States.

Yes: Abolish the death penalty

The death penalty debases human life and brutalizes society. If killing is wrong, death penalty opponents argue, killing the killer cannot be right. "If everyone took an eye for an eye," said Mohandas K. Gandhi, "the whole world would be blind." As the eighteenth-century Italian philosopher Cesare Beccaria wrote, the death penalty undermines the very purpose of the law, which is to moderate human passions and promote respect for the rights of others. "If the passions, or the necessity of war, have taught men to shed the blood of the fellow creatures," he wrote, "the laws, which are intended to moderate the ferocity of mankind, should not increase it by examples of barbarity."

The death penalty is not needed to deter crime. Whether or not capital punishment is an effective deterrent, there are other deterrents—such as life in prison without possibility of parole—that are equally effective. Moreover, because the death penalty is rarely enforced, it may not be as effective a deterrent as would be the certainty of lesser punishment. An execution is but a momentary spectacle, wrote Beccaria, far less effective in terms of deterrence than "the continued example of a man deprived of his liberty, condemned, as a beast of burthen, to repair, by his labour, the injury he has done to society."

Constitutional and moral standards evolve, and they have evolved sufficiently to allow us to give up the death penalty. The Constitution's ban on "cruel and unusual punishments" presents us with a broad concept, which we must fill in according to contemporary standards of morality. More than half the countries in the world have abolished the death penalty in law or practice, and most of the rest execute no more than a handful a year. In 1996, only five countries executed more prisoners than the United States: China, Ukraine, Russia, Turkmenistan, Iran, and Saudi Arabia—hardly an honor roll of democratic nations.

The death penalty is often applied arbitrarily or unfairly. Critics argue that members of certain groups—including minorities and the poor—are far more likely to receive the death penalty than others. The nature of a death penalty, which requires by law that a judge and jury make an individual determination about each case, practically guarantees that capital punishment will be invoked in an arbitrary and discriminatory way. Half of all prisoners on death row are minorities. Of the 227 prisoners executed in the United States between 1976 and 1994, for example, only two were whites convicted of killing non-whites.

The death penalty is irreversible, and mistakes are inevitable. Even if the death penalty is appropriate in some murder cases, it is impossible to prevent erroneous convictions and executions of the innocent. According to one study, over four hundred innocent people have been executed in the United States in the twentieth century. But the statistics don't really matter, critics of the death penalty argue—even one erroneous execution is too many.

SOURCES: Paul A Winters, ed., *The Death Penalty: Opposing Viewpoints*, 3d ed. (San Diego, CA: Greenhaven Press, Inc., 1997); Hugo Adam Bedau, ed., *The Death Penalty in America: Current Controversies* (New York: Oxford University Press, 1997); Amnesty International <http://www.amnesty.org>; Death Penalty Information Center <http://www.essential.org/dpic>.

Privacy

No area of constitutional law has created as much controversy as the **right to privacy.** The right to privacy includes not only the search-and-seizure issues discussed above, but also questions of free speech, lifestyle, sexual behavior, and abortion.

Background   The Constitution does not explicitly mention a right to privacy. But privacy is hinted at, or suggested, in several different places. The very concept of limited government suggests that the interests of the private citizen should be protected from the intrusions of government. Moreover, the Framers certainly believed that there were some aspects of private life into which the government should not intrude. The most obvious examples are the Fourth Amendment's protection of each individual's "person, papers, houses, and effects," and what the Framers called "freedom of conscience"—the right to think and worship freely.

The difficult question is whether the Constitution protects a right to privacy that goes beyond the specific guarantees of the Bill of Rights. The idea that the right to privacy was more than the sum of its parts was described more than one hundred years ago as the right "to be let alone." This formulation was picked up by Supreme Court Justice Louis D. Brandeis, who later described it as "the most comprehensive of rights and the right most valued by civilized men."[51]

Through the years, lawyers and justices have suggested that several provisions of the Constitution imply a right to privacy. Most commonly mentioned are the Fifth and Fourteenth Amendments' guarantee of due process of law, the Third and Fourth Amendments, and the open-ended Ninth Amendment, which specifies that "the enumeration in the Constitution, of certain rights, shall not be construed to deny or disparage others retained by the people." Justice William O. Douglas found the right to privacy in the "emanations" and "penumbras" of the Bill of Rights, a shadowy theory that has sparked much commentary.

Although the Supreme Court has not always been clear on the subject of privacy, its decisions can be divided according to the nature of the privacy right in question. Three strands of privacy law emerge from the Court's decisions:

Right to Be Free from Government Intrusions   The Fourth Amendment cases, discussed above, make it clear that Americans have the right to keep certain information and activities away from the government, and to be free from unwanted governmental interference. The right to keep certain matters private underlies the requirement that the government invade private spaces only when it has a real need to do so, and then only after following all appropriate procedures. Protecting the right to privacy in this sense is essential to preserving the dignity of every human being.

This conception of privacy was at the heart of the Fourth Amendment search-and-seizure cases. An example is *Rochin* v. *California,* in which the police invaded a suspect's bedroom to search for illegal drugs. The suspect, who at the time was in bed with his common-law wife, quickly swallowed the drugs in question, but three police officers "'jumped upon him' and attempted to extract the capsules." Failing to achieve their objective, the officers handcuffed Rochin and took him to a hospital, where they instructed the physicians to induce vomiting. This procedure produced two capsules of morphine. The Supreme Court reversed Rochin's conviction, holding that such police action "shocks the conscience," "is bound to offend even hardened sensibilities," and involves "methods too close to the rack and the screw to permit of constitutional differentiation."[52]

Associational Privacy The right to privacy is closely related to the right of free association. By extension, constitutional privacy also extends to personal relationships between individuals. In ruling that the government could not ban the use of contraceptives by married couples, for example, the Supreme Court relied heavily on the idea that marriage was a "sacred association." Only later did the Court extend this decision to nonmarried couples also. Allowing the police "to search the sacred precincts of marital bedrooms for telltale signs of the use of contraceptives," wrote Justice Douglas, is an idea "repulsive to the notions of privacy surrounding the marriage relationship."[53]

Autonomy: The Right of Self-Determination A third important strand of privacy—and by far the most controversial—is the right to do what you want, free from government compulsion or interference. This conception of privacy was applied early on to limit the government's ability to interfere with an individual's decisions on such essential matters as whether to have children, and how to educate children once they arrive. As early as the 1920s, for example, the Court ruled that the government could not ban the teaching of foreign languages to young children. Liberty, the Court declared, included the right to "marry, establish a home and bring up children."[54] Similarly, the Court decided two years later that the state could not force children to attend public schools, because such a law interfered "with the liberty of parents and guardians to direct the upbringing and education of children under their control."[55] And in 1942 the Court expressed similar sentiments when it prohibited the forced sterilization of habitual criminals. Although states were normally free to set the punishment for various crimes, they could not ride roughshod over matters that were "fundamental to the very existence and survival of the race," such as marriage and procreation.

It is this strand of the privacy doctrine—known as autonomy, from the Greek for "govern oneself"—that ultimately led to the 1973 abortion decision, ***Roe* v. *Wade.*** A concern for autonomy was also evident in the Court's earlier decision on contraception. In the Court's view, certain areas of private life—marriage, sexual relationships, procreation, the upbringing of children—are so important that they deserve special protection, even though they are not specifically mentioned in the Bill of Rights.

The Court's decisions in the autonomy area have left it open to serious criticism. First, the Court's reasoning is sometimes difficult to follow or downright misleading, and the meaning of privacy, and its constitutional sources, is often unclear. Second, the autonomy decisions have left the Court open to the charge of judicial activism. Without clear guidance from the Constitution, critics argue, the Court seems free to roam about unchecked, creating law virtually at will. The autonomy decisions, of course, are passionately defended by those who believe that the Constitution strongly implies the protection of privacy rights such as abortion.

Obviously the three strands of the privacy doctrine discussed above overlap. The contraception decision, for example, involves the

Norma McCorvey (left), alias Jane Roe, leaves the Supreme Court after attending the oral arguments in the 1989 case of Webster v. Reproductive Health Services. *In* Webster *and subsequent cases, the Court narrowed but did not overturn its landmark decision in* Roe v. Wade.

right to be free from government intrusion (concerns about police searches of the marital bedroom), the right of free association (the marriage relationship), and the right of autonomy (deciding whether or when to have children). That the strands of the privacy doctrine overlap is one reason that the Court's decisions in this area often appear confused or contradictory. Still, it is useful to keep these categories in mind as you think about the cases on abortion and sexual privacy.

Abortion   Few, if any, decisions have caused as much controversy, or generated as much commentary, as the Supreme Court's 1973 decision recognizing a woman's right to choose whether or not to terminate a pregnancy.[56] Drawing on its decisions regarding procreation and contraception, the Court held in *Roe* v. *Wade* that the right to privacy, whatever its specific constitutional source, is broad enough to include the abortion decision. The Court also held that regardless of when life begins in a biological, philosophical, or theological sense, the Fourteenth Amendment's guarantee of life, liberty, and property does not apply until birth.

A woman's right to terminate a pregnancy, however, is not absolute. The Court held that the state could regulate the medical procedures involved beginning in the second trimester, or fourth month, of the pregnancy, a time when abortions are medically more dangerous than if done early on. The state could ban abortions altogether beginning in the third trimester, or seventh month, at which point the fetus is capable of living outside the woman's body.

Critics of *Roe* have attempted to overturn the decision outright—a goal helped along by the appointment of five new justices by Presidents Reagan and Bush, who were both committed to reversing *Roe.* For a time it looked as if they might succeed, but support for at least the core decision in *Roe* seems to have stabilized. Meanwhile, abortion opponents have taken a different tack, imposing more and more legal obstacles in the path of a woman who seeks an abortion. The Supreme Court has upheld some of these and rejected others. In *Harris* v. *McRae,* for example, the Court upheld Congress's refusal to pay for abortions under Medicaid, which provides medical services to the poor. The Court has also upheld requirements that minors obtain consent from a parent or from a judge and that a woman consent in writing to the procedure. However, the Court has struck down state requirements that abortions be performed in hospitals, that women receive their husbands' consent before an abortion, and that only certain abortion techniques be used.[57]

The Supreme Court's 1973 decision legalizing abortion has provoked enormous controversy. Here, prolife and prochoice demonstrators clash outside the Supreme Court.

Table 4.2
Public Opinion on Abortion

Abortion should be permitted by law	Percentage Agreeing		
	Men	Women	Total
Never	10.3	12.6	11.5
Only in cases of rape, incest, or danger to the woman's life	31.1	26.7	28.9
Only when a clear need has been established	17.9	14.2	16.0
Always	38.9	45.5	42.3

Source: National Election Study, 1996.

In 1989, a bitterly divided Court ruled in *Webster* v. *Reproductive Health Services*[58] that states could require fetal testing to ensure that the fetus was under twenty-four weeks old (after which the state could prohibit the abortion), and upheld a ban on abortions in public hospitals. More important, the Court seemed poised to reject the *Roe* framework and accept far greater limitations on the abortion right. Both prochoice and prolife groups viewed the decision as a fundamental departure from earlier cases, or at least as a sign that such a departure was imminent.

The most recent major test of the abortion issue came in 1992, in *Planned Parenthood* v. *Casey.*[59] Writing for the Court, Justice Sandra Day O'Connor reaffirmed the "central holding" of *Roe,* that the state may not interfere with a woman's right to terminate her pregnancy until after the point of fetal viability. At the same time, O'Connor and two other justices rejected *Roe's* rigid trimester framework, substituting instead the test of whether a particular state regulation prior to viability "unduly burdens" the abortion right. Although O'Connor's position on this last point did not command a majority of the Court, her view does appear to be the lodestar toward which the justices are heading.

The politics of the abortion issue continue to be bitter and divisive (see Table 4.2). Under George Bush, abortion opponents succeeded in banning abortion counseling at federally funded family planning clinics and in stopping federally funded research involving fetal tissue. The first rule was upheld by the Supreme Court in *Rust* v. *Sullivan* (1991),[60] but both rules were overturned when the Clinton administration took office. Still, the abortion issue refuses to go away. Controversies have erupted over the rights of abortion protesters, the use of federal marshals to protect abortion clinics, and the funding of abortion under federal health care reform.

Sexual Privacy   Except for its decisions guaranteeing the right to use contraceptives and striking down laws banning interracial marriages,[61] the Supreme Court has never explicitly decided whether or not the states can regulate the sexual relations of married or unmarried couples of the opposite sex. Most states still have laws on the books banning a variety of sexual practices, including oral sex and anal sex, although these are rarely enforced. Most constitutional scholars believe that the Court's prior decisions would prohibit the government from interfering with a consensual sexual relationship between a man and a woman.

Many argued that the logic of the Court's decisions on contraception suggested that homosexual relations were similarly protected, but the Supreme Court ruled otherwise in 1986. In a Georgia case known as *Bowers* v. *Hardwick,* the Court held that the Constitution did not prohibit a state from imposing criminal penalties on a homosexual couple who engaged in forbidden sexual practices. The Court based its argument on the fact that laws banning homosexual sodomy were on the books in all fifty states until 1961, and in twenty-four states at the time *Bowers* was decided. Critics, including Justice Harry Blackmun, reacted harshly.

Although *Bowers* remains the law of the land, gay rights groups did achieve a major victory in 1996, when the Supreme Court invalidated a Colorado constitutional amendment that prohibited the state or any local government in the state from passing any legislation designed to protect the status of persons based on their "homosexual, lesbian or bisexual orientation, conduct, practices or relationships." The Colorado amendment "identifies persons by a single trait and then denies them protection across the board," wrote Justice Anthony M. Kennedy. "The resulting disqualification of a class of persons from the right to seek specific protection from the law is unprecedented in our jurisprudence."[62]

Summary

Civil liberties encompass the rights guaranteed by the Constitution of the United States, as interpreted by the courts and other institutions of government. Civil liberties issues include freedom of speech, press, and assembly; freedom of religion (and freedom from state-imposed religion); freedom from unreasonable searches and seizures; due process of law, especially in criminal cases; and the right to privacy, which includes a woman's right to choose whether or not to have an abortion.

The classic defense of rights appears in the writings of the English philosopher John Locke, who believed that all men were born with certain rights that could not be given or taken away. These "unalienable rights," as Thomas Jefferson wrote, include "life, liberty, and the pursuit of happiness." Later writers, including the English philosopher John Stuart Mill and Supreme Court Justice Louis Brandeis, stressed the importance to individuals and to a democratic society of allowing all persons to develop and express their own ideas and to pursue their chosen ways of life.

The Bill of Rights originally applied only to the federal government, but in the twentieth century it has been applied to the states as well. Especially in recent decades, the Supreme Court has played the central role in the protection of civil liberties, although other institutions of government—including Congress, the presidency, and the lower federal and state courts—also play important parts. Threats to civil liberties, likewise, can come from all three branches and from both the state and the national governments, although historically the states have presented the greater threat.

Exactly what rights are secured by the Constitution and how to balance individual rights against the interests of society at large have sparked great controversy. Moreover, the modern Supreme Court's emphasis on individual rights has been challenged by those who believe that rights are meaningless outside the context of community and that the community's interests should be given sufficient weight. In addition, the rights guaranteed by the Constitution often conflict with one another, forcing difficult choices.

Not surprisingly, therefore, civil liberties issues have given rise to a great number of important legal cases. Over the years the Supreme Court has taken an expansive approach to the Bill of Rights, interpreting its provisions broadly and enforcing them vigorously. The Court's activist approach in civil liberties cases peaked in the 1950s and 1960s, during the era of the Warren Court. Recently the Supreme Court has taken a more restrictive approach in civil liberties cases, narrowing some of the rights it previously recognized and refusing to recognize new rights. Still, most of the core decisions of the Warren Court remain largely intact, and Americans continue to enjoy the broad protections of the Bill of Rights.

Key Terms

Civil liberties
Civil rights
John Locke
John Stuart Mill
Bill of Rights
Habeas corpus
Due process of law
Incorporation
Warren Court
Clear and present danger test
Fighting words

Prior restraints
Free Exercise Clause
Establishment Clause
Freedom of assembly
Freedom of association
Unreasonable searches and seizures
Exclusionary rule
Miranda rights
Right to privacy
Roe v. *Wade*

Review Questions

1. What is the meaning of the term *civil liberties?* How, in common usage, do civil liberties differ from civil rights?

2. What is the source of individual rights, according to Locke and Jefferson? What are unalienable rights?

3. Why are freedom of thought and freedom of speech of special importance to civil libertarians like John Stuart Mill and Louis D. Brandeis?

4. Compare and contrast the individualist conception of rights with the communitarian conception of rights. Give examples of each.

5. Which institutions of government pose the greatest threats to civil liberties? Which institutions provide the greatest protection for civil liberties? Why?

6. Describe the important concerns that the Supreme Court must balance in deciding cases dealing with free speech, freedom of religion, privacy, and other civil liberties issues.

Suggested Readings

Abraham, Henry J. *Freedom and the Court: Civil Rights and Liberties in the United States.* 6th ed. New York: Oxford University Press, 1994.

Dworkin, Ronald M. *Taking Rights Seriously.* Cambridge, Mass.: Harvard University Press, 1977.

Glendon, Mary Ann. *Rights Talk: The Impoverishment of Political Discourse.* New York: Free Press, 1991.

Hall, Kermit L., ed. *The Oxford Companion to the Supreme Court of the United States.* New York: Oxford University Press, 1992.

Lewis, Anthony. *Gideon's Trumpet.* New York: Random House, 1964.

Lockhart, William B., Yale Kamisar, Jesse H. Choper, and Steven H. Shiffrin. *Constitutional Law: Cases-Comments-Questions.* 8th ed. St. Paul, Minn.: West Publishing Co., 1996 [with annual supplements].

McCloskey, Robert G. *The American Supreme Court.* 2d ed. revised by Sanford Levinson. Chicago: University of Chicago Press, 1994.

Mill, John Stuart. *On Liberty.* Ed. by David Spitz. New York: Norton, 1975.

White, G. Edward. *Earl Warren, a Public Life.* New York: Oxford University Press, 1982.

Internet Resources

The American Civil Liberties Union, the nation's oldest civil liberties organization at:

http://www.aclu.org/

The National Legal Center for Public Interest, an organization founded "to bring balance into the courts in the defense of citizens' rights, the freedom of private enterprise, and the reduction of excessive government regulation" at:

http://www.nlcpi.org/

Web-based legal resources, including full text of Supreme Court decisions since 1893 and links to historical cases and other legal materials at:

http://www.findlaw.com/

The National Abortion and Reproductive Rights Action League, a leading prochoice interest group at:

http://www.naral.org/

The National Right to Life Committee, a leading prolife interest group at:

http://www.nrlc.org/

5

Civil Rights

★ ★

Can a loyal and innocent American citizen be forced from home and imprisoned in a concentration camp for no reason other than his or her racial or ethnic background? It happened here, to Japanese Americans on the West Coast of the United States during World War II.

The war hysteria that swept the nation after the Japanese navy's attack on Pearl Harbor in December 1941 was particularly intense in California. The alarm was focused on the 112,000 Americans of Japanese descent—three-fourths of them American citizens—who lived there. Always the victims of racial prejudice and discrimination, Japanese Americans were especially vulnerable in the early days of the war. Many of their fellow citizens presumed them to be disloyal to the United States, and they were widely suspected—without evidence—of operating as spies and saboteurs in preparation for a Japanese invasion of the mainland.

Pressed by political leaders in California and by generals in Washington, President Franklin D. Roosevelt approved the creation of "exclusion zones" for Japanese Americans in February 1942. A month later, Roosevelt established the War Relocation Authority, which moved quickly to build and populate a series of relocation camps. Although Roosevelt had acted by executive order, Congress lost no time in passing a law to ratify his actions.

Some Japanese Americans refused to comply with the relocation policy. One of them was Fred Korematsu, who was born in the United States and lived in the San Francisco Bay area. For his disobedience, Korematsu was arrested and convicted of a criminal offense that consisted, in the words of Supreme Court justice Robert Jackson, of "being present in the state whereof he is a citizen, near the place where he was born, and where all his life he has lived."[1] There was no evidence— nor was any required—that Korematsu was in any way disloyal to the United States.

Korematsu's case went all the way to the United States Supreme Court, which rendered its decision in December 1944. Justice Hugo Black, writing for the Court, upheld Korematsu's conviction and with it the entire relocation program. Black conceded that the policy was based solely on a racial classification, but held that such classifications were constitutional if they were justified by a "compelling state interest" and if the means used were necessary to achieve the government's objective. Black had little difficulty finding that Korematsu's conviction met this test: the compelling interest involved was nothing less than the security of the United States, and the method of achieving that goal was to be left to the discretion of the military authorities.

Three justices disagreed. They pointed out that the government could have held hearings to determine whether particular individuals were security risks, and

Japanese Americans arrive from California at the Heart Mountain Relocation Center in the Wyoming desert. Internees had to endure winter temperatures of 30° below zero in makeshift buildings that could not keep out the winds.

★★

they challenged the Court's uncritical acceptance of military expertise in such matters. More to the point, the dissenters recognized that the exclusion and detention program was largely motivated by racial prejudice and hostility. The "foremost advocates of the evacuation," wrote Justice Frank Murphy, were people who for years had spread "misinformation, half-truths and insinuations" against Japanese Americans.[2] Only racial prejudice could explain why Americans of German ancestry had not suffered comparable treatment.

Korematsu v. *United States* is one of the most heavily criticized Supreme Court decisions of this century. Justice William O. Douglas, who joined the majority opinion, later wrote that "fine American citizens had been robbed of their property by racists—crimes that might not have happened if the Court had not followed the Pentagon so literally."[3] Finally, in 1988, Congress officially apologized for the episode, and approved small but symbolically important reparations payments to those victims who were still alive.

The history of race relations in America presents the problem of majority rule and minority rights in its starkest form. African Americans were transported to the American colonies as slaves; their descendants were freed by law but still face many social and economic obstacles. Native Americans were pushed off their lands, and many were massacred in the name of progress. Asian Americans and Latinos have faced prejudice and exploitation.

Other groups too have faced discrimination at the hands of those with political and economic power.

Until the 1970s, sex discrimination was permitted by the courts and encouraged by a variety of government programs. Children born out of wedlock, foreign nationals, the mentally ill, the disabled, gays and lesbians, and members of small and unpopular religious sects have all faced hostility and prejudice not because of what they do but simply because of who they are.

This legacy of discrimination and exploitation has not disappeared. Yet America in the 1990s can boast of substantial progress, both in law and in public opinion. All three branches of the federal government have cooperated to fight discrimination in education, employment, and housing. More and more minority and female candidates are running for, and winning, public office. The media and Americans in general have shown a growing awareness of the problems of minority groups.

This success has not come cheaply, however. Progress in civil rights has at times produced a dangerous backlash, especially when economic times turn difficult. Fire-breathing orators fan the flames of bigotry and discrimination, while thoughtful critics argue that an overemphasis on group membership and group status divides society and threatens to undermine individual rights and responsibilities.

This chapter explores the complex and emotional area of civil rights in law and politics. Because the current debate cannot be understood except in the context of what came before, its approach is largely historical. Its goal is to encourage thoughtful discussion and debate of some of the most difficult and contentious issues facing the United States today.

Questions to Keep in Mind

✔ *How does the American constitutional system protect the rights of racial minorities and other minority groups? How successfully does the system balance majority rule and minority rights?*

✔ *What parallels exist between the civil rights movement and the women's rights movement? Between the struggles of African Americans and those of other racial and ethnic minorities, including Asian Americans and Native Americans?*

✔ *How does the Supreme Court decide when racial classifications are appropriate? When gender classifications are appropriate?*

Basic Concepts

Definition of Civil Rights

The term **civil rights** refers generally to questions of equality under law, especially those regarding race, ethnicity, and gender. Originally applied to the rights of African Americans, the term has now been expanded to include any group disadvantaged by its minority status, and also to women, who, though technically a majority, have historically been excluded from positions of power and influence in the public and private sectors.

The Constitution and Equality

The Fourteenth Amendment—added to the Constitution after the Civil War largely to protect the rights of the freed slaves—guarantees to everyone "the equal protection of the laws." On the surface these words seem straightforward enough; they would appear to require simply that the government treat all persons equally under the law. In fact, the Equal Protection Clause is difficult to interpret and apply. Much of our current understanding of the equal protection requirement stems from a series of Supreme Court decisions dating back just half a century.

The difficulty for the Court is that government policies, by definition, treat different people differently. A person who carries out a premeditated murder is not treated the same way as someone who kills in the heat of passion. The admissions office of a state university treats a student with an SAT score of 1500 differently from an applicant who scores 1000. A wealthy citizen is taxed at a higher rate than a poor one. It is the very purpose of law to classify individuals according to their conduct or status, and to treat them differently on that basis.

You may or may not approve of the classifications noted in the preceding paragraph, but all of them are legal under the Constitution of the United States. The law requires that persons who are "similarly situated" be treated similarly, but it allows wide latitude for deciding who is similarly situated in any particular circumstance. Some forms of government classification, however, are unconstitutional under the Fourteenth Amendment. The problem is to determine which ones.

In general the courts require that all government classifications be "rational"—that is, that they be *reasonably related to some legitimate governmental purpose.* This is a very weak standard that allows for almost complete discretion on the part of Congress and the state legislatures. An age twenty-one drinking limit, for example, is reasonably related to the state's desire to cut down on traffic accidents; an age twenty or twenty-two limit might be better, but the courts leave that judgment up to the legislature. The government need not show that its classifications are perfect or even optimal (some nineteen-year-olds, surely, are more responsible drinkers than many forty-year-olds). It need only show that they are reasonable.

Some types of government classification, however, call for a higher judicial standard. When the government classifies on the basis of race or religion, for example, its actions raise immediate suspicions of illegal discrimination. Such classifications are known as **suspect classifications** and give rise to **strict scrutiny** by the courts. Under the strict scrutiny test, a suspect classification is presumed to be illegal unless the government can demonstrate that it has very good reasons for its actions, and can be justified only if the government demonstrates that the classification is *necessary* to serve a *compelling* interest—a very high standard indeed.

How do the courts decide what classifications are suspect? At least three factors weigh into the decision:

"I hate everybody, regardless of race, creed, or place of national origin!"

- *A tradition of stereotyping and discrimination.* Classifications that reflect traditional stereotypes or that have traditionally been used as the basis of unfair treatment are inherently suspect. These include race, religion, and gender.
- *Impossibility of change.* Society has recognized that individuals should not be penalized for characteristics over which they have no control, such as gender or race. But impossibility of change does not guarantee suspect status—consider age, which forms the basis of many government classifications. And some factors which can be changed (such as religion) are nonetheless suspect.
- *"Fundamental" characteristics.* Classifications that affect aspects of human personality that are judged fundamental to our existence and well-being are more likely to be treated as suspect. Thus gender is accorded a protected status, whereas hair color, eye color, and height are not.

So far the Supreme Court has recognized four suspect classifications: race, religion, illegitimacy (being born to unmarried parents), and alienage (not being an American citizen). It also imposes strict scrutiny when government classifications touch on a fundamental interest such as privacy or free speech. Gender is considered to be a "semisuspect" classification—laws that distinguish between men and women are subjected to a judicial test in between strict scrutiny and the minimum rationality requirement. The Supreme Court has refused to declare either sexual orientation or wealth to be suspect classifications.[4]

Note that although the Equal Protection Clause applies only to the states, the Supreme Court has held that the Fifth Amendment's Due Process Clause imposes essentially the same requirements on the national government.

The Perennial Challenge of Race Relations in America

Any discussion about civil rights in America must begin with the issue of race. Combating racial discrimination was the original purpose of the Fourteenth Amendment, and is at the core of modern efforts to define and enforce civil rights. Moreover, despite decades of progress in fighting racial discrimination in every area of American life, race remains a fundamental and troublesome line of division in American politics and society.

Race Relations Before the Civil War

The first African slaves were brought to the United States in the 1600s. By 1787 the slave population had grown to around seven hundred thousand, mostly in the South.[5] Already there was considerable controversy over slavery, and much agitation on both sides over its future. In July 1787—during the Constitutional Convention—Congress passed the **Northwest Ordinance,** which banned slavery in the area now encompassing Ohio, Indiana, Illinois, Michigan, and Wisconsin. But that victory for the antislavery forces did not mean they had the strength to abolish slavery. Of the original thirteen states, only Massachusetts, New Hampshire, Vermont, Rhode Island, and Connecticut had even begun to abolish slavery by 1787.

Slavery and Race in the Constitution of 1787   Even antislavery delegates to the Constitutional Convention realized that the Constitution was doomed unless the slavery issue was put off until later. The original Constitution dealt with slavery only three times, and never by name. It gave Congress the authority to abolish the slave trade, but only after 1808; provided for slaves to be counted as three-fifths of free persons for purposes of taxation and representation in the House of Representatives; and declared that any slave who escaped into a free state would not become free but would be returned to his or her owner.

By not abolishing slavery, of course, the Constitution condoned its continued existence. In the 1840s, in fact, the abolition leader William Lloyd Garrison denounced the Constitution as a "covenant with death."[6] Whether the Framers' decision to accept the existence of slavery was a sign of moral weakness or a legitimate exercise in political pragmatism is still debated.

Growing Tensions   In the seven decades between the adoption of the Constitution and the outbreak of the Civil War, the nation came face to face with the slavery question on many occasions. Each time, the nation's political leadership was able to diffuse the tension before it could develop into a full-fledged crisis.

Of the original thirteen states, six—Delaware, Maryland, Virginia, the Carolinas, and Georgia—accepted and supported slavery up to and during the Civil War. Because slavery was clearly sanctioned by the Constitution, critics focused on isolating the slave states by fighting the extension of slavery to new states and territories. The proslavery forces, meanwhile, struggled to extend slavery in the same way, by bringing into the Union new states and territories that supported the practice.

Congress's solution was to maintain a rough balance of free and slave states. The precedent was set with the **Compromise of 1820,** which allowed Missouri to join the Union as a slave state and Maine to come in as a free state. The Compromise also banned slavery in the northern territories of the west while permitting it in the southern territories, with the assumption that the states eventually carved out of the territories would be divided the same way. A similar compromise was worked out in 1850, when the territorial question again threatened to blow the nation apart. Congress also gave in to pressure from the slave states by passing and then strengthening the **Fugitive Slave Act,** which required every state to return fugitive slaves to their home states.

The **Dred Scott** *Case*   Eventually this compromise strategy began to break down. The final blow came in 1857, when the Supreme Court handed down its notorious decision in the case of ***Dred Scott*** v. ***Sandford.***[7]

Dred Scott, a slave living in Missouri, sued for his freedom in federal court, arguing that he had become a free man when his master took him into Wisconsin territory, where slavery was prohibited. The principle Scott relied on—"once free, forever free"—had already been accepted in the courts of England.

The Court rejected Scott's argument, and went much further. Chief Justice Roger B. Taney's long and complex opinion made a number of sweeping points, but the two most important were these:

- Scott's case could not be brought before the federal courts. The Constitution gives the right to sue in federal court only to *citizens of the United States,* Taney ruled; since Missouri did not regard Scott as a citizen, he was not a citizen of the United States. Moreover, Taney declared that no state was authorized to make blacks citizens of the United States, since (in his view) the Framers did not regard them as eligible for national citizenship. In language that was widely quoted out of context, Taney wrote that the prevailing opinion in the eighteenth century was that the Negro had "no rights which the white man was bound to respect."
- Scott did not become free when he entered the territory of Wisconsin, because Congress lacked the constitutional power to declare a territory free. In other words, Taney viewed the Constitution as guaranteeing the right of slave owners to take and hold slaves to any territory of the United States.

The second argument was political gunpowder. If Congress could not ban slavery in the territories, no compromise on slavery was possible. In fact, Taney's opinion declared the Missouri Compromise of 1820 unconstitutional. It made both sides more strident and undercut all efforts at reconciliation. Just over four years later, the South seceded and the nation went to war.

The Civil War The South fought the Civil War to preserve slavery and states' rights. The North fought at first to save the Union and only later to abolish slavery. On the eve of the war, Congress proposed a constitutional amendment that would have guaranteed the existence of slavery in states where it was already permitted. The amendment was too little, too late; but as late as August 1862 Lincoln still proclaimed that his "paramount object in this great struggle is to save the Union, and is not either to save or to destroy slavery."[8]

A year later, however, Lincoln came to feel that "slavery must die so that the nation might live." Congress authorized the president to declare the slaves of convicted rebels to be free, and in September 1862 Lincoln announced the **Emancipation Proclamation,** freeing all slaves in the states in rebellion against the United States effective January 1, 1863. Although as yet Lincoln had no power over the South, the proclamation's meaning and ultimate effect were clear. Once the war was over, slavery was doomed.

Race Relations After the Civil War

Reconstruction Laws and Amendments During the immediate postwar period, known as **Reconstruction,** Congress moved quickly to capitalize on its absolute power over the occupied southern states, approving three new constitutional amendments. The **Thirteenth**

Amendment, ratified in 1865, abolished slavery. The **Fourteenth Amendment,** ratified in 1868, extended citizenship to all people "born or naturalized in the United States"—regardless of race—and declared that all people were entitled to the "privileges and immunities of citizens of the United States," to the "equal protection of the laws," and to "due process of law." It also gave Congress specific power to enforce the amendment by appropriate legislation. The **Fifteenth Amendment,** ratified in 1870, guaranteed that the right to vote could not be denied or abridged on the basis of race.

The Fourteenth Amendment was clearly intended to make it illegal for any state government to treat African Americans as second-class citizens. In particular, it meant to outlaw the policies embodied in the "black codes" passed by many southern states in the immediate aftermath of the Civil War. These laws deprived blacks of many basic rights, including the right to testify in court, make contracts, travel, speak freely, and peaceably assemble.

Some backers of the Fourteenth Amendment intended that it be interpreted to apply the Bill of Rights to the states. Others believed that the amendment would simply ban discrimination based on race. There was no widespread agreement on the meaning of the amendment, however, and the language ultimately adopted was broad and vague. Thus the Supreme Court was free to interpret the amendment as it saw fit, and in a series of important decisions the justices ruled that the protections of the amendment were narrow and specific. In the 1873 *Slaughterhouse Cases,* for example, the Court held that the Fourteenth Amendment did not provide a general protection for all rights, but only for a few fundamental rights associated with United States citizenship. In the *Civil Rights Cases* of 1883, the Court ruled that the Fourteenth Amendment offered protection only from state-sponsored, as contrasted with privately based, discrimination.[9]

The Dismal Era: 1876 to 1932

The Reconstruction Amendments held great promise for African Americans. Enforcement of these newly won freedoms was immensely difficult, however, and depended largely on the presence of the federal troops who occupied the South from 1865 to 1876. Within a few years the Union's zeal for enforcing Reconstruction waned, and political power flowed back to the former slave owners.

Between 1876 and 1930, the federal government largely abandoned the cause of southern blacks, consigning the former slaves and their descendants to a life little better than slavery. Economic conditions were horrendous, with many blacks forced into subsistence farming as sharecroppers. Educational opportunities for black children beyond the basic level were essentially nonexistent, and political freedoms were more theoretical than real. The criminal

Four black sharecroppers lynched in 1908 for expressing sympathy with a black man who killed his white employer in self-defense.

A 1922 protest in Washington, D.C., in support of a federal antilynching bill. The protest failed; even the support of President Franklin D. Roosevelt a decade later could not convince Congress to pass this most basic of civil rights laws.

justice system was notoriously biased against African Americans, and lynchings were common—between 1889 and 1918 no fewer than 2,522 blacks were killed by racially motivated mob violence, while thousands more were intimidated into submission.[10]

The Jim Crow Laws At the center of southern racial policy in the post–Civil War era were the **Jim Crow laws,** passed in one state after another between 1890 and 1910. Named for a popular blackfaced character in an 1830s minstrel show, the Jim Crow laws were essentially a system of *apartheid,* requiring the separation of blacks and whites in virtually every area of public life. Schools and churches had been largely segregated for a long time, but the new laws required segregation in railroad cars and streetcars, hospitals and hotels, theaters, inns, and restaurants. Segregation was even extended to public lavatories and water fountains, conspicuously labeled "white" and "colored."

The Jim Crow laws were motivated largely by a desire to deny to blacks any degree of political or economic power, and to forestall what might have been a natural political alliance of poor whites and poor blacks against well-off whites. By appealing to racial prejudice and hatred, white elites were able to attract poor whites to their cause. Then they ensured their victory by systematically stripping blacks of all political power, including the right to vote.

Reducing the political power of southern blacks could not be accomplished directly because of the Fourteenth and Fifteenth Amendments. Southern political leaders therefore took an indirect approach. One approach was to levy a tax on individuals who registered to vote. Such "poll taxes" meant nothing to well-off whites but presented a serious burden to poor blacks. The primary effect of poll taxes was to exclude blacks from the electorate, but they also kept many poor whites from exercising their voting rights. Other tactics included the use of literacy tests and of racial violence. These techniques were extremely effective. By 1910, black registration had fallen to around 15 percent in Virginia and less than 2 percent in Alabama and Mississippi.[11]

Throughout this period the federal government stood by silently, and even lent moral support to the segregationists. The critical event was the 1896 Supreme Court decision of *Plessy* **v.** *Ferguson. Plessy* upheld racial segregation as consistent with equal protection, as long as the facilities provided for blacks were equal to those provided for whites. This infamous separate-but-equal rule remained the law of the land until 1954.

The problem with *Plessy* was twofold. First, the Supreme Court's literal reading of the Fourteenth Amendment followed the letter of the law but violated its spirit. Segregation, according to the Court, treated both whites and blacks the same way—forbidding each to intermingle with the other. Incredibly, the Court denied that segregation implied in any way that one race was inferior to the other. Second, *Plessy* revealed an utter lack of attention to the social or political realities of the day. A trip through the South could not help but reveal that the "white" and "colored" facilities were *not* equal.

Despite its backward-looking decision in *Plessy,* the Supreme Court does not deserve to shoulder the full blame for the federal government's refusal to combat discrimination against blacks in the South. Congress passed no major civil rights legislation between 1875 and 1957, and was unable to pass even a rudimentary antilynching bill. A succession of presidents offered weak leadership on civil rights at best, and at times made matters worse. Perhaps the low point came during the presidency of Woodrow Wilson, with the imposition of Jim Crow-style segregation in Washington, D.C., and in the federal civil service.

Small Signs of Progress: 1933 to 1953

The two decades from the inauguration of Franklin D. Roosevelt in 1933 to the nomination of Earl Warren to be chief justice of the Supreme Court in 1953 marked the beginnings of real movement on the civil rights front. Progress was slow, at times imperceptible, but the events of this period did lay the foundation for the great strides that would be made in the 1950s and 1960s.

Political Trends   Roosevelt's New Deal reached out to include black Americans in the Democratic coalition. This was partly a matter of principle, but mostly a result of old-fashioned politics. The many blacks who moved to the North in search of economic opportunity were welcomed by the Democratic city machines as a fertile source of votes, especially given the Republican party's apparent lack of interest in their problems and needs. The depression hit urban blacks hard and made them ready to turn away from their historical allegiance to the Republicans, the "Party of Lincoln."

It was not that the New Deal did much for civil rights. But its economic relief programs helped blacks along with everyone else, and the Democratic party, at least, seemed to have its heart in the right place. In 1935, for example, northern Democrats led a fight to pass a federal antilynching law; although unsuccessful, they were given credit for the attempt. Some New Deal programs, like the Civilian Conservation Corps and the Public Works Administration, actively worked to include African Americans.

World War II also brought momentum for change. Black soldiers, fighting in segregated units, were highly decorated, and many Americans began to wonder how these men could be asked to fight and die for a country that treated them as second-class citizens. Many Americans also bristled at Nazi propaganda, which sought to deflect attention from Germany's racial and ethnic atrocities by reminding the world of America's race problems. These slow but definite shifts in public opinion led to small but significant victories: the Democratic party, led by President Harry S Truman, adopted a pro–civil rights position in its 1948 platform, and the same year Truman issued an executive order desegregating the army.

Despite these signs of progress, the 1940s also demonstrated just how difficult it would be to eliminate racial bias from American society. For even as the country was waking up to the discrimination faced by African Americans, it was condoning or applauding the forced evacuation of Japanese Americans from their homes on the West Coast. Truman's efforts at desegregation engendered tremendous opposition, both inside and outside the armed forces. The adoption of the civil rights plank at the 1948 Democratic Convention caused a group of southern delegates to walk out of the convention. Nicknamed the "Dixiecrats," they reconvened and nominated South Carolina governor Strom Thurmond as their presidential candidate.

Legal Trends   Meanwhile, the courts were taking small steps to recognize the civil rights of African Americans. In the 1930s, lawyers from the National Association for the Advancement of Colored People (NAACP) Legal Defense Fund began to formulate the legal strategy that would chip away at the foundations of segregation and eventually bring it down completely. Their strategy was simple: rather than challenge *Plessy*'s separate-but-equal doctrine, the civil rights lawyers used it to their own advantage. They repeatedly pointed out to the courts that separate was *not* equal in the American South, and tried to make it increasingly expensive and burdensome for the southern states to maintain truly equal facilities or to deny the existence of inequality.

The NAACP lawyers were led by **Thurgood Marshall,** who would later become the first African American justice on the United States Supreme Court. Marshall and his colleagues began with southern law schools, reasoning that the justices could readily identify with the black students involved and that a successful outcome would cause little commotion or backlash. In the first case, in 1938, the Court ruled that Missouri could not operate a law school for whites while forcing black students to attend law school out of state.[12] When several southern states responded to the Missouri decision by opening up new (and inferior) black law schools, the Legal Defense Fund went to court again. This time, in 1950, the Supreme Court held that if a state operated one law school for blacks and another for whites, the two schools had to be substantially equal—not only in facilities but also in the quality of the faculty and in the overall prestige of the school. Obviously it was impossible for a state to replicate such intangible factors as a school's prestige and standing in the community, and southern schools were forced to open up their doors to blacks and other minority students.[13]

Still the states did not give in. In Oklahoma (never a slave state, but segregated nonetheless), the state admitted a single black student to its law school, but forced him to stay in a segregated area of the library, eat at separate times in the school cafeteria, and sit in an alcove area outside the classrooms. Again the Supreme Court objected, ruling that the separate-but-equal doctrine required that black students be given an opportunity to interact as equals with faculty and students.[14]

These seemingly narrow decisions laid the groundwork for a broader assault on segregation. The Texas and Oklahoma cases established that *intangibles,* such as prestige and the creation of an atmosphere conducive to learning, would count along with such tangible factors as the physical plant and teacher salaries in determining whether separate was in fact equal. Although these early decisions changed the lives of very few black Americans, they set the stage for the Supreme Court's landmark decision in the 1954 case of *Brown* v. *Board of Education.*

Brown v. Board of Education

The litigation that would be known to history as **Brown v. Board of Education** was actually a combination of six cases, from five different states and the District of Columbia. Each one presented the same legal question: Did segregated education in the public schools, even in equal facilities, violate the Constitution of the United States?

Central to the black students' case was the contention that segregated schools did not and could not provide an equal education. Relying on various social science studies, the NAACP lawyers argued that segregation stamped minority children with a badge of inferiority, which in turn damaged their self-esteem and hindered their educational progress. If the Court accepted this proposition, the separate-but-equal doctrine was as good as dead, since separate facilities by definition could not provide equal educational opportunities.

Convincing the Court to overturn a sixty-year-old decision, especially in so highly charged an area as school segregation, was no easy task. And the Court might never have come around to this position had not fate intervened in September 1953, when Chief Justice Fred Vinson died suddenly of a heart attack. Vinson, a conservative from Kentucky, had been a staunch supporter of the southern position and, as chief justice, had carried great weight among his colleagues and among the public at large. The new chief justice, appointed by the Republican Dwight D. Eisenhower, was the progressive former governor of California, Earl Warren. Warren's constitutional views were largely unknown or nonexistent. On civil rights, he was best remembered for supporting the internment of Japanese Americans during World War II. Yet once Warren became convinced of the need for an antisegregation decision, he devoted all of his considerable political skills to making sure that the Court would speak with a single, unambiguous voice.

The first *Brown* decision, written by Warren and joined by all eight of his colleagues, was delivered in May 1954. Relying heavily on the social science arguments presented by the NAACP lawyers, Warren held that "separate educational facilities are inherently unequal" and thus violated the Equal Protection Clause of the Fourteenth Amendment. At the same time, Warren also struck down school segregation in the District of Columbia, even though the federal territory was not covered by the Fourteenth Amendment. "It would be unthinkable," he wrote, "that the same Constitution" that prohibited the states from establishing segregated schools "would impose a lesser duty on the Federal Government."[15]

Recognizing that the principle established in *Brown* would cause enough controversy for one day, Warren carefully put off deciding how to go about dismantling the long-established system of segregated schools. That decision would not come until a year later, in 1955, in a decision known as *Brown II.* Rejecting any drastic measures in favor of a more gradual approach, Warren accepted the position of President Eisenhower's Justice

Southern schools before Brown v. Board of Education were separate but hardly equal, as illustrated by this 1941 photo of the Mount Zion Negro School in Greene County, Georgia.

Department and ruled that the desegregation of individual school districts would be supervised by the federal district courts. Desegregation, the Court ordered, would progress "with all deliberate speed"—whatever that meant.[16]

Although *Brown* had little immediate effect on southern schools, it had great symbolic impact. Coming as it did from a united Court, it removed the last shreds of respectability from the southern system of apartheid. The shock waves it set in motion would resonate well into the 1960s and beyond.

The Civil Rights Movement and Southern Resistance

The response to *Brown* in the Deep South—Virginia, the Carolinas, Georgia, Alabama, and Mississippi—ranged from massive resistance to deliberate foot-dragging. There were also sporadic outbreaks of violence, including murder, bombings, and beatings, throughout the South. These tactics were effective: in 1964, ten years after *Brown*, 98 percent of black students in the South still attended segregated schools.[17] The border states, meanwhile, made some progress toward implementing the *Brown* decree. Paradoxically, therefore, the first major confrontation over desegregation came not in the Deep South but in Little Rock, Arkansas.

What the Arkansas officials did was simple enough. When twelve black students tried to enter the doors of Central High School in August 1957, public officials—including the governor—blocked the doors. The students' legal representatives went back to federal court, and their case was heard in an extraordinary special session of the United States Supreme Court. The Court unanimously reaffirmed the *Brown* decision and ordered the students admitted immediately. When Arkansas officials still balked, President Eisenhower grudgingly sent in federal troops to enforce the court's order.

The Little Rock crisis marked a major turning point in the history of the civil rights movement. Eisenhower's decision to commit federal troops put the full weight of the United States government behind the *Brown* decision. It would be years before the White House and Congress would take positive action on their own, but the Court was no longer alone in its struggle to end racial discrimination under the law.

The Civil Rights Act of 1957 As the first congressional civil rights act since 1875, the Civil Rights Act of 1957 added to the momentum for real reform. The act did not make major changes in law, but it did put Congress back into the civil rights arena and provided

ECONOMICS AND POLITICS

The Racial Income Gap

Underlying the politics of civil rights is the enormous economic disparity between whites and blacks. For all the progress in civil rights law, the racial income gap has increased sharply over the past three decades. These charts provide a statistical summary of the economic problems facing racial minorities. As you examine them, think about how these numbers may have been affected by the history of race relations in the United States.

Figure 5.1 **Income Distributions in 1995 Dollars, 1970–1995**

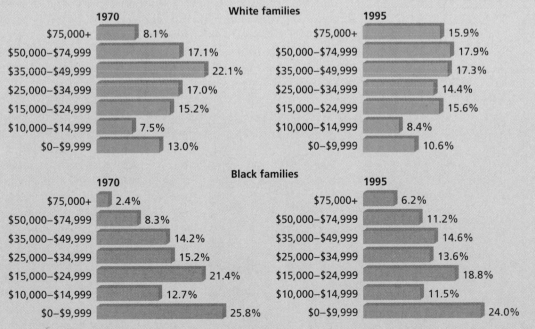

White families

1970
$75,000+	8.1%
$50,000–$74,999	17.1%
$35,000–$49,999	22.1%
$25,000–$34,999	17.0%
$15,000–$24,999	15.2%
$10,000–$14,999	7.5%
$0–$9,999	13.0%

1995
$75,000+	15.9%
$50,000–$74,999	17.9%
$35,000–$49,999	17.3%
$25,000–$34,999	14.4%
$15,000–$24,999	15.6%
$10,000–$14,999	8.4%
$0–$9,999	10.6%

Black families

1970
$75,000+	2.4%
$50,000–$74,999	8.3%
$35,000–$49,999	14.2%
$25,000–$34,999	15.2%
$15,000–$24,999	21.4%
$10,000–$14,999	12.7%
$0–$9,999	25.8%

1995
$75,000+	6.2%
$50,000–$74,999	11.2%
$35,000–$49,999	14.6%
$25,000–$34,999	13.6%
$15,000–$24,999	18.8%
$10,000–$14,999	11.5%
$0–$9,999	24.0%

SOURCE: Adapted with the permission of Scribner, A Division of Simon & Schuster from *Two Nations* by Andrew Hacker. Copyright © 1992 by Andrew Hacker.

a building block for later legislation. The bill established the Civil Rights Commission and the Civil Rights Division in the Justice Department, and gave the federal government the power to bring suits on behalf of those denied the right to vote on account of race.

From the Courts to the Streets: The Civil Rights Movement The civil rights movement was active not only in law but also in politics. A major player was the Southern Christian Leadership Conference (SCLC), led by the Reverend **Martin Luther King, Jr.** The SCLC's approach was to combine "direct action" with nonviolence—a combination that generated pressure for change, put advocates of segregation on the defensive, and created much sympathy for the protesters. The SCLC strategy was first put into place in 1955 in the Montgomery (Alabama) bus boycott—a mass protest inspired by the refusal of a black woman named Rosa Parks to give up her bus seat to a white man. "We are not here advocating violence," King declared in Montgomery. "The only weapon that we have in our hands . . . is the weapon of protest."[18] The protesters' nonviolence stood in sharp contrast to the violence practiced by some of those on the other side.

> *I still have a dream. It is a dream deeply rooted in the American dream. I have a dream that one day this nation will rise up and live out the true meaning of its creed: "We hold these truths to be self-evident; that all men are created equal."*
>
> —Martin Luther King, Jr.,
> *I Have a Dream* speech,
> August 1963

A much broader protest movement was sparked by the 1960 sit-ins, which began when four black students at North Carolina Agricultural and Technical State University defied segregation laws and asked to be served at the local Woolworth's lunch counter. The sit-in movement spread across the South, resulting in thousands of arrests and jailings. The protesters stuck to their strict code of nonviolence, and regarded jail time as an opportunity to continue their crusade.

The 1960 sit-ins inaugurated a series of actions designed to publicize the injustices forced on southern blacks. The election of John F. Kennedy later that year gave hope to many blacks—the new president was personally opposed to segregation and had won his office with the strong support of black voters—but the new administration was cautious to a fault. Kennedy refused to ask Congress for sweeping civil rights laws and took little action to protect civil rights protesters in the South.

The Reverend Martin Luther King, Jr., presents his "I Have a Dream" speech at the March on Washington in August 1963.

Civil rights leaders kept up the pressure, however, focusing in April 1963 on the militantly segregationist city of Birmingham, Alabama. Again led by King, the protesters were greeted by massive arrests—including of King himself—and brutal violence. Pictures of police officers attacking unarmed men, women, and children were splashed across national newspapers and featured on network news shows. The publicity forced President Kennedy to put civil rights on the front burner, and he sent Justice Department officials to Birmingham to arrange negotiations. The city quickly capitulated, agreeing to desegregate a wide range of public facilities. The success of the Birmingham march prompted a series of similar protests that summer, capped off in August 1963 by the

March on Washington, in which some 250,000 Americans went to the capital to demand civil rights. It was here that King delivered his famous "I Have a Dream" speech.

In the midst of these marches and demonstrations, President Kennedy at last agreed to submit a major civil rights bill to Congress. Kennedy's proposal would have banned segregation in hotels, restaurants, theaters, retail stores, and other public facilities. It would have strengthened the federal government's role in enforcing civil rights and toughened laws designed to secure voting rights for blacks. Civil rights leaders still faced an uphill climb in overcoming the opposition of southern whites, however, especially in the Senate, where the rules made it possible for a determined minority to stretch out debate and kill the bill. The fate of the bill was still an open question when Kennedy was assassinated on November 22, 1963.

In one of those strange quirks of history, the new president was perfectly poised to push through what became the Civil Rights Act of 1964. Lyndon Baines Johnson was a white southerner, whose support of the bill carried great symbolic weight—it could no longer be claimed that the bill was being foisted on the South by northern outsiders. Moreover, Johnson's connections in Washington were extraordinary. As a former majority leader of the Senate, he knew everyone and everything on Capitol Hill, and was prepared to use his knowledge to get his way politically. Moreover, Johnson was able to present the Civil Rights Act as a memorial to John F. Kennedy. Few bothered to remember that Kennedy's support of civil rights had been lukewarm until just months before his death.

The Civil Rights Act of 1964 and the Voting Rights Act of 1965 Together, the **Civil Rights Act of 1964** and the **Voting Rights Act of 1965** are the two most important pieces of civil rights legislation ever enacted. The 1964 law represented an all-out attack on racial segregation and discrimination. Despite the Supreme Court's 1883 decision in the *Civil Rights Cases,* Congress endeavored to prohibit segregation and discrimination in any business that served the public, in employment and labor unions, in all public facilities, especially schools, and in any state program that received federal funds. The 1965 Voting Rights Act banned literacy tests and other devices that had kept blacks from the voting booth; permitted federal officials to take over the task of registering voters; and required Justice Department approval (or "preclearance") for any local or state regulations that established new voting requirements or procedures. (The Act applies only in states that have a history of voting discrimination.) The United States Supreme Court quickly upheld both the Civil Rights Act and the Voting Rights Act.[19]

A key aspect of the Voting Rights Act became apparent only later, after judicial interpretation of its provisions on preclearance. Some southern states tried to dilute the impact of the Voting Rights Act by replacing single-member legislative districts with multimember or at-large districts. The

Firemen blast civil rights protesters during the civil rights rally in Birmingham, Alabama in 1963. Official violence contrasted sharply with the nonviolent tactics of the protesters, and generated much sympathy from those who watched on the relatively new medium of television.

purpose was clear—a five-member council in a city where one district was predominantly black might elect one black representative; if elections were at-large, no black candidate could get a majority. In *Allen* v. *State Board of Elections,* decided in 1969, the Court held that such changes were covered by the act and thus required Justice Department preapproval.

Four years later, the full impact of the *Allen* decision became clear. Under a series of Supreme Court decisions, states were required to reapportion all legislative bodies after every census, to maintain equal representation. In the 1973 case of *Georgia* v. *United States,* the Supreme Court held that such reapportionments were changes in voting procedures and were thus covered by the act. From then on, the reapportionment of all legislative bodies in any state covered by the Voting Rights Act was brought under the supervision of the Justice Department and the federal courts.[20]

With the full weight of all three branches of the federal government behind the civil rights movement, African Americans at last began to see progress across the South and the nation.

From Desegregation to Affirmative Action

Ending discrimination under the law did not immediately solve the problems of black Americans. The report of a federal study commission in 1968 summed up the extent of the challenge: "Our Nation is moving toward two societies, one black, one white—separate and unequal."[21] The status of school desegregation at that time underscored the problem with an approach that aimed merely to eliminate discrimination on paper. More than a decade after *Brown,* most school districts in the Deep South were still substantially segregated.

Busing Frustrated by a decade of noncompliance with its decision in *Brown,* the Supreme Court at last began to demand real progress. The key decision came in 1971, when the Supreme Court approved the use of **busing** as a way to achieve desegregation of southern school districts.

What the Court now required was known as **integration,** implying an active process of racial mixing, rather than **desegregation,** which suggested only the elimination of laws that required the separation of the races. Busing to achieve integration was first approved in Charlotte, North Carolina, but the idea quickly spread throughout the South and then across the nation. Under the law, courts could order desegregation even in states where segregation was not explicitly required by law, as long as they found that the government had intentionally brought about segregated schools. Court-ordered relief could be granted, for example, if state officials had repeatedly redrawn school attendance zones to exclude black students from predominantly white schools, or had intentionally built new schools in the middle of segregated areas rather than in boundary areas. Such conditions were found in city after city throughout the 1970s, and court-ordered busing became commonplace.

> *"Sitting at the table doesn't make you a diner, unless you eat some of what's on that plate. Being here in America doesn't make you an American. Being born here in America doesn't make you an American."*
>
> —Malcolm X, 1965

Busing sparked great controversy in the 1970s, producing strong protests and, in some cities, even violence. Within a few years, however, much of the controversy had dissipated. In many cities, the mass migration of whites to suburban school districts made busing ineffective. In other places, successful alternatives to busing created moderately integrated school systems and thus reduced or eliminated pressures for stronger measures. Across the country, moreover, busing and in-

In 1997, Bill Clinton unveiled the President's Initiative on Race, a year-long series of events involving "thoughtful study, constructive dialogue, and positive action" to create "an America based on opportunity for all, responsibility from all, and one community of all Americans."

tegration issues were pushed into the background as newer issues, such as drugs, crime, and education reform came to the fore. In recent decisions the Supreme Court has held that schools that were once desegregated but become segregated again because of shifting residential patterns are no longer subject to court-ordered efforts at integration. These decisions have all but ended the era of forced busing.[22] Still, many communities continue to operate under policies instituted in the 1970s and 1980s.

Fifty Years of Civil Rights

The past fifty years have seen unprecedented changes in the legal and political status of African Americans. Yet the civil rights movement can hardly be called a complete success.

Economically, African Americans remain far behind their white counterparts (see the box on page 121). The problems of crime, unwed mothers, teenage pregnancy, and drug and alcohol abuse all remain more acute among blacks than whites. Discrimination in employment and housing remains, and even today many urban schools are highly segregated.

The history of Topeka, Kansas, since the 1954 *Brown* decision is typical. Although there has been much progress—including a significant expansion in the African American middle class—huge areas of the city remain poor, unsafe, and largely black. Segregation became so severe that in 1979 the American Civil Liberties Union went back to court to demand new action to integrate the public schools. Joining the lawsuit, ironically, was Linda Brown, whose father had brought the original *Brown* case twenty-five years before.

"It was unrealistic to expect that we could overcome all these entrenched problems, even in forty years," commented NAACP lawyer Ted Shaw on the fortieth anniversary of the original *Brown* case. Although his comments were directed specifically at the school desegregation problem, in a way they sum up the entire civil rights movement. "It's not too late to turn this around," Shaw said. "The question is whether the commitment is there."[23]

The Civil Rights Movement Extended

The civil rights movement provided a model for other disadvantaged minorities to follow. Court decisions and congressional statutes could be modified and extended, protest marches and other forms of political expression could be copied or adapted. Every group is different, however, and faces unique historical and contemporary challenges. Some off-spring of the civil rights movement have therefore fared better than others.

Women

Women who grew up in the 1980s and 1990s may find it difficult to imagine the level of discrimination faced by women as recently as fifteen or twenty years ago. Women must still cope with a variety of forms of discrimination and sexual harassment—including the "glass ceiling," a term used to describe the real but barely visible barrier that limits opportunities for advancement to top professional and management positions. But American society and especially the American workplace is a far more egalitarian place than it once was.

Women have been seeking equal rights under the law and an equal role in American public life since the days of Abigail Adams. The first organized effort on behalf of women's rights was a convention held in 1848 at Seneca Falls, New York, which ended with the adoption of resolutions calling for equality and expanded rights for women. Two decades later, advocates of voting rights for women formed the National Women's Suffrage Association. Led by Susan B. Anthony, the suffrage movement at last achieved victory in 1920, with the adoption of the Nineteenth Amendment. Meanwhile, reformers worked in Congress and the state legislatures for the passage of laws designed to protect women from hazardous working conditions and to provide minimum wages and other basic rights on the job.

For the most part, however, courts and legislatures continued to deny women equality under the law. State laws routinely discriminated against women, barring them from certain professions, assuming their inability to handle complex financial affairs, and encouraging them to avoid public life altogether and concentrate on home, family, and children. In the 1948 case of *Goesart* v. *Cleary,* for example, the Supreme Court upheld a Michigan law that banned women from working as bartenders unless their fathers or husbands owned the bar. "The fact that women may now have achieved the virtues that men have long claimed as their prerogatives and now indulge in vices that men have long practiced," wrote Justice Frankfurter, "does not preclude the States from drawing a sharp line between the sexes."[24] In 1961 a like-minded Court sustained a Florida law that allowed women to serve on a jury only if they made a special request. "Woman," the Court declared, "is still regarded as the center of home and family life."[25]

The modern women's movement—also known as feminism—dates from the early 1960s. The movement was driven by rapid changes in the role of women in American society, especially the significant growth in the number of married women in the workforce and in the number of women attending and graduating from college. Widespread availability of contraception and abortion also played a role, allowing women to delay or avoid having children and pursue professional careers.

The efforts of the women's movement began to pay dividends early on, especially in Congress. In 1963, for example, Congress passed the Equal Pay Act, which requires that men and women be paid the same amount for equal work. In 1964, Congress banned sex discrimination as part of the Civil Rights Act. (Ironically, the protection of women under the law was originally intended as a joke, a way of bringing the entire act into disrepute. But the law did pass, and in later years was enforced by the courts with gusto.) Other important laws passed by Congress include the Education Amendments of 1972 (known as Title IX of the Civil Rights Act), which banned sex discrimination in education. In 1971, Congress finally approved the **Equal Rights Amendment,** which would have changed the Constitution to prohibit the denial of "equality of rights under law . . . on account of sex." The ERA was intensely controversial, and was ultimately defeated, but its impact was still substantial: it brought the problem of sex discrimination to public consciousness and helped define the terms of the debate.

In the early 1970s, meanwhile, the Supreme Court began to take a tougher line on sex discrimination. Previously it had allowed the states to make distinctions based on sex as long as they were minimally reasonable. Now it began to insist that such distinctions be more carefully justified. In *Reed* v. *Reed* (1971), the Court struck down a law that gave preference to men over women in deciding who was to become the administrator of an estate. In 1973 the Court invalidated a federal law that allowed male soldiers to claim their wives as dependents automatically but required women soldiers to prove that their husbands were dependent on them for support. The old assumptions and stereotypes, once sufficient for justifying discriminatory laws, were no longer enough.[26]

For a while it appeared that the Court would simply declare gender, like race, to be a suspect classification. Instead the Court adopted a slightly weaker standard. Classifications based on sex are "semisuspect": they can be justified only if they are "substantially related" to an important government interest. The real meaning of this middle-tier standard became clear only through a series of Court decisions throughout the 1970s, 1980s, and 1990s. Essentially it means that the Supreme Court will strike down laws that discriminate against either sex on the basis of "the mechanical application of traditional, often inaccurate, assumptions about the proper roles of men and women."[27]

Thus the Court set aside an Oklahoma law that allowed women to drink beer at age eighteen but required men to wait until age twenty-one; forced Mississippi to open up its all-female nursing college to men; disallowed an Alabama rule that only men could be required to pay alimony; and put an end to males-only admissions policies at state-supported military colleges. In a similar spirit, the Court ruled in 1986

Members of Local 34 of the Federation of University Employees—a predominantly female union of clerical and technical workers at Yale University—strike for pay equity, arguing that "woman's work" should be valued on the same basis as traditionally male jobs. The university eventually agreed to restructure salaries and end discrimination against women who take maternity leave.

that sexual harassment in the workplace is sex discrimination under the Civil Rights Act.[28] But the Court has also allowed Congress to mandate draft registration for men alone (reasoning that the rule was appropriate given Congress's exclusion of women from combat).

That rights are secured by law does not mean that discrimination has disappeared, of course; women still earn less than seventy-five cents for every dollar earned by men. But women (and men) who are the victims of arbitrary discrimination can now rely on a variety of legal remedies that simply did not exist two decades ago. Fear of such lawsuits, moreover, has made most employers, schools, and public institutions well aware of the need to change their attitudes and actions to avoid litigation.

Women in Politics   Women have also made strides in the political arena. In the past two decades, the number of women in Congress, for example, has grown from 15 to 59 (just over 10 percent). The number of women serving in state legislatures has grown from 604 to 1,598 (over 20 percent of the total).[29] Since 1981, America has seen an extraordinary number of firsts for women in public life: the first female Supreme Court justice (1981), vice presidential candidate (1988), and attorney general (1993), to name just a few.

It is too soon to conclude that women have achieved true equality in the public sector. Besides all of the other problems they must face, women also must confront the slowly changing attitudes, of both males and females, on questions related to sex equality. The sexual abuse of women in the United States Army, for example—revealed in a series of scandalous cases in 1997—stands as a clear reminder that women have a long way to go before they achieve true political and social equality with men.

Native Americans

Native Americans have suffered great hardships and indignities since the early days of European exploration and settlement. According to scholarly estimates, the Native American population when Columbus arrived in 1492 numbered upwards of 7 million people, 5 million in what is now the continental United States and 2 million in Alaska, Canada, and Greenland. Over the next four hundred years, the Native American population was steadily ravaged, first from new European diseases (including smallpox, bubonic plague, and typhoid), then from war, forced relocations, and genocide. By 1900 the Native American population had dropped to barely more than 350,000. Since then it has recovered significantly, due mainly to advances in medicine and public health. Today more than 2.75 million Native Americans live in North America. Another 4 million Americans claim some degree of Native American ancestry.[30]

Native Americans and the United States Government   Until this century, the policies of the United States government were markedly hostile to Native Americans and contributed greatly to their hardships and suffering. Until 1924, most Native Americans were considered citizens of foreign countries and were not entitled to the basic rights guaranteed to American citizens. Throughout the nineteenth century, the westward expansion of the United States led to vicious wars and forced many tribes off their lands and onto reservations, where they were encouraged to give up their traditional ways of life, including language, religion, and economy.

By the early twentieth century, the United States government took a more protective approach toward the Indians, though with mixed results. Federal policy, implemented by the Office (later Bureau) of Indian Affairs, emphasized three goals: to control and regulate the use of Indian land; to improve health care; and to improve educational opportunities. In this period the government sought to assimilate Indians and make them self-sufficient, largely by selling tribal lands and distributing the proceeds to individual families. Little assimilation resulted, but many tribal cultures and support systems were disrupted, leaving families even worse off than before. Federal health care programs were only a little more effective, and Native Americans remained far below the general population in terms of life expectancy and other measures of public health. Education programs were a little more successful; although most Indian schools were underfinanced and underequipped, the illiteracy rate among Native Americans dropped sharply. The vast majority of Indians also learned English, although at some cost to the viability of native languages.

The Indian New Deal   Federal policy shifted dramatically in 1934, with the passage of the Indian Reorganization Act. The government's new emphasis was on Indian self-determination and self-government. More than $100 million was spent on soil conservation, irrigation, and other programs on the reservations, and more than 1 million acres of land were added to the tribal holdings. New economic programs emphasized traditional arts and crafts, and Indian education was changed to emphasize native languages and traditions.

The Indian New Deal was not wholly successful, but it did stop the Native Americans' centuries-long decline. By the 1950s, however, the government abandoned its self-determination policy in favor of a new policy that sought to end the "special relationship" between the federal government and the tribes altogether. This so-called termination policy was extended to only a few Indian tribes, but it was spectacularly unsuccessful and sparked a strong counterreaction. By the 1960s, the termination policy had been all but abandoned.

AIM and Self-Determination   Federal policy since the passage of the 1975 Indian Self-Determination Act has once again focused on tribal self-government. The government's response was largely prompted by the activities of the American Indian Movement (AIM). Modeled on the more aggressive elements of the civil rights movement, AIM sponsored a wide range of protest activities, including the occupation of Alcatraz Island; a Thanksgiving Day demonstration at Plymouth, Massachusetts, which included painting Plymouth Rock red; and the Trail of Broken Tears—a caravan of some two thousand Native Americans who descended on Washington, D.C., to state their grievances. The AIM movement culminated in an armed confrontation with federal police at Wounded Knee, South Dakota. In the end, AIM was disbanded as a national organization, although it remains strong in some local areas. But it was a critical force in making the government come to terms with Native American concerns and in creating a strong movement for

Russell Means, founder of the American Indian Movement (AIM), at Wounded Knee, South Dakota, 1973. "AIM never died, it only changed form," Means said many years later. "Anywhere Indians are standing up for themselves whether they are struggling as individuals whose basic civil rights are being denied, as peoples whose human rights are being denied, as nations whose sovereign rights are being denied, or any combination of these factors, that's where you'll find the American Indian Movement."

Native American self-determination and for the restoration of tribal cultures.[31] Its legacy was carried out by less militant but very effective groups, such as the American Indian Law Center, which provides legal and political advice and support to tribal leaders.

American Indians Today   The legacy of four hundred years of discrimination and hardship remains a powerful force today. The average per capita income of Native Americans (including Eskimos and Aleuts) is below even that of blacks, and barely half of the average for whites. Native Americans suffer poverty not only on reservations but also in cities; in New York, for example, their average income is only 49 percent that of whites. In several states, the poverty rate among Native Americans exceeds 40 percent. In some Native American tribes, life expectancy is only forty-five years, and the leading cause of death is alcoholism.[32]

The self-determination movement does provide some hope. Native American tribes are seeking to reaffirm their rights under long-neglected treaties, and have undertaken extensive efforts to teach traditional ways of life to troubled children and teenagers. In 1994, in a dramatic and symbolic example, a Washington state judge allowed a Native American tribe to impose the traditional punishment of banishment on a desert island on two boys who would otherwise have been sent to prison.[33] Modern court decisions have upheld Native American hunting and fishing rights in territories governed by federal treaties, strengthened tribal self-government, and granted compensation for long-ago takings of Indian land and property. In recent years, however, the Supreme Court refused to allow the use of illegal drugs in Native American religious ceremonies and has required Indian tribes to comply with federal environmental regulations.

Latinos

Latinos (or Hispanic Americans) are defined not by race but by a common culture rooted in the Spanish conquests of North and South America in the sixteenth century. What draws Latinos to each other, and what separates them from Anglos and other groups, is a "larger culture of history, myth, geography, religion, education, language, and affairs of state." Although many Latinos face discrimination on the basis of skin color, last name, accent, or language, others, if they wish, can assimilate effortlessly into the larger culture.

Latinos came to what is now the United States with Columbus, and have been here ever since. Nevertheless their numbers were small until relatively recently. From one hundred thousand or so in the mid-1800s, the Latino population of the United States grew to several million early this century. Only since the 1960s, however, have Latinos come to America in massive numbers. By 1990, the Latino population had grown to 22.4 million, an estimated 1.8 to 3.1 million of whom are illegal immigrants. The Latino population is growing nearly ten times faster than the general population.[34]

Diversity   The Latino population is extremely diverse. Groups from different countries arrived in the United States at different times and under different circumstances. Each of these groups has its own history and unique cultural, economic, and political characteristics. The three largest groups are Mexican

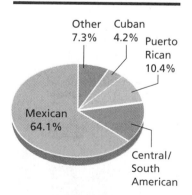

Figure 5.2 **Hispanic Ethnicities Nationwide, 1994**

Other 7.3%
Cuban 4.2%
Puerto Rican 10.4%
Mexican 64.1%
Central/South American

SOURCE: United States Bureau of the Census. *March 1994 Current Population Survey.*

Americans, Puerto Ricans, and Cuban Americans. Smaller groups include immigrants from Central and South America.

Mexicans began arriving in the United States in large numbers in the early 1900s. They came to escape difficult economic conditions, an ever-increasing population, and a great deal of political unrest and uncertainty. Today, Mexican immigrants are drawn largely by the demand for cheap labor, especially in the agricultural and service sectors. Mexican Americans are concentrated mainly in the Southwest, especially in Texas, New Mexico, Arizona, Colorado, and California.

Puerto Ricans were granted American citizenship in 1917, eighteen years after the United States acquired Puerto Rico in the Spanish-American War. Thus, unlike other Latino arrivals in the United States, Puerto Ricans are not considered immigrants and are free to come and go without immigration restrictions. Puerto Ricans came to America in significant numbers only after World War II, largely in pursuit of economic opportunity. Most Puerto Ricans living in the United States reside in large cities, especially New York and Chicago.

The arrival of Cuban immigrants in large numbers dates from 1959, when Fidel Castro seized power and created a communist regime. Most went to, and stayed in, Florida. In contrast to most Mexican and Puerto Rican arrivals, Cuban immigrants tended to be well-educated, middle-class professionals. The Cuban American community in Florida now numbers over 1 million and enjoys significant economic, political, and cultural influence.

From 1959 to 1994, anyone who was able to escape the Castro regime was permitted to immigrate to the United States. Under the threat of massive immigration from Cuba, American policy was changed to restrict Cuban immigration, and Cuban refugees caught trying to enter the United States were intercepted by the Coast Guard and denied entry.

Other significant Latino groups in the United States include immigrants from El Salvador and Nicaragua.[35]

Figure 5.3 **Diversity of Income Among Hispanic Americans, 1993**

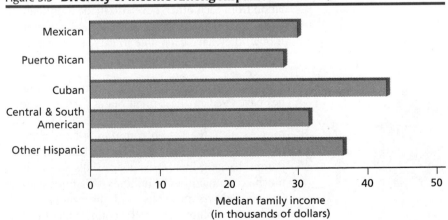

Median family income (in thousands of dollars)

SOURCE: United States Bureau of the Census; "Current Population Survey, 1994," published March 1994 at the following address: http://www.census.gov/population/socdemo/hispanic/finc94.txt.

Economic Conditions   Cuban Americans have been economically successful, but both Mexican Americans and Puerto Ricans have faced poverty and deprivation. The average family income among Cubans, for example, is $38,144—very close to the average for non-Latino whites. The average family income of Mexican Americans and Puerto Ricans, however, is only $27,879 and $25,066, respectively—just above the average income of African Americans. Not surprisingly, Mexican Americans and Puerto Ricans are concentrated in unskilled and low-skilled jobs and suffer from high unemployment. Cuban Americans are far better represented in managerial and professional positions.[36]

Education   Again with the exception of Cuban Americans, Latinos suffer from low educational opportunity and achievement. Whereas 19 percent of Cuban American adults have completed college (compared with 22 percent of whites and 12 percent of blacks), only 10 percent of Puerto Ricans and 6 percent of Mexican Americans have done so. A similar pattern holds true at the high school level. These discrepancies owe more to immigration patterns than to cultural attitudes about education.

In recent years, efforts have been made toward requiring bilingual education and preventing discrimination against Latino children in the public schools. But the struggle remains steeply uphill.[37]

Politics   The Cuban American population is heavily involved in politics. Cuban Americans are overwhelmingly conservative, a result of their flight from communism and their success in the American economic environment. In foreign policy they are staunchly anti-communist and anti-Castro. All of these factors have led Cuban Americans to embrace the Republican party in large numbers.

Mexican Americans and Puerto Ricans, by contrast, are politically more akin to African Americans. Participation in politics tends to be low. Many Mexican Americans and Puerto Ricans have little faith in the efficacy of politics. The government's role as enforcer of the immigration laws makes many Latinos even more suspicious and afraid of government officials than their African American counterparts. The diversity of Latino groups, and their geographic isolation from each other, have also made it difficult for Latinos to operate effectively at the national level, although they have been able to exercise considerable influence at the state and local levels.

Immigration Issues   Although many Latino families have lived in the United States for generations, overall the Latino community is an immigrant culture. As such, the Latino community faces many of the same problems faced by earlier immigrant groups. Lacking English language skills and without much economic muscle, millions of Latinos work in low-wage, low-status jobs, with little hope of advancement. Millions are in the country illegally. Illegal aliens cannot work legally, and are therefore especially vulnerable to exploitation and abuse. Fur-

GLOBAL
PERSPECTIVES

Immigration and Civil Rights

The large inflow of legal and illegal aliens from Latin America has fueled a long-standing debate over the status of noncitizens under American law. Feelings run strong on all sides of the issue. Not surprisingly, neither the Supreme Court nor Congress has followed a consistent policy.

In the 1971 case of *Graham* v. *Richardson*, the Supreme Court ruled that noncitizens were entitled to the full protection of the Constitution, and that the denial of welfare benefits to aliens was therefore illegal. Applying strict scrutiny, the Court held that states could discriminate against aliens only under exceptional circumstances, when such discrimination was necessary to serve a compelling state interest. The *Graham* decision followed the logic of earlier decisions on race discrimination: aliens, like racial minorities, are the victims of widespread stereotyping, prejudice, and discrimination that makes any law singling them out inherently suspect.

In the years since *Graham*, the Court has created two important exceptions. In a long line of cases beginning in 1973, the Court has upheld restrictions on aliens in public employment. Thus states can exclude aliens from jobs as state troopers or public school teachers, and from the civil service. Then, in the 1982 case of *Plyler* v. *Doe*, the justices indicated that states would have an easier time discriminating against illegal aliens. Although *Plyler* struck down a Texas law banning illegal aliens from the public schools, the Court's decision stressed the special circumstances involved in the case of children, suggesting that other forms of discrimination might be permissible.

Congress has also sent out mixed signals. Attempts to restrict illegal immigration pit those seeking to protect American jobs and taxpayers' money against both Latino groups and employers who depend on cheap immigrant labor. Attempts to enforce immigration laws strictly run the risk of trampling on the rights of aliens and citizens alike. Immigration raids, for example, can interfere with privacy rights; thus a crackdown on Islamic groups suspected of links to terrorism can trample on legitimate First Amendment speech and religion interests. The result has been a policy that has talked tough on immigration while offering only sporadic and ineffective enforcement.

For legal aliens, the United States offers a standard of living far in excess of what can be found in any Latin American country. For illegals, America may still represent a better deal than they have at home. Jobs can still be found in many border areas dependent on illegal workers. Medical care and education are still available. Perhaps most important, the fear of capture or harassment by immigration agents is often far outweighed by the hope of building a better life in the United States.

There is one other factor to consider. The Constitution itself specifies that all persons born in the United States—whether their parents are here legally or illegally—are citizens of the United States. That citizenship is permanent, can never be taken away, and can be passed on to children and grandchildren. Like millions of other immigrants before them, the prospect of a better life for their children often outweighs all other considerations.

SOURCES: Thomas Weyr, *Hispanic U.S.A.: Breaking the Melting Pot* (New York: Harper & Row, 1988); Linda Chavez, *Out of the Barrio: Towards a New Politics of Hispanic Assimilation* (New York: Basic Books, 1991).

thermore, they must live in constant fear of immigration authorities. In 1991 alone, more than a million aliens, most of them Latinos, were deported from the United States.

Recent trends have heightened Latinos' concerns. In 1994, for example, California passed Proposition 187, which blocks state aid to illegal immigrants and encourages state workers (including doctors and teachers) to report suspected illegals. Although a federal court struck down Proposition 187 as an unconstitutional attempt to interfere with the federal government's authority to make immigration laws, Latinos continue to fear that Congress will pass similarly hostile legislation. Such fears are not unfounded; the welfare reform law passed in 1996, for example, cut all illegal aliens off of welfare.

Despite their unique problems, many Latinos seek to emulate the success of earlier immigrant groups, eventually reaching economic and political parity with Anglo-Americans. But Latinos also find much in common with the experiences of African Americans, who have had less success in integrating into the mainstream. Many Latinos, like many blacks, feel they have suffered from a historic pattern of discrimination. And though Latinos can be of any race, many are dark skinned and are treated as a racial minority by many whites. In any event, many Latinos believe that their path to political and economic power has been blocked by long-standing prejudice on the part of non-Latinos.

The dual identity of Latinos as both an immigrant group and a minority group has given rise to deep divisions within the Latino community. It has also led to two very different, and at times conflicting, political strategies. On the one hand, Latino interest groups lobbied successfully for protection under the Voting Rights Act. Latinos have also been included in many affirmative action programs, and have won legal protection against discrimination. On the other hand, many Latino leaders see more hope in identifying with the Anglo mainstream. To such leaders, the road to success lies with education, self-improvement, and economic development.

One strategy that both sides can agree on is to increase political participation among Latinos, who currently register and vote at the lowest levels of any comparable group.

Asian Americans

Asian immigrants have been coming to the United States since before the Civil War. Imported to serve as cheap labor, the first Asian Americans provided the raw labor needed to build the transcontinental railroads. Later they worked in American factories and on American farms. They also worked on Hawaii's sugar plantations, both before and after Hawaii was annexed to the United States in 1896. All told, between 1850 and 1930 Asian immigrants to the United States and Hawaii numbered more than 400,000 from China and nearly as many from Japan. Smaller numbers came from the Philippines, Korea, India, and elsewhere.[38]

Asian Americans faced racial discrimination and economic exploitation. Far from home and without any sort of safety net, Asian immigrants were forced to work under difficult and degrading conditions. Still, Asians continued to come to America, hoping, like all immigrants, to find a better life for themselves or at least their children.

Although Asian workers proved useful and profitable for American industry, American labor quickly came to perceive them as a threat. In 1888, acting on a combination of racial hostility and economic protectionism, Congress passed a series of Chinese Exclusion Acts, which banned the im-

Figure 5.4 **Asian-American Ethnicities**

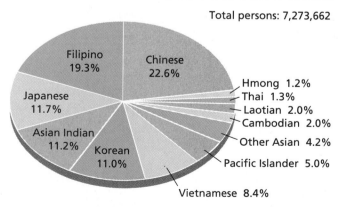

Total persons: 7,273,662

- Chinese 22.6%
- Filipino 19.3%
- Japanese 11.7%
- Asian Indian 11.2%
- Korean 11.0%
- Vietnamese 8.4%
- Pacific Islander 5.0%
- Other Asian 4.2%
- Cambodian 2.0%
- Laotian 2.0%
- Thai 1.3%
- Hmong 1.2%

SOURCE: United States Bureau of the Census, *1990 Census of Population: General Population Characteristics,* Table 48.

migration first of Chinese laborers and then of "all persons of the Chinese race," with only a handful of exceptions. One result was a dramatic increase in Japanese immigration, although the Japanese fared little better than their predecessors. In 1913, for example, California banned Japanese immigrants from land ownership; in 1922, the Supreme Court ruled that non-Caucasians were ineligible for naturalized American citizenship. Finally, in 1924, Congress passed a new immigration bill that greatly restricted all immigration and reduced Asian immigration to the vanishing point. The official quota for Japanese immigrants after 1924 was exactly one hundred people a year.

Figure 5.5 **Diversity of Income Among Asians and Pacific Islanders Nationwide**

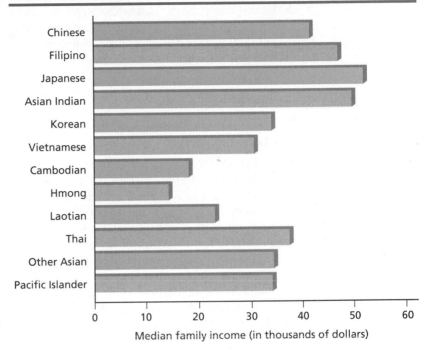

SOURCE: United States Bureau of the Census, *1990 Census of Population: Social and Economic Characteristics*, Table 111.

Discrimination against Asian Americans reached its worst point during World War II, with the exclusion of Japanese Americans from California and their internment in concentration camps. In all of this, the explicit guarantees of the Fourteenth Amendment were virtually ignored.

Recent history has been kinder to Asian Americans. Since Congress reformed the immigration laws in 1965 to reverse their bias against non-Europeans, the various Asian American communities have expanded fivefold, now numbering around 5 million. Many new immigrants come with technical or professional skills and have found great opportunities in the United States. Others, however—including many refugees from Vietnam, Laos, and Cambodia—have found the adjustment to America difficult, even traumatic.

Today the Asian American communities represent an extraordinary diversity. Each of these communities is unique, and generalizations are hazardous. Each faces its own mix of special challenges and can draw on its own set of strengths and advantages.

Still, two aspects of the modern Asian American experience are worth noting. First, discrimination against Asian Americans has not gone away. Like their nineteenth-century forebears, today's Asian Americans form a distinct and easily identifiable racial minority, and are subjected to continual stereotyping. Despite much progress, they continue to conjure up irrational fears and latent prejudices in many of their fellow citizens. When non-Asians express alarm at the number of Asian Americans attending Ivy League schools, for example, they echo the fears and hostility of nineteenth-century industrial workers. Asian Americans also face discrimination from other minority groups.

Second, the Asian American communities today encompass both great success and profound difficulties. While thousands of Asian Americans attend top-level schools and reach the highest levels of American medicine, science, and industry, millions of others remain in impoverished "Chinatowns," join violent street gangs, and struggle with daily existence. Asian Americans are held up as a model minority of overachievers, yet as a group they remain underpaid, stuck in dead-end jobs, and locked out of corporate boardrooms and top executive positions.

Nontraditional Minority Groups

Over the last few decades, groups besides clearly defined racial and ethnic minorities have also demanded recognition of the discrimination they face and have at times succeeded in obtaining relief from the government. In 1991, for example, Congress passed the Americans with Disabilities Act, which protects the disabled from discrimination in schools and in the workplace. The efforts of gays and lesbians have been less successful; they continue to face discrimination on the job and in society at large, and in 1986 the Supreme Court refused to extend constitutional protection to homosexual relationships.[39]

The gay rights issue is complicated by the distinction between protected *status* and protected *conduct,* which have traditionally been handled somewhat differently by the courts. This problem was clearly faced in the debate over gays in the military, when gay and lesbian groups objected to the "don't ask, don't tell, don't investigate" policy eventually adopted by the Clinton administration. That policy ended the military's active efforts to weed out gays and lesbians, but stopped well short of accepting homosexuality as an acceptable military lifestyle.

Affirmative Action

For decades, blacks and other minorities aimed to eliminate legally sanctioned segregation and racial discrimination. Next they turned to using the power of government to discourage racial discrimination in education, employment, and housing. Unfortunately, minorities often found that hundreds of years of slavery and discrimination had created immense burdens, leaving them far behind at the starting line. A more activist approach, many argued, was necessary.

The new remedy was called **affirmative action,** a broad term used to describe any program making distinctions based on race, gender, or disability in order to promote equality. Affirmative action programs reject the idea that equality can be achieved merely through a color-blind or gender-blind approach. They can require an organization that has engaged in proven illegal discrimination to set aside a specific number of positions for women or minorities. More commonly, such programs involve setting "goals"—less definite numbers that might or might not be achieved. The legality and desirability of any particular affirmative action program may depend on exactly how it is structured, what problems it is meant to solve, and whether there are other reasonable alternatives.

Constitutionality of Affirmative Action

Legally, affirmative action drew on the lessons of the school desegregation experience. Busing, in fact, was an early example of a program that took race into account to achieve broader goals of racial equality. The color-blind approach did not work: assigning students to the school closest to their homes without regard to race simply perpetuated the segregated system. Race-conscious busing was approved by the Supreme Court in 1971 as a court-imposed remedy for an existing constitutional violation. Whether other branches of the federal or state governments could use race-specific approaches was the central question in the 1978 case of *Bakke* v. *Regents of the University of California.*[40]

Allan Bakke, a white male, was denied admission to the University of California at Davis medical school. He was rejected, he claimed, solely on the basis of race: the school had reserved sixteen out of one hundred seats in the entering class for members of traditionally disadvantaged minority groups. Bakke claimed that an explicit racial quota system, however well motivated, was unconstitutional.

The Supreme Court, agreeing that the school could not adopt a rigid numerical quota, ordered Bakke's admission. At the same time, it approved a more flexible affirmative action approach that merely took race into account as one variable among many. It was legitimate for the school to seek out a racially diverse student body, the Court held, and the admissions process could thus give added weight to applications from minority students.

Although quotas were gone, affirmative action was not. In the years after *Bakke,* the Court upheld affirmative action in a variety of areas, including private and government employment and the distribution of broadcast licenses. In the 1980 case of *Fullilove* v. *Klutznick,* the Court also approved a federal law requiring the government to assign 10 percent of certain contracts to minority-owned firms. Such "set-aside" programs, the Court held, could be justified under Congress's power to enforce the Fourteenth Amendment. But the Court was deeply divided in *Fullilove* and in other cases, and did not always rule in favor of affirmative action. For example, the justices rejected one program that determined who would be laid off from work on the basis of race, reasoning that such a system unfairly makes specific individuals suffer the brunt of affirmative action efforts.[41]

In the 1990s, the Supreme Court has become increasingly hostile to affirmative action. In a key 1995 decision known as *Adarand Constructors, Inc.* v. *Pena,* the Court overruled its earlier rulings and held that "all racial classifications, imposed by whatever federal, state, or local governmental actor, must be analyzed by a reviewing court under strict scrutiny." Thus the government could not mandate an affirmative action program unless it could show that its actions were "narrowly tailored" to serve "compelling governmental interests." Under this standard, the Court ordered the lower courts to reexamine the constitutionality of federal set-aside programs. In the same year the Court struck down a congressional redistricting plan designed to increase the number of minority representatives in Congress, ruling that race could not be the predominant factor used in drawing congressional district lines.[42]

The Supreme Court has not been alone in restricting or repealing affirmative action programs. In 1996, for example, a federal appeals court banned racial admissions preferences at the University of Texas law school. Later the same year, California voters approved Proposition 209, which prohibits racial preferences in government hiring and public school admissions throughout the state. [43]

Affirmative Action, Pro and Con

Affirmative action has become extremely controversial in recent years. Both proponents and opponents advance forceful arguments, although they often talk past, instead of to, one another.

Proponents' arguments

Affirmative action counteracts present-day discrimination and provides a form of compensation for past discrimination. Proponents of affirmative action begin from the premise that America is not, and never has been, a "color-blind" society. "Some blacks never escaped the straight line of oppression that ran from slavery through the semicentury of sharecropping to the late mid-century migration from Southern farms into isolated pockets of urban poverty," writes Roger Wilkins. "Their families have always been excluded, poor, and without skills, so they were utterly defenseless" against recent economic and social problems. Furthermore, blacks and women have traditionally been excluded from the old-boy network that provides contacts and often jobs.

Despite the efforts of the past forty years, moreover, discrimination against minorities has not gone away. In 1991, for example, ABC's *Prime Time Live* followed two young men who were identical in every respect except one: race. The result? "In a series of encounters with shoe salesmen, record-store employees, rental agents, landlords, employment agencies, taxicab drivers, and ordinary citizens, the black member of the pair was either ignored or given a special and suspicious attention." Similarly, research suggests that a black male college graduate's share of his white male counterpart's salary dropped from 82 percent in 1979 to 72 percent in 1989.

Forcing minorities to compete on a level playing field would only continue the existing patterns of dis-

crimination. "The playing field is already tilted in favor of those by whom and for whom it was constructed in the first place," argues Stanley Fish. For example, statistical studies have shown that educational achievement is heavily influenced not only by native ability and merit but also by the educational and socioeconomic status of parents and classmates.

Evaluation of an individual's qualifications should be based on a range of criteria, including race or gender. Advocates of affirmative action argue that no one is, or should be, required to admit, hire, or promote someone who is unqualified. However, they question whether standard measures of qualifications are suitable or sufficient. For example, one scholar points out that the correlation between SAT scores and college grades "is lower than the correlation between height and weight." In many circumstances, moreover, a person's race is directly relevant to the work at hand. A police department might seek out female or black officers, for example, to better serve the needs of women or the black community. Schools might add women and minorities to the faculty to provide role models for women and minority students. Such an approach is desirable "not because it is desirable for a black boy or girl to find adult models only among blacks, but because our history has made them so conscious of their race that the success of whites, for now, is likely to mean little or nothing to them." Finally, advocates of affirmative action point out that factors other than merit, such as being a veteran or the child of an alumna, often play a role in admissions and hiring decisions.

Properly designed affirmative action programs can minimize unwanted side effects. Supporters of affirmative action recognize that such programs have unfortunate side effects. When women and minorities are given preference in admissions or employment policies, other people—white males—are left out. But affirmative action need not result in such stark contrasts between winners and losers, especially if it is coupled with other efforts designed to expand opportunities for everyone. Moreover, a less racist and sexist society would be a better society for everyone. "A nation that persists in racism and sexism," Wilkins writes, "abandons its soul and its economic strength, and will remain mired in ugliness and moral squalor because so many people are excluded from the possibility of decent lives and from forming any sense of community with the rest of society."

Opponents' arguments

Affirmative action is unfair. Every individual has the right to be judged on his or her own talents, not as a member of a group or as a means of achieving artificial goals or quotas, critics of affirmative action argue. Thus discrimination by race or sex is wrong, period, no matter how noble the intentions of those who practice it. A white male denied a job simply because of sex and skin color suffers the same harm as a black woman denied a job for the same reasons. "Why me?" a white male passed over for a job might say. "I didn't own slaves; I didn't vote to keep people on the back of the bus; I didn't turn water hoses on civil rights marchers. Why, then, should I be the one who doesn't get the job or who doesn't get the scholarship or who gets bumped back to the waiting list?"

In the end, the strongest argument against affirmative action is the simplest: the idea that "work and merit, not race or religion or gender or birthright, should determine who prospers and who does not."

Affirmative action is ineffective and actually erodes minority rights. Critics of affirmative action suggest that the beneficiaries of affirmative action are never given the opportunity to earn respect for their own actions, while whatever success they do achieve is attributed to gender or skin color instead of talent. Affirmative action programs damage the self-confidence of the beneficiaries and create resentment among those left out. Forcing minorities to make it on their own is a slower, but perhaps surer, route to success. "When blacks say we have to have affirmative action," comments the economist Glenn Loury, "it's almost like saying, 'You're right, we can't compete on merit.' But I know we can compete." Moreover, critics argue that affirmative action has divided the nation,

pitting whites against minorities and men against women. In the end, affirmative action may actually increase racism in society and harm those it is intended to help.

Race and gender are poor proxies for need. Whatever statistics may suggest, many of the recipients of affirmative action simply do not need help. "I'll be goddamned why the son of a wealthy black businessman should have a slot reserved for that race when the son of a white auto assembly worker is excluded," says one liberal Democrat. Moreover, conventional affirmative action programs include well-off minority groups while they leave out disadvantaged white subgroups. "Pennsylvania Germans . . . have a lower mean earnings, $10,339 per year, than the regulars on the affirmative action list," writes one critic. "Just because Hmongs earn a paltry $3,194, should affluent Chinese or Japanese reap benefits?"

Instead, many argue, affirmative action programs should be focused on those who are truly disadvantaged, regardless of race or gender. "It is possible to devise an enforceable set of objective standards for deprivation," writes Richard Kahlenberg. For example, college admissions officers could focus on parental income, education, and occupation. "Class preferences could restore the successful formula on which the early civil rights movement rested: morally unassailable underpinnings and a relatively inexpensive agenda," Kahlenberg concludes. "It's crucial to remember that Martin Luther King, Jr., called for special consideration based on class, not race."

Sources: Roger Wilkins, "The Case for Affirmative Action," *The Nation*, March 27, 1995, pp. 409–416; Ronald Dworkin, "Bakke's Case: Are Quotas Really Unfair?" in *A Matter of Principle* (Cambridge, Mass.: Harvard University Press, 1978), pp. 293–303; Stanley Fish, "Reverse Racism, or How the Pot Got to Call the Kettle Black," *The Atlantic Monthly*, November 1993, pp. 128–136; "Affirmative Action on the Edge," *U.S. News and World Report*, February 13, 1995, pp. 32–37; Thomas Sowell, "From Equal Opportunity to Affirmative Action," in *Civil Rights: Rhetoric or Reality?* (New York: William Morrow, 1984), pp. 37–48; Richard Kahlenberg, "Class, Not Race," *New Republic*, April 3, 1995, p. 217; Dante Ramos, "Losers," *New Republic*, October 17, 1994, pp. 24–25.

Summary

The term *civil rights* refers generally to questions of equality under law, especially with respect to race, ethnicity, and gender. Although originally applied to the rights of African Americans, the term has now been expanded to include any group disadvantaged by its minority status, and also to women, who, though technically a majority, have historically been excluded from positions of power and influence in the public and private sectors.

The Supreme Court has held that the Equal Protection Clause of the Fourteenth Amendment and the Due Process Clause of the Fifth Amendment prohibit government classifications by race, religion, and national origin unless the government can show that the classification serves a compelling governmental interest and that the classification is necessary to achieving that interest. These classifications are known as suspect classifications, and the test imposed by the Court is known as the strict scrutiny test. Classifications based on sex are held to a slightly lower standard.

The Fourteenth Amendment, ratified in 1868, was originally intended to redress the legacy of slavery and discrimination against African Americans. Early on, the Supreme Court limited the scope of the amendment, however, ruling first that it did not reach private conduct and then that it permitted segregation under the separate-but-equal standard. With the acquiescence of all three branches of the federal government, the southern states were able to impose a system of segregation and discrimination that left African Americans little better off than under slavery.

The federal government began to take an interest in the plight of African Americans during the New Deal, but real progress did not begin until 1954, when the Supreme Court outlawed segregation in the landmark case of *Brown* v. *Board of Education.* In the 1960s the civil rights movement, under the direction of the Reverend Martin Luther King, Jr., and others, spurred the executive and legislative branches to action. The result was key legislation, including the Civil Rights Act of 1964 and the Voting Rights Act of 1965, designed to protect the civil rights of racial minorities. The combination of judicial, executive, and legislative action greatly improved the legal status of African Americans and other racial minorities, but the legacy of slavery remains strong and persistent.

The civil rights movement has served as a model for other disadvantaged groups. Women, Native Americans, Latinos, Asians, gays and lesbians, and other minorities have used similar legal and political strategies to improve their lot. Some groups—for example, women—have fared well. Others—especially gays and lesbians—have been less successful.

In recent years the debate over civil rights has turned from equal opportunity to affirmative action. Minority groups argue that equal treatment is ineffective in redressing years of discrimination; instead the government and the private sector must take affirmative steps to help minorities compete. In the 1970s and 1980s, the Supreme Court upheld the constitutionality of a variety of types of affirmative action programs; in the 1990s, it has taken a more restrictive approach. Affirmative action remains controversial, and the exact dimensions of what is constitutionally and politically acceptable are currently in flux.

Key Terms

Civil rights
Suspect classifications
Strict scrutiny
Northwest Ordinance
Compromise of 1820
Fugitive Slave Act
Dred Scott v. *Sandford*
Emancipation Proclamation
Reconstruction
Thirteenth Amendment
Fourteenth Amendment
Fifteenth Amendment
Jim Crow laws
Plessy v. *Ferguson*
Thurgood Marshall
Brown v. *Board of Education*
Martin Luther King, Jr.
Civil Rights Act of 1964
Voting Rights Act of 1965
Busing
Integration
Desegregation
Equal Rights Amendment
Affirmative action

Review Questions

1. What is the meaning of the terms *suspect classification* and *strict scrutiny*? What classifications are considered suspect? Semisuspect? Why?

2. What was decided in the *Dred Scott* case? How did *Dred Scott* contribute to the growing crisis over slavery and help lead the country into civil war?

3. What were the goals of the Thirteenth, Fourteenth, and Fifteenth Amendments? Were those goals achieved between 1868 and 1950? Why or why not?

4. What was the ruling, rationale, and impact of the Supreme Court's decision in *Brown* v. *Board of Education?*

5. What is the significance of the Civil Rights Act of 1964 and the Voting Rights Act of 1965?

6. How did other minority groups, including women, model their legal and political strategies after the civil rights movement? Which groups were successful? Which were not? Why?

7. What is meant by affirmative action? Why do its supporters say that affirmative action is necessary? Why do its critics argue that affirmative action is undesirable?

Suggested Readings

Acosta-Belén, Edna, and Barbara R. Sjostrom, eds. *The Hispanic Experience in the United States: Contemporary Issues and Perspectives.* New York: Praeger, 1988.

Davis, Mary B., ed. *Native America in the Twentieth Century: An Encyclopedia.* New York: Garland Publishing, 1994.

Goldman, Roger L. *Thurgood Marshall: Justice for All.* New York: Carroll & Graf, 1992.

Kluger, Richard. *Simple Justice: The History of* Brown v. Board of Education *and Black America's Struggle for Equality.* New York: Knopf, 1976.

Lockhart, William B., Yale Kamisar, Jesse H. Choper, and Steven H. Shiffrin. *Constitutional Law: Cases-Comments-Questions.* 7th ed. St. Paul, Minn.: West Publishing Co., 1991 [with annual supplements].

Nieman, Donald G. *Promises to Keep: African-Americans and the Constitutional Order, 1776 to the Present.* New York: Oxford University Press, 1991.

Roberts, Cokie. *We Are Our Mothers' Daughters.* New York: W. Morrow, 1996.

Takaki, Ronald T. *Strangers from a Different Shore: A History of Asian Americans.* Boston: Little, Brown, 1989.

Thernstrom, Stephan, and Abigail Thernstrom. *America in Black and White: One Nation, Indivisible.* New York: Simon & Schuster, 1997.

Woodward, C. Vann. *The Strange Career of Jim Crow.* 3d rev. ed. New York: Oxford University Press, 1974.

Internet Resources

The National Association for the Advancement of Colored People, the nation's oldest civil rights organization, at:

http://www.naacp.org

The Center for Individual Rights, which has successfully brought litigation challenging a variety of affirmative action programs; also active in First Amendment cases at:

http://www.wdn.com/cir

The Martin Luther King Directory, containing secondary documents written about Martin Luther King, Jr., as well as primary documents written during King's life at:

http://www-leland.stanford.edu/group/King /#MartinLutherKing,Jr.

The National Organization for Women, leading feminist group at:

http://www.now.org

Searchable database of Supreme Court decisions and other legal and legislative information at:

http://www.findlaw.com/casecode/supreme. html

6

Political Culture

★★★★★★★★★★★★★★★★★★★★★★★★★★★★★★★★

When President Bill Clinton tried to fulfill his 1992 campaign promise to abolish the ban on gays and lesbians in the military, he did not know that he would touch off a national debate of epic proportions. On one side stood a variety of gay and lesbian groups, who regarded Clinton's promise as an important opportunity to establish themselves within the American mainstream. On the other side stood the military and its supporters, including the chairman of the Joint Chiefs of Staff and the chairman of the Senate Armed Services Committee, both of whom regarded the ban on gays as essential to military discipline and morale and thus to the national defense. In the middle stood the president, trying desperately to find a compromise that would put and keep a lid on an explosive issue.

The debate on gays in the military was more than just another Washington policy dispute. It struck a raw nerve at the very heart of American political culture—the fundamental ideas and principles on which American politics rests. Was the American conception of individual rights and personal privacy expansive enough to include those with alternative sexual lifestyles—even to the point of admitting them to the close-knit and critically important subculture of the armed forces? Or could the American community create and impose moral standards on individuals, to the point of excluding from

Colonel Margarethe Cammermeyer, who, after twenty-six years of service and a Bronze Star, was discharged from the Army in 1992 after acknowledging that she is a lesbian. In 1994 a federal judge ordered the Army to reinstate Cammermeyer; though the decision technically applied only to the pre-1993 ban on gays in the military, it cast legal doubt on the Clinton Administration's "Don't Ask, Don't Tell, Don't Pursue" policy.

the military those whose sexual orientations did not match those of the majority?

In the end, Congress and the president compromised on a policy of "Don't ask, don't tell, don't pursue." In other words, gays and lesbians would not be expelled from the military or otherwise punished as long as they did not engage in open gay and lesbian activity or otherwise bring their sexual orientation to the notice of their superiors. Questions about sexual orientation would no longer be asked routinely of military recruits, and the military would not actively investigate the sexual orientation of military personnel. Still, a soldier or sailor who advertised his or her homosexuality would remain subject to military discipline, including the possibility of imprisonment or expulsion.

The Clinton compromise seemed to please no one. Gays and lesbians, and many liberals, were unhappy because the new policy did not ban discrimination on the basis of sexual orientation. Conservatives were displeased as well, because liberals had achieved at least a symbolic victory. They also worried that even a small change in military policy might lead to a decline in morale and readiness among the troops. As for the president, by all accounts he was happy simply to have put the issue behind him.

The debate over gays in the military reaches to the core of Americans' views about morality and politics. Disagreement over this issue reflects not only differences on policy but also something deeper. More and more, American politics in the 1990s seems to turn on cultural issues, to the point where Americans on both sides of the great divide speak in terms of cultural warfare.

It is easy to pretend that the two sides in this war come from diametrically opposite political cultures. One side presses for individual autonomy even in an arena where the very life of the community may be at stake; the other side appeals to a traditional view of family, community, and military spirit. It would be difficult to imagine two groups as diverse as the gay rights marchers pressing for their full constitutional and human rights and the many soldiers and sailors who oppose their efforts.

Beneath the surface, however, the combatants in this cultural battle are not so different. Each side put its case at least partially in terms of individual rights, especially the right to privacy. Individual soldiers both for and against the ban on gays spoke in traditional terms of the importance of sacrifice, honor, and country. Both sides argued within the confines of the law, as it exists and as they hoped it will evolve.

Like every other political conflict in America, the gays-in-the-military debate took place within the boundaries of American political culture. As this chapter suggests, American political culture brings together even the most disparate viewpoints. No matter how obscured that common culture might become in the heat of battle, it rarely disappears altogether. That is why, with only the rarest exceptions, political solutions are possible even to the most bitter and divisive conflicts in American political life.

Questions to Keep in Mind

What common political and cultural values are widely shared by Americans of every political perspective? What common values do liberals and conservatives share?

Are some conflicts too deep and bitter to be bridged by political means? Is gay rights such an issue? Abortion? Pornography?

How do the ideals of American political culture compare and contrast with the realities of American political life? How can any gaps be explained?

Basic Concepts ★★★★★★★★★★★★★

Political Culture: The Unwritten Constitution

The term **political culture** refers to the "beliefs, values, and attitudes" that help shape a given society's political behavior, political institutions, and political outcomes.[1] These cultural factors are as important in determining the workings of a political system as are its formal constitution and laws. Political culture is not the same as political behavior: a community may act in ways that are inconsistent with widely accepted beliefs and attitudes. For example, a community might value free speech in the abstract, yet show little tolerance for certain controversial opinions. Even so, political culture is important, because culture may shape the way a community behaves in the long run or provide important insights into how its political system works. A community's political culture is closely linked to its history, its dominant religion or religions, and its shared assumptions about justice and morality.

Of course, neither political culture nor political institutions exist in a vacuum. Each exerts an influence on the other, and the two are often difficult to separate. The existence of social equality, for example, may favor the development of democratic political institutions. Democratic institutions, in turn, may reinforce the social equality of citizens. Thus it is often difficult to specify with precision exactly what influence political culture has had on political events. Nevertheless, many political scientists are convinced that the study of political culture comprises a kind of "unwritten Constitution" that is essential to an understanding of politics as a whole.[2]

What's Become of Rosie the Riveter?

Attitudes about the role of women in American society, like other aspects of American political culture, have changed dramatically in the past half century. During World War II, government propaganda urged women to work at "men's jobs" on behalf of the war effort; after the war, they were expected to return to their accustomed roles as housewives and mothers. The women's rights movement of the 1960s and 1970s, led by women like Gloria Steinem (shown on the right in a 1971 photo at her desk at Ms. magazine), urged men and women to treat each other as equals at home, at work, and in politics.

Nations are remarkably successful in handing down their political cultures from generation to generation, and to newly arrived immigrants as well. This process, known as **political socialization,** allows elements of a nation's political culture to remain remarkably stable over time. Still, political culture is always evolving. In the long term, it is affected by economic, demographic, and technological changes in society, and by the activities of citizens and political leaders. The mass migration of America's population from farms and villages to large urban centers in the late 1800s, for example, hardly could have occurred without some impact on political culture. The invention of television had an equally profound impact. The impact of such long-term changes, although real, is notoriously difficult to measure, and sorting out the effects of one factor from any of the others is next to impossible.

Short-term factors that lead to changes in political culture are easier to identify. A dramatic event, such as a war or an economic catastrophe, can shape political attitudes for a generation or more. Eleven months before the Japanese attack on Pearl Harbor in December 1941, for example, 88 percent of Americans opposed American entry into World War II. In October 1945—two months after the Japanese surrender—71 percent of those surveyed believed that the United States should "take an active part in world affairs." To this day, an overwhelming majority of Americans support an active role for the United States in world affairs.[3]

Cultures and Subcultures

The study of political culture focuses on what unites the people of a country rather than what divides them. Such shared values are of immense importance in any political system. Some degree of commonality is a necessary precursor to stable, democratic government, for otherwise disputes could not be settled peacefully or according to established rules. Politics in a day-to-day sense may emphasize conflict, but the very existence of a democratic political system is possible only because the participants are able to keep such conflicts within reasonable bounds. Revolutions and civil wars occur only when the members of a political community are hopelessly divided against themselves.

Because the participants in a democratic political system can easily get caught up in what divides them, they frequently take these common values for granted. The language of politics, like the language of sports, is full of military imagery: presidential "campaigns," budget "battles," partisan "warfare." In politics as in football, however, the fight takes place according to agreed-upon rules, and does not routinely degrade into mayhem. It is easy to overestimate the extent of political conflict in America by focusing on the fierceness of the struggle rather than its essence.[4]

Because analyses based on political culture emphasize a community's shared values, they tend to give short shrift to minority cultures or subcultures. The neglect of minority subcultures

To many Americans, the American flag represents the attempt to create "one nation, indivisible, with liberty and justice for all" out of the many subcultures that comprise the nation.

is particularly common in discussions of American politics, perhaps because the dominant political culture itself puts great emphasis on the idea of cultural unity. Focusing too heavily on the dominant culture not only ignores the millions of Americans who by choice or circumstance do not fit the mold, but may also contribute to both subtle and overt forms of discrimination and prejudice against minorities. Nonetheless, political culture is a useful concept, and if not misused it provides helpful insights into the nature of a political system and its people.

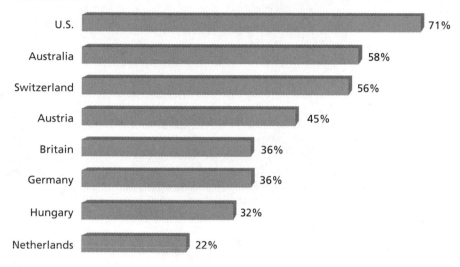

Figure 6.1 **Attitudes Toward Economic Equality in America and Europe**

Modern survey research bears out the claim that America is different. Americans are far more likely to be optimistic about their economic futures, for example, than are citizens of other countries.

U.S.	71%
Australia	58%
Switzerland	56%
Austria	45%
Britain	36%
Germany	36%
Hungary	32%
Netherlands	22%

Source: Roger Jowell, Lindsay Brook, and Lizanne Dowds, eds., *International Social Attitudes: The 10th BSA Report* (Aldershot, England: Dartmouth Publishing Group, 1993), pp. 128, 131, 132. The category labels have been altered slightly for clarity.

Is America Different?

Studies of political culture lend themselves to a comparative approach emphasizing the similarities and differences across national boundaries. Given America's colonial heritage, it is not surprising that most analyses of American political culture begin, implicitly or explicitly, by comparing the United States with Europe. The dominant theme of such analyses is that America is fundamentally different from Europe.[5]

The idea that the political culture of the United States is unique is known as **American exceptionalism.** "The Americans are in an exceptional situation," wrote the French political writer Alexis de Tocqueville, who toured the United States in the 1830s, "and it is unlikely that any other democratic people will be similarly placed." America's uniqueness, in Tocqueville's view, was the result of four factors:

- America's geographic isolation from the rest of the world.
- The relative social, economic, and political equality of the American settlers, excepting the slaves. As Tocqueville put it, "No novelty in the United States struck me more vividly during my stay there than the equality of conditions." Moreover, the Americans were "born equal" and did not need "the sufferings of a democratic revolution" to become that way.
- The absence of a single cultural, ethnic, linguistic, or religious division within the body politic, although conflict over the consequences of slavery and racial discrimination would eventually in fact create just such a division.
- The dominant influence of religion. Although there was an "innumerable multitude of sects in the United States," each worshiping God in its own way, Tocqueville observed that "all preach the same morality in the name of God."[6]

Is America Different?

For more than two centuries, scholars, politicians, and journalists have argued over whether American political culture is fundamentally different from that of Europe. As early as 1775, the great English parliamentarian and political writer Edmund Burke warned his fellow countrymen that the American people were unique; their character was marked by "a fierce spirit of liberty" stronger "than in any other people of the earth."* Alexis de Tocqueville, who coined the term "American exceptionalism," made the contrast between America and Europe the central theme of his great work, *Democracy in America.*

Although those who argue that America is different have dominated the debate, in recent years especially the American exceptionalism thesis has come under a strong challenge. Some critics argue that advocates of American exceptionalism have always overstated the differences between America and Europe; others argue that while fundamental differences might once have existed between America and Europe, in recent decades they have shrunk very nearly to the vanishing point.

Yes, America is different

Advocates of American exceptionalism, from Burke and Tocqueville to the modern era, point to several key differences between America and Europe:

There has never been a successful socialist or communist movement in America. Every European nation has seen significant socialist and communist movements over the past century. In some countries—such as Sweden and Russia—socialism or communism has dominated the political system; in others—including France and the United Kingdom—socialist parties have been viable players and have,

on occasion at least, won control of the government. In the United States, by contrast, socialism and communism have never been more than fringe movements. Advocates of American exceptionalism argue that the failure of socialism and communism is rooted in Americans' distrust of large, centralized governments.

Americans are more religious than Europeans, and their religious views are different in nature. Burke, in his 1775 speech, noted that the dominant religion in America was a Protestantism "of that kind which is the most adverse to all implicit submission of mind and opinion." Tocqueville, likewise, noted that "the religious atmosphere was the first thing that struck me on arrival in the United States," and observed that "there is not a single religious doctrine in the United States hostile to democratic and republican institutions."† The distinctiveness of American religious beliefs and practices remains clear, supporters of American exceptionalism argue. Commenting on a multinational survey, the political scientist Kenneth Wald writes: "The United States . . . was . . . the most 'religious' of countries as shown by the answers its citizens gave to the interviewers. The magnitude of American 'exceptionalism' can best be gauged by comparing the percentage of Americans who actually assigned great importance to religious belief—51 percent—with the proportion that should have done so on the basis of the pattern in other countries—a mere 5 percent."‡

Americans think differently about politics than do Europeans. Many commentators have pointed out that American politics is grounded in basic political attitudes that contrast sharply with European views. Most often cited are Americans' distrust of centralized government; their emphasis on individual rights, both economic and otherwise; and their commitment to egalitarianism. These themes, of course, are related, and were especially so in the early days of the American Republic. Those who fought the American revolution saw the centralized government in London as a defender of inequality and as a threat to individual rights. Therefore, as the political scientist Aaron Wildavsky has written, "both egalitarians and individualists could join in severely limiting the size and scope of central government."§

No, America is not different

Critics of the American exceptionalism hypothesis argue either that Americans never were that different from their European counterparts, or that any such differences have diminished in recent years—both because Americans have become more like Europeans, and because Europeans have become more like Americans.

American public policy is not that different from European public policy. Despite the traditional American antipathy toward big government, the United States has adopted a broad array of social welfare programs, including social security and programs to assist the poor and the unemployed. And while levels of American social spending do not approach those of Sweden or Denmark, they are comparable to those of Canada, Switzerland, Japan, Finland, and Australia, argues the political scientist Richard Rose. Each of these countries, Rose writes, "has the money to provide a high level of public benefits. . . . However, their governments have chosen *not* to levy taxes claiming a large proportion" of the national income.‖

The assumption that Americans' religious views are unique does not stand up to objective scrutiny. Surveys have shown differences in the aggregate between Americans and Europeans on religious matters, but these differences, when analyzed carefully, cannot be ascribed to American exceptionalism. In his analysis of survey data in the United States and England, for example, Andrew Greeley finds that the real "exception" is found among English Anglicans; "those identifying in England with non-Anglican denominations, whether Catholic or Protestant, would be as likely as Americans to believe, for example, in the existence of God and life after death and to attend church regularly." Angli-

cans, being "born into a religion almost by the fact of birth in a society," find that religion adds little to their identity and makes few demands on their behavior. By contrast, non-Anglicans, whether in America or England, find that their religion contributes a great deal to their sense of identity. But this difference, Greeley stresses, suggests an "Anglican exceptionalism," not an American exceptionalism.#

Whatever the history, Europe and America are becoming more alike. The growth of multinational corporations, advances in communications technology, and freer movement of goods and people between the United States and Europe are all contributing to a decline in American exceptionalism. Political commentators, for example, stress the parallels between Ronald Reagan's leadership in the 1980s in the United States and Margaret Thatcher's leadership in England, both of whom pursued a strong conservative agenda. More recently, analysts point to the similarities between Bill Clinton and British Prime Minister Tony Blair, both of whom took control of left-leaning political parties and moved them toward the center of the political spectrum. In an age when Europeans watch American television, phone calls to Europe cost ten cents a minute, and the Internet provides instant access to information world-wide, the continued viability of American exceptionalism—if it ever really existed—is highly doubtful.

*Edmund Burke, "Speech . . . on Reconciliation with the Colonies," March 22, 1775, in *The Works of the Right Honourable Edmund Burke* (London: George Bell & Sons, 1889), I:464.

†Burke, *Works*, I:406; Alexis de Tocqueville, *Democracy in America*, ed. J. P. Mayer (Garden City, NY: Doubleday & Co., 1969), pp. 295,289.

‡Kenneth D. Wald, *Religion and Politics in the United States* (New York: St. Martin's Press, 1987), pp. 6–7.

§Aaron Wildavsky, "Resolved, that Individualism and Egalitarianism Be Made Compatible in America: Political-Cultural Roots of Exceptionalism," in Byron E. Schafer, ed., *Is America Different? A New Look at American Exceptionalism* (Oxford: Clarendon Press, 1991), p. 122.

‖Richard Rose, "Is American Public Policy Exceptional?" in Shafer, ed., *Is America Different?*, p. 207.

#Andrew M. Greeley, "American Exceptionalism: The Religious Phenomenon," in Shafer, ed., *Is America Different?*, p. 114.

Tocqueville's analysis forms the starting point for the many later works that developed the idea of American exceptionalism. All of these works stressed that the American political culture is essentially liberal, in the classical sense of the word, placing great emphasis on rights and liberty and rejecting the feudal idea that human beings were naturally unequal. With no feudal past to go back to, Americans could avoid the European social revolutions that aimed to destroy feudal regimes. American exceptionalism thus provided an explanation as to why America avoided the extreme movements, from fascism to communism, that kept Europe in a perpetual state of convulsion.[7] As we will see, clear differences between American and European political culture continue to exist even in the modern era.

National differences in political culture have very real consequences for public policy. Widespread assumptions and attitudes about government and politics constrain the choices available to political leaders and to citizens in general. Often, the influence of political culture operates in the background, and voters and policy makers alike are unaware of its effect. Political culture also helps frame the problems and issues with which the political system must cope. Thus certain policies, such as the abolition of private property, may be so deeply in conflict with the prevailing political culture that they are never even discussed. Or a state of affairs that is seen as a problem in one culture (say, the existence of unequal distributions of wealth) may be accepted as an unalterable fact of life in another.

The American Creed

The core of America's unique political culture is an unwritten set of widely shared beliefs commonly known as the **American creed** (a creed is simply a set of beliefs). The creed is less a coherent political philosophy than a hodgepodge of political values, assumptions, and aspirations. Belief in the American creed is not universal, and Americans differ greatly in the weight and importance they place on particular elements. But the main components of the creed help to define the broad contours of American politics.

To a remarkable degree, major conflicts in American politics have revolved around different interpretations or applications of the shared values of the creed. It can thus be said that agreement on the main components of the creed makes politics possible, but disagreement on their meaning and application makes politics necessary.

Paradoxically, the components of the American creed often point in opposite directions. Some stress the sanctity and primacy of the individual, for example; others emphasize the importance of community. Few Americans ever choose between these competing elements, trying instead to reconcile them or at least to live with both.

Liberty and Individual Rights   "We have always been a nation obsessed with liberty," wrote the political scientist Clinton Rossiter.[8] From the Declaration of Independence to the modern era, the idea of liberty has been at the core of American political culture. Since liberty by definition involves individual choice, there can be no common agreement on exactly which aspects of liberty are important or how that liberty should be used. Many Americans emphasize the importance of religious freedom, freedom of speech and press, and privacy. Others focus on economic liberty and argue for minimal government regulation of business. Still others oppose all but the most essential government restrictions on individual freedom.

Closely tied to the concept of liberty is the idea of rights. Rights protect individuals from government or private coercion, creating zones of individual freedom into which no one can intrude. According to classical American political theory, individuals are born with certain rights that cannot be given or taken away. It is the purpose of government to protect and secure these rights, and care must be taken not to permit any government to limit or violate them. Jefferson described these rights as "life, liberty, and the pursuit of happiness"; the Constitution enumerates at least some of them in more detail in the Bill of Rights. Rights can also be conferred on individuals by legislative enactments or through private transactions: for example, Congress can create a right to be free from sexual harassment in the workplace, and an individual can obtain rights over a specific piece of property by purchasing it from the owner.

Competing definitions of rights and liberty are responsible for much of the political conflict in the United States today. Both sides in a political dispute commonly cast their arguments in terms of individual rights. Both supporters and opponents of abortion, for example, base their arguments on individual rights—one side on the rights of women, the other on the rights of the fetus or embryo. Likewise, both sides in the debate over prayer in the public schools put their arguments in terms of religious freedom.

Equality   The concept of equality is also central to American politics. Equality is the basis of the democratic form of government, which allows all to participate and recognizes no special privileges. It is the basis of our system of legal and constitutional rights and of the American justice system. Proclamations of equality are everywhere, from the Declaration of Independence ("All men are created equal") to the pediment of the Supreme Court building ("Equal Justice Under Law").

Even men and women of good intention cannot agree on what equality means, or what it requires. Perhaps the most common division is over how to bring about a meaningful equality among those with different social, economic, racial, and ethnic backgrounds. Some believe it is enough for the government to treat all citizens the same way, creating no artificial barriers to equality. Others argue that the government must play an active role in ensuring true equality of opportunity.

However one defines equality, American history—and American society today—is replete with examples of inequality in every sphere. Does this mean that the ideal of equality exists merely to be violated or hypocritically abandoned? Not at all. Like other features of the American creed, equality exists both as a reality and as an ideal. The American belief in equality does not erase all inequalities, but it does create a standard against which our society can be continually measured, and toward which it can continually strive.

Property and Economic Rights   The concepts of private property and economic rights are fundamental to the American creed as well. The American political system has always recognized the sanctity of private property and the importance of such values as self-reliance, competitiveness, and entrepreneurship. The value of economic rights is explicitly mentioned in the Constitution, which protects the "life, liberty, and property" of the people and provides that "private property shall not be taken for public use without just compensation."

In the twentieth century, however, property rights and economic freedoms have run up against competing concerns about the consequences of unregulated economic activity.

Especially since the New Deal of the 1930s, Americans have turned to the national government to guard against the most serious consequences of private economic power. The government's role includes protecting the losers in the economic competition through social welfare programs; protecting workers and consumers through regulation of business; breaking up private monopolies; and outlawing or restricting activities that are detrimental to the interests of society at large. But government is also relied on to promote economic growth and to protect business interests.

Drawing the line between appropriate and excessive government regulation and support of business is not an easy task. How to draw that line has become an important issue in the American political debate, as evidenced by the Clinton administration's controversial efforts in 1993 and 1994 to promote increased government involvement in the health care industry. Paradoxically, many Americans seem to support economic freedom in the abstract but to favor particular programs aimed at promoting or regulating business.

Individualism and Self-Reliance   The American emphasis on rights and liberties, including economic and property rights, created strong support for the idea that individuals ought to be able to succeed on their own. The ideals of individualism and self-reliance were embodied in the American frontier spirit and lie at the heart of Americans' reputation for optimism and a "can-do" attitude. As one nineteenth-century American put it, "Ours is a country, where men . . . can attain to the most elevated position, or acquire a large amount of wealth, according to the pursuits they elect for themselves. . . . One has as good a chance as another, according to his talents, prudence, and personal exertions. This is a country of self-made men, than which nothing better can be said of any state of society."[9]

The American belief in the virtues of self-reliance and individualism was eroded during the Great Depression of the 1930s. Under the New Deal, the United States established a social safety net—including welfare, social security, and unemployment insurance—long after such programs had been adopted in other industrialized nations. Still, as current debates over welfare suggest, Americans remain committed to the idea that individuals should take care of themselves.[10] Most Americans today believe that welfare should be used only as a temporary measure and that welfare recipients should be encouraged to work hard and become self-sufficient as quickly as possible.[11]

Law   "There is hardly a political question in the United States which does not sooner or later turn into a judicial one," wrote Alexis de Tocqueville in 1831.[12] Today, it is frequently noted that the United States has many more lawyers per capita than any other nation, and that America produces more lawsuits than any other country in the world.[13]

American political culture is deeply rooted in the rule of law, and Americans have delegated enormous authority and responsibility to courts and judges.[14] Significantly, law provides the only legitimate way for government to control the

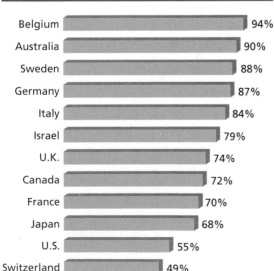

Figure 6.2 International Voter Turnout

Belgium	94%
Australia	90%
Sweden	88%
Germany	87%
Italy	84%
Israel	79%
U.K.	74%
Canada	72%
France	70%
Japan	68%
U.S.	55%
Switzerland	49%

SOURCE: Curtis Gans, Committee for the Study of the American Electorate.

behavior of individuals, and constitutes one of the only effective ways to limit the power of government and thus protect individual rights. This dual quality of law reflects both the lawmaking powers of the legislative branch and the rights-enforcing powers of the judiciary, and is the source of much confusion and conflict.

So many political questions end up in court that disputes about the law and the courts are inevitable. Moreover, Americans define law not only as what the courts actually do but also as what they *should* do. At times, therefore, the law itself provides a way of challenging controversial legal decisions. Critics of the courts can always turn to the Constitution, and even the Constitution can be challenged as violating the higher law of God or nature. In the 1850s, for example, some abolitionists criticized the Supreme Court for its rulings that slavery was permitted under the Constitution, while others took issue with the Constitution itself, arguing that the Framers' decision to condone slavery undermined the legitimacy of the document.[15]

Community The concept of community is as deeply rooted in American political culture as the idea of individual rights. The Pilgrims, for example, came to America less to advance individual freedom than to preserve the religious life of their community (despite what is often assumed, they had little tolerance for dissenters or free thinkers). Even the Declaration of Independence speaks to the importance of community, its very purpose being to proclaim the independence of the American people—as a community—from England. Although it is best remembered for its enshrinement of "life, liberty, and the pursuit of happiness," its signers ended up by pledging to each other "our lives, our Fortunes and our sacred Honor."

The importance of community shows itself in many aspects of American political culture, including the value many Americans place on sacrifice and volunteerism, political participation, and loyalty to town, state, and region. These community-based values are perhaps not as strong as they once were (political participation, for example, has declined markedly in recent decades), but the concept of community remains an essential component of the American creed and of American political culture.

Religion "The religious atmosphere of the country was the first thing that struck me on arrival in the United States," wrote Tocqueville. Although on the surface the separation of church and state appeared to diminish the influence of religion, he observed, in reality it freed religion from subservience to the government and made it an even more powerful force.[16]

Discussion and dialog among diverse groups of citizens helps build a feeling of community, and encourages individuals to work together to solve common problems.

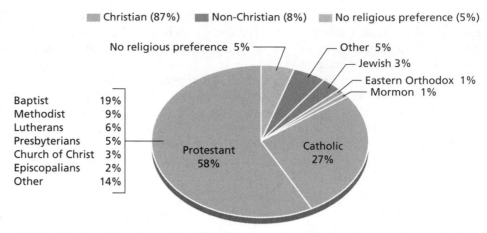

Figure 6.3 **Religious Self-Identification of Americans, 1997**

SOURCE: Frank Newport and Lydia Saad. "Religious Faith Is Widespread but Many Skip Church," *The Gallup Poll,* March 29, 1997 <http://www.gallup.com/poll_archives/970329.htm>

Religion continues to be an important force in American life and in American politics. A large majority of Americans say that religion is an important factor in their lives, attend religious services on a regular basis, and regard religious faith as critical to the future of humankind. Religious organizations and principles play a central role in the civil rights movement and in the debate over abortion. In recent years, conservative Christians (often called the "religious right") have emerged as a powerful force in national politics. Still, the centrality of religion in American life has been steadily declining over the past forty years, and American society has become increasingly secular. While only 7 percent of Americans thought that religion was "largely old-fashioned and out of date" in 1957, for example, 23 percent took that position in 1986.[17]

In spite of the multitude of religious sects in America, the dominant influence of religion in Tocqueville's day was to bring Americans together, reinforcing the values of community life. In 1830, America was overwhelmingly Protestant; only later did large numbers of Jews, Catholics, and others arrive. By the late nineteenth century the tensions between Catholics and Protestants and between different sects of Protestantism were clearly apparent, especially on such questions as whether to ban alcoholic beverages. Today, according to some analysts, religion seems to be more of a dividing than a unifying force. The Supreme Court's decisions on school prayer, pornography, abortion, and other social issues; the rise of conservative Protestantism as a political force since the 1970s; and the hard-line positions of the Catholic church on issues such as abortion and homosexuality have all contributed to the polarization of American society around religion and religious issues. As the political scientist Charles W. Dunn has noted, "religion, once a part of the glue holding American society together, now appears to be contributing substantially to society's breaking apart."[18] The divisive role of religion in America should not be overstated, however. Many controversies divide liberal and conservative wings of the same religious sect, and many forces besides religion have contributed to the breakdown of community.

Competing Values Within the Creed The American creed combines many diverse and competing elements. Although most Americans believe in some version of the creed, few make an effort to reconcile its conflicting parts. Instead, most Americans simply hold the various elements of the creed side by side, ignoring or brushing aside any contradictions that might result.

Moreover, the American creed is susceptible to very different shadings and interpretations. Although two Americans might both believe in liberty, they might define liberty in different ways. Each might profess a belief in liberty or equality, yet they might weigh these two values differently. Thus the creed not only provides a commonality of political beliefs but also helps to shape and structure political conflict.

The attempt to make American society more equal through affirmative action programs, for example, can conflict directly with the ideals of economic liberty and self-reliance. Efforts to promote unity and community through compulsory flag salutes or prayer in the public schools conflicts with the minority's rights of free speech and freedom of religion. Trying to resolve these conflicts within the American creed and create a coherent approach to political life provides the basis for the emergence of competing political ideologies, or ways of approaching political life, a subject to which we now turn.

American Political Ideologies: Liberalism and Conservatism

A political **ideology** is "a set of beliefs and opinions about how government and society should be organized and how the 'good society' can be achieved." Ideologies "help people organize specific opinions into a coherent belief system," helping them to make sense of the political world in which they live. The dominant political ideologies in the United States are **liberalism** and **conservatism**.

Few terms in the lexicon of American politics are as used and abused as these two. Like Humpty-Dumpty, many Americans seem to think that these words mean "just what I choose it to mean—neither more nor less." Often Americans use one term to mean "what I'm for" and the other to mean "what I'm against."[19]

The problem with using the words *liberalism* and *conservatism* in the American context is fourfold. First, the meaning of both terms is constantly changing, and their meaning may change completely from one era to the next. Second, the words *liberalism* and *conservatism* mean different things to different people, and few Americans use them with real consistency. Third, liberalism and conservatism are used to refer not only to specific policy preferences but also to competing *styles* of politics.[20] Finally, many Americans describe themselves as moderates or "middle-of-the road," and are uncomfortable with either ideological label.[21]

Liberalism and Conservatism: A Brief History Liberalism as a political philosophy began some five hundred years ago, during the European Renaissance. Essentially it was a broad-based challenge to the status quo in religion, politics, economics, and science. Liberalism reached its intellectual peak in the seventeenth and eighteenth centuries, in the ideas of such great thinkers as John Locke, David Hume, and Immanuel Kant.

Early liberalism was grounded on three premises. First, all ideas were to be judged by reason alone. No deference would be shown to received wisdom, popular superstition, or religious dogma. But reason could not prevail without freedom of thought and speech, and thus liberalism demanded an end to censorship and the promotion of individual liberty (hence the origin of the word). Second, liberalism embodied a deep distrust of centralized power, including both the government and the church. Finally, liberalism fostered a strong

"Society is indeed a contract . . . . It is a partnership in all science, a partnership in all art; a partnership in every virtue, and in all perfection. As the ends of such a partnership cannot be obtained in many generations, it becomes a partnership not only between those who are living, but between those who are living, those who are dead, and those who are to be born."

—Edmund Burke, 1790

belief in political equality, since natural reason and the world of ideas were, in theory at least, independent of wealth or political status.

In practical terms, liberalism developed as a broad-based assault on the existing power structures of early modern Europe. Its emphasis on freedom of thought and speech and on political equality threatened the primacy of kings and queens, fostered a massive rebellion against the rule of the Pope, and jeopardized the position of every bishop, earl, count, and duke. Ultimately, it would lead to political upheavals everywhere in Europe.

Predictably, those who had traditionally held the reins of political and religious power were unwilling to give up without a fight, and fought to conserve their position. They therefore became known as conservatives. They emphasized the value of tradition and the danger of radical change; the importance of order over excessive liberty; the importance of the naturalness of inequality rather than equality; the value of practical wisdom and experience over theoretical wisdom and philosophy; and the advantages of aristocracy (the rule of the best) over democracy (the rule of the common folk). Conservatives had a pessimistic view of human nature, and stressed the role of the church, the government, and other institutions in protecting and preserving society. Classical European conservatism is perhaps best exemplified by the English politician and writer Edmund Burke, whose most famous work was an extended diatribe on the evils of the French Revolution.

In America, the competing philosophies of liberalism and conservatism were quickly jumbled together. Having pushed the Native Americans aside, the first European settlers were able to build a new society without overthrowing an old one. Almost none of the immigrants to America had noble titles or great wealth, but almost all could quickly acquire enough land to be self-supporting. The "natural" state of these first European Americans, then, was in line with the core ideas of liberalism: they were relatively equal in power and status, largely free from religious coercion, and clearly separated from the conventions and customs of life in Europe.

Under these conditions a true conservatism could hardly develop, and liberalism became predominant almost by default.[22] The ideas of European liberalism, transmitted from the English philosopher John Locke to the American lawyer Thomas Jefferson, formed the ideology of the American Revolution. But the revolutionaries themselves were quite unlike the poor, downtrodden mobs who would later take to the streets of Paris during the French Revolution. Instead they were well-off or middle-class lawyers, farmers, and merchants. Their goal was not to destroy the existing social and economic order but—as they said repeatedly—simply to protect the rights they had enjoyed for decades as British Americans.[23]

The American patriots were thus conservative revolutionaries who fought in the name of liberalism. Given this starting point, it is no wonder that the terms *liberal* and *conservative* have little intrinsic meaning in the American context. From the beginning, Americans have used the terms *liberal* and *conservative* differently from Europeans, and through the years they have used these terms inconsistently and often arbitrarily.

Ideologies and Political Attitudes   Any attempt to identify and categorize American political ideologies in terms of attitudes about particular policies risks (or perhaps guarantees) oversimplification and distortion. Americans themselves are often uncertain about their own political ideologies, or use terms to describe themselves that do not match up neatly with the content of their beliefs. In a 1992 survey, for example, those who called themselves "liberals" were evenly split on whether the government should guarantee jobs to all; divided two to one against fighting the Persian Gulf War; and split three to one in favor of abortion choice and expanded government-provided medical care. Conservatives were more consistent, but still divided. Only about two-thirds opposed expanded medical care, while fully one-quarter felt the Persian Gulf War was not worth fighting and were in favor of abortion choice.[24]

A useful way to categorize the relationship between American political ideologies and specific policy preferences is to think in terms of policy clusters, or groups of related issues. Three clusters are particularly important: economic issues, social issues, and foreign policy issues. Within the first two of these categories, at least, it is relatively easy to classify an individual on the liberal-conservative continuum. Keep in mind, however, that inconsistency *between* these policy clusters is common.

Economic Liberalism and Conservatism   The split between liberals and conservatives on economic issues is clear. Liberals, in general, favor an active government role in regulating economic activities, redistributing wealth, and expanding programs to help the poor and middle class. Conservatives, by contrast, generally favor a more limited government role in regulating the economic marketplace. They typically oppose government efforts to impose high taxes on the wealthy or to provide the poor with more than a basic safety net. In short, liberals look to government to increase economic equality, while conservatives seek to avoid government actions that infringe on economic liberty.

The positions of liberals and conservatives on economic matters has flip-flopped over the past two centuries, causing no end of confusion. Classical (meaning eighteenth and early nineteenth century) liberals opposed government regulation of economic affairs, just as they opposed government intrusion into other areas of life. Conservatives favored a strong governmental role in protecting business from competition, and expanding what we now call the national infrastructure—roads, bridges, canals, and the like. Understanding why liberals and conservatives switched sides on these two issues is critical to understanding their current points of view.

For liberals, the change came with the industrial revolution of the late nineteenth century. As the power of large corporations grew, liberals came to believe that the major threat to individual freedom came from concentrations of private economic power—especially large corporations. The only effective counterweight to corporate power, according to liberals, was government power. Liberals thus fought for government programs to regulate banks, utility companies, and the stock markets, and to establish minimum wage levels and strict codes for worker safety.

Liberals also came to believe that government power was necessary to secure the larger public interest whenever the private marketplace breaks down. All Americans benefit from clean air and water, for example, but such "public goods" are difficult to achieve through private economic transactions alone. It is all too easy for individuals to enjoy the benefits of these goods without paying their fair share of the costs. This difficulty is known as the free-rider problem. Liberals argue that solving the free-rider problem requires the active intervention of government to set national goals and spread the burdens and benefits fairly across various groups.

Finally, liberals grew to believe that government power is frequently needed to ensure that all individuals are accorded equal dignity and respect, and to minimize the inequalities that arise from a freewheeling industrial economy. The less fortunate must be protected by government programs that provide social security for the aged, welfare and health care for the poor, and unemployment insurance and job training for those out of work. In addition, liberals stress that government must pay special attention to the needs of women and minority groups, who must deal with both present-day and past discrimination.

Since at least the New Deal, modern economic conservatism has been defined in part as a reaction to the liberal economic agenda. Conservatives place great faith in the ability of private markets to make efficient economic decisions, thus promoting economic well-being in the long run. They oppose liberals' efforts to redistribute wealth, expand the size of government, and increase the scope of government regulation. Conservatives believe that individuals should be rewarded for hard work, ingenuity, and assumption of risk, and that the incentive of the profit motive is the surest way to ensure that human beings lead productive lives that benefit the entire community.

Conservatives do not advocate a complete hands-off policy for government. For the most part, they support the basic elements of the social safety net, such as social security and unemployment insurance. They seek to reform, but not eliminate, programs providing welfare and medical services to the poor. Moreover, many conservatives favor a strong government role in supporting industry through the enforcement of a fair playing field at home and abroad, public spending on highways, and large government contracts funneled to private companies, especially in the national defense area.

Few Americans adopt a pure liberal or conservative viewpoint on economic issues. In fact, many Americans seem to support conservative ideas when dealing with abstract issues but reveal more liberal attitudes when it comes to specific government programs. Scholars describe such people as *ideological* conservatives and *programmatic* liberals. In a 1996 survey, for example, even those who most strongly believed that the "government should provide many fewer services" were divided when it came to specific issues. Some 29 percent of those in this group favored increased spending for AIDS research, for example, while 35 percent favored increased spending to help solve the homeless problem. [25]

Social Liberalism and Conservatism The liberal and conservative viewpoints on social issues are exactly the opposite of their views on economic matters. On social issues, liberals stress the individual's freedom from government restraint or coercion, while conservatives advocate a strong role for government in maintaining order and in promoting and policing the moral standards of the community. Common flash points for the liberal/conservative split on social issues include abortion, pornography, and sexual behavior. Conservatives and liberals differ also on church and state questions, with conservatives favoring government accommodation of religion and liberals backing a strict separation of church and state. Another area of conflict involves questions of criminal law, with liberals putting more emphasis on the rights of criminal defendants and conservatives focusing on the rights of victims and on the right of the larger community to be free from crime.

In some respects, the split between liberals and conservatives on social issues reflects the original, European contest between the liberal Locke and the conservative Burke. Social liberals look to the political system simply to provide an environment in which individuals can pursue their own ideas of what is good for them. Social conservatives see politics as providing an essential sense of community, which both channels individual desires and allows them to reach their highest purposes.

A Note on Foreign Policy   Some Americans define liberalism and conservatism in terms of foreign policy. Here again the two groups have flipped back and forth depending on historical and political circumstances. Before World War II, for example, liberals (led by Franklin Roosevelt) favored increased American involvement in Europe and Asia, while conservatives argued that Americans should stay out of other people's troubles. During the Vietnam era, however, liberals came to oppose American involvement in Southeast Asia, arguing that Americans should not be sent to fight except where the national interest was clearly at stake. This liberal isolationism lasted through the Reagan era, and could be seen as late as the Persian Gulf War, which many liberals opposed. At the same time, conservatives became increasingly focused on the importance of a strong military response to communism and third-world terrorism, favoring the "Star Wars" space defense program, a massive increase in the military budget, and military excursions in Grenada, Libya, and the Persian Gulf.

The end of the cold war has further confused matters. Many conservatives now favor an isolationist position. They oppose economic assistance to foreign countries, favor strict limits on immigration, and object to American military operations designed to promote democracy or human rights unless American interests, narrowly defined, are clearly at stake. Many conservatives particularly object to American involvement in operations run by the United Nations, fearing a loss of U.S. control. By contrast, many liberals now favor American involvement abroad in order to promote human rights and help the oppressed. Yet many liberals remain deeply suspicious of military interventions abroad.

American views on foreign policy are highly variable and depend greatly on the particular circumstances of any proposed involvement. They also depend on whether a liberal or conservative president is in power. At this point, it is difficult if not impossible to mark out a clear liberal or conservative position on foreign policy issues.

Other Political Ideologies   One distinguishing feature of American politics has been the relative scarcity of extremist political ideologies. Although the United States has been home to communists, fascists, Nazis, and extremists of every other type, such groups have never played a major role in mainstream politics. Three unpopular ideologies, however, are worth mentioning.

Socialism favors broad economic equality, even including government ownership of key industries. Socialism gained many adherents before the New Deal, although the thrust of its program was largely usurped by the development of the modern welfare state. Today, socialism is successful in only a few communities and rarely makes an appearance at the national level. Its unpopularity makes it a useful insult when applied to policies that redistribute wealth, increase government regulation, or extend government benefits.

Populism expresses a belief in the power of ordinary people as opposed to elite groups. The original populist movement centered on poor southern and western farmers, who organized politically in the late nineteenth century to combat what they saw as the unbridled power of businessmen and bankers. More recently, the term has been used by conservative politicians who have gained support among average Americans by railing against a perceived "cultural elite," and by liberal politicians who rail against big business interests.

Libertarianism embodies opposition to government intervention in both the economic and social spheres. To the dismay of many libertarians, their ideology has been linked with extremists like Lyndon Larouche, who have combined a belief in minimal government with a variety of unrelated conspiracy theories and other inflammatory arguments.

Ideology as Political Style   Distinguishing between the political views of liberals and conservatives is difficult. Both self-described liberals and self-described conservatives show relatively little consistency either within or between the economic and social categories discussed above. This overall sense of confusion has led some political scientists to focus not on the issue components of ideology but on liberalism and conservatism as political *styles*.

Simply put, these scholars argue that liberals and conservatives see the world differently. In particular, liberals tend to support proposed changes in public policy while conservatives are more resistant to change; and liberals tend to be more open-minded toward new ideas, while conservatives are more cautious. Some of these stylistic differences are essentially apolitical—they describe an individual's approach to life in general rather than to politics in particular. But they may have profound implications for the way individuals relate and react to politics.[26]

One problem with the concept of ideology as political style is that those who are commonly identified as liberals and conservatives do not always act in accordance with these stylistic descriptions. Thus the conservative Newt Gingrich advocates what he describes as a "revolution" in the federal government's role in American life, while many liberals find themselves defending the status quo.

The Dark Side of American Politics

Americans justly take pride in many aspects of their political culture. American democracy, with its commitment to rights and its dedication to law, has become a model for many other political systems and a beacon of hope for countless more. But America can hardly claim to be without its political dark side. The best that can be said is that, over time, some of the negative aspects of American political culture have changed for the better. An accurate rendering of American political culture must include its historical and contemporary blemishes.

Intolerance and the Pressure to Conform

In some respects, America has never been especially tolerant of those belonging to minority groups or expressing minority opinions. Even the Puritans, who left England in search of religious freedom, were intolerant of those who disagreed with them. The intolerance of the early settlers reached a peak in 1692, when nineteen innocent people were executed and many more persecuted at the Salem Witch Trials. Many others were forced to leave the Massachusetts Bay colony because their religious freedom was not respected by the ruling majority.[27]

Intolerance of minority groups and minority viewpoints has persisted throughout American history. Tocqueville noted that there was no country in which "there is less independence of mind and true freedom of discussion than in America." Not that the unpopular speaker had anything to fear from the law; instead he was subjected to "all kinds of unpleasantness and everyday persecution" from his fellow citizens and "denied everything, including renown." So complete was the majority's ability to stifle dissent, according to Tocqueville, that censorship in the United States was far more effective than in even the despotisms of Europe.[28]

Although Tocqueville's point may be overstated, especially if applied today, it perhaps explains why Americans are far more tolerant of unpopular ideas in theory than in practice. Seventy-five percent of Americans express support for the view that the majority has a duty to respect the rights of the minority, for example, whereas only 18 percent believe that a community should allow the American Nazi party to use its town hall for a public meeting, and only 23 percent believe that a group should be allowed to use a public building in order to denounce the government.[29]

Examples of public intolerance for minority viewpoints can be found in every era. In the 1950s, for example, Senator Joseph McCarthy (R-Wisc.) led a campaign to purge alleged communists from positions of influence—whether in Washington, Hollywood, or elsewhere. McCarthy was spectacularly unconcerned about the truth of his accusations, and ruined the lives and careers of thousands of loyal Americans. Eventually, he went too far and ended in disgrace. He is best remembered now for inspiring the term "McCarthyism," which is generally applied to any political witch-hunt based on ideology or expedience and unsupported by facts.

Senator Joseph McCarthy (R-Wisc.) lashes out at critics and communists during the 1954 Senate investigation of the United States Army. McCarthy's intolerance and underhanded tactics added a new term—McCarthyism—to the American political vocabulary. Eventually McCarthy overreached and was discredited, but intolerance and paranoia remain potent factors in American political life.

Today the pressure to conform can be seen in efforts to limit the discussion of certain ideas and to restrict speech deemed offensive to minorities and women. These efforts—dubbed the "political correctness" movement by their critics—have had some impact, especially on certain college campuses.

Distrust

A healthy distrust of government is one of the strong points of American politics. It lies behind our efforts to divide power among several levels and branches of government, and contributes to the protection of our rights and liberties. Sometimes, however, feelings of distrust cross over the thin line that separates skepticism from cynicism, alienating Americans from government and undermining democracy.

Nearly three-quarters of all Americans, for example, believe that the government is run for the benefit of "a few big interests looking out for themselves." Sixty percent believe that the government wastes a lot of money. When asked to decide whether big government, big business, or big labor will be the biggest threat to the United States in the future, more than half the public choose big government.[30] These numbers are down sharply from levels of trust in government expressed just twenty or thirty years ago.[31]

Cynicism and distrust do not necessarily mean hopelessness. H. Ross Perot's success in gaining 19 percent of the popular vote in his 1992 presidential campaign revealed not only the breadth and depth of Americans' alienation from government but also the extent to which American voters want to believe that solutions are possible. In Perot's case, the proposed solution was a folksy, multibillionaire businessman who talked about fixing the nation as if it were a cranky old car. But Perot's campaign also

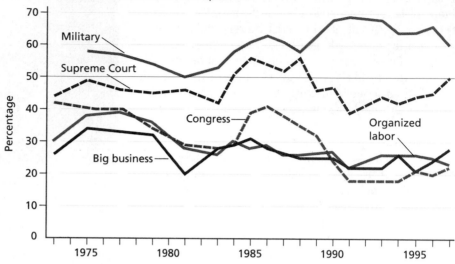

Percentage of respondents who indicate "a great deal" or "quite a lot" of confidence in the institution in question.

Figure 6.4 **Confidence in U.S. Institutions**

Sources: Frank Newport and Lydia Saad, "Confidence in Institutions: *The Gallup Poll Monthly*, April 1994, p. 6; Frank Newport, "Small Business and Military Generate Most Confidence in Americans," *Gallup Poll*, August 15, 1997, http://www.gallup.com/poll/news/970815.html.

demonstrates just how easily a charismatic figure can rise to power, backed by those who are alienated from government and politics and who seek—or at least respond to—extreme or simplistic solutions.

Paranoia and Conspiracy

Conspiracy theories have always played a part in American politics. During the Revolution, for example, colonial orators engaged in a feeding frenzy of conspiracy talk, blaming the oppression of the colonies on the "corrupt, Frenchified party," a "junto [*sic*] of courtiers and state-jobbers," "tyrannic *bloodthirsty*" ministers, or the "monied interest"—to name just a few of the alleged wrong-doers.[32] In the 1890s, southern politicians whipped up poor farmers with talk of a conspiracy involving Jews, Catholics, Wall Street, and English banking interests. In the 1930s, the radio preacher Father Charles E. Coughlin attracted millions with a message that blamed the depression on "the filthy gold standard," "the vested interests of wealth and intellect," "international bankers," and those who would "help America forget its Anglo-Saxon origins." Much of Coughlin's rhetoric had a distinctly anti-Jewish theme: gold was the "slave standard of the Rothschilds," while the city of Washington would one day be called "Washingtonski." In the 1950s the blame fell on communists, and anyone with pacifist or left-wing connections was an easy target.

Our own time is hardly free of what one historian has called the "paranoid style in American politics."[33] An entire industry has been created out of the search for conspiracy in the assassination of John F. Kennedy. Similar attention has been paid to the fate of Americans taken prisoner in Vietnam. In recent years, critics of the Clinton administration talked openly of a conspiracy to cover up the facts surrounding the death of presidential aid Vincent Foster, while Hillary Clinton blamed a "right-wing" conspiracy for the scandals that plagued her husband's presidency.

Multiculturalism and American Political Culture

American political culture, like American society itself, has survived and prospered through two centuries of growth and transformation. From a small country with a relatively homogeneous population of Anglo-Saxon Protestants (along with black slaves and Native Americans who were excluded from all social and political power), America has grown into a continental nation composed of an enormous number of racial, ethnic, and religious groups. Throughout the centuries, the American creed and the ideals of American democracy have helped keep the nation together—one culture out of many cultures.

The unifying tendencies of American political culture stand in marked contrast to the experiences of other nations. Across the globe and the centuries, political systems have been shaken by ethnic, religious, and cultural conflicts. In Canada, French-speaking *Quebecois* clash with their English-speaking compatriots. In Belfast, Catholics have clashed with Protestants. In the former Yugoslavia, Croats, Muslims, and Serbs are kept apart only by the presence of NATO troops.

In recent years, political culture seems to have become a divisive force in the United States as well, although certainly not to the same extent. This is not the first time in our history that culture has played such a role, but the pervasive influence of "culture wars" has been distressing to many Americans who believed, or wanted to believe, that the United States was different. Still, debates about multiculturalism can also be seen in a more positive light, as a reflection of the increased participation of various racial, ethnic, and religious groups in public life.

The Melting Pot

For centuries, America's ability to absorb and assimilate a wide variety of distinct national, ethnic, and religious groups was a point of great pride. America was the great **melting pot,** where men and women of all origins and descriptions became simply "Americans." As the English commentator James Bryce put it one hundred years ago, American "institutions, habits, and ideas" exercised an "amazing solvent power . . . quickly dissolving and assimilating the foreign bodies that are poured into her mass."[34]

The idea that Americans were a new breed, quite distinct from their (mostly European) forebears, dates back to revolutionary times. Its power was greatly enhanced a century later, when waves of immigrants passed through entry points such as Ellis Island to take up a new life. For those immigrants, and especially for their children, the ethnic and national identities of Europe belonged to the past. Conventional American clothing replaced their former dress, old languages were dropped quickly in favor of English—without an accent, if possible—and old customs were discarded or adapted to fit the American mainstream. In an act of great symbolism, many immigrants even changed their names to make them sound more "American," turning Jacobson into Jackson, or Giradelli into Gordon.

To generations of new Americans, the melting pot became an ideal, a source of hope and future success. In Europe, their ethnic identity and poverty had made them targets of discrimination, deprivation, and violence. They eagerly cast their old identities aside in favor of a newfound status and freedom as, simply, Americans.

The Meltdown of the Melting Pot   In this century, the ideal of the melting pot has come under heavy scorn and criticism from two sources: the children and grandchildren of immigrants, who rekindled a sense of pride in their ethnic and national identities; and disadvantaged minorities, who saw the melting pot as a device designed by the dominant majority to subjugate minority cultures.

That their children and grandchildren would take great pride in traditional customs and practices would have struck most immigrants as laughable. Yet their descendants have eagerly reclaimed their ethnic identities, merging them into their American identities. They have returned to traditional religious practices, studied the languages their forebears had abandoned, learned native songs and dances, even changed their names back to the original forms. Generations of Americans now aspired to be "hyphenated" Americans—Italian-American, Irish-American, Polish-American, Chinese-American.

To these Americans, the melting pot seemed a way to wipe out all traces of their ethnic identity in favor of an all-encompassing Anglo-Saxon culture. Their new metaphors of choice were not the melting pot but the **salad bowl** or **mosaic.** Their goal was not to create a homogeneous American culture but to foster a truly pluralistic society that can accept and revel in its ethnic, religious, racial, and national diversity.

The melting pot has also been scorned by blacks, Hispanics, Native Americans, and other disadvantaged minorities. For these Americans, the melting pot was powerful enough to erode their traditional cultures but not strong enough to dissolve the discrimination they faced as a result of skin color. Unlike other immigrant groups, for example,

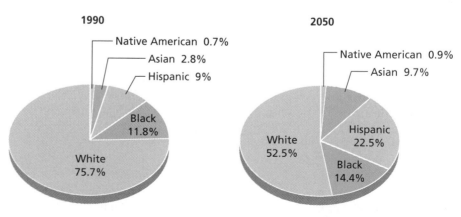

Figure 6.5 **Share of U.S. Population by Race/Ethnicity, 1990 and 2050 (projected)**

1990

Native American 0.7%
Asian 2.8%
Hispanic 9%
Black 11.8%
White 75.7%

2050

Native American 0.9%
Asian 9.7%
Hispanic 22.5%
Black 14.4%
White 52.5%

Sᴏᴜʀᴄᴇ: U.S. Bureau of the Census.

blacks had not fled Africa in search of freedom and opportunity but had been torn away from their native lands and brought to America as slaves. Even after emancipation, white society did not allow blacks to enjoy the benefits of assimilation. Native Americans were not immigrants at all, and for them too the melting pot served only to facilitate and even justify the destruction of their traditional way of life.

The Idea of Multiculturalism

These two critiques of the melting pot theory both rejected the idea of a single American culture in favor of a community of subcultures—an idea known as **multiculturalism.** The versions of multiculturalism that arose from each of these critiques are very different, however. The first sees the larger American culture as existing compatibly with each of the many subcultures, allowing "hyphenated" Americans to move effortlessly between their ethnic and American identities without damage to either one. The second is more controversial, since it sees the larger culture as inherently unfriendly to minority subcultures, and indeed as responsible for much of the economic, social, and cultural deprivation that has afflicted minority groups in the United States.

The latter critique presented by multiculturalism is essentially this. American culture has been dominated by those in power—Anglo-Saxons, whites, males, heterosexuals, the wealthy—who have shaped that culture to preserve their own power. To do so it was necessary to denigrate and degrade any and all competing cultures. Thus the white male culture (to use a favorite shorthand) systematically stripped minority groups of their own cultures, depriving them of their self-esteem and creating a permanent subservience. As the New York State Task Force on Minorities put it in 1989, "African-Americans, Asian-Americans, Puerto Ricans/Latinos, and Native Americans have all been the victims of an intellectual and educational oppression that has characterized the culture of the United States and the European American for centuries."[35]

The multiculturalists therefore set out to reclaim the minority cultures. They publicized the nearly forgotten history of blacks, women, Native Americans, and others. They called for the public recognition of minority holidays (such as Martin Luther King Day), and for public acknowledgment of the crimes perpetrated against minorities in the present and past. They instituted minority-based and bilingual curricula in American classrooms at every level and created university-based programs in women's studies, African American studies, Native American studies, gay studies, Chicano studies, and more. They brought minority perspectives into textbooks and anthologies, and into the public media. They called on America to come to terms with both the good and the bad side of its history and traditions.

Some, of course, went further, turning multiculturalism into an all-out attack on traditional Western culture. Not surprisingly, this form of multiculturalism has generated a fierce reaction. Conservatives delight in pointing out what they see as the most absurd excesses of the multiculturalist movement; since conservative academics and the conservative press represent precisely the white male perspective denounced by multiculturalists, these attacks serve only to feed the fire. Those with extreme views on either side thus succeed in creating a cycle of escalating rhetoric, generating much heat with little light.

A Liberal Multiculturalism?

Between the two extremes of a radical multiculturalism and a hostile conservatism, and often obscured by the smoke of battle, lies a middle ground. It is possible to embrace both the individual subcultures that make up the United States and the broader tradition of American culture. In fact, a true multiculturalism is possible within—and perhaps only within—a democratic system such as America's, which at least aspires to a respect for individual rights, human dignity, and the rule of law.

The key to this middle-of-the-road multiculturalism lies in the broad aspirations of the American creed and the American political tradition. "Our task," as the historian Arthur M. Schlesinger has written, "is to combine due appreciation of the splendid diversity of the nation with due emphasis on the great unifying Western ideas of individual freedom, political democracy, and human rights. These are the ideas that define the American nationality—and that today empower people of all continents, races, and creeds."[36] However poorly the United States has lived up to them, the ideals of the Declaration of Independence and the Constitution point the way toward an acceptance of different religious, ethnic, racial, and cultural traditions within the larger umbrella of American politics.

Summary

The term *political culture* refers to the "beliefs, values, and attitudes" that help shape a given society's political behavior, political institutions, and political outcomes. A community's political culture is closely linked to its history, its dominant religion or religions, and its shared assumptions about justice and morality.

Many influential studies of American political culture emphasize the differences between America and other nations, especially those of Europe. Following Alexis de Tocqueville, advocates of the American exceptionalism thesis argue that American political culture is the result of a unique set of historical factors unlikely to be reproduced elsewhere. These factors include America's geographical isolation; the economic, social, and political equality of the early settlers; the absence of a single cultural, ethnic, or linguistic divide; and the dominant role of religion.

The essential elements of American political culture are found in the American creed—a loosely connected set of values that includes liberty and individual rights, equality, property and economic rights, respect for law, and attachment to the community. The various components of the American creed are frequently at odds with one another, and Americans often disagree over the meaning and weight that should be given to its diverse elements. Nevertheless, the American creed plays a powerful role in shaping political attitudes and public policy.

Disagreements over the meaning of the American creed have given rise to distinct worldviews or ideologies—most notably, liberalism and conservatism. Although these ideologies play an important role shaping the national political debate, they are difficult to define with precision and few Americans fall clearly into one camp or the other. Some political scientists have attempted to define ideology in terms of style rather than substance, an approach that helps explain some of the inconsistencies within both the liberal and the conservative camps.

American political culture is not expressed only in positive terms. For centuries, Americans have been prone to intolerance and distrust, and even paranoia. A belief in conspiracy theories has marked American politics since the eighteenth century. Americans have revealed a disturbing tendency to force others to conform to the values and viewpoints of the majority, often with tragic results.

An important current controversy in American political culture involves the idea of multiculturalism. To many multiculturalists, the dominant political culture in America excludes or diminishes the distinct political cultures of minority subgroups. Advocates of multiculturalism stress that American political culture is really the culture of the dominant majority. Critics of the multiculturalist approach stress the importance of bringing minority groups into the mainstream of American political culture.

Key Terms

Political culture
Political socialization
American exceptionalism
American creed
Ideology
Liberalism
Conservatism
Socialism
Populism
Libertarianism
Melting pot
Salad bowl (or mosaic)
Multiculturalism

Review Questions

1. What is political culture?

2. What is meant by American exceptionalism? In what senses is American political culture distinct from that of Europe?

3. What is the American creed, and what are its essential elements?

4. How are liberalism and conservatism defined in the American context? What values do American liberals and conservatives share? How do liberals and conservatives differ?

5. What is the dark side of American political culture? How are these negative attitudes related to the elements of the American creed?

6. What are the essential features of the debate over multiculturalism? How do the metaphors of the melting pot and the salad bowl or mosaic help illuminate—or cloud—the debate?

Suggested Readings

Berger, Arthur Asa, ed. *Political Culture and Public Opinion.* New Brunswick, N.J.: Transaction Publishers, 1989.

Edsforth, Ronald, and Larry Bennett. *Popular Culture and Political Change in Modern America.* Albany: State University of New York Press, 1991.

Hartz, Louis. *The Liberal Tradition in America.* New York: Harcourt, Brace, 1955.

Huntington, Samuel P. *American Politics: The Promise of Disharmony.* Cambridge, Mass.: Belknap Press of Harvard University Press, 1981.

McClosky, Herbert, and John Zaller. *The American Ethos: Public Attitudes Toward Capitalism and Democracy.* Cambridge, Mass.: Harvard University Press, 1984.

Sanders, Arthur. *Making Sense of Politics.* Ames: Iowa State University Press, 1990.

Schlesinger, Arthur M., Jr. *The Disuniting of America.* New York: W. W. Norton, 1992.

Shafer, Byron, ed. *Is America Different? A New Look at American Exceptionalism.* Oxford: Clarendon Press, 1991.

Tocqueville, Alexis de. *Democracy in America.* Ed. J. P. Mayer. Garden City, N.J.: Doubleday, 1966.

Internet Resources

Web page of C-SPAN's Alexis de Tocqueville Tour, featuring information and links relating to the great French political writer at:

http://www.c-span.org/alexis/

CIVITAS, an "international organization for civic education" which "aims to strengthen effective education for informed and responsible citizenship in new and established democracies" at:

http://civnet.org/civitas/civitas.htm

Interesting and eclectic collection of conspiracy-based web sites at:

**http://www.yahoo.com/Government/Politics/
Political Opinion/Conspiracy/**

7

Public Opinion

★ ★

Throughout the summer of 1983 the United States and other western nations stood idly by while millions of Ethiopians were literally starving to death. Although well aware of the impending disaster, the Reagan administration was reluctant to send aid to a nation ruled by a hostile, Marxist regime. Washington officials expressed concern about the logistics of any relief effort, and suspected that much of the problem was not the availability of food or money but the conduct of the Ethiopian government. Any aid that was sent to Ethiopia, they believed, was as likely to end up on the black market as in the mouths of starving children.

Politically, the Reagan administration's foot-dragging carried little risk. Although the Ethiopian crisis had been amply covered in the print media, the American people had shown little interest. To most Americans, the famine "was a distant event. . . . Most Americans . . . were given to a certain sense of doom about Ethiopia: men, women, and children had starved there for ages and probably always would. 'We'd all seen the pictures hundreds of times before,'" as one television news producer put it.

Everything changed on the evening of October 23, 1983, when NBC News broadcast a segment called *The Faces of Death in Africa*. The spot consisted mainly of pictures of unimaginable horror:

> *In the forefront . . . stretched thousands of drought-stricken people, some of them nearly skeletons. Naked babies huddled next to mothers with dry breasts. Most of the multitude sat or lay in the sand. Beyond, wizened men carrying sticks for walking trudged aimlessly. Now and then at a rumor of food, groups of children would scamper off, but many others were too near death to move. At one point a three-year-old, last of one mother's children, died before the camera's lens. . . . Nothing was more revolting than the unrelenting scourge of flies. Swarms of them preyed on the eyes and mouths of the bloated, bony children, too weak to brush their tormentors away.*

The broadcast set off a political earthquake of the highest magnitude. Thousands of viewers called NBC News, asking how they could help. Other television networks picked up the story, which seemed to "roll across the country, gathering force." Relief agencies in America and around the world were overwhelmed with donations and offers of assistance.

Within days, the United States government made a 180-degree policy shift. The White House authorized the use of two cargo planes and sent $51.2 million worth of food. The Agency for International Development sprang into action. Congress responded by authorizing millions in drought relief, as did scores of other countries. The worldwide relief effort was under way.

"On most big issues the government leads and public opinion follows," wrote Robert J. McCloskey of Catholic Relief Services. "Certain gut issues have the capacity to turn that process around. We are now witnessing a singular example." Asked to explain the shift in public opinion, one Canadian official put it succinctly. Most people do not read the reports of the United Nations Food and Agriculture Organization, he pointed out, "but they do watch television."

Television's impact on public opinion cuts both ways; in Somalia, news photos of U.S. casualties helped focus opposition to American involvement and may have contributed to President Clinton's decision to withdraw the troops in early 1994.

Self-government requires a more active role for the people than merely participating in annual or biannual elections. The people have both a right and a duty to let the government know how they feel on the major issues of the day, and the government has a corresponding right and duty to listen and respond. If popular involvement in the democratic process were limited to voting on election day, self-government would be an empty shell.

The Framers were deeply ambivalent about the role of public opinion in popular government. They knew that public opinion was easily swayed by passion and emotion, and by the short-term self-interest of the majority. Yet they also knew that a politically engaged public was the only reliable check against corruption and tyranny. The challenge was to devise a system of government that would respond to public opinion when appropriate and resist it when necessary.

When it works as planned, the American system allows the people to engage their leaders in an ongoing dialogue. Final decisions are left to the leadership, at least until election day, but the entire process is informed by a constant interchange of information between the people and the government. Politicians watch the ebb and flow of public opinion the way sailors watch the tide, ever alert to subtle shifts in the public mood that might call for adjustments in course.

All of this presumes that the public is aware of key political issues and that individuals are able to reach thoughtful decisions about public controversies. At a minimum, citizens must be informed enough to judge their representatives' actions and ongoing fitness for office. The public can learn about politics from many different sources, most importantly the print and broadcast media. But politicians and interest groups also play a role in shaping public opinion, both directly and indirectly.

In their efforts to shape public opinion, politicians and interest groups can easily cross the line between keeping the public informed and manipulating public opinion for their own narrowly conceived benefit. Efforts to influence public opinion can thus turn into a damaging cycle, in which politicians respond to ill-advised demands that they themselves have created.

This chapter explores the uneasy relationship between public opinion and democracy. It considers the nature of and influences on public opinion; the state of public opinion in the United States today; and the various techniques by which politicians and analysts measure public opinion.

Throughout, the overriding concern is to explore the dilemma that the Framers so clearly identified: how to balance the need for political leadership of the people with the need for political responsiveness to the people.

Questions to Keep in Mind

☑ *What is public opinion? What forces influence the formation of public opinion?*

☑ *How can public opinion be weighed and measured? What are the practical and theoretical problems of using opinion polls to gauge public opinion?*

☑ *How did the Framers view public opinion? How did they seek to ensure that the government would be responsive, but not overresponsive, to public opinion?*

Basic Concepts ★ ★ ★ ★ ★ ★ ★ ★ ★ ★ ★ ★ ★

By definition, a democratic political system must be aware of and respond to **public opinion**. Note that it is not enough that people have opinions, or that they express them. The government must constantly endeavor to be aware of what the people are saying, and to respond to the public's concerns and demands. A government that fails to make these efforts cannot be considered a democracy in any real sense.

The Concept of Public Opinion

The term *public opinion* is used in two general senses. In one sense it simply means "the opinions of the people," usually as measured through some sort of formal or informal survey. Successful politicians are extraordinarily good at sensing subtle shifts in the opinions of their constituents. Scholars and political analysts have developed sophisticated tools—the most important of which is the public opinion poll—for measuring how the public feels about any given issue. Even so, gauging public opinion is as much art as it is science, and much depends on the skill and honesty of those who carry out polls and interpret the results.

> *"You may fool all the people some of the time; you can even fool some of the people all the time; but you can't fool all of the people all the time."*
>
> —Abraham Lincoln, to a caller at the White House

Often, *public opinion* is used in a quite different sense, as if the public were a single, living entity capable of having a particular opinion on any given subject. This mythical public is capable of deliberation and discussion, and, like a single person, can eventually reach a considered judgment. "Public opinion forced the nominee to resign," "the success of the bill will depend on how it is received by the public," and "public opinion demands an investigation" are all examples of this usage.

This second usage is hardly precise, or scientific, but it does reflect the way politicians and pundits think about public opinion. There are times when a very high proportion of the people seem to reach a common agreement on an issue, and demand specific action on the part of the government or of a particular official. To define such a moment of agreement in precise terms is perhaps less important than to recognize and understand its impact on government officials and political players. An example occurred in February 1968, during the Vietnam War, when North Vietnam launched the Tet Offensive. North Vietnamese troops marched all the way to Saigon and attacked the American embassy; in the end, they were turned back. Despite the ultimate failure of the offensive, the strength and ferocity of the North Vietnamese attack shocked both the American people and the American military. The media reported Tet as a great military defeat, and public opinion turned against both President Lyndon Johnson and the war. In January 1968, Johnson's approval rating was 48–39 percent positive; in March, it had dropped to 35–52 percent negative. Public support for the war collapsed and never recovered.[1]

The Framers and Public Opinion

The Framers' view of public opinion was directly connected to their views on representative government and to their conception of the public interest. "The genius of republican liberty," wrote James Madison, "seems to demand on one side, not only that all power should be derived from the people, but that those intrusted with it should be kept in dependence on the people, by a short duration of their appointments." The problem, of course, was that the people were not always the best judge of the public interest, at least in the short term; they were too easily swayed by emotion, and too likely to ignore the rights of the minority or to disregard the long-term interests of the community. For the Framers, the central problem was to design a government that was both responsive to public opinion, yet not slavishly dependent on it.

Thus the Framers gave the people a direct role in the election of the House of Representatives, but only an indirect role in electing the Senate and the president. They protected the freedom of speech, press, and assembly, but insulated key governmental decisions from the direct or immediate influence of the public. (Even members of the House of Representatives serve for two full years between elections; members of the Senate and other branches serve even longer terms.) They insisted on the separation of powers, to protect against ill-considered reactions to public demands and to promote a slow, deliberate approach to policy making.

Measuring Public Opinion

The most obvious way to measure public opinion is by taking a **public opinion poll,** in which a representative sample of the population is surveyed on particular questions (see the discussion later in this chapter). Many polls, such as those sponsored by the major news organizations, are reported to the public. Others, such as those conducted by political candidates or office-holders, are used to dictate political strategy and are closely guarded.

Polls are not the only way to measure public opinion, and probably are not the best way to gauge how strongly the public feels about an issue or how public opinion might change under the influence of a determined effort (by the president, for example) to change the public's views. Another method of taking the public pulse, borrowed from the advertising industry, is to conduct "focus groups," in which a small panel of citizens engage in a discussion, guided by a moderator. Their reactions and responses are closely monitored by experts trained to interpret and analyze the results.

Other methods of measuring public opinion take advantage of high technology. One such method uses a handheld device on which viewers of, say, a presidential speech can dial their agreement or disagreement on a continual basis. A more common technique, used by many television and radio shows, allows members of the audience to "vote" on a given issue using a 900 phone line.

Despite the availability of such high-tech approaches, most politicians still rely on old-fashioned methods or gut instinct. Members of Congress watch their mail closely, and make frequent visits home to talk with friends and constituents. They (or their staffs) actively monitor media coverage of important issues, both at home and in Washington—including call-in radio talk shows and letters to the editor. They also watch for evidence of citizens "voting with their

Public opinion polling has become the dominant method for measuring public attitudes on politics.

feet"—by actions, rather than words. Falling ridership on buses, for example, is probably a good indicator of the public's dissatisfaction with the public transportation system. The amount that voters are willing to contribute to a political cause may be a better indicator of their support than any poll.

No one method of measuring public opinion is entirely accurate, and it is easy to misread public opinion through carelessness or error. It is also easy, and quite common, for politicians and interest groups to manipulate public opinion or deliberately distort it. A radio talk-show host who asks his viewers whether they favor "government assistance to welfare queens" will get a very different response from one who asks whether the audience favors "help for those who cannot help themselves." Representatives who want to show how popular they are may enlist their supporters to flood the office with letters, and then report "overwhelming" public support.

Such distortions and deceptions are useful mainly because of the **bandwagon effect:** a voter who sees that "everybody" is supporting a particular candidate or issue may fall in line simply because he or she wants to be part of the group. The opposite—known as the **underdog effect**—can also occur: a candidate or issue may drop so low in the polls that voters show support out of sympathy.

Political Socialization

Like religious traditions and family recipes, attitudes about politics are passed along from parents to children, from one generation to the next. The process by which such attitudes are transmitted from one generation to another is known as **political socialization**. Political scientists find it useful to distinguish between *direct* socialization and *indirect* socialization. Direct socialization transmits information and beliefs that are explicitly political. Indirect socialization transmits information and beliefs that, while not inherently political, may nonetheless have an effect on political attitudes and practices.

Political Socialization in Children   Although political socialization occurs throughout life, it is particularly important in childhood and adolescence. Political values and ideas are taught to children at a remarkably early age, often without conscious effort. Even very young children learn the importance of obeying the rules set down by parents and teachers. Two- and three-year-olds are well aware of rudimentary concepts of property and justice; "it's mine" and "that's not fair" are staples of any playground conversation. But the key period for the development of political attitudes seems to occur in elementary and middle school. "By the time youths enter ninth grade," conclude the political scientists M. Kent Jennings and Richard G. Niemi, they "have established what are presumably stable opinions about the nation and the political system in which they live." Although attitudes about the political system in general form early, views on specific political controversies develop later, probably in late adolescence.[2] Children learn about politics from many sources, including:

   Family. Children receive their initial exposure to political ideas from their families. Many ideas are transmitted in a way that masks their political content, to both adults and children alike. Treating children as responsible and valued members of a family, for example, reinforces the political idea that all human beings deserve to be treated with dignity. Requiring children to obey their parents teaches respect for authority. Older children are exposed to direct political socialization by listening to family discussions, or perhaps through direct teaching. The absence of family discussions about politics, of course, sends its own message.

Even children's stories often contain an underlying political message, often so subtle that parents are unaware of what is being taught. For example, one researcher argues that the popular children's books by Dr. Seuss contain a clear political message: the characters in his books "possess an un-self-conscious magic that permits them to determine their own existences and sometimes to reshape their worlds. . . . This control over one's destiny extends to all individuals, no matter how insignificant or small, to the point that political authority figures are frequently denigrated as foolish and arrogant."[3]

In general, parents exercise a strong influence on the development of their children's political attitudes. In one study, high school seniors were asked to identify themselves and their parents as Democrats, Republicans, or independents; 59 percent said their party affiliation was the same as that of their parents. However, students were more likely than their parents to be political independents. Research also suggests that there is at least some degree of similarity between parents' and students' views on public policy issues, especially if the issues in question are "tangible and of unusual prominence."[4] In particular, attitudes toward the political parties and views on race seem to be socialized early in life, when the direct influence of parents is at a maximum.[5]

The direct influence of parents over the political attitudes of their children begins to wane as the child reaches adolescence—just as he or she begins to develop a real awareness of politics. In these later years, political attitudes are more heavily influenced by individuals and institutions outside the family. But parents continue to play an indirect role in shaping political attitudes, since they are heavily responsible for choosing their children's social environment—where they live, what schools they attend, where they attend religious services, even who their friends are. Thus parents and children may share political attitudes because they share a common social environment. Finally, some similarities between the political attitudes of parents and children can be traced to their common racial, regional, socioeconomic, and religious backgrounds.[6]

Schools. Like families, schools influence political attitudes both directly and indirectly. Direct influences include the curriculum, classroom rituals (such as the pledge of allegiance), conversations with teachers, and extracurricular activities. Indirect influences come from fellow students, who typically make up the student's circle of friends and peer group. The influence of friends and peer groups on political attitudes is discussed in the next section.[7]

Both public and private schools in the United States place a high priority on educating students to be good citizens. Since the earliest days of the Republic, American schools have tried to ensure that students have the "loyalty, vision, and skill" necessary to participate in a democracy.[8] Schools provide courses in American history and government, often depicting past leaders as heroes and past events in a highly favorable light. They initiate children in the forms of participatory democracy through student council elections and other political activities. They teach children to obey rules and authority figures. "Much of what is called citizenship training in the public schools does not teach the child about the city, state, or national government," concludes one study, "but is an attempt to teach regard for the rules and standards of conduct of the school." Research suggests that formal high school civics classes have little influence on political views, probably because such courses largely repeat messages that students have heard before. Thus such courses may have more impact on students who have not previously been exposed to mainstream political values.[9]

Schools can also be used to promote specific political viewpoints. The racial integration of public schools, for example, was justified not only with reference to the rights of minority students but also as a way of encouraging racial tolerance in the larger society. Schools were a major focal point of the Reagan administration's "Just Say No" campaign against illegal drugs. Today, school-based programs attempt to discourage teen pregnancy, encourage sexual responsibility, and reduce the transmission of AIDS and other diseases. Many of these programs have generated tremendous controversy over whether and how they should be implemented.

Education itself has a clear influence on political attitudes and behavior. For example, individuals with high levels of education are more likely to vote and to believe that they can influence the political system, and are more likely to be tolerant of those with different opinions, including atheists and socialists.[10] Isolating the impact of education from other factors that influence opinion is difficult, however, because educational achievement is associated with many other variables that influence political attitudes.[11]

Religious institutions. Churches, synagogues, and other religious institutions can play a critical role in the political socialization of children. Because church or synagogue affiliation is a matter of the parents' free choice, religious institutions in general serve to reinforce lessons taught at home, and, to a lesser extent, in school. Like schools, religious institutions socialize children directly—for example, through sermons and Sunday school lessons—and indirectly, through the influence of peer groups and adult members of the organization.

Peer Groups. Friends and classmates also play an important role in political socialization. In particular, peer groups can reinforce or undermine political views learned at home. Separating the influence of peer groups from that of parents is difficult because of the indirect role parents play in shaping their children's social environment.[12]

The influence of high school peers is especially clear on age-specific issues and on those that depend on skills or abilities that develop late in childhood. In the 1960s, for example, children's views on whether eighteen-year-olds should be allowed to vote were influenced more by friends than by family. Similarly, attitudes on political efficacy—that is, on whether individuals can influence the political system—seem more heavily dependent on peer groups than on parents.[13]

The Media. The impact of the media on political attitudes is apparent even in childhood. Television, for obvious reasons, is particularly important. Children absorb political attitudes from television long before they can read or write. For example, the PBS show "Barney," which is aimed at preschool children, features a friendly purple dinosaur interacting with an ethnically and racially diverse group of young children. The show contains clear, if uncontroversial, political elements, stressing tolerance, equality, and concern for others. Older children are exposed to political information explicitly, through news shows, situation comedies, and other programs. Like their parents, they may get most of their political information from the television set.

How Adults Form Political Opinions   Political learning does not stop after high school or college. Although an individual's fundamental approach to life and politics is largely fixed at an early age, specific attitudes change and evolve over the course of a

Conservative talk radio megastar Rush Limbaugh, whose daily show reaches an estimated 15 to 20 million Americans a week. Talk
radio has been blamed for lowering the level
of public debate and credited for inspiring the
conservative revolution of the 1990s; whatever its impact, it provides an important new
channel for political communication and
political participation.

lifetime. Political attitudes in adults are shaped by a number of different forces, including
one's social and economic circumstances; external events; and the media.

Economic and Social Circumstances. A person's economic and social position plays a
major role in determining the political learning experiences that he or she will have. An
upper-class individual who has never known anyone on welfare is likely to have different
views on the subject than someone who has been on welfare. A person who has never experienced race or sex discrimination is unlikely to have the same views as one who has.

Political attitudes based on life experiences are typically reinforced by one's friends and
social relations. "Because people in a particular social category, for the most part, make
friends with 'their own kind' of people," write Richard E. Dawson and Kenneth Prewitt,
"the views they hear outside the home are usually very much like the ones they hear at
home." Moreover, social groupings "serve as reference points and filters for the individual's
understanding of the world of politics."[14]

External Events. Specific political events—especially those that involve trauma or upheaval—can have an important influence on an individual's political views. The impact of
such events can be difficult to measure; for one thing, different groups can perceive the same
event differently, and an external event can thus reinforce group differences. Still, an event like
the depression of the 1930s or the Vietnam War cannot help but influence political attitudes.

Even ordinary experiences can make a difference. As Dawson and Prewitt point out,
children are taught that a police officer is a "friendly, fair, and trustworthy helper." A later
encounter with the police may undermine that lesson. In general, one's adult experiences
tend to confirm or adjust the political lessons of childhood.[15]

The Media. The media are a major factor in adult socialization. "Much of what the
average person learns about political norms, rules, values, events . . . comes of necessity
from the mass media," writes Doris A. Graber. Some citizens rely on the media simply for
the raw material from which opinions are made; others accept directly the attitudes and
opinions that the media express.[16]

The evidence suggests that the media have the least impact on those whose political opinions are based on personal experiences or personal values. Conversely, "the least informed and least interested citizens are most likely to reflect the viewpoints expressed in the media, particularly television."[17]

The media's impact on political attitudes is discussed more fully in Chapter 11.

Public Opinion and Democracy

At a minimum, democratic government requires that the public be able to express its views on politics and that the government be compelled to listen and respond. But except for those rare circumstances in which public opinion is clear, unified, and unambiguous, the relationship between public opinion and democratic government is tenuous at best. Two general problems can be identified. First, the views of some citizens or groups may be more influential than the views of others, and may be even more powerful than the views of the majority. Second, on many issues the government may influence, as well as respond to, public opinion.

Public Opinion and Majority Rule   At the most basic level, democratic government presupposes that the views of the majority will have a major influence on government decision making. Most obviously, the majority is able to express itself through the electoral process, choosing government officials who best represent its point of view. In addition, when a clear majority of the people expresses itself forcefully and consistently on a major question of public policy, its influence on policy makers can be enormous.

Elections do allow the majority to make its presence felt, at least in a general way. Over the long term, public policy is generally consistent with the political values and priorities of the majority. However, elections are a blunt instrument, ill suited to influencing particular policy decisions. Voters faced with a choice between two candidates or parties must often accept a package of policy positions, of which they agree with only some. Election results are thus highly ambiguous, even when they result in a landslide for one party or the other.

For the most part, however, the majority's ability to influence specific public policies may be far less than democratic theory might predict. Advocates of the elite theory of democracy point out that a number of factors operate to weaken the influence of majority opinion:

- *A minority often feels strongly about an issue.* A minority can often overcome majority opinion simply because it cares deeply about an issue. A determined minority is more likely than the majority to express its views, to express its views strongly, and to punish officeholders who defy its wishes.[18] For example, the defeat of the Equal Rights Amendment for women in the 1970s, despite the fact that a majority of Americans supported it, may have been due to the intensity with which opponents fought the proposal.[19]
- *A minority is likely to be organized and well funded; the majority, disorganized and poorly funded.* As we will see in the next chapter, people in the minority are likely to compensate for their lack of numbers by forming an organized interest group to focus their efforts. Such groups are often well funded and can become very powerful. The National Rifle Association, for example, has used its considerable resources to fight gun control, often succeeding in the face of the general public's overwhelming support for such

programs. The problem is that those who support gun control are not organized to nearly the same extent, nor is the general public as concerned about the issue as gun control opponents.

* *Those holding minority opinions may have disproportionate access to the media.* Influencing public opinion requires access to the mass media. One way to gain such access is through paid advertising in newspapers or in the electronic media. Groups with access to sufficient resources can thus influence public opinion out of proportion to their numbers. In 1993 and 1994, for example, health insurance companies engaged in an expensive and effective public relations campaign against proposed health care reforms that they perceived to be against their interests. Groups on one side or another of a political issue may also have disproportionate access to free media.

The Government and Public Opinion   Communication in a democracy is a two-way street. Public officials do not merely sit back and respond to public opinion. Instead they continually communicate with the people. Presidents hold news conferences and make public speeches; members of Congress send newsletters to their constituents, and hold town meetings and other events on visits home. Both the White House and Congress regularly provide journalists with information to report to the people.[20]

Politicians and government also work actively to mold public opinion, either in support of actions already taken or to build momentum for policies they wish to see adopted. In 1990 and 1991, for example, the Bush administration built support for the Persian Gulf War through presidential speeches and news conferences and with daily briefings from the Pentagon. Likewise, in 1993, the Clinton administration waged an active effort to convince Americans to support the reduction of trade barriers with Canada and Mexico.

Politicians have an obligation to keep the citizenry informed; otherwise, the people could not play a meaningful role in government. Political leaders typically have access to information that the public does not have, and can bring both expertise and experience to the public debate. In principle, public debates among leaders who offer a fair interpretation of available evidence can help the public reach more informed and thoughtful decisions. In practice, however, leaders who attempt to educate the public face numerous difficulties. They must try to explain complex, often controversial proposals to a vast audience whose interest in and understanding of policy making may be quite limited. The more specific and complete their explanations, moreover, the more they risk alienating various groups of voters. Thus politicians often prefer to outline broad policy goals while leaving complex details to the experts. Instead of making a case for their own proposals, they may instead rely on discrediting their opponents' arguments. They may resort to emotional appeals, incomplete disclosure of facts, and even outright deception in an effort to shape public opinion in their favor.

The Bush administration's successful efforts to persuade the public to support the Persian Gulf War, for example, frequently included the selective use of information. Pentagon news conferences highlighted U.S. "smart bombs" that were able to hit their targets with amazing precision, thus demolishing military targets without injury to civilians. One bomb was even shown entering the smokestack of an Iraqi military installation. But Pentagon officials carefully avoided showing images of actual suffering and harm, and closely guarded reporters' access to the battlefield.[21]

If they are unable to persuade the public to adopt their position on a controversial issue, politicians must face a difficult choice: do they follow their own convictions or give in to those of the public? Following public opinion is not always the right decision. As John F. Kennedy put it in a speech to broadcasters, "the politician's desire for reelection . . . [may] cause [him] to flatter every public whim and prejudice—to seek the lowest common denominator—to put public opinion ahead of the public interest."[22]

PARTICIPATORY DEMONOCRACY
1. CHOOSE WHAT IS REALLY TO BLAME.
2. CALL A RADIO TALK SHOW. 3. DENOUNCE LOUDLY.
4. GO ON WITH YOUR DAY KNOWING YOU'VE DONE YOUR BIT.

Public Opinion and Political Participation

Questions about public opinion are closely linked to questions about political participation. Not only does citizen involvement in politics help to make politicians aware of how the public feels; it also demonstrates the strength and intensity of public opinion. Politicians can and will ignore opinion polls if they believe citizens do not hold their views strongly or do not care much about the issues involved, but a flood of angry letters and telephone calls or an army of political protesters is more difficult to ignore. Citizens may also participate in politics in order to try to influence other citizens, especially in an election year.

Citizens in a democracy have many opportunities to participate in politics. These range from simply following political events, to trying to convince others how to vote, to engaging in political protest marches. Table 7.1 lists some of the ways in which Americans participate in politics, along with the percentage who take advantage of each form of participation.

Citizen involvement can make a difference. Consider the impact that Ross Perot and his followers had on Congress's response to the federal budget deficit. Public opinion polls had shown for years that the public believed the growing deficit was a problem, but voters did little more than express their concerns to poll takers. After Perot raised the issue in 1992,

Table 7.1
Forms of Political Participation, 1996

Watched any television program about the presidential campaign	76.1%
Voted	48.9
Talked to people and tried to show them whom to vote for	29.3
Allocated $3 of federal taxes to campaign fund	12.8
Wore campaign button or put bumper sticker on car	9.9
Attended political meetings or rallies	6.1
Gave money to a party or candidate	5.5
Worked for a party or candidate	2.8

SOURCES: *Statistical Abstract of the United States,* 1997, table 464; National Election Study, 1996.

however, the climate in Washington changed dramatically. The difference was not a change in public opinion but the mobilization of public opinion to political action. Perot's supporters joined his "United We Stand" organization, donated money, turned out for political rallies, and eventually voted in huge numbers for their third-party candidate. Although Perot's star declined, the issue he rode to power did not go away, and was eventually embraced by both major political parties.

American Public Opinion: A Snapshot

Politicians, pollsters, and public opinion scholars constantly try to measure Americans' views on politics and public issues. Although the methods of polling and other measurement techniques are well established, the task is not an easy one. First, public opinion is constantly changing, especially on issues such as presidential popularity and support for specific proposals. Second, it is easier to tabulate the results of poll questions than to figure out what to ask in the first place and how to interpret those results appropriately.

This section presents a broad overview of American public opinion. Its goal is not to present a complete picture of Americans' views on every issue, but to highlight and illustrate key divisions within the body politic.

Political Knowledge and Awareness

Most Americans are poorly informed about even the most basic facts of political life. One-quarter of Americans surveyed in 1989 did not know who the vice president was; one-third did not know which party controlled the House of Representatives; and nearly one-half did not know who controlled the Senate. A majority could not identify the first ten amendments to the United States Constitution as the Bill of Rights, and nearly three-quarters did not know the name of their own representative in Congress.[23] In addition, many Americans either have no position on many public issues or refuse to say what their position is.

The public's lack of political knowledge is nothing new. A 1947 study (see Figure 7.1) revealed even lower levels of political knowledge. In that year, one-third of those surveyed could not identify the vice president, and less than one-third could correctly identify the Bill of Rights. Awareness of which party controlled the House and Senate was roughly the same as in the 1989 survey, although the 1947 group did a little better at identifying the name of their representative.[24]

A significant number of Americans do not even have an opinion on major issues of the day. In a 1996 survey, 14 percent of all Americans had no opinion on whether the government should provide more or fewer services, for example. But less than 2 percent had no opinion on welfare reform, which was a major issue in the 1996 campaign, while only about 1 percent had no view on abortion.[25]

Not surprisingly, knowledge about politics is directly related to educational achievement. Only 18 percent of those with a grade school education knew who William Rehn-

Figure 7.1 **Still Uninformed After All These Years: Political Knowledge in 1947 and 1989**

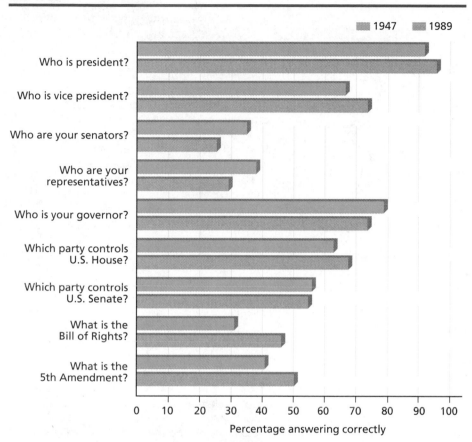

SOURCE: From Carpini & Keeter, *Public Opinion Quarterly 55:* (Winter 1991): 583–612. Reprinted by permission of the University of Chicago Press.

quist was, for example (he is the Chief Justice of the United States Supreme Court), while 42 percent of those with a college degree could identify him.[26]

Whether the public's general lack of knowledge on political questions poses a threat to self-government is a matter of debate. Many political scientists believe that candidates and parties can provide the electorate with sufficient information on key issues to allow for intelligent choices.[27] Others think that voters may have a better sense of issues than is revealed in their responses to direct questions. One researcher, for example, points out that "people who cannot define either *affirmative action* or *deregulation* may have fairly sophisticated notions about these matters. They know about government price controls on some goods and services and fully understand the burdens faced by people hampered in finding a job because of race or gender."[28] Others scholars, however, argue that the American public is too uninformed to make intelligent political choices.[29]

Public Opinion Around the World

How do American attitudes on social and political issues compare with those of citizens of other democracies? Consider these examples, drawn from surveys in thirteen countries in the early 1990s. For many of the questions, results were not reported in every country.

Interest in politics. Americans are generally more interested in politics than their counterparts in other democracies. Forty-one percent of Americans say they are "very" or "fairly" interested in politics; only Australia, eastern Germany, Britain, and Israel boast higher or comparable numbers. By contrast, only 30 percent in Northern Ireland, 32 percent in Italy, and 34 percent in the Irish Republic are "very" or "fairly" interested in politics.

Economic policy. Only 62 percent of Americans believe that government should "tax the rich"—fewer than in any other country. And only 44 percent believe that government should provide jobs for all—more than in Australia (42 percent), but far less than in Hungary (89 percent), Israel (88 percent), Italy (85 percent), and Norway (84 percent). America also ranks at the top in the number of citizens who believe that "large differences in income are necessary for prosperity"—31 percent, as against 26 percent in Britain, 24 percent in Germany, and 15 percent in the Netherlands. Significantly, the United States, Hungary, and Switzerland are the only nations in which working-class citizens are more likely than salaried workers to believe that income inequalities are necessary.

Americans' views on state ownership of various industries are also striking. Only 6 percent of Americans believe that electric utilities should be state-owned, for example, compared with 19 percent of western Germans, 26 percent of Britons, and 37 percent of Australians.

Spending priorities. Asked what they would like the government to spend "much more" money on, more Americans chose education than any other category. Australians also chose education as their top priority. By contrast, citizens in other countries made the following choices: environment (western Germany); health care (Great Britain, Hungary, Italy); pensions (Northern Ireland). Norwegians split evenly between the environment and health care.

Religion and "family values." Americans reveal stronger religious feelings than citizens of any other nation (although Poland is tied for first). Americans are also at the top in believing that "married people are happier than unmarried people." On other issues Americans line up more closely with their counterparts elsewhere. Roughly the same percentage of Americans believe that gay couples should have the right to marry (11 percent) as in western Germany and Great Britain (13 percent).

Civil liberties. How tolerant are Americans of those with different political beliefs? Compared with citizens of other democracies, not very. Only 48 percent of Americans said they would "definitely allow" others to take part in a protest meeting "against a government action they strongly oppose." Only Hungarians were less tolerant (47 percent), whereas Britons, Norwegians, and Israelis all checked in at over 65 percent. Americans were somewhat more likely to allow publication of views they opposed (42 percent), but still ranked third lowest out of the ten countries surveyed.

SOURCE: Roger Jowell, Lindsay Brook, and Lizanne Dowds, eds., *International Social Attitudes: The 10th BSA Report* (Hants, England: Dartmouth Publishing Co., 1993).

Liberals and Conservatives

As we saw in Chapter 6, the terms *liberal* and *conservative* are at best loosely defined in the American context. Few Americans line up on one side or the other of the liberal/conservative divide across all issue areas. Many Americans describe themselves as moderates or refuse to classify themselves altogether.

When asked to place themselves on a seven-point scale from "extremely liberal" to "extremely conservative," for example, almost half of all Americans placed themselves in the middle position or answered "don't know" or "haven't thought much about it." Only 4.6 percent of those surveyed described themselves as either "extremely liberal" or "extremely conservative," and only 21 percent more chose "liberal" or "conservative." In all, nearly 75 percent chose "moderate," "slightly" liberal or conservative, or no answer (see Figure 7.2).[30]

Even those who classified themselves as "extremely" liberal or conservative do not line up consistently behind the liberal or conservative position on controversial issues. For example, one would expect conservatives to support private medical insurance over a government insurance plan that would cover all medical expenses for everyone. Yet only three-fourths of those who called themselves "extremely" liberal favored government health insurance, while only two-thirds of self-described extreme-conservatives favored a system of completely private insurance.[31]

Similarly, the conventional wisdom suggests that liberals would favor increased government services and spending in the areas of health and education, while conservatives would oppose it. While liberals are in fact more likely than conservatives to favor government services and spending, there is much inconsistency in both camps. Thus only 47 percent of liberals favored increased social spending, while only 55 percent of conservatives favored decreased spending. Fully 18 percent of liberals and 17 percent of conservatives found themselves on the opposite side of what the standard liberal and conservative positions would suggest.[32]

There is also much inconsistency on the abortion issue. Seventy-one percent of self-described liberals favor a woman's right to terminate a pregnancy under all circumstances, but 12 percent of liberals would never permit abortions or would do so only in cases of rape, incest, or when the life of the mother is threatened. Conservatives are more divided; nearly half of those responding actually favor abortion rights under all circumstances or when the need for the abortion has been "clearly established"; only 13 percent of self-described conservatives would ban abortions altogether.[33]

Inconsistencies among liberals and conservatives on these questions reflect in part the differences between social liberalism and conservatism and economic liberalism and conservatism. Consider the question of whether "the government in Washington is getting too big for the good of the country and the individual person." In a 1992 poll, nearly 40 percent either had no opinion or said "it depends"; of those who did respond, a majority of both liberals and conservatives agreed that the government is getting too big—liberals by 31 percent to 23 percent, and conservatives by 46 percent to 14 percent. These numbers suggest that many Americans feel

Figure 7.2 **Ideological Self-Identification of Americans, 1996**

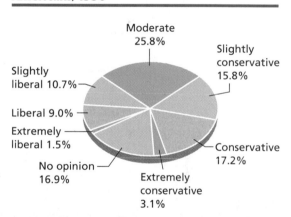

SOURCE: National Election Study, 1996.

Bill Lann Lee, President Bill Clinton's nominee to be the assistant attorney general for civil rights. Lee's outspoken support of affirmative action led the Senate to block the appointment, prompting Clinton to invoke his power to fill the position through temporary "recess appointment," making Lee the first Asian American ever to hold so high a position in the Justice Department.

the government is getting too big in some respects but not in others, and it is likely that liberals and conservatives have different reasons for feeling the way they do. Social liberals might well fear government interference with individual rights of free speech and privacy, while economic conservatives might fear government involvement in economic activities.[34]

Attitudes by and About Race

Race is an important factor in understanding American public opinion. First, whites and blacks have very different political attitudes across a wide range of issues. Second, attitudes *about* race and racial issues play an important role in shaping public policy and electoral politics.

Attitudes by Race   African Americans comprise approximately 12 percent of the population. As Table 7.2 indicates, their political attitudes differ sharply from those of

Table 7.2
The Race Gap: Whites and Blacks on Selected Political Issues

	Whites	*Blacks*
Favor government health insurance?	35.4%	52.6%
Agree that government should ensure that all citizens have a job?	21.6	47.1
Agree that the best way to fight crime is to address social problems rather than focusing on catching and punishing criminals?	28.3	36.2
Agree that civil rights leaders are pushing for progress "too slowly"?	11.7	37.4
Agree that U.S. should be more concerned with matters at home?	23.6	31.8
Have more confidence in the national government than in state or local government?	28.2	35.9
Agree that women and men should have an equal role in business, industry, and government?	78.4	78.4
Agree that abortion should always be permitted?	42.5	42.3
Describe self as Democrat?	34.5	64.2
Describe self as Republican?	31.9	3.5

SOURCE: National Election Study, 1996. Data on civil rights progress is from National Election Study, 1992.

whites. As expected, African Americans tend to favor government intervention to solve social problems and guarantee the economic well-being of its citizens. African Americans are less inclined than whites to favor American intervention abroad, perhaps because a disproportionately large number of African Americans serve in the armed forces. African Americans are overwhelmingly Democratic in party affiliation and voting behavior; as Figure 7.3 indicates, more than nine in ten African Americans who voted in 1996 opted for President Bill Clinton, although nearly half did not vote.[35]

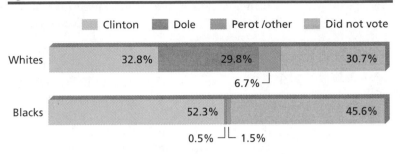

Figure 7.3 **The 1996 Vote: Whites and Blacks**

Source: National Election Study, 1996.

The differences between the attitudes of African Americans and whites at least partly reflect differences in education and socioeconomic status. Thus as African Americans climb the socioeconomic ladder, they become less supportive of government welfare programs. However, African Americans with higher levels of education tend to be *more* supportive of government programs in health and education than those with lower educational achievement. Neither income nor education has much effect on African Americans' attitudes toward government policies aimed specifically at racial minorities.[36]

There is considerable diversity of opinion among African Americans, as Table 7.2 suggests. African Americans are generally more liberal than whites on economic questions and more isolationist when it comes to foreign policy. On social issues such as abortion and the role of women in American society, African Americans' views resemble those of whites. African Americans are divided on questions of affirmative action (see Table 7.3), with only around half believing that "government should make every effort to improve the social and economic position of blacks." Moreover, support for affirmative action has fallen since the early 1970s, when more than three-quarters of African Americans supported such programs.[37]

Table 7.3
Affirmative Action

Question: Should there be special consideration for each of the following groups to increase their opportunities for getting into college and getting jobs or promotions?

	Percentage Agreeing	
Group	Blacks	Whites
Blacks	62%	25%
Women	62	26
Hispanics	57	22
Asians	48	18
Native Americans	65	34

Source: *Newsweek*, February 13, 1995, p. 37.

Research indicates that Latinos are slightly more likely to classify themselves as liberals than non-Latinos, and are more likely to identify with the Democratic party. Moreover, these differences persist even after taking income, education, and other factors into account.[38]

Attitudes About Race The nation has come a long way since the 1940s and 1950s, when overt racial prejudice and discrimination were acceptable practices to many Americans. In 1942, for example, white Americans favored separate schools for black and white children by 66 to 30 percent. By 1985, they favored integrated schools by 92 to 7 percent. Similarly, in 1942 only 42 percent of whites believed that blacks were "just as intelligent" as whites; by the 1980s, more than 75 percent felt that differences between the races were not inborn.[39] Even so, African Americans continue to perceive a great deal of prejudice in the world around them; in a 1989 study, for example, 26 percent of blacks believed that over half of white Americans "personally share the attitudes of groups like the Ku Klux Klan toward blacks." In 1992, nearly one-third of blacks reported that there had been "not much" change "in the position of black people in the past few years."[40]

It may be possible to explain this apparent paradox. Although conventional measures of white attitudes toward blacks show marked improvement in racial tolerance, in practice many whites flee neighborhoods and schools when large numbers of mostly poorer African Americans move in. Also, most white Americans have little tolerance for affirmative action or other programs designed to help racial minorities. While 45 percent of whites believe that "generations of slavery and discrimination" have made it difficult for blacks to work their way out of the lower class, for example, over two-thirds express strong or moderate agreement with the view that "Irish, Italians, Jewish and many other minorities overcame prejudice and worked their way up. Blacks should do the same without any special favors."[41]

Table 7.4
The Gender Gap: Men Versus Women on Selected Political Issues

	Men	*Women*
Favor government health insurance?	34.5%	40.5%
Agree that government should ensure that all citizens have a job?	20.8	29.2
Agree that government should address crime problem by solving social problems rather than by focusing on arresting and convicting criminals?	26.7	32.6
Agree that civil rights leaders are pushing for progress "too slowly"?	13.9	16.2
Agree that U.S. should be more concerned with matters at home?	22.8	26.7
Trust the national government more than state and local governments?	29.7	29.0
Agree that men and women should have an equal role in business, industry, and government?	78.1	78.1
Agree that abortion should always be permitted?	38.9	45.5
Describe self as Democrat?	31.5	43.6
Describe self as Republican?	32.6	24.5

Source: National Election Study, 1996. Data on civil rights progress is from National Election Study, 1992.

The Gender Gap

A statistical profile of men's and women's attitudes on politics reveals clear differences between the two groups. It should be kept in mind, however, that in political terms the two genders are far more alike than they are different. Other factors— race, religion, social class, and education, to name just a few—are more important than gender in determining political attitudes. Moreover, the **gender gap** between men and women reveals itself only on certain political issues, and not always those that one would expect (see Table 7.4).

The biggest gaps between the political attitudes of men and women involve the role of government, with women favoring a larger role for government in social programs. For example, women are more likely than men to believe that the government should provide every citizen with a job. Women and men are equally likely to agree that women should have an equal role in business, industry, and government, although women are more likely to support a right to abortion under all circumstances.

These differences in issue positions are reflected in the voting booth. In 1996, for example, women were significantly more likely than men to vote for Bill Clinton, and significantly less likely to vote for Robert Dole (see Figure 7.4). In general, women are more likely than men to identify themselves as Democrats and less likely to identify themselves as Republicans.[42]

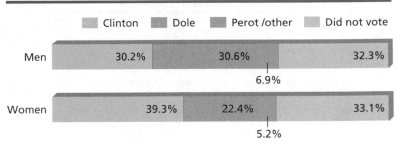

Figure 7.4 The 1996 Vote: Men and Women

Clinton | Dole | Perot /other | Did not vote

Men: Clinton 30.2%, Dole 30.6%, Perot/other 6.9%, Did not vote 32.3%

Women: Clinton 39.3%, Dole 22.4%, Perot/other 5.2%, Did not vote 33.1%

SOURCE: National Election Study, 1996.

Religion, Age, and Income

Other factors—including religion, age, and socioeconomic status—also play a role in determining political attitudes. This is to be expected, since these factors are associated with differences in family attitudes and in an individual's social environment.

As Table 7.5 and Figure 7.5 suggest, the political attitudes of Protestants, Catholics, and Jews vary greatly. On average, Protestants tend to be more conservative on both economic and social issues than Catholics, although Catholics are slightly more likely to favor U.S. intervention abroad. Both Protestants and Catholics are far more conservative than Jews, at least on most issues. However, summarizing the political attitudes of the three major religions masks a

The Promise Keepers, which describes itself as a "Christ-centered ministry dedicated to uniting men through vital relationships to become godly influences in their world" has attracted thousands of Americans to prayer meetings large and small, including a much-publicized march on the Mall in Washington, D.C.

Table 7.5
Religious Groups on Selected Political Issues

	Protestant	Catholic	Jewish
Favor government health insurance?	34.8%	39.8%	28.6%
Agree that government should ensure that all citizens have a job?	23.7	25.3	25.0
Agree that government should address crime problem by solving social problems rather than by focusing on arresting and convicting criminals?	27.7	30.4	33.3
Agree that civil rights leaders are pushing for progress "too slowly"?	14.4	14.7	16.9
Agree that U.S. should be more concerned with matters at home?	24.9	23.9	15.2
Trust the national government more than state and local governments?	26.2	32.3	42.9
Agree that men and women should have an equal role in business, industry, and government?	73.6	83.2	94.1
Agree that abortion should always be permitted?	38.3	38.8	70.6
Describe self as Democrat?	35.3	41.1	63.6
Describe self as Republican?	33.8	24.9	6.0

SOURCE: National Election Study, 1996. Data on civil rights progress is from National Election Study, 1992.

Figure 7.5 **The 1996 Vote: Protestant, Catholic, Jewish**

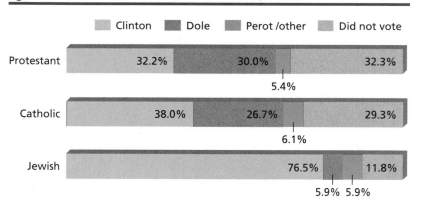

SOURCE: National Election Studay, 1996.

great deal of disagreement within each group, especially with respect to Protestants and Catholics.

Other factors that influence political attitudes are age and income. For example, 51 percent of Americans under the age of 45 favor a woman's right to choose an abortion under all circumstances, compared with only 39 percent of Americans aged 45 or older. Similarly, 42 percent of the wealthiest Americans, but only 27 percent of the poorest, believe the government is getting too powerful.[43]

Tracking Public Opinion: The Power of Political Polling

One could not have even the briefest encounter with the American political scene without confronting the political poll. The president's approval and disapproval ratings, charted on a monthly basis, are widely analyzed and reported. A presidential race produces dozens of polls every week, so many that some newspapers and magazines publish a "poll of polls" to allow their readers to keep track. Organizations like the American Institute of Public Opinion (the Gallup Poll) follow Americans' attitudes on issues such as abortion and gun control, and keep close account of the public's confidence in government agencies and institutions. Polls are widely used by business organizations, government agencies, and, of course, political parties and campaign organizations.

Political polls appear on almost a daily basis, yet they are poorly understood and often misinterpreted. What follows is a crash course in political polls: how and why they work, why they are sometimes wrong and often abused, and how they help, and hinder, the workings of the democratic process.

Why Polls Work

A political poll is nothing more than a projection about the beliefs and behaviors of a large group of people based on a survey of a small—sometimes very small—sample of the overall population. Properly done, a poll can provide a reasonably clear snapshot of public opinion at a given moment.

Sampling and Sample Size   The idea of **sampling** is routine and familiar. A doctor who seeks to measure blood glucose needs only a few drops of blood; the results of the tests on the sample can be presumed to reflect the patient's overall blood chemistry. Likewise, a federal meat inspector need not test every single animal carcass to be reasonably sure that a supplier's meat is free from contamination.

Political polling works the same way. Suppose the pollster wants to measure the number of Americans who approve of the way the president is doing his job. Instead of trying to survey every person in the United States, the pollster might decide to survey every tenth person, or every hundredth, or every thousandth. If the sample so obtained is representative of the population as a whole, it should be possible to obtain reasonably accurate results without having to survey everybody.

Scientific Sampling.   For a poll to yield accurate results, the individuals surveyed must at least roughly resemble a cross section of the general public. To ensure a representative sample, modern pollsters typically see to it that the sample population contains approximately the right mix of races, income groups, men, and women. At a minimum, good polling technique requires that the sample population be checked for representativeness. For example, suppose that the sample population for a given poll (drawn at random) was found to be 20 percent African American. Since African Americans make up only 12 percent of the population, the results of such a poll would have to be regarded with great caution.

Polls used for specific purposes may make further modifications to the sample population. For example, a poll used to predict election results may exclude from the sample those who are unlikely to vote. Such polls of "likely voters" are frequently seen around election time, and are generally better at predicting the election results than polls that do not make such an adjustment.

Sample Size.   The next question is, *How few people can a pollster survey and still be reasonably assured of accurate and meaningful results?*

The answer may be surprising. Excellent estimates of public opinion in a nation of 250 million citizens can be obtained with as few as 1,200 or 1,500 respondents. Passable results, at least for some purposes, can be obtained with as few as two or three hundred. Of course, obtaining meaningful results from such numbers assumes that everything else about the poll is done carefully and well.

Are Public Opinion Polls Bad for Democracy?

Public opinion polls have become a staple of political life in the United States. The news media report them; politicians and officeholders depend upon them; political scientists find them a useful and at times indispensable research tool. But are public opinion polls really good for democracy? Do they help or hinder the political process? Advocates of the direct democracy model argue that polls are an excellent way to inform the public and to encourage politicians to respect the views of the people. Those who are more comfortable with the representative model of democracy contend that polls encourage politicians to follow the people rather than lead them, undermining the advantages built into the American constitutional system. Whichever side is right, one thing is sure — polls will remain an integral part of the political process until researchers find a better way to measure the public pulse.

Public opinion polls undermine democracy

Many polls are meaningless or misleading. Although public opinion polls possess an air of scientific precision, many provide inaccurate results, and some are consciously designed to deceive the public. Moreover, even scientific polls require careful and cautious interpretation. Yet even the most responsible news organizations rarely do more than provide a quick report of poll results, and citizens frequently lack the sophistication or information necessary to put the polls in the proper perspective. If poll results do not accurately reflect public opinion, any contribution they might make to the democratic process is necessarily suspect.

Polls encourage citizens to conform to the majority viewpoint, and discourage independent thinking. Analysts from Tocqueville on have commented on the American tendency to think in packs; by clearly identifying the majority viewpoint on a given issue, polls make it even less likely that individuals will make up their own minds. A candidate with low poll numbers, for example, might be dismissed by many voters as a hopeless cause, whatever his or her merits. Likewise, a minority viewpoint on public affairs might be denied due consideration by voters who feel the public's mind is already made up.

Polls discourage voter turnout, and contribute to citizen apathy. If the results of an election can be predicted in advance, many voters will decide that voting is a waste of time and energy. This problem is particularly serious in presidential election years, since a predicted presidential landslide may discourage voters from turning out to participate in important state and local races. Moreover, an overemphasis on polls diverts the citizens' attention from the substance of public policy, encouraging voters to think of political races as sporting events instead of as a vital debate on public issues.

Polls encourage politicians to follow the people, rather than lead them. The Framers wanted political leaders to conduct public policy in the public interest, but not necessarily to follow the majority. They sought to design a system in which politicians would help shape public opinion by analyzing issues thoroughly and then carefully explaining their views to their constituents. In a polling culture, however, the tables are turned; politicians make policy to match the opinions of the majority, however ill-conceived or ill-informed those opinions may be. When the congressional Republicans designed the "Contract with America" in 1994, for example, they selected issues known from polls and focus groups to be popular with the electorate. Carried to the extreme, politicians may be disinclined to make any decision that does not have their pollsters' seal of approval. President Bill Clinton, for example, once used poll results to help determine the politically most advantageous place to take a vacation.

Public opinion polls are vital to democracy

By providing reliable data on the views of the public, polls keep politicians in line and in touch. Supporters of public opinion polls argue that polls are vitally necessary to ensure a close linkage between the people and their leaders. In the old days, officeholders spent much of their time in their home districts and were keenly in touch with the sentiments of the people. Modern politicians, by contrast, spend much of their life in Washington and need polls and focus groups to ensure that they know what their constituents think about public issues. When politicians rely on polls, moreover, they are less likely to fall prey to special interest groups and lobbyists who seek to use public policy to benefit the few instead of the many.

Polls keep voters educated, informed, and interested. Combined with various other sources of information and opinions, polls provide the citizenry with an easy way to keep up with public issues. Even the "horse race" polls conducted before presidential elections serve the vital purpose of keeping voters interested in the ongoing contest. And while many polls are unscientific or biased, voters are smart enough and sophisticated enough to evaluate the value of particular poll results and to distinguish between the useful and the unsound.

Polls provide a workable substitute for direct democracy. As it now stands, when Republicans and Democrats disagree on a particular issue, they each present their case to the American people, then sit back and let the poll results resolve the question. The process, in effect, allows the people, rather than the politicians, to determine public policy. When President Bill Clinton fought with congressional Republicans over Medicare and other budget issues in 1995, for example, the public's clear stand in support of the president—expressed through public opinion polls— forced the Republicans to back down and moderate their proposals. This method of resolving public issues actually improves on direct democracy, since it allows political leaders to frame key policy questions and gives them an opportunity to present their arguments and viewpoints to the people. The result is sound public policy and a healthy democracy.

If only 200 to 1,500 respondents are needed to obtain a picture of the entire American population, does it follow that proportionally smaller numbers can be used to obtain a snapshot of the city of Chicago, or of the student body of a large university? The answer is no. The size of the overall population is almost irrelevant to the size of the survey.

Many Americans find it difficult to understand why the necessary sample size does not decrease in proportion to population. A simple analogy might help.

If an environmental scientist needed one drop of water from a swimming pool to test for contaminants, he or she would not need any more than that amount to test a small pond, or even Lake Erie—provided, of course, that the contaminants were randomly distributed throughout all three bodies of water.

Accuracy of Polls   Typically, poll results are given as precise numbers. For example, a newspaper might report that the president's approval rating stands at 53 percent. Somewhere in the fine print the paper might state that the poll results are "plus or minus 3 percentage points." This means that there is only a 5 percent chance that the poll results are not within 3 percent of the correct number for the entire population.

The "confidence interval" is almost completely dependent on the size of the sample (not, as we have seen, on the size of the underlying population). A survey of 1,200 people yields results that are within 3 percentage points of the correct figure 95 percent of the time. A survey of only 400 people yields results that are accurate to within 5 points of the real figure 95 percent of the time.

Why Polls Go Wrong

Everything to this point has been based on the assumption that the only errors in a poll come from statistical deviations due to sample size. As we will see, this assumption is not always justified. Many other things can also go wrong:

Political Bias   Any poll conducted by an organization that has an interest in the result should be regarded with great suspicion. Such polls can be tinged with all sorts of problems, but the fundamental one is that the poll taker is interested less in scientific accuracy than in how the poll's results can be used to help or hinder a particular cause.

If media polls consistently show a candidate ten points behind, for example, be wary of a poll conducted by the underdog's campaign that suddenly shows a shift in momentum. Even if this claim is based on a real poll and not entirely made up, the poll results are very likely flawed. Likewise, polls released by interest groups may be biased one way or the other for political effect.

Sample Bias   Polls that are too small, or those in which the sample is not properly chosen, are prone to erroneous results. Such **sample bias** is not usually a problem in major national polls, but it may affect local polls or those conducted on a low budget.

The most famous example of sampling error was the 1936 *Literary Digest* poll that predicted a major defeat for Franklin Roosevelt in the presidential election of that year. The sample population was huge—2 million postcard ballots were returned. The problem was that the pollsters drew their sample from telephone books and auto registration lists. People who owned telephones or cars in 1936 turned out to be much likelier than their poorer counterparts to vote Republican. Thus the sample was biased, and the results were spectacularly wrong—Roosevelt won by a landslide.

Response Bias   Even if a sample is well chosen, problems may arise if the *actual responses* drawn from the sample do not yield a reasonable cross section of the population. Such problems are known as **response bias.**

The 1936 *Literary Digest* poll, for example, suffered from response bias as well as sample bias. Among those who received a ballot, Roosevelt supporters turned out to be less likely to return the postcard than those who supported his Republican challenger.

Another problem is that voters may consciously lie to a researcher or may refuse to participate. When asked whether they voted in a recent election, for example, some respondents are too embarrassed to admit that they did not vote. Similarly, some voters may be reluctant to admit that they are voting for a par-

ticular candidate. When the ex–Ku Klux Klansman David Duke ran for the Senate in Louisiana in 1989, for example, preelection polls showed him with only 30 percent of the vote; on election day, he received 44 percent.[44] Finally, those who refuse to participate in a poll may affect the outcome. Likewise, polls understated the number of voters who supported H. Ross Perot in 1992, perhaps because Perot's supporters included a disproportionate number of citizens who were alienated from the political system and hostile to the media.

Question Design   The best that a poll can do is return reliable answers to the questions posed. The usefulness or accuracy of a survey may depend on how questions are worded or on the quality of the overall survey design. For example, when Americans are asked whether they support more assistance for the poor, around 65 percent say yes. When asked whether they support more spending on welfare, however, only 19 percent agree.[45]

Sometimes question wording is designed to influence the results of a survey. For example, a survey prepared by the Planetary Society, a group that supports increased expenditures on space exploration, recently asked the following question:

> *President Clinton and Vice President Gore have emphasized their commitment to promoting high-technology research and development, arguing that the economic, environmental, and scientific future of the United States is at stake. Do you believe the Clinton Administration should fund more space research and exploration as a vital and integral part of America's overall technological base?*

Another problem is overall survey design. If women are asked, "Have you ever been the victim of sexual harassment?" they might give one answer. Suppose, however, that the actual survey looks like this:

1. *Please indicate which of the following, in your opinion, constitute sexual harassment:*
   Threats involving sex
   Unwanted sexual advances

The 1975 Public Affairs Act: Never Was— But Not Forgotten

Who says Americans don't pay attention to public policy? More than four out of ten persons surveyed in a recent national poll had a definitive opinion when asked whether the 1975 Public Affairs Act should be repealed.

One problem: There is no 1975 Public Affairs Act. There never was. Pollsters made it up—naughty them! Still, 43 percent of those surveyed took a position aye or nay when asked whether the phony act should be repealed. (The remainder had no opinion—the smarties.)

Actually, it's not the first time that Americans have been gulled by the 1975 Public Affairs Act. Nearly seventeen years ago, George Bishop, a political scientist at the University of Cincinnati, first included questions about repealing the fictitious act in surveys of Cincinnati-area residents.

"We had the sense that people weren't at all well informed about many policy issues but give opinions to appear to be informed or simply to be cooperative," Bishop said. "So we decided to give them a real red herring"—and the 1975 Public Affairs Act was born.

"The simple fact is that on a lot of big policy issues, there really isn't any informed public opinion," Bishop said.

To honor the twentieth (un)anniversary of the 1975 Public Affairs Act, the [Washington Post] added a twist to Bishop's classic test of pseudo-opinions.

In a recent *Washington Post* national survey, the [Post] asked three slightly different versions of a question about repeal of the fictitious 1975 Public Affairs Act to three separate randomly selected groups.

The first version was Bishop's original question. In the second version, the words "President Clinton says" replaced the original "Some people say" in the introduction. The introduction to the third version read: "Republicans in Congress say. . . ."

You guessed it: More than half of those questioned offered an opinion when given a partisan cue. And Democrats were far more likely to support repeal of the phantom act (and Republicans to oppose) when told Clinton favored repeal—but Republicans were far more likely to favor repeal when clued that congressional GOPers favored dumping it.

SOURCE: *Washington Post,* February 26, 1995, p. C5.

> *Unwanted touching*
> *Sexually suggestive remarks*
> *Jokes with sexual themes or overtones*
> *"Whistling" or other unwanted sexual behavior*
> 2. *Have you ever been the victim of sexual harassment?*

The results of the second survey are likely to be very different from the first. Some women respondents may be reminded of various incidents of sexual harassment by the first question, prompting them to respond "yes" instead of "no" to the second.

Which of these two polls yields the more useful result is a matter of debate. The point here is that when one survey shows only a small percentage of women have been the victims of sexual harassment, and another gives a much larger figure, the differences might be explained by differences in question wording or questionnaire format.

Asking the Wrong Question, or the Right Question at the Wrong Time Polls, like computers, can do only what you ask them to. Often the problem with a poll is not that it has failed to measure public opinion accurately but that it has asked the wrong question or the right question at the wrong time.

In politics, timing is everything. A poll conducted the weekend before an election, even if it is perfectly designed and executed, cannot measure public opinion on election day. In a close race, a few days can make a big difference. Timing problems afflicted the famous 1948 Truman-Dewey race, in which the polls seemed to indicate a decisive Dewey victory. In those days, when poll results were reported by mail and tabulated by hand, it took a full ten days to conduct a poll. Thus the latest preelection poll was ten days out of date on election day. Some analysts have suggested that the polls were not wrong, but that Truman simply closed the gap.

Pollsters confidently predicted that Harry Truman would lose the 1948 presidential election, leading the Chicago Tribune's *headline writers to jump to the same conclusion. "Ain't the way I heard it," was Truman's response.*

Drawing the Wrong Conclusion Interpreting poll results takes great skill. It is essential to know what a particular poll has measured and what it has not.

One problem is that polls, like snapshots with an inexpensive camera, produce blurry, two-dimensional images devoid of depth and movement. For a single poll to judge the depth with which people hold their beliefs, or the likelihood that they will change their opinions in response to changing conditions, is very difficult. A poll on attitudes toward prayer in the schools, for example, might find an overwhelming majority in favor of the practice. Knowing that, however, tells us very little about the school prayer issue as a factor in American politics. What we need are the answers to other questions. How strongly do supporters and opponents of school prayer feel about the issue? How important do the two sides view the issue compared with others? Are public attitudes likely to shift or remain relatively stable? Which side of the controversy is more likely to use the issue in evaluating candidates on election day?

Answers to these questions can be obtained with sophisticated polling techniques, but most polls do little more than report a single finding. As President George Bush discovered when he was defeated in the 1992 election, less than two years after enjoying 90 percent approval ratings, sometimes that finding is of little lasting consequence.

Polls are among the most useful tools for measuring public opinion. When used carefully, they can provide important insights into what Americans think at any given time. Moreover, polls provide politicians with a way to keep up with their constituents and thus increase the opportunities for citizens to influence their government. Wrongly used, however, polls can produce misleading and even meaningless results. Moreover, an overreliance on polls may lead public officials to avoid using their own judgment, and may tempt presidents and politicians to design their policies in order to maximize short-term gain over the long-term public interest. These themes are taken up in Chapter 13.

Summary

The term *public opinion* is used in two general senses. In one sense it simply means "the opinions of the people," usually as measured through some sort of formal or informal survey. In the other it is used as if the public were a single, living entity capable of having a particular opinion on any given subject. This mythical public is capable of deliberation and discussion, and, like a single person, can eventually reach a considered judgment.

Public opinion can be measured in a variety of ways. The most common scientific methods include public opinion polls and focus groups. Politicians also rely on old-fashioned methods, such as watching their mail, talking with constituents, and monitoring media coverage.

Political attitudes develop through a process known as political socialization. Even very young children are exposed to political concepts, and many political attitudes are fully formed by late adolescence. The primary agents of political socialization include family, school, peer groups, and the media. Political attitudes are also shaped by race, gender, and social class, and by exposure to external events.

Public opinion plays a critical role in shaping government decisions. The people have many opportunities to voice their opinions through participation in various political activities. However, the government may not always be influenced by the majority. Those in the minority may be better financed and organized, and may have easier access to the media. Moreover, public officials do not merely sit back and respond to public opinion. Instead they work actively to mold public opinion, either in support of actions already taken or to build momentum for policies they wish to see adopted. While it is entirely appropriate for political leaders to educate and inform the public, political leaders may also try to manipulate public opinion through the use of incomplete or misleading information or through appeals to emotion.

Researchers have conducted extensive studies of American public opinion. In general, Americans are poorly informed about specific political issues, although whether they are able to make valid judgments despite their lack of political awareness is a matter of debate. Most Americans are centrists, and most do not express their views in an ideologically consistent manner. Political attitudes are affected by such factors as race, gender, education, religion, age, and income.

Most analyses of public opinion are based on public opinion polls, in which the views of the entire population are based on those of a small sample. Polls can be very useful to both political scientists and political strategists, but they are not always accurate and must be regarded with caution. Problems with political polls can include sample bias, response bias, and bias related to question wording or survey design. Even if these technical problems are overcome, pollsters must be sure to ask the right questions at the right time, and to analyze their results with care.

Key Terms

Public opinion
Public opinion poll
Bandwagon effect
Underdog effect
Political socialization
Gender gap
Sampling
Sample bias
Response bias

Review Questions

1. What is public opinion? Describe how the term is used in two different senses.

2. How do individuals learn about politics? What factors are most important in shaping the political attitudes of children? Of adults?

3. How well informed are Americans about politics? What role does ideology play in shaping political attitudes?

4. How do individuals make their views known to the government and to other citizens? Why are the views of some groups more influential than those of others?

5. How do public officials help to shape, or manipulate, public opinion?

6. How do public opinion polls work? What are some of the problems that make polls inaccurate?

Suggested Readings

Asher, Herbert. *Polling and the Public: What Every Citizen Should Know.* Washington, D.C.: CQ Press, 1988.

Conway, M. Margaret. *Political Participation in the United States.* Washington, D.C.: CQ Press, 1991.

Erikson, Robert S., and Kent L. Tedin. *American Public Opinion: Its Origins, Content, and Impact.* 5th ed. Needham Heights, MA: Allyn and Bacon, 1995.

Jennings, M. Kent, and Richard G. Niemi. *The Political Character of Adolescence: The Influence of Families and Schools.* Princeton: Princeton University Press, 1974.

Key, V. O. *Public Opinion and American Democracy.* New York: Knopf, 1964.

Mayer, William G. *The Changing American Mind: How and Why American Public Opinion Changed Between 1960 and 1988.* Ann Arbor: University of Michigan Press, 1992.

Miller, Warren E., and Santa A. Traugott. *American National Election Studies Data Sourcebook, 1952–1986.* Cambridge, Mass.: Harvard University Press, 1989.

Internet Resources

Well-respected commercial polling firm, with presidential approval ratings and other survey data at:

http://www.gallup.com

Guide to the National Election Studies at the University of Michigan, which has surveyed American voters since 1948 at:

http://www.umich.edu/~nes/nesguide/nesguide.htm

The Pew Research Center for the People and the Press, an independent political research group that studies Americans' attitudes toward press, politics, and public policy issues at:

http://www.people-press.org/

The National Opinion Research Center at the University of Chicago, which features the General Social Survey, a broad-based survey of Americans' attitudes and behaviors on a variety of social issues at:

http://www.norc.uchicago.edu/

★ 8 ★ Interest Groups

By all accounts, the case of *Sharon Taxman* v. *Board of Education of Piscataway* was destined to become the definitive affirmative action case of the 1990s. Taxman, a white teacher in the Business Department at Piscataway High School in Piscataway, NJ, had lost her job in 1989, when the Board of Education voted to reduce the number of teachers in the department by one. Taxman had exactly the same seniority as another teacher, Debra Williams, who is black. In keeping with the Board's affirmative action policy, adopted in 1975, the Board decided to keep Williams and terminate Taxman. The Board admitted that Taxman and Williams were "two teachers of equal ability" and "equal qualifications", but defended its decision based on the need for a culturally diverse teaching staff. Taxman, claiming racial discrimination, brought suit in federal court.

Both the district court and the Third Circuit Court of Appeals had little difficulty finding in favor of Taxman. "The harm imposed upon a nonminority employee by the loss of his or her job is so substantial and the cost so severe," the court concluded, "that the Board's goal of racial diversity, even if legitimate . . . may not be pursued in this particular fashion."

The *Taxman* case presented two problems for those who support affirmative action. First, many of those who favored affirmative action in general had difficulty defending it on the facts of this particular case. Second, advocates of affirmative action feared that the specific nature of the *Taxman* case greatly increased the likelihood that the Supreme Court would use the case to strike out at affirmative action in gen-

Sharon Taxman

eral—especially since a majority of the justices had made it very clear that they had doubts about the constitutionality of such programs.

As the Supreme Court convened for its October 1997 term, *Taxman* was one of the most closely watched cases on the Court's agenda. The *National Law Journal* called the case the "major lightning bolt" of the upcoming year. "This could be the biggest affirmative action case of the decade," commented one employment law scholar. "The biggest fear is the court will say you can hardly ever take race into account, and that would be a devastating blow to public and private affirmative action programs."

Then, in late November 1997, a coalition of civil rights groups announced an even bigger lightning bolt. Led by the NAACP Legal Defense Fund, the civil rights groups announced that they had reached an agreement with the Piscataway School Board to finance around 70 percent of the $433,500 needed to settle the case—and that Sharon Taxman had accepted the offer. Because the case was settled, it was summarily dropped from the Supreme Court's agenda.

Settling cases once they reach the Supreme Court's docket is rare enough; but the way this case was settled forced legal scholars to scratch their heads in search of a similar precedent. Paying the money was worthwhile, said a spokesman for the American Civil Liberties Union, because "this was a bad case for a decision on the bigger issues of affirmative action." The civil rights groups' logic was clear enough—they could at least live to fight another day, hopefully in a case with better facts. But in the process, the groups seem to have invented a new way for interest groups to participate in the American political process.[1]

The *Taxman* case, like so many other controversies, shows the extraordinary influence that interest groups have in American political life. Interest groups provide ordinary citizens with a way to combine with other citizens to amplify their influence on politics and increase the likelihood that their interests will prevail. Thus interest groups must be nurtured and protected, both to secure the fundamental rights of the citizenry and to ensure that the system itself runs smoothly; without interest groups, ordinary citizens would lose much of their ability to affect the processes of government.

Yet interest groups also pose serious challenges to democratic politics. As James Madison warned in *Federalist* No. 10, interest groups can easily turn into factions, putting their own interest above the rights of others and the long-term interests of the community. Moreover, interest groups do not represent a cross section of the people. Groups representing corporate interests, for example, are more numerous, better funded, and perhaps more influential than those representing the general public. A small but well-funded group can often outmaneuver or outweigh a large but poorly organized group.

Interest groups interact with all three branches of the national government, with political parties, and with state and local governments. They are active in influencing public opinion and in campaign politics. Like most things, interest groups and lobbyists are neither all good nor all bad. Enhancing their contributions while controlling their dangers is one of the great challenges facing those who would reform and improve the democratic process in America.

Questions to Keep in Mind

What roles do interest groups play in a democracy? What advantages and disadvantages do they offer for self-government?

How does the Framers' constitutional design promote and/or hinder the influence of interest groups in the United States?

Basic Concepts

An **interest group** is a voluntary association of citizens who share a common economic or ideological interest. Interest groups attempt to influence governmental decision making in a variety of ways. Interest groups participate in the electoral process by contributing time, money, or ideas. They also try to influence what candidates do once they are elected.

Political scientists differentiate between *interests* and *interest groups.* An interest is a group of citizens who share a common set of concerns and goals—for example, farmers. Interest groups are the formal organizations that recruit members, publish newsletters and magazines, hire professional staff, and register as lobbyists on Capitol Hill. An example of an interest group is the American Farm Bureau Federation. The key difference between interests and interest groups is that interest groups are *organized,* whereas interests are not.

Interest groups are sometimes known as lobbying groups, or simply lobbies. The term derives from efforts to influence lawmakers in the lobby of the House or Senate, as they entered the legislative chamber for a vote. Interest groups are also known as pressure groups, because they attempt to put pressure on the government.[2]

The Framers and Interest Groups

The Framers recognized that different groups of citizens had different interests, and that the right to pursue those interests was fundamental to the preservation of liberty. Yet allowing citizens to pursue their interests freely raised two critical issues. First, the interests of different groups of citizens were frequently in conflict; government policies that served the interests of one group could threaten the interests, or even the rights, of another group. Second, the interests of a group of citizens—and even the interests of the majority of citizens—could be bad for society in the long run.

According to James Madison in the *Federalist* No. 10, groups of citizens who pursue government policies adverse to the rights of other citizens or to the long-term interests of the community are known as factions (see Chapter 2, p. 40). Since factions could not be prevented without threatening liberty, Madison proposed instead that they be rendered harmless. Small factions could simply be outvoted, while large factions could be neutralized by creating a large republic and by instituting a decentralized representative system.

Madison's claim that a minority faction could be dealt with easily ("it may clog the administration, it may convulse the society, but it will be unable to execute and mask its violence under the forms of the Constitution") may seem naive to modern scholars. We know that narrowly based interest groups can exercise power far out of proportion to their numbers. They may do so by expending huge sums of money to influence representatives and the public or by taking advantage of the federal government's large, decentralized structure to apply pressure at key points. Interest groups also benefit greatly by aligning themselves with friendly congressional committees and executive agencies, creating small but influential power centers within the government.

Some modern scholars have therefore extended Madison's critique of factions, arguing that small factions can be just as dangerous as large ones. Central to this argument is the claim that such groups can pursue their own interest at the expense of the public. For supporting evidence, scholars can point to any number of governmental programs that benefit the few at the expense of the many. Consider the countless loopholes in the federal tax code, each of which benefits some special group. Or the thousands of unjustified "pork-barrel" projects enacted every year, by which members of Congress improve the lives of their own constituents at the expense of everyone else. All in all, it is difficult to argue against the proposition that local, narrow, or parochial interests can distort national programs and undermine national priorities.

The key assumption behind the arguments of Madison and his modern followers is that there is a "public interest" that can be determined independently of the political process, through reasoned analysis. Such a claim cannot be proved or disproved, but must be adopted or rejected on faith. Once accepted, Madison's picture of the ideal representatives follows automatically: citizens "whose wisdom may best discern the true interest of their country and whose patriotism and love of justice will be least likely to sacrifice it to *temporary or partial considerations*."[3]

But what exactly is the public interest in the Madisonian sense? Studying Madison does not usually give us answers to modern public policy problems. But it does tell us that the public interest is that which is in the long-term interests of the whole community, provided that it does not infringe on the rights of any member of the community. Modern Madisonians thus look to protect the entire community and each individual from the influence of both large and small groups.

Pluralists and Elitists

Balancing the Madisonians are those who unabashedly embrace the idea of pluralism—the view of society as composed of a multitude of overlapping but well-defined groups. Citizens interact with government and with society not as isolated individuals but as members of those groups. Each group seeks to advance its own interest, and in doing so clashes with all the others. Out of this general melee arises the public interest.

Pluralist theorists do not believe that the public interest emerges magically or mysteriously. They simply reject the idea that there is a public interest that can be identified outside the democratic process. As long as the democratic process is functioning properly, the public policy that emerges from the clash of group interests will be the public interest. Outside of politics, they believe, there can be no way of identifying or articulating the public good.

Of course, pluralist theorists recognize that the democratic process is often skewed and unbalanced. Some groups have more power than others, and some groups have no power at all. For example, women, African Americans, and other minorities were badly underrepresented throughout most of American history, while business interests, many argue, have been overrepresented. For these theorists, pluralism is less a description of how American politics really works than a goal of how it should work.

Thus the government need not be simply a neutral referee between interest groups, but might properly seek to create a level playing field, reducing the power of some groups and increasing that of others. It might limit the amount of money that groups can contribute to political candidates, for example, or create public access channels on cable television to ensure that all groups have an opportunity to be heard. Moreover, certain government institutions—most notably the courts—might develop a special role in the protection and advancement of group interests that are otherwise shut out of the political process. Some pluralists, in fact, cite the increased power of previously underrepresented groups as a positive feature of the modern pluralist system.

Despite these gains, however, many political scientists question whether a system of interest group pluralism can ever exist on a truly level playing field. Because they believe that a system of interest group pluralism inherently favors the well-off and well-connected at the expense of other citizens, these theorists are known as elitists. For all the gains of underrepresented groups, they claim, American society continues to ignore a growing underclass of citizens who lack resources, skills, and political power. Despite the proliferation of consumer groups and environmentalist groups, they add, American business continues to dominate the American political system.

Echoes of Madison are found among liberals and conservatives alike. Both are apt to criticize the interest group system for favoring elite interests over those of the common people. Conservatives typically speak in terms of a "cultural elite" that includes well-educated Washington insiders, liberal journalists, academic policy "wonks," and liberal interest group professionals. Liberals are more likely to denounce the wealthy, big business, and industrial trade groups. Both sides join in denouncing foreign lobbyists and nameless "influence peddlers." Both agree that the government rarely reflects or advances the interests of the general public.

As a general rule, however, it can be said that liberals see a greater need for adjustments and modifications of the political marketplace to ensure equal opportunity for all groups to participate, whereas conservatives are likelier to oppose such restrictions. Still, the debate over pluralism can create strange bedfellows. First Amendment absolutists joined with conservative pluralists, for example, to assert the right of corporations to participate in unfettered political debate. Their opponents (claiming to speak in the public interest) favored government restrictions on such speech in an effort to blunt the effects of corporate money.

Types of Interest Groups

Interest groups are most commonly classified according to the policy areas in which they operate or the causes they represent: agriculture, business, labor, environmental or consumer protection, and the like.[4] An alternative, proposed by the political scientist Jack L. Walker, is to distinguish between groups on the basis of their history and social structure. Such an approach focuses on how and why groups evolved, the nature of their memberships, and the relationship between the members' goals and the groups' activities.[5] Broadly speaking, groups can be classified under four types—profit sector, nonprofit sector, mixed sector, and citizens' groups.

The two approaches are fully compatible with one another. Within each of the four broad categories it is possible to separate groups in the traditional way, according to issues and causes.

Profit Sector Groups Profit sector groups, which represent particular industries or occupations, were among the first to form. Comprising a wide array of economic interests, they make up nearly 40 percent of all interest groups.[6] Profit sector groups include organizations representing agriculture, labor, business, and a variety of professions.

The large number of profit sector groups and their considerable influence at every level of government provides elite theorists with powerful evidence to support their claims that the interest groups do not operate on a level playing field. However, it should be noted that there is as much competition among the various profit sector groups as there is between the profit sector

Figure 8.1 **Labor Union Membership**

SOURCES: Harold W. Stanley and Richard G. Niemi, *Vital Statistics on American Politics*, 3rd ed. (Washington, D.C.: CQ Press, 1992), Table 6–11, p. 190; *Statistical Abstract* 1997, Table 688, p. 440; U.S. Bureau of Labor Statistics, *Employment and Earnings*, January issues.

and other groups. Not only is there competition between business and organized labor, but there is also considerable friction among the various parts of the business community. Large umbrella organizations—such as the National Association of Manufacturers or the United States Chamber of Commerce—rarely find all of their members united behind a single position. More specialized trade groups commonly fight among themselves on key issues.

Even though business interests generally opposed health care reform in 1994, for example, business groups were originally split into a host of competing factions on all sides of the issue.[7] Similarly, business groups split on whether to support the North American Free Trade Agreement in 1993, depending on whether they saw opportunities or dangers in reduced trade barriers with Canada and Mexico.

Nonprofit and Public Sector Groups   Nonprofit and public sector groups, which represent the not-for-profit sector of the economy and related professional associations, make up about one-third of all groups.[8] Many of these groups sprang up in the twentieth century in response to increased government activities in education, social welfare, and recreation. At the same time, the growth in the size of government and the increasing professionalization of the government workforce gave rise to groups representing public employees at all levels of government. Examples of nonprofit and public sector groups include the American Heart Association and the American Federation of State, County, and Municipal Employees. Also included in this group are lobbying organizations representing various governmental entities, such as states and cities.

Mixed Sector Groups A small percentage of groups are mixed sector groups, which include members from both the profit and nonprofit sectors. The American Hospital Association, for example, includes both nonprofit and for-profit hospitals. Likewise, the National Association of Broadcasters includes members representing public as well as commercial television and radio stations. Such mixed groups comprise less than 6 percent of all groups.[9]

Citizens' Groups A large and rapidly growing number of groups can be classified as citizens' groups. Citizens' groups are open to all, regardless of occupation or industry affiliation.[10] Thus their memberships are typically more diverse than those of other groups, although many are organized around narrow goals or specialized constituencies. According to pluralists, the rise of citizens' groups provided an important counterweight to the already-powerful lobbies representing corporate inter-

Labor-union membership has steadily declined over the past few decades, but campaign contributions from labor PACS have increased sharply, ensuring that labor remains a major player in national, state, and local politics.

ests. While many citizens' groups have become quite influential, their ability to counteract the efforts of business groups is limited. First, they have far less money to spend than business groups. Second, citizens' groups often represent only a part of the citizenry. When consumers' groups fight for increased government safety standards for automobiles, for example, they must face the reality that many Americans oppose such laws on the ground that they limit individual choice and impose high costs on drivers.

Citizens' groups comprise nearly one-quarter of all groups. Among the most important are these:

Civil Rights Groups. Many groups exist to promote the civil rights of their constituents. The first important civil rights group was the National Association for the Advancement of Colored People (NAACP), formed in 1909 (although general references to African Americans as "colored" are now considered insensitive and insulting, the group retains its name, partly as a monument to its role in the civil rights struggle). Traditionally, civil rights groups have been characterized by a widespread membership base, a broad range of activities and issue concerns, and a close public identification between the formal group and its broad membership. The views of the NAACP, for example, are frequently (but not always correctly) taken to be an expression of the views of African Americans in general.

The success of the NAACP and its allies in the civil rights movement inspired the creation of a host of similar groups that act on behalf of other citizens. These include women's rights groups, such as the National Organization for Women (NOW); groups representing Hispanics and Native Americans; and religious groups. Ironically, as its imitators have gained power

Vice President Al Gore and Costa Rican president Jose Maria Figueres (center) discuss global warming at an international conference in Kyoto, Japan. Although foreign nations are barred by U.S. law from making campaign contributions, their representatives frequently meet with American officials to discuss issues of common concern.

the NAACP itself has been rocked by internal divisions, scandal, and a growing gap between its leadership and the rank and file of the African American community.

Because civil rights groups often represent unpopular causes, they sometimes take their claims to court as well as to legislatures. The NAACP pioneered this strategy in the 1930s, and it has been widely adopted by women, other minorities, and, most recently, gay and lesbian groups. Thus in 1994 gay and lesbian groups convinced the Colorado Supreme Court to strike down a state constitutional amendment that would have banned local laws protecting gays and lesbians.[11]

Most groups in this category have been clustered at the liberal end of the political spectrum. In the last few years, however, many similar groups have sprung up on the conservative side.

Environmental Protection. Groups such as the Environmental Defense Fund, the Sierra Club, and the National Wildlife Federation take an active interest in the environment. Such groups have been extremely successful in convincing Congress to pass tough legislation protecting the air, land, and water, as well as endangered species and habitats. Although environmental groups are hardly new—the Sierra Club was founded in 1892—they have grown tremendously in recent years. Membership in the Sierra Club itself, for example, more than doubled between 1981 and 1989.[12]

Consumer Organizations. Consumer groups include the Consumers' Union, the Public Interest Research Group (PIRG), and the Air Passengers' Association. These groups have grown up not in response to government activity but in order to urge the government to take action. PIRG, for example, was started by the consumer advocate Ralph Nader on the basis of his success as an individual in lobbying for increased government regulation of automobile safety and other consumers' issues.[13]

Single-Issue Groups. Many groups have been formed to fight for a single issue. Such groups are found on both sides of the political divide. Examples include groups advocating or opposing abortion rights; protecting the rights and interests of the homeless, battered spouses, and children; and promoting efforts to reduce drunk driving. Single-issue groups can be particularly effective if their opposition is diffuse, poorly organized, or nonexistent, because these groups can marshal enormous energy and focus it on a single concern. When such groups oppose each other, however—as on the abortion issue—they may simply frustrate each other.

Although not technically a single-issue group, the American Civil Liberties Union (ACLU) can be classified under this heading. All of its activities are focused toward protecting the various provisions of the Bill of Rights, especially freedom of speech, separation of church and state, defendant rights, and personal privacy. The ACLU has had great success in the federal courts, although in recent years it has been countered by groups advocating conflicting values, such as victims' rights or competing interpretations of the Bill of Rights.

The latter category includes groups that stress the need for government accommodation of religion under the Free Exercise Clause of the First Amendment in cases where the ACLU emphasizes the separation of church and state under the Establishment Clause.

The entry into politics of a number of religious groups has caused considerable controversy in recent years. Like the ACLU, these groups often have a fairly broad, although interrelated, agenda. Conservative Christian groups like the Christian Coalition, Focus on the Family, and Concerned Women for America have received most of the attention, but liberal religious groups have also sprung up. An example is Bread for the World, which fights poverty and hunger across the globe.[14]

Other Citizens' Groups. One of the most important private interest groups is the American Association of Retired Persons (AARP), which despite its name welcomes the membership of anyone over fifty, retired or not. The AARP entices members with low membership fees, specialized insurance programs, and various discounts. It is extremely active in working to preserve and expand such programs as social security and Medicare.

More than 30 million Americans—many of whom are not retired—belong to the American Association of Retired Persons. Besides its political lobbying efforts, the AARP sends its members Modern Maturity *magazine and offers them medical, homeowners, and automobile insurance; a mail-order pharmacy; special pricing for on-line computer services; and, of course, hotel and motel discounts.*

Public Versus Private Interest Groups   A group that serves only the interests of its members is properly classified as a **private interest group**. However, almost every interest group serves both the private interests of its members and its own view of the public interest. Moreover, many groups justify their actions and issue positions by claiming that they are serving the public interest. When environmentalists clashed with oil industry interests over whether to build the trans-Alaska pipeline, for example, both sides claimed to be acting for the public good—environmentalists by protecting the wilderness, oil companies by feeding Americans' need for new energy sources.[15] Does it make sense, then, to try to separate public interest groups from private interest groups?

Some political scientists think so. Jeffrey Berry, for one, has attempted to provide a neutral definition of a **public interest group**. In Berry's view, a public interest group is one that pursues policies that do not directly or disproportionately benefit the economic interests of its members. Some public interest groups pursue collective goods, such as world peace or clean air, that benefit all of society. Other public interest groups pursue government policies that benefit individuals who do not belong to the group. For example, the Children's Defense Fund (CDF) seeks material benefits for children, for example, but it can be classified as a public interest group because the children of its members or supporters do not benefit disproportionately from those benefits (indeed, the middle-class supporters of the CDF receive almost none of the benefits obtained by the organization).[16]

Berry's definition of public interest groups does not depend on any particular conception of the public interest. For example, whether groups like the American League to Abolish Capital Punishment or the Christian Coalition serve the public interest is a matter of great controversy; in both cases, the members of the group might have very different views from the public at large. However, both groups qualify as public interest groups under Berry's definition.

Many public interest groups are poorly funded, at least compared with the business groups they often must fight. Thus they must rely extensively on volunteer work and grass-roots activities, and look for ways to generate free publicity and new members. Public interest groups often find success in "outsider" strategies, which emphasize such activities as protest marches and demonstrations. Because many public interest groups represent unpopular causes, they have often had greater success in the courts than in the legislatures.

Many groups act part of the time as private interest groups and part of the time as public interest groups. Often, the group's pursuit of the public interest is merely a by-product of its primary activity. In other cases, however, private interest groups do seem to pursue collective goods even at the expense of their members' economic interest. When the American Medical Association fights for government policies to restrict cigarette smoking, for example, its actions resemble those of a public interest group. Doctors, as a group, do not benefit disproportionately from such policies, and may actually lose income as the population becomes healthier.

WHEN IT'S BUDGET CUTTING TIME, THEY ALWAYS START WITH THE EASIEST TARGETS.

The Children's Defense Fund (CDF) fits the definition of a public interest group; it aims to protect all children, whether or not their parents belong to the organization.

Interest Groups in American Politics

Although American society has always been divided into competing and cooperating interests, the development of formal interest group organizations began only in the late 1800s. The first formal interest groups were organizations of farmers, such as the Grange (or Patrons of Husbandry), founded in 1867. Farmer's groups were followed by the organization of workers into labor unions in the late 1800s.[17]

These organizations—like the many groups that followed—developed in response to changing social, economic, technological, and political conditions. Farm organizations, for example, developed in response to the depression of the 1870s, which was particularly devastating to farmers in the South and West. Similarly, labor unions developed after the industrial revolution created a permanent wage-labor force with little political or economic power of their own.[18]

Not all interest groups are formed as a reaction to changes in the political, social, and economic order. Some groups exist to bring about such changes. The original purpose of the League of Women Voters, for example, was to fight for women's right to vote. As with many movements for social change, the leaders of the women's suffrage movement were in the unenviable position of having to recruit members who were not yet aware that they needed the organization or that they could benefit from it. Little wonder, then, that the formation of such groups has been heavily dependent on the emergence of dedicated and charismatic leaders—such as Susan B. Anthony—who can project a vision of the future and mobilize an indifferent constituency.

New interest groups are continually forming, even in the modern era. The 1980s, for example, saw the emergence of gay and lesbian interest groups, largely in response to changing social mores and attitudes. The health care crisis of the 1990s, similarly, sparked a proliferation of health care groups advocating a larger or smaller role for government.

At the same time, new circumstances may push established groups out of the picture or reduce their influence. Labor unions, for example, have declined in membership and political power over the past few decades as new labor patterns have emerged. Other groups simply evolve as times change. The National Association of Manufacturers (NAM) started life in 1895 to help expand foreign trade opportunities for American business; only later did it evolve into a general probusiness lobby.[19]

Interest Group Membership

Political scientists have long argued about why people join interest groups. On the surface, the answer might seem obvious: individuals join groups to promote their own interests or to advance causes they believe in. Alternatively, they may join groups to enjoy various social benefits. These factors may be summed up under three headings:

*   *Material benefits.* Under the traditional theory, groups exist in large part to advance the material well-being of their members. Thus individuals or firms join a group to advance their own economic interests. A business might join the National Association of Manufacturers (NAM) in order to support the group's efforts to improve the business climate, and thus the firm's bottom line. Or a professor might join the American Association of University Professors (AAUP) in order to support the association's efforts to preserve academic tenure.[20]
*   *Social incentives.* Some people join associations because they enjoy the group's activities in a social sense. They like going to annual meetings or conventions, enjoy doing volunteer work in the company of others, or find political protests or demonstrations exhilarating and fun. They might also enjoy the prestige that comes with group membership. Conversely, individuals might join groups in response to social pressure from their family, friends, or coworkers.[21]
*   *Ideological incentives.* Perhaps the most important reason that individuals join groups is that they believe in what the group stands for and want to contribute to its success. They join political groups, that is, for the same reason they contribute to charitable causes. There is ample evidence to suggest that many individuals are strongly motivated by ideology or political philosophy to join groups such as the ACLU, the Sierra Club, or the many abortion groups on both sides of the issue.[22]

Members and Entrepreneurs   The traditional explanation assumes that individuals come together spontaneously in support of personal or political goals. In practice, such bottom-up mobilization is the exception, not the rule. Many groups, as the political scientist Jack Walker explains, "are begun at the instigation of leaders of large corporations or government agencies," and are established through the efforts of "entrepreneurs" who then recruit others to the cause.[23] These entrepreneurs are often single-minded "zealots" who give up the prospects of monetary gain to realize their dreams. The leaders of an organization, once it is established, can devote themselves to recruiting members.[24] The critical role

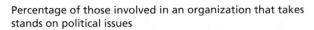

Percentage of those involved in an organization that takes stands on political issues

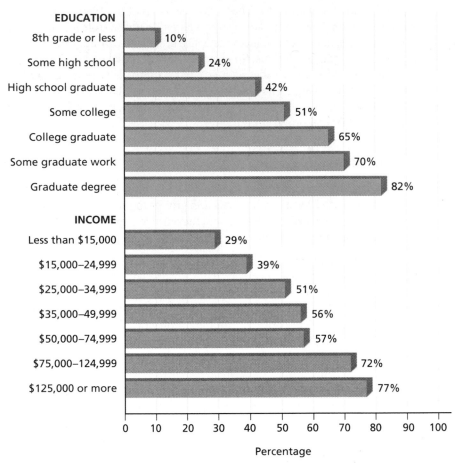

Figure 8.2 **Organizational Involvement of Demographic Groups**

Percentage of those involved in an organization that take stands on political issues

SOURCE: Kay Lehman Schlozman, "Voluntary Organizations in Politics: Who Gets Involved?" in William Crotty, Mildred A. Schwartz, and John C. Green, *Representing Interests and Interest Group Representation* (Lanham, Md.: University Press of America, 1994), p. 76.

of entrepreneurs helps explain the growth of social movements, which typically arise before their mass constituencies are aware of the need for their existence.

The Free-Rider Problem   Recognizing that groups play an active role in recruiting and retaining members helps explain what economists call the **free-rider problem**. Simply put, on close examination it is often illogical for an individual to join a group, even one that works to advance his or her self-interest. When the National Taxpayers' Union (NTU) works to lower income taxes, for example, everyone benefits—whether or not they are members of the NTU. Because lower taxes are a collective good available to members and nonmembers alike, it would seem more logical to let others join the group, and then reap the benefits anyway. This paradox is known as the free-rider problem.[25]

The possible ways around the free-rider problem are several. One explanation recognizes that members of groups do in fact receive special benefits that are not available to nonmembers. Most groups provide various material benefits to their members, including hotel and travel discounts, journals and newsletters, insurance packages, legal services, and the like. Other groups provide accreditation or legitimacy to their members; some professional groups go so far as to provide the equivalent of certification in a specific field. Some groups, such as labor unions operating under a "closed shop" rule, can effectively force individuals to join.[26]

Another approach is to emphasize the nonmaterial benefits that individuals gain from group membership. These include the social and ideological incentives discussed earlier. At bottom, it seems clear that individuals do not act out of purely material motives, but do value the nonmaterial benefits of belonging to a group.

Access to Interest Groups An important part of the elitist critique of pluralism is that some groups of citizens are systematically underrepresented in the ranks of interest group members. Political scientists have long recognized that interest group membership in the United States has a distinct middle-class bias, and that the poor, by contrast, are poorly represented. According to one study, seventy-three percent of Americans with incomes over $75,000 a year are affiliated with a political organization, compared with only twenty-nine percent of those with incomes below $75,000. Likewise, rich and middle-class Americans have more free time and more highly developed political skills than their less affluent counterparts.[27]

What Do Interest Groups Do?

In general, interest groups serve as intermediaries between the citizenry and the government. The activities of interest groups include the following.

The Power of Information Interest groups spend a great deal of time, money, and energy on information-related activities. The information flows both from the membership to the government, and from the government to the membership. Increasingly, interest groups also communicate directly with the public at large.

Informing the Government. Interest groups provide information to the government both officially (through congressional hearings, formal comments on proposed government actions, court briefs, and membership on advisory committees) and informally (through contacts with government officials, members of Congress and congressional staff, and informal correspondence).

Interest groups provide two kinds of information to the government. First, they supply government decision makers with information on how proposed or actual policies will affect their particular subgroup of the population. A government tax policy may inadvertently hurt certain farmers, for example; a farmers' association may be able to point this out early on and allow Congress to take corrective measures. Second, interest groups may provide technical information to supplement the expertise of legislative and executive officials and staff. A congressional committee might ask the American Association for the Advancement of Science for help in drafting complex provisions related to biotechnology, or a court might learn more about how the college admissions process really works by reading a brief submitted by the American Association of Colleges. Sometimes the material that interest groups prepare for the government is quite detailed and extensive. Much of the groundwork for the health care reform proposed by the Clinton administration, for example, was done by interest groups.

Informing the Membership. Most interest groups carefully monitor government actions of consequence to their memberships, transmitting the information by way of newsletters, magazines, telephone hot lines, seminars, conventions, personal contacts and the Internet. Access to such information may be an important material benefit to members.

Communicating with the Public. Interest groups also try to influence the government by appealing beyond their members to the general public. To that end, groups may use press releases, background briefings for the media, and appearances on radio and television news shows. They may also take their cases directly to the public through print or broadcast advertising. Group-sponsored information campaigns rarely present a neutral version of the facts. They frequently appeal to emotions rather than reason; and sometimes they offer information as factual that is actually either misleading or simply false.

Lobbying Congress and the Executive   Interest groups allocate much of their time and energy to trying to influence the legislative and executive branches through a wide variety of activities.

Insider Lobbying. Insider lobbying depends on one-on-one contacts between interest group representatives and government officials. Interest group lobbyists may capitalize on long-standing personal relationships with key decision makers. In the old days, lobbyists would improve their chances by backing up their arguments with fancy dinners, expensive gifts, and other direct incentives, although some of this has been eliminated by stricter ethics rules. Still, money (especially in the form of campaign contributions) plays an important role.[28]

Outsider (or Grassroots) Activities. Another way to influence government agencies—especially Congress—is through **outsider lobbying**—generating phone calls, postcards, and letters from constituents for or against a particular measure. Sometimes the members of an interest group generate such contacts spontaneously. More often, such campaigns are carefully orchestrated. Probably the most effective letters at least *appear* to be spontaneous, but typically an interest group uses preprinted postcards or standardized letters. Some groups, taking advantage of new technology, have instituted 900 telephone numbers that automatically generate a letter and charge the caller's phone bill for a contribution to the sponsoring group. Many groups also organize trips to Washington for consultation with government officials or for protest marches and demonstrations.[29]

Formal Participation in Government. Increasingly, the government has recognized and formalized the participation of interest groups in the decision-making process. In setting up a government commission, for example, Congress often mandates that representatives of the public (in practice, representatives of interest groups) play a prominent role. Interest groups are routinely invited to give formal testimony before congressional committees, and are directly involved in creating and supporting congressional caucuses (informal groups of legislators who share common interests).

Coalition Building. Interest groups are often unable to muster enough support on their own to influence public decision makers. Thus the ability of interest groups to build broad-based coalitions in support of their goals is crucial. Some coalitions are natural, and persist over time. Other coalitions are formed for a specific purpose, and last only briefly.

Some coalitions that look as though they should work in fact do not, usually because the various groups involved are unable to avoid pursuing their own conflicting interests. Environmental coalitions sometimes fail because pragmatists and purists cannot reconcile their conflicting approaches. Other coalitions that look as though they should not work in fact do, simply because the players are willing to work together for a common goal. In Florida, for example, environmentalists worked with beer wholesalers to defeat a bill that would have required seven-ounce beer bottles. Environmentalists were opposed to the extra waste such a bill would produce; beer wholesalers were opposed to the extra packaging costs they would incur.[30]

Government by Subgovernment. The power of interest groups to influence government policy is greatly enhanced by the decentralized structure of American political institutions. Because power is dispersed among so many individuals and institutions, virtually every interest group can find powerful friends somewhere in government. Such alliances can operate with great autonomy and independence.

The most important players in the Washington power structure are congressional subcommittees and executive agencies. As we will see in later chapters, both the legislative and executive branches are highly decentralized. Congress is divided into hundreds of *subcommittees,* each of which exercises power over a narrow field of policy, while the executive bureaucracy is divided into even more bureaus, offices, and agencies, each with a specific mandate and purpose. Moreover, the subcommittees and their related agencies work closely together in both developing and implementing policy, and generally share a common set of priorities and purposes. Thus the House Subcommittee on Livestock, Dairy, and Poultry (a subcommittee of the Agriculture Committee) works closely with the Department of Agriculture (DOA) to support federal programs to aid dairy and livestock farmers. Not surprisingly, the chairman of the subcommittee in 1997–1998 was a congressman from California, a leading dairy state, while the ranking Democratic member was from Minnesota, also a leading producer of agricultural products.

It should come as no surprise, then, that the American Dairy Association—an interest group made up of dairy farmers—would find a receptive welcome from both DOA and the Livestock Subcommittee. And since the policy decisions made by this triumvirate are unlikely to be overturned either by the full Congress or by the White House, it is able, in effect, to make government livestock and dairy policy all by itself.

Combinations of like-minded executive agencies, interest groups, and subcommittees are known as **subgovernments.** They arise from the increasing complexity of government and the consequent tendency toward specialization in and out of government. A subgovernment, according to the political scientist Richard Rose,

- is focused on a particular policy area, such as education, defense, or transportation;
- includes representatives of more than one branch of government;
- is relatively stable through time;
- involves continuous bargaining among its members; and
- tends to resist direction from outside organizations such as the White House.[31]

Because three key players take part in each subgovernment (a congressional subcommittee, an interest group, and an executive agency), and because they are difficult for outsiders to penetrate or influence, subgovernments are also known as *iron triangles*.

The subgovernment system has obvious implications for the behavior of interest groups. First, interest groups seek out allies in both the executive and legislative branches, allowing them to operate almost exclusively on friendly turf. Second, interest groups typically avoid direct confrontations with opposing groups, since they are unlikely to win while playing on someone else's field. A better strategy is to try to neutralize the policies of opposing subgovernments by creating countervailing policies through a different subgovernment.

Some political scientists discount the importance of subgovernments. Hugh Heclo, for example, suggests that a better model involves loose "issue networks." In contrast to subgovernments, issue networks involve many participants, none of whom dominates the others. The participants are less interested in shaping policy for their own material benefit than in fulfilling their "intellectual or emotional" commitments. Moreover, issue networks "operate at many levels, from the vocal minority who turn up at local planning commission hearings to the renowned professor who is quietly telephoned by the White House to give a quick 'reading' on some participant or policy." In short, advocates of the issue network approach see Washington as more fluid and less clearly structured than do those who favor the subgovernments model.[32]

Going to Court   An interest group that is unable to have its way in Congress or the state legislatures—perhaps because other interest groups are simply too powerful—can sometimes achieve success by taking its case to court. In modern times the courts have shown great sympathy to minority interest groups, especially those that for one reason or another are frozen out of the policy-making process. Congress has actually encouraged this trend by making it easier for interested parties to get into court, and by continually enacting vague legislation that must be applied and interpreted by the judicial branch.

Politically Disadvantaged Groups. Groups that espouse unpopular positions or are underrepresented in the political process often find it useful to go to court. The American Civil Liberties Union, for example, won a Supreme Court case against prosecuting flag burners. Subsequently, a majority in Congress voted to overturn the decision, but the Court ruled again in favor of allowing protesters to burn the flag. Other groups that have used the courts effectively include racial and religious minorities, women, and groups representing prison inmates and the institutionalized mentally ill.

The legal approach is not always effective. In recent years, a more conservative Supreme Court has been reluctant to rule against legislative majorities in favor of underrepresented groups. Gay rights groups, for example, suffered a serious setback in 1986 when the Supreme Court refused to extend constitutional protection to homosexual conduct.[33] Likewise, civil rights groups have met with one defeat after another in cases involving affirmative action; in 1995, for example, the Court cast doubt on the constitutionality of federal set-aside programs designed to aid minority businesses (see the discussion in Chapter 5, p. 137).

A defeat in court does not preclude further appeals to the legislative and executive branches. After the Supreme Court held in 1974 that pregnancy benefits were not required under federal laws governing health insurance, for example, women's groups successfully lobbied Congress to reverse the decision.[34] Similarly, in 1991, a coalition of civil rights groups succeeded in overturning a series of Supreme Court decisions that had hampered enforcement of civil rights.[35] The legal strategy does carry a serious risk, however. An adverse Supreme Court decision may create a precedent that hardens opposition to the group's position not only in the judicial branch but in the legislative and executive branches as well. Because a judicial setback may be harder to reverse than a defeat elsewhere, liberal interest groups in particular have become more selective in deciding what cases to bring before the Supreme Court.

Use of the Courts by Conventional Groups. Unpopular and underrepresented groups are not the only ones to go to court. Research suggests that the groups most likely to use the courts are "the wealthy and established groups that seek court favor for conservative purposes," including the protection of members' business or professional interests.[36] The reasons are clear: going to court costs a great deal of money, and is an especially appropriate strategy when large amounts of money are at stake. In addition, despite much discussion of Supreme Court cases like *Brown* v. *Board of Education* that shake up the status quo, the nature of the legal process makes it easier to use the courts to maintain existing social and political arrangements than to create new ones. As Walker points out, "If a group has been buffeted about by the winds of political change and stands to be blown around in the future by changes in administrations, then having precedent on its side can be an enormously stabilizing force."[37]

Money and PACs   Most interest groups have associated **political action committees** (PACs), which make campaign contributions to congressional and other candidates. These contributions typically do not buy votes, but they do buy *access*. During the 1990 deliberations over the Clean Air Act, for example, the vice president of General Motors met with a key member of Congress for four hours, while the Sierra Club got only thirty minutes.[38] PACs are limited by law to contributing a maximum of $5,000 per candidate per election. Most PACs donate to incumbents, regardless of party, because incumbents are more likely to win than their opponents (in part because incumbents have better access to PAC money). Some PACs cover their bets by contributing to both the incumbent and the challenger. The role of PACs is discussed more fully in Chapter 10.

The Power to Protest   Another important way that interest groups can influence politics is by engaging in highly public forms of political protest. "Taking to the streets" is a time-honored way for citizens to make their feelings known both to the government and to their fellow citizens. Some political protests occur spontaneously and provide a way for unorganized interests to express themselves in the political process. The urban riots of the 1960s, for example, clearly brought into focus the problems of America's cities in a way that would have been impossible through the ordinary forms of lobbying. Other political protests are carefully orchestrated by organized interest groups. The civil rights marches of the early 1960s, for example, were tightly organized by groups such as the Southern Christian Leadership Council.

Political protests are closely associated with the activities of social movements, such as the civil rights movement. In some cases, spontaneous political protests may lead to the creation or strengthening of organized pressure groups, as clients take their political activities from the streets to the corridors of power in Washington.

The Changing Character of Interest Groups

The behavior and character of interest groups have changed dramatically in recent decades. These changes are directly related to the broader changes in American politics and government since the 1950s. In particular, interest groups have had to adapt to the tremendous expansion of federal government power in every area, to the increasing complexity of government policy issues and the decentralization of power in Washington, and to the declining strength and influence of the major political parties. In addition, interest groups have taken advantage of advances in technology to expand their power and influence.[39]

Responses to the Expansion of Federal Power

Proliferation of Interest Groups   The sheer number of interest groups has increased dramatically over the past several decades as the federal government has broadened its agenda. When the federal government's role in shaping health policy was small, for example, a few key interest groups (such as the American Medical Association) were sufficient. In the 1990s, by contrast, the federal government is the dominant player in the health policy arena, and scores of interest groups have risen to the occasion. Active health policy interest groups now include representatives of the elderly, the poor, and the uninsured; labor unions; education groups; and hospitals, doctors, and other health care professionals.

Another reason for the increased number of interest groups is the mobilization of new groups that had never before been involved in lobbying activities. Such groups include universities, state and local governments, gays and lesbians, and groups representing women and disadvantaged minorities.

As more and more groups have become involved in the governing process, they have increasingly congregated in Washington. Older groups have moved their headquarters to

Conservative Christians— like these members of the Christian Coalition—are among the many citizens who have formed specialized interest groups in the 1980s and 1990s.

Washington, or opened large Washington offices to cope with their increased focus on lobbying activities.

Responses to Increased Complexity and Decentralization

Rise of Single-Issue Groups   As new groups have formed, they have become increasingly specialized. A narrow policy focus allows a group to fit more easily into the decentralized subgovernment structure, and gives it more clout over policy issues that demand great expertise. Moreover, single-issue groups may find it easier to attract and organize a loyal membership base and attract media attention. The first factor has given rise to single-issue groups in areas such as health care and environmental protection. The second has encouraged the proliferation of groups focused on high-profile issues such as abortion and gay rights. Sometimes the two factors operate together to produce ultra-specialization: one active player in the health policy area is the Gay Men's Health Crisis, Inc., which bills itself as "the oldest and largest AIDS organization in the U.S., providing services, education and advocacy for men, women, and children with AIDS."[40]

Sometimes a single-issue group finds that its issue has disappeared from under it—either because the group was hugely successful or because it failed completely. Instead of dissolving, such a group can often change its focus. For example, the National Association for the Reform of Abortion Laws (NARAL) worked in the 1960s to convince the states to create more liberal abortion regulations. When *Roe* v. *Wade* made abortion legal in all fifty states, NARAL changed its name and focus (but not its initials) and became the National Abortion Rights Action League.

Increased Penetration of Interest Groups into the Formal Structures of Government
Over the years, the government has encouraged interest groups to take on official or semiofficial roles in the political process. These roles go beyond participation on government boards and advisory commissions and informal relationships with congressional committees. Many federal programs, for example, require and encourage the participation of citizens' groups in the decision-making process. The Senate now routinely relies on the professional judgment of the American Bar Association in evaluating judicial nominees. Some federal laws are enforced by groups or citizens authorized to act as "private attorney generals," bringing lawsuits on behalf of the public. Many interest groups, in fact, receive federal funding in the form of grants or contracts, allowing them to dispense with their memberships altogether, becoming, in effect, private extensions of Congress or the executive branch.

Increased Role of Lawyers and Specialized Lobbyist-Law Firms   As policy issues become more complex, lawyers must play an increasingly bigger role in the lobbying process. The Washington "lawyer-lobbyist" is nothing new, but their enormous numbers are unprecedented. In addition, whereas lawyer-lobbyists used to be seasoned Washington lawyers who could put their experience and contacts to good (or profitable) use, they are now being recruited out of law school for that very purpose.

Responses to the Declining Strength of Political Parties

Campaign Finance   Political action committees (PACs), which are often extensions of interest group organizations, play a major role in providing campaign funds to congres-

Figure 8.3 **Number of Political Action Committees, 1974–1995**

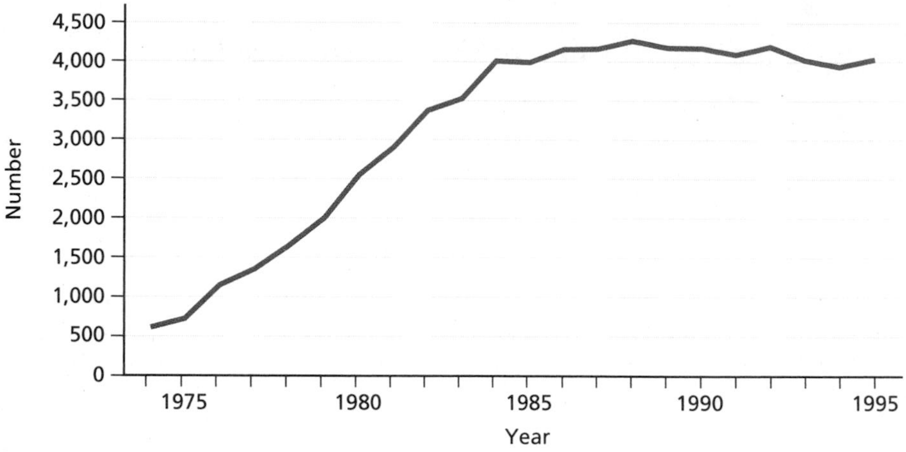

SOURCES: *Statistical Abstract of the United States*, 1997, Table 468, p. 292; 1994, Table 454, p. 291; 1992, Table 442, p. 274; 1988, Table 456, p. 253.

sional and other candidates. The funds replace the money that was previously raised by the political parties. PACs are controversial because of their tendency to support incumbents, and because of the possibility (or at least the appearance) of vote-buying.

Campaign Activities Since many political activists are affiliated with interest groups rather than with the traditional political parties, candidates often find it useful to establish good working relationships with friendly groups in order to attract loyal campaign workers and advisers. Liberal interest groups now play an important role in providing staff support to Democratic candidates, and conservative groups play a similar role for many Republican candidates. One interest group that has sparked considerable controversy for its work on behalf of Republican candidates is the officially nonpartisan Christian Coalition, which actively supports candidates who favor a conservative line on issues such as abortion, gay rights, and school prayer.

Responses to Advances in Technology

Small "mom and pop" groups have become increasingly important. Anyone with a computer, fax machine, telephone, and some office space (even at home) can become an effective lobbyist. By taking advantage of high-tech equipment, small interest groups can greatly enhance their ability to influence the political system. Advanced technology decreases the overhead involved in producing newsletters, coordinating letter-writing and telephone campaigns, and managing fund-raising and membership tasks. Not only can small, low-budget operations compete with larger, better-funded groups, but they may actually be better able to compete because they can be more flexible and more focused.

High technology is a contributing factor in the proliferation and specialization of interest groups. Small overhead makes a wide membership base unnecessary and allows a group to concentrate on a narrow issue that attracts a small but determined following.

The Bureaucratization of Interest Groups

In the past few decades, interest groups have become an integral part of the Washington establishment. Professional staff members move effortlessly between private sector lobbying jobs and positions in government, either on the Hill or in the executive branch (at higher levels, as the next section suggests, new ethics rules make such moves less effortless). Interest group staff members may also move easily from one interest group to another, representing children one year and farmers the next. Rarely are the power players amateur members of the associations they represent. More likely they are full-time, professional Washington insiders.

This is not to suggest that all lobbyists are "hired guns" who have little interest in the groups they represent except a weekly paycheck. Many are deeply committed to the causes they espouse. Young men and women come to Washington to work for agencies or organizations that match their own political viewpoints, at least in a general way. Then their views are confirmed or even hardened by the constant reinforcement of political warfare, and their job prospects are largely limited to the agencies or organizations within their political network and experience. Exceptions occur, but it is far more likely that a staffer will move within either the liberal or conservative network than between them.

The political views of an organization's professional staff are thus influenced at least as much by the culture and subcultures of Washington as by the actual members of the organization. Increasingly, Washington interest groups have come to believe that they should not simply reflect the views of the membership but actively help to shape them. As issues become more numerous and more complex, it becomes more and more the job of the Washington office to identify the issues that affect the membership, and to interpret and explain those issues to the members in ways they can understand.

Ironically, it is now possible for the Washington office of an association and the membership at large to find that their interests and viewpoints have grown apart! Usually discovered only after some sort of crisis, this divergence of interests can lead to dramatic confrontations. Members may quit, reducing the organization's budget (and the number of employees), and forcing the Washington office to decide whether to close the gap.

In the late 1970s, for example, the American Civil Liberties Union faced a severe crisis when it decided to defend the right of the American Nazi Party to march in the predominantly Jewish suburb of Skokie, Illinois. The ACLU's position was entirely consistent with its mission to protect the First Amendment, and with the views of the organization's leadership and Washington staff. However, a large part of its membership felt differently. Many ACLU members were Jewish, and had joined not purely out of concern for the First Amendment but to support a broader liberal agenda. They were appalled that their dues money was going to defend avowed Nazis. Torn between its historical mission and its membership, the ACLU chose the former, suffering a severe reduction in dues revenue and a consequent shrinkage in its operating budget.

A similar incident, although with different results, occurred in 1989. The American Association of Retired Persons decided to lobby Congress to pass the Medicare Catastrophic

Does Interest Group Pluralism Promote Democracy?

The debate over whether the interest group system promotes or hinders democracy has occupied political scientists for more than four decades. On the one side are the pluralists, who believe that the interest group system provides the best and perhaps the only mechanism for effective popular government. On the other side are their critics, who argue that the interest group system is systematically biased in favor of certain groups, most notably the well-off and well-connected.

At its heart, the controversy over pluralism raises the same set of issues faced by the Federalists and Antifederalists in the 1780s. In the *Federalist* No. 10, James Madison dismissed Antifederalist concerns about the disproportionate influence of small factions; such groups, he wrote, would be easily controlled by the democratic process. Both pluralists and their critics agree that Madison understated the importance of small groups in the political process, but the two sides propose very different ways of dealing with them. Pluralists would balance the influence of small groups by forcing them to compete with numerous other groups; their critics insist on more aggressive measures to ensure that interest groups are not allowed to achieve their purposes at the expense of the public.

Yes: Interest groups promote democracy

To pluralists, restricting the freedom of interest groups is both wrong and unnecessary. Instead, they argue that the interest groups system is the only way to determine and achieve the public interest. Moreover, they deny that the system is hopelessly biased in favor of a "governing elite."

Democracy is about bargaining and compromise, not a simplistic notion of majority rule. Like Madison, pluralists resist the idea that democratic politics is well served by the simple process of majority rule. Instead, they contend, a viable democracy should allow all citizens to have a say in the making of public policy, and provide a mechanism through which those in power can modify and adapt policy to serve the interests of all, and not only those of the majority. By allowing a variety of interest groups to influence the political process at various points, the interest group system forces policy makers to consider a wide range of perspectives and to develop policies that many different groups can live with. Thus, one group might be influential in the legislature, while another might find success in the bureaucracy or in the courts. In any event, the fundamental right of free association cannot be abridged in any democratic society.

No single "governing elite" runs the country. In a famous study of politics in New Haven, Connecticut, in the 1950s, the political scientist Robert A. Dahl found that different groups were active and influential in different areas of policy, and that no one group controlled policy making across the board. As Jeffrey M. Berry summarizes Dahl's findings, "Although most citizens might be apathetic about most issues, many do get interested in the issues that directly affect them. Businessmen were very active in urban development; teachers, school administrators, and the Parent Teacher Association (PTA) were involved in school politics. Politicians, always on the lookout for supporters, would court groups, trying to build their own resources. Consequently groups representing different interests were not only active, but their support was sought and their views carried weight." Dahl's conclusions, though based on research in one city some forty years ago, still represent a valid analysis of the American political system.

The rise of citizens' groups and other public interest groups balances the interest of corporate and other elites. Although corporate and professional interests do contribute large sums of money to politicians and although their views carry great weight, the influence of these elite groups is counterbalanced by the presence of citizens' groups and other public interest groups. Despite their enormous lobbying effort, for example, tobacco companies have consistently lost ground to antismoking and health groups. Likewise, industrial interests have been unable to stymie the environmentalist movement, which carries great weight with lawmakers and which has won major victories for clean air, clean water, and the protection of wetlands and of endangered species.

The public interest can be determined and achieved only through the clash of interest groups. The test of a democratic political system, in the end, is whether it carries out policies that advance the interests of the public. But there is no magic way to determine the public interest. Pluralists argue that a democratic system must, by definition, leave the determination of the public interest up to the people. But because every group of citizens has its own view of the public interest, the only effective way to determine the public interest is through the competition and cooperation of interest groups. Those who attack pluralism on the grounds that interest group politics creates policies that run counter to those of the public must provide some other mechanism to resolve the fundamental question— who decides what is and is not in the interests of the public?

No: The interest group system is a threat to democracy

Critics of pluralism fall into three camps. One group condemns the interest group system because it allows a small "elite" to rule the country. A second group admits that many Americans—perhaps even a majority— benefit from interest group politics, but argues that the system's "middle-class bias" excludes the poor and the disadvantaged from gaining their fair share. A third group suggests that interest group politics operates mainly to reinforce the *status quo*, making political

change difficult and strengthening the position of those who already hold power and influence.

The interest group system is biased in favor of the rich and the well-connected. It is hardly difficult to prove that corporations and the well-off dominate the system of interest group politics. "The flaw in the pluralist heaven," wrote the political scientist E. E. Schattschneider in 1960, "is that the heavenly chorus sings with a strong upper-class accent."[2] In sheer numbers and in the amount of money contributed to politicians, groups representing businesses far outweigh groups representing other interests. The influence of the "haves" is seen in countless policies adopted by the government—including a variety of general and specialized corporate subsidies that total hundreds of billions of dollars a year.

The system allows the middle class to prosper at the expense of the poor and disadvantaged. Many critics of pluralism focus not on the system's supposed bias toward the rich, but on its bias *against* the poor. In a word, they argue that the interest group system is heavily weighted toward the middle class. The tax system, for example, is rife with tax breaks that primarily benefit those in the middle class. Thus, home owners can deduct mortgage interest, but renters cannot deduct rent. The reason for the middle-class tilt in the system is easy to see—the have-nots in American society are poorly organized and lacking in resources; furthermore, their inability to move the system creates discouragement and disillusionment and makes it even less likely that they will participate.

Politics under the interest group system is fundamentally resistant to change. Many groups were created to protect existing benefits, not to seek new ones; senior citizens' groups, for example, were formed largely to dissuade the government from making changes in social security and Medicare. On the whole, as the political scientist Theodore J. Lowi has written, the interest group system is inherently conserv-

(continued)

ative—that is, resistant to new ideas and to the influence of new groups.‡ Thus except under extraordinary circumstances, the American political system permits only minor, or incremental, changes. A politician who attempted to make wholesale changes in American education, for example, would face the wrath of countless well-funded and well-entrenched education groups, from the American Federation of Teachers to the National School Boards Association—and probably give up the effort.

Even if the interest group system were not biased, it discourages politicians from pursuing the broader interests of the nation as a whole. Even if all groups were represented equitably, critics contend, the pluralist system would still suffer from a fatal flaw. Interest group politics encourages politicians and policy makers to look at public policy from the point of view of satisfying particular group inter-

ests, instead of from the perspective of the public interest. The outcomes of such a process, as Lowi noted, are chaotic and even contradictory. Governments based on interest-group pluralism "cannot plan," he wrote in 1969. "Planning requires law, choice, priorities, moralities." The interest-group system, by contrast, "replaces planning with bargaining."§ So too, say critics of pluralism, the interest group system abandons any effort to take a long-term view of the whole society, substituting the dubious process of interest group bargaining for the public interest.

*Robert A. Dahl, *Who Governs?* (New Haven: Yale University Press, 1961); Jeffrey M. Berry, *The Interest Group Society*, 3rd ed. (New York: Longman, 1997), p. 10.
†E. E. Schattschneider, *The Semi-Sovereign People* (New York: Holt, Rinehart, and Winston, 1960), p. 35.
‡Theodore J. Lowi, *The End of Liberalism*, 2d ed. (New York: Norton, 1979).
§Ibid., p. 101.

Coverage Act of 1988. The act replaced private insurance to supplement Medicare with a government-sponsored program. Under the act, supplemental insurance was supplied to everyone on Medicare; recipients were charged according to their ability to pay. As part of a compromise, the AARP agreed that the program would be completely funded by the elderly, at no additional cost to young or middle-aged taxpayers.

The Catastrophic Coverage Act was a catastrophe for the wealthy and middle-income elderly. Under the old system, they received Medicare and then could buy their own supplemental insurance. Under the new plan, they were *forced* to buy supplemental insurance and, worse yet, had to pay a premium to cover the poor elderly who could not afford to pay. For the wealthy and middle-class elderly, the result was more or less the same coverage at much higher cost.

Overall, the act was arguably in the interests of retired people, as the AARP's position suggested. The problem was that the AARP's membership base was precisely the middle-class and wealthy elderly (or soon-to-be-elderly) who were hit hardest by the new plan. The membership rebelled, flooding congressional offices with thousands of letters a week and subjecting the AARP to a relentless torrent of abuse. A year later, the AARP officially reversed its position, went back to Congress, and obtained a repeal.[41]

These examples are isolated, but they reflect a growing trend: Washington interest groups are often more liberal—or more conservative—than the memberships they represent. A related problem is that interest groups may reflect the views of their dues-paying members, but not of the broader groups they claim to represent. The National Organization for Women, for example, is not representative of all American women, and the National Rifle Association is not representative of all gun enthusiasts. Since the perception that a group represents a base broader than its dues-paying membership is critical to its ability to wield power, groups have an incentive to close, or at least hide, the gaps between themselves and their broader constituencies.

The traditional assumption that interest groups directly represent the views of the broader citizenry must, at a minimum, be carefully qualified. Many Americans seem increasingly skeptical of "special interest groups" and may have reached the conclusion that interest groups are just another part of the Washington establishment.

Interest Groups and Ethics

The role of interest groups in American politics raises serious ethics questions for government officials and lobbyists alike. Moreover, the **Ethics in Government Act of 1978** made minimum ethical standards a matter of law, and included both civil and criminal penalties for violations. However, critics argue that the standards established by the Ethics in Government Act are far too weak and permit widespread unethical activity to continue unabated.

Ethical issues involving lobbying fall into two categories: the trading of money and other favors for preferential treatment; and the "revolving door" between the government and outside pressure groups.

Lobbying and Money

Money may or may not be the root of all evil, but it is certainly at the heart of ethical issues in lobbying. Simply put, campaign contributions and gifts from lobbyists to government officials present the obvious danger that money will be traded for favors, in the form of preferential legislation or special treatment. The problem is especially acute in the case of Congress, since many members depend on political action committees to supply the large sums of money needed for their reelection campaigns.

Since 1925, it has been illegal for a corporation to give a federal executive official a gift, loan, or anything else of value. Various statutes and congressional rules regulate gifts to executive and legislative officials and require public disclosure of various financial transactions.[42] These restrictions have eliminated some of the old-fashioned ways of doing business; lobbyists no longer roam the halls of Congress handing out envelopes stuffed with $100 bills. But current rules contain big loopholes and provide many opportunities for questionable activities. In the late 1980s, for example, congressional ethics investigators found that five senators had acted improperly or exercised poor judgment when they met with a federal bank regulator and urged him to withdraw a regulation limiting certain real estate investments by savings and loans. The regulation, it turned out, was especially damaging to the Lincoln Savings and Loan, whose owner was Charles Keating. All five senators had received large campaign contributions from Keating; one had received more than $1 million over the course of his career. Exposure of the deal led to a long investigation by the Senate Ethics Committee, which eventually found one senator guilty of breaking ethics rules and the other four of giving "the appearance of being improper" or simply of "poor judgment." The "Keating Five" scandal led to calls for tighter ethics rules and congressional campaign finance reform but resulted in no definite action.[43]

A broader scandal erupted in the midst of the 1996 presidential campaign, when it was revealed that foreign governments had made illegal contributions to the Democratic National Committee in an effort to influence the outcome of the election (later reports revealed that smaller amounts of money also found their way into the coffers of the Republican National Committee). Although the parties returned the money in question, these revelations brought into focus for many Americans the potentially dangerous influence that interest group money can have on the political system.

Interest groups have always been involved with political contributions, but the problem became especially acute in the 1980s and 1990s, after federal campaign finance reforms limited individual contributions but created loopholes through which interest groups, acting through political action committees (PACs), could provide large amounts of money to political candidates. Between 1977 and 1994, for example, PAC contributions to House and Senate candidates increased by some 500 percent. Interestingly, the pattern of PAC contributions shows that interest groups are interested less in electing friendly candidates than in obtaining access to those who are likely to win. Thus PAC contributions to Republican candidates increased dramatically after the Republicans gained control of Congress in 1995. In 1993–1994, when the Democrats controlled Congress, the Republicans picked up only 49 percent of PAC contributions. In 1995–1996, after they gained control, the Grand Old Party's share of PAC contributions increased to 63 percent.[44]

As if the problem of PAC giving was not bad enough, the situation was compounded in the mid-1990s by the emergence of so-called "soft money" contributions to the major political parties. Because these dollars are donated not to candidates or campaigns but to the parties themselves—ostensibly for non-campaign-related activities—they are technically exempt from federal campaign contribution limits. By the 1995–1996 election cycle, soft money giving had grown to a staggering $263 million. Philip Morris, a major tobacco company, led the list with contributions of over $3 million—nearly 85 percent of which went to the Republicans.[45]

Trading votes for money is clearly improper, at least if done explicitly. But it is not improper for interest groups or individuals to contribute to congressional or presidential campaigns, nor is it improper for politicians to look after the interests of their constituents. When a longtime contributor asks his or her representative to sponsor a particular piece of legislation, it may be wholly appropriate for the representative to comply. Much depends on context and circumstance.

In any event, there is little doubt that under current law and practice "money not only can make the difference but can make a huge difference," as the Republican pollster

Richard Wirthlin puts it. "People make decisions based upon the way they see the world, and the way they see the world is conditioned by the information they have; and money can influence not only the information they have but also the perceptions they have, and therefore influences who wins and loses."[46]

The Revolving Door

In Washington, as elsewhere, contacts are the key to power. Being on intimate terms with key political figures is perhaps the greatest asset a lobbyist can have. And there is no better way to achieve it than to have been a key political figure yourself. Hence the revolving door: the back-and-forth movement of powerful insiders between top government positions and private lobbying organizations.

The Ethics in Government Act aimed to shut the **revolving door,** or at least partly close it. Under current law, senior government officials are barred from lobbying their former agencies for one year. Other restrictions limit former government officials from trying to influence the government on matters on which they participated while in government service. In addition, an executive order issued at the beginning of the Clinton administration barred senior White House officials from

- lobbying during the five years after they leave government any agency where they have served or which they have had any responsibility for as a member of the White House staff;
- engaging in any activity on behalf of any foreign government at any time after they leave government service; or
- representing any foreign government or foreign corporation in any way within five years of being involved in a trade negotiation on behalf of the U.S. government.[47]

The Ethics in Government Act has ended the most obvious and outrageous abuses of the revolving door, but it has hardly eliminated the problem altogether. Government officials still routinely move from top positions in government to powerful and well-paid positions in the private sector. For example, despite the Clinton administration's strict ethics guidelines for White House aides, a number of individuals who worked for Clinton in Arkansas or during the transition period before he took office accepted lucrative positions as lobbyists and have used their White House connections on behalf of paying clients.[48]

Summary

Interest groups are voluntary associations of citizens that attempt to influence governmental decision making in a variety of ways. The members of a particular interest group typically share a common economic or ideological interest. The first formal interest groups were organizations of farmers, such as the Grange (or Patrons of Husbandry), founded in 1867. Farmers' groups were fol-lowed by the organization of workers into labor unions in the late 1800s.

Interest groups are most commonly classified according to the policy areas in which they operate or the causes they represent: agriculture, business, labor union, environmental or consumer protection, and the like. An alternative, proposed by the political scientist Jack L. Walker, is to distinguish between groups on the basis of their history and social structure. Walker classifies interest groups as profit sector, nonprofit sector, mixed sector, or citizens' groups.

A complementary approach is to distinguish between public and private interest groups. According to the political scientist Jeffrey Berry, a public interest group is one which pursues policies that do not directly or disproportionately benefit the economic interests of its members. An example of a public interest group under these criteria would be the Children's Defense Fund.

Individuals join interest groups for a variety of reasons, including material, social, and ideological benefits. Typically, interest groups are founded by entrepreneurs, who establish the organization first and seek members second. The leaders of an interest group use a variety of methods to recruit and retain members. Understanding that individuals get both material and nonmaterial benefits from interest groups helps explain the free-rider problem, which asks why individuals would join a group when they could get many of the benefits without the costs of joining. In the aggregate, however, interest group membership does not reflect American society as a whole, but is disproportionately biased toward the middle and upper classes.

Interest groups participate in a variety of different activities. Most important, they act as conduits of information between the people and the government, in both directions; lobby the executive and legislative branches on behalf of particular legislation or regulations; work with congressional subcommittees and executive agencies as part of a subgovernment; bring court cases; and donate money to political campaigns.

Interest groups have changed greatly in recent decades, in response to changes in the size and structure of government, in the nature and role of political parties, and in technology. They have also been subjected to new, tighter ethics rules imposed on both lobbyists and government officials.

Whether interest groups strengthen or weaken American democracy remains a topic of debate. Those who follow in the tradition of James Madison argue that interest groups threaten to undermine democracy by leading government away from the pursuit of the public interest. Those in the tradition of pluralism, by contrast, argue that interest groups play a vital role in ensuring fair and broad representation of all Americans before their government.

Key Terms

Interest group
Private interest group
Public interest group
Free-rider problem
Insider lobbying
Outsider lobbying
Subgovernments
Political action committees (PACs)
Ethics in Government Act of 1978
Revolving door

Review Questions

1. What are interest groups? What is the difference between organized and unorganized interests in society?

2. How do political scientists classify interest groups? How are public interest groups distinguished from private interest groups?

3. What roles do interest groups play in the American system of government? How do interest groups interact with the three branches? With the electoral process?

4. How have the roles of interest groups changed in recent decades? What are the causes of these changing roles?

5. What ethical concerns are raised by interest group activities? How have government rules and legislation sought to allay these concerns?

6. Why do the followers of James Madison fear the influence of interest groups? Why do pluralists argue that interest groups are vital to democratic government?

Suggested Readings

Berry, Jeffrey M. *Lobbying for the People: The Political Behavior of Public Interest Groups*. Princeton: Princeton University Press, 1977.

Cigler, Allan J., and Burdett A. Loomis, eds. *Interest Group Politics*, 4th ed. Washington, D.C.: CQ Press, 1995.

Key, V. O. *Politics, Parties, and Pressure Groups*. 5th ed. New York: Thomas Y. Crowell, 1964.

Lowi, Theodore J. *The End of Liberalism: Ideology, Policy, and the Crisis of Public Authority*. New York: W. W. Norton, 1969.

Olson, Mancur, Jr. *The Logic of Collective Action: Public Goods and the Theory of Groups*. Cambridge, Mass.: Harvard University Press, 1965.

Verba, Sidney, Kay Lehman Schlozman, and Henry E. Brady. *Voice and Equality: Civic Volunteerism in American Politics*. Cambridge, Mass.: Harvard University Press, 1995.

Walker, Jack L., Jr. *Mobilizing Interest Groups in America: Patrons, Professions, and Social Movements.* Ann Arbor: University of Michigan Press, 1991.

Wilson, James Q. *Political Organizations.* New York: Basic Books, 1973.

Internet Resources

Lists of and links to nearly 600 political interest groups at:

http://www.politicalindex.com/sect10.htm

Project Vote Smart, which collects performance evaluations of members of Congress by various interest groups, at:

http://www.vote-smart.org/ratings/

The non-partisan Center for Responsive Politics, which provides information on campaign contributions by hundreds of political action committees representing various interest groups, at:

http://www.crp.org/spnew.htm

★9★
Political Parties

Running for political office is never easy, but for minor party candidates the road is particularly uphill and steep. Minor party candidates have no established voter base, are usually underfunded, and must struggle to attract media recognition and coverage. Just getting on the ballot is difficult; in most states, minor party candidates must run an obstacle course that requires them to obtain thousands of signatures, each of which can be checked and potentially ruled invalid by the major party officials who control the state elections office.

Consider Pennsylvania, for example. When Robert B. Surrick sought to run for justice of the Supreme Court in 1993 on the Patriot party ticket, he had to obtain the signatures of 56,641 Pennsylvanians—2 percent of the total number of votes received by the candidate who won more votes than any other at the last general election, whether for state or national office. Surrick was forced to carry this heavy burden even though his party was a direct offshoot of the presidential campaign of H. Ross Perot, who won nearly one million votes the year before.

Surrick and the Patriot party challenged Pennsylvania's strict ballot access rules in federal court, claiming that they violated the Equal Protection Clause of the United States Constitution. The court agreed, ruling that the 2 percent rule was arbitrary and illogical, and thus unconstitutional.

Surrick and the Patriot party may have won the battle, but they lost the war. Despite its ruling in their favor, the court made it clear that the state had broad authority to set the rules for ballot access. The state had legitimate interests in avoiding "ballot clutter" and keeping frivolous candidates off the ballot, the court noted. Thus it could impose heavy burdens on minor party and independent candidates.

"While it is true that third parties do play a significant role in our country's political development," the court concluded, the interests of third parties must be balanced against the interests of the state. Moreover, Pennsylvania could legitimately distinguish small political parties from those that have "historically established broad support." Small parties trying to make the giant leap to major party status thus have to overcome a catch-22: until they can document "historically established broad support," they can be relegated to minor party status; but until they are accorded major party status, achieving such support may be next to impossible.[1]

Reform party candidates Ed Zschau, Richard Lamm, and Ross Perot, who vied for the party's 1996 nomination. Not surprisingly, the winner was Perot, whose personality and money helped put the party on the map after the 1992 election.

★ ★

Political parties were essential to the development of modern democracy. They helped bring politics to the people, providing an effective way for the people to participate in government. Parties simplified the choices available to voters, and allowed voters in different parts of the country to come together for common purposes. They provided key links between the electoral process and the governmental process, and between the executive and legislative branches. In sharp contrast to interest groups, as the political scientist E. E. Schattschneider argued in 1960, parties aimed to bring together a majority of voters into a coalition designed to advance the public interest.[2]

American political parties today, however, are but distant cousins to their counterparts of earlier eras. For 150 years, the American party system was closely controlled by party leaders and local party bosses, who could count on virtually automatic support from an electorate accustomed to voting a straight party line.

To many voters, switching parties, even in a single election, was tantamount to treason. Parties today are far weaker. Party bosses have been stripped of their dictatorial powers, in favor of a chaotic but open system in which all Americans can participate. Many Americans now vote a "split ticket" and would regard straight party voting as an abandonment of their civic duty to vote on the basis of issues and candidates. Yet these trends, combined with lower voter turnout, the rise of television, and the growth of interest groups, have also increased the power of extremist groups within the major parties and opened the door to third-party or nonparty candidates, such as H. Ross Perot in 1992 and 1996.

The transformation of American political parties and of the American party system has proceeded apace with changes in other aspects of American politics. This chapter traces the changes in the party system and links them to broader changes in the system as a whole.

Questions to Keep in Mind

▸ *What is meant by the American "party system"? What are the characteristics and functions of American parties?*

▸ *How does the modern American party system differ from the party systems of the past?*

▸ *How do parties contribute to self-government? Why are some analysts concerned about the declining influence of parties?*

Basic Concepts ★ ★ ★ ★ ★ ★ ★ ★ ★ ★ ★ ★ ★

A **political party** is a broad organization of officeholders, party workers and activists, and rank-and-file voters whose goal is to win elective offices and control the institutions of government. Parties can be distinguished from interest groups by their focus on winning elective offices and by their emphasis on uniting various groups and interests into a broad and successful coalition.[3]

American political parties consist of small national organizations and even smaller state and local affiliates; national and state political figures who give the parties both formal and informal leadership; and thousands of citizens who support the parties financially and through volunteer work. In addition, millions of Americans simply identify with a particular party or support it zealously or occasionally at the polls.

The Framers and Political Parties

The Framers viewed political parties with disdain, equating them with petty intrigues and decrying their corrosive effect on reasoned decision making. They equated political parties with factions—groups of citizens bound together to advance their own interests at the expense of the public (the word "party" derives, after all, from "part"). In the *Federalist Papers* and in their other writings, the Framers almost always used the word in a negative way.

The Framers, however, knew nothing of political parties in the modern sense. The Federalists and Antifederalists were not political parties, but informal collections, as one scholar puts it, of "local groups, factions, leaders and cliques." The creation of modern political parties in the early 1800s was, at least in part, an effort to find a substitute for the kind of factional warfare that had characterized politics in the early days of the Republic.

At their best, modern political parties work toward the broad political goals favored by the Framers. They bring order and stability to the political system by integrating the mass of voters into the system while providing structure and predictability. They reinforce the Framers' theory of representation by giving voters the opportunity to make choices between competing conceptions of the public interest, and they provide a mechanism to move political decision making away from the state and local level and toward the national arena. At their worst, of course, political parties can heighten the differences between groups of voters, and reinforce the voters' tendency to act on emotion rather than reason.

The Framers' evaluation of modern political parties would thus depend on the role parties play in the American political system. In a word, if parties make it easier and more likely that voters will form factions and abandon the public interest, they present a danger to American democracy. If, however, they help combat what James Madison called "the mischiefs of faction," they may do the political system a great service.

The Idea of a Party System

Political scientists focus not just on the activities of individual political parties, but also on how the various major and minor parties interact with one another and how those relationships change over time. The set of relationships between the political parties of a particular country at a given moment in time is known as a **party system**.[4]

Party systems vary from country to country, and over time within a country. A party system is characterized by the number and relative influence of the major and minor parties, the extent to which the parties can control their own candidates and officeholders, the relative stability of the governing coalition, and the degree to which the parties inspire loyalty and commitment from the voters.

The dynamics of a particular party system depend on both legal and cultural factors. Perhaps most important are the laws and rules governing the selection of candidates for public office. For example, the **winner-take-all system** prevalent in the United States encourages the creation of a kind of party system very different from the **proportional representation (PR)** method used in most European countries. In most American elections, whoever wins the most votes—even without an absolute majority—wins the election. Losing candidates, by contrast, win nothing. In a PR system, the percentage of seats a party controls in the legislature approximates the percentage of votes received in the election. Thus a party that receives 10 percent of the votes nationwide would be allotted 10 percent of the seats in parliament. (The actual numbers may not match exactly. In particular, most PR systems establish a floor below which no seats are assigned. A party with only 2 percent of the popular vote might receive no seats at all; more popular parties would have proportionally higher representation.)

By rewarding parties that win relatively small percentages of the vote, PR systems encourage the creation of many small parties. The American system, by contrast, discourages the creation of small parties and strengthens the two major parties.

Cultural factors are important, too. Are voters generally centrist, or do their political views tend toward one extreme or the other? Are they responsive to single-issue parties, or do they prefer a more general approach? Do typical voters identify strongly with a particular party and remain loyal to that party over time? Or do they remain independent, and commonly vote for candidates of different parties?

Role of Parties in Democratic Government   Political parties are not essential to a functioning democracy. No political parties existed in the United States before the adoption of the Constitution, and even today many elections for school boards, judgeships, and other local offices are contested on a nonpartisan basis. But political parties do make it easier for ordinary citizens to participate in politics, and may make democracy more efficient, stable, and legitimate.

At the broadest level, political parties contribute to democratic government by fulfilling these key functions:

- *Providing a mechanism for mass participation in politics.* "Competition among political parties," as the political scientist V. O. Key wrote, is "the only way so far contrived" by which the people can "give or withhold their consent to authority." In this classical viewpoint, parties play an essential role in allowing the mass of ordinary citizens to participate effectively in the political process. However, not everyone agrees that parties truly empower all citizens, especially in the United States; the political scientist Walter Dean Burnham, for example, stresses that American parties have always been "overwhelmingly middle-class in organization, values, and goals," thus leaving other voters—and especially the poor—essentially unrepresented.[5]

- *Simplifying political choices and clarifying alternatives.* The average citizen has limited time and energy to devote to politics. Parties reduce complex or difficult decisions to clear-cut choices between two or more alternatives. Thus they enable citizens to express their views on candidates or issues in a convenient shorthand that captures the essence, if not every detail, of their general philosophy of government.

- *Consolidating and articulating the positions of the majority and the minority.* In a large and diverse country, it is easy for the citizenry to be divided into numerous factions or interest groups, with none commanding a majority of the electorate. By identifying key issues and forcing diverse groups to work together to gain control of the institutions of government, parties provide a mechanism that allows those in the majority to express and implement their views. In addition, the party system provides a way for those in the minority to express their views and to challenge for control of the government.

- *Bridging the separation of powers.* In earlier periods of American history, the political parties helped to bridge the constitutionally mandated gap between the legislative and executive branches. Before 1968, Congress and the White House were usually controlled by the same party. Under such circumstances, parties provided a key link between the policy-making branches and helped prevent inefficiency and stalemate. In the modern era, however, divided government has become the norm. Since 1969, the same party has controlled the White House and both houses of Congress for only six years. Under a divided government, parties reinforce, rather than bridge, the gap created by the separation of powers.

- *Integrating local or regional politics into a national system.* Without political parties, politicians and voters in different states may have little in common, making national politics inefficient and national decisions difficult. Parties provide a key link among local, state, and national political systems and make it easier for politicians from different parts of the country to work together for a common purpose.

- *Legitimating political decisions and political conflict.* When a national political party wins control of the machinery of government, it can plausibly claim to act on behalf of the majority of the nation—giving its decisions the aura of legitimacy. Equally as important, parties provide a way of channeling political conflict, ensuring that opposition to the policies of the government are not seen as challenges to the political system itself. By channeling conflict into elections, parties may moderate that conflict, decreasing the likelihood of violence and civil war.

The American Party System

The United States has traditionally had a two-party system. Generally speaking, that is, only two major parties have existed at any given time in American history. For more than a century, the major parties have been the Democrats and the Republicans.

The Democratic and Republican parties have survived so long because they have been extremely adaptive to changing circumstances. Both are and have always been broad coalitions of diverse interests, united by a common but often hard-to-define core. Rarely have the parties defined themselves except in the most general terms. Still, as a British journalist once wrote, "Parties have characters. . . . We should feel the weave of the parties between our thumbs and

Two-Party Versus Multiparty Systems

The American two-party system has inspired praise bordering on reverence from political scientists and politicians alike. "The fundamental requirement of accountability" in a democratic system, wrote a committee of the American Political Science Association in 1950, "is a two-party system in which the opposition acts as critics . . . presenting the policy alternatives that are necessary for a true choice in reaching public decisions." A two-party system ensures that parties "appeal to the general public broadly on matters of general interest," rather than to special interest groups or narrow factions.

Comparatively speaking, however, two-party systems are the exception, not the rule. Most democracies—including Italy, Israel, the Scandinavian countries, and Germany—have *multiparty systems.* Under the electoral system known as proportional representation, parties can gain parliamentary seats by winning relatively small proportions of the vote. Following the 1997 elections in Norway, for example, the parliament consisted of representatives of the following parties:

Labour party	65 seats
Progress (antitax) party	25 seats
Christian People's party	25 seats
Conservative party	23 seats
Centre (Agrarian) party	11 seats
Left Socialists	9 seats
Left (liberal)	6 seats
Independent	1 seat

To control a majority of seats and thereby be able to form a government, even the largest party in a multiparty system must typically enter into a coalition with smaller parties. In the Norwegian case, for example, at least two parties would have to combine to form a majority.

Whether a two-party or a multiparty system is better is impossible to say; much depends on the individual country. Parties in Sweden, Norway, Finland, and Germany have had little difficulty in forming stable coalition governments in the post–World War II era; the Italian party system, by contrast, has been marked by confrontation and animosity, resulting in fifty-three different governments since 1945! Israel, likewise, has run into difficulties at times with its fragmented and deeply divided multiparty system. Israel has two major parties at roughly even strength, but neither with a majority. Thus various small parties hold the balance of power in Israel's parliament and have often been able to extract concessions from the major parties in exchange for support. At other times, Israel has been forced to resort to a highly volatile and unstable coalition between the two major parties.

The main advantages of a multiparty system are that voters have clear electoral choices, and that small groups of voters can be directly represented in the national legislature. Parties in a multiparty system can afford to be different; in fact, many small parties thrive on their distinctiveness. The Norwegian Centre party, for example, appeals almost exclusively to farmers. With only around 7 percent of the vote, the party could hardly compete at the national level in a two-party system. In the Norwegian system, however, the party can provide a clear and effective voice for its constituency. American farmers, by contrast, must choose between Democrats and Republicans, neither one of which is centrally focused on agrarian issues.

Supporters of the multiparty approach also point out that such a system might increase voter turnout, since it provides a viable alternative to voters who do not want to vote for either major party. The presence of minor parties can also help "clarify the policies, programs, and the lines of accountability of the major parties," writes Theodore J. Lowi. Finally, if more than two parties competed for the presidency, the odds would be high that the election would be thrown into the House of Representatives, forcing presidents to court members of Congress before the election and increasing the possibility of effective cooperation between the two branches afterward.

SOURCES: Theodore J. Lowi, *The Personal President: Power Invested, Promise Unfulfilled* (Ithaca, N.Y.:Cornell University Press, 1985), pp. 195–208; W. Phillips Shively, *Power and Choice: An Introduction to Political Science,* 4th ed. (New York: McGraw-Hill, 1995), pp. 209–212. Data from the Norwegian election of 1997 updated by author.

forefingers. We should be able to rub them and know their texture, or, to change the image, to smell and taste them, and know their vintages. Parties have color, they have bouquet, they have flavor."[6] This section gives some sense of the character of the American party system.

The Two-Party System   The two-party system can be traced back to the earliest days of the Republic, when the nation split between the Federalists and the Antifederalists. The Democratic and Republican parties have been the predominant parties since the Civil War era.

Why Two Parties? Two factors have contributed to the existence and persistence of the two-party pattern. First, the rules and laws that govern the American electoral system discourage the creation of third parties and make it difficult for them to achieve real success. Even gaining access to the ballot can be a problem for a new party. Typically, parties that have never been on the ballot before must obtain thousands of signatures, each of which must withstand the scrutiny of major party officials searching for the most minor technical errors. Once on the ballot, a third party candidate must actually win a majority of the votes cast, or at least more than anyone else, to claim success. In American electoral politics, winning is everything; there is usually no reward for second place.

Second, American political culture is not conducive to the formation of narrowly focused parties. Multiparty systems are more likely to form in countries that are deeply splintered along regional, ethnic, religious, economic, or cultural lines. Although American politics is hardly free from such tensions, different groups generally have been able to join together in broad-based, inclusive parties to work for their common interests.

Third Parties in American History. Third parties have often played a key role in American politics, especially in raising important issues that the major parties were unwilling or unable to confront. The Republican party, created in 1854 as an antislavery party, quickly became a major party in its own right, toppling and absorbing the Whig party.

Even the most successful third parties in American history have generally found that real achievements were possible only through a merger with a major party. Thus the American Independent party, which nominated Governor George Wallace of Alabama on a states' rights, antibusing, and anticrime ticket in 1968, was largely absorbed into the Republican party under Richard Nixon. Similarly, the Progressive party, which achieved some success in the 1920s under the leadership of Wisconsin Senator Robert La Follette, was folded into the Democratic party under Franklin D. Roosevelt.

Party Identification   **Party identification** refers to the voters' tendency to associate with a particular political party, or with no political party. Party identification can be strong or weak and can be expressed in a variety of ways. In some states, voters may select a party affiliation when they register to vote. Other ways to express party identification are by giving money to the party, attending party functions, and participating in a primary election. Alternatively, party identification may be simply a question of whether a voter feels an affinity with one party or the other.

When political scientists measure party identification, they typically measure it in this last, weakest sense. Even so, 35 percent of Americans classify themselves as independents (or independent Republicans or Democrats). By contrast, 34 percent call themselves strong or weak Democrats, and 31 percent strong or weak Republicans. In all, only 31 percent of Americans classify themselves as strong Democrats or strong Republicans.[7]

Party identification has a strong impact on voters' decisions. In 1996, for example, 84 percent of self-described Democrats voted for Democratic presidential candidate Bill Clinton, while 80 percent of self-described Republicans voted for Republican candidate Bob Dole. In the 1994 congressional elections, the numbers were similarly lopsided: fully 90 percent of Democrats and 93 percent of Republicans stayed with their party's candidate.[8]

The number of voters who strongly identify with one party or the other has not changed dramatically over the past forty years. However, the number of independent voters is greater today than in the past. Overall, the number of independents has increased from 23 percent in 1952 to 35 percent in 1994, while the number identifying as strong or weak partisans has dropped from 75 to 65 percent. The evidence suggests that the American electorate was slightly more parisan in 1996 than in 1992.[9]

The Weakness of American Political Parties   Although the two major parties have shown great staying power, they are weak in comparison with political parties in other countries and have become even weaker in modern times. American parties are particularly weak in that they lack the internal cohesion and discipline to carry out policies systematically or over the long term. The weakness of American political parties stems from two principal factors: the constitutional framework in which the parties operate, and the rules governing nominations and elections.

The American constitutional system weakens political parties through both the separation of powers and federalism. In other democracies, a political party need only control the lower house of parliament to carry out its program. Even to begin making policy, by contrast, an American party must gain control of both the House and the Senate, and, unless they have enough votes to override a presidential veto, the White House as well. Even then, the party's efforts can be frustrated by the federal courts or the states.

The rules governing nominations and elections also tend to weaken the parties' ability to enforce cohesion and discipline. Compared with parties in other democracies, American parties have relatively little influence over candidates and elected officials. If a candidate or official deviates from the party line, the party can do little about it. Renomination and election depend not on the party leadership but on the candidate's ability to attract a personal following. Promotion to higher office depends on the candidate's electoral skills and on his or her per-

Table 9.1
Party Identification of the Adult Population, 1952–1994

	SD	WD	ID	Ind	IR	WR	SR	A
1952	22	25	10	6	7	14	14	3
1962	23	23	7	8	6	16	12	4
1972	15	26	11	13	11	13	10	1
1982	20	24	11	11	8	14	10	2
1992	18	18	14	12	12	14	11	1
1994	15	19	13	10	12	15	16	1

SD = Strong Democrat; WD = Weak Democrat; ID = Independent Democrat; Ind = Independent; IR = Independent Republican; WR = Weak Republican; SR = Strong Republican; A = Apolitical.

NOTE: Numbers may not sum to 100 due to rounding.
SOURCES: Warren E. Miller and Santa Traugott, *American National Election Studies Data Sourcebook, 1952–1982* (Cambridge, Mass.: Harvard University Press, 1989), p. 81; *Statistical Abstract of the United States,* 1994, p. 286.

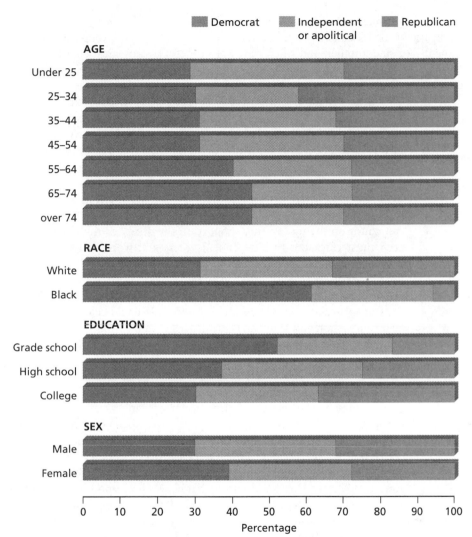

Figure 9.1 **Political Party Identification, 1994**

NOTE: Independent category includes those who describe themsleves as independent Republicans or independent Democrats. Republican and Democratic categories include strong and weak identifiers.

SOURCE: 1997 *Statistical Abstract,* Table 460, p. 287.

sonal relationship with the president or other officials. A member of Congress must answer to his or her constituency at home—not to the party leadership in Washington, the president, or local party officials. Candidates are not typically dependent on the party for money or support, and are free to modify or reject the official party position on any issue.

The system is very different for candidates and public officials in most other democracies. In England, for example, nomination for public office depends entirely on maintaining a good relationship with the party leadership. Likewise, a disloyal member of Parliament has almost no chance of gaining a cabinet position, becoming prime minister, or receiving a knighthood or other honor.

Decentralized Character of American Political Parties. Both major American parties are actually broad coalitions of state and local parties. These state and local parties operate independently of one another, and often have very different ideological characteristics. Many southern Democrats, for example, are ideologically closer to northern Republicans than to northern Democrats.

To accommodate these diverse elements, American political parties must be relatively open, avoiding specific "litmus tests" for party membership. The various state and local parties need to work together only when organizing the party leadership in Congress and during a presidential campaign. At other times, they can go their separate ways.

Centrist Character of American Political Parties. The existence of a weak, two-party system practically guarantees that American political parties will seek the middle of the road, at least in the long term. Neither party can count on the unwavering support of a majority of the electorate, so each must reach out to independent voters and weak party identifiers. Moreover, every four years the major parties must try to hold together broad and diverse coalitions across the fifty states. Both of these considerations put a premium on inclusiveness and compromise.

Twenty years ahead of his time, the conservative Barry Goldwater ran as the Republican candidate for president in 1964. Backers of President Lyndon Johnson, playing on the voters' fear that a vote for Goldwater would risk nuclear war, countered Goldwater's slogan with their own: "In your heart you know he might."

Consider abortion, for example. Although Republicans are generally against abortion and Democrats are generally in favor of personal choice, these lines are hardly absolute, and both parties include candidates and officeholders on both sides of the debate. Moreover, both parties have made an effort to reach out to voters who are ambivalent on abortion or who take a centrist position. In the 1992 campaign, the Republicans made a major point of allowing prochoice speakers to appear at their national convention (unfortunately for the Republicans, this point was largely lost on the general public, who focused instead on the stream of "profamily" speakers). In 1988, George Bush softened his position on abortion, suggesting that the law refrain from punishing women who seek abortions. And in 1992, Dan Quayle, admitting that he would support his daughter if she decided to obtain an abortion, called for dialogue and education rather than a hard line. Similarly, candidate Bill Clinton struggled to tone down his party's prochoice position, calling abortion a "necessary evil" and advocating programs that reduced the number of abortions while keeping them legal.

There are clear differences between the Democratic and Republican parties. But neither party is a bastion of ideological purity, and both must guard against adopting extremist positions that would endanger their ability to appeal to a majority of the electorate.

Party Structure   The Republican and Democratic parties are organized along similar lines, although there are differences at the level of detail. The rules under which each party operates are set by its national convention, held in every presidential election year. The conventions are best known for selecting and adopting the parties' presidential and vice presidential candidates and for adopting the party platforms, or statements of policy and principle. But they are also responsible for setting forth the rules under which the party operates and for overseeing the operations of the party in a general way.

The day-to-day responsibilities of the two parties are handled by national committees. The Democratic National Committee (DNC) consists of 404 members, including the top-ranking man and woman in each state party; 200 additional members apportioned among the states on the basis of population and Democratic vote in the last presidential election; and a variety of other state and national politicians and party activists. The Republican National Committee (RNC) has only 165 members, appointed on the basis of equal representation for each state (each state, along with the District of Columbia, Guam, Puerto Rico, and the Virgin Islands, has three representatives: a national committeeman, a national committeewoman, and the state party chairman). Both the DNC and the RNC are headed by a national chairperson (the RNC sticks with the more traditional title "chairman"). The chairpersons of each party are officially elected by the national committees, although the party in control of the White House traditionally leaves the selection of the chair up to the president.

Both the Democratic and Republican committees are major operations, with large budgets and numerous full-time employees. A major function of the committees is to raise money, especially for congressional and presidential campaigns. Under federal law, the party committees are authorized to spend approximately $12 million each in "coordinated party expenditures" on behalf of their presidential nominee. The parties spend far larger amounts (so-called "soft money") for party-building activities, which are supposed to include voter registration, get-out-the-vote drives, and the like. In practice, the line between "hard" and "soft" money is often difficult to determine. Large amounts of money are also channeled to state and local parties for similar efforts.[10]

Party Activities   Above all, American political parties exist to contest and win elections. To do so, the parties must maintain their loyal base of voters and expand their appeal to independent voters and to those who lean toward, but are not committed to, the other side. These are complicated tasks that require considerable planning, money, time, and effort. Much of the work is handled by individual candidates and campaigns; other chores are the responsibility of the party itself. Among the many tasks that lie behind a successful political party are these:

- *Nomination of candidates.* The nomination of candidates for public office is a political party's primary function. Parties typically select their candidates through *primary elections,* in which candidates are selected directly by the voters. For state and local elections, however, there is often a shortage of candidates to compete in primary elections. In that case, party leaders must actively recruit candidates to run on the party ticket. If there is an incumbent officeholder, the primary election is often little more than a formality.
- *Fund-raising.* A party needs money to meet its operating budget and to spend on behalf of its candidates. Operating expenses, which swallow up a high percentage of state and local party budgets, include rent, utilities, postage, and paid staff, as well as the cost of holding party functions. Candidate-related expenses include support services (such as research, polling, and policy development), and special services, such as voter registration and get-out-the-vote drives. State and federal laws limit direct expenses for particular candidates (which must be charged to the campaigns themselves), but loopholes allow the parties to get around these restrictions fairly easily. Popular fund-raising activities include direct mail campaigns, telethons, and social events.

Eight Republicans squared off in the 1996 New Hampshire primary, the traditional start of the primary season. The winner was political commentator Pat Buchanan (far right), who eventually lost the republican nomination to Kansas senator Bob Dole (fifth from left).

- *Attracting and keeping voter loyalty.* Political parties must have a base of loyal voters who are committed to supporting the party's candidates against all comers. Such voters also tend to be active in party functions, and may also be a source of campaign contributions. Because the support of these voters is so important, parties must avoid taking positions that alienate them, and must deliver on the issues and programs most vital to their core constituencies. Often the need to keep the party loyalists happy creates problems in appealing to the general electorate on election day, since ordinary voters might be opposed to the positions and policies favored by party activists.

- *Research and strategy.* The party organizations work closely with elected officials and candidates to develop issue positions and overall political strategy. Exactly how this process works depends on whether the party is in power or in opposition, whether an election is imminent or far off, and whether elected officials provide strong or weak leadership. In the 1994 midterm elections, for example, congressional Republicans focused on making the vote a national referendum on the Clinton administration's proposals on health care and other issues. In 1996, by contrast, much of the planning and strategy work was handled, or at least coordinated, by the White House.

- *Media relations.* Inevitably, the parties must spend a great deal of time and energy making sure their message is getting through, and a large part of this effort involves local and national media. Party leaders appear regularly on television talk shows like *Meet the Press* and *Face the Nation,* issue press releases concerning the activities of their own party or of the opposition, and meet formally or informally with reporters and editors to provide background information. When money is available, the parties also use paid media—such as radio or television ads—to get their points across.

Parties in the American Political System

The influence of the major political parties is seen in every aspect of the American political system. The role of the parties is discussed in several other chapters of this book.

What follows is a brief summary that presents a quick glimpse of the pervasiveness of parties and partisanship in American politics.

The White House   By tradition, the president is recognized as his party's unofficial leader. He appoints the party chairman (who directs the operations of the party itself), rewards the party faithful with executive and judicial appointments, and campaigns across the country for his party's candidates. By default, his program is the party's program, and he sets the tone and substance of the party's message to the voters.

Presidential leadership in party matters is limited, however. The number of presidential appointments not subject to civil service rules (which preclude partisan considerations) numbers only a few thousand. The number of judgeships varies according to the number of vacancies, but is never enormous. Presidential influence on Congress is also limited. When party control of the White House and Congress is divided, presidents are lucky to prevail on more than half the congressional votes on which they take a clear position. When one party controls both branches, presidents do better, but they still lose 20 to 25 percent of the time.[11]

A popular president can wield great power and find great support among members of his own party who hope to benefit from the president's success. An unpopular president will find the job of drumming up party support even more difficult than usual. In the modern era, even incumbent presidents cannot count on their party's nomination for re-election, and may have to fend off challengers in a string of primaries. No president since Lyndon Johnson has actually been denied renomination (Johnson pulled out of the race when he did less well than expected in the first primary), but both Jimmy Carter in 1980 and George Bush in 1992 faced serious challenges.

If presidents feel frustrated about their lack of control over their own political party, they can take comfort from the fact that they can operate with great freedom from the party organization. Presidents may do little for their parties, but their parties also do little for (or to) them.

Congress   Party influence in Congress varies greatly depending on circumstances. Except in rare circumstances, the majority party bands together to vote as a bloc for the leadership positions, having first chosen those leaders from among themselves. On key votes, the party leaders in both the House and Senate can often pull uncertain members along through bargaining and persuasion, although they lack the ability to do so consistently. Over the past twenty-five years, the percentage of House votes in which a majority of one party votes against a majority of the other party (so-called **party unity votes**) has gone up sharply. In the 1970s, less than half of all House votes pitted the two parties against one another; in 1995, by contrast, at the height of the partisan conflict between President Bill Clinton and the congressional Republicans, party unity voting rose to an astonishing 73 percent. Although still high by historical standards, party unity voting dropped in 1996 to only 56 percent of all votes. A similar trend appears in Senate voting, with party unity votes rising to a high of 69 percent in 1995, before dropping back to 62 percent.[12]

In general, party unity in Congress has been increasing since 1970, as the Republican and Democratic parties have grown more ideological and confrontational. Party unity scores under Speaker Newt Gingrich reached the stratosphere in 1995, at least early on. House Republicans were unanimous on 73 of the first 139 roll call votes in the 104th

Congress; on only 13 votes did 10 or more Republicans defect from the party line.[13] Similar numbers were racked up in the Senate. Party unity should not be exaggerated, however. Although Speaker Gingrich was able to impose strict discipline on his troops in his 1995 effort to pass the "Contract with America," Senate Republicans helped to slow or scuttle some of the more controversial aspects of the contract.[14]

The Courts   In theory, partisanship is not supposed to enter into the judicial realm, where judges are appointed for life and are presumed to be above party politics. In practice, however, presidents typically appoint judges who belong to their own political party. Over 90 percent of Jimmy Carter's and Bill Clinton's judicial appointees were Democrats; 94 percent of Reagan's appointees, and 88 percent of Bush's, were Republicans. However, the number of judicial appointees who were active in party politics prior to their nomination to the bench is slightly lower in the Clinton era than in earlier years.[15]

Whether judges reflect their partisan backgrounds once on the bench is a complex question, better left for a later discussion of the courts.

Parties and Party Systems in American History

The history of American political parties can be divided into distinct eras, or historical party systems. Each era is marked by a relatively stable alignment of voters and parties, usually with one party in a dominant position; by a distinct set of key political issues dividing the parties; and by a widely shared understanding of the broad contours of the American constitutional system. Each of these party systems (five in all before the modern era) lasted for thirty or forty years, if not longer.[16]

The Idea of Realignment

The transitions from one party era to another have generally been marked by intense periods of political activity and conflict. Scholars disagree on the exact beginning and end points of the historical party systems, and thus over the exact length of these transitional periods. Nevertheless there is general agreement that periods like the Civil War and New Deal eras represent major turning points in American political and constitutional history, and that the nature of party politics after such episodes is markedly different from what came before.[17]

Periods of transition between the historical party systems have been described as **realignments**. Each realignment period has been marked by one or a series of **critical elections**, in which the issues involved seemed vitally important, voter interest and participation was unusually high, and ideological differences between the parties gave voters a clear choice. In general, periods of realignment have been marked by economic or social crisis, and have centered around one or more key issues, such as whether the government should allow slavery or how the government should respond to an economic emergency.

The atmosphere of crisis that surrounds one or more critical elections causes many voters to abandon their traditional party attachments. At the same time, a large bloc of new voters is suddenly drawn into the system. Thus the realignment can involve a massive shift in the relative strength of the major parties, or even the disappearance of one major party and the creation of a new one. A newly crowned majority party may sweep into Washington with a new agenda and a new mandate, dramatically changing the shape of public policy and recasting the broad outlines of the constitutional system. Realignments may produce major constitutional questions and provoke serious constitutional crises, for example, or bring about fundamental changes in the relationship between the states and the federal government, the government and the private sector, or the White House and Congress.

> *"I am not a member of any organized party—I am a Democrat."*
>
> —Will Rogers

The political attachments forged during a critical election do not dissolve easily. They reflect deeply held moral and political principles and basic feelings of right and wrong, and can guide a person's voting behavior for a lifetime. As a result of such lasting partisan attachments, the victorious party can typically look forward to ruling for an extended period, broken only by occasional losses brought about by war, scandal, or economic downturn. Elections that appear as temporary deviations from the normal voting pattern of the electorate are known as **deviating elections**.

As time goes on, the relevance of the previous realignment on political attitudes and voting behavior becomes increasingly remote. Old voters die, taking their partisanship with them to the grave. New voters may continue to vote as their parents did, but only out of habit, not from deep-seated conviction. For many new voters, politics seems irrelevant, and participation drops. Differences between the two parties may seem small or unimportant, and the issues that so excited the older generation may seem outdated or irrelevant to their children and grandchildren. When the party system reaches this stage of weakened partisan attachment, it is said to be in a state of **dealignment**. Under such conditions, the electorate may be ripe for another realignment.[18]

The First Party System

The origins of the first national party system can be seen in the debate over the ratification of the Constitution. For the first time, Americans were involved in a nationwide political campaign, with contests over the Constitution in every state. Although the different state contests were hardly coordinated in a modern sense, the focus was not wholly local. Supporters of the Constitution took the name Federalists; opponents were known as Antifederalists.

The Federalist-Antifederalist split spilled over into the new government. The Federalists' leader was Alexander Hamilton, George Washington's first secretary of the treasury. A natural political operator, Hamilton devised a clear political program and worked to secure support for it both within the executive branch and in Congress. Hamilton quickly became the leader of a distinct group in the capital, and his program was rapidly adopted. Hamilton's group supported a strong national government, led by a powerful executive branch, and generally backed the interests of business and industry. Among the policies they supported were federal assumption of state debts resulting from the Revolutionary War; a protective tariff, making it more difficult for foreigners to compete with American businesses; wholesale sell-offs of public lands; and the creation of the first Bank of the United States. The Federalists also pursued a strongly pro-English foreign policy.[19]

Hamilton's successes sparked the creation of an opposition movement, led by James Madison in the House of Representatives. Taking the name Democratic-Republicans (or just Republicans) instead of Antifederalists, Madison's group was at first defined simply by its opposition to Federalist policies. But the Federalists' strong support among the wealthy classes and their general distrust for popular majorities created a clear opportunity for the Republicans, who were able to win support by appealing directly to the people. By 1793, over 80 percent of the House was clearly affiliated with either the Federalist or the Republican cause.

Between 1794 and 1800, both sides built links between their factions in the capital and their supporters in the states. Gradually, Federalists and Republicans established connections with local politicians, coordinated candidate selection and election activities, and built up a general following. The two parties also created national and local press organs designed to promote their viewpoints. Although the Federalists dominated early on, handily winning the election of 1796, by 1800 they were deeply divided and facing a united and well-organized opposition. The election of 1800 was bitter and divisive, and ended in the House of Representatives. Ultimately, Thomas Jefferson won out over his Federalist rival, and the Federalists were swept from office.

The election of 1800 marked the beginning of the end of the first party system, although the second party system did not organize itself for several decades. During that time the Federalist party gradually withered away, and the Republicans became less of a party and more of a loose governing coalition. Gone were the tensions of the 1790s, which had fueled the growth of both parties. Party loyalty was weak among both voters and politicians, and there were few professional politicians whose fortunes depended solely on political success. Many defeated Federalists simply gave up and went home, while the victorious Republicans lost any incentive to build a permanent party structure. The first party system did not so much die as evaporate.[20]

The Second Party System

The decline of the Federalist party led to a succession of Republican presidents, all from Virginia and all with little real opposition. This "Era of Good Feeling" lasted from 1800 until the election of 1824.

With no obvious Virginian to follow James Monroe to the White House, the Republicans in Congress were unable to agree on a presidential candidate. Thus the election of 1824 was something of a free-for-all. Four presidential candidates emerged—two nominated by state legislatures, one chosen by the Republicans in Congress, and one nominated by himself. The contest came down to John Quincy Adams and Andrew Jackson, although neither was able to muster a majority of the electoral vote. In the end, the decision was left to the House of Representatives, which chose Adams.

The 1824 election was so chaotic and evoked so little public interest that it did little to rejuvenate the party system. But the close race heightened interest in upcoming presidential contests and led to the formation of a variety of party organizations at the state and local levels. The Jacksonians took the name "Democrats"; over time, their opponents became known as "Whigs." Progress in the building of a new party system was sporadic and uneven, and took place not in a single critical election but over the series of elections between 1824 and 1840. By then, two major parties had emerged—the Whigs and the Democrats. Virtually every state of the Union could boast a competitive two-party system, focused on the presidential election but affecting every political contest. For the first time, the political parties sought and found a loyal following among the mass of voters. Now both voters and politicians grew to identify with one or the other of the two major parties, and to view political issues and candidates in partisan terms.

In the three decades between 1828 and 1860, the Democrats were the majority party, the Whigs a decided minority. The Democrats controlled the White House and both houses of Congress for twenty-two of these thirty-two years; they controlled the White House for twenty-four and the Senate for twenty-eight years. The Whigs were competitive in all parts of the country and among all classes of citizens, however, and many of the elections in this era were close.

The Democrats and the Whigs were divided more by style than by substance. The Democrats, led at first by Andrew Jackson and always reflecting his influence, cast themselves as the party of the people and dramatized their opposition to economic and political elites. Jackson opposed the Bank of the United States, for example, and played up his opposition to the United States Supreme Court. Thus the Democratic party appealed to small farmers and newly arriving immigrant groups. But it also drew support from southern plantation owners, and historians have debunked the idea that Whig supporters were primarily men of wealth.[21]

The second party system differed from the first party system in several important respects. Together these differences were fundamental and make it possible to conclude that the parties of the second party system were the first "modern" political parties:

- *Presidential candidates were selected by national nominating conventions instead of by the congressional caucus.* In theory, the convention system took power from the politicians and gave it to the people. In practice, the system took power from members of Congress and gave it to professional politicians. The convention system was pioneered by the Antimasonic party in 1827 and quickly became the standard method of nominating presidential candidates.
- *The major parties became elaborate and formal organizations instead of fleeting arrangements of convenience.* The process of selecting delegates to the national convention began with local caucuses and party committees, and fostered the creation of formal organizational structures at every level. Party structures also developed in response to the increasing number and frequency of elections during this period. The party organizations were labor-intensive and grew rapidly.
- *The focus of the parties shifted from making policy to winning elections.* The emphasis in the first party system was on winning elections in order to strengthen party control of the legislative and executive branches. Party efforts thus had a strong policy orientation, and the differences between the parties were great. The professional politicians of the second party system, by contrast, were more interested in winning elections than in making policy. Between 1824 and 1856, for example, both the Whig and Democratic parties sought to avoid a sharp confrontation over slavery, an issue that divided both parties internally and thus presented a serious threat to the entrenched party leadership.

- *Political participation grew and the parties inspired great loyalty from voters and politicians alike.* The new political parties put a premium on participation and loyalty. Participation in elections grew from under half the eligible electorate in 1824 to over 80 percent in the 1840s. Millions of voters participated in party activities or attended party-sponsored social events. In time, voters developed loyalty toward their party, and began to vote strictly along party lines no matter what the office or who the candidates.

The second party system, like the first, did not last long. Instead of merely withering away, however, it imploded under the stress of the slavery question and the coming civil war. The civil war crisis resulted in a critical realignment that saw the death of the Whig party, the transformation of the Democratic party, and the birth of a new party, the Republicans. The institutional forms created by the second party system, however, would characterize the American party system until the modern era.

The Third and Fourth Party Systems

Political scientists divide the years between 1860 and 1932 into two distinct eras. The third (or Civil War) party system grew out of the Civil War and lasted until the realignment of 1896. The fourth party system lasted from 1896 until the New Deal realignment of the 1930s.

The dominant political parties throughout this period were the same—the Democrats and the Republicans. The Republican party was created in 1854, with the explicit and sole purpose of containing and eventually destroying slavery. The Republican party grew at a phenomenal pace, quickly displacing the Whigs and winning the presidency in 1860. The Democratic party survived, although in a greatly weakened condition; after the Civil War, its strength was largely confined to the South.

The third party system was delicately balanced between the Republicans and the Democrats. Although the Republicans controlled the White House for twenty-eight of the thirty-six years between 1860 and 1896, they controlled the executive branch and both houses of Congress for only twenty of those years.* Moreover, many elections in this era were excruciatingly close: in 1876, the Republican Rutherford B. Hayes received a minority of the popular vote but won by a single electoral vote; in 1880, the Republican James Garfield won by just seven thousand out of nearly nine million votes cast. The split between the two parties followed the sectional lines that had divided the nation during the Civil War: the Republicans were the party of the North, the Democrats the party of the South. The Democrats were also strong among Catholic immigrant groups in the North. The main policy differences between the parties in this period involved industrial development, with Republicans favoring high tariffs on imported goods to foster domestic industries.

Republicans solidified their control of the national government during the fourth party system, which lasted from 1896 to 1932. Their control of Congress and the executive branch was more complete than in the previous era, and their margins of victory were generally larger. During this thirty-six-year period, the Republicans controlled the White House for twenty-eight years, and the executive and legislative branches together for twenty-four years. Every presidential election won by the Republicans during this period

*The two years of Union Party control in the Thirty-ninth Congress (1865–1867) are included in the Republican total.

was won by a comfortable margin. The Republicans were the dominant party in every part of the country except the South.

The divisions between the parties in this period were complex. The Republicans represented a broad coalition of western farmers, midwestern reformers, and eastern financial and manufacturing interests. Early in this period the Republicans pushed forward a reformist agenda that included government regulation of railroads and other industries, but by the 1920s they were following a general laissez-faire, or hands-off, policy toward business. The Democrats were also divided as to the appropriate uses of governmental power. In foreign affairs the Democrats took a more interventionist approach, especially when Woodrow Wilson led the nation into World War I. The Republicans leaned increasingly toward an isolationist policy in foreign affairs.

In form and structure, the parties of the third and fourth party systems largely followed the pattern set in the second party system. There were differences, however, the most important of which were these:

Chicago's Richard Daley—"The Boss"—shown here after winning the Democratic primary for mayor in 1955. The last of the big city machine bosses, Daley ruled Chicago, and the Illinois Democratic party, for the next 25 years.

- *The growth of urban "machine" politics.* The late nineteenth and early twentieth century was a period of large-scale immigration and industrialization, both of which fostered the growth of America's cities. Party leaders found it especially profitable to integrate the immigrant groups into the party machinery, creating a fiercely loyal and powerful base. Cities, counties, and even entire states routinely came under the power of party "bosses" who controlled patronage jobs and city services. Well-run party machines organized cities ward by ward and block by block, and powerful bosses could deliver their territories on election day to the national ticket.
- *The importance of regionalism.* One legacy of the Civil War was the distinctly regional character of the party system. This regionalism reached a peak in the period just before the New Deal. Generally speaking, the Democratic party held an overwhelming advantage in the South, whereas the Republicans controlled the Northeast. Only in the border states, the Midwest, and the West was there a semblance of competition between the two parties. To take just one example: excluding 1912 (in which the Republican party split and there was a three-way race for the White House), nearly 85 percent of the total electoral votes won by the Democratic party between 1896 and 1928 came from the southern and border states.[22]
- *Overwhelming power of industrial and economic elites.* Until the New Deal of the 1930s, both political parties were under the strong influence of powerful elite interests, especially big business. Less privileged groups—small farmers, workers, and blacks, in particular—found few sympathetic ears. The major exception was in the 1890s, when rural populists seized control of the Democratic party and sought a coalition with the urban working class under William Jennings Bryan of Nebraska. Urban workers found little attraction in Bryan or his platform, however, and the opportunity vanished. The power of economic elites after 1896 was, if anything, even greater than before.

The fourth party system lasted until the 1930s. With the election of President Franklin D. Roosevelt in 1932 and his reelection in 1936, the fifth (or New Deal) party system was born.

The Fifth (or New Deal) Party System

The New Deal party system came into being in the midst of the worst economic depression in American history. In sharp contrast to its predecessors, the Roosevelt administration believed in a strong federal role in supervising and regulating the nation's economy. It reached out to the very groups that the previous party system had systematically ignored. The implications of the New Deal and its aftermath for both the nation and its political parties were nothing short of fundamental.

From 1932 until 1968, the Democrats were the dominant party in the nation. Combining their traditional base in the South with new support among farmers, workers, blacks, and other beneficiaries of the New Deal, the Democrats won every presidential election in this period except in 1952 and 1956. They controlled the executive branch and both houses of the legislative branch for twenty-six of these thirty-six years. Democrats sponsored a variety of New Deal programs involving government intervention on behalf of workers, farmers, and consumers, and established the government's "safety net" of programs to protect the poor, the unemployed, and the elderly. After 1948, the Democrats turned increasingly toward the protection of blacks and other minorities, a policy shift that eventually helped undermine the party's traditional support among southern whites.

The fifth party system brought about significant changes in the nature of American party politics. Ironically, the policies of the New Deal helped weaken the role of both major parties in American politics:

- *Nationalization of politics.* Over the long term, the new activism of the federal government weakened the power of local party leaders. Before the New Deal, local party

In the 1939 classic film **Mr. Smith Goes to Washington**, *Jimmy Stewart stars as a naive country bumpkin who becomes a United States Senator and then takes on the corrupt political leaders in control of his home state. Released during the New Deal, the movie reflected public concerns that the political system was controlled by party bosses and powerful economic elites.*

bosses held sway by providing patronage jobs and other services to their constituents; now benefits flowed directly from Washington. State and local parties were further weakened by national policies designed to impose national standards and national norms—the most obvious but by no means the only example being civil rights.

- *Weakening of political parties.* As the federal government's expanded role became an accepted way of political life, the very success of the New Deal operated to weaken the political parties, Democratic and Republican alike. By the 1960s, government benefits such as social security and unemployment compensation were no longer tied to the success of the Democratic party, but became permanent "entitlements." The economic stability and prosperity of the 1950s and 1960s further weakened the bonds that held together the old New Deal coalition.

The Modern American Party System

At some point between 1960 and 1980, the old New Deal party system gave way to the modern party system. The transition was gradual rather than dramatic, and in some ways is still ongoing. In part, the modern party system represents merely an extension of trends that were evident even at the height of the New Deal system. In other ways, the modern party system represents a brave new world whose contours are as yet unclear and whose features are still evolving.

Above all, the modern American political system is characterized by a sharp decline in the power of parties and party leadership. As little as thirty years ago, parties and party leaders still exercised great power over both the people and the politicians. In the modern era, the power of the leadership is weak and sporadic at best. The decline of parties is evident across a range of political institutions and at every level.

- *Weakened partisan attachments and the rise of split-ticket voting.* Past party leaders commanded great loyalty from the voters. With a loyal electorate and a strong party organization, they could deliver the votes to candidates for positions from water commissioner to president. Only the catastrophe of a critical realignment could shake the leadership's hold on the reins of power.

  Today, many voters display little loyalty to either major political party. Instead of voting a straight party ticket, voters today often make individual judgments on each race. **Split-ticket voting** is common, and more and more Americans describe themselves, or at least act, as political independents.

- *Divided government.* A natural consequence of the decline of straight-ticket voting is **divided government**. In the past, one party typically controlled both the White House and Congress, and usually the majority of state governments as well. In the modern era, divided government has become the norm. Between 1969 and the present (counting Bill Clinton's term through 2001) the Democrats and Republicans have divided control of the presidency and at least one house of Congress more than 80 percent of the time.

- *Disappearing influence of state and local party leaders and political bosses.* In the past, politicians knew how important it was to keep state party leaders and local party officials happy. Now most politicians have established independent bases of support, both in Washington and at home, and can afford to thumb their noses at the local leadership.

Was There a Realignment in the 1990s?

The 1990s have been a dramatic roller-coaster ride for the nation's two major political parties. The Democratic party's impressive victory in 1992 gave it control of the White House and of both branches of Congress for the first time since 1980; Democrats claimed a broad mandate for new policies, including the creation of a new federal health-insurance system. By 1994, however, the Democrats were in disarray; the Republican party, led by Georgia representative Newt Gingrich, capitalized on voter discontent with politicians in Washington and seized control of Congress for the first time in forty years. For a brief moment the Republicans were ascendant, but in 1996 the Democrats regrouped, with president Bill Clinton defeating Republican candidate Robert Dole and becoming the first Democrat to win a second full term in office since Franklin Roosevelt in 1937.

The shifting momentum throughout the 1990s has led both parties—and some analysts—to claim that the American party system has undergone a realignment for the first time since the 1930s. At the same time, many political scientists doubt that a realignment has occurred, or will ever occur again.

Yes, the 1990s were a period of realignment.

Those who suggest that a realignment has indeed taken place point to four main pieces of evidence:

The shift in party control of the major branches of government, especially Congress. The Democratic stronghold on Congress lasted from 1954 until 1994, and was one of the characteristic features of the post-New Deal party system. The Republican victory in 1994 was thus a highly significant event. And although the Republicans' grip on Congress is by no means unbreakable, even a shifting balance of power between the two parties in the House is itself indicative of a major change in the party system. Meanwhile, the presidency—solidly under Republican control throughout most of the 1980s and all of the 1990s—has become highly competitive.

Major changes in each party's regional base. The Republicans, once a non-entity in the South, have now emerged as the dominant party in the region. As recently as 1990, Southern Democrats outnumbered Southern Republicans in the House by 95 to 47; by 1997, Republicans had moved ahead by 83 to 66. Likewise, the Republicans have made major gains in the West; outside of California, the Grand Old Party now leads in the House by 28 to 13 seats, compared with a Democratic advantage of four seats in 1990. The Republicans have made similar gains in the presidential and senatorial contests, as well as in governorships and lesser state offices.

Changes in individual and group voting behavior. The changes in partisanship among key population groups in the 1980s and 1990s have been dramatic. Between 1984 and 1992, for example, 33 percent of self-described conservatives voted Democratic; in 1994 and 1996, that number dropped to well below 25 percent. Likewise, the percentage of southern whites who voted Democratic dropped from around half in the 1980s to barely a third in 1994. There have been swings toward the Democrats as well, though they are less dramatic: 61 percent of voters without a high school degree voted Democratic between 1984 and 1992, compared with 68 percent in 1994 and 1996.*

The transformation of public policy. As in previous periods of realignment, all of these changes in voting behavior and in the strengths and weaknesses of the parties have led to significant changes in public policy. The "Republican revolution" of 1994 forced President Bill Clinton to move significantly toward the right in a number of areas—agreeing to pursue a balanced budget, abandoning his quest for national health insurance, and embracing a variety of tax cuts. Even before 1994, Clinton adopted a number of positions which had previously been advocated by Republicans—taking a tougher stance on crime, for example, and pushing for a major overhaul of the welfare system.

Even if the Republicans do not maintain their control of Congress, and even if they do not recapture the White House, much of their agenda has already been enacted into law. Moreover, the Republicans have defined the terms of the debate, forcing the Democrats to follow suit.

No, the 1990s were not a period of realignment.

As impressive as these arguments are, many political scientists doubt the existence of a 1990s realignment. Although they do not deny the validity of the arguments presented by the other side, these analysts argue that the American political system has changed so fundamentally since the post-New Deal era that a classical realignment is no longer even possible. They point, in particular, to these differences between the modern era and past periods of realignment:

Voters show little real loyalty to either party, and seem to favor divided government Unlike in the past, modern voters are fickle; many are apt to change their party preferences from one election to the next, and even to split their vote between the two parties when voting for different offices in the same election. Thus many analysts believe that the 1980s and 1990s are a period not of realignment, but of *dealignment*. Moreover, exit polls taken after the 1996 election suggested that many Americans were not unhappy about this divided result; fully 38 percent of the electorate told pollsters that it is better for the country to have divided government than to have the same party control both the legislative and executive branches.[†]

The 1994 and 1996 elections lacked the intensity characteristic of critical elections. Although voter turnout in 1992 was higher than in any presidential election since 1968, it dropped sharply in 1996, when, for the first time since 1924, under half the eligible electorate bothered to vote. Even in 1994,

when the Republican "Contract with America" outlined the party's policy goals in sharp contrast to the positions of the Democratic party, voters were largely uninterested. A November 1994 poll revealed that only 34 percent of Americans had even heard of the Contract, much less knew what it contained.[‡]

Despite a great deal of noisy rhetoric, the two parties are close together on most issues. In sharp contrast to prior realignments, when the parties presented the voters with a clear choice on at least one critical issue, there are relatively few meaningful differences between the Republican and Democratic parties today. Clinton and the congressional Republicans have agreed on the major outlines of the federal budget, on the welfare overhaul, on crime legislation, and on cutting taxes. Although the parties have different views on some social issues (such as abortion and affirmative action), on other issues the differences are more apparent than real. For example, President Clinton embraced the idea of voluntary school prayer, as long as it is not sponsored by the government, and has advocated various mechanisms to keep children from viewing pornography on the Internet.

Recent elections provide little useful guidance as to what will happen next. In past realignments, a major victory by one party in a critical election ushered in a long period in which politics was stable and predictable. By contrast, the elections of the 1990s have resolved nothing. Future elections are likely to be decided not by a continuation of existing patterns, but by short-term and idiosyncratic factors—such as the state of the economy, the popularity of particular candidates and office-holders, and the occurrence of political scandals or foreign policy crises.

*Walter Dean Burnham, "Realignment Lives: The 1994 Earthquake and Its Implications," in Colin Campbell and Bert A. Rockman, *The Clinton Presidency: First Appraisals* (Chatham, NJ: Chatham House Press, 1996), p. 378; "Who Voted For Whom in the House," *The New York Times*, November 7, 1996, p. B3.
†CNN *National Exit Poll*, November 5, 1996
<http://allpolitics.com/1996/elections/natl.exit.poll/index2.html>
‡*The Gallup Poll Monthly*, November 1994.

Most important, local party leaders have lost the power to control the nominations process for local, state, and national offices. Under the old system, a member of Congress who did not pay proper deference to the party boss at home could wind up bumped off the ticket and forced to run as an independent. Now, because almost all party nominations are determined by primary elections, a politician can safely ignore party bosses.

- *Rise of third party and nonparty candidates.* The 1992 candidacy of the Texas billionaire H. Ross Perot was the most successful third party campaign since 1912. In reality, Perot's "United We Stand America" movement was not a party at all. It held no convention, adopted no platform, and existed less to nominate Perot than to support his already-existing candidacy. Perot created a number of new state parties in order to comply with ballot access requirements, but his campaign was a completely personal one and left little in the way of a lasting organization or structure.

  Perot's success as a protest candidate was due to several factors beyond the millions in personal funds that he pledged to the campaign. Although many Americans were uncomfortable with Perot himself, most were willing to vote for a man and not a party. Television provided Perot with a way of reaching millions of Americans without the need for an extensive network of party workers and connections. Whatever else Perot proved, he demonstrated that the right candidate at the right time could actually win a presidential election as an independent or third party candidate—an unthinkable notion as little as a generation ago.

- *Increasing influence of interest groups and intraparty factions.* The declining influence of party leaders on the nominations process created a vacuum that others have moved in to fill. For instance, in the Republican party of the late 1980s and early 1990s, Representative Newt Gingrich (R-Ga.) developed an extremely well funded political action committee—known as GOPAC—which helped recruit, train, and fund candidates for House seats across the country. When Gingrich's efforts paid off in 1994, he was rewarded with an army of new representatives who were fiercely loyal both to him and to his ideological program. Thus Gingrich was able to enforce strict loyalty from and control over his troops.[23]

  Gingrich's success in galvanizing the Republican party in 1994 does not signal a return to the earlier era of strong party bosses. Instead, it underscores the weakness of traditional party leaders, who must now cope with highly powerful factions—or groups within parties—which are becoming increasingly strident and ideological, making it even more difficult for the parties to remain inclusive, broad-based coalitions. As the Republican party has become increasingly conservative in recent years, for example, the differences between its competing conservative factions have become increasingly pronounced.

Democrats and Republicans Today

All of these factors have contributed to shaping the modern Democratic and Republican parties. The two parties differ in their ideological character and in their demographic and geographical bases.

Ideological Character of the Democratic and Republican Parties In recent years Republican officeholders and candidates have become increasingly conservative; the once-viable liberal wing of the party has virtually disappeared, and even moderate Republicans have become endangered species. That most Republican politicians are conservatives does not mean that they are united, however. The Republican party comprises an uneasy coalition of traditional economic conservatives, who favor a reduced role for the government, and the "social issues" right, which draws its strength especially from religious groups like the Christian Coalition. Complicating the mix is a new wave of conservatives, led by House Speaker Newt Gingrich, who attempt to combine "a sophisticated social science perspective on the future, a free market economic analysis of the present and moral values firmly rooted in the past." These diverse factions within the party have very different interests and agendas, and keeping them together presents a continuing challenge to the Republican leadership.[24]

"THE DEMOCRATIC PARTY TODAY CHANGED ITS NAME TO 'THE REPUBLICAN PARTY.'"

The Democratic party is similarly divided between traditional liberals and a centrist wing led by the Democratic Leadership Council (DLC), once chaired by Bill Clinton. The first group favors a continuation and extension of New Deal and 1960s policies on economic issues, civil rights, education, welfare, and the environment. The second group favors a more pragmatic blend of policy reforms and new initiatives designed to cope with these and other issues such as health care, industrial competitiveness, crime, and immigration. The difficulty of keeping these two wings of the party in balance is perhaps best symbolized by Clinton himself, whose policies and proposals combined a mix of traditional democratic initiatives, such as increasing the minimum wage, with newer approaches, such as welfare reform and a review of affirmative action.

Geographical Strengths and Weaknesses of the Parties. The Republican Party of the 1990s has built on its strong base in the west and south. The party has won five of the eight presidential elections between 1968 and 1996, and in 1994 won control of both houses of Congress for the first time in forty years. The "Grand Old Party" can now count on a solid base in what analysts call the "Republican L," an area comprising twenty-six states sweeping from Alaska to the Rocky Mountains, then through the plains states and the South.* Together, the "L" states provide 223 of the 270 electoral votes needed to win the presidency. In

---

* The twenty-six states include the eleven states of the Confederacy (Virginia, North Carolina, South Carolina, Georgia, Florida, Alabama, Mississippi, Tennessee, Arkansas, Louisiana, and Texas), plus Kentucky; five Plains states (Oklahoma, Kansas, Nebraska, South Dakota, and North Dakota); and nine Rocky Mountain and western states (New Mexico, Arizona, Utah, Colorado, Wyoming, Montana, Idaho, Nevada, and Alaska). (Source: telephone interview with Rhodes Cook, *Congressional Quarterly,* April 21, 1995.)

Figure 9.2 **Political Typology**

Core Republican	15%	Moralists	Middle-aged; middle income; favor "traditional" moral values
	12%	Enterprisers	Affluent; educated; predominantly men; pro-business; anti-government
Republican-leaning	7%	Libertarians	Highly educated; affluent; predominantly white men; pro-business, anti-government, anti-welfare, but highly tolerant, low on religious faith, cynical about politicians
	14%	New Economy Independents	Average income, young to middle-aged, mostly female; conflicting values (for example, pro-environment but not believers in government regulation)
Apolitical	6%	Embittered	Low income, low education, middle-aged; old ties to Democrats gone but feel unwelcome in the Republican Party; distrust government, politicians, corporations
	10%	Bystanders	Young; urban; poorly educated; little interest in news or politics
Democratic-leaning	7%	Seculars	Uniquely nonreligious; educated; relatively affluent; some Republican sympathies; believe strongly in personal freedom
Core Democrat	8%	New Dealers	Older; blue-collar; financially comfortable; religious; moderately hawkish
	9%	Partisan Poor	Very poor, disadvantaged; more than one-third non-whites; very religious; socially intolerant; want more government spending on the poor
	12%	New Democrats	Mostly female, average income and education; not intolerant, but reject discrimination as a major barrier to black progress; more pro-business than other Democratic groups, but also pro-government and environmentalist

SOURCE: Pew Research Center for the People and the Press at http://www.people-press.org/fit.htm

J. C. Watts of Oklahoma, who was elected to the U.S. House of Representatives in 1994 as the first African American Republican from south of the Mason-Dixon line since Reconstruction.

1980, Ronald Reagan won every state in the "L" except for Georgia, which was his opponent's home state; in 1984 and 1988, he and George Bush won every state. The party won only seventeen of the "L" states in 1992, largely due to opposition to Bush and support for the independent Ross Perot, and only eighteen of the "L" states in 1996, due mainly to the weakness of candidate Bob Dole. Significantly, Dole won only one state—Indiana—outside the "L."[25]

The Democratic Party's strength, conversely, now lies on the two coasts and in the industrial states of the upper Midwest. But the Democrats dominate in few states, and, despite Clinton's two victories, still face tough fights in traditional strongholds like New York and Ohio. Since the Republicans can win the presidency by combining the "L" states with California, victory in the nation's largest state is almost a prerequisite to Democratic success at the national level. Yet California is often a battleground, with neither party able to count on consistent success.

The Democratic and Republican Coalitions The Democratic party's core of support remains grounded in the groups that made up the enormously successful New Deal coalition: African Americans, union members, the poor, Jews, Catholics, and liberals. Republican support is strongest among conservatives, the affluent, and white Protestants. Southern whites, once steadfast Democrats, have become increasingly Republican. Beginning in the 1960s, the Republican party has managed to chip away at Democratic support among all of these groups except African Americans. By contrast, the Democrats have picked up support only among southern blacks, whose right to vote was ensured only after passage of the Voting Rights Act of 1965.

The kinds of voters who traditionally vote Democratic are concentrated in America's cities; Republican voters are clustered in the suburbs and countryside. As the nation's population basis has shifted to the suburbs over the past three decades, Republican strength has grown accordingly. By 1988, the Republicans' edge in the suburbs was large enough to cancel out the Democrats' edge in the cities. Add to that the Republicans' small lead in rural America, and the result is enough to explain the Republicans' recent success.

Summary

A political party is a broad organization whose goal is to win elective offices and control the institutions of government. The set of relationships between the political parties of a particular country at a given moment in time is known as a "party system." The nature of a party system is affected by the nature of the constitutional system and by cultural factors.

Parties play many roles in a political system. They provide a mechanism for mass participation in politics; simplify political choices; consolidate and articulate the position of the majority and the minority; and legitimate political decisions and political conflict. In the United States, the parties also help bridge the separation of powers and integrate local and regional politics into a national system.

The American political system has been characterized almost from the beginning as a two-party system. The two major parties today, the Republicans and the Democrats, have dominated the party system since the Civil War. Both major parties can be described as weak, decentralized, and centrist. Both are loose affiliates of state and local parties, presided over by a national committee and ultimately responsible to a national convention held every four years.

The history of American political parties can be divided into distinct eras, or historical party systems. The transitions from one party era to another have generally been marked by intense periods of political activity and conflict, known as realignments. Scholars disagree on the exact number and duration of these realignment periods, although a realignment clearly occurred in the 1850s and 1860s, and during the New Deal era of the 1930s. Realignments are associated with dramatic shifts in voter loyalty and in party control of the institutions of government, and major changes in public policy.

American parties developed over the first half of the nineteenth century and reached their heyday in the late nineteenth and early twentieth centuries. In this period, the party system was marked by strong urban machines, and controlled by powerful party bosses. Voters were intensely loyal to the parties, and split-ticket voting was uncommon.

The realignment of the 1930s brought the Democratic party to power, led by President Franklin D. Roosevelt. The Democratic coalition comprised a broad array of different groups, including southern whites, northern blacks, and urban workers. The Democrats dominated American politics from 1932 until 1968, only occasionally yielding control to the Republicans.

The transition to the modern party system began in the 1960s. The parties in the modern system are weak, both in terms of voter loyalty and in the degree of control they can exercise over candidates and elected officials. Moreover, the modern era has seen a steep rise in the number of independent voters, and split-ticket voting is common. As a result, many scholars believe that the modern system is incapable of a realignment in the classic sense, and is best described as dealigned. However, dramatic elections—such as the Republican takeover of Congress in 1994—continue to fuel speculation about the next realignment.

Key Terms

Political party
Party system
Winner-take-all system
Proportional representation (PR)
Party identification
Party unity votes
Realignments
Critical elections
Deviating elections
Dealignment
Split-ticket voting
Divided government

Review Questions

1. What is a political party? How do parties differ from interest groups?

2. What is a party system? How do cultural and legal factors influence a party system?

3. What roles do political parties play in a democratic political system?

4. What are the major characteristics of the American party system? Consider the number and character of parties and their relationship to the government.

5. What is party identification, and how has Americans' party identification changed over the past few decades?

6. Define *realignment* and *dealignment*. Why do many scholars believe that the modern period is an era of dealignment rather than realignment?

7. Describe the differences between the modern Democratic party and the modern Republican party in terms of ideology and voter support.

Suggested Readings

Beck, Paul Allen. *Party Politics in America.* New York: Longman, 1997.

Burnham, Walter Dean. *Critical Elections and the Mainsprings of American Politics.* New York: W. W. Norton, 1970.

Key, V. O. *Politics, Parties, and Pressure Groups,* 5th ed. New York: Thomas Y. Crowell, 1964.

Maisel, L. Sandy, ed. *Political Parties and Elections in the United States.* 2 vols. New York: Garland Publishing, 1991.

Milkis, Sidney M. *The President and the Parties: The Transformation of the American Party System Since the New Deal.* New York: Oxford University Press, 1993.

Pomper, Gerald M. *Passions and Interests: Political Party Concepts of American Democracy.* Lawrence: University Press of Kansas, 1992.

Shafer, Byron E. *The End of Realignment: Interpreting American Electoral Eras.* Madison: University of Wisconsin Press, 1991.

Sorauf, Frank J., and Paul Allen Beck. *Party Politics in America,* 6th ed. Glenview, Ill.: Scott Foresman, 1988.

Internet Resources

An exhaustive list of American political parties, major and minor, at:

http://pslab11.polsci. wvu.edu/polycy/psparty.html

The Democratic Party web site at:

http://www.democrats.org

The Republican Party web site at:

http://www.rnc.org

The Reform Party web site at:

http://reformparty.org

★ 10 ★
Campaigns and Elections

It was the greatest roller-coaster ride in the history of American campaign politics. H. Ross Perot entered the 1992 presidential campaign on February 20, 1992, with an appearance on *Larry King Live*. Perot declared that he would consider entering the race if his supporters could gather the signatures to put him on the ballot in all fifty states.

Immediately dismissed by the news media and the political experts, Perot took the nation by storm. By mid-May he was actually leading in a CNN poll, with 34 percent of the vote against 30 percent each for Bill Clinton and George Bush. By June his campaign was reeling, both from disorganization and from the candidate's propensity for gaffes and misstatements. In July he more or less endorsed Bill Clinton, although not officially, and dropped out of the race. In the fall Perot reentered the race, ending up with 19 percent of the vote—the most for a third party candidate since 1912.

Perot, of course, was no ordinary candidate. One of the wealthiest men in America, he backed his campaign with a bankroll of $100 million. He had won national attention for his work on behalf of American prisoners of war in Vietnam and for his successful rescue of employees held prisoner in Iran. And his lack of ordinary political skills was, for the most part, an advantage with an electorate fed up with politics and politicians as usual.

In the end, Perot emerged as mainly a protest candidate. But the outcome of his 1992 race, and his political future, are not the real issues. Perot's candidacy seemed to bring into focus the extraordinary changes in the American electoral system since the days when a few old men met in smoke-filled rooms to select the candidates for president. In one stroke, Perot's 1992 performance revealed the weakness of modern political parties, the enormous importance of money in American elections, and the uses and abuses of the media—especially the "new media"—in modern politics. By tapping into the discontent and alienation of millions of voters, Perot's candidacy also underscored the emergence of a powerful, if as yet unfocused, political force.

The United States has more elections than any other nation. Every four years we elect a president and a vice president. Every two years we elect the entire House of Representatives and one-third of the Senate. In addition, various elections are held in every state and in most towns and cities. These include elections for state legislature, governor, school board, water commissioner, mayor, and judgeships.

Elections are as American as apple pie, or maybe more so. Students begin electing class officers as early as the primary grades, and continue on through college. Labor unions, college faculties, corporate shareholders, and interest groups large and small select their leadership through the ballot. But too many elections—like too much apple pie—can be detrimental. Elections are a poor way to protect the rights of minorities, and they may encourage decisions based on emotion rather than reason, and on short-term interests rather than the long-term view.

Taking his case directly to the people, 1992 presidential contender H. Ross Perot announces his candidacy on the **Larry King Live** *television program*

Moreover, critics of the modern American electoral system raise a host of doubts about whether campaigns and elections truly serve the goal of rational self-government. They note that voters are poorly informed about even the most basic political issues; that campaigns are waged and won not with reasoned arguments but with emotional slogans and packaged advertising; and that the overwhelming influence of money reduces politicians to fund-raisers and increases the power of wealthy candidates and political action committees. Not surprisingly, critics point out, the number of Americans who decide not to vote usually exceeds the number who do.

In theory, elections should provide the people with their best opportunity for self-government. In reality, whether elections always advance American democracy is unclear. This chapter explores the nature of American campaigns and elections, the overwhelming importance of money and media, and the persistent problem of low voter turnout. Throughout, its goal is to examine whether the electoral system provides a meaningful opportunity for the people to govern themselves.

Questions to Keep in Mind

☑ *How did the Framers view the role of elections in a democracy? What kinds of decisions did they leave to the people? What kinds were left to the people's elected representatives?*

☑ *What kinds of voters are over- or underrepresented in the electoral process? What effects might higher rates of participation have on election outcomes and representation?*

☑ *Why do fund-raising and media politics play such important roles in modern campaigns? How do money and media influence the decisions of the electorate?*

Basic Concepts ★★★★★★★★★★★★★

Elections serve three major purposes in an organization or political system.

First, and most obviously, they provide a mechanism for selecting leaders and for helping to set the broad course of public policy. Whether elections are the best method for making such decisions is an open question; it depends on the nature of the decision, the commitment of the electorate, and the availability of alternate mechanisms. For the most part, American elections are used to select leaders and thus influence policy only indirectly. In many states, however, elections are used as a way for voters to pass legislation directly or to ratify decisions made by their elected representatives.

Second, elections provide a key check on public officials. Merely knowing that an election will be held may profoundly affect the behavior of political leaders. At a minimum, even the remote possibility of electoral defeat might dissuade an elected official from pursuing policies that the majority opposes. More commonly, the need for constant reelection might lead the official to court voters actively and constantly. Asking successful politicians why they worry about reelection is like asking the rich why they clip coupons: that's how they got where they are in the first place.

Finally, elections serve to legitimize the exercise of political power. Citizens who have a say in the governmental process may be more likely to accept the regime as lawful and more likely to obey its rules and regulations. Having the chance to participate in political decision making may strengthen the bonds between the citizen and the government, and may create stronger feelings of community among those participating.

So important are elections to political legitimacy that nondemocratic regimes routinely go through the charade of holding elections to bolster the government's standing both at home and abroad. More positively, a regime that is truly seeking to become democratic can gain instant legitimacy by holding elections that are in fact free and fair, often under the supervision of international authorities or independent observers.

Texans hold elections for state and local judges and for a variety of other offices, including constable. Critics charge that Texas voters must cope with a dizzying array of choices and decisions, making informed voting difficult if not impossible.

The Framers and Elections

The Framers recognized the value of elections in any system of popular government: only "frequent elections," wrote James Madison, could ensure that the government would have "a common interest with the people."[1] But the Framers were equally convinced of the need to avoid a system of government that gave the people too direct a role in government. Thus, they rejected the idea of annual elections for members of the House of Representatives, preferring a two-year term, and gave the people only an indirect role in the election of the president and the Senate. They allowed the people no direct role in making laws, requiring them to act at all times through their elected representatives, and removed federal judges from the electoral process altogether.

In other ways too, the Framers sought to structure elections so as to limit the direct role of the people in their government. The combination of large electoral districts and a small House of Representatives was designed to ensure that members of Congress would be "men who possess the most attractive merit and the most diffusive and established characters"—men whose "wisdom may best discern the true interest of their country, and whose patriotism and love of justice will be least likely to sacrifice it to temporary or partial considerations."[2] Moreover, each member of Congress would represent a broad and diverse constituency, and would therefore be unable to devote his energies entirely to the protection or promotion of a particular group or interest. In short, the Federalists' goal was to implement a system of government closely akin to the model representative democracy.

The Antifederalists, by contrast, believed that elections should promote direct democracy. They believed that representatives should stand for election every year, continually repeating the adage that "where annual elections end, tyranny begins."[3] They called for legislative bodies made up of many members each representing a small and relatively homogeneous district. Finally, they wanted the electoral process to facilitate the election of ordinary citizens, not a professional political elite.

Despite the Federalists' victory in the constitutional debate of 1787–1788, elections in the United States do not always follow the representative democracy approach. At the state and local levels, citizens frequently vote directly on public issues, and public officials commonly represent small districts and must endure very frequent elections. Many state judges are elected, and some are subject to recall by popular vote. Moreover, even at the federal level, modern elections often take on the trappings of direct democracy, with candidates laying specific policy choices before the voters or promising to follow where the majority leads.

Elections Under the Constitution

The Right to Vote   The original Constitution left it to the states to decide who would have the right to vote. The only limitation on the power of the states existed in the Constitution's vague guarantee that each state have a republican form of government, a requirement that the federal courts have never enforced. Originally, most states limited the franchise to white males over twenty-one who owned a small amount of property (often fifty acres of land or the equivalent). The property requirements were dropped in most states in the period between the Revolutionary and Civil Wars.[4]

In 1870, however, the Fifteenth Amendment to the Constitution banned restrictions on the right to vote based on race. Similar amendments extended the franchise to women in 1919 and to eighteen-year-olds in 1971. The constitutional right to vote extends to every election, state and federal. In general the Constitution gives the states the authority to set the qualifications for voting, although Congress can override the states and set qualifications for voting in federal (meaning presidential, senatorial, and congressional) elections.[5]

The Fifteenth Amendment had little real impact until the 1960s. Before then, state officials easily evaded the amendment and limited the voting rights of African Americans. One common method was to establish literacy tests as a condition for voting. Racially biased examiners would find ways to let illiterate whites pass the test while failing even the most literate African Americans. Another technique was to impose a tax on voter registration. Such **poll taxes** discouraged many poor blacks from trying to participate. A third approach was to set various literacy and property requirements, but then adopt a "grandfather clause" exempting those eligible to vote in 1867 and their descendants. The Supreme Court upheld both literacy tests and the poll tax, but nullified the use of grandfather clauses as an obvious effort to evade the Fifteenth Amendment.[6]

Only in the modern era has real progress been made on voting rights for African Americans and other racial minorities. In 1944, for example, the Supreme Court ruled that blacks could not be excluded from political primaries.[7] But the big breakthrough for southern blacks did not come until Congress passed the **Voting Rights Act of 1965.** Intended to enforce the Fifteenth Amendment in a meaningful way for the first time, the act prohibited virtually all racial discrimination in elections and established a means for the federal courts and the Department of Justice to enforce those requirements. The Supreme Court upheld the act in 1966.[8] Congress has renewed and extended the Voting Rights Act several times in the past three decades.

One Person, One Vote.   The Constitution requires that a population census be taken every ten years. After each census, the number of seats allotted to each state in the House of Representatives must be recalculated, and the size and shape of congressional districts within each state must be redrawn to reflect population changes. Seats in state and local legislatures are similarly affected. This process is known as **reapportionment.**

Before 1962 the Supreme Court stayed out of the political thicket of drawing legislative districts, whether for the House of Representatives or for state and local districts.[9] All such matters were simply left to the discretion of the states, which, over the years, had used their power to draw district lines in order to benefit or hurt particular political, racial, or economic groups. This practice is called *gerrymandering* in honor of Vice President Elbridge Gerry, who, as the governor of Massachusetts, was credited with inventing the practice.

THE GERRY-MANDER.

The original "gerrymander," a congressional district designed to favor the Democratic party at the expense of the Federalists, was signed into law in 1811 by Massachusetts governor Elbridge Gerry. The district, tracing its way through what is now suburban Boston, was said to resemble a salamander—hence the name.

In the cases of *Baker* v. *Carr* (1962) and *Reynolds* v. *Sims* (1964) the Supreme Court at last decided to intervene.[10] At issue were gross disparities in the population of legislative districts in Tennessee, Alabama, and several other states. The largest Senate district in Alabama, for example, had some forty-one times as many residents as the smallest, and the largest House district had sixteen times as many. Such a scheme gave far greater power to voters in less populated districts.

In its sweeping opinion in *Reynolds,* the Court held that state legislative districts had to be apportioned on the basis of population, a principle known as "one person, one vote." Later cases extended the principle to the United States House of Representatives and to city and county councils as well. The only exception now is the federal Senate, whose makeup (two senators from each state) is specifically mandated by the Constitution. Mathematical perfection in drawing district lines is not required, however, and the Court has allowed slight deviations from the one-person-one-vote rule, when justified by a satisfactory explanation. In 1971, for example, the Court approved deviations from mathematical equality in order to respect town boundaries.[11]

Because reapportionment has direct consequences for the political power of competing groups, recent cases have caused considerable controversy. In 1986, for example, the Court ruled that the Constitution prohibited gerrymandering to benefit members of a particular political party.[12] In 1995 the Court held that congressional redistricting schemes were unconstitutional if race was the predominant factor motivating the state legislature's action.[13]

General Elections and Primary Elections American elections fall into two broad categories. **Primary elections** (or **primaries**) pit candidates from the same political party against each other in a battle for the party's nomination for a particular office. **General elections** involve candidates from different parties competing for the office itself. *Special elections* are held whenever necessary to fill a position left vacant by death or resignation.

Primaries were invented in the early twentieth century as a way to reduce the influence of party bosses. Instead of candidates being selected in "smoke-filled rooms," they would be chosen by ordinary voters. Primaries proved very popular and are used today in most states. Some states hold *open primaries,* in which voters decide on election day whether to vote in the Democratic, Republican, or third party primary. Other states hold *closed primaries,* in which only those voters who have affiliated with a particular political party can vote in that party's primary. Except in the case of the presidential election, primary voters directly select the party's candidate for office. In presidential primaries, voters select delegates to the national party conventions, which in turn select the nominees.

Many primary elections, especially for state and local offices, are virtually uncontested. Many general elections are also uncompetitive or involve only token opposition to an incumbent candidate.

Presidential Elections: The Long and Winding Road

American presidential elections resemble an Olympic marathon. Winning the presidency requires extraordinary stamina, tremendous organizational skills, and a great deal of money. Above all, perhaps, surviving the obstacle course that leads to the presidency requires that the candidate possess an overwhelming desire to win—the kind of personal drive and ambition that political journalists like to call "fire in the belly."

Qualifications for the Presidency   An old saying has it that "anyone in America can run for president" (another saying suggests that "anyone" has). In fact, *almost* anyone can become president. The Constitution provides only that the president be a natural born citizen of the United States (that is, a person born in the United States or whose parents are American citizens); at least thirty-five years old; and a resident of the United States for fourteen years. In practice most presidential candidates have had considerable political experience, although military figures, such as Dwight D. Eisenhower or Ulysses S. Grant, have often made a successful run for the White House in their first political campaign. In recent years, presidential candidates have often stressed their *lack* of Washington credentials: three of the four presidents from Carter to Clinton were state governors, and only one (Bush) had served in Congress—and then only for a single term.

Presidential Two-Term Limit   The Twenty-Second Amendment, ratified in 1951, bars the election of a president more than twice, in effect, an eight-year term limit on the presidency. The original Constitution contained no such limitation, but George Washington, discouraged and tired after an eventful second term, refused to run a third time. The tradition started by Washington lasted until 1940, when, on the brink of World War II, President Franklin D. Roosevelt ran for and was elected to a third term. Roosevelt was elected for a fourth term in 1944, although he died a few months later.

   In the wake of the Roosevelt presidency, Congress turned President Washington's rule of thumb into a constitutional mandate. Since 1951, only four presidents—Eisenhower, Nixon, Reagan, and Clinton—have been elected twice. Toward the end of the Reagan presidency, there was talk of repealing the two-term rule, but no action was taken. Supporters of the presidential term limit argue that any other rule could create a "monarchy for life," effectively undermining democracy. Opponents point out that the abolition of the two-term rule would eliminate the difficulties encountered by "lame-duck" second-term presidents.

The Electoral College   Technically, presidents are selected not by the people directly but by members of the **electoral college,** who are in turn selected by the people on election day. Each state is allotted a number of electors equal to its total number of senators and representatives, with the District of Columbia allotted three. California has the highest number of electoral votes, with fifty-four; eight states (including the District of Columbia) have the minimum of three.

   The Framers designed the electoral college system as an alternative to either direct popular election of the president or election by Congress or the state legislatures. The first alternative was rejected as too democratic ("It would be as unnatural to refer the choice of [the president] . . . to the people as it would to refer a trial of colors to a blind man," said Virginia's George Mason); the second was rejected because the Framers could not agree among themselves as to which legislative body or bodies should be entrusted with the job.[14]

   When citizens vote, of course, they pull a lever or mark a ballot labeled with the names of the presidential candidates. The names of the candidates for the electoral college are typically listed in smaller print and mean nothing to the average voter. Although the details of the process are left up to the individual states, in general each presidential candidate presents a slate of potential electors. The candidate who wins the majority of votes in the state then receives all of its electoral votes, meaning that the candidate's entire slate of electors is named to the electoral college. This *winner-take-all* system is used in every state except Maine, which chooses one elector from each congressional district, plus two from the state at large.

Should the Electoral College Be Abolished?

Americans have elected their presidents by means of the Electoral College since the days of George Washington. Originally designed to provide a forum where delegates chosen by the people could debate and deliberate on the various candidates for president, the system quickly became little more than an accounting device—a way of counting the votes for president by state, rather than at the national level. Over the years, many have suggested that it be abolished in favor of a direct popular vote, with the presidency going to the candidate receiving the largest number of votes. Others defend the system as a valuable tradition and argue that it continues to serve important purposes.

Yes, the Electoral College should be abolished.

The Electoral College has been much criticized for being anachronistic, overly complex, and fundamentally unfair. Among the leading arguments against the system are these:

The Electoral College violates the principle of "one person, one vote." Elections for every office but the presidency are conducted on the principle that each person's vote should count equally in determining the result. In the Electoral College, by contrast, the votes of those in small states count more than those of voters in large states. Since each state is guaranteed a minimum of three electoral votes, the smallest states are overrepresented in the electoral college. Thus Wyoming, with less than 0.2 percent of the total U.S. population, has 0.5 percent of the electoral votes. This difference may seem small, but together the influence of the small states can be meaningful: the sixteen smallest states (including the District of Columbia) account for only 6 percent of the population, but 10 percent of the electoral votes—an overrepresentation of more than 25 electoral votes.

The electoral college encourages candidates to concentrate on only the largest states. When the legendary bank robber Willie Sutton was asked why he robbed banks, he replied "Because that's where the money is." By the same token, presidential candidates concentrate their efforts on the biggest states because that's where the votes are. Together, the five largest states (California, New York, Texas, Florida, and Pennsylvania) control 167 electoral votes—31 percent of the total, and 62 percent of the number needed to win the presidency. Theoretically, a candidate could win the election simply by winning the biggest eleven states.

A candidate with a minority of the vote can win the election outright. This is perhaps the most serious objection to the electoral college, since it seems to violate the basic principle of majority rule. It has actually happened twice in American history, in 1876 and 1888.

To see how it is possible for the loser in the popular vote to win in the electoral college, consider a hypothetical election held in only three states, each with 25 electoral votes. In States A and B, the Republican candidate ekes out a victory, winning each of the two states by a margin of 10,000 votes out of 10 million cast. In State C, however, the Democratic candidate wins in a landslide, by a margin of two million votes. The Democratic candidate thus wins the popular election by a margin of 1,980,000 votes, but loses in the electoral college by 50 to 25.

The Electoral College disfavors third parties or independent candidates without a regional base. A third party or independent candidate whose strength is focused in a few states can hope to win those states. One whose strength is spread out will likely win no electoral votes.

In 1992, for example, independent candidate H. Ross Perot won nearly one out of five popular votes cast. Since his strength was spread out over all 50 states, however, he won no electoral votes. Perot's best state was Maine, where he received 30 percent of the vote.

Contrast Perot's performance with that of American Independent Party candidate George Wallace in 1968. Because Wallace's support was concentrated in the South, he was able to turn his 13 percent of the popular vote into a respectable 8 percent of the electoral vote.

No, keep the Electoral College.

Despite these criticisms, the Electoral College has its defenders. Supporters of the system point particularly to the virtues of counting votes on a state-by-state basis. Besides their general loyalty to tradition, supporters point to these arguments:

The Electoral College forces candidates to build broad national coalitions, demonstrating substantial strength across the country, and encourages candidates to think about the nation as a whole. In a direct election system, candidates can "run up the vote" in a few large states and thus cover up their weaknesses elsewhere. Under the Electoral College, they have to have broad appeal from Maine to Hawaii. The system also helps ensure that candidates think about the specific concerns of voters in states across the land.

Supporters of the Electoral College liken the system to the method used to determine the World Series champion. The winning team is not the one that scores the highest total number of runs, but the one able to win consistently—four games out of seven. In the famous 1960 World Series, for example, the New York Yankees scored huge margins of victory in their three wins, but lost the series anyway.

The Electoral College protects the two-party system. By giving third parties no reward unless they can mobilize a broad coalition across the country, the Electoral College helps preserve the American two-party system, which has been a major feature of our political system since the early 1800s, and which has well served American democracy.

The Electoral College sustains voter interest and adds to the drama of the campaign. The current system provides an added dimension to the election, making it far more interesting both throughout the campaign and on election night. With less than half the electorate turning out to vote, anything that keeps voters involved is worth preserving.

The Electoral College gives small groups of voters—who might otherwise be ignored—an important part in the election. In a direct election, candidates could safely ignore small groups of voters, concentrating instead on the largest voting blocs. Under the Electoral College, however, small groups of voters can make the crucial difference in key states. Thus while candidates might safely ignore dairy farmers in a national election, their interests must be taken into account in states like Wisconsin. The same is true of Jewish voters in New York, Mexican-Americans in Texas, and gays and lesbians in California.

By turning a close race into a landslide, the Electoral College can confer legitimacy on a new administration. A candidate who narrowly wins a number of large states can end up with a far larger majority in the electoral college than in the popular vote. In 1960, for example, John Kennedy barely squeaked by Richard Nixon in the popular vote, winning by less than 120,000 votes out of nearly 70 million cast, yet won decisively in the electoral college, by 303 to 219 electoral votes. The exaggeration effect is particularly extreme when there are more than two candidates in the race. In 1992, for example, Bill Clinton won 69 percent of the electoral votes but only 43 percent of the popular vote.

Far from being a problem, this exaggeration of the victory margin allows a new administration to claim a national mandate, increasing the chances of effective governance.

The Electoral College is no more antiquated or undemocratic than the Senate. Many of the arguments used against the Electoral College could equally be applied to the Senate, where voters are not represented by population and where small coalitions frequently frustrate the majority. Yet those who passionately oppose the Electoral College rarely criticize the Senate. Supporters of the Electoral College point out that both institutions guard against the tyranny of the majority, protect small groups of voters, and, in general, contribute to American democracy.

Figure 10.1 **Popular Vote Cast for President, 1972–1996**

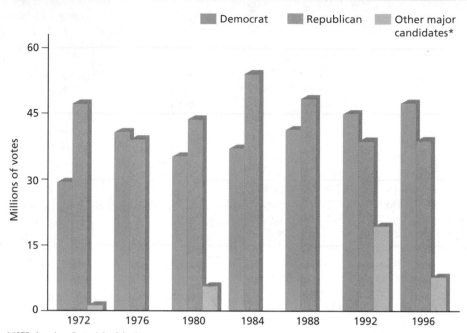

* 1972: American Party, John Schmitz
1980: Independent, John Anderson
1992: Independent, H. Ross Perot
1996: Reform Party, H. Ross Perot
SOURCE: U.S. Bureau of the Census; *1997 Statistical Abstract,* Tables 437 and 438, p. 271.

The winning electors meet in their respective states to cast their ballots for president. The results are then sent to Washington, where they are officially counted in the presence of Congress. The entire process is form without substance, however, since the electors are carefully selected by the political parties and candidates and are pledged, by law or tradition, to support particular candidates.[15] For practical purposes, the significance of the electoral college lies not in the details of the procedure but in the fact that the presidential decision is made on a state-by-state, rather than on a national, basis.

A candidate needs a majority of electoral votes, or 270 out of 538, to win the presidency. If no candidate musters a majority in the electoral college, the election is decided by Congress, under special rules outlined in the Constitution. The House of Representatives chooses the president from among the top three vote-getters in the electoral college. Each state delegation is allowed to cast one vote, with a majority of the total number of states necessary for victory. At the same time, the Senate chooses the vice president from among the two highest vote-getters, with each senator having, as usual, one vote. Congress has had to decide the presidential election twice in American history—in 1800 and in 1824.

The continued existence of the electoral college disturbs many political scientists and commentators, but a popular groundswell against the institution has never developed.

Moreover, the two major parties have a clear incentive to preserve the electoral college system, since it effectively locks out most third party candidates. But the electoral college has its supporters, and not only among those who are bound by tradition. Supporters argue that the system's tendency to exaggerate the margin of victory, especially in three-way races, confers legitimacy on a candidate who wins a narrow victory in the popular vote or (in a three-way race) commands less than a majority of the vote. Supporters also point out that by concentrating the impact of minority voters in a few key states, the system helps maximize their impact on the electoral process.

The fact that the presidential nominations process and the general election itself are conducted on a state-by-state basis profoundly affects the candidates' overall strategy and tactics. Candidates do not set out to win a majority of the popular vote; instead they must seek victories in particular states and hope to win enough states to create a national victory.

Stages of a Presidential Campaign   The long road toward winning the 270 electoral votes needed for election to the presidency officially begins in Iowa. In January of a presidential election year, Iowa voters meet in local caucuses to begin the process of selecting delegates to the national nominating conventions. The first primary election is traditionally held in New Hampshire, in early February.

Iowa and New Hampshire mark the beginning of the official presidential campaign, but the real campaign stretches back months, or in some cases years. An early start is essential because running a successful presidential campaign requires large quantities of money, volunteers, and support. The bulk of the primary and caucus season is now compressed into February, March, and April, meaning that a candidate's organization and fund-raising apparatus must be in place long before.[16] As candidate Phil Gramm observed before the 1996 race, "You're going to have to raise all this money early, you're going to have to run in fifteen or twenty states at the same time, without being the party nominee, without having every political operative in the party working for you." To be taken seriously, Gramm estimated, each prospective Republican candidate would have to raise "upwards of $25 million" before the primary season had even begun.[17]

The season of caucuses and primaries lasts from January until June. The process ultimately produces delegates to the national nominating conventions in July or August. The victorious candidates then select their vice presidential candidates—subject to virtually automatic confirmation by the conventions—and the campaign begins. (The traditional kickoff of the presidential campaign is on Labor Day, in early September. In the old days, it was said that the campaign did not begin in earnest until after the World Series, but in modern times we are lucky if there is a World Series and if it is over before the election itself.)

An independent or third party candidate must follow a course very different from that of the major party candidates. The candidate must get his or her name on the ballot in all fifty states, a challenging process that involves collecting thousands of signatures and complying with a formidable array of state election laws. The candidate must also establish sufficient credibility to generate news coverage and guarantee participation in any debates. All the while, the candidate must raise large amounts of money, a process that typically involves a catch-22: it is difficult to raise money until the candidacy is credible, and it is

Democratic convention rules adopted after 1968 guaranteed that delegates would represent a broad cross-section of America—including women and racial minorities.

difficult for the candidacy to become credible without raising money. In 1992, of course, H. Ross Perot sidestepped these difficulties by spending his own money.

Party Nomination Rules and Procedures   As late as 1968, the process of selecting presidential candidates to run under a party's banner remained under the control of party leaders. After that, changes in Democratic party rules and various state laws shifted control to the party's general membership, through participation in state and local caucuses and primary elections.

Delegate Selection. In the caucus system, delegates are selected at a state convention, whose membership is determined by a series of local meetings or conventions.[18] In a presidential primary, the voters directly choose delegates to attend each party's national nominating convention. Delegates are typically pledged to vote for a particular candidate, at least on the first convention ballot. The rules governing primary elections vary from state to state.

Prior to 1972, primaries were used mainly as a way for candidates to demonstrate to party leaders that they could successfully appeal to rank-and-file voters. John F. Kennedy, for example, used the West Virginia primary in 1960 to prove that a Catholic could win in the Protestant state of West Virginia—a clear sign that the nation was ready to elect a Catholic president. Richard Nixon likewise used the 1968 Republican primaries to shake the "loser" image he had acquired through defeats in the presidential election of 1960 and the California governor's race in 1962. By contrast, a candidate without evident weaknesses and whose strength was well known to party leaders had no need to enter the primaries. Vice President Hubert Humphrey, for example, won the 1968 Democratic nomination without competing in a single one.

The role of presidential primaries began to change after the 1968 convention, when the Democratic party named a commission, headed first by George McGovern and then by Donald M. Fraser, to recommend reform of its candidate selection procedures. The **McGovern-Fraser Commission** adopted rules mandating that the selection of delegates to the national nominating convention be more open and representative, goals most easily accomplished by holding caucuses or primary elections. After 1968, therefore, real control over the nominations process passed to those participating in caucuses and primary elections.

The increased importance of primaries at first affected the Democratic party more than the Republican party, largely because the Republican rules maintained a large role for party leaders and professionals. In recent years the Democrats have tried to deemphasize primaries somewhat, reserving more convention seats for party leaders and replacing primaries with caucuses in several states. Even so, the importance of primaries in the delegate selection process in both parties remains overwhelming.

The National Conventions. Each major party holds its national convention in the summer before a presidential election. The formal purpose of the convention is to select the party's candidates for president and vice president and to decide on a "platform," which states the party's positions on various issues. In the modern era, however, the convention merely ratifies the choice made by the voters in state primaries and caucuses. Every convention since 1952 has selected its presidential candidate on the first ballot; in all but a handful, the results have been a foregone conclusion. The conventions do approve a party platform, or statement of policies and principles, but the platform-writing process is typically controlled by the presidential nominee (who controls a majority of the delegates), and in any event the nominee is free to reject or ignore specific provisions of the platform. (In 1996, Republican candidate Bob Dole publicly boasted that he had not even read his party's platform.) In both parties, the selection of a vice presidential running mate is left entirely to the discretion of the presidential nominee, subject technically to ratification by the convention delegates.

If the conventions do not deliberate on the selection of a candidate and for the most part merely ratify the platform, what purpose do they serve? In effect, the conventions have become huge media events, providing the parties with free television time to kick off their campaigns for the presidency. They also provide a reward for loyal party workers, who typically enjoy the experience of being a delegate or alternate. And why not? They get to hobnob with the party's leadership, are wined and dined for nearly a week, and feel a part of history while experiencing firsthand the excitement and pageantry of the convention spectacle.

Bob Dole (right) and Jack Kemp, the Republican presidential and vice-presidential candidates in 1996. The Republican ticket trailed President Bill Clinton and Vice President Al Gore from early on, and never closed the gap.

The General Election Campaign Running a presidential campaign is a vast undertaking. Candidates must put together a campaign organization, from the inner circle down to local volunteer workers. They and their staffs must devise a campaign strategy, determine key themes, and coordinate with state and local candidates and campaign organizations. They must plan a backbreaking schedule of campaign events, write major speeches, prepare for debates, and develop issue positions. They must conduct research (including polling and focus groups), develop paid media spots, and work to get their message across through free media.

Debates. Debates have become so important to the modern presidential campaign that it may be hard to believe that they are a modern invention. The first presidential debate was held in 1960, between Richard Nixon and John F. Kennedy (the famous Lincoln-Douglas debates of 1858 took place in a campaign for a U.S. Senate seat, not the presidency). The next series of debates was held in 1976, between Jimmy Carter and Gerald Ford. Since then debates have become a standard part of presidential races.

Whether there are debates, what their number and format are, and whether any third party candidates will participate are points to be negotiated among the presidential campaigns, the news media, and sponsoring organizations such as the League of Women Voters. Presidential candidates are not required to participate in debates, but today a candidate's refusal to participate in a debate would itself become a campaign issue, and it is hard to imagine a candidate refusing to participate. Conventional wisdom holds that debates are of most benefit to young, untested challengers and of least benefit to older, established incumbents. The former have much to gain in a debate; the latter have everything to lose. For example, it is often said that Kennedy's success in the 1960 debate helped assure voters that despite his youth he was qualified to be president, whereas Richard Nixon's poor performance hurt his image as a capable, experienced leader.

Obviously, debates are more important to the candidate who is behind than to the candidate who is ahead, because they may provide a way to close the gap. But objective research does not bear out the claim that debates categorically benefit challengers over incumbents. First, it is difficult to isolate the impact of debates on the final outcome of the election from all the other influences on the voters. Although debates clearly influence the public's views in the hours and days after the event, their impact seems to fade after that time. Second, the value of debates to a campaign seems related more to individual performance and circumstances than to any categorical rule. Often the impact of a debate is determined by a single gaffe or a single great line. In 1976, for example, Gerald Ford said that Poland was a "free country," which made him appear to know nothing about foreign policy. In 1980, Ronald Reagan scored points when he responded to attacks by Jimmy Carter with the line "There you go again." In 1988, Michael Dukakis lost points when, after being asked how he would feel if his wife were raped, he responded with a cool and calculated statement on public policy rather than with an emotional statement.

The public's evaluation of a candidate's performance in a debate may be greatly influenced by news coverage and commentary afterward. Voters surveyed immediately after the debate in which President Ford made his infamous remark on Poland showed that Ford had won by 11 percentage points. Later polls, conducted after voters were exposed to news coverage of the issue, showed Ford losing by 45 percentage points. Debates typically have little impact on the candidates' fortunes, however. Polls taken after the first Kennedy-Nixon debate in 1960, for example, showed an improvement for Kennedy of a modest 3 percentage points.[19] Likewise, the 1992 and 1996 debates did little to affect the outcome of the elections.[20]

The evidence suggests that how a candidate looks during a televised debate may greatly affect the public's perception of who wins and who loses. Television viewers of the 1960 Kennedy-Nixon debate were apparently influenced by the appearance of the candidates: Nixon had hurt his knee on the way to the studio, looked "tired and nervous," and used only light makeup that did not hide his five o'clock shadow, whereas Kennedy looked relaxed, tanned, and well rested. By contrast, many radio listeners believed that Nixon had actually won the debate.[21]

Congressional, State, and Local Elections

Congressional Elections   Congressional elections are held every two years, with the entire House of Representatives and one-third of the Senate up for reelection. Congressional elections are held independently in each state and congressional district, although individual races often combine both local and national themes. When a congressional election coincides with a presidential election, for example, it may be heavily influenced by the presidential campaign. When a congressional election is held in an off year—that is, between presidential elections—it often serves as a referendum on the first half of the president's term.

Between 1955 and 1992, congressional elections were marked by the dominance of the Democratic party and an extremely high victory rate for incumbents. During that forty-year span, the Democrats controlled the House of Representatives continuously and the Senate for all but six years. In 1994, however, Republicans took advantage of President Bill Clinton's unpopularity and the voters' angry mood to take control of both chambers.

The political earthquake that shook Washington in 1994 overturned much of the conventional wisdom concerning congressional elections. Still, that conventional wisdom provides a useful starting point for understanding the 1994 election and its implications for the future.

Political analysts offered several different explanations for the Democrats' control of Congress over the previous four decades. First, they noted that former Speaker of the House Tip O'Neill's famous dictum that "all politics is local" applied more to congressional than to presidential elections. Presidential campaigns centered on broad ideological themes, whereas congressional elections tended to focus on local issues and on the candidates themselves. Second, analysts pointed out that the Democrats enjoyed extraordinary advantages as a result of incumbency. Sitting members of Congress enjoyed free mailing privileges, for example, and a great deal of free publicity. They could also win votes by doing favors for constituents or by obtaining federal money for their districts. Above all, incumbents were able to attract a great deal of money, much of it from political action committees. In the 1990 House elections, for example, incumbents raised an average of nearly $450,000, whereas challengers could muster little more than $100,000. Not surprisingly, of the 407 incumbents seeking reelection, only 16 (3.9 percent) were defeated.[22] Third, some commentators argued that divided government was perfectly logical for voters who embraced conservatism in the abstract (expressed in the presidential race) but who nonetheless favored specific government programs and benefits (guaranteed by the congressional vote).

The 1994 election turned at least some of this analysis on its head. Republicans successfully nationalized the election, running on a program known as the Contract with

Elections in Other Democracies

Elections differ in both style and substance from one democracy to another. The electoral system of each country, like that of the United States, reflects both legal and cultural factors. Here is an international sampling of electoral customs, laws, and practices, intended not to provide a complete picture of any one system but simply to reflect the extraordinary diversity in electoral systems across different democracies. Some of these diverse practices might well be imported into the U.S. system; others would be unconstitutional, or so clearly at odds with our traditions and political culture that they would be inappropriate in the American context.

United Kingdom. British elections are held every five years, or whenever Parliament dissolves itself by majority vote. In general, the majority party can control when Parliament is dissolved, and tries to choose the optimal date for dissolution. "The Prime Minister can call the election at a time when voters are feeling prosperous and when the government is riding high in the polls," writes Dennis Kavanaugh, a professor at Nottingham University. "By 1959, and certainly by 1964, opinion-poll findings of voting intentions were a major influence on a government's decision on when to go to the country." Such strategy doesn't always work; of the last twelve dissolutions, the party in power has won seven and lost five. "Of course," adds Kavanaugh, "without control of the timing the government party might have done even worse."

Another important distinction is that the entire election campaign in Great Britain lasts just three weeks compared with a year or longer in the United States.

Scandinavia. Sweden, Norway, Finland, and Denmark all require television stations to provide free coverage of special campaign events, including debates. Paid television advertising has recently made its debut in Scandinavia but remains a minor factor in the campaign. Television provides three types of programs: hourlong interviews with the leaders of the major parties; one or two issue-oriented debates; and, finally, a major debate between party leaders a few days be-

fore the election. Rules allowing every party represented in Parliament to participate in these programs improve the fortunes of minor parties. In Denmark, every party is allowed to participate in the final televised debate, often producing chaos.

Japan. Long-standing Japanese tradition frowns on candidate-centered campaign activities, favoring party activities instead. All campaign activities by parties and candidates alike are limited to a fifteen-day "official campaign period," and all house-to-house canvassing is prohibited. In addition, as the political scientist Gerald L. Curtis writes, "There are restrictions on candidate speech-making activities and a prohibition on the distribution by candidates of written materials (handbills, newsletters, campaign buttons, and so on) except for those the election law expressly permits. These sanctioned materials include some 35,000 postcards and, depending on the size of the district, between 60,000 and 100,000 handbills. . . . Candidates can display their campaign posters only on government-provided poster boards; they may use a specified number of additional posters to publicize the time and place of a planned speech." In the extremely unlikely event that these rules were adopted in the United States, it seems clear that the Supreme Court would nullify every one as a violation of the First Amendment.

Australia. "The exceptional feature of Australian electoral life," writes Colin A. Hughes of the University of Queensland, "has been compulsory voting." All Australian citizens are legally required to vote, under penalty of a $20 fine. Similar compulsion is used in Belgium, Spain, and Greece (Italy does not require its citizens to vote, but it stamps DID NOT VOTE on the identification papers of nonvoters). Not surprisingly, Australian turnout rates are high, hovering around 96 percent of the eligible electorate. The low fine for not voting, lax enforcement of the compulsory voting rule, and a variety of legal excuses account for the roughly four percent of Australians who do not vote.

SOURCE: This discussion draws on the following chapters from David Butler and Austin Ranney, *Electioneering: A Comparative Study of Continuity and Change* (Oxford: Clarendon Press, 1992): Dennis Kavanaugh, "The United Kingdom," pp. 71–72; Peter Esaiasson, "Scandinavia," pp. 210–212; Gerald L. Curtin, "Japan," pp. 223–225; and Colin A. Hughes, "Australia and New Zealand," pp. 92–94. See also David Glass, Peverill Squire, and Raymond Wolfinger, "Voter Turnout: An International Comparison," *Public Opinion* (December 1983/January 1984), pp. 49–55.

America. The Republicans turned incumbency against many officeholders, arguing that entrenched politicians were the problem in Washington, not the solution.

The Republicans' success at nationalizing the 1994 congressional elections prompted the Democrats to try a similar approach in 1996. Democratic candidates across the nation sought to tie Republican candidates to the now-unpopular Speaker Newt Gingrich, and to the Republican leaderships' proposals to slow the growth of spending on Medicare and education. To some extent, the Democrats succeeded, winning back around twenty of the seats they had lost in 1994. In other ways, however, 1996 represented a return to form; incumbents fared far better than in 1994, with only twenty-one losing their seats compared to thirty-four. Finally, the 1996 electorate made it clear that its preference was not for radical change, as the victorious Republicans had claimed after 1994, but for continued divided government, though with the Republicans and Democrats exchanging places in the White House and Congress.[23]

State and Local Elections America holds more elections than any other country. Besides federal elections, Americans have the opportunity (or duty, or burden) of participating in state and local elections. These include major campaigns for governor and lieutenant governor along with elections for state legislatures, judges, state cabinet officials, city and county councils, mayors and county executives, school boards, district attorneys, and the proverbial dogcatchers.[*]

State election laws and procedures are highly variable. In general, turnout in state and local elections is lower than in national races, so many states time their elections to coincide with presidential or congressional elections. At the local level, campaigns are often won or lost on the basis of personal reputations, campaign organization, fund-raising, and one-on-one politicking. Statewide races, especially in large states, resemble national elections in their emphasis on paid and unpaid media, debates, and other efforts to reach large groups of voters.

Initiatives, Referenda, and Recall. All federal elections are to select individual officeholders. At the national level, voters never make direct choices on particular laws or policies, nor even on constitutional amendments. The federal emphasis on restricting voters to the choice of individuals rather than specific policies derives from the Framers' efforts to filter democratic choices through representatives rather than allow for direct popular rule.

By contrast, several states permit and encourage direct citizen involvement in lawmaking decisions. An **initiative** allows citizens to place a proposed law on the ballot by petition, for approval or rejection by the electorate. In some states, initiatives must be submitted to the legislature for approval prior to being voted on by the people. A **referendum,** by contrast, is proposed by the legislature, then voted on by the people. **Recall** allows voters to remove state elected officials by majority vote. Typically, recalls first require a petition signed by 10 to 40 percent of the electorate.

Twenty-one states allow some form of initiative; thirty-four allow or require some form of referendum; fifteen allow recall of some or all elected officials. Many of the states allowing these direct forms of citizen involvement are located in the western half of the country. California, in particular, has frequently created national shock waves through initiatives, referenda, and recalls. For example, in 1996 California voters approved Proposition 209, an initiative designed to end state-sponsored affirmative action programs.

---

[*] The village of Mariemount, Ohio, still elects a town crier.

The Modern Campaign

Modern campaigns are enormously expensive operations. They require paid staff, huge travel budgets, specialized consultants, and the latest in technological wizardry. But above all they demand large amounts of money to provide access to media, especially in the form of paid television commercials. Thus money and media in modern electoral politics are inextricably linked.

Money

The total amount of money spent in local, state, and national elections amounts to billions of dollars. In a single presidential election, the candidates and the major parties spend, in all, over $500 million.[24]

Why do campaigns cost so much? Although television advertising is the most visible expense, campaigns face many other costs. These include printing and mailing costs, rent for campaign headquarters, telephone charges, consultants and paid staff workers, computers, and office supplies. In a study of thirty high-cost races in Seattle, Washington, in 1989, media advertising took roughly one-third of the total campaign budgets, printing and mailing another third, personnel about one-sixth, and everything else another sixth. Media can take a larger chunk of campaigns in large states.

Does money make a difference in political campaigns? It certainly makes it more difficult for challengers to unseat incumbents; even in 1994, for example, congressional incumbents outspent challengers by nearly five to one, and more than ninety percent were re-elected.[25] But money is not the only reason incumbents do well, nor does it guarantee success.

Vice President Al Gore appears at the Hai Lai Temple outside Los Angeles. Gore's appearance sparked a scandal when it was revealed that the event was a Democratic fund-raiser, and that several Temple nuns had destroyed important documents relating to fund-raising irregularities.

Campaign Finance Before 1974 The connection between money and politics is hardly new. In Thomas Jefferson's day, for example, politicians were generally expected to pay their own campaign expenses, not to mention the expenses of holding office. Two presidential campaigns and eight years of the presidency nearly bankrupted Jefferson, who ultimately had to sell his books to the government to remain solvent—in the process starting the Library of Congress.[26] Other politicians began soliciting help from government employees and from people who sought government employment. The practice of trading campaign contributions for government jobs and contracts was known as the "spoils system," and became a staple of nineteenth-century politics.

By the 1850s the parties had hit upon another major source of campaign funds: wealthy businessmen who were making large sums of money in the emerging industrial economy. By the turn of the century, such men were contributing huge amounts of money, especially to the Republican party. Between 1896 and 1900, for example, nearly 90 percent of Republican presidential campaign funds were contributed by New York City business interests.[27]

In the twentieth century, a new source of funds arose, especially for the Democrats: big labor. The major unions were solidly behind Franklin Roosevelt's New Deal and benefited greatly from laws like the National Labor Relations Act of 1935. Labor unions helped the Democrats with direct contributions as well as "in kind" contributions, which included voter registration drives, get-out-the-vote efforts, and other volunteer activities.

By the 1960s, major political campaigns were largely financed by wealthy individuals, large corporations, and large labor unions. The system reached its peak in 1972, during the Nixon-McGovern campaign. One Nixon contributor, the insurance executive W. Clement Stone, gave over $2 million. In all, 1,254 individuals gave a total of $51.3 million to the two major parties—an average of over $40,000 a person. As the Watergate investigations subsequently showed, the 1972 election was full of irregularities and illegalities, including money laundering, cash contributions, and other efforts to hide the sources of campaign funds. The spirit of the age was perhaps best symbolized in the Senate Watergate Committee's discovery that the Nixon reelection campaign once accepted a paper bag filled with cash.

Federal efforts to regulate and control campaign contributions before the 1970s approached the problem from three directions: elimination of the spoils system, restrictions on individual and corporate contributions, and requirements for public disclosure. Each time the federal government acted, however, political contributors found ways around the system. The first approach was partially successful, although the practice of awarding ambassadorships and other top government jobs to big contributors remains to this day. The other two approaches were basically ineffective.

Modern Campaign Finance Reform Congress approved stronger reform measures only after the campaign finance scandals of the 1960s and 1970s. Modern campaign finance reform began with the passage of the **Federal Election Campaign Act of 1971.** The heart of the 1971 reform focused on tightened disclosure and spending requirements. Another 1971 law established the Presidential Election Campaign Fund, which provides for public funding of presidential campaigns. Under the 1971 law, which is still in effect, taxpayers are allowed to allocate $1 (now $3) of their taxes to the fund, which is then turned over to the presidential candidates for campaign expenses.

The Federal Election Campaign Act provided an enormous amount of information on campaign finance practices, and helped investigators uncover the irregularities of Nixon's 1972 campaign, which led to the Watergate affair. Watergate inspired even more ambitious reforms, known as the **Federal Election Campaign Act Amendments of 1974.** The 1974 package, which forms the basis of current campaign finance

Table 10.1
Median Expenditures of House Candidates in Contested Races, 1996

Winning incumbents	$491,103
Losing challengers	$235,912
Winning challengers	$483,462
Losing incumbents	$822,983
Open-seat winners	$527,895
Open-seat losers	$376,942

NOTE: "Contested races" are defined as those in which the winner received less than 60 percent of the two-party vote.

SOURCE: Compiled from data provided by the Center for Responsive Politics.

law, included limits on campaign contributions; on independent expenditures on behalf of a particular candidate; and on the amount that individuals can spend on their own campaigns. The law also established limits on the amount that candidates can spend in House and Senate races, and extended public financing of presidential elections to include a matching grant system for primary elections and grants to parties to help fund their nominating conventions. Finally, it created an independent federal commission, known as the Federal Elections Commission (FEC), to oversee enforcement of the act. Two members of the FEC were to be appointed by the president, two by the House of Representatives, and two by the Senate.

The new law also eased limits on political action committees (PACs). PACs are organizations set up to raise money and to distribute it to various candidates and parties. For years, PACs had provided a way for corporations and labor unions to evade the federal ban on direct contributions: they simply set up independent committees, then encouraged their employees or members to make contributions. However, the growth of PACs was limited, since neither corporate funds nor union dues could be used to set up or administer an independent PAC.

The 1974 act removed this limitation. The idea behind the repeal was that PACs would replace big contributors as a major source of campaign funds, allowing small donors to pool their resources to amplify their influence. Individuals were limited to contributing $5,000 to any one PAC, and PACs were limited to contributing $5,000 to any one campaign.

Since 1974, the number of PACs and their influence on campaign finance have increased tremendously (see the discussion in Chapter 8).

Buckley v. Valeo: The Supreme Court Speaks. The 1974 reforms were immediately subjected to a legal test. Those who challenged the new law argued that its limits on expenditures and contributions violated the First Amendment, and that the makeup of the FEC violated the separation of powers.

In the 1976 case of **Buckley v. Valeo**, the Court rendered a split verdict. The Court struck down the Federal Election Campaign Act's limits on independent expenditures and on personal expenditures by the candidates and their families. Since campaign money is spent largely to communicate ideas, the Court said, such limits were direct limits on free speech. The Court also struck down the makeup of the FEC, holding that Congress could not directly appoint members of the executive branch.

But the Court did uphold limits on campaign *contributions,* ruling that the free speech value of contributions was largely symbolic. "By contrast with a limitation upon expenditures for political expression," the majority wrote, "a limitation on the amount of money a person may give to a candidate or campaign organization . . . involves little direct restraint on his political communication, for it permits the symbolic expression of support evidenced by a contribution but does not in any way infringe the contributor's freedom to discuss candidates and issues."[28]

The New Rules of the Game. After the *Buckley* decision and some additional amendments to the Federal Elections Campaign Act, the new rules of the game were set. Briefly summarized, here is the state of current federal campaign finance law:[29]

• *Public funding of presidential campaigns.* Major party candidates who accept public funding automatically receive federal campaign funds (a little over $60 million in 1996). Candidates accepting these funds are barred from spending additional money on the general election campaign. Third party candidates and candidates in the major

Figure 10.2 **PAC Contributions to Congressional Candidates, 1994–1996**

With the Republican takeover of Congress in 1994, PAC giving shifted sharply toward the Republican side. Note especially the shifts in defense industry and abortion interest group contributions.

■ 1996 ■ 1996
■ 1994 ■ 1994

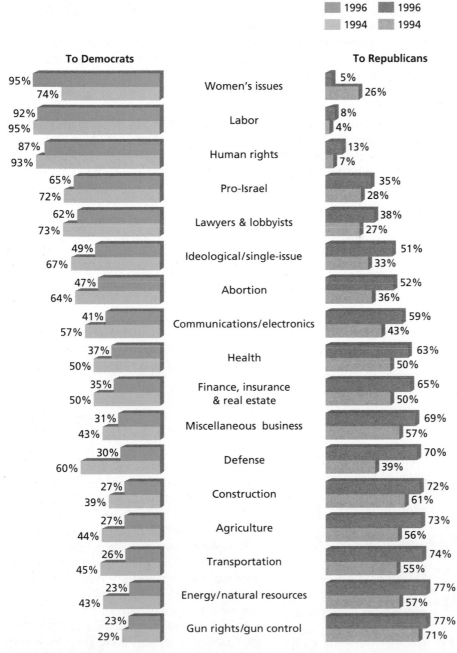

To Democrats	Category	To Republicans
95% / 74%	Women's issues	5% / 26%
92% / 95%	Labor	8% / 4%
87% / 93%	Human rights	13% / 7%
65% / 72%	Pro-Israel	35% / 28%
62% / 73%	Lawyers & lobbyists	38% / 27%
49% / 67%	Ideological/single-issue	51% / 33%
47% / 64%	Abortion	52% / 36%
41% / 57%	Communications/electronics	59% / 43%
37% / 50%	Health	63% / 50%
35% / 50%	Finance, insurance & real estate	65% / 50%
31% / 43%	Miscellaneous business	69% / 57%
30% / 60%	Defense	70% / 39%
27% / 39%	Construction	72% / 61%
27% / 44%	Agriculture	73% / 56%
26% / 45%	Transportation	74% / 55%
23% / 43%	Energy/natural resources	77% / 57%
23% / 29%	Gun rights/gun control	77% / 71%

SOURCE: Center for Responsive Politics.

party primaries also receive public funding according to a complex formula that depends on the number of votes won.

- *Individual contributions* are limited to $1,000 per candidate per campaign, and $5,000 per PAC per year. Thus by contributing both to a candidate's primary and general election campaign, an individual can contribute $2,000.
- *Individual contributions* are capped at $25,000 a year. This includes contributions to candidates and PACs. It also includes unrestricted contributions to party organizations, but not contributions used for "party-building" purposes, such as voter registration drives and "get-out-the-vote" efforts. Even the limit on contributions to candidates and PACs is difficult to police, however; a 1991 *Los Angeles Times* investigation turned up sixty-two individuals across the country who had exceeded the limit, apparently without being challenged by the FEC.[30]
- *PAC contributions* are limited to $5,000 per candidate in the primary election and $5,000 per candidate in the general election. There is no overall limit on the total amount a PAC can contribute to all candidates.
- *Contributions from the political parties* are limited to $5,000 per candidate, though the major party senatorial campaign committees are allowed to contribute $17,500 to each senate candidate.
- *Independent expenditures* by individuals and PACs are unlimited. An individual or PAC can underwrite campaign commercials on behalf of a particular candidate, as long as these expenditures are made without the knowledge or cooperation of the candidate or campaign they are intended to help. In 1994, for example, PACs favoring term limits on congressmen spent at least $56,000 in a successful effort to defeat Speaker of the House Tom Foley in Washington state.[31]
- *Campaign spending by the candidates themselves* is unlimited. This rule gives a great advantage to wealthy candidates, who can fund their own election campaigns. However, presidential candidates who accept public funding may not add additional funds from their own pockets.

The Failure of the Post-Watergate Reforms

The 1974 reforms changed the way American political campaigns were financed, and between 1976 and 1984 the system seemed to work fairly well. By the 1990s, however, the post-Watergate campaign finance reforms were in shambles. The collapse of the system occurred primarily because candidates of both parties learned to exploit various loopholes in the system, and because the Federal Election Commission lacked the resources necessary for meaningful enforcement of the laws. Among the loopholes, inadequacies, and difficulties of the current system are these:

The Extraordinary Influence of PACs. Both the $5,000 limit on individual contributions to PACs and the $5,000 limit on PAC contributions

"THIS IS AMERICA, SON, WHERE ANYBODY WITH TWENTY MILLION BUCKS TO SPEND COULD END UP BEING PRESIDENT."

to particular campaigns are easy to work around by simply increasing the number of PACs. Today, a well-funded candidate can receive hundreds of thousands of dollars in PAC contributions. Many of these PACs represent only a single corporation, effectively allowing an end-run around the federal ban on corporate contributions. In 1995–1996, for example, Representative Charles Schumer (D–NY) received over $300,000 in PAC contributions—including donations from PACs representing Merrill Lynch, Morgan Stanley, Chase Manhattan, and American Express. He also received contributions from the National Association of Letter Carriers, the American Postal Workers Union, and the National Association of Postmasters.

"Soft Money." Money contributed to state parties or to the "party-building" activities of the national parties, but used to influence federal campaigns, is known as "soft money." In theory, soft money must be spent to promote the parties, rather than individual candidates, but in practice it has been impossible to prevent the parties from using soft money however they wish. A 1996 study by the campaign reform group Common Cause found that television ad campaigns financed by soft money were prepared and controlled by the presidential campaigns of Bob Dole and Bill Clinton; promoted the parties' candidates or attacked the opposition; and were targeted to run in key presidential election states such as California and Ohio.[32]

Soft money has become the tail that wags the dog of campaign finance. In the 1995–1996 campaign cycle, the two major parties raised over $260 million in soft money—more than twice the amount allotted to them by public funding. Individual and corporate contributors, freed from the limits imposed by federal law, have opened up their checkbooks in staggering amounts. In 1994, Amway Corporation gave $2.5 million to the Republican party; in 1996, various tobacco interests contributed more than $5 million to the two major parties.

It was in pursuit of "soft money" that President Bill Clinton hosted White House "coffees" for large contributors. Although federal law bans the solicitation of funds on federal property, Clinton claimed that these functions were legal and appropriate, since, he argued, no direct requests for money were made. Whether or not the White House coffees violated the letter of the law, for many Americans they came to represent a return to the pre-Watergate style of campaign finance.

Figure 10.3 **"Soft Money" Giving to National Parties, 1996 Election**

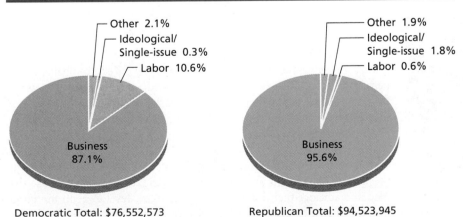

Other 2.1%
Ideological/ Single-issue 0.3%
Labor 10.6%
Business 87.1%

Other 1.9%
Ideological/ Single-issue 1.8%
Labor 0.6%
Business 95.6%

Democratic Total: $76,552,573   Republican Total: $94,523,945

Source: Center for Responsive Politics

International Contributions. Federal law bans campaign contributions by foreign nationals. Thus, after the 1996 elections, the Democratic National Committee (DNC) was forced to return a $250,000 contribution from a Korean corporation. The ban on foreign contributions is riddled with loopholes, however. It is perfectly legal for American companies owned by foreigners to make campaign contributions (the $250,000 contribution returned by the DNC would have been legal if it had been made not by the Korean corporation, but by its U.S. subsidiary). It is also lawful for foreign citizens to make campaign contributions if they are legally resident in the United States. Thus the DNC kept a $450,000 contribution from an Indonesian couple who returned to their home country shortly after the election.

The Rich Candidate Exemption. The Supreme Court's decision lifting all limits on a candidate's contribution to his or her own campaign has given a great advantage to wealthy candidates. The best-known beneficiary of this rule is Ross Perot, who was able to spend as much of his own money as he wanted on his 1992 presidential bid. This rule has benefited wealthy candidates, who have a clear advantage over their opponents if they are willing to spend their own money to get elected. Still, money does not guarantee success: Republican candidate Michael Huffington spent $28 million of his own money in the 1994 California Senate race, but lost to Senator Dianne Feinstein—though just barely.[33]

The Future of Campaign Finance Reform.   The campaign finance scandals that developed during and after the 1996 election seemed to provide an opportunity for meaningful campaign finance reform. According to a 1997 poll, Americans favored every important campaign finance reform proposal on Capitol Hill, and supported a ban on "soft money" by a margin of almost three to one. However, most of those surveyed also believed that "special interests will always find a way to maintain their power in Washington" no matter what laws were passed.[34] The public's skepticism on the value of even the best-intentioned reform may help explain why the campaign finance reform movement quickly lost momentum. Congressional hearings on the subject became bogged down in partisan wrangling, and no action was taken.

Mary Matalin and James Carville—the political equivalents of Romeo and Juliet—tie the marriage knot. Matalin was a major player in George Bush's 1992 reelection bid; her soon-to-be-husband was a key adviser to Bill Clinton.

Media

Campaign politics is dominated as never before by the electronic media, especially television. In a very real sense, the media now provide the playing field on which elections are won or lost. But the ground under that playing field is rapidly shifting, with the development of new media technologies and a growing level of sophistication among candidates, media advisers, and voters.

The 1990s have seen fundamental shifts in the role of the media in presidential campaigns and in the way candidates react to and use the media to advance their interests. Whether these developments are good for the American people or for the democratic process remains very much an open question.

A bus—not a train—was the focus of the Clinton-Gore campaign's "whistle-stop" tour in 1992. By using a bus, the campaign hoped to suggest that Clinton and Gore, in contrast to the aristocratic George Bush and the billionaire H. Ross Perot, were men of the people.

The Media As Stage   In the early days of television and radio, the media's role was mainly to report on campaign events and developments. Occasionally, candidates would schedule live radio or television appearances. Later, candidates began to purchase time on commercial radio and television stations for campaign advertisements. For the most part, however, the candidate's personal appearances—duly reported in the press—were the centerpiece of the campaign. As late as 1948, for example, Harry Truman's main campaign vehicle was a whistle-stop train tour across the nation.

Candidates still engage in exhaustive (and exhausting) personal appearances, although the train has been largely replaced by the airplane and the modern whistle-stop takes place on an airport runway. The difference is that virtually all such events are designed to generate media interest and coverage, thus dramatically expanding the number of voters who see and hear the candidate. The candidate's thirty-minute airport stopover—like every other aspect of a modern campaign—is not designed for the benefit of the immediate audience but for the national and local evening news audiences.

The Media As Critics and Scorekeepers   The decline of parties in the modern era has made the electoral process infinitely more complicated and confusing than in the past. Popular involvement in the nominations process means that voters have to choose among as many as a dozen candidates of the same party. Weakening partisan attachments mean that voters must weigh the strengths and weaknesses of the major party nominees, instead of relying on party labels or endorsements.

As the power of the party bosses fell, the media stepped in to fill the gap. Establishing themselves as intermediaries between the candidates and the people, the major television and print media took it upon themselves to screen the candidates—"to inspect their character, their charisma, their competence, their skills, [and] their electability."[35] The media began to play a key role in winnowing the presidential field and handicapping the race.

Given the media's central role in the campaign, their judgments could easily become self-fulfilling prophecies. A candidate thought to have no chance of winning would be ignored by the press, would never be seen by the public, and thus would have no chance of winning. If the media decided that a campaign was losing momentum, press coverage would focus on the momentum issue and the campaign would in fact lose momentum.

In the 1992 campaign, for example, the media decided early that Senator Paul Tsongas of Massachusetts was not a serious candidate. When Tsongas announced his candidacy, only three dozen reporters showed up, and when he went to Iowa, none of the regular press corps followed him. Tsongas actually won the New Hampshire primary, with 33 percent of the vote, but the media decided that runner-up Bill Clinton was the real winner. Clinton's feat had been to survive intense media flaps over his alleged affair with the nightclub singer Gennifer Flowers and his alleged draft-dodging during the Vietnam War. Ironically, Clinton's "victory" in New Hampshire was accomplished largely by beating the media critics at their own game. By confounding the media's own predictions that his campaign was over, Clinton's survival became the big story of the New Hampshire primary.[36]

Bypassing the Mainstream Media   The media's role changed profoundly, and perhaps forever, on February 20, 1992, the night Texas billionaire H. Ross Perot appeared on CNN's *Larry King Live* interview program. Perot hinted that he might be persuaded to run for the presidency, but only if the voters in all fifty states acted on their own to put him on the ballot. Much of Perot's appeal seemed to be his direct approach, bypassing the media, the major parties, and any other middlemen. That his campaign was dismissed by media critics and Washington pundits only served to increase its credibility.

Perot did not invent the idea of bypassing the mainstream media, but he did come to symbolize it. Moreover, his success was copied by the other candidates in the race and will serve as a blueprint for the future.

In bypassing the mainstream media, Perot had the great advantage of being able to draw on virtually unlimited personal funds. But he also had access to a host of new technologies that together have the potential to transform American electoral politics. Among the methods used by Perot and others to bypass the mainstream media were these:

- *Direct television.* The *Larry King Live* appearance was only the first of many occasions when Perot took his case directly to the people. Toward the end of the campaign, he bought thirty-minute slots on national television to pitch his case directly.

    Other candidates learned that with a little effort they could get on television for free. Appearances on talk shows, television "magazines" like *Sixty Minutes,* and specialized cable stations all allow the candidate to make a more or less direct pitch to the public. Clinton even appeared on Arsenio Hall's show, playing his saxophone.

- *The local press.* Candidates have also learned that local news shows are usually thrilled to have a presidential candidate on live, and are likely to ask easy, open-ended questions. With modern technology, candidates can give interviews to dozens of local stations across the country from a single location.

AN **OUTSIDER-PARTY** CANDIDATE IS FORCED TO ADMIT THAT HE ONCE VISITED WASHINGTON, D.C.

- *The tabloid press.* Alternatives to the major networks and the mainstream print media are rapidly emerging as an easy way to reach the public. On television, shows like *Hard Copy* and *A Current Affair* are willing to showcase stories the major networks refuse to touch. In print, magazines like the *Star* and *People* play a similar role. Magazines and newspapers outside the political mainstream—such as the *American Spectator* and the *Washington Times*—also take up stories that the regular press leaves alone. But the tabloid press is often less accountable than the mainstream media, rarely makes an effort to present both sides of the story, and may sacrifice accuracy in pursuit of flashy headlines.

- *Radio and TV talk shows.* Another "new media" outlet is talk radio and television. Radio and TV hosts, such as the conservative Rush Limbaugh, provide another significant mechanism by which candidates can take their case directly to the people. Local radio shows can also play an important role.
- *The Internet.* For the 1996 election, several presidential campaigns established Internet "home pages" featuring candidate biographies and other information. Although used by only a tiny fraction of voters, these electronic outposts may be forerunners of an important campaign tool of the future.

The role of the new media is discussed in more detail in Chapter 11.

Using the Media   The new media age has changed not only the style of political campaigns but also their substance. To succeed, candidates need to be highly skilled in the art of media manipulation.

Sound Bites and Visuals. Campaign strategists realize that their total exposure on the average nightly news broadcast will be less than a minute—sometimes only a few seconds. It is critical to ensure that those few seconds present the candidate in the best light and that they allow the candidate to talk on a topic of his or her own choosing. These brief statements by a candidate or public official are known as sound bites.

Television producers are trained to pick out highlights that have strong visual appeal, or that show drama or confrontation (these are known colloquially as visuals). A well-organized campaign will see to it that the candidate continually repeats the same theme over and over on any given day, thus ensuring that no other message makes it to the television screen. Even better, the message should be packaged as a brief sound bite and backed up by a strong visual image.

If the campaign has done its job, television producers will have no choice but to show what the campaign wants them to show. If the campaign has slipped up, the entire day's message will be lost or, worse yet, replaced by an image showing the candidate at his or her worst.

Negative Campaigning. One way to attract attention, from both voters and the media, is to "go negative." Direct attacks on the opposition inject a sense of drama into the campaign and can be easily packaged into usable sound bites or paid advertisements. Moreover, negative campaigning may force the opposition candidate into a defensive position, as journalists press for a response or rebuttal. Once the opponent does respond, he or she has lost the chance to dominate the day's news coverage.

Negative campaigning does carry risks. For one thing, it takes attention away from the positive aspects of one's own campaign. It can also increase voter cynicism and turn off potential supporters. Most seriously, from the candidate's point of view, negative campaigning may produce sympathy for the opposition and may inspire brutal counterattacks.

One way to diffuse the adverse effects of negative campaigning is to use humor to sugarcoat the pill. An advertisement used against former Ku Klux Klan leader David Duke in the 1990 Louisiana governor's race, for example, used the *Jeopardy* game show ("I'll take Former Nazi Buddies for $50") to sugarcoat a bitter message—allowing Duke's opponents to attack him without creating a hint of sympathy.

Rapid Response. One lesson put to good use by George Bush in 1988 and Bill Clinton in 1992 is the necessity of responding rapidly to opponents' charges and criticism, and to do so in a way that does not detract from the campaign's own message. The key is to minimize the impact of a negative story by dealing with it within one news cycle—typically, on the same day. The responsibility for rapid response in the 1992 Clinton campaign was left

Negative campaigning is nothing new. In the 1884 presidential race between the Democrat Grover Cleveland and the Republican James G. Blaine, both sides got into the act. The Democrats charged Blaine with corruption; the Republicans accused Cleveland (truthfully, it turned out) of fathering a child out-of-wedlock. Gleeful Republicans sang a new song: "Ma, ma, where's my Pa/Gone to the White House, Ha Ha Ha!"

to George Stephanopoulos, later a White House aide. As one reporter recalls it, Stephanopoulos's response to George Bush's acceptance speech at the Republican National Convention came before Bush had even delivered the speech! [37]

Combating negative campaigning is not always so easy, mainly because the opposition can be equally skilled in responding with a counterstrategy. In most cases, however, it is better to respond quickly and be done with an issue than to let an accusation simmer.

The Direct Approach: Paid Advertising   An effective but expensive way to reach voters is to purchase time on television and radio for campaign advertising. Advertisements range from fifteen-second commercials highlighting a candidate's name and basic message to thirty-minute "infomercials" that have the tone and feel of ordinary programming. The infomercial approach can be effective, although the cost of such programs is so high that they are useful only for campaigns where money is no object.

Political advertising has been the subject of intense controversy. Critics charge that commercials allow candidates to be sold like soap (in recent years, some political commercials have become so negative that the comparison seems unfair to soap). Advertising emphasizes emotion over reason and image over issues, according to critics, and gives well-heeled candidates (especially incumbents) an overwhelming advantage. Suggested remedies include requiring television stations to provide free advertising time, banning commercials of less than five minutes' duration, and educating voters to look past the advertising to more substantive issues.

Some scholars take a more benign view of political advertising. The communications expert Kathleen Hall Jamieson, for example, argues that political advertising should be viewed as an integral part of a candidate's overall campaign message. Focusing on paid advertising over the course of a campaign "can reveal a campaign's fundamental coherence or incoherence." The vigilance of the printed press and of the opposition party makes it unlikely that candidates can successfully use paid advertising to lie, about either their own views or their opponents'. In the end, she writes, political advertising "legitimizes our political institutions by affirming that change is possible within the political system, that the president can effect change, that voters can make a difference."[38]

Voters

All of the energy, money, and effort put into election campaigns is directed toward one goal: winning the support of voters. Before they can vote, of course, voters must decide whether to vote. This section examines who votes and who does not, and how voters make their decisions.

Voter Turnout

Although voting is only one of many ways that Americans can participate in politics, it is perhaps the most important. The existence of a free and robust electoral system is central to any definition of democracy. It is also essential to the citizen's own feelings of empowerment and involvement in public life and to ensuring that his or her interests and preferences are taken into account by government officials. Voting thus plays both a substantive and symbolic role in legitimizing and preserving democratic government.

Figure 10.4 **Voter Turnout in Presidential Elections 1888–1996**

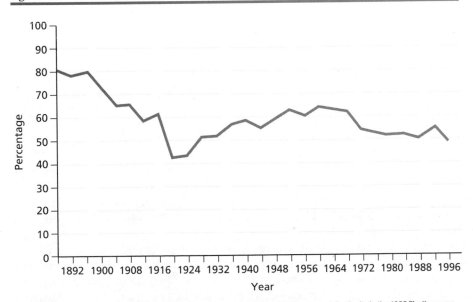

Source: Data from Paul R. Abramson, John H. Aldrich, and David W. Rohde, *Change and Continuity in the 1988 Elections,* rev. ed. (Washington, D.C.; CQ Press, 1991), pp. 89,91; United States Census Bureau.

Over the last century, **voter turnout**—measured as the percentage of eligible voters who choose to vote—has dropped sharply. A century ago, more than 80 percent of eligible voters showed up to vote in presidential elections. Turnout dropped sharply in the early part of the twentieth century, reaching lows of just above 40 percent in the 1920s. Turnout increased steadily until 1960, when it reached nearly 65 percent. It has dropped again over the past four decades, however, and dropped below 50 percent in 1996. Turnout in congressional, state, and local elections, and in primary elections, is even lower than that. Such statistics put the United States near the bottom of the international voter participation list, just ahead of Switzerland.

Who Votes and Who Doesn't   It is relatively clear who votes in the United States and who does not. The typical voter is older than thirty-five, has attended college, is employed in or retired from a white-collar job (or is a housewife), is reasonably well off economically, and is white. The typical nonvoter is young, has not been to college, is unemployed or employed in a blue-collar job, is poor, and is a member of a racial or ethnic minority. These profiles, of course, are drawn from statistical data, and are not meant to imply that there are no poor voters or that every college graduate votes. However, the likelihood that a person will vote increases dramatically as one moves up the educational and socioeconomic ladder, and across racial lines. (Unless otherwise noted, all figures in the following discussion are drawn from the presidential election of 1996.)

Age. Although the extension of voting rights to eighteen-year-olds in 1970 was hailed as a major extension of civil rights, in fact only 31.2 percent of all eligible voters under twenty-one actually turn out. The numbers rise steadily among older voters, reaching a maximum with the sixty-five to seventy-four age group, which turns out at a rate of 70.1 percent. Voters over seventy-five still turn out in high numbers, although the effects of age and illness begin to take their toll.

The tendency of younger Americans not to vote reflects a decline in the importance of voting as a cultural norm. Young voters have always been less likely to vote than their older counterparts, but today's young voters are less likely to vote than young voters of the past. Moreover, voter turnout among young voters dropped sharply in 1996, even compared to 1992. Whereas overall turnout was down around 7 percent, turnout among voters aged 21 to 24 dropped by more than 12 percentage points, to barely one-third of those eligible.

Employment, Education, and Income. As one moves up the socioeconomic ladder, the likelihood of voting increases dramatically. This tendency can be seen in statistics based on employment, education, and income, all three of which are closely linked to one another. Voters from families with incomes of over $40,000 report turnout rates upwards of 70 percent. Turnout rates steadily decline with income until, among the very poorest Americans, reported turnout rates are well below 50 percent. Likewise, 73.0 of those who completed at least one year of college reported voting in 1996, compared with 49.1 percent of those who attended high school for four years and only 28.1 percent of those with eight or fewer years of formal education.

Race. Almost 60 percent of whites report having voted, compared with barely 50 percent of blacks. Turnout among Hispanic voters is even lower than among blacks, a reported 26.7 percent. Lower turnout rates among racial minorities can be explained almost completely by the fact that blacks and other minorities tend to be poorer and less well educated than whites. Thus when blacks and whites with similar family incomes are compared, their reported turnout rates are roughly comparable.

Figure 10.5 **Voter Turnout Among Whites and Blacks by Family Income, 1992**

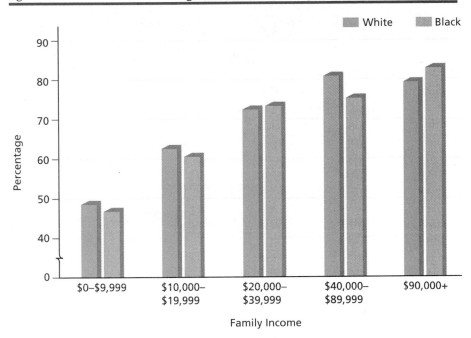

Source: National Election Study, 1992.

Explaining Nonvoting   Why do so many Americans fail to vote? Why do so many more stay away from the polls than in the past?

People do not vote for one of two reasons: they find the *costs* of voting (in time and energy) too high, or they find the *benefits* of voting too low.

The High Costs of Voting. Voting is not a particularly difficult or time-consuming act. Still, many people find it inconvenient. If voting were made easier for them, they might participate.

For some citizens—perhaps 5 percent of the electorate—voting is literally impossible. Some are hospitalized or bedridden. Others may have been called away on an unexpected trip, or find it difficult to get to the polls on election day because of work (Americans, as a group, are squeezed for time; many find it hard enough to carry out their day-to-day responsibilities, much less vote).[39] Little can be done about these nonvoters. Expanding the hours that the polls are open might help a little. Eventually, advances in technology might permit voting by telephone—from work, a hospital bed, or Tokyo. For the present, however, this "frictional nonvoting" (so-called because, like friction in a mechanical system, it cannot be avoided) must simply be accepted as a fact of life. In any event, even if the cost of voting in time and energy could be reduced to almost zero, most experts believe that turnout would grow by only a few percentage points.

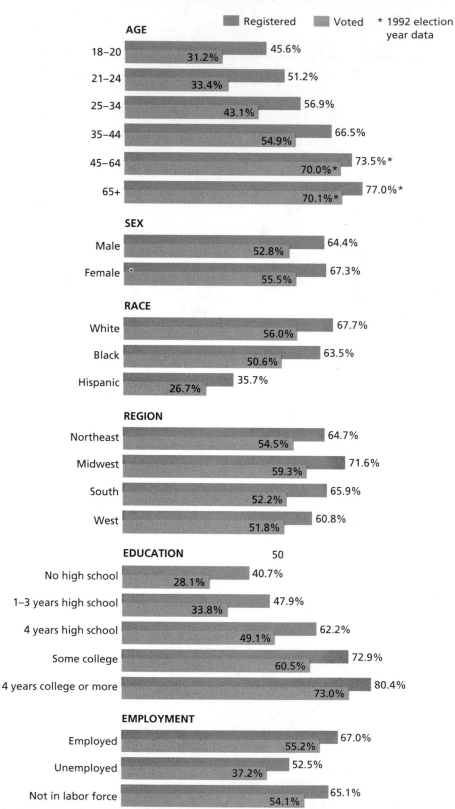

Percentage of the voting-age population who registered/voted in the 1996 presidential election

■ Registered ■ Voted   * 1992 election year data

AGE

18–20   45.6%   31.2%
21–24   51.2%   33.4%
25–34   56.9%   43.1%
35–44   66.5%   54.9%
45–64   73.5%* 70.0%*
65+   77.0%* 70.1%*

SEX

Male   64.4%   52.8%
Female 67.3%   55.5%

RACE

White   67.7%   56.0%
Black   63.5%   50.6%
Hispanic 35.7%   26.7%

REGION

Northeast 64.7%   54.5%
Midwest   71.6%   59.3%
South   65.9%   52.2%
West   60.8%   51.8%

EDUCATION   50

No high school   40.7%   28.1%
1–3 years high school   47.9%   33.8%
4 years high school   62.2%   49.1%
Some college   72.9%   60.5%
4 years college or more 80.4%   73.0%

EMPLOYMENT

Employed   67.0%   55.2%
Unemployed   52.5%   37.2%
Not in labor force 65.1%   54.1%

Figure 10.6 **Registering and Voting, 1996**

Percentage of the voting age population who reported registering/voting in the 1996 presidential election

SOURCE: 1997 *Statistical Abstract,* Table 462, p. 288.

Some citizens do not vote because they are not registered to vote. Among registered voters, the actual turnout rate is fairly high. Recent laws have tried to make it easier for citizens to register to vote. A federal law passed in 1993, known as the "motor-voter" bill, requires states to allow citizens to register to vote at the same time they apply for or renew their driver's licenses. The new law also requires states to allow registration by mail, and provides that registration forms must be available at various state and local agencies that serve the public.[40] Projecting the impact of such laws is not easy, but studies have suggested that they will increase turnout by somewhere between 4 and 15 percentage points, adding between 7 and 29 million voters.

The total number of Americans whose nonvoting can be attributed to the high costs of voting is probably about 20 to 30 million. That still leaves the bulk of the nonvoters—around 60 million, or around 30 percent of the potential electorate—to be accounted for.

The Low Benefits of Voting. These 60 million Americans do not vote because they do not find it worth their while to do so. In other words, they perceive the benefits of voting as so low as to be not worth the cost.

- *"Why Should I Bother?"* Although many Americans view voting as an important act of citizenship, many obviously do not. Citizens who feel disconnected from society at large find little reason to vote. The importance of social connectedness as a predictor of voting behavior helps explain why young, poor, and unemployed or underemployed citizens turn out in far fewer numbers than their older, wealthier, and better-employed counterparts. Middle-aged professionals who own their own homes have strong incentives to vote, and may feel some pressure from friends and colleagues to do so. Unemployed twenty-year-olds are unlikely to experience either set of pressures.[41]

  On the whole, however, the past few decades have seen little if any decline in the number of Americans who believe that participating in the political process is a citizen's duty. Similarly, there has been little decline in Americans' interest in politics. Thus the decline in voter turnout cannot be attributed to declining levels of either civic duty or political interest.[42]

- *"My Vote Won't Matter."* Many Americans do not bother to vote because they feel their vote will not make a difference. This simple sentiment can actually mean one of three different things.

  Some who say their vote won't matter realize that the odds that their one vote will affect the outcome of any particular race are virtually nil. No presidential or statewide race has ever been decided by a single vote. When a local race is decided by one vote, it is a rare enough occurrence to qualify as national news.

  Others who believe their votes don't count are actually saying that *it doesn't matter which candidate wins.*

"AND THEY WONDER WHY WE DON'T VOTE...."

The number of voters expressing such views has increased markedly over the past few decades. For example, the number of Americans who think that elections make the government pay a good deal of attention to what the people think has declined from 65 percent in 1964 to only 42 percent in 1992. Moreover, increasing numbers of Americans distrust government; in 1992, for example, 63.2 percent of the American public expressed the view that the government could be trusted to do what is right never or only some of the time. More than two-thirds of all Americans believe that government is "run by big interests," and over 40 percent believe that "many" in the government are "crooked." Studies indicate that declining feelings of trust in government could account for as much as half of the decline in voter turnout over the past three decades.[43]

- *Declining Party Identification.* Americans who strongly identify with one or the other of the major political parties are much more likely to vote than those who are independent or apolitical. In 1992, for example, reported turnout among strong partisans was 78.8 percent, compared with only 49.6 among independents and apoliticals. In 1980, according to scholarly estimates, the declining partisanship of the electorate accounted for a drop of 2.5 percentage points compared with 1960 turnout levels (out of a total decline of 10.2 percentage points). Since 1980, however, turnout among strong partisans has declined, and in 1992 declining partisanship accounted for only 1.9 percentage points out of a total decline of 11.7 percentage points since 1960. Thus declining party identification has had only a small impact on voter turnout.

Does Low Voter Turnout Matter?   In the end, the important question is whether massive nonvoting really matters. This question can be broken down into three parts. First, what effect would proposed (or recently enacted) changes in registration and voting procedures have on the makeup of the electorate? Second, how would the election results change if nonvoters were somehow persuaded to participate? Finally, irrespective of changing outcomes, what effect does nonvoting have on the representation of diverse individuals and groups?

Expanding the Electorate. As we have seen, the American electorate does not represent an accurate cross section of the population as a whole. On average, the electorate overrepresents white, well-off, well-educated, and older voters. It underrepresents minorities, the poor, the poorly educated, and the young.

> *"The people might be better served if a party purchased a full half hour of radio and TV silence during which the audience would be allowed to think quietly to themselves."*
>
> —Adlai Stevenson, 1952

Reversing the evident biases in the makeup of the active electorate has provided a major justification for state, federal, party-sponsored, and private initiatives to expand voter registration and ease the voting process. Increasing registration (and, it is hoped, turnout) in inner-city areas has been a particular goal of those who would like to see poor and minority citizens better represented in the voting booth and in policy making.

Unfortunately, research suggests that increasing the number of voters by even a substantial amount will do little to redress the problem of bias in the voting population. The reason is not hard to find. Low turnout groups (such as African Americans) are underrepresented not only among people who do vote but also among those nonvoters who are *most likely* to become voters. In other words, African Americans and other low-turnout groups are *heavily overrepresented* among the large group of nonvoters who would not respond to initiatives designed to expand the electorate.

Changing Election Results? Paradoxically, studies suggest that increasing the participation rate of nonvoters would have little real impact on election results in any event. Forced to choose, nonvoters tend to support the major party candidates in roughly the same proportions as voters.

On the surface, this conclusion appears to contradict both expectations and experience. As we have seen, nonvoters do not represent a cross section of American society, but instead are drawn disproportionately from among the "have nots"—racial minorities, the poor and unemployed, the young and poorly educated. Since the members of such groups have traditionally supported the Democratic party, it stands to reason that an increase in voter participation would benefit the Democrats and hurt the Republicans. In fact, strategists in both parties have acted on this assumption for years. In 1994, for example, the Republican governor of California vetoed a state law implementing the federal "motor-voter" bill, which sought to increase turnout by easing the registration process.

The reality is more complex. Many nonvoters, it seems, have made a conscious and rational decision that *neither mainstream party* has their interests at heart. Although on the surface the Democratic party is the party of the poor and dispossessed, many nonvoters have concluded that the Democrats' support of social programs is aimed less at bringing about fundamental changes in the system than at maintaining order and assuaging the consciences of the middle class. To these nonvoters, both the Democrats and the Republicans are more interested in serving special interests and in placating the middle class than in serving the true interests of the social and political underclass.

To some scholars, American nonvoters display a keen sense of the realities of American politics. Unlike most nations of Europe, the United States has no socialist or workers' party, nor even a party that supports the basic overhaul of the current social and economic order. Without such an alternative, many citizens simply choose to stay home.

Is Low Voter Turnout a Sign of Moral Decay? Does the low rate of voter turnout reflect negatively on the American political system? Is it a sign of moral and political decay?

Some analysts suggest precisely the opposite. Low voter turnout, they argue, is at least partly a reflection of voter contentment and satisfaction with the system. Citizens with nothing to complain about and with no desire to change the system need not expend their energies on politics and can focus on more important things.

There is little real evidence for this position. Certainly the nonparticipation of some citizens is a sign of contentment, but for the most part nonvoters represent the least contented segments of the population. Low voter turnout is more a sign of alienation and disaffection than of happiness and satisfaction.

Does Low Voter Turnout Frustrate Equal Representation? When a group of potential voters does not turn out at the polls, politicians have little incentive to take their interests into account. Before passage of the Voting Rights Act, for example, southern politicians had no need to address the interests of African Americans. To this day, low voter turnout among minority groups makes it easier for politicians to ignore them when it comes to making key decisions.

The converse is also true: groups that have high rates of voter turnout may have a disproportionate influence on political decisions. High voting rates among older Americans, for example, is one reason why most politicians regard cuts in social security as unthinkable.

Voting Behavior

How do Americans who do vote decide how they cast their ballots? What factors influence voters' decisions to vote for or against a particular candidate? These questions have been the focus of much study, both by political scientists and by political consultants.

The factors influencing voter choice can be divided into short-term and long-term ones. Long-term factors include political ideology, political party affiliation, and socioeconomic status. Short-term factors include the individual candidates, specific issues, and recent party performance. The results of any particular election can be viewed as a combination of the long-term trend plus or minus a short-term deviation.

Long-Term Factors: Party and Ideology   As we have seen in earlier chapters, many Americans identify closely with one or the other of the major political parties. Many Americans also define themselves in ideological terms, placing themselves somewhere along the liberal-conservative spectrum. Unless short-term factors create reasons to do otherwise, these voters use party and ideology to guide their choice at the voting booth.

Historical research suggests that party and ideology do determine the votes of many Americans. At any given time, party loyalty and ideology provide a baseline of the "expected vote" for each party. The actual vote in any election can then be viewed as a deviation from this norm. Such deviations can easily be large enough to decide the election.[44]

The importance of party as a factor in determining voter choice has declined over the years. At one time, most voters chose a straight ticket—voted for one party down the line. Today, split-ticket voting is common. Still, party identification plays an important, if not always determinative, part in voting decisions.

As earlier chapters have indicated, party identification and ideology are correlated with voters' race, gender, and socioeconomic status, as well as with feelings on key political issues.

Short-Term Factors: Candidates, Issues, Party Performance   Any given election is decided by swing voters, whose loyalty to the parties and ideological orientation is weak or nonexistent. These voters are likely to be influenced by a variety of factors.

Candidate Image. Many voters make up their minds on the basis of how they perceive the individual candidates. Is the candidate seen as a strong or weak leader? A person of strong or weak character? A person who is likable or unlikable? The importance of such considerations helps explain the emphasis candidates place on both positive and negative television advertising and on news coverage.

Of course, a voter's image of a candidate does not exist in a vacuum. It is influenced by party identification and ideology. Thus a conservative (or Republican) voter might perceive a conservative (or Republican) candidate as a strong leader. But personal issues clearly have an independent influence on voter choice. The 1994 Senate campaign of Republican Michael Huffington in California, for example, suffered greatly when it was revealed that Huffington had hired an illegal alien as a nanny—this despite his strong support for a tough anti–illegal immigration measure on the ballot at the same time.[45]

Specific Issues. In any given election, one or more issues may take precedence over all others, significantly impacting the final vote. In bad economic times, for example, voters are likely to punish the party in power and turn to the opposition. Exactly that happened in 1980, when a damaged economy clearly contributed to the defeat of President Jimmy Carter. Two years later, the "Reagan recession" helped congressional Democrats win back many seats.

ECONOMICS AND POLITICS

The Political Business Cycle

Conventional wisdom has long asserted a close connection between economic policy and the government's desire for reelection. Since voters are greatly influenced by the state of the economy, that is, governments are likely to tailor their economic policies in order to ensure that the economy is strong right before an election. This relationship between economic performance and the electoral calendar is known as the political business cycle.

The political business cycle theory is based on several assumptions about both voters and governments. As for voters, the theory assumes that voters seek economic benefits; that they reward governments that provide those benefits; and that they are shortsighted, taking into account only the economy's performance in the very recent past. As for governments, the theory assumes that they desire reelection; that they can alter the economy's performance through economic policy; and that they therefore alter the economy to maximize the electoral benefits. In particular, the political business cycle theory asserts that governments will trade off the long-term health of the economy in favor of short-term gains around election time.

The idea of a political business cycle, proposed as early as 1939, has been subjected to extensive testing both in the United States and Europe. Despite its theoretical appeal, however, researchers have failed to show a clear relationship between economic performance and the electoral cycle. Scholars have pointed to several explanations for their inability to prove the existence of the electoral business cycle:

- *Try as they might, governments cannot control the economy in the short run.* A growing number of economists attack one of the central assumptions of the political business cycle theory: that governments have the ability to manipulate economic performance. This inability may be the result of institutional factors—in the United States, for example, many key economic decisions are made by the Federal Reserve Board, which is not an elected body. Or it may be that the economic tools available to the government do not work very well, or that timing the impact of government policies is extremely difficult. No matter: either conclusion effectively undermines the political business cycle theory.

- *Voters may not be shortsighted.* The political business cycle argument assumes that voters do not remember past economic performance and do not look forward to the long-term impact of government economic policy (or, at least, that such considerations are outweighed by short-term factors). One school of economists attacks this view directly, arguing that voting behavior is based on "rational expectations" of future performance. "When voters have foresight, as well as hindsight," writes one scholar, "the government cannot simply stand on a good economic record. It must also promise a bright economic future."

- *Governments may not always have an incentive to maximize short-term economic benefits.* A more sophisticated critique of the traditional political business cycle model argues that governments seek to maximize short-term economic gains only when they have to—that is, only when they face stiff electoral competition from the opposition. If the government feels secure that it will be reelected, in other words, it may pursue policies designed to maximize long-term economic well-being, even at the expense of short-term performance. A test of this model on the nine British elections between 1964 and 1992 seems to provide some preliminary evidence of such a strategy.

Researchers' failure to demonstrate the existence of a traditional political business cycle does not mean that governments are not trying to manipulate the economy in the short term. "For incumbents," comments a former chairman of the president's Council of Economic Advisers, "a little better performance before November at the cost of a lot of trouble later on still appears to be a good deal."

SOURCES: Michael S. Lewis-Beck, *Economics and Elections: The Major Western Democracies* (Ann Arbor: University of Michigan Press, 1988); Kenneth A. Schultz, "The Politics of the Political Business Cycle," *British Journal of Political Science* 25 (1995); pp. 79–99.

The economy is not the only issue that can influence voter choice. Domestic policy, especially health care, was an important issue in 1992. Anger toward corruption and mismanagement in Washington fueled the Republican landslide of 1994. Foreign policy issues can also play a role, as in 1968, when concerns over Vietnam spilled over into the presidential election, and in 1984, when the cold war and defense issues helped boost Ronald Reagan.

Party Performance. Americans have a way of rewarding or punishing the party in power when times are good or bad. In the long term, of course, voter evaluation of party performance translates into party loyalty. Thus the Democrats found it useful to "run against Hoover" for years after the unfortunate depression-era president had left office. But evaluation of party performance can also have a short-term impact. The Watergate scandal, for example, hurt the image of the Republican party so badly that Democrats were able to make strong gains in the House and Senate elections of 1974, and win the White House in 1976. Likewise, voter discontent over the Democrats' handling of health care and other issues undoubtedly hurt the party in the 1994 midterm elections.

Summary

Elections are central to the existence of any modern democracy. They provide a direct opportunity for citizens to control who governs, helping to ensure that the government operates in the interests of the majority. They provide a key check on the conduct of public officials. And they increase the legitimacy of the government and its decisions. American elections come in two varieties: primary elections, in which a political party's nominees for public office are selected; and general elections, in which candidates of different parties compete for election to those offices. In some states and localities, voters also have the opportunity to vote on specific legislative proposals and to remove candidates from office.

The Constitution guarantees the right to vote to virtually every American, regardless of race, religion, or gender. The right to vote has been further secured by congressional legislation, most importantly the Voting Rights Act of 1965. The Supreme Court has held that every American has the right to be represented equally. Thus seats in all legislative bodies except for the United States Senate must be apportioned roughly equally on the basis of population.

The most visible election campaign in the United States is the quadrennial run for the presidency. American presidential elections are held in two stages. In the first, candidates from each party run in a series of state caucuses and primaries. On the basis of these caucuses and primaries, delegates are selected to the national nominating conventions, which in turn select each party's nominee. In the second stage, the major party candidates (and any third party or independent candidates) run in the general election. The general election, in reality, is a series of statewide contests, with each state allotted a number of electoral votes equal to its total number of senators and representatives. The candidate who wins a majority of the electoral votes wins the election.

Modern campaigns require access to the media, and access to the media requires large sums of money. Presidential general election campaigns are publicly funded (with federal matching funds provided for the primary campaigns). Congressional candidates receive no public money. Congress has placed limits on the amount that individuals and political action committees can contribute to federal campaigns, and many states have put limits on contributions to state and local candidates. The present law has many loopholes, however.

Media campaigns involve a tug of war between the candidates and the journalists. Journalists attempt to expose the faults and foibles of the candidates, while the candidates attempt to manipulate the news media to place themselves in the best possible light. Much modern campaigning involves efforts to bypass the national press corps altogether. Examples include appearances on radio and television talk shows, and interviews with local journalists. Another major focus of modern campaigning is paid advertising, mainly on radio and television. Recent elections have seen a sharp, and to some people disturbing, increase in negative campaigning.

The targets of all of these efforts, of course, are the voters. In recent years the American electorate has been shrinking, with turnout down to less than 50 percent in presidential races and under 40 percent in congressional, state, and local races. Evidence suggests that education, income, and age appear to be the most significant variables associated with turnout rates. Nonvoters do not participate for one of three reasons: they cannot vote; they find the costs of voting (in time and energy) too high; or they find the benefits too low.

In the end, voters make up their minds based on both long- and short-term factors. Long-term factors include party identification and voter ideology. Short-term factors include key issues, and the perceived performance of the president and the parties.

Key Terms

Poll taxes
Voting Rights Act of 1965
Reapportionment
Primary elections (or primaries)
General elections
Electoral college
McGovern-Fraser Commission
Initiative
Referendum
Recall
Federal Election Campaign Act of 1971
Federal Election Campaign Act Amendments of 1974
Buckley v. *Valeo*
Voter turnout

Review Questions

1. Define *general election* and *primary election.* What is the difference between a closed primary and an open primary?

2. How does the Constitution protect the right to vote and the right to equal representation? How were these goals advanced by the Voting Rights Act of 1965?

3. How are presidential campaigns funded? Congressional campaigns? What limits does federal law place on campaign contributions and expenditures by individuals and by political action committees?

4. What roles do the media play in American elections? How do candidates attempt to manipulate the media? How do they attempt to circumvent it?

5. Who votes and who does not? How does turnout in the modern era compare with years past? What factors may account for these trends?

Suggested Readings

Alexander, Herbert E. *Financing Politics: Money, Elections, and Political Reform.* 4th ed. Washington, D.C.: CQ Press, 1992.

Campbell, Angus, Philip E. Converse, Warren E. Miller, and Donald E. Stokes. *The American Voter.* New York: Wiley, 1960.

Flanigan, William H., and Nancy H. Zingale. *Political Behavior of the American Electorate.* 8th ed. Washington, D.C.: CQ Press, 1994.

Jamieson, Kathleen Hall. *Dirty Politics: Deception, Distraction, and Democracy.* New York: Oxford University Press, 1992.

———. *Packaging the Presidency: A History and Criticism of Presidential Campaign Advertising.* 2d ed. New York: Oxford University Press, 1992.

Nie, Norman H., Sidney Verba, and John R. Petrocik. *The Changing American Voter.* Enlarged ed. Cambridge, Mass.: Harvard University Press, 1979.

Pomper, Gerald. *The Election of 1996; Reports and Interpretations.* Chatham, N.J.: Chatham House Publishers, 1997.

Teixeira, Ruy A. *The Disappearing American Voter.* Washington, D.C.: Brookings Institution, 1992.

Internet Resources

Comprehensive election news from America and around the world at:

http://www.klipsan.com/elecnews.htm

The Federal Election Commission, with information on federal election laws, campaign contribution and spending reports, and more, at:

http://www.fec.gov/

11

The Media

On Saturday, January 17, 1998 reporter Michael Isikoff and his editors at *Newsweek* magazine held in their hands the journalistic scoop of the decade. After a year-long investigation, Isikoff was ready to go public with allegations that President Bill Clinton had engaged in a sexual relationship with a twenty-one-year-old White House intern named Monica Lewinsky, and had then conspired with others to cover up the story by persuading Lewinsky to lie under oath. That morning, Isikoff had obtained a tape recording of conversations between Lewinsky and a friend, Linda Tripp, in which the former intern provided explicit details about her alleged affair with the president.

With the deadline for Monday's issue fast approaching, *Newsweek* had to decide whether to publish what it knew or to delay the story for one more week in order to check its facts. Isikoff argued for publication, but his editors hesitated. For one thing, the tape recorded conversations between Lewinsky and Tripp gave no insight into the alleged White House cover-up; for another, the editors were concerned that the magazine had never talked directly with Lewinsky, and therefore had no chance to check her credibility. In the end, *Newsweek* made the painful decision to hold off.

Enter Matt Drudge, the editor of an Internet-based gossip sheet called *The Drudge Report.* On Monday morning, Drudge reported *Newsweek*'s decision not to print the Lewinsky story, effectively bringing the story into the open. On Tuesday, the *Washington Post* became the first mainstream media outlet to report the story. At that point, the Lewinsky scandal exploded onto the political scene, saturating the newspapers, the airwaves, and the Internet as well.

In the view of many media-watchers, the Lewinsky story marked a dramatic shift in power from the traditional media—such as newspapers and television—to the new media, and especially the Internet. "It really shows the game has changed forever," commented one analyst. "On the Internet, everyone is a publisher, but they are not held accountable to the same rules . . .

Whereas *Newsweek,* which is a responsible news organization, painfully fact-checks their story as they should, on the Net no one cares. Rumor runs rampant, and the need for fact checking and expectations are different."[1]

Newsweek's editor-in-chief expressed himself in more personal terms. "It hurt like hell," he complained. "But given the magnitude of the allegations and the information we had at the time, I'm convinced we acted responsibly."[2]

The media play a critical role in any democratic system of government. Without a free and active press, the people would find it difficult to know what their

government was doing and impossible to follow the issues or participate meaningfully in public debate. Candidates and public officeholders would find it hard to communicate effectively with their constituents. And the people would lose an important channel for communication with their government.

Yet like other institutions that provide a connection between the people and their government, the media create as many problems as they solve. The extraordinary powers of the media are concentrated in a very small number of individuals and corporations, who, by constitutional design, are subject to minimal outside control. Most media organizations are operated for profit, not for the public interest; news organizations may fulfill essential political functions, but their primary purpose is to sell newspapers or advertising spots. Thus the media may avoid unpopular topics, or provide only shallow coverage of complex issues. There is no guarantee that the media's news reporting will be complete, accurate, or unbiased.

The Framers recognized the importance of a free press as a check on the power of government. In the age of radio and television, however, the power of the media has gone far beyond what the Framers envisioned. A candidate for president whom the media do not regard as "serious" is likely to be ignored by the major network news shows, and, as far as the election is concerned, may as well not even exist. He or she could turn to paid advertising, but the enormous cost of national television time precludes all but the very wealthy or the very well connected. With one story about a politician's sex life, the Washington press can destroy a career. An inaccurate or misleading news story may sidetrack or stall a successful campaign.

Equally troubling is the possibility that candidates and officeholders will manipulate the media, advancing their own interests at the expense of the people. A president who wants to lead the nation to war may conduct what amounts to a massive public relations campaign, using all the techniques and tricks perfected by the Madison Avenue purveyors of soap and diet soda. A successful media campaign may sway public opinion, at least in the short term, substituting for and eclipsing any kind of rational policy debate.

This chapter examines the relationship between the media and American democracy. Its central focus is on whether the media facilitate or stand in the way of responsible popular government.

Questions to Keep in Mind

☑ *Do the media do an effective job of keeping the people informed on public issues? Do they do a fair and impartial job of reporting the news?*

☑ *Why does the Constitution place so high a value on freedom of the press?*

☑ *How do candidates and politicians manipulate or bypass the mainstream media? Do such efforts help solve the problem of media power, or make matters worse?*

Basic Concepts ★ ★ ★ ★ ★ ★ ★ ★ ★ ★ ★ ★ ★ ★ ★

Few institutions have changed so dramatically over the course of this century as the American media. The very word *media* reflects the emergence of new technologies—first radio, then television, now computers and fax machines—that have revolutionized American politics. Today, the media comprise a wide range of individuals and organizations who provide information and entertainment to the American public and the world. The media include conventional news and entertainment outlets, such as newspapers, magazines, book publishers, network and local television, radio, and news wire organizations (such as the Associated Press). They also include less traditional news and entertainment sources, such as cable television, religious broadcast networks, television or AM-radio talk show networks, specialized newsletters, and the Internet.

Analysts and politicians often distinguish between the **print media** (newspapers and magazines) and the **electronic media** (radio and television). The term *press* dates from the days when all media were print media, and still survives in some usages ("press conference," "press corps," "press secretary"). It is rarely used in any precise sense.

It is also useful, especially in election years, to distinguish between *free media* and *paid media*. The former, as the term suggests, includes any publicity gained for free—on news broadcasts or talk shows or in print stories. The latter includes television commercials or print advertisements that must be paid for out-of-pocket.

Technological changes are quickly creating new forms of media. The **new media** comprise a wide range of information sources that take advantage of new technologies such as computers and fax machines. Examples include newsletters with late-breaking news sent directly by fax, electronic editions of major newspapers and magazines on the World Wide Web, and news groups on the Internet. The new media hold out the promise of a society in which information is available to everyone and in which ordinary citizens operate as both consumers and producers of the news. However, the new media also pose serious problems of accountability, accuracy, and access.

The Constitution and the Press

The Framers specifically and categorically protected the freedom of the press under the First Amendment to the Constitution, which states that "Congress shall make no law abridging . . . the freedom of the press." Originally the First Amendment applied only to the actions of the federal government, and provided no protection against the states. Since 1931, however, the Supreme Court has applied the protection of the Free Press Clause to the states as well as the federal government.

Exactly what the Framers meant by freedom of the press, and exactly what they intended to accomplish by including the Free Press Clause in the First Amendment, is a matter of considerable dispute. Some scholars have argued that the Framers wanted to wipe out laws that made it illegal to criticize the government, and to outlaw any and all forms of government licensing or censorship. Other scholars take a more restrictive view of the First Amendment, arguing that its purpose was merely to protect the states from the national government and that it had little to do with a general theory of freedom of expression.[3]

Over the past sixty years, the Supreme Court has developed an expansive reading of the First Amendment that provides broad protection for the press. The Court's reading has rested on two general principles. First, the Court has underscored the importance of freedom of the press in order to promote self-expression and self-development. Second, the Court has stressed the importance of freedom of the press as an essential component of self-government. The first theme has led the Court to protect all forms of artistic and literary expression. The second has led to broad protections of politically motivated speech, and strict limits on the power of the government to prevent or punish criticism of politicians and government officials.

In general, the constitutional protection of the press is identical to its protection for free speech. With a few technical exceptions, freedom of the press is nothing more than an extension of the right of the citizens to speak freely on matters of public and private interest. Accordingly, the freedom of the press can be limited in circumstances—such as the publication of obscenity—where freedom of speech could also be limited (see Chapter 4, pp. 89–93).

The constitutional issues of most interest to the organized press involve questions of prior restraints, libel, and special privileges or access.

Prior Restraints   Fundamental to the First Amendment's protection of the press, as interpreted by the Supreme Court, is a virtual ban on prior restraints. A **prior restraint** is an order from a judge or other government official, issued *before* publication, that blocks or censors specific information or a particular story. The government may be able to punish certain types of material *after* publication, but it can rarely prevent publication altogether.

Prior restraints are allowed only in extraordinary circumstances—such as when, in wartime, a newspaper attempts to publish the whereabouts of troop ships already at sea. One case that qualified for a temporary prior restraint occurred in 1971, when the Nixon administration tried to stop the *New York Times* and the *Washington Post* from publishing the details of the "Pentagon Papers," a top-secret report on American actions in the Vietnam War. After a full hearing, the Supreme Court lifted the ban, ruling that the government had failed to meet its difficult burden of proof. Another temporary injunction was issued by a federal district court in 1979 when the *Progressive* magazine threatened to reveal how to make a hydrogen bomb. (After the government found out that the information in the article was available elsewhere, it dropped the case).[4]

The Supreme Court's strict refusal to allow prior restraints except in the most extraordinary circumstances is vital to the free operation of the American press. Essentially this rule bans administrative or judicial supervision of the day-to-day operations of the working press, effectively insulating the press in most cases from direct government pressure.

The Supreme Court has also ruled that the government is powerless to *force* the press to run a particular story. In a 1974 case, the Court invalidated a Florida law compelling newspapers to publish replies to negative stories about political candidates.[5]

Libel   The publication in writing of false statements that injure a person's reputation may give rise to a suit for damages. Such statements are known as **libel.** Libel suits are an old remedy available to private individuals (and corporations) who suffer at the hands of the press. (*Slander* is essentially equivalent to libel, except that the words in question are spoken rather than written. Slander suits are less common than libel suits, because individual defendants rarely have enough money to make a lawsuit worthwhile.)

The Supreme Court recognized in 1964 that the threat of libel suits could give rise to a "chilling effect" on the free press, which might grow overcautious in fulfilling its legitimate responsibilities. Thus the Court held that *public officials* could not recover for libel unless they could show not simply that the statements made about them were false but also that they were made with *actual malice*—that is, with knowledge that they were false or with reckless disregard for whether or not they were true. In reporting about public officials, therefore, newspapers need not worry that an occasional good-faith error will land them in court.

Later the Court extended the actual malice rule to *public figures*—that is, individuals who are well known to the public—as well as to public officials. Only occasionally is a newspaper so irresponsible that a libel suit by a public figure is successful.[6]

Special Access and Privileges In modern times, reporters have tried to convince the government to grant them special access to newsworthy events and other privileges not accorded to the general public. In general, they have been unsuccessful. Except in a few technical cases, the Supreme Court has refused to extend freedom of the press beyond the freedom of speech granted to everyone. Reporters have had better luck in Congress and the state legislatures.

Three issues are particularly important. First, reporters have tried to claim a special right to attend government meetings or other functions and report on them to the general public. Although the Supreme Court has recognized that most criminal proceedings must be open to the public, it has refused to extend any special privileges to members of the press. Government agencies are free to make life easier for reporters, for example by providing special press seating or background briefings, and they usually do. But if the government can exclude the public from a particular proceeding, it can exclude the press, too.

Second, reporters have tried to claim the right to refuse government orders to release information obtained from confidential sources. The government cannot force anyone to divulge any information except according to established procedures, such as a judicial or congressional subpoena. The Supreme Court has refused to grant a special privilege to reporters in this area, although several states have established such a privilege by statute. Congress is usually reluctant to compel such testimony for political reasons, though constitutionally it could do so. In 1992, for example, a congressional committee made noises about forcing National Public Radio reporter Nina Totenberg to disclose her source for the leak of FBI reports on Anita Hill, who had accused Supreme Court nominee Clarence Thomas of sexual harassment. When Totenberg refused to give in, Congress backed off.

Finally, news organizations argued unsuccessfully in a 1978 case that law enforcement agencies could not constitutionally search newsroom files, even with a search warrant, for materials related to a crime investigation. Again the Supreme Court found no special privilege for the press, but this time Congress intervened, passing a law in 1980 that banned newsroom searches unless the news organization or its members were suspected of wrongdoing.[7]

Electronic Versus Print Media   Although the radio and television media have First Amendment rights, the Supreme Court has permitted more government regulation of the broadcast industry than of the print media. For one thing, the Court has upheld government regulation and licensing of television and radio stations, recognizing that the number of broadcast frequencies is limited and that the absence of regulation would create chaos. In addition, the Court has approved government regulation of the *content* of radio and television broadcasts in order to serve the public interest. Government regulation of broadcast stations is handled by the Federal Communications Commission (FCC).[8]

Few object to government licensing of broadcast stations. Government regulation of the *content* of broadcasts, however, is another matter. The Court's rationale for allowing such regulation is twofold. First, the limited number of television and radio stations makes regulation necessary to accommodate the First Amendment rights of the public by encouraging free and open debate. Second, radio and television programs are more likely than newspapers to reach unwilling or inappropriate audiences, such as children.

Technology is quickly undermining both arguments for the different treatment of print and electronic media under the Constitution. Cable television allows a much wider range of program options than conventional broadcast technology—up to five hundred or more stations in the near future is not unlikely. Moreover, new technologies like digital and cable radio, digital audio and video, and special computer chips to screen out unwanted programming will eventually make it easier to exclude unwilling or inappropriate audiences without government regulation.

For the moment, however, Congress is free to impose at least some regulations on the television industry. Under the **equal time rule,** for example, television stations that sell commercial time to one candidate for office must offer the same opportunity to other candidates for the same office. Stations must also offer the opposition party the chance to respond to a major presidential address (routine news coverage of political events is not subject to the same rule, however). Other restrictions include a requirement that stations sell commercial time to candidates at the lowest rate charged to any advertiser, although in practice this rule is frequently violated: an FCC audit of twenty stations that sold commercial time to candidates in 1990 revealed that four out of five stations ignored the lowest-rate rule. Television stations can also be prohibited from showing "indecent" material that in other contexts would be covered by the First Amendment.

Perhaps the most controversial federal rule governing broadcast content was the **fairness doctrine,** which required stations that broadcast "controversial issues of public concern" to provide "reasonable opportunities for the presentation of conflicting viewpoints." The doctrine also gave any identified person or group that was attacked on the air an automatic right of rebuttal. The right of reply provision was upheld by the Supreme Court, even though the Court declared unconstitutional a similar restriction on the print media.

The fairness doctrine was suspended by the FCC in 1987, partly because cable and satellite technologies had greatly expanded the number of available communications channels. A congressional effort to overrule the FCC was vetoed by President Ronald Reagan. The equal time rule and restrictions on offensive material remain in effect.[9]

Political Roles of the Media

The influence of the media pervades the American political system. In fact, it is difficult to see how democratic politics could be conducted at all without some form of mass communication, be it newspapers as in the old days or television today. A survey of the various roles played by the media in the American system of government makes clear the media's enormous impact. Some roles played by the media are obvious and well known. Others may be less apparent or even surprising. One thing is clear: The media are not simply passive sources of information. Whether purposefully or not, they shape the news as they report it, profoundly affecting both politics and public policy.

The Media As a Source of Information   The most basic function of the media is to provide the people with information about public affairs. Obviously, much of the information transmitted over the airwaves or printed in newspapers has little or nothing to do with government or public affairs. But a surprising amount is related, directly or indirectly, to politics.

How Americans Get Their News.   More Americans watch television than read a newspaper. In fact, more Americans watch television than know how to read at all. Nearly 99 percent of American households have at least one television set, and many have more. More than half the nation's households subscribe to cable television.

Not surprisingly, then, more Americans get their news from television than from any other source. The typical combined audience for the evening news shows on ABC, CBS, and NBC is about 50 million, split almost evenly among the three. Even larger audiences tune in for local news broadcasts. CNN now attracts a significant audience, rising to as high as a 10 percent share during breaking news stories. PBS provides a nightly look at the news in depth in the NewsHour, which attracts a small but influential audience.

All told, nearly 60 percent of Americans get their news primarily from television, and only 20 percent rely mainly on newspapers. Moreover, Americans find television news more credible than print sources by a factor of nearly three to one.[10]

That television has an important influence on public opinion, and hence on politics and public policy, is clear. Exactly what that influence is, however, is hard to say. Some scholars have argued that television acts mainly to reinforce existing beliefs and, in this and other ways, is a conservative force in American political life. Among low-income individuals, for example, those who watch a great deal of television are more likely to classify themselves as middle class than those who watch little television. This blurring of class distinctions presumably occurs because viewers identify with the predominantly middle-class culture depicted on television.[11] Another study suggested that when television news coverage of poverty focused on "close-up depictions of personal experience," it reinforced the belief that the poor were to blame for their own problems.[12]

Other researchers, however, suggest that television can act as an important force for change in American society. For example, one study concluded that media stories about the dangers of nuclear energy were responsible for a sharp decline in public support for nuclear power plants.[13]

Pinning down the exact size and nature of the media's influence on public opinion would be difficult. First, as one media scholar concludes, the effects of mass media are "highly complex and elusive," and hard to measure.[14] For example, it is difficult to separate the impact of media coverage of a presidential speech on public opinion from the impact of the speech itself. Second, the media frequently give the public what it wants to hear, creating a chicken-and-egg problem. Did the media generate the hype over the O. J. Simpson murder trial? Or did they simply respond to the public's demand for more coverage about something it was interested in already? Probably the answer is both, but it is impossible to reach any precise conclusions.

Window on Government. The media perform an important function by closely watching the various activities of the government. In a large, modern nation like the United States, it is neither possible nor desirable for every citizen to follow the diverse affairs of government in person. It is far more efficient and practical for society to delegate that responsibility, or at least some of it, to members of the professional media.

The news media are not simply a passive window on government, however. Instead, they play an active role in selecting and filtering the news that is reported or covered. Research suggests that the media tend to show familiar faces; fewer than fifty people—including the president, leading presidential candidates, major congressional figures, cabinet members, leading state and local political figures, and various celebrities—dominate news coverage. The media prefer to cover stories that are new and dramatic, especially if they have good pictures to go with them.

The media's emphasis on dramatic stories often leads to disproportionate coverage of conflict and violence. It also means that the media may miss "the underlying causes and likely consequences and the major issues involved" in major stories. Television coverage of the Vietnam War protests, for example, focused "more closely on specific acts of protest than on the issues that gave rise to the protests." Likewise, when the media covers international terrorism, "information about specific terrorist acts is not accompanied by information about related historical, economic, or social antecedents."[15]

For the most part, media coverage of politics tends to be reactive. White House reporters, for example, typically wait around for the president or his aides to do or say something, then report on it. A similar approach marks coverage of the State and Defense Departments. The reason for such an approach is clear: most of what happens in these institutions takes place behind the scenes, away from the journalists. As a result, the executive branch is typically able to dictate the media's agenda on any given day. This passive role may frustrate White House reporters, however, adding to the tension between the president and the White House press corps and possibly leading to negative coverage. When White House reporters do get the chance to pursue a story actively, chances are the story involves conflict or scandal, both of which can provide dramatic news footage even without the cooperation of the White House.

Congress receives less attention from the news media than does the executive branch. Unlike the White House, Congress provides no single focal point for media attention; on a given day, important events may be happening on the floor of both Houses and in half a dozen committees. Moreover, much of Congress's work involves the details of writing legislation, which is harder to package in a news story than a presidential speech or press con-

Modern press conferences—such as this one held by President Bill Clinton—are nationally televised media events. With the nation watching, presidents must be very careful what they say and how they say it. By contrast, presidential press conferences before the age of television were informal, private affairs; during Franklin Roosevelt's presidency, reporters were not allowed to quote the president or even name him as a source. Not surprisingly, press conferences were held much more frequently in the past than in the modern era.

ference, especially on television. When the media does cover Congress, the emphasis tends to be on dramatic hearings or inflammatory rhetoric rather than the nuts-and-bolts of pending legislation.

Coverage of interest group activity is similarly reactive. In general, interest groups must make the media come to them, by holding press conferences, political demonstrations, or other media events. All told, "pseudo-events"—those created specifically to attract media coverage—account for seventy percent of all television news coverage.[16]

An alternative form of news coverage is provided by C-SPAN, the Cable-Satellite Public Affairs Network. Much of C-SPAN's programming consists of simply putting a camera before the government. Its commentary-free coverage includes congressional debates and hearings, White House and other high-level press conferences and news briefings, and campaign speeches and events. A similar approach is often taken by Court Television, a cable network that broadcasts live trials from around the country.

The conventional wisdom suggests that the print media provide both broader and deeper coverage of issues than the electronic media. A leading newspaper—such as the *New York Times*—may contain around 25,000 words of national and international news coverage. The average 30-minute network newscast, by contrast, contains only around 4,000 words. "The average news story on television takes about a minute, just enough time to announce that an event has taken place and present a fact or two about it," writes Doris Graber. "Complex stories may have to be scratched entirely if they cannot be dramatically condensed."[17]

Very few American read the *New York Times*, however; most rely on local or regional papers, which offer far less detailed coverage of important issues. For example, a study comparing network news coverage in January 1995 with coverage by the *Atlanta Constitution* and the *Des Moines Register* found that the networks covered many fewer national and international subjects than the newspapers. But many of the stories provided by the newspapers were "very brief," and the newspapers provided less coverage of some important national and international issues. For example, the study found that ABC's *World News Tonight* actually provided more coverage of the national welfare debate than did the newspapers.[18]

Entertainment. Much of the news industry exists not simply to inform but also to entertain. The information and entertainment industries have become increasingly intertwined in recent years, driven by relentless competition within the news industry. The results range from the leavening of news shows with entertainment elements (CNN's *Headline News,* for example, includes a "Hollywood Minute" every half hour) to presentations that are as much entertainment as they are news, including network "news magazine" shows such as *Sixty Minutes.* News spills over into entertainment also in the various documentaries, docudramas, made-for-TV movies, and talk shows that use current issues and news stories both to inform and to entertain.

Much of what is on television news shows and in the print media has little or nothing to do with politics. But any news story—even stories on sports or entertainment—may have political implications.

Interpreting and Analyzing the News. The media do not simply report the news. They also provide a great deal of analysis, expert commentary, speculation, and editorial opinion. The same newspaper might contain a report on a presidential tax proposal, an analysis of the political climate surrounding the proposal and the likelihood of congressional approval, a "what this means to you" piece putting the proposal in perspective, an op-ed column praising the plan, and an editorial condemning it. Television and radio programs might contain the same sort of mix, although the different kinds of stories are typically interwoven.

Shaping the Agenda. By choosing what issues to cover and how to cover them, the media play an important role in shaping the nation's political agenda. Press coverage of the AIDS epidemic, for example, brought the disease to the attention of the general public and eventually led to government action on several fronts. Scholars have noted that the media play both an "educating" and a "packaging" role in shaping the agenda. That is, the media not only bring new information to policy makers and the public but also "make some choices more politically palatable" by "organizing issues, options, and rationales." Finally, the media may help set the agenda by playing the role of facilitator, "providing the forum to link public demands and political decision makers, or among interested political actors."[19]

The Media As Bulwark Against Government Abuse of Power

Identifying and exposing corruption and abuse of power among government officials and political candidates is a time-honored role for the American media. "The freedom of the press," proclaimed the Virginia Bill of Rights in 1776, "is one of the great bulwarks of liberty, and can never be restrained but by despotic governments." In adding the First Amendment to the Constitution, wrote the Supreme Court Justice Hugo Black, the Framers made it clear that "the press was to serve the governed, not the governors. The Government's power to censor the press was abolished so that the press would remain forever free to censure the Government. The press was protected so that it could bare the secrets of government and inform the people. Only a free and unrestrained press can effectively expose deception in government."[20]

Besides serving an important public purpose, press reporting on political scandals also sells. Who would buy a newspaper with headlines like "Politician faithful to spouse," "Mail delivered on time," and "Senator votes according to public interest"? Reporters need scandal and corruption stories to get their byline on the front page, and editors, producers, and publishers need them to attract readers and viewers.

To many critics, the American media's emphasis on sex and corruption has become an obsession. Thus it should come as no surprise that much of the American media focus on digging up stories involving sex, corruption, and massive inefficiency (and not just the American press; the British press is truly obsessed with sex scandals, especially those that come complete with pictures of key members of the royal family). *Sixty Minutes,* which often contains at least one report showing government at its worst, is consistently among the most-watched shows on television.

But investigative journalism, properly defined, encompasses more than sex and corruption. It includes all news stories that probe beyond official press conferences and news releases and rely instead on unofficial sources of information to cast light on public issues. Examples include stories on the real lives of welfare mothers, investigations into the way medicine is practiced in the United States, and undercover pieces on life inside a youth gang or drug ring.

A good investigative news story is built up piece by piece, exactly as a prosecutor might assemble the evidence for a criminal trial. Reporters must rely on a wide variety of sources, some of whom provide access to classified or confidential documents and some of whom provide eyewitness testimony. Many of these witnesses are of uncertain reliability, and some will speak only on condition that their names are not released. The reliability of witnesses is made even more uncertain when news organizations exchange money for information, a practice that most major news organizations shun but that others—like *Hard Copy*—rely on routinely. The most responsible news organizations do not go public with a story unless and until they are satisfied that the story is true, or at least highly plausible. Failure to adhere to such standards not only may bring the news agency into disrepute, but may even result in an expensive libel suit.

Smaller, more partisan, and more sensationalist newspapers and magazines, including many found on the Internet, take a more combative approach, and might be willing to go forward with a story that is less well documented or substantiated. Sometimes such stories turn out to be genuine "scoops." Others quickly fade for lack of interest or evidence. Stories that start off in the alternative press are closely monitored by the major newspapers and media organizations, which may conduct their own investigations into the matter and then report the story themselves. One such

"...THEN A SUPERMARKET TABLOID HEARD ABOUT ALL THOSE "WASHINGTON SLEPT HERE" SIGNS...AND MY POLITICAL CAREER WAS HISTORY..."

case occurred in 1993, when the conservative magazine the *American Spectator* published an article on the alleged extramarital affairs of President Bill Clinton while he was governor. The story went nowhere for a week or two, until CNN reported the *Spectator's* charges and the *Los Angeles Times* published an independent analysis based on their own reporting. Soon the story was in every major paper and on every major television and radio show.

Investigations that begin life as news stories may be taken over by public prosecutors or by Congress. The Iran-contra affair, in which several members of the Reagan administration were implicated in connection with an attempt to trade arms for hostages in the Middle East—began with a news story in a Beirut paper, was picked up by the American press, and eventually led to both a major congressional investigation and a seven-year inquiry by a special prosecutor.

The Media As a Participant in Politics

The media are not simply observers of the American political scene. They are also active participants. In various ways, both deliberately and inadvertently, the media often *make* the news instead of simply reporting it.

Influencing Opinion. Every newspaper and most television stations and networks make some attempt to influence public opinion. Newspapers do this explicitly through editorials and opinion pieces, and indirectly through the choice and depth of news coverage. Television stations achieve the same result through occasional editorials, news broadcasts, documentaries, and talk shows.

There is no question that the way the media present the news has a tremendous impact on public opinion. The real questions are whether this influence is systematic and deliberate, and whether it is politically biased in one direction or the other. The question of media bias is taken up later in this chapter.

Advocacy Journalism. Most major newspapers and broadcast news organizations confine their advocacy to the editorial page or to special opinion segments, although critics often suggest that political bias is frequently reflected in an organization's news stories or in the tone of its coverage. Many specialized journals and radio and television talk shows take an entirely different approach, admitting, or even boasting about, their partisan point of view.

Important magazines exist on both sides of the political divide. *Commentary,* the *American Spectator,* and the *National Review,* for example, are conservative. The *Nation, Dissent,* and the *Progressive* are liberal or leftist. Other journals are more difficult to classify, but are highly opinionated and explicitly seek to influence opinion. The *New Republic,* which at one time was socialist, later turned liberal, and is now generally regarded as neoconservative, typically contains a wide variety of different viewpoints.

Journals of opinion have their equivalents on radio and television. The popular talk show host Rush Limbaugh, for example, is an unabashed conservative. Major television stars like Oprah Winfrey and Geraldo Rivera rarely shrink from expressing their mainly liberal viewpoints.

Finally, many highly specialized journals are literal or figurative extensions of interest group organizations. Examples include *Modern Maturity,* published by the American Association of Retired Persons (AARP), and *American Hunter,* published by the National Rifle Association (NRA).

The Media As the Voice of the People

Media communication is a two-way street. Just as the people need the media to follow the government, politicians and public officials rely on the media to keep abreast of the public pulse. The media plays this role in many ways.

Public Opinion Polls. News organizations routinely sponsor public opinion polls and other, less scientific methods of tracking public opinion. After the 1994 victory of congressional Republicans, for example, the news media conducted several polls designed to determine the "meaning" of the electorate's decision. Such polls undoubtedly have some effect on political leaders, although they may simply duplicate the numbers that the politicians' own polls already produce.

Letters to the Editor. Politicians and public officials are avid readers of the letters column in their local papers. Letters to the editor frequently reflect the genuine concerns of the public, or can at least confirm or cast doubt on a politician's sense of what his or her constituents are thinking.

Political parties and politicians often use the letters column as a way of making it *appear* that public opinion is moving one way or another on an issue, or to generate support for one side or the other. A letter to the editor praising the local congressman as a great American may be genuine, but it may also be generated by the congressman's own supporters as part of an organized effort. Of course, the same applies to a letter suggesting that the congressman could best serve his country by resigning from office.

Call-in Shows. In recent years the radio and television call-in show has achieved great prominence. Politicians often appear on such shows to face the public directly, and more often monitor such shows to keep track of public opinion. In most cases, however, such shows attract only a narrow segment of the population (usually those who agree with the host), and cannot be relied on as an accurate guide to public opinion.

Nevertheless, call-in shows can play a key part in getting across a message to the government. In 1991, for example, radio talk show hosts spearheaded an onslaught of protest and helped delay a proposed congressional pay raise.

Coverage of Interest Group Activities. By publicizing the activities of interest groups, the media help transmit the groups' messages to Washington, D.C. Television coverage of the 1963 civil rights protest marches in Birmingham, Alabama, for example, was a critical element in convincing President John F. Kennedy to back federal civil rights legislation. Likewise, television coverage of the anti–Vietnam War protests helped convince government officials of the growing public opposition to the war.

The message that the media transmits to the government may or may not reflect the views of the majority of the people. Interest groups and activists who are skilled in the art of attracting media attention may be successful at convincing the government that their views are shared by far more Americans than might really be the case. Just as the media may distort the picture that Washington sends to the people, they may also distort the picture that the people send to their government.

The Media and the Government: Watchdog or Lapdog?

The role of the American press has changed greatly over the past two hundred years. In the early Republic, the press made no pretense of objectivity, openly acting as boosters for one political party or another. The limits of early-nineteenth-century technology precluded the emergence of a national press, although Washington newspapers assumed obvious prominence in political circles. Political debate was open and robust, even raw, with the press acting less as moderators than as active participants.

The nature of the American press changed slowly over the next 150 years. Technology—first the telegraph, then telephones, computers, and satellites—allowed the emergence of a national press corps. Slowly the idea of journalism as a *profession* developed, bringing with it new standards of conduct and ethical behavior. Newspapers began to draw clear lines between fact and opinion, and made the unbiased dissemination of information their highest priority. Although newspapers were still known informally as "Democratic" and "Republican" until well into the twentieth century, these designations largely reflected the editorial policy of the management rather than news coverage.[21]

Media Versus Government

The combination of the Vietnam War and the Watergate scandal of the second Nixon administration (1972–1974) fundamentally changed the American media. The decline of the pre–World War II partisan press had taken much of the bite out of the Washington press corps, and left the media in a generally friendly and supportive role toward the government. The press showed particular respect for presidents and even more for the presidency, although it should be pointed out that a furious John F. Kennedy once canceled the White House subscription to the *New York Herald-Tribune.* Still, there was an informal agreement among the newspapers not to show Franklin D. Roosevelt in a wheelchair, and not to discuss extramarital affairs and other presidential peccadilloes. Deference to the presidency even extended to public matters. During the 1962 Cuban missile crisis, for example, the *New York Times* noted troop movements and other unusual activities, deduced that a crisis was brewing in Cuba, and even speculated correctly that nuclear missiles were involved. Before printing the story, their reporter checked with the White House, whereupon the president himself called the publisher of the *Times* and asked him not to run the story. The story never appeared.[22]

The media's approach to covering the Vietnam War started out the same way. By 1968, however, correspondents in Vietnam began to sense that the government was not telling the whole truth. The defining moment came in 1968, when North Vietnamese forces launched an offensive over the Tet, or Vietnamese new year, holiday. Enemy troops reached the American embassy in Saigon before being turned away, sending shock waves through the military and the press corps alike. Although the Tet offensive was repulsed, American journalists reacted as if the U.S. Army had been defeated. The reaction of the war correspondents can be attributed to their shock at seeing the enemy put up so strong an attack, and their sudden sense that the war was not going as well as the American military had been telling them. Media coverage of the antiwar protests at home and intense probing of the Johnson administration's Vietnam policy seemed to put the government and the press into a constant state of tension.

Relations between the media and the government might still have recovered had Johnson's successor been someone other than Richard M. Nixon. Nixon had had a confrontational relationship with the press for decades. In 1962, for example, after losing the California gubernatorial election, Nixon told the press corps that "you won't have Nixon to kick around anymore." Once Nixon became president, his rapport with the press went from bad

The most enduring image of the Tet Offensive was this cold-blooded execution of a North Vietnamese prisoner by a South Vietnamese soldier. The photograph helped erode the American public's support for our ally, and for the war.

to worse. The president and his subordinates were obsessed with secrecy, and made attacks on the press a staple of both the 1968 and 1972 campaigns. In 1972, Nixon lashed out at the "so-called opinion leaders of this country" for failing to recognize "the necessity to stand by the President of the United States when he makes a terribly difficult, potentially unpopular decision." Vice President Spiro Agnew, meanwhile, denounced the media as "nattering nabobs of negativism." Eventually, the press began to suspect, and then prove, that the administration was telling outright lies about Vietnam and Watergate.[23]

The media's exposure of the Watergate scandal turned the Washington press corps into minor folk heroes. The two *Washington Post* reporters who broke the story, Bob Woodward and Carl Bernstein, wrote a best-selling book about their adventure, complete with a mysterious source identified only as "Deep Throat" (the nickname came from a well-known porn film). Woodward and Bernstein's book, *All the President's Men,* was turned into a Hollywood blockbuster starring Robert Redford and Dustin Hoffman as the intrepid journalists.[24]

Watergate and Vietnam did not transform the role of the American press by themselves or overnight. The media's confrontational attitude reflected the American public's general sense of distrust in authority, a feeling especially pronounced among the young and the well educated, both of which were well represented in the Washington and Vietnam press corps. That sense of distrust, moreover, was exacerbated by the government's own handling of both domestic and foreign policy. The polarization of American society between Establishment and anti-Establishment factions could also be seen in the attitudes of key government officials, who increasingly took a circle-the-wagons approach to public and press relations.

Dustin Hoffman and Robert Redford played the reporters Carl Bernstein and Bob Woodward in the 1976 movie All the President's Men.

Despite the surface antagonisms between the media and the government, researchers suggest that the era of advocacy journalism may already have peaked. In the modern era, reporters and government officials are increasingly dependent on one another. Indeed, the appearance of antagonism between reporters and government officials may actually serve the purposes of both—presidents and members of Congress can score points with their constituents by attacking the media, while reporters can gain instant stardom and increased credibility by taking on the government.

Government Versus Media

Although the conventional wisdom sees the media as a check on public officials who might abuse their authority and betray the public trust, in practice the media can be extremely useful to officials at every level of the government. To be successful, in fact, politicians and government officials must learn to cultivate, and manipulate, the reporters and editors who are supposed to keep them in line.

Politicians have been trying to manipulate the news media since the days of Presidents Washington and Jefferson. President Franklin D. Roosevelt was a masterful radio performer, and Richard Nixon was a pioneer in trying to master the new medium of television. It was under Ronald Reagan, however, that the art of media politics seemed to reach new heights. Reagan, a former actor, capitalized on his own skill at presentation and delivery. He seemed particularly adept under pressure: his dry one-liners on the day he was nearly assassinated endeared him to millions of Americans of all political persuasions. (To his wife, Reagan said, "Honey, I forgot to duck!" To his doctor, he remarked, "I hope you're a Republican.")

Media politics is a subtle art and takes many forms. The following is a brief survey of terms and techniques.

Media-Bashing. Presidents and other politicians have learned to blame the media for the nation's problems, thus neatly deflecting criticism from themselves. This technique has been used more effectively by conservatives than by liberals, perhaps because there is a widespread perception that the media are biased toward the left and against the right. More recently, however, liberals too have learned the fine and useful art of blaming the messenger.

Examples of media-bashing are legion. Richard Nixon blamed the media for America's problems in Vietnam, alleging that an antiwar press eroded morale at home and undermined the war effort. In 1992, conservatives argued that the nation's poor economic performance during the Bush years was caused by the media's obsession with bad economic news. Likewise, the Clinton administration eagerly embraced the idea that urban crime could be blamed on violent television shows and rock lyrics; and, when Clinton was attacked for his alleged "womanizing," Hillary Clinton responded by denouncing the Washington press corps for ruining her family's Christmas holiday.

Media-bashing works because the American people have little respect for or confidence in the press as an institution. A 1997 poll, for example, revealed that 35 percent of Americans had "a great deal" or "quite a lot" of confidence in television news, compared with 62 percent who had "some" or "very little" confidence. Newspapers fared about the same.[25] On the other hand, polls taken after the Persian Gulf War showed that 72 percent of the public felt that the press had shown respect for the military's security concerns, and 75 percent believed that the press did enough to respect the privacy of families of American soldiers.[26]

News Management. Politicians and government officials can use the media to their own advantage by carefully manipulating and managing the news. Sometimes this is done subtly, and with great skill. In other cases it is done bluntly, and boorishly. In any case, it usually works.

Because everything the president does or says is news, the White House is in the best position to manipulate the media. Others, including members of Congress and executive officials, can practice the same art to a lesser degree. Likewise, private interest groups try to manipulate the press into covering their stories in the most favorable light.

The ways and means of news management are too numerous and complex to deal with systematically, but a few illustrations will provide a general sense of how the game works. When President Reagan returned from a major trip to the Soviet Union, for example, he went immediately to Capitol Hill to report on his activities, not even stopping at the White House. Reagan arrived in Washington precisely as the network news shows were going on the air. They naturally carried his dramatic arrival in the presidential helicopter, and his speech, live. The timing of the episode was no coincidence; the entire affair was perfectly orchestrated by the president's staff, who even added a last-minute meeting with the prime minister of Belgium to delay the president's arrival until the desired moment.

Presidents and others can also manipulate the media through the skillful control of classified or confidential information. This method works best in wartime, when security restrictions and military censorship make the news media almost completely dependent on the government for access to news. The Bush administration's handling of the Persian Gulf War was in this respect exemplary, and accounts for at least some of the president's unprecedented 90 percent approval ratings at the time. The Pentagon carefully chose its most telegenic and articulate officers to conduct daily briefings, then presented a very selective version of the news. While the American public was given awesome photographs of "smart bombs" that could find the opening in a smokestack, it was given little or no chance to see the bombs that missed their targets, or malfunctioned, or were simply old-fashioned and "dumb." Similarly, the Pentagon systematically overstated the success rate of the Patriot antimissile missile, leading both Israelis and Americans to the false sense that American technology was providing an effective shield over Jerusalem and Tel Aviv.

Perhaps the ultimate pair of media manipulation techniques are the **sound bite** and the **visual.** The first consists of packaging a politician's message into a short, succinct, and memorable phrase guaranteed to make the news shows. Sound bites have gradually shrunk in length and now are rarely longer than ten seconds. Sound bites can be used as an answer to a reporter's question, as part of a policy statement, or in any other context where the television camera lights are on and the news shows are waiting.

Visuals, as the name suggests, are attempts to picture the politician or government offi-

Figure 11.1 **The Declining Presidential Audience, 1969–1992**

On average, the number of Americans watching presidential press conferences has declined over the years. In part, the bigger audiences of the past reflect higher levels of public participation in government. But they also reflect the fact that there used to be only three major television networks—and no cable stations—and all three typically carried press conferences live.

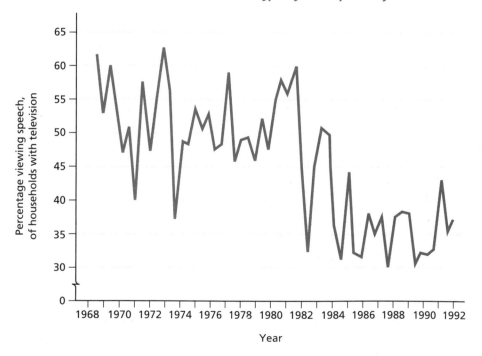

SOURCE: Nielsen Media Research, cited in Samuel Kernell, *Going Public: New Strategies of Presidential Leadership,* 2d ed. (CQ Press, 1993), p. 114. Reprinted with permission of Nielsen Media Research.

cial in the best possible light when he or she appears on television. Candidates and officials often hire media consultants to polish their image before the cameras. Nothing is left to chance, including makeup, clothing, and setting. Good staff work ensures that the candidate or official is presented to the cameras against an appropriate backdrop, and in a favorable visual setting.

Visuals are very important, because studies have confirmed that television watchers are more strongly affected by what they see than by what they hear. Thus a good politician pays as much attention to how he or she will look as to what he or she is saying. Here is how the CBS reporter Leslie Stahl described a typical day in President Jimmy Carter's 1980 campaign:

> What did President Carter do today in Philadelphia? He posed, with as many different types of symbols as he could possibly find.
>
> There was a picture at the day care center. And one during the game of bounce ball with senior citizens. Click, and another picture with a group of teenagers. And then he performed the ultimate media event—a walk through the Italian market.
>
> The point of all this, obviously, is to get on the local news broadcasts and in the morning newspapers. It appeared that the President's intention was not to say anything controversial. . . . Simply the intention was to be seen.[27]

Both sound bites and visuals can backfire, of course. A slip of the tongue or an unfortunate misstatement can end up being repeated endlessly on every news program; an ill-chosen or unplanned background scene may make a candidate look silly, insensitive, or worse. President George Bush and Vice President Dan Quayle seemed particularly susceptible to visual and verbal gaffes. During the 1991–1992 recession, a picture of Bush on a golfing vacation seemed to imply complete unconcern with the plight of average Americans. During the 1992 campaign, pictures of Bush touring the disaster caused by Hurricane Andrew in Florida made him look somehow responsible for the carnage. And Quayle, of course, had to suffer through endless reruns of his misspelling of the word *potato* when a carefully staged media event in a public school turned into a fiasco as the vice president chided a young student for forgetting the final "*e.*"

Bypassing the National Press Corps. Every president and candidate is followed by representatives of the major national media outlets. These reporters are typically bright, well informed, and hard to intimidate. They have heard every message before, and they know every technique of media manipulation and control. Tough and cynical, they can defy even the most expert attempts to manipulate them or to manage the news.

One answer to this problem is to make an end run around these seasoned reporters and go directly to the representatives of the local media. Local reporters and editors are often awed and excited by the presence of the president or of a major candidate. They may lack detailed knowledge of issues and events, and are typically more willing to accept advice and direction from the campaign or White House staff. They will be much more likely to display respect to the president or candidate, and will probably ask relatively uncontroversial, or "soft," questions. Moreover, local reporters are often willing to do whatever it takes to get a few minutes with the president or with a candidate, and may agree to avoid certain topics or even to accept pre-edited video tape. The result is free media exposure that approaches the style and impact of commercial advertisements.

Should Criminal Trials Be Televised?

The Constitution guarantees a public trial to every criminal defendant. The Framers well understood the dangers of secret justice and wanted to ensure that the legal system remained open to public scrutiny. But would the Framers have approved of television in America's courtrooms? Supporters view televised trials as merely an extension of the public-access rule; critics argue that television distorts the trial process and leads to unjust verdicts and sentences.

Televised trials were virtually unknown in the 1970s, but by the mid-1990s more than three-quarters of the states—but not the federal government—allowed cameras in their courtrooms. Today, criminal trials have become a staple of television programming. Legal commentators and analysts abound, and one cable network—Court TV—is dedicated almost exclusively to broadcasting newsworthy trials.

The O. J. Simpson case and other highly sensational trials of the mid- to late-1990s have caused many Americans to reconsider the wisdom of allowing cameras inside America's courtrooms.

Yes, keep cameras in the courtrooms.

Advocates of cameras in the courtoom make several important arguments:

Television in the courtrooms merely extends the constitutional principle of public trials. "I doubt that the Founding Fathers would have allowed—had there been cameras and televisions available in the 1700s—the print media, the sketch artists, and the general public into the courtroom, but not the television camera," says Rikki Klieman, a leading defense attorney who is now a commentator for Court TV. Supporters of television trials argue that televised trials merely give every American the chance to view court proceedings that are already open to the public. "If you take cameras out of the courtroom," said Judge Lance Ito, who presided over the O.J. Simpson criminal trial, "then you hide, I think, a certain measure of truth from the public."

Televised trials lead to more justice. Although televised trials have been blamed for unjust results in a few highly publicized cases, supporters of cameras in the courtrooms insist that television improves the overall level of justice in America's courts. "Openness and public access" are "the ultimate guardian[s] of fairness in our judicial system," writes Frances Kahn Zemans of the American Judicature Society. The presence of cameras, for example, forces both judges and attorneys to be on their best behavior. In her experiences as a trial lawyer, reports Klieman, "there were those few judges—two in particular that I remember with not so fond memories—that would act judiciously only when in front of the camera." Moreover, television exposure of the negative side of the justice system can lead legislators and judges to make necessary changes and improvements.

Television improves public confidence in the judicial system. With public confidence in the media at shockingly low levels, the public cannot rely on news reporters to ensure that trials are fair and just. "The public cannot simply rely on newspaper coverage of major trials," says Klieman, "for the newspapers have a way of distorting the truth. After all, we all watched O. J. trying on the gloves, and we could make an independent determination that they did not fit. Yet, the following morning, some commentators remarked that 'the gloves fit snugly.'" Without television coverage of the 1991 rape trial of William Kennedy Smith, adds Frances Zemans, many Americans would have simply assumed that Smith's acquittal was due to his family connections and high-priced attorneys. "Having had the opportunity to weigh the evidence as it was actually presented in the courtroom, the public could make reasonable judgments."

Television coverage can be restricted when necessary. Some aspects of the criminal justice system should not be televised. At times, for example, the identity of witnesses or victims must be kept confidential. But judges have the power to limit television coverage in such cases. Moreover, several states have enacted laws that allow witnesses to opt out of being televised if they so choose.

Television should not be blamed for sensationalizing highly controversial cases. The media circus that surrounded the O. J. trial was largely blamed on television. But media circuses existed long before cameras were even invented, and lawyers played to the general public as early as the eighteenth century. The 1970 "Chicago Seven" trial—which involved protesters arrested at the 1968 Democratic Convention in Chicago—involved "the kind of outrageous behavior that those" who "looked only at the Simpson trial can hardly imagine," writes Zemans. "It was total chaos. . . . I can assure you that everyone in that courtroom—the defendants, the attorneys and the judge—was playing to the audience and each other." If lawyers and judges play to the cameras, the solution is to change their behavior, not to remove the cameras.

No, cameras do not belong in the courts.

Some critics of cameras in the courtroom would ban televised trials altogether. Others would permit television in some cases, but not others, leaving great discretion to the trial judge. In any event, these critics agree that cameras can and do pose a danger to the judicial process in many cases.

Cameras provide the public with a distorted view of the judicial process. Because television networks cover only "newsworthy" trials, the trials presented on television are not representative of how the American justice system really works. Viewers of the Simpson trial—with its multi-million-dollar defense team, extraordinary length, and dramatic outcome—might not realize that most criminal defendants plead guilty; are represented by overworked and underpaid attorneys; and lack the resources needed to challenge the evidence brought forward against them by the government.

Cameras change the way judges, lawyers, and witnesses behave, usually for the worse. "Of those few judges having television experience who chose to respond to [a] California survey, sixty-five percent of them noticed a change in the lawyers' behavior, while forty-seven percent noticed a change in the behavior of witnesses," reports Judge Stanley Weisberg of the Los Angeles Superior Court, who has presided over several high-profile cases. "Much of this change in witness behavior was deemed to be negative." Although judges can control this behavior to some extent, their performance too is affected by the presence of television cameras.

Very few Americans watch trials in their entirety; the rest must depend on pictures and commentary provided by the news media. In theory, televised trials provide Americans with the opportunity to view unfiltered images of a trial. In practice, television simply gives reporters and commentators a visual tool to back up their own judgments and analyses. Television "feeds the public only those pictures the news media deems important or relevant, followed by unnecessary color commentary," according to Judge Weisberg. "Under these circumstances, the general public cannot fully appreciate the workings of our judicial system."

Television makes it harder to seat juries and more difficult to keep them focused only on the events of the trial itself. Although jurors can be instructed not to discuss a trial and not to watch television coverage, some contamination of a jury is inevitable unless the jury is sequestered—an expensive and difficult burden, especially in a long trial. Even worse, if a retrial is necessary—for example, because

(continued)

of a mistrial—the chances of finding an unbiased jury become even lower. Because of this, some judges resist television coverage in cases in which the chances of a mistrial are higher than normal.

Television coverage invades the privacy of innocent parties, especially witnesses. Although privacy rights are often overridden by the demands of the criminal justice process, the particular nature of television coverage makes the potential for invasion of privacy far more consequential. In the age of televised trials, the intimate details of peoples' lives and their deepest emotions can be instantly exposed to an audience of millions across the nation.

All too often, television captures dramatic moments of testimony through close-ups and tight camera angles that attract viewers at the expense of those who did not choose to become public figures. Although television cameras routinely avoid revealing the identity of jurors, witnesses are not so lucky.

SOURCES: Charlotte A Carter, *Media in the Courts* (Center for State Courts, 1981); Criminal Law Symposium: Television Coverage of State Criminal Trials, *St. Thomas Law Review* 9 (Spring 1997): 506–516; Frances Kahn Zemans, "Public Access: The Ultimate Guardian of Fairness in Our Judicial System," *Judicature* 79 (January–February 1996), 173–175; S. L. Alexander, "The Impact of *California* v. *Simpson* on Cameras in the Courtroom," *Judicature* 79 (January–February 1996): 169–172.

Another approach is to appear before the national media only in carefully controlled situations, rather than in free-for-all press conferences or unrehearsed, informal encounters. Television and radio talk shows—especially CNN's *Larry King Live*—are a favored venue, used especially well in 1992 by the independent candidate H. Ross Perot. Another alternative is to appear on a national or local call-in show with a friendly host, fielding questions not from experienced and cynical reporters but from ordinary Americans, who are more likely to be respectful and to ask soft questions.

Cultivating the National Press Corps. A final technique aims not to avoid the national media but to co-opt them. A president can win favor with the national press by catering to their needs and desires and by establishing an informal, friendly relationship. No one was better at this than Franklin Roosevelt, who held frequent off-the-record press conferences and treated the press corps almost as colleagues. No one was worse than Nixon, who seemed unable or unwilling to overcome his adversarial relationship with the press.

In recent years, especially since Watergate, it has become increasingly difficult for a president to cultivate the national press. For one thing, the press corps is now much larger than it once was. For another, as we have seen, modern reporters now seem to view their job as a check on the government, and thus are wary of entering into too close a relationship. Many organizations have even adopted strict ethics rules that bar reporters from accepting gifts or other amenities from the government.

Are the Media Biased?

A common complaint, especially among conservatives, is that the national media are biased in favor of liberal programs and policies. This viewpoint has found support in some academic studies, although the case is far from ironclad. It seems reasonably clear that news reporters and editors are personally more liberal than their average reader or viewer, and in general do not represent a cross section of the American populace. What is less certain is exactly how these personal characteristics affect the media's presentation of the news.

Moreover, other scholars suggest exactly the opposite: that the media are biased in the conservative direction. The major media are almost entirely owned by large corporations, they point out, giving the media a clear stake in the outcomes of debates that might adversely affect corporate interests. Moreover, they note that the nation's newspapers are overwhelmingly conservative in editorial outlook.

A Liberal Bias?

Several studies have shown that the members of the national media are not representative of the nation as a whole. The most well-known are a series of analyses by S. Robert and Linda S. Lichter and their colleagues. In one study, the Lichters interviewed 238 journalists at what they described as "the nation's most influential media outlets: the *New York Times,* the *Washington Post,* the *Wall Street Journal, Time, Newsweek, U.S. News and World Report,* and the news organizations at CBS, NBC, ABC, and PBS." The survey included reporters and correspondents, columnists and news anchors, department heads, bureau chiefs, editors and producers, executives, and others. The Lichters compared their results with a survey of 216 executives at major corporations.

The Lichters found that, on average, members of what they called the "media elite" hailed from big cities in the northeast and north-central states; came from well-off, highly educated families; and were distinctly secular—or nonreligious—in outlook and practice. Half expressed no religious affiliation; only 8 percent attended church or synagogue weekly; and 86 percent seldom or never attended religious services.

Politically, the Lichters found the media elite to be distinctly left-of-center. Self-described liberals outnumbered conservatives by 54 to 17 percent (the remainder described

MEDIA BIAS QUIZ –
HOW MANY PEOPLE REALLY ATTENDED THE RECENT PRO-LIFE RALLY IN WASHINGTON, D.C.?

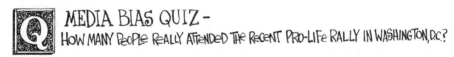

7
PRO-CHOICE ESTIMATES

200,000
U.S. PARK POLICE ESTIMATE
AS REPORTED BY THE DEATH SERVING
LYING, BIASED, ULTRA-LIBERAL MEDIA.

12,497,000,000
PRO-LIFE ESTIMATES

Joe Heller ©1770 GREEN BAY PRESS GAZETTE

themselves as "middle of the road"). Between 1964 and 1976, less than 20 percent of the journalists interviewed supported *any* Republican candidate for president. A large proportion of the journalists also expressed liberal viewpoints on social and economic issues. For example, only 25 percent of those interviewed agreed with the idea that homosexuality is wrong, while more than two-thirds expressed support for government action to reduce the income gap between the rich and the poor. By contrast, the business executives in the control group showed a distinct rightward tilt. Some 60 percent of the executives believed that homosexuality was wrong, while only 29 percent favored government action to reduce the income gap.

The Lichters did not claim that the journalists' liberal tendencies translated deliberately or automatically into a liberal bias in their reporting and coverage. Instead they concluded only that "the media elite's conscious opinions seem to be partly reflected in the ways they subconsciously structure reality," thus indirectly affecting the way they present the news. In studying such issues as nuclear power, busing for integration, and the energy crisis, the Lichters found that the journalists were "consistently one-sided" in their reportage.[28]

Critics have disputed the Lichters' methods and conclusions, charging, in effect, that the Lichters found in their surveys exactly what they were looking for. Much of the criticism centers on technical issues, such as the soundness of the Lichters' survey research techniques. Critics point out that other studies have found that most journalists and reporters are "moderates," or "not very political."[29]

Moreover, critics charge that the Lichters have confused professional values with political bias. The majority of American journalists do share a common set of political beliefs, but it is a mistake to regard these views as "liberal" or, indeed, to view them simply within the context of the current political debate. Instead reporters and editors reflect the deeply held convictions of the journalism profession. These convictions include a belief in the power of information and in the need for free and open political debate; a commitment to exposing inefficiency, dishonesty, and corruption in high places, especially in government; and an almost visceral distaste for hypocrisy of any kind. These views can be characterized as "reformist," but they do not translate into automatic opposition to conservatives (or Republicans) or automatic support for liberals (or Democrats).

Finally, even if journalists are biased in their own views, it is by no means clear that they allow their personal beliefs to control the way they report the news. A reporter's personal political views are not the only factor that determines whether and how a story will be reported—and may not even be a major factor. Probably more important, for example, is the need to present the news in a way that sells newspapers or increases viewership in a highly competitive environment. One of the reasons so many reporters focus on "bad news" is that bad news sells.

> "You don't tell us how to stage the news, and we don't tell you how to cover it."
>
> —Sign on the door of Larry Speakes, White House Press Secretary during the Reagan administration

A Conservative Bias?

Some critics charge that the media are biased in a conservative direction, especially when dealing with issues involving business. These critics note that the media are largely owned by big corporations, and that both the electronic and print media are dependent on advertising revenue from big business as their lifeblood. As an example, critics point to the reluctance of some newspapers and magazines to devote sufficient attention to the hazards of using tobacco. They also note the overwhelming tendency of newspapers to endorse conservative over liberal candidates.[30]

Like charges of liberal bias, these charges of conservative bias are largely unproved. Undoubtedly examples of bias in both directions exist, but whether a clear trend exists in one direction or another remains a matter of debate.

Pack Journalism

Whether true or not, the idea that the media are biased is reinforced by **pack journalism**—the media's habit of attacking a story in unison, like a pack of wolves. An all-out media assault on a story can easily turn into a feeding frenzy in which reporters seem to lose all sense of individual responsibility. Then the story can take on a life of its own, with discussions of whether the story deserves such intense coverage left only to academics and media critics.

Many factors contribute to pack journalism. Probably the most important are the relatively small number of truly big news stories available at any given time, the small size and closeness of the national press corps, the tight deadlines and intense pressure surrounding every story, and the fierce competition between news organizations. In this atmosphere, decisions on what is "newsworthy" are not made by individual journalists sitting alone in their offices, but in a sort of informal, collective judgment of the press corps as a whole. Typically, coverage of the story is greatly affected by the consensus view of how important the story is or how seriously it should be taken.

When George Bush chose Dan Quayle as his running mate in 1988, for example, all the elements were in place for the journalists' pack instincts to take hold. The reporters had been in New Orleans for a week covering an uneventful Republican convention, and were desperately looking for a big story. Bush had kept his vice presidential decision as a closely guarded secret, thus magnifying the tension. The national press corps already knew Quayle well from his service in the Senate and did not regard him as a political heavyweight. Thus from the beginning, the story behind the Quayle story seemed to be whether he had the political experience and savvy to stand as a serious candidate for vice president.

The press corps' initial sense of the story affected its coverage throughout the 1988 campaign and, indeed, for the entire Bush presidency. Every time Quayle made a verbal gaffe, it automatically appeared in every newspaper and on every network news show. Stories about Quayle's lackluster college career and his reliance on family connections rather than personal merit became staple news features, whereas the same stories about politicians regarded as more serious were disregarded or downplayed.

Interestingly, when events suddenly demonstrate that the media's consensus judgment on an issue or candidate is wrong, the story may be greatly magnified in importance. Thus when Bill Clinton surprised the media by surviving the 1992 New Hampshire primary despite allegations of marital infidelity, his survival itself became the story. Clinton was transformed overnight from an also-ran to the "Comeback Kid," and his campaign picked up a momentum that it never lost.

Whether or not the media are biased in one direction or the other, their role in the American political system is hardly neutral or passive. In deciding what is news and how to

Going Their Own Way

Journalists do not always travel in packs. When Federal Reserve Chairman Alan Greenspan testified on Capitol Hill in June 1995, for example, press reports differed so widely that it was hard to believe that all the journalists had attended the same hearing. Here is a sampling of headlines:

"Greenspan Hints at Interest Rate Cut"

—Nashville Banner

"Change Unlikely in Interest Rates; Greenspan Dampens Speculation on Cut"

—The Sun, Baltimore

"Cautious Greenspan Hints at a Cut in Rates"

—The Star-Ledger *of Newark, N.J.*

"Interest Rate Cut Not on Horizon, Greenspan Hints"

—Los Angeles Daily News

One thing Greenspan really did say to one senator:

"If I say anything which you understand fully, I probably made a mistake."

—Associated Press

present the news, in investigating candidates and public officials, in their direct efforts to persuade the public, and in their efforts to measure the public pulse and to report on the activities of interest groups and individual citizens, the media shape the broad contours of democratic politics. The ability of public officials and candidates to manipulate or circumvent the media and talk directly to the public should, in theory, be good for democratic politics; but political figures are typically more interested in putting themselves and their policies in the best possible light than in engaging in a genuine dialogue with the public. Modern media politics, when all is said and done, is a far cry from reasoned and deliberative government by discussion.

Summary

The media comprise a wide range of individuals and organizations who provide information and entertainment to the American public and the world. Analysts and politicians often distinguish between the *print media* (newspapers and magazines) and the *electronic media* (radio and television). The past few decades have seen the development of many new forms of media, including the Internet and the World Wide Web.

The First Amendment to the Constitution guarantees the freedom of the press. As interpreted by the Supreme Court, the Constitution bans most forms of prior restraints on the press, except in the most unusual circumstances. It also makes it difficult, but not impossible, for public officials and public figures to recover damages for libel. However, the Constitution provides few special privileges to the press; for example, it does not allow the media access to government meetings closed to the public. In general the print media have been more free than the electronic media, which have long been regulated on the theory that broadcast frequencies were a scarce resource that had to be managed in the public interest. In recent years, however, technological change has undermined much of the rationale for treating the electronic media differently from the print media.

The news media play many important roles in American politics. First and foremost, the media are a major source of information. More Americans get their news from television than from any other source. The media provide a window on the government, interpret and analyze developing stories, and filter out stories they deem unimportant. In all of these ways, the media help to shape America's political agenda. Second, the media play an important role as a check on the power of the government. Media reporting frequently exposes government wrongdoing, from minor snafus to major scandals. Third, the media can be a participant in politics, actively seeking to influence public opinion and to change the status quo. Finally, the media provide a mechanism by which the people can communicate with their government.

The history of the relationship between government and the media has been a tumultuous one. During and after World War II, the media's relationship with the government was largely friendly and supportive. The Vietnam War and the Watergate scandal fundamentally changed this relationship, however. The press and the government eventually came to see each other as adversaries, creating a confrontational attitude on both sides. In the past twenty years, politicians have turned from open hostility toward the press to a more complex and subtle approach to media manipulation and management.

Critics have charged that the American media are biased, either toward the left or the right side of the political spectrum. In any event, the media frequently run in packs, attacking a story relentlessly and in unison. The media's tendency to practice *pack journalism* reinforces the view that the media are biased and helps undermine public confidence in the news media.

Key Terms

Print media
Electronic media
New media
Prior restraint
Libel
Equal time rule
Fairness doctrine
Sound bite
Visual
Pack journalism

Review Questions

1. How does the Constitution protect the freedom of the press? How and why do the courts treat the electronic media differently from the print media?

2. What are the political implications of the media's tendency toward consolidation and corporate ownership?

3. What roles do the media play in the American political system?

4. How do the media influence public opinion and public policy?

5. What is the nature of the relationship between the government and the media, and how has that relationship changed in recent decades?

6. Why do some critics argue that the media are biased? What is the nature of the media's alleged bias, and what evidence supports this claim?

Suggested Readings

Ansolabehere, Stephen, Roy Behr, and Shanto Iyengar. *The Media Game: American Politics in the Television Age.* New York: Macmillan, 1993.

Graber, Doris A. *Mass Media and American Politics.* 5th ed. Washington, D.C.: CQ Press, 1996.

Graber, Doris A., ed. *Media Power in Politics.* 3d ed. Washington, D.C.: CQ Press, 1994.

Kennamer, David. *Public Opinion, the Press, and Public Policy.* Westport, Conn.: Praeger, 1992.

Lichter, S. Robert, Stanley Rothman, and Linda S. Lichter. *The Media Elite.* Bethesda, MD: Adler, 1986.

Spitzer, Robert J., ed. *Media and Public Policy.* Westport, Conn.: Praeger, 1993.

Internet Resources

A listing of various news and media web sites at:

http://www.yahoo.com/News and Media/Politics/

The New York Times, the nation's "newspaper of record," at:

http://www.nytimes.com

CNN political news at:

http://www.allpolitics.com/

The Drudge Report, an off-beat source of rumors, gossip, and political news not necessarily reported in the mainstream media (made famous by breaking the Monica Lewinsky story) at:

http://www.drudgereport.com

12 ★ Congress

On the surface, William Weld seemed uniquely qualified to serve as the American ambassador to Mexico. A second-term governor, Weld had a working knowledge of Spanish, national stature, and extensive experience, not only in the Massachusetts state house, but also as a United States attorney. Weld was also a Republican—a perfect choice, the White House reasoned, to help build a bridge to the congressional leadership in the wake of the 1996 elections.

What neither Weld nor Clinton had counted on, however, was that the nomination would trigger an intense response from Sen. Jesse Helms (R-N.C.), the influential chair of the Senate Foreign Relations Committee, which would have to confirm Weld's appointment. Even before the nomination was official, Helms announced his opposition and stated flat out that he would not even schedule a confirmation hearing. Helms accused Weld of being "unqualified" for the position because of his support for the legalized medical use of marijuana and for the distribution of clean needles to heroin addicts, and because of his allegedly weak record in drug cases while a United States Attorney. Pundits suggested that Weld's support for abortion and his ambition to be president in the year 2000 were more relevant factors.

What the White House had planned as a peace offering now turned into a nasty fight within the Republican Party. Weld resigned as governor to campaign full time for his hoped-for post, and the president

watched as Weld and Helms attacked each other, catching other Republicans in the crossfire. Although Clinton never pulled his support from Weld, neither did he give the fight his full attention. Weld accused Helms of "ideological extortion"; Helms charged Weld with "threatening that unless his nomination to Mexico is moved [to the Senate floor], he will begin a war within the Republican Party."

In the decentralized power structure of the Senate, Helms, as a committee chair, exercised full control over the committee's agenda and was thus able to block the nomination by refusing to schedule a hearing. The only way out was if a majority of senators signed a petition forcing the nomination to the floor. But such a move was discouraged by the Republican Senate leadership, which had no difficulty in choosing to support a powerful member of the Senate over a former governor of Massachusetts.

Five months after it began, Weld's quest was over. But would there be fallout, in the form of a revision of the Senate rules that give such extraordinary power to one person? Probably not. "The ultimate power of chairmen, in general, may make people think twice," said Senator Joseph R. Biden, Jr. "But no hard feelings."[1]

Congress, and especially the House of Representatives, is often described as "the people's branch" of government. Members of the House, wrote James Madison, would have "an immediate dependence on, and an intimate sympathy with, the people."[2] Senators were originally appointed by the

Bill Weld (right) and Jesse Helms share a civil moment before a meeting of the Senate Foreign Relations Committee.

state legislatures, but after 1913 they too were elected by the people. It is in Congress, therefore, that the idea of self-government should find its clearest and most vital expression.

The Framers did not believe that Congress should simply mirror the will of the people. Instead the purpose of representation was "to refine and enlarge the public views by passing them through the medium of a chosen body of citizens, whose wisdom may best discern the true interest of their country." Moreover, both the Senate and the presidential veto power were designed to protect minority interests and to prevent hasty or ill-considered actions on the part of the people's representatives.

Members of Congress are expected to represent not only the national interest, but also the interests of their local constituencies. The direct representation of the states in the original Constitution reflects this concern, as does the very fact that congressional districts never cross state lines. Yet James Madison, at least, sought to overcome the localism that pervaded American politics in the 1780s. For him the public interest was most decidedly the national interest and could be attained only in a large republic, with a small House of Representatives and large legislative districts (see the discussion of *Federalist* No. 10 in Chapter 2).

The theoretical ambiguities of Congress's role—balancing national and local interests, the need for representation against the Framers' desire to avoid direct democracy, and the power of the majority against the rights of minorities—are matched by ambiguities in practice. The twentieth century has seen both ebbs and flows in the power of the congressional leadership and in the power of Congress relative to the executive branch. Strong leadership allows Congress to govern more effectively but reduces its ability to address the needs and wants of the many interests in American society. Weaker leadership strengthens the role of the people's representatives but may compromise Congress's ability to compete with the White House or to develop coherent policy.

Whether Congress can govern, and the relationship between congressional government and popular government, are the major themes of this chapter. The stakes are high, for if effective representative government cannot be found in Congress, it probably cannot be found anywhere in the American constitutional system.

Questions to Keep in Mind

- *How well does Congress represent the majority? How well does it represent minority interests?*

- *How do Congress and the executive branch check and balance one another?*

- *Can Congress address the nation's problems effectively and efficiently? What are Congress's strengths and weaknesses as an institution?*

Basic Concepts ★ ★ ★ ★ ★ ★ ★ ★ ★ ★ ★ ★ ★

Congress Under the Constitution

The Constitution lays out the structure and powers of Congress in some detail. Although the role of Congress in the American political system and the rules under which it operates have grown over time, there is much about the modern Congress that the Framers would recognize and embrace.

Constitutional Powers of Congress   The Constitution grants all legislative power to the Congress. The president's formal functions in the legislative process, as Justice Hugo Black once put it, are limited to "the recommending of laws he thinks wise and the vetoing of laws he thinks bad."[3] Although the president's informal powers give him a central role in the legislative process, the fundamental authority to make the law remains with Congress.

The Constitution grants Congress many specific legislative powers. In addition, as established in the 1819 case of *McCulloch* v. *Maryland* (see Chapter 3), Congress can exercise powers implied by the Constitution, and has broad authority to make all laws "necessary and proper" to carrying out its powers.

Congress's functions are not limited to the legislative process. Congress also oversees the activities of the federal bureaucracy in an effort to ensure that its laws are implemented effectively. Through the impeachment process, Congress provides a check on judicial and presidential corruption and abuse of power. Moreover, the Constitution gives the Senate the responsibility of approving presidential appointments of judges, ambassadors, and many executive officials, and of ratifying treaties with foreign nations.

> *"You are apprehensive of monarchy; I, of aristocracy. I would therefore have given more power to the President and less to the Senate."*
>
> —John Adams to Thomas Jefferson, December 6, 1787

Election of a New Congress   A new Congress is elected every two years, in even-numbered years. The first session of a Congress begins in January following the election, and lasts until Congress adjourns, usually in the fall. The second session begins the following January, again lasting until the fall, when new elections are held. If necessary, the president can call a third (or special) session between the elections and the start of the next Congress in January. Ever since the first Congress in 1789, each two-year Congress has been referred to by number. Thus the Congress that sits from January 1999 to January 2001 is the 106th Congress.

Bicameralism   Congress is designed on the principle of **bicameralism**—that is, it consists of two chambers, the Senate and the House of Representatives.

The Senate consists of two members from each state, for a total of one hundred members. Senators serve six-year terms, staggered so that one-third of the Senate is up for re-election at every two-year election cycle.

The House consists of 435 voting members, with the number of representatives for each state based on population. In addition, there are five nonvoting members, from American Samoa, the District of Columbia, Guam, Puerto Rico, and the Virgin Islands. Members of the House are elected in even-numbered years and serve two-year terms.

The House of Representatives is typically referred to simply as "the House." The two chambers together are known as Congress, although the term *congressman* or *congress-woman* always refers to a member of the House, never to a senator. Members of the House are also known as representatives, members, or MCs, which stands for "members of Congress." Congress, because it is physically located on Capitol Hill in Washington, is often referred to by Washington insiders as "the Hill"—as in "I think we'll run into trouble on this on the Hill."

The Constitution requires that all legislation and all federal expenditures be approved by both the Senate and the House of Representatives in exactly the same form, down to the very last word; then they must be presented to the president for acceptance or veto. A presidential veto can be overridden only by a two-thirds vote of each chamber.

Congressional Districts   The Supreme Court has ruled that congressional districts within a state must have roughly the same population (see the discussion of reapportionment in Chapter 10). However, because each state must have at least one representative and because congressional districts cannot cross state lines, the size of districts in different states varies, at times considerably. For example, Montana's single member of Congress represents approximately 862,000 people, whereas Wyoming's single member represents only 487,000. The number of representatives allotted to each state, as well as the size and shape of congressional districts, is adjusted every ten years to keep up with population changes recorded in the census. As of 1997, each member of Congress represented, on average, just over 600,000 people.[4]

Qualifications of Members   According to the Constitution, members of the House of Representatives must be at least twenty-five years old and must have been a citizen of the United States for at least seven years. A senator must be at least thirty years old, and a citizen for at least nine years. Both senators and representatives, when elected, must be inhabitants of the state from which they were elected.

Table 12.1
Differences Between the House and the Senate

House	Senate
CONSTITUTIONAL POWERS AND CHARACTERISTICS	
Larger (435 members)	Smaller (100 members)
Elected from local districts	Elected statewide
Two-year term	Six-year term
Originates tax bills	Approves treaties, presidential appointments
Power to impeach president and other officers	Conducts impeachment trials
TRADITIONAL POWERS AND CHARACTERISTICS	
Stronger leadership	Weaker leadership
More formal atmosphere	Less formal, "clubby" atmosphere
Structured debate	Debate unlimited unless 60 senators approve cloture motion
Lower prestige, visibility	Higher prestige, visibility
Many members specialize in one policy area	Less specialization

A 1969 Supreme Court decision made it clear that neither the states nor Congress can add to the Constitution's three qualifications of age, citizenship, and residency. A1995 decision struck down state efforts to limit members of Congress to a maximum number of terms in office.[5]

Differences Between the House and the Senate The House and the Senate differ in origin and purpose, in their constitutional responsibilities, and in structure and style.

Origin and Purpose. The creation of a bicameral legislature was a compromise between the large states and the small states, and between those who wanted the legislature to represent the people and those who wanted it to represent the states. James Madison, who preferred a one-house legislature apportioned on the basis of population, defended the arrangement that the Convention ultimately agreed upon on the grounds that any other arrangement likely to command the support of all the states would be "still more objectionable."[6]

Flanked by supporters, Senator Carol Moseley-Braun (D-Ill.) announces the introduction of the Violence Against Women Act, passed by Congress in 1994. Their high prestige and visibility allow senators to command the attention of the news media.

Nonetheless, Madison argued, the two-house system did have certain practical advantages. The two houses would provide an effective check on one another, reducing the chances that Congress would "yield to the impulse of sudden and violent passions" and take away the rights of the people. The members of the Senate, who would be more experienced than their House colleagues and who would serve longer terms in office, would also provide a degree of experience and stability not likely to be found in the House ("Every new election in the States," Madison noted, "is found to change one half of the representatives").[7] Finally, the Senate would be small enough to serve as a council of advisers to the president, especially on matters of foreign policy.

To make the Senate more independent of electoral majorities, the Framers provided that members of the Senate would be appointed by the state legislatures and would serve a six-year term. Members of the House, by contrast, would serve a two-year term and would be elected directly by the people. In addition, while the entire House would come up for reelection every two years, only one-third of the Senate would stand for reelection each election cycle. The Seventeenth Amendment, ratified in 1913, provided for the direct election of senators by the people.

Responsibilities. The legislative powers of the two houses are identical for most purposes. Either house can initiate legislation, and both must concur in the final passage of any bill. Exceptions exist, however, in the areas of taxation, foreign affairs, executive appointments, and impeachment.

The Framers followed the English practice by requiring that the popularly elected lower house initiate all revenue bills. The Framers saw this as an essential check on government, preventing "taxation without representation." The Senate can easily circumvent this requirement, however, by amending a minor House tax measure as it sees fit. In 1981, for example, the Republican-controlled Senate initiated the major tax cuts sought by the Reagan administration.[8] Even so, Senate initiation of tax measures remains the exception.

POLITICS LIGHT

Congressional Humor

Members of Congress, like lawyers, are an easy target for jokes. Many Congress jokes and lawyer jokes are unfair, of course, but both have a long history. Unbridled Congress-bashing may be linked to voter cynicism and to the institution's low standing with the American public, but congressional humor also reflects the essential democracy of American political culture. As long as the public is free to laugh at those who govern them, the prospects of tyranny are probably pretty dim.

Here are a few Congress jokes, drawn from some of America's best political humorists:

It could probably be shown by facts that there is no distinctly native American criminal class except Congress.

—Mark Twain

Senate, n. A body of elderly gentlemen charged with high duties and misdemeanors.

—Ambrose Bierce

Senatorial Courtesy: "If ye let me talk I'll let ye sleep."

—Finley Peter Dunne

A toy company is now "making action figures modeled after the U.S. Senate, and they're pretty realistic—each Senator is sold separately."

—Jay Leno

When Congress makes a law, it's a joke; and when Congress makes a joke, it's a law.

—Will Rogers

Suppose you were an idiot. And suppose you were a member of Congress. But I repeat myself.

—Mark Twain

Congress also typically follows the tradition of having the House approve all spending bills prior to the Senate.

To provide stability in foreign policy, the Framers gave the Senate alone the power to ratify treaties. Reflecting their view of the Senate as a council of advisers to the executive, they gave the Senate the power to approve presidential appointments, including judges. Finally, the Framers gave the House the sole power to impeach the president and other public officials, but left to the Senate the power to conduct the actual trials and remove officials from office.

Structure and Style. With 435 members, the House must conduct its business with great formality. Thus it is organized as a hierarchy, with the leadership and committee chairs exercising great power. The House imposes strict limits on how long any given issue can be debated and how long individual members can speak. The large size of the House of Representatives also means that members are assigned to only a few committees—and usually to only a single major committee. Thus members of the House tend to have expertise in a single issue area, and can focus more specifically on matters of detail. Few members of the House become nationally known personalities.

The small size of the Senate and its tradition of unlimited debate and deference to individual members make for a sharp contrast with the House. The atmosphere of the Senate is often described as being more like a club than a legislative body. The leadership in the Senate, as we have seen, is much weaker than in the House. Senators have traditionally placed great weight on maintaining cordial relations with one another and on preserving strong personal relationships even between political rivals. Senators typically serve on several committees, and most are generalists rather than specialists. Finally, senators are likelier than their House counterparts to become well-known national figures; an individual senator can more easily command the attention of the media than a rank-and-file member of the House, and may be better poised to move into a national leadership role. Three of the four vice presidents between 1976 and 1996, for example, were chosen from among the ranks of current senators.

A trademark of the Senate is its rule permitting unlimited debate on virtually every issue. Debate can be limited only by a vote of three-fifths of the membership (sixty senators). This procedural rule creates the opportunity for the **filibuster**—a deliberate attempt to prevent passage of legislation by debating it to death. Senators can also block or delay action on a bill by forcing votes on countless amendments. The pros and cons of the filibuster reflect the tension between direct and representative democracy. At times, the filibuster simply frustrates majority rule, nullifying the will of the people. At other times, however, the filibuster provides a way for the minority to ensure that its objections are taken seriously and to prevent unwise or ill-considered legislation.

An example of a recent filibuster occurred in 1995, when 43 senators were able to prevent the majority from approving Dr. Henry Foster, whom President Bill Clinton had nominated for the position of surgeon general. The record for the longest filibuster was set in 1957 by Senator Strom Thurmond of South Carolina, then a Democrat, who spoke for 24 hours and 18 minutes in opposition to a civil rights bill.[9]

Parties, Organization, and Leadership. The political parties play the central role in the organization of each house. At the beginning of each congressional session, the majority party in each house sets the rules; determines the number of committees and subcommittees; selects the committee and subcommittee chairs; and appoints the other leadership positions. There are differences in these matters, however, between the House and Senate.

The top leader in the House of Representatives is the **Speaker of the House**. He is assisted by the **House majority leader** and by the majority whip and his or her deputies. Together, the leadership is responsible for managing the day-to-day business of the House; setting the agenda and presiding over the floor debate, and, when necessary, maintaining party discipline and unity. The precise duties of each of the leadership positions fluctuate over time, depending on the style and personalities of the major players. Speaker Newt Gingrich, for example, delegated almost complete responsibility for managing his party's legislative agenda to the majority leader, Dick Armey (R-Tex.).

The leadership structure of the Senate is more complicated. Under the Constitution, the president of the Senate is the vice president of the United States, although he rarely serves in that capacity except on ceremonial occasions or to break a tie vote on an important issue. There is also a president *pro tempore* (or *pro tem*), who serves as president of the Senate when the vice president is not there. The president *pro tem* is largely a ceremonial post, and is generally held by a senior member of the majority party. By law, the president *pro tem* is third in the line of presidential succession, after the vice president and the Speaker of the House.

The real leader of the Senate is the **Senate majority leader.** His duties are similar to those of the Speaker of the House, but he has few formal powers and is viewed by other senators more as a colleague than as a superior. Thus, the majority leader must lead by persuasion rather than by force. The Senate majority leader is assisted by the whip and the whip's aides.

In both the House and Senate, the bulk of the day-to-day work is done in committees. In general, committees allow Congress to consider a wide range of legislation efficiently and to develop greater levels of expertise in particular policy areas. But the committee system, as we will see, may also enable individual members and special interest groups to exercise a disproportionate degree of influence on public policy.

How a Bill Becomes a Law

The German Chancellor Otto von Bismarck once suggested that there were two things no one should watch being made: legislation and sausage. And, in fact, the legislative process is extraordinarily daunting and complex. The following discussion of how a bill becomes a law deals only with basic rules and procedures. In practice, as we will see, the legislative process is full of horse trading, informal negotiations, interest group involvement, and media politics. Nor does the process end with the enactment of a law: to the contrary, the process of applying and interpreting the law, both by agencies and courts, is only beginning.

A detailed example of one bill's tortuous route through both houses appears in the box on pages 336–337.

Introducing Legislation The idea for a new law may come from the President or lower executive officials; from individual members of Congress or their staff; or from interest groups or private citizens. The proposed legislation may address a societywide problem, such as poverty or pollution, or it may serve the interests of some narrow group. In any event, an idea is proposed, a bill is drafted, and the legislative process begins.

Technically, only a member of Congress can introduce legislation, and only in his or her own chamber. In practice, many bills are proposed, developed, and even written by the White House or an executive agency, and introduced by a friendly representative or senator. They are known as "administration bills," and although often defeated or modified substantially, they are rarely ignored entirely. Other bills are written largely by or with the advice of interest groups.

Referral to Committee(s) Once introduced, a bill is sent by the speaker to one or more committees for consideration. The committees, in turn, usually send the bill on to specialized subcommittees. The subcommittees investigate the issue, often hold formal hearings, and modify the bill as they think appropriate. In a formal *markup* session, the subcommittee makes changes to the original bill and takes a formal vote on whether to approve it.

Figure 12.1 **How a Bill Becomes a Law**

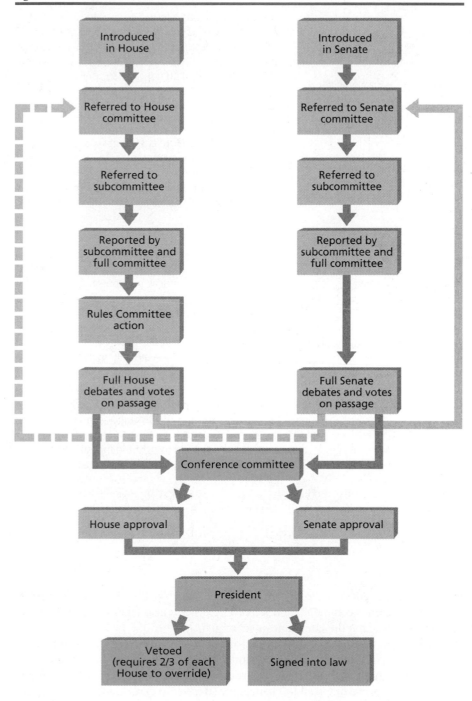

How a Bill Becomes a Law: The Case of the 1994 Assault Weapons Ban

The Omnibus Crime Control Act of 1994 contained a ban on the sale and possession of nineteen kinds of assault weapons. The legislative history of this measure stretches back over five years.

Background. Advocates of gun control began to focus their energies on banning semiautomatic assault weapons after a series of tragic incidents, including the 1989 massacre of five school children in Stockton, California, by a man using a Chinese AK-47. In response, Presidents George Bush and Bill Clinton banned the importation of assault weapons, but between 1989 and 1993, gun control advocates pushed Congress to pass legislation banning the sale and possession of assault weapons as well.

The key players. On the one side stood a coalition of gun-control groups, led by Handgun Control, Inc., and the Coalition to Stop Gun Violence. A leading figure in both groups was Sarah Brady, the wife of former White House Press Secretary James Brady, who was seriously wounded in the 1981 assassination attempt on Ronald Reagan. Also supporting the assault weapons ban were various law enforcement organizations. On the other side stood the National Rifle Association (NRA). One of the most powerful single-interest groups in Washington, the NRA boasts a membership of around 3.3 million gun enthusiasts and an annual budget of $90 million. Also opposing the control of assault weapons were representatives of the gun industry.

Early White House support. Responding to the public's growing concern about crime, President Clinton announced his support for a ban on assault weapons as part of a broad anti-crime package in a White House Rose Garden ceremony on August 11, 1993.

Congressional developments. Clinton's anti-crime package—minus its proposed ban on assault weapons—was introduced by Joseph Biden (D-Del.) and Jack Brooks (D-Tex.), chairmen of the Senate and House Judiciary Committees, respectively. The House committee promptly approved the bill, known as H.R. 3355, and sent it to the House floor, which passed it on November 3—though still with no assault weapons bill included.

Meanwhile, the Senate debated the crime package. Among the many amendments adopted by the Senate was the ban on assault weapons, proposed by Senator Dianne Feinstein (D-Cal.). Gun control opponents decided not to fight the measure in the Senate, but in conference and in the House instead. On November 19, the Senate incorporated its own measure into H.R. 3355 and approved it. It requested the appointment of a conference committee.

Once approved, the bill goes back to the full committee, which holds a further markup session and makes its own recommendation. The same process also takes place in the other house of Congress, either at the same time or subsequently.

The leadership in each house plays an important role in deciding which committee or committees will consider a bill. Congressional leaders know that some committees will be more sympathetic than others to a particular bill, and may steer legislation one way or another to improve or lessen its chances for success. In general, committee opposition to a bill dooms its chances for success. Most bills, in fact, never make it out of com-

Surprise in the House. After a delay of almost six months, the House returned to consideration of the crime bill. On April 25, 1994, Representative Charles Schumer (D-N.Y.) introduced a bill to ban assault weapons. The bill was approved by the Crime Subcommittee and the full Judiciary Committee, despite the opposition of Chairman Brooks. On May 5, the House shocked Congress watchers by approving the ban by a vote of 216-214. The bill was added to H.R. 3355, which was still awaiting conference.

Conference. The conference committee met in June 1994. The NRA and its allies fought fiercely behind the scenes to excise the assault weapons ban. Informal negotiations between the House, the Senate, and the White House dragged on into July, stalled by Democratic disagreements over the assault weapons ban and other parts of the bill. Finally, on July 28, 1994, the conference committee agreed on a deal.

After conference. The conference committee's recommendation still had to be approved by both houses, so the NRA had one final chance to kill the bill. It found unusual allies in the congressional black caucus and other civil rights groups, who were upset because the conference committee had deleted provisions dealing with racial bias in death penalty sentencing. Between them, the anti–gun control and civil rights groups could muster enough votes to keep the conference bill off the House floor.

Reenter the president. With the entire crime bill now in jeopardy, President Clinton reentered the fray, stepping up attacks on the NRA and its allies. "Do not let us pull another Washington, D.C., game here and let this crime bill go down on some procedural hide-and-seek," he declared. Meanwhile, a "brigade of lobbyists" from both sides made their case to fence-sitting lawmakers.

The final chapter. Despite the efforts of the White House, the House voted 210 to 225 on August 11 to keep the final bill from coming to a floor vote. Clinton and Democratic leaders promised to "fight and fight and fight" for reconsideration; ten days later, after a weekend of "marathon negotiations," a new compromise was reached. Republicans agreed to support the assault weapons ban in return for a $3.3 billion reduction in spending on crime prevention programs.

The House adopted the conference agreement on August 21; the Senate followed suit on August 25. The bill was formally sent to the White House on September 12 and signed by the president the following day. It is now known as P.L. (Public Law) 103-322.

SOURCES: *Congressional Quarterly Weekly Report,* various issues; *Congressional Quarterly Almanac,* 1993; Robert J. Spitzer, *The Politics of Gun Control* (Chatham, N.J.: Chatham House Publishers, 1995).

mittee; of the more than 10,000 bills introduced in the 102d Congress (1991–1993), for example, only 590 became public laws. All but a few of the bills not approved were killed at the committee stage.[10]

In recent years, bills have frequently been referred to more than one committee for consideration. Some twenty-three committees, for example, worked on the 100th Congress's trade bill. Partly, multiple referrals reflect the increasing complexity of federal laws, which may impact the jurisdictions of several different committees. By expanding the number of legislators and interest groups involved in the consideration of a bill, multiple referrals also promote public discussion of important issues, increase access to the legislative process, and encourage consideration of alternative approaches. Multiple referrals can also strengthen the leadership by weakening the influence of particular committees or subcommittees and by fostering competition and conflict between committees. New rules imposed by the Republican leadership in 1995, however, limited the Speaker's ability to make multiple referrals.[11]

Reports   In addition to approving the text of the bill, the committee or subcommittee with primary responsibility for the bill also prepares a report to accompany it. The report contains required information on the economic and budgetary impact of the proposed legislation, as well as a great deal of supplementary information that is useful for administrative agencies and courts that need to interpret the meaning of the bill down the road. Reports also contain "nonstatutory controls," which are unofficial instructions from the committee to the administrative agencies.

Rules Committee   With some exceptions, every important bill proposed by a House committee must go to the **rules committee,** a special committee that determines how the bill will be handled on the floor (that is, by the full House). The rule specifies the amount of time spent on debate and whether the measure can be amended before the floor vote. The nature of the rule can make passage of the bill easier or harder, and if the rules committee refuses to approve any rule, the bill is in most cases effectively dead. The majority party leadership generally exercises close control over the rules committee.

Floor Debate and Vote   At last the measure is brought to the floor of each house, debated, and voted on. Floor debate rarely changes anyone's mind—although there are exceptional occasions when it does—but it does give undecideds an opportunity to make up their minds. Floor debate serves three additional purposes. First, it completes the legislative record (or "legislative history") of the proposal, providing useful guidance for courts and agencies who must apply and interpret the law if passed. Second, it provides an opportunity for policy questions to be discussed and debated in a highly public setting, giving members of Congress the chance to make their views known to their constituents and focusing the public's attention on the matter in question. (Floor debates are shown on the C-SPAN television network, and debates on important issues are usually given prominent coverage on news broadcasts.) Finally, floor debate provides the opportunity for the full House or Senate to consider amendments to the committee version of a bill.

Conference   To become law, the identical bill must be passed by both chambers. If the House and Senate have passed different bills on the same subject, their differences may be resolved by a **conference committee** made up of members of both houses. The final version of the bill as approved by the conference committee must be approved by both houses on a strict up-or-down vote, with further amendments not permitted.

Conference committees involve much politicking and considerable compromise. For example, the 1995 law restricting the federal government from imposing unfunded mandates on the states nearly foundered when the House and Senate could not agree on two key provisions. On one issue, the House accepted the Senate version; on the other, fellow Ohioans Rob Portman of the House and John Glenn of the Senate met privately for weeks and eventually forged an acceptable compromise.[12] Once the conference committee has agreed on a compromise bill, rejection by the House or Senate is rare.[13]

A modern trend is to use conference committees to insert new material, which has not been approved by *either* house, into a bill. Technically, the insertion of new material into a conference bill violates the rules, but the rules are not enforced unless members object.

To the White House Finally, the bill is sent to the White House for signature or **veto** by the president, who has ten days to decide. If the president does nothing, the bill goes into effect. However, an unsigned bill does not take effect if Congress has adjourned by the tenth day, giving presidents the opportunity to make a "pocket veto" in the last days before Congress adjourns simply by doing nothing.

Veto Override If the president does veto a bill (except by pocket veto), the bill is returned to Congress for possible override. Overriding a presidential veto is very difficult, because it requires a two-thirds vote of each house. Between 1993 and 1996, President Bill Clinton vetoed seventeen bills, and the Congress was able to override only one. Historically, Congress has been able to override less than 5 percent of all bills vetoed by the president.[14]

Budget and Revenue

Among the most important powers of Congress is the power of the purse. Only Congress can impose taxes, and only Congress can authorize the expenditure of money. The president plays an important role in the budgetary process, but the final decisions are up to Congress.

Congressional approval of expenditures is a two-step process. In the first step—**authorization**—Congress creates the legal basis for government programs. Authorizations bills establish the rules governing the expenditure of funds, and may put limits on how much money can be spent and for how long. In the second step—**appropriation**—Congress determines the actual amount of money that can be spent each year. The amount of money appropriated may be less than, but can never exceed, the amount previously authorized.

Many federal programs—including social security, Medicare, and veterans' benefits—operate under broad, open-ended authorizations that place no limit on the amount of money that can be spent. Such programs, which comprise roughly two-thirds of the federal budget, are known as **entitlements,** because the government is obligated to provide services or benefits to any person who qualifies under the law. Changing the amount of money on such programs requires changes in the underlying authorization. Other federal programs, by contrast, involve purely **discretionary spending,** meaning that Congress can shrink or expand them each year through the appropriations process, without changes to the underlying authorizations. Discretionary spending includes a wide variety of programs, such as national defense, prisons and law enforcement, environmental protection, and employment and training programs. Discretionary spending makes up roughly one-third of the federal budget, split half and half between foreign affairs (including the military) and domestic programs.

The Budget Process The president is required by law to send a budget proposal to Congress every year. Congress then adopts its own budget resolution, which sets out overall spending limits and targets by budget category. Since the 1980s, Congress and the White House have struggled to try to reduce the federal budget deficit—the difference between

Figure 12.2 **The Budget Process**

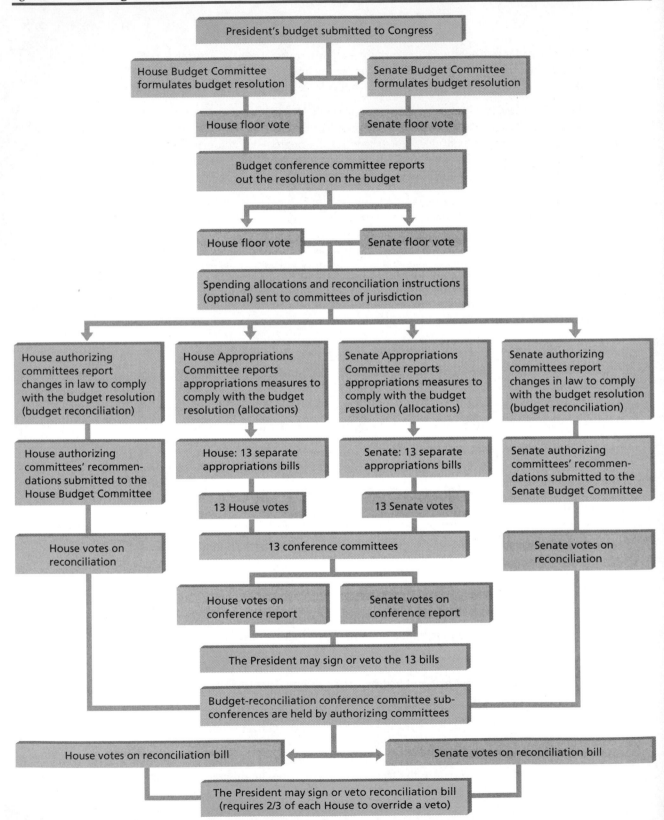

the amount the government receives in taxes and the amount it spends on various programs. Under the 1990 budget agreement, a projected budget deficit does not invoke automatic budget cuts. Instead, Congress is required to maintain strict limits on discretionary spending; other causes of the deficit do not count. If, for example, a recession increases unemployment and thus raises government spending on unemployment insurance, the resulting increase in the deficit is ignored.

Any new expenditures on discretionary domestic spending must be on a pay-as-you-go basis. That is, Congress cannot spend more in one area unless it either cuts spending from another area or raises taxes. A host of rules ensures that final appropriations fall within the overall budget agreement targets.

The budget agreement has made the funding of new federal domestic programs extremely difficult. Critics argue, however, that the new agreement fails to get at the heart of the problem—because it specifically exempts entitlement programs from its provisions. Any new spending that does not result from a specific congressional appropriation or from a change in the rules of entitlement programs is simply not covered by the agreement.

The 1990 budget agreement and a 1993 tax increase had some effect in reducing the budget deficit, but what really helped was the steady and solid growth of the American economy, which raised incomes (and thus tax revenues) and a remarkably low inflation rate, which kept down interest payments on the debt. In 1996, Congress and the White House agreed on a plan to eliminate the deficit by 2002; by 1998, the deficit had disappeared by itself, and the two sides were debating how to spend the projected surplus. Congressional Republicans sought tax cuts; President Clinton urged modest new social programs.[15]

Both sides agreed, however, that the government will not continue to run surpluses forever. The problems lie in social security and Medicare—federal programs which provide retirement income and health care benefits to the elderly. Early in the twenty-first century, the retirement of the "baby-boom" generation will put enormous strains on both programs. The long-term health of the federal government's balance sheet, experts agree, depends on reforming these highly popular programs.

The disappearance of the deficit has undermined support for a Balanced Budget Amendment to the Constitution. The strongest argument of those who supported such an amendment—that Washington would bring down the deficit only under the compulsion of a constitutional rule—has been brushed aside by events.[16]

Representing the People

The concept of representation is central to any modern conception of democracy. In the American system, the branch of government most clearly designed to provide effective representation for the people is Congress, and especially the House of Representatives. Exactly what constitutes effective representation has always generated considerable debate, however, both in the Framers' time and our own.

The Federalists and Antifederalists, as we saw in Chapter 2, had very different notions of representation. For the Antifederalists, the goal of representation was to ensure that

Should Congressional Terms Be Limited?

Unlike the president of the United States, who is limited by the Constitution to two terms in office, members of Congress can be reelected indefinitely—as long as they continue to win the support of their constituents on election day. In the mid-1990s, however, several states adopted laws imposing congressional "term limits," usually six or twelve years for House members and twelve for senators. In 1995, the Supreme Court ruled all such limits—whether imposed by Congress or by the states—to be unconstitutional; so fundamental a change in the American system of government, the justices concluded, could be imposed only by constitutional amendment.* Alternatively, term limits could be adopted voluntarily. In 1998, for example, the advocacy group U.S. Term Limits asked all House candidates to sign a pledge stating that they will not serve more than three two-year terms.

The term limits debate is important not only because it involves an issue of current interest, but also because it strikes at fundamental issues in American politics. What is the ideal form of political representation? What is the proper relationship between members of Congress and their constituents? Why do members of Congress continue to be elected at high rates despite the public's lack of confidence in Congress as a whole? Keep these issues in mind as you consider the two sides of this important debate.

Yes, term limits would improve the political process.

Supporters of term limits make several key arguments:

Term limits would negate the advantages of incumbency and allow for a fair contest between competing candidates. Advocates of term limits begin with the undeniable fact that members of Congress enjoy extraordinary job security—despite the constitutional requirement that they stand for reelection on a regular basis. Although a considerable number of incumbents were defeated in the 1994 elections, voters returned to form in 1996, reelecting over 95 percent of those who ran. The assumption that such high reelection rates represent the public's satisfaction with Congress ignores the many advantages of incumbency—including access to PAC dollars, lots of free publicity, an efficient staff, and uncounted opportunities to do favors for constituents—that make defeating a sitting member of Congress an all but Herculean task.

Term limits would reduce the influence of special-interest lobbyists. One reason for the high reelection rate, as we have seen, is that lobbyists pay large sums of money—in the form of PAC contributions—to gain access to members of Congress. As one state legislator put it, "Lobbyists thrive on having pet 'good ol' boy' and 'good ol' girl' legislators they can go to for a vote when they need to. These relationships are built up over years of camaraderie developed through dinners, drinks, basketball and football tickets, evenings of 'harmless' little poker games . . . and most importantly through campaign contributions."† The adoption of term limits would mean that legislators would have less time, and fewer incentives, to build up such relationships. Knowing that they will be returning home in at most six years, legislators could focus instead on the interests of the public.

Term limits would eliminate "career politicians" and help ensure that members of Congress truly represent the people. Backers of term limits see the ideal member of Congress as a "citizen-legislator" who goes to Washington for a brief period but who remains firmly grounded in his or her life and career in the district. By contrast, most members of Congress are career politicians, and many have lost touch with the men and women who elected (and keep electing) them. Thus term limits are seen as a way to reform Congress, making it more representative of and responsive to the people. "As long as Congress is run by professionals," writes one supporter of term limits, "Washington will operate essentially the same way."‡

The vast majority of Americans want term limits. The American people have conclusively demonstrated their strong and consistent support of the term limits principle. Before term limits were invalidated by the United States Supreme Court, term limits had been approved in twenty-three states. Public opinion polls show that the vast majority of voters support term limits and are more likely to support a candidate who pledges to limit his or her own term. That the same voters keep reelecting their own representatives demonstrates not that the public is against term limits, but that contests between incumbents and challengers are not fair fights.

No, term limits are not the answer.

Opponents of term limits often admit that Congress is a less-than-perfect institution, but they insist that arbitrary restrictions on voters' choices would only make matters worse. In particular:

Term limits are fundamentally undemocratic. The Framers rejected the idea of term limits even for the presidency (the tradition that a president serve only two terms was initiated by George Washington and broken only by Franklin D. Roosevelt on the eve of World War II; it was made a constitutional rule in 1951). In the *Federalist* No. 72, for example, Alexander Hamilton categorically rejected the "idea of disabling the people to continue in office men who had entitled themselves, in their opinion, to approbation and confidence; the advantages of which are at best speculative and equivocal, and are overbalanced by disadvantages far more certain and decisive." For democracy to function well, voters must be trusted to make decisions on who is fit or unfit for congressional office. Limiting their choice by imposing arbitrary term limits violates the democratic principle.

Term limits would increase the power of unelected bureaucrats and congressional staff and of special-interest groups. Members of Congress who have served in Washington for a long time develop considerable expertise in various policy areas, opponents of term limits argue, enabling them to manage their staff, weigh the conflicting claims of lobbyists, and conduct effective oversight of the bureaucracy. Inexperienced legislators will be forced to

depend on staff members—who *are* Washington professionals—and will be prone to being misled or manipulated by more seasoned bureaucrats and lobbyists. If term limits were adopted, argues the former presidential aid Hodding Carter III, "about 50 percent of the House and Senate would at all times be filled with trainees, just beginning to learn the ropes."§

Term limits would deprive the nation of its wisest and most experienced legislators. Opponents concede that term limits would rid Congress of self-serving, incompetent, and corrupt legislators. But they would also force out a large number of men and women who have proven their wisdom, dedication, and integrity over many years of service. As one opponent puts it, "where surgical strikes are needed to eliminate the incompetent or corrupt, the term limitation uses carpet bombing in the hope that in the resulting carnage, some of the guilty will suffer along with the innocent."‖ Given the difficulty and complexity of the tasks facing the government, the value of experienced leadership cannot be underestimated.

What the American people want is good government, not term limits. The success of the term limits movement, opponents claim, is not so much an endorsement of the concept as an effort by the public to latch onto any idea that might help restore confidence in government. If the problem is PAC money, the answer should be campaign reform; if the problem is an unresponsive Congress, the answer should be to "vote the bums out"—as the voters did in 1994. Many of the goals of the term limits movement are laudable, opponents agree, but the term limits idea is merely a quick fix that will cause more problems than it solves.

*U.S. Terms Limits v. Thornton, 112 S. Ct. 1842 (1995).
†George Wingard, "Term Limits Keep Lobbyists from Plying Legislators," Eugene (Or.) Register-Guard, March 25, 1997.
‡Doug Bandow, "Bias for Incumbents," Washington Times, October 17, 1996.
§Hodding Carter III, "Limits on Congressional Terms: A Cure Worse Than the Disease," Wall Street Journal, October 4, 1990, p. A21.
‖Ross K. Baker, "Quack Therapy for Democracy," Los Angeles Times, October 10, 1990, p. B7.

members of the legislature would reproduce the opinions and policy preferences of the people. Ideally, members of the legislature would act as "instructed delegates," mirroring as closely as possible the will of their constituents. To ensure that the legislature would broadly reflect a cross-section of the people, the Antifederalists called for a large legislature; to keep the legislators in line with the views of the people, they called for annual elections.

The Federalists, by contrast, rejected the instructed delegate model outright. Instead, they viewed representation as a mechanism for filtering the will of the people. Ideally, legislators would be chosen for their capacity to "refine and enlarge" the views of the people. Under the Federalists' approach, legislators would not necessarily reach the same conclusion on public issues as would the people themselves, but they would have a better chance of discerning the true public interest. The Federalists argued that these goals were best served by creating a relatively small House and a separate Senate, and by holding elections no more often than every two years.

The Electoral Connection

Even with elections held every other year, the constant pressures of electoral politics are an inescapable fact of life on Capitol Hill. Members of the House face an almost permanent campaign; even Senators, who serve six years at a time, are never far removed from the demands of electoral politics. Reelection pressures may influence how members of Congress vote and how they spend their time, both in Washington and at home. Above all, many members of Congress must work constantly to raise the money needed for expensive media campaigns.

For many scholars of Congress, the "electoral connection" is the starting point for any understanding of how the institution works. Whatever their ultimate goals, such scholars argue, members of Congress must begin by getting themselves elected and reelected. For some, reelection is simply a means to a more noble end, such as serving the public interest or achieving important public policy results. For others, reelection is almost an end in itself, providing continued access to perks and power. Either way, one way to understand Congress is to assume that reelection is the immediate goal of every member. "Whether narrowly self-serving or more publicly oriented," writes the political scientist Morris Fiorina, "the individual congressman finds reelection to be at least a necessary condition for the achievement of his goals."[17]

In any event, the electoral model provides important insights into how and why Congress works. The "electoral connection" permeates every aspect of congressional life. The desire for reelection influences not only floor votes on controversial issues but also a representative's choice of committee assignments and thus his or her legislative interests and oversight activities. The electoral model also helps explain why members of Congress place so much emphasis on serving their constituents (that is, on serving potential voters) and on advancing the goals of key interest groups.

From the Framers' point of view, of course, the key question is not what motivates members of Congress but whether the system as a whole represents the people and whether it is able to achieve the public interest.

Who Sits in Congress?

From a demographic point of view, members of Congress are hardly a mirror of the nation. There are only fifty-one women in the House (11.7 percent), and only nine in the Senate. As for racial minorities, there are only thirty-eight blacks in the House (8.7 percent) and only one in the Senate; there are also eighteen Hispanics (4.1 percent) and three Asians and Pacific Islanders (0.7 percent) in the House, and two Asians and Pacific Islanders and one Native American in the Senate. Women and minorities are very underrepresented not only in overall numbers but also with respect to leadership positions.[18] Congress is also unrepresentative in other ways. Nearly half of all members in the House and Senate combined are lawyers, for example, and nearly as many come from the fields of business and banking. On the whole, members of Congress are wealthier, better educated, and older than the people they represent.

Differences between Congress and the general public in age, education, and wealth would not have alarmed and might even have pleased the Federalists, who expected the national government to be a kind of natural aristocracy (see the discussion in Chapter 2). Nor would the Framers have been surprised by the underrepresentation of women and minorities.

Congressional Voting

Do members of Congress vote the way their constituents want them to? In part, at least, they do, if only to get reelected. But the influence of voters is limited, indirect, and uncertain.

The most important predictor of congressional voting patterns is the representative's political party. Differences between Republicans and Democrats are predictable and substantial, and party voting has increased in recent years (see Figure 12.3). Deviations from straight party voting are often due to regional factors, especially defections from the party line by conservative southerners. According to one study, the combination of political party and region can explain as much as 85 percent of all recorded votes. Party voting reflects constituent concerns, at least in a general way, since many voters take the two parties' positions into account at election time.

Voting in Congress, however, is influenced by many factors besides constituent pressures. These include the representative's own views on important matters; the influence of interest group lobbyists and PACs, especially on less visible issues; pressure or guidance from the White House and congressional colleagues; and the advice of congressional staff members.

On occasion, members of Congress may take their constituents' views into account directly. This happens only when (1) voters have a definite opinion on an issue, (2) the issue is of overriding concern to at least a key portion of the constituency, (3) the representative finds out—and cares—how the voters feel, and (4) other factors—such as partisan pressures or the representative's

Maxine Waters (D-Cal.), chair of the Congressional Black Caucus.

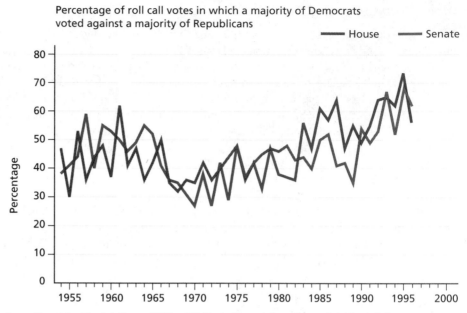

Percentage of roll call votes in which a majority of Democrats voted against a majority of Republicans

Figure 12.3 **Party Unity Votes, 1994**

SOURCE: *Congressional Quarterly Almanac* (1996), p. C22. Used with permission of Congressional Quarterly Press.

own strong feelings—do not get in the way. For all these conditions to exist on more than a few issues for any one member of Congress is unusual.

That members of Congress rarely act as the instructed delegates of their constituents does not mean that the people do not exercise control over their representatives. Most members of Congress do worry about whether individual votes can be used against them by opponents at election time. Evidence suggests that representatives frequently try to anticipate when a vote could get them in trouble with the electorate. Similarly, many members of Congress seek to preserve their ideological credentials by maintaining consistent voting patterns, as measured by various liberal or conservative interest groups.

In any event, the instructed delegate model is not the only legitimate approach to analyzing whether members of Congress are responsive to their constituents. An alternative model suggests that the people act "more like tax auditors, who notice when things are seriously out of line, than like drill sergeants, who direct troops to march left and right in precise formations." According to this view, the people may play an essentially passive role up to a point, reelecting their member of Congress on a seemingly automatic basis.[19]

Representation and Casework

An important sense in which members of Congress represent their constituencies is by advancing their interests within the federal bureaucracy. Such activities, known as **casework (or constituent service),** occupy a substantial part of the workload of the typical representative's personal staff.

Constituents contact their representative with all sorts of requests. Many seek advice and counsel about how to navigate through the federal bureaucracy—most commonly, to obtain social security disability coverage or obtain help with immigration matters. Constituents also seek congressional assistance with military matters (getting emergency leave or discharge, for example) and for help in dealing with various federal agencies. The congressional office can provide guidance to the constituent, help clear away red tape, and expedite agency action. The emphasis is usually on making the process easier for constituents to cope with, rather than on affecting the substantive results of agency decisions.

A significant proportion of the requests to congressional offices involve matters that are clearly not within the jurisdiction of the federal government. Many Americans, when faced with a problem involving state or local government, nonetheless feel most comfortable turning to their member of Congress. Thus congressional offices routinely field requests for help in zoning matters, child custody cases, and local tax matters. Many citizens call their representative with personal problems wholly outside the scope of any government agency—including financial and family crises. The most the congressional office can do in those cases is to provide a sympathetic ear and a referral to the public or private agency best able to offer assistance.

Most members of Congress are eager to help constituents in any and all circumstances. Routine requests to agencies for help in solving constituent problems may occupy staff time, but they rarely call for a member's personal attention. Constituent service builds loyalty among the voters, and helps cement a House member's image as a powerful force in Washington (excellent casework, according to one estimate, can swing up to 5 percent of the vote on election day).[20] Agencies, of course, are usually willing—if not happy—to help out, anxious to stay on the good side of the institution that controls the purse strings. Most agencies have set up special offices to handle congressional inquiries and often give such inquiries priority attention. Most casework requests can be handled expeditiously and successfully, and, in any event, the member will at least get credit for the attempt.

Casework matters more to some members of Congress than others. Senator Alfonse D'Amato (R-N.Y.), for example, has built an enormous reputation as a can-do senator,

"Let's never forget that the constitution provides for three equally important branches of government; the legislative and the other two."

largely from his focus on constituent service; so has Senator Strom Thurmond (R-S.C.). Whether or not a member of Congress emphasizes casework is largely a function of necessity and inclination. Those in marginal districts—especially districts in which the natural majority belongs to the opposition party—will try to make up in service what they might lack in issue support. Others emphasize casework because it fits in with their conception of their role as the representative of the people.

In theory, casework ought to provide an excellent window on the day-to-day workings of the federal bureaucracy, and thus ought to be a useful source of information for Congress. Occasionally, in fact, constituent complaints lead directly to congressional investigations and efforts to reform the way the government works. But far more often casework activity is carried on quite separately from oversight. The reason is clear: casework, by and large, is the province of members' personal staffs, whereas oversight is in the domain of the committees and subcommittees. Moreover, most members of Congress see casework as primarily an electoral activity, not as part of their substantive work.[21]

At its best, casework can be justified as the essence of representation. Providing favors for a constituent who is also a campaign contributor, however, can raise serious legal and ethical questions. Providing favors for a campaign contributor who is not a constituent raises questions that are even more troubling. For a discussion of these issues, see Chapter 8.

How Congress Really Works

The realities of life in Congress go far beyond the institution's rules and procedures. This section aims at describing and illustrating how Congress really works.

The Modern Congress in Context

Before 1995, the weakness of congressional parties was taken for granted. "Few policy statements are adopted by the U.S. congressional party meetings," wrote one analyst, expressing the conventional viewpoint. "The parties neither pronounce nor enforce party discipline. While members usually do want to vote with their party, they are entirely free to vote differently, and usually show less party cohesion than is found in other democratic legislatures."[22] Members of Congress do not need the support of their national party to win reelection or to maintain their power base in Washington.

The separation of powers makes presidential control of the legislature just as problematic. In a parliamentary system, writes the political scientist Richard Rose, the legislature must endorse the legislative program offered by the prime minister and the cabinet: "A Prime Minister can threaten a member of Parliament who persistently votes against the party with expulsion and virtually certain electoral defeat because of the loss of the party's endorsement." A British prime minister once compared an unruly member of parliament to a barking dog, and warned him to shape up or "he may not get his dog license renewed when it falls due."

Although rank-and-file members of the British Parliament have more power than in days gone by, they are far more dependent on the executive branch than their American counterparts. Presidents have few carrots and even fewer sticks to use to bring members of

Congress into line. The president cannot prevent a member from being reelected (although some have tried), and can exercise little influence over the member's career. Because of the separation of powers, the president cannot even count on his party having a majority in either house of Congress. And even when the president's party does control the legislative branch, there is no guarantee that Congress will follow the president's lead—a lesson learned early by President Bill Clinton.[23]

The Revolution of 1995?   The Republican victory in the congressional elections of 1994 cast doubt on these conventional viewpoints. Led by Representative Newt Gingrich (R-Ga.), the congressional Republicans presented to the voters the clear party platform known as the Contract with America. More than three hundred candidates for Congress signed the pledge, and Gingrich promised a House vote on all ten provisions of the contract within the first one hundred days of the 104th Congress.

When the Republicans gained control of Congress, Gingrich claimed a mandate for the contract and proceeded to make good on his promise of bringing its provisions to the House floor. The House Republicans' burst of legislative activity involved approval of nine of the ten contract provisions; only a proposal to impose congressional term limits was turned down. During this period, the House leadership imposed a high degree of party discipline; in half of the first 139 House votes in 1995 the Republicans were unanimous, for example, as they were in 54 of the Senate's first 73 votes. In only 13 of the first 139 House votes did more than ten Republicans defect from the party line.[24]

The early days of the 104th Congress were not unique in American history, in terms of either legislative accomplishments or party discipline. Similar episodes have occurred several times in American history, although (unlike 1995) usually under strong presidential leadership. The classic example was the original "First One Hundred Days," led by Franklin D. Roosevelt in 1933. In the midst of the economic emergency of the Great Depression, Roosevelt prevailed upon Congress to pass a host of new laws. The pattern was emulated by several later presidents, including Lyndon Baines Johnson and Ronald Reagan.

Rather than marking a major sea change, the Republican takeover of Congress in 1995 can be seen as the culmination of a fifteen-year trend toward stronger leadership in the House of Representatives. Gingrich's strength as Speaker was amply demonstrated in 1997, when he and his supporters put down a coup attempt by young Republican members who objected to the budget deal worked out between the White House and the congressional leadership.

The Death and Revival of Congressional Leadership

Imposing control over the many committee and subcommittee chairs and even over individual members is no easy task. Because congressional leaders are not elected by the nation as a whole, strong leadership raises important questions of representativeness and accountability. Yet some degree of leadership is necessary to maintain order in Congress, to focus the institution's energies on the most pressing national problems, and to avoid the fragmentation of policy on behalf of narrow groups and special interests.

In the nineteenth century, congressional leaders—especially the Speaker of the House—wielded great power over rank-and-file members. Then, in 1910, ordinary

A (Mercifully) Brief History of Congressional Pay Increases

Controversy over congressional pay started almost from the beginning. Here are a few highlights from history.

1789:

The first Congress has to decide how much to pay itself. James Madison, recognizing the conflict of interest, suggests a constitutional amendment to delay congressional pay raises until after the next election. The amendment is eventually ratified—but not until 1992!

Meanwhile, Congress decides to pay itself $6 a day. This princely sum causes an outcry from the public and press, which points out that members of the British House of Commons receive under a dollar a day. Congress also pays itself $6 for every twenty miles traveled—or 30 cents a mile. The total pay package works out to around $900 a year.

1816:

Legislation raising congressional pay to $1,500 a year causes a public outcry. Members of the Georgia delegation are burned in effigy. The 1816 elections are a disaster for incumbents.

1873:

Under cover of night, Congress raises its pay by 50 percent, from $5,000 to $7,500. The pay raise, moreover, is made retroactive for two years. Again the public takes vengeance against this "salary grab," defeating 96 of the 202 Republicans in the House and handing control over to the opposition Democrats.

1932–1933:

At last setting a good example, Congress votes itself a pay cut to express sympathy with Americans caught in the midst of the Great Depression. In 1932 the pay rate goes down from $10,000 to $9,000; in 1933 it is reduced even further, to $8,500.

1935:

Congress restores its pay to the pre-depression level of $10,000. The depression itself continues.

1955:

Congress raises its pay a whopping 80 percent, setting an all-time record. Members are now paid $22,500 a year. The rest of the country is doing well, too, so few complain.

1967:

Congress turns pay matters over to an independent commission, which is to recommend pay increases every four years. Congress can reject the commission's recommendations by passing a resolution to that effect. Political pressures cause it to do just that in 1974 and 1976.

1987:

The House votes to block a pay increase proposed by the commission—but a day too late. This legislative sleight-of-hand allows members to claim that they voted against a pay increase while pocketing the money anyway.

1989:

Congress votes itself a big pay raise, nearly 40 percent for House members and nearly 10 percent for senators. The raise for members of the House is accompanied by new limits on how much members can earn from speeches and other outside earned income.

1992:

At long last, Madison's constitutional amendment becomes law. Congressional pay raises can no longer become effective until after an election has passed. Still, on January 1, 1993, yet another congressional pay raise goes into effect, raising a member's annual salary to $133,600.

SOURCE: Adapted from *Congressional Quarterly 1989 Almanac* and *Congressional Quarterly Weekly Reports*, January 2, 1993.

members of the House revolted, implementing reforms that stripped the speaker of much of his power. The real power now spread downward to the committee chairs, who often ran their committees with ruthless discipline. The era of strong committee chairs lasted until 1974, when a group of House Democrats elected in the wake of the Watergate scandal successfully fought for reforms that took power away from the leadership and the committee chairs, and gave it to subcommittees, individual members, and the entire Democratic membership. By 1980, the power of the House leadership was at its lowest point since the early days of the Republic.

The Counterrevolution of the 1980s   The election of Ronald Reagan and a Republican Senate in 1980 created the conditions for a revival of the House leadership. As the sole remaining bastion of Democratic power in Washington, House Speaker Thomas P. ("Tip") O'Neill (D-Mass.) marshaled his troops in opposition to Reagan's policies. Although Reagan successfully led Congress early on, O'Neill quickly proved a strong match for the popular president.

Long after Reagan and O'Neill had departed the scene, the House leadership continues to consolidate its power. The long-term trend toward a strengthening of the House leadership over the past fifteen years is the result of at least four key factors:[25]

- *Increased partisanship in the House.* The fundamental problem facing the House Democratic leadership for decades was the ideological split between northern and southern Democrats. Northern Democrats were more liberal, southern Democrats more conservative, especially on matters of race and social policy. The 1980s saw a great increase in the voting power of African Americans, especially in the South, and consequently the election of many progressive southern Democrats. That gave the Democratic leadership a coherent ideological base from which to operate. In the 1990s, the election of large numbers of conservative Republicans, especially from the South, continued the trend, which culminated in the 1994 Republican victory.
- *New House rules that strengthened the leadership.* A variety of reforms in the 1980s and 1990s helped strengthen the party and House leadership, mainly by allowing the Democratic majority to present a more unified opposition to Republican presidents. In the 1980s, for example, the Speaker was given the power to nominate the majority-party members of the rules committee. New Republican rules in 1995 moved in two directions at once, both opening up the process of congressional decision making and strengthening the power of the leadership.[26]
- *The deterioration of relations between Congress and the White House.* The cold war between President Bush and the congressional leadership in 1991–1992, coupled with the national recession and the presidential campaign of 1992, created incentives for Democrats to cooperate in passing a variety of major bills in the teeth of White House opposition or with only grudging White House acceptance. Many of the bills were vetoed, and congressional Democrats lacked the strength to override, but the efforts did represent the first successful attempt at congressional governance in decades. Congressional opposition to White House pressure persisted even when the Democrats regained control of the White House in 1993, and reintensified when Republicans gained control of Congress in 1995.

The increasing power of the party leadership occurred simultaneously with the growth of power of the individual subcommittees. Thus there are currently two distinct power centers in Congress: the leadership, which plays a major role in shaping legislative-executive relations and in lining up party support for highly publicized issues; and the subcommittees, which continue to predominate in particular policy areas, especially in routine matters.

Consider, for example, medical research. In developing research priorities and budgets for the National Institutes of Health (NIH), the congressional health subcommittees operate with great independence from the leadership. When it comes to a highly controversial issue like whether to allow research on fetal tissue, however, the action shifts to the full Congress, and the leadership—and the White House—play a far greater role.

Committee and Subcommittee Government

To suggest that the work of Congress is the work of its committees would be an exaggeration. Yet in institutional terms, congressional committees are nothing less than little legislatures, serving as centers of policy making, agency oversight, and public debate.

The committee system undoubtedly increases Congress's efficiency and allows individual members to develop their expertise in particular policy areas. But committee and subcommittee government raises troubling questions. By design, committees and subcommittees are not representative of Congress as a whole, much less of the American people. Committees and subcommittees are easily influenced by powerful interest groups and allow individual members the chance to favor their own constituents, often at the expense of the public at large.

Government by Subgovernment   Because committees and subcommittees are so important, members of Congress devote much of their legislative energy to their committee and subcommittee assignments. Subcommittees take primary responsibility for identifying areas of concern, compiling information through investigations and legislative hearings, and debating and negotiating proposed legislation. Such legislation is then sent to the full committee and, if approved, to the full House or Senate.

Most bills reported out of subcommittee contain only a handful of controversial provisions, and are typically approved by the full committee with only minor changes. Further fine-tuning takes place on the floor, and in negotiations with the other house and with the White House. Especially in the House, the bulk of the final product remains largely as it was when it left the subcommittee.

Given the complexities of the modern world and the tremendous scope of legislation passed by Congress, the committee system makes good sense. A bill on health policy or antitrust law, for example, contains material far too technical for the average member of Congress to understand without extraordinary effort. It is not reasonable to expect that such a bill can be written and revised on the House floor.

The decentralized nature of much of Congress's day-to-day decision making, however, presents a number of difficulties. Bills approved by one subcommittee may work at cross purposes to bills approved by another, yet both may be enacted into law. Subcommittee bills are often framed by *subgovernments* (or *iron triangles*), consisting of subcommittees, agencies, and interest groups that share a common interest (see the discussion in Chapter 8). Even in this age of stronger leadership, individual senators and representatives—especially committee and subcommittee chairs—are still able to exercise tremendous influence over the content of legislation.

Committee Assignments   Committee assignments are of great importance to members of Congress. For some, being on the right committee is purely a matter of electoral politics; a representative from a rural district, for example, might want to serve on the House Committee on Agriculture. For others, choice committee assignments provide the opportunity to focus on legislative areas of interest or importance, or to gain power within Congress.[27]

Every member of Congress is assigned to various standing committees—usually one major committee and one or more lesser committees. Senior representatives from the majority party may serve as committee chairs. Within a representative's major committee, he or she generally will be assigned to one key subcommittee. The subcommittee then becomes the major focus of the member's legislative activities. In all there are 20 committees with 86 subcommittees in the House, and 20 committees with 68 subcommittees in the Senate. There are also four joint committees.

Localism: Me First   From the earliest days of the Republic, observers of American politics have pointed out that, in the words of former Speaker Tip O'Neill, "All politics is local."[28] The House Republicans' success in "nationalizing" the 1994 elections by running on a unified platform is an exception to the rule, although whether it marks a new pattern in American politics is hard to tell. Either way, individual representatives and senators are often focused on securing passage of legislation that will help their constituents and their campaign contributors. To take just one post-1994 example: When the Senate Environment and Public Works Committee approved a bill giving states new power to limit the importation of garbage from other states, it included a number of provisions designed to serve the constituencies of particular members. Senator Bob Graham (D-Fla.), for example, persuaded the committee to exempt at least twenty Florida counties from any state laws restricting dumping. Senator Joseph I. Lieberman (D-Conn.) secured an exemption for Connecticut communities that contracted with public service authorities for trash disposal. And Senator Dirk Kempthorne (R-Id.) convinced his colleagues to reinstate an exemption from groundwater monitoring rules for small landfills in rural areas receiving low annual amounts of rainfall—a category that included a number of sites in Idaho.[29]

A bill designed to benefit a single state, locality, or even corporation—especially a wasteful or unnecessary spending measure—is known as a "pork barrel" project, or just plain "pork." Whether or not a particular measure qualifies as pork, of course, is a highly subjective question. Frequently, influential senators or representatives—especially those who serve on the appropriations committee—simply funnel money that will be spent anyway to their home states or districts. Thus Senator Ted Stevens (R-Alaska), in one of the most dramatic efforts of its kind, managed to have a new desert warfare unit based in his home state! But the all-time champion in this regard is probably Senator Robert Byrd (D-W. Va.), the former majority leader of the Senate. In 1994, for example, Byrd managed to steer one-quarter of the money appropriated for special highway projects to his home state. The ability of individual representatives to pull off such maneuvers is reinforced by the fact that other representatives are trying to do the same thing. "Some lawmakers," wrote one reporter with reference to the Byrd highway money, "are reluctant to challenge Byrd or other top appropriators publicly for fear that their requests . . . in the future will go unfulfilled."[30]

Interestingly, most congressional initiatives designed to benefit a particular state or district are not contained in legislation. Instead most laws leave specific decisions on which communities are harmed or helped up to the executive agency that implements the legislation. Influential members of Congress then use various methods to persuade the agency to accommodate their wishes. This less public and more subtle process is, as we will see, a part of the congressional oversight process.

Pork barrel spending raises serious questions for representative government. The design of the federal system—particularly the equal representation of the states in the Senate—reflects the long tradition of local-mindedness among members of Congress. Moreover, "bringing home the bacon" remains a time-tested way of winning votes and raising money at home.

More problematic is the growing tendency of members of Congress to trade legislative favors to special interest groups for PAC contributions. Direct trades are illegal, of course, but the informal exchange of campaign money for legislation is common. Such arrangements are mutually beneficial both to the legislators and to the interest groups, but often serve no public purpose.

Staff: The Unelected Representatives Much of the real work of Congress is done not by the members themselves but by their staffs. Over the past three decades the number of staffers working on Capitol Hill has grown dramatically. In 1947, House and Senate staffers totaled 5,451. Today, the total is more than 16,000, including members' personal staff, committee staff, and congressional support agencies.[31]

The growth of the congressional staff in the decades after World War II reflected two major trends. The first was the growth in the size and scope of Congress's responsibilities; the second was the corresponding growth in the size and power of the executive bureaucracy. Congress needed more staff both to do its own job effectively and to maintain its ability to provide an effective check on executive power. Staff cuts imposed by the Republican leadership in 1995 reflected their overall philosophy of smaller government.

The long-term growth in congressional staff has led some to worry that these "unelected representatives" are usurping power that should be exercised only by the elected representatives of the people. Others complain that even if the staff has not usurped the members' power, its growth has still changed Congress for the

Senate Majority Leader Trent Lott (R-Miss.) ponders advice from a member of his congressional staff.

worse, principally by making it more difficult for members themselves to deliberate on and decide public policy.

The first concern is without much foundation; the second is probably overstated. The relationship between staff and member is very much akin to that between lawyer and client: the staff have much freedom of action, but are constantly aware of the need to stay within the broad boundaries set by their chiefs. If a staff member wants to stay employed, he or she will make sure that the final product is generally in line with the member's attitudes and priorities.[32]

Overseeing the Bureaucracy

The tremendous expansion of the federal government's role and responsibilities since the New Deal would have been impossible without broad delegations of legislative power to the federal executive branch. Congress lacks not only the time and energy to handle every detail of government policy making but also the necessary expertise. It must depend heavily on the federal bureaucracy for the implementation of its programs.

Legislation passed by the modern Congress, therefore, is typically general and open-ended. Executive agencies are authorized to fill in the details as they implement the law. In doing so, the agencies create rules and regulations, which have the status of law; interpret and apply key provisions of the underlying legislation; make decisions regarding the application of the law to particular individuals or corporations; and exercise judgment on exactly where and how to spend federal funds. These activities, as we will see in Chapter 14, constitute the day-to-day work of the federal bureaucracy.

Having delegated so much power to the bureaucracy, Congress has then sought ways to control it. Foremost among these, from the congressional perspective, is the oversight process. **Congressional oversight** is defined by one scholar as congressional "review after the fact, . . . [including] inquiries about policies that are or have been in effect, investigations of past administrative actions, and the calling of executive officers to account for their financial transactions."[33] Oversight in this narrow sense is closely bound up with the legislative process (since such inquiries may lead to the passage of new legislation) and the budget process (since they may lead to new restrictions or priorities in the expenditure of funds). Oversight, like much else that Congress does, is largely carried out by subcommittees. The same subcommittee–agency–interest group triangles that work together in the legislative process also predominate when it comes to oversight.

Committees and subcommittees carry out their oversight responsibilities in a number of ways. First, both members and staff actively monitor agency activities on an ongoing basis. Second, oversight committees and subcommittees engage in periodic, regularly scheduled reviews of agency programs, particularly when programs require reauthorization. Third, agency activities are scrutinized whenever the need or opportunity arises, for example when the Senate considers the appointment of a new administrator or when a scandal is revealed by the press. Depending on the circumstances, congressional oversight can be carried out by means as informal as a friendly phone call or as formal as a full-blown investigation, complete with lawyers, subpoenas, and sworn testimony.

Ultimately, oversight provides a mechanism for Congress to influence the implementation of policy by the executive branch. Congress can exercise its influence informally, giving the agency a gentle push and suggesting that it change its ways. If the agency is stubborn, Congress may threaten to hold up or reduce other agency programs, or otherwise apply informal pressure on the agency to comply. As a last resort, the Congress can always adopt special legislation forcing the agency to comply with its demands.

Probably the fastest-growing—and least understood—means of congressional oversight are so-called nonstatutory controls. These are semiformal instructions to executive agencies that appear outside of statutes (laws) passed by Congress. They typically appear in the reports that accompany every piece of congressional legislation, and are often used by the House and Senate Appropriations Committees to provide specific directions for the expenditure of federal funds. Thus while the law itself might simply appropriate a given amount for airport construction, the committee might indicate in the accompanying report its specific instructions for where airports should be constructed.[34]

Oversight is generally thought of as an adversarial process. The oversight hearings that receive media attention, for example, usually feature a spirited confrontation between a senator or representative and an embattled agency head. Especially when the legislative and executive branches are controlled by opposite parties, such episodes may involve cabinet secretaries or even White House officials, and may focus on fundamental questions of domestic and foreign policy. The 1987 Iran-contra hearings—featuring the testimony of Lieutenant Colonel Oliver North and National Security Adviser John Poindexter—were a particularly dramatic example.

It is tempting to conclude from such examples that congressional oversight typically pits the legislative branch against the executive for control of public policy. In reality, however, the picture is more complicated. Agencies—especially those involved in controversial areas—are often caught in a tug-of-war between their official executive masters and their unofficial congressional overlords. More often than not, their sympathies lie not with the White House but with Congress. That should not be surprising: after all, as we have seen, congressional subcommittees and executive agencies generally work closely together and share common assumptions about and commitments to public policy. Some 75 percent of congressional oversight committees and subcomittees, for example, are sympathetic to the agencies they watch over. Congressional oversight is thus rarely directed at the heart and soul of an agency, but only at specific disagreements over the way a particular program is being carried out.[35] Oversight, far from being a way of checking the executive bureaucracy, is often a way of supporting and expanding their activities.

Evaluating the Modern Congress

Most Americans hold Congress in low regard. Public support for Congress as an institution has dropped sharply in recent years; in the 1990s, the number of Americans who approve of the way Congress is doing its job has hovered around 20 percent, near the all-time low. Public dissatisfaction with Congress has fueled the popularity of the term limits movement, and was at least partly responsible for the massive Republican gains in the 1994 congressional elections.

Public criticism of Congress tends to focus on two sets of issues. First, many Americans feel that members of Congress are out of touch with the daily concerns of their constituents. That view has been strengthened over the past decade by a host of major and minor scandals, but it also reflects a deeper sense that members of Congress are beholden to special interests and do not effectively represent the interests of their constituents. Second, many Americans have come to believe that Congress, as an institution, cannot govern effectively. The popular term for Congress's apparent inability to deal with many of the nation's problems is *gridlock*—a permanent state of legislative inaction in the face of the nation's serious and mounting problems.

Scholars too have been concerned with these two questions. Is Congress representative? Can Congress govern?

Is Congress Representative?

Congress can be regarded as representative or unrepresentative of the American people depending on one's definition of representation. As we have seen, the average member of Congress is very unlike the average constituent in terms of demographic and socioeconomic statistics. Moreover, the evidence suggests that members of Congress rarely receive clear directions from their constituents on how to vote. The typical member of Congress is very concerned, at most, with a few key issues, and with the needs and interests of particular groups of voters within his or her constituency. Often working at cross-purposes to the member's duty

Figure 12.4 **Trends in Congressional Job Rating**

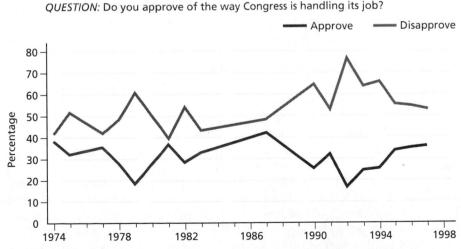

Note: When multiple surveys were conducted in the same year, figures represented averages calculated by the author.

Source: The Gallup Poll <www.gallup.com/poll/data/congjob.html>

to represent his or her constituents is the need to curry favor with potential campaign contributors, including PACs and wealthy individuals who do not live in the district.

In other senses, however, Congress can be seen as representative of the public interest. The open and decentralized nature of congressional decision making enables all groups and interests to find some degree of representation in Congress. Some groups have more influence than others, of course, but few interests are without any representation at all. Members of Congress also play an important role in directly representing the interests of individual constituents through casework and other techniques.

Moreover, it is not clear whether members of Congress ought to represent the views of their constituents directly and unreservedly. The Framers clearly intended for Congress to represent the long-term public interest, rather than the short-term or parochial interests of their constituents. A larger problem may be that Congress is too responsive to the pressures of constituents, contributors, and interest groups, and unable to act in ways that benefit society in the long run. When members of Congress refuse to raise taxes, for example, or refuse to tamper with social security benefits, they may be giving their constituents exactly what they want—and disregarding the long-term problems of the budget deficit in the process.

Can Congress Govern?

The Framers of the Constitution approved of checks and balances, but they also believed in effective and efficient government. Many modern critics of Congress worry that the current system contains too many checks and balances and not enough efficiency.

Many factors have been put forward as contributing to Congress's apparent inability to govern, although none seems sufficient to explain the problem:[36]

- *Divided government.* The White House and both houses of Congress have been controlled by the same party for only six of the past thirty years (counting through 1998). However, recent scholarship has cast doubt on the assumption that divided government prevents effective cooperation between the executive and legislative branches. The political scientist David Mayhew, for example, argues that divided government has made little or no difference in the amount of legislation enacted into law.[37] Divided governments have passed many important laws, and unified control—as President Clinton learned during the health care reform battle of 1994—is no guarantee of success.
- *Fragmentation of authority.* The congressional reforms of the 1970s splintered Congress into scores of powerful committees and subcommittees, weakening the congressional leadership and arguably making decisive action impossible. The 1970s reforms clearly strengthened the power of individual members and subcommittees, but developments in the 1980s and 1990s seem to have restored strong leadership, especially in the House. The Senate, to be sure, is harder to lead—but it always was.
- *Interest group politics.* The ability of special interests to frustrate legislative efforts aimed at the public interest is taken as a truism of American politics. In particular, the dependence of many members of Congress on PAC contributions to their campaigns gives powerful interest groups leverage over efforts to enact a wide range of reforms. However, several political scientists have pointed out that interest group opposition to legislative reform can be overcome with effective congressional or presidential leadership—as, for example, in the case of the tax reform act of 1986.[38]

Congress's difficulties are partly of its own making, of course; reform of the legislative branch could not hurt. Reformers have focused on four areas: strengthening the leadership, simplifying the committee structure, streamlining the legislative process, and improving the style and substance of floor debates. But the causes of gridlock in Washington go far beyond Capitol Hill, and include the weakness of the political parties, the nature of the electoral system, and the state of the presidency. Ultimately, gridlock may have as much to do with the people as with their government.

Whether or not Congress can govern, then, is perhaps the wrong question. Under the separation of powers system, the lawmaking authority is shared between the legislative and executive branches; in modern American practice, important functions of government have been delegated to courts and executive agencies. Whatever difficulties the American system of government is suffering from, it seems inappropriate to lay the blame on the legislative branch alone.

A broader assessment of the question must await the discussions of the next three chapters—on the presidency, the bureaucracy, and the courts.

Summary

The United States Congress is a bicameral legislature, consisting of the House of Representatives and the Senate. The House has 435 voting members, each of whom is elected to serve a two-year term. The large size of the House puts a premium on strict rules and procedures. The leadership has great control over the timing and nature of the debate on proposed legislation. The smaller Senate is organized much more informally than the House, and the leadership is much weaker. The rules and traditions of the Senate give great power to individual senators, and make it relatively easy for a minority to block proposed legislation. Except in a few areas specified by the Constitution, the legislative powers of the House and Senate are identical.

Proposed legislation must navigate a difficult and complicated route through both houses of Congress. Although only members of Congress can formally introduce legislation, many bills are written by the executive branch or with the advice of interest groups. Most proposed legislation is referred to one or more committees or subcommittees, which investigate the issue, work out and approve the specific language of the bill, and write a report that explains the bill and addresses its costs and benefits. On approval by committee, proposed legislation is debated and voted on by the full House and Senate. Differences between the bills approved by the two houses are worked out in a conference committee, whose work must be approved once again by both houses. Finally, the proposed legislation is sent to the president, who can approve or veto it. Presidential vetoes can be overridden by a two-thirds vote of each house.

A major task for Congress is approval of the federal government's annual budget. Congress begins by approving overall budget targets for the year, after which the appropriations committees work out the details within each policy area. Two-thirds of the federal budget consists of entitlements—money that must be paid to individuals as a matter of law. One-third of the budget is discretionary spending, and can be increased or decreased through the budget process. Approval of spending in each policy area requires a two-step process: in the authorizations process, Congress creates the legal basis for government programs and establishes the rules governing the expenditures of funds; in the appropriations process, Congress approves actual expenditures. Congressional spending bills, like all other legislation, must be presented to the president for approval or veto.

For many scholars of Congress, the starting point for understanding how the institution works is the electoral connection—the members' constant need to raise money and shore up public support in preparation for reelection. Without frequent elections, it is hard to see how Congress could be responsive or accountable to the people. Even so, many analysts doubt whether Congress is truly representative of the people. The members of Congress do not resemble their constituents in race, gender, education, and wealth, and do not necessarily vote as their constituents would want them to. Yet members of Congress do represent the interests of individual constituents through the process of casework, also called constituent service.

The realities of how Congress works cast further doubt on the representative nature of the institution. Congressional parties are relatively weak—even the extraordinary coherence of the Republicans in the House of Representatives after 1994 did not last long and did not carry over into the Senate. The party leadership frequently finds it difficult to translate the interests of the majority into a coherent legislative program. Instead, power in Congress is decentralized, spread out among countless committees and subcommittees. Each committee or subcommittee is responsive to a different set of interest groups and executive officials, leading to the existence of subgovernments (or iron triangles), which dominate the legislative process. Moreover, members of Congress often serve the interests of their local communities or constituents, arguably disregarding the national interest in the process.

A key role of Congress is oversight of the federal bureaucracy. Congressional oversight is defined as "review after the fact, . . . [including] inquiries about policies that are or have been in effect, investigations of past administrative actions, and the calling of executive officers to account for their financial transactions." Congressional oversight is rarely an adversarial process, but it can provide a key check on the powers of the executive branch.

In recent years, Congress has come under scathing criticism from scholars and the public alike. Both have questioned whether Congress can govern and whether it is truly representative of the people. The answers to both questions are more complicated than might appear at first glance. Congress indeed has difficulty governing directly, but its difficulties are as much the result of larger forces in American politics as they are of problems within the institution itself. Understanding whether or not Congress can govern, therefore, must await analysis of the other institutions of the federal government, particularly the presidency.

Whether or not Congress is representative depends to a great degree on one's definition of representation. To people who subscribe to the direct democracy model, Congress does a poor job of representing the people. The Framers of the Constitution, however, believed in the necessity of making Congress's accountable to the people while at the same time giving it the freedom to pursue the national public interest. There is much evidence that the modern Congress has not achieved that balance, but no obvious or easy solution is in sight.

Key Terms

Bicameralism
Filibuster
Speaker of the House
House majority leader
Senate majority leader
Rules committee
Conference committee
Veto

Authorization
Appropriation
Entitlements
Discretionary spending
Casework (or constituent service)
Congressional oversight

Review Questions

1. What are the basic functions of Congress in the American system of government?

2. Discuss the similarities and differences between the House of Representatives and the Senate.

3. Briefly summarize the process by which a bill becomes a law, as well as the process by which Congress approves the annual federal budget.

4. How does the desire for reelection influence the activities of members of Congress? How does the electoral connection make Congress more, or less, representative?

5. What are the powers of the congressional leadership? What factors limit the leadership's power?

6. What are the strengths and weaknesses of the congressional committee system?

7. What is congressional oversight and how is it carried out?

Suggested Readings

Aberbach, Joel D. *Keeping a Watchful Eye: The Politics of Congressional Oversight.* Washington, D.C.: Brookings Institution, 1990.

Congressional Quarterly's Guide to Congress, 4th ed. Washington, D.C.: CQ Press, 1991.

Davidson, Roger H., and Walter J. Oleszek. *Congress and Its Members,* 6th ed. Washington, D.C.: CQ Press, 1998.

Dodd, Lawrence C., and Bruce I. Oppenheimer, eds. *Congress Reconsidered,* 6th ed. Washington, D.C.: CQ Press, 1997.

Dodd, Lawrence C., and Richard L. Schott. *Congress and the Administrative State.* New York: Wiley, 1979.

Fiorina, Morris P. *Congress: Keystone of the Washington Establishment,* 2d ed. New Haven: Yale University Press, 1989.

Fisher, Louis. *The Politics of Shared Power: Congress and the Executive,* 3d ed. Washington, D.C.: CQ Press, 1993.

Internet Resources

Official U.S. House web site at:

http://www.house.gov

Official U.S. Senate web site at:

http://www.senate.gov

Thomas, the Library of Congress's source of legislative information, including bill tracking, at:

http://thomas.loc.gov/

CapWeb, the "Internet Guide to Congress," at:

http://www.capweb.net/

Roll Call, comprehensive source of news and comment on congressional activities, at:

http://www.rollcall.com

★ 13 ★
The Presidency

Can an ordinary citizen bring a lawsuit against a sitting president of the United States? Surprisingly, that question did not reach the United States Supreme Court until 1997, when the justices were asked to resolve the matter in the case of *Clinton* v. *Jones.*

The case arose out of an alleged incident in May 1991, when Bill Clinton was governor of Arkansas and Paula Corbin Jones an employee of the Arkansas Industrial Development Commission. According to Jones's allegation, she was persuaded to visit Governor Clinton in a hotel suite, where he made "abhorrent" sexual advances that she "vehemently rejected." Jones further claimed that her superiors at work punished her for rejecting the governor's advances and that "various persons authorized to speak for the President" had later defamed her by calling her a liar and insisting that the incident had never occurred.

These salacious allegations, although of great interest to the tabloid press, were of no interest to the Supreme Court. For the Court, the question presented by the case was less sensational, but more important in the long run. Could the president be sued while in office for an incident that occurred before he became president? Or did the dignity of the office and the overwhelming importance of the president's duties "immunize" him from suit, at least until after he left office?

Clinton v. *Jones* presented, in a nutshell, the dilemma of presidential power. The Framers of the Constitution sought to ensure that the president of the United States would

Paula Corbin Jones

be strong enough to lead the nation in war and peace, in prosperity and depression. As Justice Robert Jackson wrote in 1952, the presidency concentrates executive authority "in a single head in whose choice the whole nation has a part, making him the focus of public hopes and expectations. In drama, magnitude and finality his decisions so far overshadow any others that almost alone he fills the public eye and ear."[1]

Yet the Framers also wanted a government "of laws, and not of men." Although the president "is placed [on] high," said James Wilson at the Constitutional Convention of 1787, "not a single privilege is annexed to his character; far from being above the laws, he is amenable to them in his private character as a citizen, and in his public character by impeachment."[2] In no way was the president to be a king.

The Supreme Court weighed these competing arguments and sided with Paula Corbin Jones. Although the presidency occupies a "unique position in the constitutional scheme," wrote Justice John Paul Stevens for a unanimous Court, "the litigation of questions that relate entirely to the unofficial conduct of the individual who happens to be the President poses no perceptible risk" to the presidency or to the nation. As long as cases involving the president are "properly managed" by the federal courts, they should not impose an undue burden on the president's time or attention, or compromise his ability to lead the country.

The Supreme Court's decision, although a defeat for the White House, made it clear that

★ ★

the president, like Paula Corbin Jones, was just another citizen of the United States. And Jones, "like every other citizen," had the right to have her day in court.[3]

The creation of the presidency was one of the great innovations of the Constitution. Despite their troubled experiences with King George III, the Framers recognized that effective government required "energy in the executive," a single individual who could exercise bold leadership and be held responsible for failures and disasters. Yet an individual with such powers needed to be closely guarded, and the Framers obliged with a host of constitutional checks and balances. Above all, they forced the president to share power with Congress, and limited the presidential term in office to four years, after which the president would have to stand for reelection.

The paradox of the modern presidency precisely mirrors the Framers' efforts to create a strong but not omnipotent leader. Americans expect an enormous amount from their president: they hold the chief executive responsible for peace and prosperity, for dealing with the nation's problems and crises, and for keeping America strong in the world. They regard the president as an embodiment of the nation's hopes and ideals, and impose extraordinarily high standards on the president's character and private life. Yet for all of this, neither the American constitutional system nor the American people give the president powers commensurate with these responsibilities and expectations.

This chapter has two main goals. The first is to analyze the complicated relationship between the president and the other branches of government—especially the Congress and the executive bureaucracy. The second is to examine the impact of the presidency on the theory and practice of modern democracy.

Questions to Keep in Mind

☑ *How did the Framers seek to ensure that the president would have the power to administer the government effectively? How did they try to ensure that presidential power would not be abused and that abuses could be checked?*

☑ *How has the nature of the presidency evolved over time? What does the political scientist Richard Rose mean by the "postmodern" presidency?*

☑ *How can the president maximize the power and authority of the office and become an effective leader? What resources can the president call on in battles with the other branches and with the executive branch bureaucracy?*

Basic Concepts

The Framers and Executive Power

The Framers of the Constitution knew about the dangers of unchecked executive power from firsthand experience. All had lived through the upheavals of the 1760s and 1770s, and most had fought in the war for independence. "The history of the present King of Great Britain is a history of repeated injuries and usurpations, all having in direct object the establishment of an absolute Tyranny over these States," Congress had proclaimed in 1776. In effect, the Declaration of Independence was a bill of indictment against King George III for repeated abuses of power.

Yet the men who gathered in Philadelphia in the summer of 1787 to write the Constitution also knew the dangers of government by committee. For eleven years the nation had been run by Congress, without a chief executive, and the results were frightening and depressing. The war with England was nearly lost because of Congress's inefficiency; the future Chief Justice John Marshall remembered especially the bitter winter at Valley Forge, when the continental army nearly froze and starved to death. The years after the peace had seen economic collapse and national drift. "For forms of government let fools contest," wrote Alexander Hamilton in *Federalist* No. 68. "That which is best administered is best."[4]

The Framers' task was to create a presidency strong enough to govern effectively, yet not so strong that it would infringe on the powers of the other two branches or on the rights of the people. Striking that balance has become even more difficult as the nation and the presidency have evolved. Now, as in the time of the Framers, the challenge is both to restrain the president's power and to ensure that it can and will be used for the benefit of the people.

Constitutional Powers of the Presidency

The Constitution outlines the powers of the presidency primarily in Article II. Along with a number of specific powers there are several open-ended provisions that presidents have used to expand the scope and authority of the office. A brief survey of the president's constitutional powers is given below, with more discussion later in the chapter.

Executive Powers   The Constitution declares that "the executive Power shall be vested in a President of the United States of America" and requires the president to "take Care that the Laws be faithfully executed." The **Executive Power Clause** and the **Take Care Clause** make the president the chief executive of the United States.

As chief executive, the president has the power and the duty to carry out the laws of the United States. For the most part, however, Congress has vested the power to enforce the laws in various executive officials; criminal laws, for example, are enforced by the attorney general and the Department of Justice. In practice, the president typically has limited authority to interfere in the decisions of subordinates, who are often fenced in by their duty to the law or their dependence on congressional committees, which control their budgets.

Because the executive bureaucracy is so large and complex, the president's day-to-day managerial responsibilities are more theoretical than real. Yet the president can exercise substantial influence over the federal bureaucracy, both through the appointments process and by ongoing management efforts. Presidents Reagan and Bush, for example, required agencies to clear new regulations through the Office of Management and Budget, an agency tightly controlled by the White House. In matters of particular concern, moreover, the president can often exercise direct power over the bureaucracy. For example, upon taking office President Bill Clinton ordered the National Institutes of Health to reduce restrictions on the use of fetal tissue for medical research.[5]

The Constitution also gives the president the power to pardon offenses against the United States. A presidential pardon, whether before or after conviction, completely clears the offender's record under the law. Perhaps the most controversial pardon in American history was Gerald R. Ford's September 1974 pardon of Richard Nixon for any crimes he committed or might have committed while in office.

Appointments   In addition to appointing executive officers and ambassadors, the president also nominates federal judges, including justices of the Supreme Court. High-level presidential appointments must be confirmed by the Senate.

On taking office, a new president must fill approximately three thousand executive positions, including six hundred appointments requiring Senate confirmation. The president usually takes a personal interest in only a handful of key positions, the most important being the top members of the White House staff and the heads of the executive departments (which comprise the cabinet). The bulk of the recruitment job is delegated to a team of presidential assistants working directly for the president.[6] The president's executive appointments comprise a mixed lot of politicians, friends of the president, party loyalists, lawyers, and government and academic experts.

Perhaps a president's most enduring legacy is his appointments to the federal judiciary. Federal judges serve for life, and thus can outlast a president by two or three decades. William O. Douglas, for example, remained on the Court for more than three decades after the death of Franklin D. Roosevelt, who had appointed him in 1939. Lower court judges are generally appointed after consultation with senators of the president's party in the affected states.

The president can fire any executive official whose term is not fixed by law, and even then he can usually dismiss an official "for cause," such as misconduct in office.[7] Judges can be removed from office only by impeachment.

Legislative Powers   The president's official powers in the legislative process are threefold. Most important, the president has the power to veto any law passed by Congress. The president's veto can be overridden only by a two-thirds vote of *each* house. The veto power gives the president a key weapon in negotiations with Congress over pending legislation. The president also has the right to recommend legislation to Congress and, when necessary, can convene Congress in special session.[8]

These official powers barely scratch the surface of the president's real legislative powers, which are discussed below.

Commander in Chief   The Constitution makes the president the "Commander in Chief of the Army and Navy of the United States." Although only Congress can declare war, the

Commander in Chief Clause gives the president both the authority to commit troops to battle and direct authority over the top military commanders. Throughout American history, presidents have initiated minor military operations without a formal declaration of war, and often without any specific congressional authorization. Since World War II, presidents have initiated or escalated even major wars without a congressional declaration of war.

When North Korea invaded South Korea in 1950, for example, President Harry Truman committed American troops to the conflict without seeking congressional approval. Instead Truman urged the United Nations to condemn the North Korean invasion and to call on member nations to help South Korea defend itself. Then, claiming that the UN action gave him all the authorization he needed, Truman sent 1.8 million American soldiers to Korea; more than 50,000 were killed in action. Similarly, Presidents John Kennedy, Lyndon Johnson, and Richard Nixon fought the war in Vietnam for more than twelve years—at a cost of 50,000 more soldiers—without a formal declaration of war. Instead the war was fought at first without any congressional statement of approval, and then on the authority of the Gulf of Tonkin Resolution, a hastily considered congressional measure that authorized the president to take "all necessary measures to repel any armed attack against the forces of the United States and to prevent further aggression."[9]

In the years since Vietnam, Congress has repeatedly tried to reassert its constitutional authority over foreign policy. In 1973, for example, Congress passed the War Powers Resolution, which proclaimed that Congress should play a key role in determining when military action is appropriate and necessary. The formal provisions of the War Powers Resolution have not worked well, however, and presidents have continued to commit American troops into hostile situations on their own authority.

Even when presidents do consult with Congress on matters of war and peace, they rarely do so on an equal basis. President George Bush consulted extensively with Congress before the Persian Gulf War, for example, and even asked for specific congressional authorization to conduct the war. But he did not ask Congress's permission before sending U.S. troops to the Persian Gulf in preparation for war, and thus put the legislature in the difficult position of having to vote on the matter after American soldiers were already in the field.[10] (For a complete discussion of war powers, see Chapter 17.)

Foreign Affairs   The Constitution gives the president the power to make **treaties**—or formal agreements with other nations—subject to approval by two-thirds of the Senate. The president also has the power to appoint ambassadors, with the consent of the Senate, and to receive ambassadors from foreign nations. By tradition and interpretation, however, the president's powers in the foreign arena are considerably broader than this list might suggest.

The president's power to receive ambassadors, for example, implies the power to recognize foreign governments.[11] Thus Jimmy Carter recognized the People's Republic of China and "derecognized" the government of Taiwan. Supreme Court decisions have recognized that the president alone makes treaties; the Constitution gives the Senate only the opportunity to ratify or reject a treaty after the fact. And the president alone can break (or "abrogate") a treaty, with or without the consent of the Senate.

Moreover, in many cases the president can conclude agreements with foreign nations without seeking a formal treaty or Senate approval. Although such **executive agreements** are not mentioned in the Constitution, they have become an essential part of the conduct of modern foreign policy (the Reagan administration, for example, concluded some twenty-eight hundred executive agreements). Executive agreements are useful for handling routine matters, or for filling in the details of policies already adopted by law or in a Senate-approved treaty, and since 1937 the Supreme Court has accepted such agreements as constitutional. In 1981, for instance, the Court upheld an executive agreement with the Iranian government that secured the release of American hostages held in Tehran for over a year. However, the Court has not spelled out any precise boundaries defining exactly when executive agreements are appropriate and when formal treaties are necessary.[12]

Ever since the time of George Washington, presidents have claimed broad and at times exclusive powers in foreign affairs, a position backed by the Supreme Court in the 1936 case of *United States* v. *Curtiss-Wright Export Co.* In an extraordinary opinion, the Court held that the president's powers in foreign affairs arose directly from the nature of sovereignty, and were essentially unlimited. Although later Court opinions cast doubt on the scope of *Curtiss-Wright,* presidents have invoked the case routinely whenever their foreign affairs powers have been challenged in court.[13]

Finally, presidential power in foreign affairs is naturally strengthened by the president's authority as commander in chief. Gunboats, as many presidents have learned, often make very effective instruments of policy. The presidential authority to control the use of America's nuclear arsenal only increases the president's already formidable powers in foreign policy.

Extraconstitutional Powers of the President

The Constitution is not the only source of presidential power. Certain powers have accrued to the president by tradition, and many others have been delegated to the president by Congress.

Chief of State   In the absence of a king or queen, the president has assumed the position of chief of state—standing as a representative of the United States to foreign nations and as a symbol of the nation's sovereignty at home. The president acts as chief of state when performing certain ceremonial functions, such as lighting the national Christmas tree or throwing out the first baseball on opening day, and is accorded the respect and honors due a head of state, including the traditional twenty-one-gun salute.

Crisis Manager   Americans expect the president to take charge in times of crisis, both international and domestic. At such times the presidency assumes great importance, in both real and symbolic terms.

A host of federal laws also grant the president a wide array of powers in times of domestic or international emergency.

Economic Manager   One of the president's most important domestic functions is—or is perceived to be—the management of the national economy. The state of the national economy is often a critical factor in determining the president's popularity and political success or failure.

Ironically, most analysts agree that the president's real power over the economy, at least in the short run, is limited at best. The two tools that governments can use to manage the economy are the federal budget (fiscal policy) and the amount of money in circulation

Franklin D. Roosevelt fulfills his ceremonial duties as chief of state by throwing out the first ball on opening day, 1940. On the right are Joe Cronin, manager of the Boston Red Sox, and Bucky Harris, manager of the Washington Nationals.

(monetary policy). Although the president has some influence in these areas, both fiscal and monetary policy are by law committed to other government institutions.

The federal budget, of course, is determined by Congress. The president has the authority to submit a proposed budget and can lobby hard for personal spending and taxing preferences. But Congress can mold and shape the president's proposal to its own liking, and often ignores the presidential budget altogether. Moreover, the nature of the modern federal budget makes it difficult to use as a tool for managing the economy. More than half of the budget is for uncontrollable expenses, such as interest on the national debt or entitlement programs that are guaranteed to all eligible citizens. It is difficult to predict the size of the federal surplus or deficit, much less use it as an economic tool.

The president has even less authority over monetary policy, which is the province of the Federal Reserve Board (the "Fed"). The president appoints the chairman of the board and several other members, but their term in office is fixed and does not coincide with the president's. About all the president can do to influence the Federal Reserve is to make speeches designed to put pressure on them to keep the economy moving—for example, by keeping interest rates low.

No one would suggest that presidential actions have no impact on the economy. In 1981, for example, President Reagan's insistence on a tax cut and defense spending increases, combined with the unwillingness of congressional Democrats to make major cuts in domestic spending, led to an economic boom and massive government deficits. In 1991 the combination of tax increases and the outbreak of the Persian Gulf War depressed the economy and led to a two-year recession. But more often than not the consequences of presidential action are unintended and unpredictable.

" ...AND YES, WE MUST CONTINUE TO EXPLORE NEW WAYS TO GENERATE REVENUE.."

Over the long term, presidents may have a more substantial influence over the course of the economy, especially when they are able to lead Congress in passing major legislation. Roosevelt's New Deal, for example, clearly changed the American economy in profound ways—regulating industry and banking, protecting and encouraging the growth of labor unions, assisting farmers, and creating a social safety net with programs like social security, unemployment insurance, and bank deposit insurance. The trend toward deregulation, begun by Jimmy Carter and carried further by Ronald Reagan, brought about fundamental change in the airline, trucking, and telecommunications industries.

At least in the short term, however, the president's role in the economy resembles that of a cheerleader rather than a manager. A president who can convince the public that good times are ahead can bolster consumer and business confidence and stimulate economic growth. But the president is often faced with difficult economic choices and trade-offs, even in this cheerleading role. Powerful interest groups may advocate conflicting policies: American consumers typically favor lower interest rates, for example, making it easier to buy houses and cars; the bond markets often push for higher rates to keep inflation under control.

World Leader　The president of the United States is the acknowledged leader among the leaders of the world. For decades American leadership of what was called the "free world" grew out of the cold war conflict between the United States and the Soviet Union. With the global collapse of communism, American leadership comes from its economic and military power.

As the Persian Gulf War of 1991 indicated, only the United States has the ability to send overwhelming military force abroad on short notice. Although modern sensibilities encourage the involvement of America's allies in such conflicts, typically under the auspices of the United Nations, in practice American (meaning presidential) leadership is essential. The United States can also use its influence to help mediate regional conflicts—for example, in the Middle East. Of course the world need not follow the president's lead. Bill Clinton's efforts to push Europe to a greater involvement in the Balkans in 1993 failed, largely because Clinton would not act without a strong European commitment.

American economic leadership is shared with other industrialized countries, especially Japan and Germany, but the size of America's economy and the stability of the American political system guarantees the United States a dominant role.

Party Leader　By tradition, presidents have been recognized as the leader of their political party. They appoint the party chair, give the party direction and focus, and represent the party to the public. Barring disaster, a first-term president can expect the party's nomination for a second term and can control the party platform and the convention program.

The president's role as party leader has weakened as the parties themselves have declined in power and influence. Although no sitting president has been directly denied his party's nomination since Chester Alan Arthur was rejected in 1884, primary challenges to the incumbent are now the rule. Lyndon Johnson in 1968, Gerald Ford in 1976, Jimmy Carter in 1980, and George Bush in 1992 all faced strong opposition from within their own party. Johnson, after winning the New Hampshire primary by only a narrow margin, dropped out of the race.

In the modern era, the president's role as party leader is more a function of public perceptions than of party governance. Although individual candidates may run "against the president," in general the fortunes of the president's party are tied to those of the president. A successful president is a godsend to state and local parties; a failed or failing president can be a crushing burden.

Informal Powers and Presidential Leadership

Even taken together, the formal powers of the presidency are not extraordinary. Presidents must share the power to make law with Congress, and the power to enforce the law with the courts. In many cases they can act only through their subordinates, in whom Congress may place specific legal authority. Presidents have a freer hand in foreign affairs, but still they must deal with enemies and allies abroad, and congressional and other critics at home.

The secret to effective presidential leadership, according to the political scientist Richard Neustadt, lies not in the formal powers of the office but in its informal powers—especially the power to bargain and the power to persuade.[14] Alone, bargaining and persuasion hardly seem like powers at all. But the president has unique advantages in any negotiation. The key to presidential leadership is to use those advantages effectively.

In particular, Neustadt identified three key sources of power as the president bargains with and attempts to persuade officials in Washington and around the world:[15]

- *The bargaining advantages inherent in the job.* Presidents cannot govern alone, but they do possess considerable power on a day-to-day basis. There are nominations to be made, bills to be signed, money to be spent. Presidents are thus in a position to trade favors for cooperation or threaten retaliation for the opposite. Skillfully used as bargaining chips, the formal powers of the presidency can be multiplied many times over.
- *The expectations of others regarding a president's ability and will to use the various advantages they think the president has.* A president who has proven the ability to win the political game will reassure friends and frighten enemies. That is why it is so important for a president to earn and keep the confidence of Washington insiders, including members of Congress and influential media commentators. The power of a president who is seen as wounded or ineffective can evaporate overnight.
- *The views of others as to how the public views the president and how the public will view them if they support or oppose the president.* Washington insiders can read public opinion polls and are loath to cross a popular president. On the other hand, when presidential popularity drops, so does the president's influence in Washington.

Taken together, the president's strengths in the process of bargaining and persuasion are known as political capital. Like money, political capital must be spent wisely and can dissipate quickly.[16]

Presidents and Politics

Presidents have provided hundreds of hours of amusement over the years. Here are a few gems.

Silent Cal. Calvin Coolidge was known for being a man of few words. Once a society woman sat down next to the president and said, "You must talk to me, Mr. Coolidge. I made a bet today that I could get more than two words out of you." The president replied, "You lose."

The Kennedy wit. John F. Kennedy was known for his quick wit. On receiving an honorary degree at Yale University, for example, he quipped, "It might be said now that I have the best of both worlds—a Harvard education and a Yale degree." His description of Washington, D.C., is still quoted: "A city of southern efficiency and northern charm." Kennedy deflected comments about his father's great wealth by telling one audience: "I have just received the following wire from my generous Daddy: 'Dear Jack: Don't buy a single vote more than necessary. I'll be damned if I'm going to pay for a landslide.'"

War story. The president's role as commander in chief has given rise to many notable stories. One of the most famous involves Abraham Lincoln. When a temperance committee came to the White House and demanded that Lincoln fire General U. S. Grant, Lincoln asked why. "He drinks too much whiskey," was the reply. "Well," said Lincoln, "I wish some of you would tell me the brand of whiskey that Grant drinks. I would like to send a barrel to every one of my other generals."

The also-rans. Would-be presidents have also contributed to the leavening of American politics. In 1916, Republican candidate Charles Evans Hughes followed the election returns at his hotel in New York City. Early returns seemed to indicate victory, and Hughes, with the election apparently in hand, went to bed. But later returns from the West Coast gave the victory to Hughes's opponent, President Woodrow Wilson. When a reporter called Hughes's room in the early hours of the morning, he was told, "The President has retired." The reporter shot back: "When he wakes up, tell him he is no longer President."

One of Republican Alf Landon's more memorable lines from the 1936 campaign against Franklin D. Roosevelt was this: "Wherever I have gone in this country," he announced, "I have found Americans."

Eisenhowerese. Like many presidents before and some since, Dwight D. Eisenhower sometimes had trouble with words. Ike's rambling style was parodied by one reporter in a rewrite of the Gettysburg Address. "I haven't checked the figures," it begins, "but 87 years ago, I think it was, a number of individuals organized a government setup in this country, I believe it covered certain eastern areas, with this idea they were following up, based on a sort of national independence arrangement."

The vice presidency. No office has evoked as much humor as the vice presidency. The satirist Finley Peter Dunne said of the vice presidency: "It ain't a crime exactly. You can't be sent to jail for it, but it's a kind of a disgrace." Vice President John Nance Garner, who served under FDR, said the job "wasn't worth a bucket of warm spit." But perhaps the ultimate comment on the vice presidency came from Thomas Riley Marshall, who served as vice president under Woodrow Wilson. "Once there were two brothers," the story begins. "One ran away to sea, the other was elected Vice President, and nothing was heard from either one of them again."

Adapted from Paul F. Boller, Jr., *Presidential Anecdotes* (New York: Oxford University Press, 1981); Paul F. Boller, Jr., *Presidential Campaigns* (New York:Oxford University Press, 1984); Leonard C. Lewin, *A Treasury of American Political Humor* (New York: Dell, 1968); Arthur Power Dudden, *Pardon Us, Mr. President! American Humor on Politics* (South Brunswick and New York: A. S. Barnes and Company, 1975); and Thomas Riley Marshall, *Recollections* (Indianapolis: Bobbs-Merrill, 1925).

Tracking Political Capital: Presidential Approval Ratings   The president's political capital can be tracked by following the public's perception of how well the chief executive is performing on the job. Such polls, which have been taken since 1935, constitute a kind of political stockmarket average—giving the entire country a monthly reading of how the president is doing.

Presidents' approval ratings are usually highest at the beginning of their term. Having just elected a president to office, the public is naturally confident that the person can and will do the job. As Figure 13.1 illustrates, however, approval ratings typically decline over time, although crisis situations, especially in foreign policy, typically produce short-term boosts.

That is why a president's first year in office is so critical. With political capital at a maximum, the president must take advantage of the opportunity to push proposals through Congress. Early in his first year, for example, Ronald Reagan built on a nearly 70 percent approval rating to push through a massive tax cut and a major defense buildup, changes that brought about dramatic transformations in federal policy. Two years later, Reagan's popularity had sunk by half, to 35 percent, and his power went with it.

Of course, popularity alone is no guarantee of policy success. In the early part of his second term, Reagan built up high approval ratings, but made little effort to affect policy except in the area of tax reform. Reagan's strategy seemed designed to cultivate popularity for its own sake, and was often counterproductive in policy terms. Likewise, George Bush made little effort to turn his unprecedented 90 percent popularity rating after the 1991 Gulf War into real policy initiatives.

Boosting Presidential Popularity   Because high approval ratings greatly increase the president's bargaining power, modern presidents often go to great lengths to improve their standing with the people. However, the president's opponents can use many of the same techniques to undermine the president's popularity ratings.

"Going Public." Presidents can often gain by taking their case directly to the public. "Going public" typically involves a media campaign designed to improve the president's image and build popular support for the president's programs.[17] A media campaign can include televised speeches and press conferences, tours across the country, paid television commercials, and appearances on network and cable TV talk shows. Theodore Roosevelt had the "going public" aspect of the presidency in mind when he called the office a "bully pulpit" (the "bully" in the phrase means first-rate.)[18] The various techniques of media campaigning are also available to the president's opponents, however. In the 1994 health care debate, for example, opponents of the Clinton plan successfully countered the president with television commercials of their own.

Foreign Policy as Photo Opportunity. A variant of going public involves using foreign policy events to boost presidential support and thus maximize the president's bargaining power. Summit meetings, whether with Russian leaders or European and Japanese heads of state, can be particularly impressive and helpful. The president can tightly control press and public access, making sure to be shown only in the best light (there are exceptions, as when international television caught George Bush collapsing and vomiting at a Japanese state dinner). Summit meetings provide instant stature, making the president look most presidential. They also provide an opportunity for revealing major (or apparently major)

Figure 13.1 **Presidential Approval Ratings, 1953–1997**

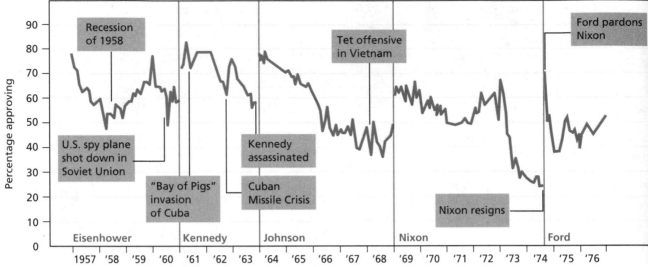

SOURCE: Gallup Polls.

breakthroughs in foreign policy, even though such deals are almost always negotiated beforehand.

Minimizing Expectations. Since a fundamental problem facing the postmodern presidency is that the public's expectations of presidential performance are often too high, a simple remedy is for the president to reduce the public's expectations of the office. President Reagan turned reduced expectations into a philosophy of government, arguing that the government could not manage the economy successfully and would do better by getting out of the way. Much more common is the use of reduced expectations as a tactical device. When President Clinton went to his first economic summit, for example, he deliberately downplayed the chances for major breakthroughs on trade issues. When a minor breakthrough occurred, Clinton looked like a hero.[19]

Unfortunately, most presidents are in the habit of raising public expectations instead of lowering them. On the day of the Oklahoma City bombing in April 1995, for example, Bill Clinton promised flatly that the government would catch the perpetrators. "When we do," he declared, "justice will be swift, certain, and severe." In this case, Clinton was right; two years later, Timothy McVeigh was convicted of the crime and sentenced to death. Even so, both catching and punishing criminals are largely beyond the power of the White House.[20]

Achieving Real Policy Results. Politics is about governing, and in the end a president is judged on results. Aside from short-term blips, public attitudes toward the president are most influenced by the nation's economic performance. The prosperity of the 1980s made Ronald Reagan a popular president, and the recession of 1991–1992 doomed George Bush.

It would be nice if presidents could do well by doing good. The problem is that the nation's long-term (or even medium-term) economic health often requires measures that produce short-term pain. Hence every president has a great incentive to produce short-term economic prosperity, leaving the consequences to the next president. But the public interest, as Madison argued in *Federalist* No. 10, requires a long-term approach.

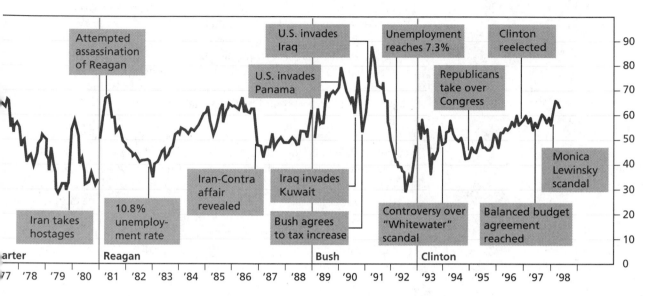

Leadership and Presidential Character   Historians and political scientists have long argued over whether presidents make history or history makes presidents. Can a president's personality or character lead to triumph even when the flow of history seems to be going the other way? Can personality or character destroy a presidency even when the forces of history are flowing in the right direction? As with many such controversies, the truth lies somewhere in the middle, although exactly where is hard to tell. We only have one president at a time, and any effort to sort out the influence of history from the influence of personality requires speculation, supposition, and guesswork.

Calvin Coolidge was the ultimate "passive-negative" president. When he died, the writer Dorothy Parker quipped, "How could they tell?"

Among political scientists, the leading proponent of the importance of presidential character is James David Barber. "Who the president is at a given time can make a profound difference in the whole thrust and direction of national politics," Barber has written. "Even the most superficial speculation confirms the common sense view that the man himself weighs heavily among other historical factors."[21] Barber's goal was to figure out an easy way of classifying presidential character and of giving that classification some predictive value.

Barber's approach stressed two key aspects of presidential personality. First, he identified presidents as active or passive; this dimension asks how much energy the president invests in the presidency. Second, he identified presidents as positive or negative; this dimension asks whether the president is someone who "has fun in political life . . . a kind of register of felt satisfaction." These two characteristics, Barber argued, were so essential to anyone's orientation toward life in general that they could not fail to play an important role in shaping a presidency.[22]

Barber's two dimensions gave rise to four types of presidents: active-positives, such as Franklin D. Roosevelt, John F. Kennedy, and Bill Clinton; active-negatives, such as Lyndon B. Johnson and Richard Nixon; passive-positives, such as William Howard Taft and Ronald Reagan; and passive-negatives, such as Dwight D. Eisenhower and George Bush.

How useful is Barber's analysis? Placing a president or potential president into one of Barber's categories gives us some insight into the person's style and approach to the job; combined with other data, Barber's approach may help us understand, or even predict, presidential success or failure. Barber's predictions about Richard Nixon, for example, were amply borne out by the Watergate scandal. But many political scientists have come to doubt whether Barber's approach has yielded real insights, or has had real predictive power, in the two decades since Nixon left the White House.[23]

The Evolution of the American Presidency

In two hundred years the presidency has grown from a relatively weak institution to a position of apparently awesome power. Scholars have divided the growth of the presidency into three stages: the traditional presidency, the imperial presidency, and the postmodern presidency.

The Traditional Presidency: Low Expectations, Low Performance

As created by the Framers, the **traditional presidency** was a modest office in terms of both power and prestige. Although there were several key exceptions, presidents from Washington (1789–1797) to Hoover (1929–1933) used their constitutional powers sparingly and made little effort to expand the authority of the office. The traditional presidency was dominated by Congress, at times to the point of embarrassment. James Madison, for example, was able to convince Congress to declare war on Great Britain in 1812 under the banner of "Free Trade and Sailors' Rights!" But having persuaded Congress to declare a naval war, Madison was unable to persuade it to increase the size of the navy until it was too late to make a difference.

The weakness of the traditional presidency was more a function of the weakness of the federal government than of anything else. The American role in foreign affairs was limited to staying out of what George Washington called "entangling alliances" with European powers. The federal government's role in national affairs was hardly more exciting. It was expected to coin money, deliver the mail, regulate the coastal waterways, deal with the Indian tribes, and perform a variety of other mundane tasks. Some urged the federal government to assist in the building of roads, canals, bridges, and other internal improvements, but even those were highly controversial.

Until well into the twentieth century, presidential prestige was equally unimpressive. Presidents were surrounded by tiny staffs and moved about freely with little concern for security. John Quincy Adams retired from the presidency to the House of Representatives, which he considered a promotion. Grover Cleveland answered the newly installed White House phone himself, and Woodrow Wilson typed his own letters.[24]

To overstate the weakness of either the national government or the presidency in the century and a half before 1933, however, would be a mistake. The Framers did not envision a "do-nothing" presidency. On the contrary, they viewed the efficient administration of the laws as one of the primary functions of government and saw a one-person presidency as the best way to achieve their goal. Moreover, several presidents did push at the envelope of their powers. Thomas Jefferson purchased the Louisiana territory on his own authority. Andrew Jackson single-handedly destroyed the Bank of the United States, an institution that had strong congressional support. Abraham Lincoln acted without advance congressional approval to put down the rebellion in the South, calling out federal troops, enlisting volunteers, and closing southern ports. Theodore Roosevelt built the Panama Canal and drove Congress to pass legislation creating the national forest reserves and doubling the national parks. But these strong presidents were the exceptions, not the rule. Most of the traditional presidents were weak, unambitious, and unmemorable.

The Rise of the Imperial Presidency:
High Expectations, High Performance

The office of the presidency was transformed in the 1930s and 1940s by Franklin D. Roosevelt. Not coincidentally, the New Deal and World War II had also transformed both the role of the federal government in domestic affairs and the role of the United States in world affairs. The presidency benefited from both developments.

In domestic affairs, the New Deal both demonstrated and enhanced the powers of the presidency. Using the medium of radio to take his case directly to the American people, Roosevelt created a new conception of federal and presidential power. The vastly expanded role of the federal government in economic and social policy required a corresponding increase in the size of the federal bureaucracy, and the size and complexity of the federal role forced Congress to delegate increasing amounts of power to the White House. In turn the president expanded his executive office, creating both the Bureau of the Budget (later the Office of Management and Budget) and an expanded White House staff.

The growing international crisis of the 1930s and the outbreak of World War II further strengthened the presidency. Roosevelt moved on his own to increase the American commitment to the defense of Europe and pushed Congress to improve America's readiness to fight if necessary. The Japanese attack on Pearl Harbor in 1941 only increased Roosevelt's prestige at home and abroad.

So great was Roosevelt's transformation of the presidency that he was able to break the 150-year-old tradition that limited a president to a maximum of two four-year terms. That tradition, started by George Washington to prevent the presidency from taking on the trappings of monarchy, was pushed aside by the new conception of the presidency as the source of indispensable leadership in both domestic and foreign crisis.

The New Deal and World War II ushered in the era of what the historian Arthur Schlesinger, Jr., called the **imperial presidency.**[25] Presidential power and influence reached its zenith in the 1960s and 1970s, under Presidents Kennedy, Johnson, and Nixon. The power of the imperial presidents was enormous, both at home and abroad. They enjoyed near-royal treatment wherever they went, traveled on military jets and helicopters, and made internationally televised visits to foreign lands. They led the nation through a period of unprecedented prosperity. They kept the Soviet Union in line, meeting the challenge of communism.

The imperial presidents learned to control, ignore, or intimidate foreign enemies and political opponents alike. President Kennedy faced down the Soviets during the Cuban missile crisis and committed American soldiers to Vietnam. President Johnson used a variety of strong-arm tactics to persuade Congress to pass his Great Society programs, along with the Civil Rights Act of 1964 and the Voting Rights Act of 1965. When he saw the need for increasing American involvement in Vietnam, Johnson exaggerated an incident in the Gulf of Tonkin to bully Congress into granting its overwhelming approval.

The imperial presidents were not all-powerful. President Kennedy had trouble pushing his programs through Congress, and presided over the disastrous Bay of Pigs operation, an unsuccessful effort to invade Cuba and depose Fidel Castro. President Nixon ran up against strong opposition to parts of his domestic agenda from the Democratic leadership in Congress. While it lasted, however, the imperial presidency was an awesome institution. Presidential powers in domestic and international affairs were exceeded only by the public's expectations for the office and for the individuals who occupied it.

Eventually, however, the imperial presidents overreached themselves. Presidents Kennedy and Johnson led the nation into a major war in Vietnam without securing popular support, and Johnson deceived the nation about the scope and prospects of American involvement. Nixon presided over an administration that flouted the law and the Constitution, illegally and unethically manipulating the electoral process and repeatedly passing false or half-true information to the American people. When all of this erupted into the Watergate scandal, Nixon was forced to resign in disgrace, inflicting a serious wound on the imperial presidency.

The reaction to the imperial presidency would reduce the power and authority of the office, but it would do little to reduce the public's expectations of the presidency.

John F. Kennedy confers with advisers during the Cuban missile crisis in 1962. At the height of the imperial presidency, Kennedy could afford to deal with Congress, the press, and even the Russians from a position of strength.

The Postmodern Presidency: High Expectations, Low Performance

Presidents since Gerald Ford have faced a difficult dilemma: for the most part, they have lacked the power to achieve what the public expects of them. The political scientist Richard Rose has called this uncomfortable state of affairs the **postmodern presidency.**

The public still expects the president to keep the nation strong both at home and abroad. It also looks to the White House for leadership on a wide range of social issues, including crime, drugs, AIDS, and health care. It even holds the presidency responsible for coping with natural disasters and other national emergencies (when Hurricane Andrew struck southern Florida in August 1992, for example, many blamed George Bush and the government for responding too slowly).

The problem is that the president's powers have not grown to match the public's expectations. In fact, the postmodern presidency is constrained by all kinds of forces the chief executive cannot hope to control.

Changing World Order In the immediate post–World War II era, American power was unmatched. The only rival was the Soviet Union, and it was kept at bay by the threat of American military force. America's allies in Europe and Asia were dependent on the United States for military protection and for economic prosperity, and third-world countries and nationalist movements everywhere were held in check by the superpower conflict.

The collapse of communism and the rise of Europe and Japan as economic powers have fundamentally changed the power equation. Although America is now the only superpower, it is often powerless to control regional or local conflicts, or unwilling to pay the price that would be necessary if it chose to do so. The United States was able to push Iraq out of Kuwait, for example, but it failed to bring down the regime of Saddam Hussein. Although the Persian Gulf War demonstrated the willingness of the American people to support a short and successful war, whether they would endorse a long and difficult conflict where American interests were not directly at stake is extremely doubtful.

The beleaguered George Bush seemed to symbolize the postmodern presidency. He was attacked even by members of his own party—as in this campaign commercial for Pat Buchanan—especially for breaking his "No New Taxes" pledge.

Finally, the nation's economic strength now depends on maintaining strong relationships with a host of foreign partners. Both the European Community and Japan are now major economic players, and the United States must also compete with a host of economic rivals, including Singapore, China, South Korea, and Taiwan. The president must bargain with our allies on trade and pressure them on economic policy, often with limited success.

Renewed Congress The lessons of Vietnam and Watergate were not lost on Congress. In the wake of those crises, the legislative branch acted to strengthen its hand in economic and foreign policy. The War Powers Resolution of 1973 gave Congress a bargaining chip in foreign crises. The Budget Control and Impoundment Act of 1974 gave Congress a greater role in the budget process and made it less dependent on the president's proposals. By 1976, intelligence oversight committees sought to limit the president's ability to conduct covert foreign policy, and congressional staff agencies like the Congressional Budget Office ended the president's monopoly on economic information.

The end of the imperial presidency also brought an important shift in Congress's attitude toward presidential power. Having nearly impeached one president, Congress was emboldened to fight the White House in both domestic and foreign affairs. This tendency was heightened by the division of party control of the two branches, although it persisted even during the first two years of the Clinton administration, when the Democratic party controlled both the legislative and executive branches. Congress demands a major voice in foreign policy, rewrites presidential budgets with impunity, and routinely fights with the White House on domestic matters. The modern Congress is much more willing to buck the president on judicial and executive appointments than it was two decades ago, even in the absence of partisan conflict.[26]

The Watchdog Role of the Press Watergate made heroes out of *Washington Post* reporters Bob Woodward and Carl Bernstein, and led reporters to focus on their role as watchdogs over the government, especially the White House. Whereas their predecessors covered up Franklin Roosevelt's paralysis and winked at President Kennedy's sex life, modern reporters pride themselves in investigating every story and exposing every presidential flaw or foible. The adversarial role of the press is apparent in presidential press conferences, in which reporters vie to ask embarrassing questions or raise awkward subjects.

The post-Watergate role of the press has made life difficult for other institutions of government also, including Congress and the courts (press exposure helped create the House banking scandal, for example, and nearly torpedoed the appointment of Clarence Thomas to the Supreme Court). But the White House, as the intense coverage of the Paula Jones and Monica Lewinsky scandals demonstrate, has suffered the most from press scrutiny.

Figure 13.2 **Presidential Success History, 1954–1996**

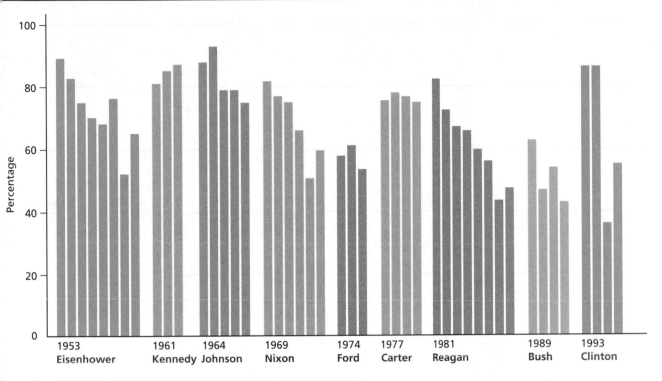

SOURCE: *Congressional Roll Call,* 1996, p. C4. Used with permission of Congressional Quarterly Press.

The Tyranny of Economic Forces   Although presidents routinely claim credit for a strong economy, recent decades have clearly demonstrated that the state of the American economy is largely out of the president's hands. In part, this is because the president is only one of many government officials whose decisions affect the economy: Congress, the Federal Reserve Board, the Bureau of Labor Statistics, and countless other agencies also play a role. It is also because the economy, as more and more economists have come to believe, has a mind of its own and cannot easily be controlled from Washington. The decisions of Wall Street traders and London bankers, as well as those of corporate leaders and ordinary consumers, all have an impact on the nation's economic well-being. Some economists argue that the government can influence the economy over the long term—for example, by implementing an industrial policy in which the government works with major industries to improve coordination and cooperation in research and development. And surely governmental tax and spending policies influence the economy in the long run. But all such influences are indirect and unpredictable.

Ironically, the presidential tendency to claim credit for a strong economy contributes, in the long run, to the public perception of presidential weakness. For sooner or later, when the economy turns downward, it will be the president who gets the blame.

"I had a better season than he did."

—Babe Ruth, in 1930, justifying his request for a higher salary than President Hoover

Loss of Moral Authority   Unquestionably the postmodern presidency has lost much of the aura that the office once enjoyed. With presidents under constant media scrutiny and persistent partisan attack, postmodern presidents simply do not command the level of respect enjoyed by their predecessors. The decline in the moral authority of the presidency is all of a piece with Americans' declining respect for authority figures of all kinds. Still, the developments over the past few years would have shocked past presidents and publics alike.

The decline in the respect accorded the presidency was apparent in the 1980s and early 1990s. Ronald Reagan countered criticism by joking that he had left orders to be woken up in case of any emergency, "even during cabinet meetings"; a preelection edition of *Saturday Night Live* in 1992 depicted George Bush groveling in the oval office, begging the American people not to make him a "one-termer." But all of this pales by comparison to the allegations, snide remarks, jokes, and ridicule directed at President Bill Clinton. During his first term, a U.S. Air Force general publicly denounced Clinton as a "draft-dodging . . . gay loving . . . pot-smoking . . . womanizer,"[27] and the president was the subject of a sexual harassment suit by Paula Jones; during his second term, he was forced to undergo detailed questioning about his sex life in a deposition in the Jones case, and subjected to an embarrassing and highly public investigation of his alleged sexual affair with Monica Lewinsky. During the Lewinsky scandal, the intimate details of the president's real or alleged sex life became a staple topic of news reports and political conversation. There is of course nothing wrong with (or new about) reporting presidential scandals, but the degree of disrespect and the lack of countervailing displays of deference are, from a historical perspective, striking.

In addition, every presidential action is analyzed and dissected in terms of campaign strategy and public relations tactics—a practice immortalized in the 1998 movie *Wag the Dog,* in which a president's aides create a war for the purpose of distracting attention from a brewing scandal. In the early stages of the Lewinsky investigation, life imitated art, as some of President Clinton's critics suggested that his decision to mobilize U.S. troops for possible air strikes against Iraq was motivated by a desire to distract the public from the scandal. Whether or not public policy is driven by such considerations, the constant repetition of such commentary has eroded the aura of presidential authority.[28]

In summary, the postmodern presidency is marked by an imbalance between the public's expectations of the presidency and the realities of presidential power. As Rose puts it, "The resources of the White House are not sufficient to meet all of the President's . . . responsibilities."[29] Although Rose emphasizes the declining power of the presidency in the international arena, the president's power has declined in the domestic arena as well.

The President and the Administrative Process

Franklin D. Roosevelt's original White House staff consisted of a few old friends, a valet, an executive clerk, and two personal secretaries. Roosevelt also employed the "brain trust," a loosely organized collection of academics and lawyers who wrote speeches, drafted legislation, and provided the president with general advice. Not a single member of the brain trust held an official White House position, although several found jobs in various executive departments. Despite its lack of size and pretension, Roosevelt's team managed to implement and oversee the ambitious programs of the early New Deal.[30]

By the end of Roosevelt's first term, the strain of trying to manage the growing national bureaucracy was beginning to show. In 1936, therefore, Roosevelt appointed a commission under the direction of Louis Brownlow to study the problem and recommend a "simple but effective machinery" to enable the president "to exercise managerial control" over the executive branch. The Brownlow Commission reported back in 1937 with a clear diagnosis: "The President needs help." The commission recommended the appointment of up to six presidential assistants, who "should be possessed of high competence, great physical vigor, and a passion for anonymity."[31]

Congress authorized the president to reorganize the executive branch in 1939, and Roosevelt acted quickly to adopt the Brownlow Commission's report—and more. Roosevelt's plan called not only for the appointment of six presidential assistants but for the establishment of a new agency, to be called the **Executive Office of the President (EOP).** Under Roosevelt, the most important components of the EOP were the White House Office and the Bureau of the Budget (BOB). The White House Office comprises the many advisers and assistants that make up the White House staff. The BOB was charged with helping the president to prepare his annual budget. But from the beginning it also played a key role in program coordination and development. In 1970 the Bureau of the Budget was renamed the **Office of Management and Budget (OMB),** and its duties were expanded to include assisting the president with the management of various federal programs.[32]

The White House Office and the Office of Management and Budget remain the principal components of the Executive Office of the President. Over the years, however, both agencies have expanded in size and responsibilities. Presidents have also created various other agencies and brought them under the EOP umbrella. Currently, the EOP includes among its many

Figure 13.3 Executive Office of the President

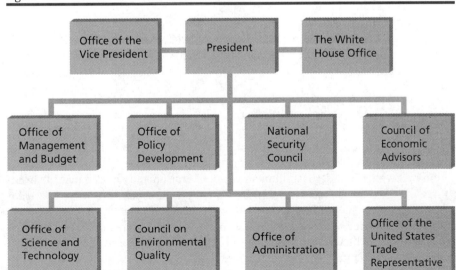

agencies the Office of the Vice President, the National Security Council, the Council on Environmental Quality, the Office of the United States Trade Representative, and the Office of Science and Technology Policy. As of 1994, the EOP staff numbered 1,595, including 396 in the White House office and 531 in the Office of Management and Budget.[33]

Organizing the White House

All presidents face two great managerial challenges. The first is to organize the White House itself, bringing together their various advisers, assistants, and agency heads into a coherent and capable team. The second is to use that team to coordinate and to some degree control the activities of the hundreds of agencies that make up the executive branch.

In theory, the only purpose of the White House staff is to assist and advise the president. In practice, every president's first task, as one presidential scholar puts it, is "to devise strategies and tactics of management for making the White House staff work effectively." Every president approaches the task differently, and every White House staff reflects the personality and style of the individual at the top. But the White House staff is also an institution, with traditions and a history of its own, and it shapes and constrains the president in turn. Whether the president can control the staff is, in the words of one former White House aide, "a measure of the President's effectiveness and the confidence that will be given him by the American people."[34]

The Inner Circle   At the center of power sits the president and a handful of key senior advisers, who can be members of the White House staff, top agency officials, or even private citizens. They are often men or women whom the president has known for a long time and in whom he has complete confidence and trust. Franklin Roosevelt, for example, relied heavily on the advice of Felix Frankfurter, then a professor at the Harvard Law School. John Kennedy confided in his brother Robert, who served as attorney general. George Bush frequently sought advice from Secretary of State James Baker, and Bill Clinton has often discussed key decisions with his wife, Hillary, a lawyer.

The inner circle of power is rarely a static place. Over time, changing relationships and external events may bring new people into the inner circle or cast others out. A dramatic example occurred in 1996, when presidential adviser Dick Morris was forced to resign his White House job after news reports that he was involved in a long-term affair with a Washington prostitute.

The Cabinet   The idea that the heads of the major government departments should meet together as a Council of State to advise the president was discussed, and rejected, by the Constitutional Convention. Thus the Constitution makes no mention of a formal body to assist and advise the president. Immediately on taking office, however, President George Washington met with Alexander Hamilton and James Madison and decided that the heads of the three executive departments should constitute an informal advisory group. This group became known as the **cabinet.**

As Washington conceived it, the cabinet was to be a collegial body that would meet together and with him to discuss issues and make policy recommendations. However, cabinet meetings quickly degenerated into opportunities for conflict. The key players were Hamilton and Thomas Jefferson, who would soon leave the government and become leaders of rival political factions. Washington's new cabinet was more harmonious but less talented, and he came to rely less and less on its advice. John Adams, who followed Washington in the presidency, distrusted his cabinet altogether.

After these shaky beginnings, the cabinet never became an independent body with real collective power. As the historian R. Gordon Hoxie has explained, the president is not bound to follow the cabinet's advice or even to consult the cabinet. Nor does the cabinet play a formal administrative role, since presidential orders are transmitted directly to the individual department heads.[35] Although the cabinet sometimes meets as a group, more often its members are separately engaged in running their respective departments.

Positions with cabinet rank generally carry with them a certain amount of prestige and visibility. Because members of the cabinet work directly for the president, they usually have direct access to the president, at least on an occasional basis. Much depends on the temperament of the president and on the president's relationship with particular cabinet members, however, and feuds or rivalries between the president and certain department heads are common.

One reason that the cabinet has rarely functioned as a cohesive advisory group is that presidents typically do not choose their cabinet members on the basis of how well they will work together. Instead they use their cabinet appointments to pay political debts, reassure particular interest groups, or promote diversity in government. President Bill Clinton's second-term cabinet, for example, included two African Americans, one Latino, and four women. The appointment of Robert E. Rubin (formerly co-chairman of the investment firm of Goldman, Sachs and Co.) as treasury secretary was intended, at least in part, to reassure Wall Street, while the appointment of William S. Cohen, a Republican, as secretary of defense was at least partly intended to ease relations with the Republican Congress on military matters.

Chief of Staff   A relatively recent innovation is the position of White House chief of staff. The chief of staff serves as a kind of presidential office manager. The duties of the chief of staff include scheduling the president's time, setting the president's agenda, and controlling access to the Oval Office. In theory, chiefs of staff exercise no independent authority but act only in the name of the president. In practice, their access to the president and ability to act as gatekeepers make them powerful figures in their own right.

Every president since Franklin Roosevelt has employed a chief of staff, in fact if not always in name. Chiefs of staff are necessary, according to the political scientist Samuel L. Popkin, "because a president's time must be rationed, decisions must be paced, and access by the staff and cabinet need to be refereed." In addition, "chiefs can sometimes learn what presidents cannot. As John Kennedy's staff found out during the Cuban Missile Crisis, only when the president is absent from a meeting will assistants challenge their bosses; in front of the president, assistants will not contradict or question their immediate superiors."[36] But as the Watergate incident demonstrated, chiefs of staff can become dangerous when they become so powerful that the president is isolated from those who would provide essential advice and criticism directly to the president.

The Nonmanagerial Presidency

In theory, a major task for any president is to coordinate and control the activities of the many executive agencies. For example, more than sixty agencies are involved in formulating and car-

rying out federal drug policy. Ensuring that they pursue common goals, avoid waste and duplication, and work together effectively is the responsibility of the Office of National Drug Control Policy, a White House agency whose director is informally known as the nation's "drug czar."

Even in the relatively focused area of drug policy, however, coordination and control are often undesirable or impossible. Each individual agency answers not just to the president but to Congress and the courts as well; presidential attempts to make major changes in the policies of a particular agency may run afoul of the law or provoke a strong reaction from interest groups or congressional committees.

Neither the president nor the president's staff has the time, energy, or resources to keep up with everything going on in every executive agency. As a practical matter, moreover, the president is well advised to stay out of most interagency disputes. "Avoiding involvement in tedious arguments and no-win conflicts conserves political capital," observes Richard Rose. Because they have relatively little to gain in political terms from the nuts-and-bolts of executive management, presidents tend to avoid such matters altogether. In the 1960s, for example, a presidential commission urged Lyndon Johnson to focus on coordinating the activities of federal, state, and local agencies. Johnson chose to ignore the suggestion. As a presidential aide put it, "It's bad enough being President without having to be Governor of Alabama and Mayor of New York City too."[37]

A complete discussion of presidential management of the executive branch appears in Chapter 14.

The President and the Legislative Process

Franklin D. Roosevelt's summary of the president's role in the legislative process is still true. "The president proposes," Roosevelt said, "but Congress disposes."[38] Roosevelt's maxim has held true for strong presidents and weak ones, for presidents whose party controls Congress and for those who must deal with opposition leadership.

FDR is remembered as a very strong president, and his first one hundred days—during which he persuaded Congress to pass a host of New Deal programs—remain a standard to which other presidents still aspire. But Roosevelt's views on Congress were born of bitter experience. Like every other president before or since, he found dealing with Congress to be a constant, but necessary, struggle.

The president can exercise influence at every stage of the lawmaking process. Actually controlling the process, however, is far more difficult.

Agenda-Setting: The Power to Propose

Historically, the White House has been the dominant force in setting the congressional agenda. This has been especially so in budgetary and economic matters, since Congress usually uses the presidential budget as a starting point for its own negotiations (the process has broken down since the Reagan years, and Congress now routinely ignores the presidential blueprint in favor of its own). Presidents can also put major policy initiatives on the congressional table, and can weigh in with their own proposals on pending matters.

On occasion, Congress can wrest the agenda-setting power from the White House. For Congress to take and sustain the initiative requires a combination of a weak president and a determined congressional leadership. In the early 1970s, for example, the Democratic Congress capitalized on the weakness of the late Nixon and early Ford presidencies to pass a number of important pieces of reform legislation, including the War Powers Resolution of 1973 and the Budget Control and Impoundment Act of 1974. In 1995, Newt Gingrich led Congress in its consideration of the ambitious provisions of the Contract with America.

Typically, presidents are most ambitious and successful in their first year in office. Following the "first one hundred days" model, many modern presidents have used the momentum of their election victory to send Congress a major legislative package embodying the promises and purposes of their campaigns. Like Roosevelt, succeeding presidents have often given these packages colorful names designed to capture the new administration's goals. Roosevelt's New Deal was followed by Truman's Fair Deal, Kennedy's New Frontier, Johnson's Great Society, and Nixon's New Federalism.

In 1981, for example, Ronald Reagan followed up his landslide victory with an ambitious package designed to reduce federal taxes, cut domestic spending, and strengthen the armed forces. Using his enormous popularity and his considerable lobbying skills, Reagan put together a coalition of Republicans and conservative Democrats and pushed the heart of his proposal through Congress. In 1993, Bill Clinton took office with an even more ambitious agenda, calling for major shifts in federal budget priorities; higher taxes and spending cuts to reduce the deficit; reforms in health care, welfare policy, and campaign finance; and new investments in education and training. With Democratic

The president's power to set the national agenda was amply demonstrated in 1993, when Bill and Hillary Clinton proposed sweeping health care reforms. Though ultimately defeated, the Clinton plan occupied Congress's attention for over a year.

majorities in both houses, Clinton was able to succeed with at least some of his proposals, although much of the original package was lost, modified, or delayed.

Once presidents decide to propose a bill, they can call on the vast resources of the federal bureaucracy, along with their own aides and advisers, to draft the actual legislation. At one time the ability to command such resources gave presidents an upper hand in their dealings with Congress, since the legislative branch lacked the staff expertise to compete with the executive branch. Increases in congressional staff and the creation and expansion of congressional staff agencies like the Congressional Budget Office and the Congressional Research Service have largely overcome the presidential advantages in that area.

Lobbying

It is not enough to propose a bill. Lacking an automatic majority in Congress, presidents must actively campaign to get their proposals passed into law. Here they must rely on their informal powers.

- *Campaigning.* Generating public support for a president's plan, or at least negating public opposition, is critical. Presidents can accomplish this objective with televised speeches and press conferences, campaign-style tours across the country, and interviews on national and local talk shows and news broadcasts. The vice president and key cabinet officials are likewise expected to join in the publicity campaign, especially to generate the support of voters in their home states and of particular interest groups over which they have influence.
- *The veto power.* Properly handled, the veto power can be used as a lever and multiplied in effectiveness. The veto can be a tool to help build legislation as well as a weapon to destroy it; by threatening to veto a bill unless certain conditions are met, for example, the president might be able to insist on those conditions. Likewise, by threatening to veto a bill favored by Congress, the president might prevail on the legislature to pass another bill that would otherwise be shelved or defeated.

  Whether used as a tool or a weapon, the veto is a blunt instrument. The president can sign or veto a bill passed by Congress, but cannot change it. Thus often the president must decide whether to veto an entire bill simply to excise one offending part. The president's position is further weakened by the modern congressional tendency to lump numerous provisions into a single bill. It is not unusual for modern legislation to consume hundreds or thousands of pages, and the $1.5 trillion budget is divided up into only thirteen individual appropriations bills.

  Recent presidents have tried to sharpen the veto ax by calling for a "line item veto," which would allow the president to strike out individual items from the large appropriations bills. The line item veto is currently exercised by forty-three of the nation's governors, and would represent a major addition to the presidential arsenal. In 1996, Congress at last passed a law giving the president an effective line item veto, although the constitutionality of this provision is in doubt. [39]
- *Campaign support.* Popular presidents can wield great influence within their own party by offering to campaign on behalf of a particular member of Congress or by threatening to withhold such support. Presidential support is particularly helpful in raising money for local campaigns and in generating enthusiasm and media coverage. Popular presidents can also boost their party's chances in general, especially when they are on

Presidential Versus Parliamentary Systems

The principle of the separation of powers distinguishes the American system of government from the parliamentary system, which is the form of government in the United Kingdom and in most of the world's democracies.

In America, the legislative and executive branches are constitutionally and politically independent, although of course they must get along with each other to achieve any kind of successful governance. Under a parliamentary system, the legislative and executive branches are fused together. At the apex of power is the prime minister, who is a member of the legislative branch and is directly elected by his or her legislative colleagues. Below the prime minister is the cabinet, which consists of the various department heads, all of whom are also members of parliament. At the bottom of the pyramid are the rank-and-file members of parliament. Although the prime minister is the chief executive officer, most countries also have a separate head of state, whether a king, queen, president, or chancellor. Depending on the system, the head of state may also have significant political power.

To Americans fed up with a system that allows and encourages unending battles between the legislative and executive branches, and which has elevated delay and inaction to an art form, the parliamentary system often appears as an attractive alternative. Specific proposals to modify the separation of powers principle have been floated periodically, although they have generated little more than academic interest. The parliamentary system does have certain advantages, but it is hardly perfect.

A parliamentary system can be more efficient than a presidential system, but it can also pose a more serious threat to liberty. A parliamentary system in which one party controls a majority in parliament—as is usually the case in Great Britain—is an awesome force. When the majority party elects its leader as prime minister, it effectively pledges its full support, and the prime minister can thus pursue broad policy initiatives with little need to compromise outside the majority party. Add the fact that the courts are typically weaker in parliamentary systems than in the United States, and there are few effective barriers to the government's power. Unfortunately, such a system also makes it easier for the government to pursue a foolhardy policy or to trample the rights of the minority. Recently, for example, the British Parliament decided to amend centuries of legal practice by ruling that a criminal defendant's refusal to testify can be regarded as evidence of guilt. Almost certainly, the American system would doom such a law to oblivion. If it managed to emerge from Congress, it would either be vetoed by the president or struck down as unconstitutional by the Supreme Court.

Parliamentary systems have their own mechanisms for avoiding rash or foolhardy policies. Perhaps the most important is the role of the cabinet, which must generally debate and approve all major policies. Most parliamentary systems also encourage spirited public debates, and many require the prime minister and other government officials to appear before parliament to answer questions on a regular basis. Ultimately, of course, any democratic regime must answer to the people; if the prime minister's party loses the confidence of the nation, its days in power are numbered.

Parliamentary systems can be fragmented, disorganized, and too dependent on small minority parties. In a parliamentary system with many political parties, it is usually difficult for one party to gain a majority in parliament. It is then necessary for a group of parties to form a coalition government. Such coalitions may include very small parties—even a single member of parliament—which must be kept happy if the government is to survive. Such parties can often exact policy concessions that are unpopular, and can bring down the government by walking out in the midst of a crisis. The American system may be less efficient than a well-functioning parliamentary system, but it is much more efficient than a parliamentary system that breaks down on a regular basis.

SOURCE: Richard Rose, *The Postmodern Presidency: George Bush Meets the World*, 2d ed. (Chatham, N.J.: Chatham House, 1988), pp. 62–70.

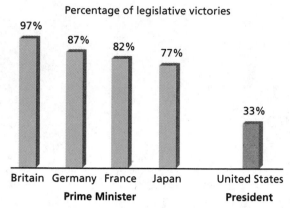

Figure 13.4 Success of Presidents and Prime Ministers in Enacting Legislation

A comparison of the success rates of presidents and prime ministers in convincing the legislature to pass legislation clearly reveals the consequences of congressional independence under the separation of powers.

Percentage of legislative victories

Britain	Germany	France	Japan	United States
97%	87%	82%	77%	33%
Prime Minister				President

SOURCE: Richard Rose, *The Postmodern Presidency: George Bush Meets the World*, 2d ed. (Chatham, N.J.: Chatham House, 1991).

the ticket. This "coattail" effect, however, is usually small. An unpopular president may be of little help to a congressional candidate, of course, and may even be counterproductive. When Bill Clinton's popularity dropped in 1994, for example, political wags suggested that he bully congressional Democrats by threatening to campaign *for* them.*

Presidents too can benefit from these electoral alliances. Members of Congress elected with presidential support or on the president's coattails may show some gratitude, at least in the beginning. Moreover, presidents can advertise a congressional election victory as evidence of their own power and influence. Since presidents may lose from an alliance with a losing campaign, however, they are often very careful about whom they support and when. Thus Bill Clinton passed up the opportunity to campaign in the 1993 special senatorial election in Texas, knowing that a Democratic defeat was close to inevitable.[40]

- *"Schmoozing."* An often overlooked way to generate congressional support involves bringing senators and representatives into the White House and giving them access to the perquisites of power that the president can provide. Intimate White House meetings, private phone calls, and rides on Air Force One can be intoxicating, even to jaded politicians. At a minimum, the VIP treatment prevents members of Congress from feeling neglected or taken for granted.

- *Arm-twisting and palm-greasing.* Perhaps the most direct approach is to encourage key members of Congress to support the president by conferring benefits on those who cooperate and punishing those who do not. A helpful member of Congress may get presidential help on a favorite bill, or get a nice pork project for his or her district. A recalcitrant member might be punished by withholding such benefits. In modern times, however, presidents are severely handicapped in their ability to hand out carrots and sticks. Congress has increasingly restricted presidential discretion in the administration of the laws, and the electoral independence of most members of Congress has greatly limited the president in this area.

*Governor Ann Richards of Texas actually did ask the president not to campaign on her behalf in her 1994 reelection bid.

The White House and the People

The Framers designed the office of the presidency to stand above the people. The president was elected by the people only indirectly, through the Electoral College, and served the relatively long term of four years before standing for reelection. In both foreign and domestic policy, the president was to serve as a check on popular authority; the presidential veto, as Alexander Hamilton explained, would furnish "a salutary check upon the legislative body, calculated to guard the community against the effects of faction, precipitancy, or of any impulse unfriendly to the public good, which may happen to influence a majority" of the legislative branch.[41] The Framers' conception of the presidency was embodied in the person of George Washington, who though beloved by the people was surely not one of them.

The first president who styled himself as a man of the people and who drew on the people as a source of political power was Andrew Jackson, who was first elected to the office in 1828. A popular war hero, Jackson reconceived the presidency as a democratic office—the only person (except for the vice president) elected by all the people of the United States. The common people were Jackson's "blood relations," explained Martin Van Buren, who was Jackson's vice president. Jackson believed that "to labour for the good of the masses was a special mission assigned to him by the Creator and no man was ever better disposed to work in his vocation in season and out of season."[42]

Jackson's conception of the presidency transformed the office and provided a model that his successors have been happy to follow. As long as the presidency represented a check on popular government, presidential power was suspect and uncertain. Once presidential power could be conceived as an expression of the people's will, its potential was extraordinary. To their already impressive list of powers presidents could now add the ability to speak in the name of the people, to stand for the majority and against the various factions represented by Congress.

Popular support for the presidency was a key factor in the growth of presidential power during the course of the twentieth century. Presidents like Franklin Roosevelt and John F. Kennedy drew on and cultivated the backing of the people. Presidencies built on the support of the people, however, were highly vulnerable when that support was withdrawn. Both Lyndon Johnson and Richard Nixon learned that lesson the hard way, falling from grace and from power with unsettling speed.

If popular faith in the White House helped create the imperial presidency, the decline of popular support has helped shape the postmodern presidency. The scandals of Vietnam and Watergate and a persistent malaise, undermined popular suuport for the White House in the 1970s and 1980s. Presidents seemed to be caught in a deepening spiral; their reduced power made it difficult for them to maintain popular support, and their declining support in turn reduced their power. More recently, however, a strong economy combined with reduced popular expectations of the office have allowed President Clinton's poll ratings to remain high, even in the grip of personal and political scandals.

After 200 years, the presidency remains a paradox. Designed at least in part as a check on the will of the people, it is now dependent on the people for its political power. Learning how to draw on popular support without turning the presidency into an ongoing popularity contest remains the great challenge that postmodern presidents must face.

Should Presidents Serve a Single Six-Year Term?

The idea that the president should serve a single six-year term—with no possibility of reelection—has been around since the Constitutional Convention of 1787. It has been introduced in Congress as a constitutional amendment at least 160 times since 1826, and has been endorsed by some fifteen presidents.

Arguments for a six-year term

"Politics is bad." A president's reelection campaign is distracting and costly, proponents argue, and interferes with the president's main job, which is to look out for the best interests of the nation. "One of the main advantages of the six-year term is the elbow room it would give a president to make hard choices in the public interest without nagging doubts as to whether his decisions would affect his reelection chances," argues Jack Valenti, who served as an aid to Lyndon Johnson. In general, proponents argue that the six-year term would allow presidents the opportunity to get to work immediately and to make

the right decisions without regard to short-term electoral consequences.

Bureaucracies stay, presidents come and go. "A president now spends his first three years in office just establishing control over the bureaucracy," says former Attorney General Griffin Bell, who served under Jimmy Carter. "The current four-year term is actually too short to achieve any of the major changes and improvements that a president should accomplish." A six-year term would avoid abrupt policy changes both at home and abroad and give the nation the time it needs to judge the president's policies and proposals.

Advancing presidential credibility. As it now stands, first-term presidents find it difficult to persuade their audiences that they have the public interest at heart. "I think that if I had a six-year term, without any possibility of reelection, it would be an improvement," said Carter during his presidency. "No matter what I do as president now . . . a lot of the things I do are colored through the news media and in the minds of the American people by, Is this a campaign ploy or is it genuinely done by an incumbent president in the best interest of our country without any sort of personal advantage involved?"

The difficulty of maintaining public support. To govern effectively in the modern age, presidents must keep their popularity ratings high. But every re-

Summary

The Framers of the Constitution sought to create a presidency that was strong enough to govern effectively yet not so strong that it would infringe on the powers of the other two branches or on the rights of the people. Striking that balance between a powerful presidency and a constrained presidency remains a major challenge in American politics.

The formal powers of the presidency are outlined in Article II of the Constitution, and supplemented by a wide range of powers

delegated to the president by Congress. These formal powers include the power to execute the laws and to "take care" that the laws be faithfully executed; to appoint executive officials and federal judges; to propose and veto legislation; to command the armed forces of the United States; to make treaties and send ambassadors to foreign nations; and to receive ambassadors and thus recognize foreign governments. The president's appointment and treaty-making powers are generally subject to the approval of the Senate.

The Constitution is not the only source of presidential power, cent president has found the public fickle and unreliable, and has seen his popularity ratings rise and fall with great volatility. A six-year term would reduce the importance of short-term public support to the president's success in office and increase the importance of long-term factors. Writes the political scientist Bruce Buchanan: "A president decoupled from public opinion would cast off a dependency which inhibits more than it helps."

Arguments against a six-year term

"Politics is good."   It is not at all clear that removing electoral accountability would produce better presidential decisions all or even most of the time," writes Buchanan. "The case can be made that forcing leaders to explain themselves, defend their decisions, and rally support is a useful discipline, more likely to yield quality results on the average than isolated, unaccountable decision-making."

Presidents do not have to spend all their time campaigning.   Presidents are free to limit the amount of time they spend on partisan politics or delegate some of those responsibilities to others. In any event, writes Buchanan, time spent campaigning is also time spent "establishing and maintaining a relationship with the American people"–that is "a central presidential responsibility, not an irrelevant diversion."

Six years may be too many, or too few. President Woodrow Wilson put this point best: "A four-year term is too long for a President who is not a true spokesman of the people, who is imposed upon and does not lead," he argued. "It is too short a term for a President who is doing, or attempting, a great work of reform, and who has not had time to finish it. To change the term to six years would be to increase the likelihood of its being too long, without any assurance that it would, in happy cases, be long enough."

The lame duck problem.   Critics worry that a six-year president would become a "lame duck" immediately upon taking office. Ronald Reagan, they point out, was far more successful in his first term than in his second; his supporters even toyed with the idea of repealing the Twenty-second Amendment, allowing him to run again and ending his lame duck status. "Unless public support is convertible into electoral clout for the president and those who support him, it becomes significantly less effective as a political resource," Buchanan writes. "Under a single six-year term, a president might well be 'free to draw his strength from other sources.'" But unless some source of power suddenly appeared, such a president might become the political equivalent of a hundred-pound weakling.

Source: Bruce Buchanan, "A Six-Year One Term Presidency: A New Look at an Old Proposal," *Presidential Studies Quarterly* 18 (1988), pp. 129–141.

however. Presidents have also accrued a number of powers by tradition or through congressional delegation. These include the president's role as chief of state, crisis manager, economic manager, world leader, and party leader.

To be truly successful at governing, presidents need to combine their formal and informal powers into a blend that maximizes their ability to lead. According to the political scientist Richard Neustadt, the most important informal presidential powers are the power to bargain and the power to persuade. Although these might not seem like formidable powers, skillful and

popular presidents can use the advantages of the office to give them tremendous leverage over other decision makers, both at home and abroad. In modern times, presidents have frequently "gone public," appealing directly to the people in an effort to reach other decision makers.

Many presidents have found, however, that the resources of the presidency are not sufficient to fulfill the public's expectations of the office. The political scientist Richard Rose describes this condition as the *postmodern presidency*. The relative weakness and high expectations of the postmodern presidency stand in sharp contrast to earlier periods in American history. The *traditional presidency* was relatively weak, but expectations of the office were low. The *imperial presidency,* which stretched from Franklin D. Roosevelt to Richard Nixon, was strong both at home and abroad, and was able to live up to the people's high expectations of the office.

To lead effectively, the president must preside over both the executive branch and Congress. Managing the executive branch is no easy task. In the years since Franklin D. Roosevelt, presidents have expanded the role of the White House staff and of the Executive Office of the President, but they have never been truly successful in managing the executive bureaucracy. Some political scientists now suggest that presidents should abandon altogether the effort to be the nation's chief executive, and should content themselves with being the nation's chief political officer instead.

Presidents have been somewhat more successful in leading Congress, although only for brief periods of time. A president's major influence over Congress is the power to set the agenda. Presidents have also learned to lobby Congress, using both carrots and sticks to get what they want. Still, presidents have rarely been able to exercise a strong hand in dealing with Congress, especially after the first year in office. On several occasions in recent years, moreover, Congress has taken the initiative away from the White House and set an agenda for itself.

The American political system continues to struggle with the paradox of the presidency. Even in the twentieth century, the office of the presidency reveals both the strengths and weaknesses that the Framers built into it. At its best, the presidency can wield tremendous power on behalf of the people and the public interest. At its worst, the presidency can become so strong that it threatens the rights of the people, or, more commonly in modern times, so weak that it is unable to protect them.

Key Terms

Executive Power Clause
Take Care Clause
Commander in Chief Clause
Treaties
Executive agreements
Traditional presidency
Imperial presidency
Postmodern presidency
Executive Office of the President (EOP)

Office of Management and Budget (OMB)
Cabinet

Review Questions

1. What are the formal powers of the presidency?

2. What are the informal powers of the presidency?

3. What is Richard Neustadt's conception of presidential power? Why are the powers of bargaining and persuasion important?

4. Why is presidential popularity important? How can presidents maximize their popularity?

5. What does Richard Rose mean by the postmodern presidency? How does the postmodern presidency differ from the traditional and imperial presidencies?

6. How have presidents tried to improve their ability to manage the executive branch? Why do some analysts argue that the president should abandon the effort?

7. What is the president's role in the legislative process? How can presidents maximize their chances of success in Congress?

Suggested Readings

Burke, John P. *The Institutional Presidency.* Baltimore: Johns Hopkins University Press, 1992.

Jones, Charles O. *The Presidency in a Separated System.* Washington, D.C.: Brookings Institution, 1994.

Milkis, Sydney. *The President and the Parties: The Transformation of the American Party System Since the New Deal.* New York: Oxford University Press, 1993.

Nelson, Michael, ed. *The Presidency and the Political System,* 5th ed. Washington, D.C.: CQ Press, 1998.

Neustadt, Richard. *Presidential Power: The Politics of Leadership.* New York: Wiley, 1960.

Rose, Richard. *The Postmodern Presidency: George Bush Meets the World,* 2d ed. Chatham, N.J.: Chatham House, 1991.

Skowronek, Stephen. *The Politics Presidents Make: Leadership from John Adams to George Bush.* Cambridge, Mass.: Belknap Press of Harvard University Press, 1993.

Internet Resources

The official White House web site, with links to other government agencies, at:

http://www.whitehouse.gov

The Center for the Study of the Presidency, dedicated to the study of the presidency, government, and politics, at:

http://www.cspresidency.org

Links to the presidential libraries at:

http://www.yahoo.com/Art/Humanities/History/ Archives/Presidential Libraries

Hear recorded voice samples of nineteen U.S. presidents, going back to Grover Cleveland, at:

http://www.msu.edu/vincent/presidents.html

14

The Bureaucracy

It was "the largest jigsaw puzzle in the world," according to FBI investigator Ken Maxwell. Reconstructed in an abandoned hangar in Calverton, N. Y., from some 30,000 pieces of wreckage and debris was TWA Flight 800, a 747 jumbo jet that crashed into Long Island sound just minutes after take-off on July 17, 1996. It took ten months, ten thousand staff hours, and the combined work of countless federal, state, and local officials and agencies to recover and rebuild the plane—all to try to figure out what had happened and how to prevent it from happening again.

Sixteen months after the accident, National Transportation Safety Board (NTSB) Chairman Jim Hall convened a nationally televised public hearing on the crash of TWA Flight 800. For nearly a week, government officials and representatives of the private sector detailed the massive effort to recover and identify the bodies of the victims and the wreckage of the plane; to investigate the possibility of criminal or terrorist activity or of an accidental missile attack; and to study the possible causes of the accident and potential solutions to prevent future occurrences.

While some Americans watched the hearings with nothing but admiration for the extraordinary efforts of federal, state, and local officials, others were more cautious. The hearings also revealed a number of problems commonly associated with government agencies. The NTSB investigation overlapped with a parallel investigation by the Federal Bureau of Investigation; for the most part, the two agencies worked together, but there were signs of competition and duplication. Many of the victims' families complained

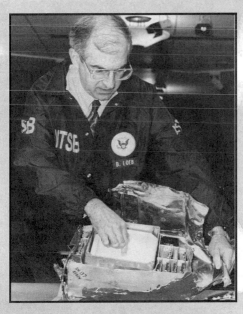

A National Transportation Safety Board official examines the voice cockpit recorder of the "black box" from the ill-fated TWA Flight 800.

that the government could have done more to help them in their time of crisis. And most seriously of all, it soon became apparent that the Federal Aviation Administration (FAA)—the agency charged with overseeing the airline industry and implementing the safety regulations of the NTSB—had been less than zealous in pursuing the NTSB's recommendations on preventing another catastrophe like Flight 800.

Although their investigation was not conclusive, the NTSB investigators believed that the crash of Flight 800 was caused when a spark ignited flammable fuel vapors in the aircraft's center wing tank. For decades, the FAA and the airline industry had assumed that the only way to prevent such explosions was to eliminate all sources of ignition. Early in its investigation, however, the NTSB recommended that steps be taken to reduce the flammability of fuel vapors. Although these suggestions had been made almost a year before the Flight 800 hearings, the FAA had yet to turn them into law. Meanwhile, the FAA's suggested voluntary inspection program had gone nowhere—the industry had inspected the fuel tanks on only a few of the hundreds of 747s currently in operation.

When he got the chance, NTSB Chairman Jim Hall put the FAA's feet to the fire. "What should I tell people when they ask me should I be flying the 747?" he demanded of an FAA official and an industry representative. "If you gentlemen can tell me what you have been doing, I'd like to know." Under the weight of Hall's questioning, the FAA's go-slow attitude began to crumble. "There is no doubt we are going to do something," said an FAA official, although he did not say exactly what. Still, Hall and others saw movement in the FAA's position. "In the ongoing investigation," he told reporters, "the most encouraging thing here is I see a change of attitude on the part of the FAA and Boeing."[1]

Bureaucracies are large organizations that make it possible to carry out programs of a size unmatched by any enterprise before the modern age. Government bureaucracies allow the nation to wage war on a modern scale, provide social security and welfare benefits to millions of people, and collect billions of dollars in taxes.

Ideally, bureaucracies provide a means by which government policy can be carried out fairly and efficiently. The bureaucracy's hierarchical organization and reliance on rules provide accountability and protect against corruption and bias. However, these very advantages can make bureaucratic government seem rigid, inefficient, and unaccountable.

The challenge of bureaucratic government precisely mirrors the larger challenge of government itself. The bureaucracy must be given the authority and capacity to carry out the many tasks expected of a modern government. At the same time, however, a way must be found to control the bureaucracy and keep it in check, ensuring that unelected officials do not abuse their power or overstep the legitimate bounds of their authority.

Although the bureaucracy is mainly housed in the executive branch, all three branches have a role in supervising its activities. Thus the bureaucracy has become a focal point for the constitutional competition between the White House, Congress, and the courts. Agencies owe their existence, and their annual budgets, to Congress; yet they must also respond to political priorities imposed by the White House, and to legal requirements imposed by the judiciary. Through it all, the bureaucracy must deal with pressure from various interest groups—some of which seek to frustrate its activities, others to promote them. Finally, the bureaucracy stands on the front lines of the nation-state relationship, working with state and local authorities to address their various concerns while at the same time ensuring that federal mandates are met.

It is easy to fall into the common habit of blaming the bureaucracy for all that is wrong with American government, and of giving it little or no credit for what goes right. The real picture, however, is far more complicated. Understanding what the bureaucracy is and what it does, and evaluating its impact on American political life, are the purposes of this chapter.

Questions to Keep in Mind

What are the primary characteristics of the bureaucratic form of government? What are its strengths and weaknesses?

How do the three branches of government check and balance the power of the bureaucracy?

How, and under what circumstances, does the bureaucracy help promote, or undermine, the public interest?

Basic Concepts

Of the nearly 4 million people who work for the United States, exactly 542 are elected by the American people. Of the rest, a little over a million are soldiers and sailors. The others—nearly three million—can best be classified as bureaucrats.*

The word **bureaucracy** literally means "rule of offices" (*bureau,* in French, means "office"). It refers to the maze of offices, agencies, departments, and divisions that characterizes any modern government, or, for that matter, any large and complex organization. Some form of bureaucracy is essential to the administration of the programs carried out by modern governments.

Contrary to popular assumptions, most federal bureaucrats do not work in Washington. And the number of state and local workers far outpaces the number of federal workers.

Characteristics of Bureaucracy

A bureaucratic system is marked by a number of distinctive characteristics:

- *Hierarchy.* Power in a bureaucracy is exercised from the top down, at least theoretically, forming the pyramid structure so familiar from organization charts. Officials at any given level are responsible to those immediately above them, and eventually up the chain of command to the top. In turn, officials supervise the activities of those below.
- *Specialization.* As one moves down the bureaucratic pyramid, the officials and offices become more specialized. Conversely, as one moves up the ladder the officials and offices are responsible for ever broader areas of responsibility. For example, the secretary of state is responsible for all of foreign policy. Beneath the secretary are a number of assistant secretaries, each with responsibility over a particular part of the world or a specific area of policy. One, for instance, is the assistant secretary for Near Eastern and South Asian affairs. The assistant secretary's subordinates include five deputy assistant secretaries, an executive director, two special assistants, a public affairs adviser, an economic affairs director, and nine directors with responsibilities for a particular country or countries in the Middle East or South Asia.
- *Division of labor.* Bureaucracies divide power not only vertically but also horizontally. For example, a federal agency might have separate offices to handle personnel matters, accounting, purchasing, and data processing. These horizontal divisions of labor typically cut across the vertical divisions. Thus the Office of Personnel Management handles a variety of personnel matters for all federal agencies, whether high or low on the bureaucratic pyramid.

  Individuals or bureaus that provide specialized services to other members of the bureaucracy are known as *staff officers* or *staff agencies.* Those that perform the actual functions of the organization are known as *line officers* or *line agencies.* The origins of

---

*For the record: as of 1993, federal civilian employment totaled 2,847,000. Of these, 796,000 worked for the Department of Defense and 852,000 for the U.S. Postal Service. In addition, there were 1,056,000 active duty military personnel.

these terms is military: an army lieutenant who commands men and women in the field is a line officer; a colonel in charge of transportation services is a staff officer.

- *Rules.* The bureaucratic model favors rule-based decision making, leaving minimal room (again, in theory) for individual discretion. Rule-based decision making goes hand in hand with specialization and the division of labor. Decisions made at one level of the hierarchical chain of command must be carried out by people below. Likewise, policies developed by specialized offices (such as personnel or accounting) must be implemented across the board.

Public Versus Private Bureaucracies   Governments are hardly the only institutions of modern life that rely on bureaucratic structures to get things done. Bureaucratic forms characterize the operations of all large-scale organizations, including corporations, universities, and hospitals. As the political scientist James Q. Wilson points out, a corporation like McDonald's restaurants is as much a bureaucracy as any government agency. McDonald's "regulates virtually every detail of its employees' behavior by a complex and all-encompassing set of rules," writes Wilson. "Its operations manual is six hundred pages long and weighs four pounds. In it one learns that french fries are to be nine thirty-seconds of an inch thick and that grill workers are to place hamburger patties on the grill from left to right, six to a row for six rows. Then they are to flip the third row first, followed by the fourth, fifth, and sixth rows, and finally the first and second. The amount of sauce placed on each bun is precisely specified."[2]

What distinguishes private from public bureaucracies is not their organizational structure or style but the constraints under which each must operate. The manager of a fast-food restaurant, for example, might be authorized to dismiss an irresponsible employee and hire a new one virtually on the spot. A government manager, by contrast, might be required to follow a complex procedure designed to protect the rights of government employees—including issuing a warning, giving formal notice of dismissal, even allowing the worker an opportunity for a hearing. The difference lies not in the nature of bureaucracy but in the fact that McDonald's and the government have put different requirements on their managers.

The most important difference between government and private bureaucracies is that private companies are organized to achieve maximum efficiency (that is, profits), whereas government bureaucracies are forced to serve many different goals, some of which may conflict with one another. When a private company buys a product from a supplier, it is concerned (at least in theory) only with quality and price. A government bureaucracy may also be asked to consider fairness to minority businesses and may be forced to go through elaborate procedures to avoid the possibility that one supplier may gain an unfair advantage. The government bureaucracy may well be less efficient than its private counterpart, but not because it is a bureaucracy.

Growth and Reform of the Federal Bureaucracy

The development of both private and public bureaucracies was largely a nineteenth-century phenomenon. In the beginning, the United States government was decidedly small and unbureaucratic, reflecting its minimal responsibilities. In 1802 the entire government establishment in Washington comprised 291 government officials. The White House consisted of the president and a personal secretary. The home office of the State Department employed 10 officials, the entire Treasury Department just 89. There was no Justice Department, only the attorney general, and he had no staff.

Growth of the Federal Bureaucracy

The federal bureaucracy began to grow in the 1820s, during the era of President Andrew Jackson. The driving force was the establishment of the first mass political parties. Politicians quickly realized that a government job was the perfect way to reward the party faithful, and Jackson began the practice of dismissing the government workers appointed by his predecessors and appointing his own loyalists in their place. Jackson defended his approach as a way to limit corruption by creating "rotation in office," but friends and critics alike recognized that Jackson's explanation was largely pretext. "To the victor belong the spoils" was the way one senator put it, giving the practice a name: the **spoils system**.

The increasing responsibilities of the national government over the next fifty years provided constant pressure for the expansion of the executive branch. The spoils system became ever more elaborate and involved a growing number of people. By the 1880s, there were some 130,000 government employees. Critics charged that the system led to "incompetence, inefficiency, [and] corruption," and calls for reform grew louder and more insistent.[3]

Reforming the Bureaucracy: Then and Now

When a frustrated office seeker assassinated President James A. Garfield in 1881, pressure for reform of the spoils system became irresistible. In 1883, Congress passed the Pendleton Civil Service Reform Act, the first of many laws designed to reform the executive branch. The **Pendleton Act** aimed not only to end the spoils system but also to modernize and professionalize the administration of national policy. That meant the creation and implementation of a bureaucratic system.

The Pendleton Act insulated civil service workers from party politics and mandated that government jobs be offered on the basis of merit. Although top-level political appointees could still be appointed on a partisan basis, most government workers were covered under the new rules. Over the next few decades, the executive branch continued to grow, increasingly stocked with professional employees who made government work their career (the creation of the federal retirement system in 1923 greatly increased the incentive for employees to stay on). By the 1920s, 80 percent of the 560,000 government employees worked in the civil service.

The emergency conditions of the Great Depression and World War II created pressures to relax civil service rules, so the government could bring in experts quickly and on a temporary basis. However, in 1938 and again at war's end, Congress acted to strengthen the civil service system. Further reforms were adopted in the 1950s and 1970s.

The goal of all these reforms was to streamline, professionalize, and depoliticize the federal bureaucracy. Unfortunately, these aims often conflicted with one another, making effective reform difficult. To ensure that government employees were not dismissed for partisan reasons, for example, Congress imposed complex and rigid procedures that make removal even of incompetent workers difficult. In addition, Congress frequently tried to piggyback unrelated goals on civil service reform legislation. For example, at the end of World War II Congress passed legislation requiring that military

> *"When in charge, ponder. When in trouble, delegate. When in doubt, mumble."*
>
> —James H. Boren, advice to bureaucrats

veterans be given a preference on hiring decisions—a policy that directly contradicts the principle that hiring decisions should be based on merit alone.[4]

The Bureaucracy Today   In keeping with the general principles of the Pendleton Act, civil servants today are hired under the merit system, often on the basis of an examination. Once they fulfill a probationary period, they are granted tenure in office, and can be removed only under set procedures. Promotions and pay raises are also based on merit or on other nonpartisan criteria, such as seniority.

The civil service system has succeeded in creating a permanent workforce that is largely immune to partisanship. According to many critics, however, the system may work too well: they see the federal bureaucracy as a permanently entrenched fourth branch of government that is inefficient, unresponsive, and undemocratic. These criticisms will be examined later in the chapter.

Political Appointees. The top leadership in virtually every government agency is appointed by the president, subject to the advice and consent of the Senate. These "political appointees," numbering around two thousand, are exempt from the requirements of the civil service act and serve either at the pleasure of the president or for a specified period. Many political appointees are newcomers to Washington, or at least to their agencies, and are generalists rather than experts in any particular field.

Technically, most decisions of the federal bureaucracy are made in the name of the political leadership. In practice, however, senior civil servants do most of the work and much of the decision making. Unlike the political appointees, the top civil servants are seasoned experts, well versed not only in their fields but in the ways of Washington. They quickly become indispensable to their political superiors and can then exercise extraordinary behind-the-scenes influence. The political appointees are then said to have been "captured" by their agencies or, more colorfully, to have "gone native"—meaning that the political appointees are effectively controlled by people who are technically their subordinates.

There are exceptions, of course, especially in agencies that are highly visible or command the direct attention of the president. Such agencies can become battlefields, in which civil servants and the political leadership slog away at each other, with Congress often enlisting the civil servants as surrogate warriors. Ultimately time is on the side of the civil service, since they (and some members of Congress) stay forever while presidents come and go.

Protecting the People's Rights. The tremendous expansion of the national government's role after 1880, and especially after 1932, greatly increased the interactions between the people and the national bureaucracy. Citizens dealt with government agencies to pay their taxes and to receive social security or other benefits. Businesses were increasingly forced to put up with government regulation, inspections, and licensing procedures. These developments raised two concerns. First, the power of the government to impose fines or penalties and to withhold valuable benefits made it necessary to design procedures to ensure fairness and protect individual rights. Second, the possibility that powerful interest groups could exercise undue influence over government decisions made it necessary to create rules that would open up the decision-making process to all citizens.

In 1946, therefore, Congress passed the **Administrative Procedures Act (APA).** The APA established clear procedures that government agencies must follow when creating rules or making decisions in individual cases. Above all, the APA requires that citizens have the opportunity to be heard. Depending on circumstances, the right to be heard might mean only that citizens be given the right to comment on proposed rules or regulations to be issued by the executive branch, or it might amount to a formal hearing, complete with lawyers and administrative law judges. The APA also authorized citizens to appeal adverse decisions of the federal bureaucracy to the federal courts, which are empowered to enforce the requirements of the APA and other laws and to protect individual rights.[5]

Other important laws designed to protect the liberties of the people include the **Freedom of Information Act (FOIA),** which gives scholars, the news media, and ordinary citizens access to much of the information held by the government; the Government in the Sunshine Act, which compels agencies to open many of their meetings to the public; and the Whistle Blowers Protection Act, which mandates that agencies may not punish an employee who reports fraud, waste, corruption, and abuses within the bureaucracy.

Organization of the Federal Bureaucracy The modern federal bureaucracy comprises a wide variety of organizations, including cabinet-level departments, **independent agencies,** regulatory commissions, and government corporations. Most of the agencies of the federal government are housed within one of fourteen cabinet-level departments, which together employ more than 90 percent of all nonmilitary federal employees.[6]

Many small and specialized agencies operate independently, outside of any cabinet department. Examples include the Federal Reserve Board (Fed), the Environmental Protection Agency (EPA), and the National Aeronautics and Space Administration (NASA). Some agencies, although located within a cabinet agency, are nonetheless granted a great deal of independence under the law. Examples include most of the federal regulatory commissions, such as the Food and Drug Administration (FDA), which is located within the Department of Health and Human Services, and the Occupational Safety and Health Administration (OSHA), which is part of the Department of Labor.

President Bill Clinton introduces his second-term cabinet in December 1996. Clinton's cabinet selections stressed diversity, with prominent places for women, African Americans, and Latinos.

POLITICS LIGHT

Investigating Native Customs in Washington

Written over three decades ago, this humorous account of the culture of Washington, D.C., remains surprisingly current.

When visiting a strange country like Washington, it's incumbent on us responsible ace newsmen to file what we call a "backgrounder." You know, a lengthy review of annual rainfall and grazing conditions with a few paragraphs about quaint native customs thrown in to sex things up a little.

Well, Washington is several miles square and about as tall, say, as the Washington Monument, give or take a little. The winters aren't too hot. Neither is the rest of the climate. The natives, in general, are sullen.

While the outside world refers to it as "Washington," the natives call it "the District," short for "District of Columbia." They think of themselves as "experts." The population, at the moment, consists of 998,762 experts and two tourists from Canton, Ohio, who, on being interviewed, said they hadn't the foggiest notion of what was wrong with U.S. foreign policy.

The main industries are eating, drinking, and talking. The major import and export—indeed, the staple of the economy—is money. . . . The local unit of currency is "the Million Dollar." Usually written "$1 million." Many of these, however, are required to purchase anything. . . . In recent years, a new denomination, "the Billion Dollar" (written "$1 billion") has come into wide use. And lately one even hears "the Trillion Dollar" mentioned on occasion. But only in referring to the national debt. . . .

Lesser denominations, such as "the Thousand Dollar" or "the Hundred Dollar" have, like the old French centime, virtually disappeared from circulation. And the only place the natives use real money, such as the dollar, is after office hours. Indeed, any mention of real money tends to make the natives restless. . . .

Despite the obvious need for a drastic currency reform, however, the local economy is booming. Everywhere the visitor looks, new buildings are going up. And when you realize that the natives neither manufacture nor produce anything of salable value, this expansion is all the more fantastic.

The new buildings are, of course, all being constructed in the Four-square Monolithic Style of modern native architecture. The natives, it is believed, pour a solid cube of concrete, hollow out the inside, and stick a flagpole on top. . . .

Congressional deregulation of the cable television industry disappointed many consumers, who faced higher basic cable rates after the government eased its rules.

Let us now refer to the social structure of the country. . . . The best known of the local tribes are, of course, the Solons, occupying the strategic heights of Capitol Hill, and the Presidents, who live on the flats perhaps a mile away. . . . Lesser known are the numerous other interesting tribes of the flats, such as "State," "Commerce," "Interior," "NRA" [National Recovery Agency] (now extinct), and so forth. While nominally joined by treaty to the Presidents, these lesser tribes devote most of their energies to battling each other. . . .

The young warriors of each tribe are prepared for leadership in these devious wars by . . . complex rituals. . . . [Two] of the simpler forms will be discussed here: Leaking [and] Copy-to-ing. . . .

Leaking is practiced only at the highest levels in each tribe. When a mistake is made, Subchief X announces quickly that no mistake was made. Then he Leaks the inside information to the Columnists (a tribe of local historians of tremendous importance) that in reality it was a horrendous mistake. And that Subchief Y made it. When three or more Columnists print the leak, it becomes known as a fact. And Subchief Y is stripped of one secretary, his leather couch, and four buttons from his phone.

Copy-to-ing is practiced on the lowest levels. Should Al Z, a young native working under Chief Y,

make a minor slip, he will immediately receive fourteen interoffice memos from his fellow tribesmen. Such as: "Al, I was very sorry to see us get in that awful bind. But I did warn you at Staff beforehand. Perhaps something can still be saved from the wreckage."

At the bottom of each memo is typed: COPY TO CHIEF Y. While no chief could possibly read all the scores of copies of memos he receives each day, the psychological damage on Al Z of these words, COPY TO CHIEF Y, can only be imagined. . . .

With all this intertribal and intratribal warfare, the natives, understandably enough, have little interest in the outside world, except as its events affect their internecine quarrels. Indeed many modern anthropologists feel that if the natives could ever be knit into one homogeneous unit, their skill and deviousness in the arts of warfare would inevitably mean that Washington would soon come to rule the world.

As of now, however, this danger appears extremely remote.

SOURCE: Arthur Hoppe, "Interesting Native Customs in Washington and Other Savage Lands," in *The Love Everybody Crusade* (New York: Doubleday, 1963).

Managing the bureaucracy from the White House is no easy task, and several agencies—including the Executive Office of the President and the White House staff—exist in part to help the president handle his managerial role. A discussion of the president's administrative functions appears later in this chapter.

The Federal Bureaucracy Under the Constitution

Not surprisingly, the Constitution says little about the federal bureaucracy. The development of large-scale bureaucratic structures came long after the Founding period, and the Framers of the original document could not anticipate the problems and challenges such a system would create. Moreover, the Constitution has never been amended to reflect the growth of the administrative state or to address the issues raised by modern bureaucratic government.

Bureaucracy in the Original Constitution   The Framers did not expect the president to govern alone. The Constitution specifically recognized that there would be several executive departments and that the government would be carried out by various "officers of the United States," who would generally be appointed by the president with the "advice and consent" of the Senate. Besides the power of appointment, the Constitution gave the president the power to require "the principal Officer in each of the executive Departments" to provide a written opinion on any relevant subject. The actual establishment of the various departments, however, was left to Congress.

Executive Branch or Third Branch?   The Constitution places all executive power in the president. Thus it would seem that the president should be able to exercise control over all executive agencies and their decisions. However, the relationship between the White House and the executive agencies is not so simple.

Do Agencies Owe Their Primary Allegiance to the President or to the Law? From early on the Supreme Court recognized that Congress could charge executive officials below the president with specific duties under the law. When Congress created such duties, federal officers were expected to comply with the law regardless of their own, or the president's, views.

In 1958, for example, the Supreme Court ruled that the secretary of state could not refuse to issue passports to citizens who refused to answer questions about whether they had ever been communists. Executive officials often do have discretion, however; thus in 1984, the Court ruled that the secretary of state could refuse to grant passports for travel to Cuba.[7]

On rare occasions, executive officers may be forced to choose between fulfilling their moral or legal duty as they see it and obeying a specific presidential order to the contrary. One recourse is to stand up to the president, resigning if necessary. Another is to follow the president's directive and allow the injured party to seek redress in court.

Independence of Regulatory Boards and Commissions. The Supreme Court has long recognized the constitutionality of regulatory boards and commissions. For constitutional purposes, these agencies are distinguished by the fact that their leaders do not serve at the pleasure of the president, but for a fixed term or under conditions set out by law. Typically, the heads of such agencies can be removed from office only for specific cause, such as misconduct or inability to fulfill the duties of the office. The Supreme Court upheld the validity of such limitations on the president's removal power in 1935, holding that President Franklin Roosevelt could not remove a member of the Federal Trade Commission except in accordance with law. In 1958, the Court extended this ruling to cover a member of the War Claims Commission who was appointed to a life term, even though the relevant statute said nothing at all about the removal power.[8]

More recently, the Court has expressed concerns about congressional delegations of power to agencies that seem more beholden to Congress than to the president. In a 1986 decision, the Court held that Congress could not grant executive power to an officer who could be removed only by act of Congress. Such an arrangement, the Court said, violated the separation of powers.[9]

Delegation of Power   The growth in the scope of the federal government's activities after 1880 and the growing complexity of federal programs made it increasingly difficult for Congress to keep up with its responsibilities. Congress soon learned the advantages of delegating legislative power to the executive agencies, which had the time, resources, and expertise to deal with broad and complicated issues.

The Supreme Court recognized as early as 1892 that the Constitution limits Congress's ability to delegate legislative power to the executive. This limit—known as the **delegation doctrine**—does not come from any specific constitutional provision but rather from the principle of the separation of powers. In practice, however, the Court gave Congress broad authority to let the executive agencies "fill up the details" of its general laws. Although the Court did strike down two New Deal laws on the grounds that they gave the president "unlimited authority" to determine policy, it soon reversed course and began approving wholesale delegations of legislative power to the president.[10] Thus the delegation doctrine has had little practical impact since the 1930s.

In 1944, for example, the Court upheld the Emergency Price Control Act of 1942, a wartime act that authorized the Office of Price Administration (OPA) to set maximum prices for various consumer goods. The delegation of power in this case was particularly broad; the OPA administrator was given no guidelines or limits except to fix prices that "in his judgment will be fair and equitable and will effectuate the purposes of this Act." These standards, the Court ruled, were "sufficiently definite and precise" to meet the requirements of the Constitution.[11]

The claim that Congress has exceeded its authority to delegate power arises every so often, but the Supreme Court has shown no inclination to go back to its New Deal–style scrutiny of such problems. It is fair to conclude that today there are no legal obstacles to broad delegations of congressional power to the executive.

What the Bureaucracy Does and How It Does It

The executive bureaucracy is involved in every aspect of government activity, from writing laws to punishing offenders. The following is a quick survey of the various roles played by the federal bureaucracy.

Administering the Law and Managing Programs

Programs do not administer themselves. Nor do laws, rules, and regulations apply themselves. Carrying out federal programs and applying the law to particular cases are the primary functions of the federal bureaucracy.

Many of the activities of the executive bureaucracy are familiar. The Internal Revenue Service (IRS) collects taxes. The post office delivers the mail. The National Park Service manages the national parks. The Coast Guard patrols the shoreline, assists those in trouble, and inspects suspicious vessels. The activities of the federal bureaucracy are as varied as the programs they carry out.

In many cases, agencies must coordinate their activities with local or state agencies, or supervise the implementation of federal programs by state and local authorities. For example, most federal welfare programs are run by the states under federal grants, which are managed and overseen by the federal Department of Health and Human Services.

Policy Development

Whether the idea for a government program arises within the executive bureaucracy, in the White House, in Congress, or in the private sector, it is a fair bet that executive branch personnel will be involved in the development and drafting of legislation. When Congress and

Are Bureaucracies Dangerous?

If newspaper editorials, campaign rhetoric, and the complaints of ordinary citizens are to be believed, the bureaucracy does not do anything very well. Bureaucratic horror stories are now commonplace, and public confidence in the public sector has sunk to dreadful lows. Almost nine in ten Americans think that "people in the government waste a lot of money we pay in taxes," while almost two-thirds believe that the Internal Revenue Service "frequently abuses its powers."*

There are indeed real problems with the bureaucratic style of government. But any assessment of bureaucratic government must weigh it against the real alternatives, which are far less desirable in practice than most Americans might think. Here are two sides of the story.

Yes, bureaucracies are dangerous.

The bureaucracy is probably the most criticized part of the government. Among the common complaints:

Bureaucracies are rigid and unresponsive.
Excessive rigidity is the classic bureaucratic problem. One of the key justifications for bureaucratic government is to rid the government of favoritism, corruption, and bias by creating clear and enforceable rules to guide government decision making and by establishing complex procedures to prevent official corruption. An unfortunate side effect is the government's inability to recognize and do something about the inevitable cases that do not neatly fit existing rules. Bureaucracies can also be unresponsive—attempting to deal with the government often leaves the average citizen exhausted and exasperated. Phone lines are continually busy; clerks and receptionists are unfriendly; officials are unhelpful or unsympathetic. A recent study by the Internal Revenue Service, for example, found that only 26 percent of callers could even get through to its telephone tax advice line.

Bureaucracies are inefficient. Another common criticism of the bureaucracy is that it is inefficient. Like rigidity, inefficiency arises largely from the attempt to prevent corruption and bias. For example, bureaucracies typically generate mountains of paperwork (much of it in triplicate) in an effort to ensure that rules and procedures are closely followed. Work is often divided among more than one agency, causing duplication and waste, and diffusing responsibility. And government bureaucracies are bloated: according to one study, the ratio of administrators to staff members at government research labs was almost twice as high as in comparable private-sector facilities.†

Bureaucracies routinely outlive their usefulness. Bureaucracies do not die, nor do they fade away. It is extremely difficult for the federal government to eliminate a program that is firmly entrenched both in Congress and in the bureaucracy, even if that program has proven ineffective or counterproductive. To take one extreme case, the Federal Board of Tea Testers—established in 1897 to set standards for teas imported into the United States—was not abolished until 1993.

Bureaucracies allow individuals to ignore the moral consequences of their actions. A particularly serious criticism of bureaucratic government was made by the political philosopher Hannah Arendt, who studied the role of the Nazi bureaucrat Adolf Eichmann in the mass murder of European Jews during the Holocaust of World War II. Arendt pointed out that the structure and style of a bureaucracy make it easy for government officials to separate their actions from the *moral consequences of those actions.* In other words, a man who would recoil in horror at the prospect of killing another human being face-to-face finds no difficulty in signing a piece of paper that sends millions of innocent people to their deaths.

The force of Arendt's argument was particularly clear in the case of Nazi Germany, but it applies in a less horrific fashion in any bureaucratic environment. Government bureaucracies all too often deal with people as numbers, or as legal generalities, or as mere names and addresses. The structure of bureaucracies divides up responsibility for specific actions, making it difficult to assign blame (or credit) to any one individual. Finally, bureaucracies tend to create and use language in ways that obscure reality. Nazi Germany, as Arendt points out, specifically devised "language rules" to provide cover for those involved in the process of mass murder. Thus "killing" became "final solution," "evacuation," or "special treatment." Much bureaucratic speech is simply ludicrous rather than reprehensible. But the distinctive language of the bureaucracy is used to conceal or disguise reality even in the United States. When the Pentagon speaks of "collateral damage" instead of civilian casualties, for example, it comes perilously close to the kind of language rules that Arendt described.

No, don't blame the bureaucracy.

A few commentators have avoided the crowd and taken up the challenge of defending the bureaucracy. Among their arguments:

Bureaucracies make things happen. The massive and complex government programs we have come to expect and rely upon would be impossible without the bureaucracy. Many of those who criticize bureaucracy in general have nothing but praise for the military—without considering that America's armed forces comprise the largest bureaucracy in the world. Whether invading Kuwait or delivering social security checks, the bureaucracy's tasks are monumental. And despite the conventional wisdom, most of those tasks are carried out successfully.

Bureaucracies bring expertise to government. Whenever Congress passes a law, whole armies of lawyers, accountants, and policy advisers stand ready to advise their clients on how to maximize the benefits and minimize the burdens of the new legislation. To avoid disaster, the government must constantly evaluate its programs and be always ready to make adjustments and modifications when neces-

sary. Such a task is far beyond the capabilities of Congress or the generalist political leadership in the executive branch. The tax code of the United States already runs to thousands of pages, and virtually every sentence and phrase is the subject of intense scrutiny and legal debate. Only a well-staffed and highly qualified bureaucracy can cope with the daily challenges such a program presents.

Bureaucracies provide stability and predictability. Even bad government programs or regulations can be overcome if they are stable and predictable. Affected parties can learn how to get around such problems, or at least learn to live with them. On the other hand, even good reforms may cause serious problems if they are implemented haphazardly or inconsistently. Government programs that are handed over to the bureaucracy are notoriously stable. Although this can mean that programs outlive their usefulness, more often it means that programs are enforced consistently over time. Such stability is especially reassuring to the business community, which abhors uncertainty.

Much of what the bureaucracy gets blamed for is not its fault. Blaming the IRS for America's tax system is like blaming the messenger; the tax agency's job is not to create the tax code, but to enforce it. Much of the complexity and unfairness in the tax code that Americans routinely complain about should be blamed on Congress, not the IRS. Likewise, government agencies are often understaffed, subjected to rigid reporting requirements, and forced to pursue conflicting goals—all of which make it difficult for them to do their jobs efficiently and effectively.

Consider the question of efficiency. Many Americans believe that private-sector delivery services, such as Federal Express, are more "efficient" than the U.S. Postal Service. But the postal service must operate under a number of cumbersome constraints that its private sector counterparts are free to ignore. Congress, for example, has traditionally chosen to

(continued)

build a post office in every small town, regardless of the economic value of such facilities. Congress has also mandated that first-class postage be set at a uniform rate throughout the entire country—including Alaska and Hawaii. If we could measure precisely such goods as "maintaining honest behavior, producing a fair allocation of benefits, and generating popular support," writes the political scientist James Q. Wilson, "then we would be in a position to judge the true efficiency of a governmental agency and decide when it is taking too much time or spending too much money achieving all that we expect of it. But

we cannot measure those things nor do we agree about their relative importance, and so government will always appear to be inefficient compared to organizations that have fewer goals."‡

Gallup Poll Monthly (September 1993), p. 31; "Public by 3 to 1 Margin Believes IRS Abuses Its Powers," *Gallup Poll* (October 1997).
†James Q. Wilson, *Bureaucracy: What Government Agencies Do and Why They Do It* (New York: Basic Books, 1989), p. 113.
‡Ibid., p. 318.
SOURCES: James Q. Wilson, *Bureaucracy: What Government Agencies Do and Why They Do It* (New York: Basic Books, 1989); Charles T. Goodsell, *The Case for Bureaucracy: A Public Administration Polemic* (Chatham, NJ: Chatham House Books, 1994).

the White House are controlled by the same party, such cooperation between the two branches may be open and explicit. Even when the two branches are divided, however, executive officials often cooperate with key members of Congress or key subcommittees. Moreover, Congress requires the executive branch to write numerous official reports and to respond to countless official and unofficial inquiries, some of which may be useful in the development of new legislation or in the modification of existing law.

In any event, no congressional hearing on proposed legislation would be complete without the input of relevant members of the executive branch. While it is usually the political appointees who testify rather than the civil servants, the testimony itself is typically prepared by bureaucratic experts, who thus exert considerable influence.

To facilitate the development of effective policy, all government agencies devote considerable effort to conducting research and collecting and analyzing data. At a minimum, such activities are necessary to determine the effectiveness of agency programs and to improve agency services.

Some government agencies devote much or all of their efforts to the collection and analysis of data. The Bureau of Labor Statistics, for example, collects and publishes information about the economy, such as unemployment and income levels. The Center for Disease Control keeps tabs on public health statistics, such as the number of AIDS cases or measles outbreaks.

Rule-Making and Regulation

Once a law is passed, its meaning must be clarified and its details filled in. Congress usually leaves those jobs to the executive branch. Agency directives designed to clarify or implement laws passed by Congress are known as **rules,** or informally as *regulations.* Rules have the force of law, and violating them can lead to civil or criminal penalties, including imprisonment.

Agency rules and regulations must comply with the Constitution and with any specific guidelines imposed by Congress. In addition, agency rule making must follow the procedural requirements of the Administrative Procedures Act and any other relevant statutes or executive orders. Proposed rules must be published in the *Federal Register* at least sixty days before formal adoption, except under urgent circumstances. During this "notice and comment" period, interested parties have an opportunity to express their views on the proposed rule, usu-

---

FEDERAL EMERGENCY MANAGEMENT AGENCY

⟶ *CFO Bulletin*

OFFICE OF FINANCIAL MANAGEMENT

NUMBER 20   NOVEMBER 17, 1993

ALL FEMA EMPLOYEES

Subject: AUTHORIZED RETURN HOME TRAVEL DURING EXTENDED TEMPORARY DUTY (TDY) ASSIGNMENT.

This CFO Bulletin is to clarify recent discrepancies regarding authorized return home travel for FEMA personnel on extended TDY assignment.

FEMA allows employees on extended TDY assignments to return home once every 30 to 45 days at government expense. Disaster Assistance Employees (DAE's) assisting in presidentially declared disasters may also be returned home once every 30 to 45 days.

With the approaching holidays, it has come to our attention that some employees would rather travel to alternate locations instead of returning home. Even though the alternate travel may produce a cost savings to the government, the Federal Travel Regulation does not allow FEMA the flexibility to reimburse travel expenses to alternate locations. Employees may only be authorized to return to his/her official duty station or place of abode.

Bureaucracies often become rigid, as illustrated in this 1993 memo denying FEMA employees the opportunity to travel where they wanted for the holidays.

ally in writing. A rule or regulation that fails to comply with any of these requirements can be challenged in court. In general, courts show great deference to an agency's interpretation of laws that apply directly to its own function, although they are occasionally willing to strike down a rule or regulation, especially if it clearly violates Congress's intent.[12]

Congressional subcommittees often make it clear to the executive agencies how they want specific rules and regulations written. Typically, agencies have little choice but to comply, although high-level conflicts sometimes arise between the legislative and executive branches. In

SOURCE: Compiled from successive volumes of the *Federal Register* (Washington, D.C.: U.S. Government Printing Office).

extreme cases, Congress can override agency decisions by passing a new law. For example, in 1977, Congress overrode the Food and Drug Administration's ban on the artificial sweetener saccharin despite concerns that the artificial sweetener caused cancer in laboratory animals.[13]

Interpreting and Applying the Law

To comply with the law, affected parties need to know what the law means and how it applies in their particular circumstances. No set of rules and regulations can take every possible case into account, and difficult cases inevitably arise. For example, the National Labor Relations Act protects the right of "employees" to organize labor unions and bargain collectively with their employers. However, the act specifically exempts "supervisory employees." But exactly who qualifies as a "supervisory employee" is not clear. When the United Auto Workers sought to organize foremen at the Packard Motor Car company into a union, the National Labor Relations Board (NLRB) had to decide whether foremen were "supervisory employees" within the meaning of the law. Although foremen had the power to discipline workers and to recommend promotion and demotion, they did not have the power to hire and fire; thus the NLRB ruled that they were not supervisory employees and were entitled to organize a union.[14]

Many such ambiguities are resolved in a friendly way, through consultation and negotiation between the agency and the affected parties. Other disputes are handled through "private letter rulings," which provide a definitive written interpretation of the law for the affected parties to follow. Sometimes, however, the agency and the client cannot reach agreement, and more formal and more confrontational procedures are called for.

In such cases the agencies engage in the process of **adjudication.** Acting like a court, the agency gives the affected party the opportunity to present arguments and evidence in a more-or-less formal hearing. The procedural requirements for such hearings vary greatly,

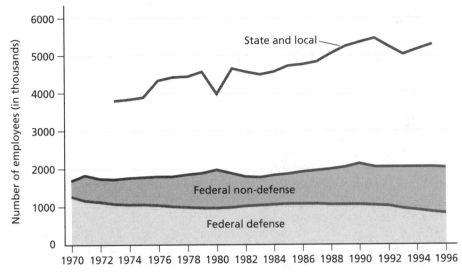

Figure 14.2 **The Shifting Burden: Federal vs. State and Local Employment**

Note: Federal defense category includes civilian employment only. State and local figures exclude educational employees; some years estimated.

Source: 1997 *Statistical Abstract,* Tables 508, 537, pp. 322, 349.

depending on the seriousness of the issue, how much money is in dispute, and other considerations; hearings can range from a one-on-one meeting with an agency representative to a courtroom-like proceeding in front of an administrative law judge. Agencies usually try to settle such disputes using informal methods, and resort to more formal procedures only after other avenues have been exhausted.

Adjudication proceedings are also appropriate when agencies seek to punish wrongdoing.

Going to Court

Really serious disputes between an agency and those affected by its decisions may end up in federal court. The courts have the authority to review all agency rules and decisions brought before them. Depending on the nature of the issue, lawyers from the Justice Department might assist the agency lawyers or take over the case altogether.

In general, any party adversely affected by an agency decision can appeal to the federal courts. In the case of the foremen's union, the Packard Company eventually took its appeal to the United States Supreme Court. However, the Court upheld the National Labor Relations Board's decision that the foremen had the right to organize.

Program Evaluation

Congress requires every agency to keep detailed records of its various programs and to evaluate them on an ongoing basis. In addition, such studies may be required by the political or civil service leadership with each agency, or by the president. Both Congress and the executive branch also rely on outside consultants, analysts, and scholars for program evaluation.

Controlling the Bureaucracy: A Job for All Three Branches

No modern government could function without vesting great authority in the unelected government officials who comprise the bureaucracy. Ensuring that the bureaucracy remains generally subject to the political will of the people, expressed through their elected representatives, thus becomes a critical task.

Although on the organizational charts the bureaucracy sits under the command of the president, in reality all three branches play a role in checking and controlling the actions of the "fourth branch." Moreover, conflicts among the three branches are frequently fought on the bureaucratic battlefield.

Together, the three branches do an effective job of making sure the bureaucracy does not run roughshod over the rights and pocketbooks of the citizenry. At the same time, however, the three branches typically have very different goals and priorities, which unavoidably leads to confusion and conflict.

The View from the White House

Every modern president has struggled to find a way to manage the gargantuan federal bureaucracy. Of all the president's roles, that of chief executive may be the most difficult in practice. In dealing with the bureaucracy, the president faces three main problems: first, finding out what the various agencies are up to and obtaining the best advice from subordinates (this is much more difficult than it sounds), second, getting the bureaucracy to obey presidential orders down the line, and third, coordinating the activities of many different agencies, each of which has its own agenda and is in rivalry with all the others.

Information   Information flows down through a bureaucracy far more easily than it bubbles up, and bad news (that is, evidence of incompetence, corruption, and inefficiency) is especially unlikely to find its way to the top. The reason is not hard to find: the hierarchical structure of the bureaucracy makes every official responsible for the mistakes of people below, so an official who sends bad news up the line about subordinates risks damaging his or her own reputation as well.

Coordination and Control   Harry S Truman is said to have commented on how tough it would be for Dwight D. Eisenhower to be president after having been an army general for so long. "He'll sit here," Truman said, tapping his desk, "and he'll say, 'Do this! Do that!' *And nothing will happen.* Poor Ike—it won't be a bit like the Army. He'll find it very frustrating."[15]

The army, of course, is the largest bureaucracy in the world, but Truman's point is still well taken. A president who expects orders to be followed to the letter and without hesitation is living in fantasyland.

Even the most explicit presidential orders are subject to interpretation by officials all the way down the line. Political appointees and civil servants learn to be experts at the subtle arts of disobedience and delay. Few have the nerve to disobey the president directly, or on a matter of major importance, but on smaller or on-going matters there is more room for maneuver. A big problem is that the president often finds it difficult to follow up on orders, to make sure they are being followed in spirit as well as to the letter.

Presidents also have the opposite problem: keeping the bureaucracy from running away with a policy problem without adequate White House review. The vast majority of bureaucratic decisions do not require explicit White House approval or notification. Others require only pro forma White House involvement. On most issues, most of the time, the bureaucracy functions with a great deal of independence, which leads to policies that are duplicative and wasteful (when more than one agency performs the same function), contradictory or incoherent (when different agencies work at cross-purposes), or contrary to the policies of the administration (when one or more agencies takes a position that contradicts that of the White House).

The explosion of the Challenger spacecraft in 1986 was a tragic example of the bureaucratic principle that "bad news doesn't travel up." Later investigations revealed that scientists' concerns about the spacecraft's design were not communicated to NASA officials.

Looking for Solutions   As the responsibilities of both the federal bureaucracy and the presidency have grown, these problems have become worse. Presidents have become increasingly suspicious and distrustful of the permanent bureaucracy—including even their own cabinet appointees. Increasingly, they have turned for help to the White House staff and to presidential staff agencies (see the discussion in Chapter 13).

The expansion of the size and influence of the White House staff has caused its own set of problems, however. The White House is becoming increasingly bureaucratic itself, and now displays many of the same problems as the rest of the government. It has become more and more difficult for presidents to hear clearly above the chatter of even their closest advisers, or to exercise control even over the White House. When it was discovered that Lieutenant Colonel Oliver North was running a major foreign operation out of the National Security Agency in the 1980s, for example (the so-called Iran-contra affair), President Reagan claimed to know nothing about it. Whether Reagan knew or not, the very fact that his claim was even superficially plausible testifies to the increasing size and complexity of the White House staff.

Ironically, *too much* presidential coordination and control may lead to the politicization of decisions that should be made on a nonpolitical basis. Thus both the agencies and the Congress have legitimate, as well as political, reasons to undermine presidential efforts to keep the bureaucracy on a tight leash.

Congress and the Bureaucracy

If the problem with presidential management of the bureaucracy is too little control, the problem with congressional management might be too much. Congressional committees

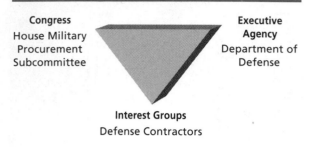

Figure 14.3 **Iron Triangles: An Example**

Congress
House Military
Procurement
Subcommittee

Executive Agency
Department of Defense

Interest Groups
Defense Contractors

and subcommittees, as we have seen, spend a large amount of their time and energy overseeing and influencing the operations of the federal government (see the discussion in Chapter 12).

On a day-to-day basis, Congress is often better equipped than the White House to oversee the functions of the bureaucracy. Unlike White House management, congressional oversight is decentralized, and specialized committees and subcommittees usually have the time, expertise, and resources to monitor the activities of the agencies under their jurisdiction. Equally important, they have the carrots and sticks necessary to influence specific agency behavior.

Unfortunately, subcommittee oversight is not an effective way to manage the executive branch. For one thing, agencies and their congressional subcommittees typically share common interests and a common worldview, creating a fox-in-the-chicken-coop style of management. Because different agencies are overseen by different subcommittees, congressional oversight does little to counter duplication and policy incoherence, and provides few effective mechanisms for encouraging cooperation between agencies or for making tough choices between competing programs. Moreover, agencies often find themselves under the scrutiny of two or more congressional subcommittees, and can often use the resulting confusion to increase their own autonomy and independence.

Congressional oversight does serve several important functions, however. Most important, it helps ensure that public policies are carried out under the supervision of the elected representatives of the people. Congressional oversight also encourages public awareness of and involvement in the day-to-day operations of the government, and provides a window into bureaucratic mismanagement or corruption.

Law, Courts, and Agencies

A final institutional check on the power of the bureaucracy comes from the courts, which play the essential role of ensuring that the agencies obey both the Constitution and all relevant statutes.

Judicial review of agency actions falls into two broad categories. First, the courts make sure that in carrying out their functions the agencies follow all required *procedures*. Second, the courts make sure that the *substance* of the agencies' decisions is consistent with the powers delegated to them by Congress.

Procedural Review   All agency actions, no matter how trivial, must be carried out according to law. Injured parties can appeal agency actions that violate the required procedures to the federal courts.

In reviewing the procedural aspects of an agency's actions, the courts look to three relevant sources. First, all agency actions must be consistent with the Constitution. If the Occupational Safety and Health Administration carries out a search of a factory, for example, its procedures must follow the requirements of the Fourth Amendment, which bans "unreasonable searches and seizures."[16] Second, all agency actions must follow the dictates of the Administrative Procedures Act, originally passed in 1946, which sets out clear procedures for agency rule making and adjudication, as well as any specialized requirements set out by Congress in other legislation. Finally, agencies are typically required to follow procedures imposed by presidential order or adopted voluntarily.

The courts have been especially vigilant in requiring the agencies to follow rules designed to allow public participation in the decision-making process and to ensure that agencies act only after hearing all sides of an issue. In the making of general rules or regulations, it is enough for the agency to allow for written comments. In the making of a specific determination on an individual case, a full, trial-like hearing is often required.

Few of the millions of actions taken by the federal bureaucracy actually go to court, of course. For the most part, agencies have assimilated relevant court decisions into their daily procedures and follow them as a matter of course.

Substantive Review   Courts are also authorized to review the substance of agency actions to ensure that they remain within the limits set by Congress. In practice, courts give the agencies wide latitude to interpret congressional statutes as they see fit. Only when the agency has clearly transgressed the will of Congress do the courts step in.

A recent case nicely illustrates the courts' role in reviewing agency actions. In 1992, the Supreme Court upheld a Department of Health and Human Services (HHS) rule that banned abortion counseling at family planning clinics that received federal funds; a federally funded clinic was expressly barred from referring a pregnant woman to an abortion provider, even upon specific request.

The HHS rule in question was adopted to implement a congressional statute that prohibited the use of federal money "in programs where abortion is a method of family planning." The statute said nothing whatsoever about abortion counseling. Accordingly, the HHS rule was challenged on the grounds that it exceeded Congress's intent and meaning in passing the original statute. In support of their argument, opponents of the rule pointed out that the original statute was passed in 1970, and was enforced without any restrictions on abortion counseling until the HHS rule was passed in 1988.

The Supreme Court upheld the rule against a variety of legal arguments.[17] The HHS rule would not be struck down as an abuse of administrative discretion, the Court said, "if it reflects a plausible construction of the plain language of the statute and does not otherwise conflict with Congress' expressed intent."*

The Ironies of Judicial Oversight   In the end, it is ironic that the courts play so important a role in the supervision of the federal bureaucracy. For the courts, no less than the bureaucracy, are both unelected and unaccountable to the democratic process. Perhaps that is why the courts have been reluctant to substitute their own judgment for that of the agencies, preferring to focus their efforts on policing agency procedures—especially procedures that maximize public involvement in the decision-making process. Furthermore, critics have argued convincingly that the federal courts are ill equipped to deal with complicated questions of social policy.

---

* In 1993, President Bill Clinton rescinded the controversial abortion counseling rule.

Moreover, the very idea of judicial control of agency action conflicts with the principle of *political* control of the bureaucracy. The more the courts interfere with agency actions, the less power the president and the cabinet have over key decisions. Judicial control thus may displace, rather than supplement, executive control of the bureaucracy.

Properly applied, however, judicial and executive control can work together. Under this theory, the president's role is to foster "coordination and centralization, making it easier for the government to act with dispatch," and counteracting the natural inertia of the bureaucracy. The focus of the courts should be on ensuring that the executive branch is not permitted to make the ultimate decisions "in determining the breadth of its own legal authority."[18]

Summary

The word *bureaucracy* refers to the web of offices, agencies, departments, and divisions that is characteristic of any large, modern organization. Bureaucracies are marked by a hierarchical arrangement of offices; by specialization and a division of labor; and by the use of rules as the basis for decision making. Bureaucracies are as much a part of large private organizations as of large public organizations, although public and private bureaucracies differ in key ways, especially in the nature of the constraints under which each is forced to operate.

The growth of the federal bureaucracy dates from the Pendleton Act of 1883, which sought to end the spoils system and create a nonpartisan executive workforce. The federal bureaucracy grew steadily over the next fifty years, and then exploded during the 1930s and 1940s and afterward. Although Congress gave the bureaucracy new responsibilities, it also created new checks on bureaucratic power, including the Administrative Procedures Act and the Freedom of Information Act.

Today the federal bureaucracy is made up of many different kinds of agencies, including cabinet-level departments, the Executive Office of the President and the White House staff, regulatory agencies and commissions, government corporations, and various government commissions, advisory groups, and hybrid agencies. The agencies are engaged in every aspect of government activity, including the management of programs, policy development, administration of the laws in individual cases, and program evaluation. Many government policies are implemented according to rules issued by government agencies, or are applied to individuals through the process of adjudication.

The original Constitution made little provision for bureaucracy. Thus the growth of the bureaucracy has created a number of difficult constitutional questions, such as whether Congress can force public officials to carry out specific duties under the law, regardless of whether the president approves; whether Congress can create "independent" agencies, which are free from the direct control of the White House; and whether Congress can delegate broad legislative powers to government agencies. For the most part, the Supreme Court has been flexible in permitting Congress to exercise its discretion in these and other matters.

Analysts have identified a number of disadvantages and advantages of bureaucracy. Critics charge that bureaucracies are excessively rigid and inefficient; that government agencies tend to outlive their usefulness; that bureaucracies are unresponsive to the citizenry; and that the bureaucratic form of government makes it easy for government officials to ignore the moral consequences of their actions. There is some truth in all of these charges, but the problems of the bureaucracy are often misattributed or overstated. Analysts also point out that bureaucracies allow for the management of complex undertakings and provide stability and predictability in the administration of the government.

The paramount concern about bureaucracies in a democratic system is to find a way to check and balance the power of unelected government officials. In the American system of government, all three branches play a role in helping to keep the bureaucracy in check, with varying degrees of success.

Key Terms

Bureaucracy
Spoils system
Pendleton Act
Administrative Procedures Act (APA)
Freedom of Information Act (FOIA)
Independent agencies
Delegation doctrine
Rules
Adjudication

Review Questions

1. What are the characteristics of the bureaucratic system?

2. What distinguishes public from private bureaucracies?

3. What were the goals of the early efforts to reform the executive branch? Of modern efforts?

4. What roles does the bureaucracy play in the American system of government?

5. What are the advantages and disadvantages of bureaucracies?

6. How does each of the three branches help to check and balance the power of the bureaucracy?

Suggested Readings

Bennett, Linda L. M., and Stephen Earl Bennett. *Living with Leviathan: Americans Coming to Terms with Big Government.* Lawrence: University Press of Kansas, 1990.

Gellhorn, Walter, Clark Byse, Peter L. Strauss, Todd Rakoff, and Roy A. Schotland. *Administrative Law: Cases and Comments,* 8th ed. Mineola, N.Y.: Foundation Press, 1987.

Heclo, Hugh. *A Government of Strangers.* Washington, D.C.: Brookings Institution, 1977.

Light, Paul C. *Thickening Government: Federal Hierarchy and the Diffusion of Accountability.* Washington, D.C.: Brookings Institution, 1995.

Rourke, Francis E. *Bureaucracy, Politics and Public Policy.* Boston: Little, Brown, 1984.

Seidman, Harold, and Robert Gilmour. *Politics, Position, and Power,* 4th ed. New York: Oxford University Press, 1986.

Wilson, James Q. *Bureaucracy: What Government Agencies Do and Why They Do It.* New York: Basic Books, 1989.

Internet Resources

Web sites for various federal government agencies at:

http://lcweb.loc.gov/global/executive/fed.html

The Federal Register, official U.S. government publication containing proposed rules, notices, and other material issued by various government agencies, at:

http://law.house.gov/7.htm

The "Federal Page" at the *Washington Post,* covering the Washington bureaucracy, at:

http://www.washingtonpost.com/wp-srv/national/fedcomm.htm

15

The Courts

On the surface, *City of Boerne* v. *Flores* was all about religious freedom. The case involved the St. Peter's Catholic Church, built in 1923 near San Antonio, Texas, and reflecting the mission-style architecture of the period. Some seventy years later, the church building was no longer large enough to suit its congregation; on a typical Sunday morning, some forty to sixty parishioners were unable to find seats. Thus, St. Peter's planned to renovate and expand its facilities.

Under the city's historic preservation law, however, changes to the building could be made only with the approval of the city authorities. Those authorities balked, however, citing the historic nature of the structure, and refused a permit. Thereupon, the church brought a lawsuit, charging that the city's actions violated the Religious Freedom Restoration Act of 1993 (RFRA), enacted by Congress and designed to stop government authorities from trampling on the religious freedoms of the citizenry. Although the city's goal of historic preservation was legitimate, the church argued, it could not be pursued at the expense of the First and Fourteenth Amendment rights of the members of the church.

Despite these overarching issues, the legal question presented to the Supreme Court of the United States in 1996 centered not on religion, but on whether Congress or the Supreme Court would have the final word on matters of constitutional interpretation. Congress's approval of RFRA was designed to override the Supreme Court's 1990 decision in *Employment Division* v.

The Church of St. Peter the Apostle, in Boerne, Texas.

Smith, in which the Court had ruled that the state of Oregon could fire a Native American employee who used peyote, an illegal hallucinogenic drug, as part of a religious ceremony. Reversing earlier decisions that required the states to show a "compelling interest" before overriding religious freedoms, the Court now held that otherwise-legitimate laws were not rendered unconstitutional simply because they interfered with the religious practices of certain individuals. "The right of free exercise" of religion, the Court concluded, "does not relieve the individual of the obligation to comply with a 'valid and neutral law.'"

RFRA, in effect, sought to force the Court to reinstate the compelling-interest test. Relying on its power to enforce the Fourteenth Amendment "by appropriate legislation," Congress declared that no governmental entity could "substantially burden" religious freedom unless it could show that its actions served a "compelling governmental interest," and that there was no other way to achieve that interest without burdening religious freedom.

The justices, in *City of Boerne,* however, rejected Congress's effort to substitute its constitutional judgment for that of the Court. Congress's power to enforce the Fourteenth Amendment comes into play only if the Fourteenth Amendment has been violated, they ruled; since the Court found no such violation in the case of St. Peter's church, Congress had no power to act. Congress's determination that constitutional liberties were at stake, in other words, carried no weight if the Court did not agree. "Simply put," wrote Justice Scalia, "RFRA is not designed to identify and counteract state laws likely to be unconstitutional because of their treatment of religion."

In the end, *City of Boerne* was just the latest episode in the long-standing power struggle between Congress and the judiciary. "When the Court has interpreted the Constitution," wrote Justice Scalia, "it has acted within the province of the Judicial Branch, which embraces the duty to say what the law is." He concluded, "Courts retain the power, as they have since *Marbury* v. *Madison*, to determine if Congress has exceeded its authority under the Constitution."[1]

The United States relies more on courts than any other nation. "There is hardly a political question in the United States," wrote Alexis de Tocqueville in the 1830s, "which does not sooner or later turn into a judicial one."[2] What was true in Tocqueville's time is even more true today. American courts are called on not only to administer justice in particular cases but also to make broad policy decisions that in other democracies would be left to the elected representatives of the people. In the past thirty years alone, the United States Supreme Court and numerous lower courts have made key decisions on racial segregation, abortion rights, obscenity and pornography, affirmative action, and school prayer. The Courts have transformed the way state and local police departments operate; forced dramatic changes in prisons, mental hospitals, and school systems; and overhauled the apportionment of Congress and the state legislatures.

All of this action has created tremendous controversy. Some critics of the courts have simply objected to the substance of the decisions, characterizing them as too liberal and arguing for a more conservative approach. Others have taken exception to the courts' approach to judicial decision making, arguing that the courts have become too ideological or too political. Still others complain that the federal courts have usurped the legitimate powers of the states.

In the 1980s, the courts became a battleground in the ideological war between American liberals and conservatives. Presidents Ronald Reagan and George Bush made clear their desire to reshape the judiciary in a more conservative image, provoking a series of fights with the more liberal Congress over judicial appointments and civil rights legislation. These battles peaked with fights over the nominations of Robert Bork and Clarence Thomas to the Supreme Court in 1987 and 1991, respectively. Bork's nomination was rejected by the Senate, but Thomas was permitted to take his seat.

The relatively conservative appointments by Bush and Reagan, not only to the Supreme Court but also to the lower courts, caused a clear shift to the right in judicial decision making, a shift that has not been reversed even though the Democrats have controlled the White House since 1993. Liberals have objected to court decisions on civil rights, the death penalty, economic regulation, and the separation of church and state. Yet many conservatives continue to regard the Court as both too liberal and too likely to interfere with the decisions of democratic legislatures.

Despite criticism from all sides, the courts continue to command extraordinary respect from the American people, at least in comparison with other government institutions. Yet the place of these unelected institutions in a democratic system of government is awkward and unusual, to say the least. The purpose of this chapter is to explore and evaluate the role of the courts in the American political system.

Questions to Keep in Mind

How do the courts protect the rights of minorities? How do they protect the rights of the majority as well?

What is the meaning of judicial review? What are the implications of judicial review for democratic government?

What is the relationship between the federal judicial system and the states? How do the federal courts advance the interests of the federal government and of the nation as a whole against the interests of the various states?

Basic Concepts ★ ★ ★ ★ ★ ★ ★ ★ ★ ★ ★ ★ ★

The American Judicial System

The federal government has its own judicial system, distinct from the judicial systems of the fifty states. The Constitution and the laws of the United States set out the **jurisdiction,** or scope of authority, of the federal courts. Cases that do not fall within the jurisdiction of the federal courts may be handled by the state courts, under the applicable state laws and state constitution.

Both the state and federal courts handle civil and criminal cases. Civil cases are ordinarily disputes between private individuals, corporations, or organizations, although the government can be involved as a party. Typical civil cases include disputes over automobile accidents, contracts, divorce, and real estate. Civil cases usually, but not always, involve money damages. Criminal cases, which are considered to involve offenses against society itself and not merely individual actual victims, pit the government (state or federal) against an individual or corporation. Examples include murder, rape, arson, theft, and espionage. In criminal cases, the prosecution (that is, the government) must prove that the defendant is guilty "beyond a reasonable doubt." On conviction, a criminal defendant can be fined, imprisoned, or even executed.

The power of the federal courts under the Constitution extends only to "cases and controversies." Thus the federal courts do not give **advisory opinions** on issues that arise outside the context of an actual legal dispute.[3]

The Federal Judicial System The Constitution established only the Supreme Court of the United States, and left the creation and organization of the lower federal courts to Congress. It also gave Congress the authority to determine the number of justices on the Supreme Court.

The organization of the federal court system has changed over the years. Currently, there are two levels of federal courts below the Supreme Court—some 649 federal district courts, and thirteen courts of appeals. Most cases are resolved at the district court level; and

The Supreme Court of the United States, in an official portrait from October 1994. Seated, from left to right: Antonin Scalia, John Paul Stevens, William H. Rehnquist, Sandra Day O'Connor, and Anthony Kennedy. Standing, left to right: Ruth Bader Ginsburg, David Souter, Clarence Thomas, and Stephen Breyer.

Federal District Judge Susan Webber Wright, who dismissed Paula Jones's sexual harassment suit against President Bill Clinton in April 1998, two months before the scheduled trial date.

most of those that are taken to higher courts are resolved at the court of appeals level. The Supreme Court decides only around three hundred cases a year, with fewer than one hundred involving oral arguments and full written opinions.

Federal judges serve for life, and cannot be removed except by impeachment. Although several lower court judges have been removed for misconduct, no Supreme Court justice has ever been removed from office, and only one—Justice Samuel Chase in 1805—has ever been impeached by the House and tried by the Senate. When the charges against Chase were shown to be politically motivated, he was acquitted.

State or Federal Court? Every state, and every federal territory, has its own judicial system. The state and territorial court systems operate independently of the federal court system and handle the bulk of the nation's legal business.

Deciding whether a case should be brought in state or federal court is often a difficult matter that depends on highly complex rules and statutes. In general, state courts handle all disputes unless a specific reason allows the federal courts to become involved. For example, the federal courts deal with crimes against the laws of the United States, cases in which the United States is a party, and cases involving claims made under federal law. The federal courts may also hear cases between citizens of different states.

Occasionally a case is so important that *both* the state and the federal courts may become involved. That occurred in 1992 and 1993, when the Los Angeles police officers who beat Rodney King were acquitted in state court, then retried in federal court under a charge of violating King's civil rights. The federal jury returned convictions of two of the four defendants. The Supreme Court has long held that such double trials do not violate the Fifth Amendment's prohibition against double jeopardy.

Selection of Judges

"A judge is a lawyer who knows the governor," according to an old joke. Although there is some truth in that remark, in reality the process by which judges are selected varies greatly among the states, between the state and federal governments, and even within a particular state. The results of the judicial selection process are critical not only because the administration of justice depends greatly on the quality of the judges selected, but also because American courts make many decisions that in other countries fall to the legislative or executive branches.

In the appointment of federal judges, a balance is sought between allowing some degree of democratic control and ensuring that those selected have both the qualifications and characteristics to operate independently of public opinion. That is why the Framers gave the power of appointing judges to the president, but required Senate confirmation (the House of Representatives was left out of the process entirely). To preserve their independence, federal

Los Angeles police officers are caught on video-tape beating suspect Rodney King. A state jury acquitted four of the officers on assault charges, but a federal jury later convicted two of them for violating King's civil rights. According to the Supreme Court, such double trials do not violate the Constitution's double jeopardy clause.

judges serve for life, unless impeached and convicted by the House and Senate. In the more than two hundred years of American history, only thirteen federal judges have been impeached: two resigned, four were acquitted, and seven were removed from office.

Although the constitutional requirements for appointment are the same for every level of the judiciary, in practice the process differs for district court, appeals courts, and Supreme Court nominees.

District Court and Court of Appeals Judges   The president rarely participates actively in the selection of lower-court judges. Instead, such decisions are typically delegated to officials in the Justice Department or to White House legal advisers. In the Clinton administration, candidates for appointment to the lower bench came from recommendations by Democratic senators in the affected state or states (if there were no Democratic senators, the administration sought recommendations from Democratic representatives or from state Democratic leaders). Because of the need for confirmation by the Senate, the administration consulted closely after 1994 with Republican senators, especially Judiciary Committee Chairman Orrin Hatch (R-Utah).[4]

Because the judiciary has become a point of contention between liberals and conservatives, in recent years the Senate has taken a more active role in scrutinizing lower-court nominees. Moreover, under divided government Senate confirmation of lower-court judicial nominees is hardly automatic. For example, the Democratic-controlled Senate confirmed 92.1 percent of President Bill Clinton's judicial nominees in 1993 and 1994; by contrast, the Republican-controlled Senate confirmed only 65.9 percent of Clinton's nominees between 1994 and 1997.[5]

Another problem brought on by the increasingly controversial nature of judicial nominees has been the imposition of long delays in the process of Senate confirmation of nominees. During the Republican Nixon administration, for example, it took the Democratic

Senate, on average, less than 26 days to confirm a nominee after his or her name was referred to the Judiciary Committee. The Democratic Senate in 1987–1988, by contrast, took an average of 79 days to confirm nominations sent up by Ronald Regan; President Clinton has faced similar delays (73 days) in the Republican-controlled Senate. In some cases, the long delays have been tantamount to rejection by the Senate.[6]

After nomination, judicial nominees are evaluated by a panel of the American Bar Association (ABA), which rates the candidate as well qualified, qualified, or not qualified; nominees judged not qualified face an uphill battle for Senate confirmation. After the ABA panel reports, the Senate Judiciary Committee holds hearings and votes its approval or disapproval. The final decision, however, is up to the full Senate.

Compared with hearings for Supreme Court justices, Judiciary Committee hearings for lower-court judges are often brief, even cursory.

Supreme Court Justices Appointments to the Supreme Court are among the most important presidential duties and may constitute a president's most enduring legacy. Yet opportunities to appoint new justices are hardly plentiful: there have been 112 Supreme Court judges in American history, an average of just two for every four-year presidential term. No wonder that presidents take Supreme Court nominations very seriously and often play a personal role in the selection process.

In recent years the Supreme Court has been sharply divided on a number of key legal issues, and presidents have tried to use the appointment of new justices to influence the Court's decisions one way or the other. Several nominations in the 1980s and early 1990s provoked great controversy as well as bitter fights in the Senate. Critics of Judge Robert Bork, who were concerned about the nominee's conservative views on the right to privacy and other issues, managed to defeat his nomination in 1987. A similar effort in 1991 to derail the nomination of Judge Clarence Thomas, who also held strong conservative views and who was charged with sexually harassing a former employee, failed by four votes. The controversy surrounding these and other nominations led President Bill Clinton to avoid divisive nominees and concentrate on men and women who could easily win Senate approval.

The process of selecting a Supreme Court justice depends on the particular president and the political situation, but an average version based on the last several administrations would go something like this:

- The process begins with the Office of Legal Policy (OLP) in the Justice Department. The OLP confers with the White House staff, members of Congress, state and local politicians, bar associations, law professors, and other interested parties and compiles a list of potential nominees. Some are on the list because the administration expects them to advance its ideological agenda on the Court; others, because they have earned the respect and admiration of the legal community; still others, because they have the support of influential senators or of key opposition leaders and could expect easy confirmation by the Senate.
- The Justice Department forwards the long list to the White House, where senior presidential advisers winnow it down to two or three names. The short list might still contain both controversial and noncontroversial names, leaving the final choice of political strategy to the president. The names on the short list are sent to the Federal Bureau of

Investigation (FBI), which conducts background checks, and perhaps to the American Bar Association for informal evaluation. The final decision is made by the president, usually after meeting with the candidates in White House interviews, and is announced in a formal "photo opportunity" and press conference.

- The nomination is formally sent to the Senate for approval. The matter is referred to the Senate Judiciary Committee, which conducts an investigation into the nominee's background and legal views. The committee then holds formal hearings, which may take days and which may include dozens of witnesses. The centerpiece of the hearings is the nominee's own testimony; by tradition, nominees do not comment on legal questions that may come before the Court, but they do give general answers indicating their judicial philosophy and approach.

- Meanwhile, the press corps descends in a swarm to uncover every fact about the nominee's life and career. If the nomination is controversial, both sides may conduct extensive lobbying efforts, including television ads and direct mail campaigns designed to influence public opinion, and thus the Senate. Interest groups friendly to the Senate majority party may work closely with Senate staff to help or hurt the nominee's chances. It was just such a collaboration that brought Anita Hill to testify about alleged sexual harassment in the Thomas hearings.

- The Senate Judiciary Committee votes up or down. Either way, the nomination is usually sent to the full Senate for final approval. More lobbying and politicking take place, with interest groups and the White House bearing down on fence-sitting senators. The White House may use all the leverage available to make deals with key senators. Eventually the Senate votes. If the nominee is confirmed, he or she is sworn in as a justice of the United States Supreme Court; if not, the process must begin all over again.[7]

Characteristics of Federal Judges   Until the Carter administration (1977–1981), securing an appointment as a federal judge depended above all on being well connected politically. Griffin Bell, who served as attorney general under Carter, described how he had earlier come to be a judge. "[It] wasn't difficult," Bell said. "I managed John F. Kennedy's presidential campaign from Georgia. Two of my oldest friends were the senators from Georgia. And I was campaign manager and special unpaid counsel for the governor."[8]

Not surprisingly, the federal judiciary before Carter was not very diverse. Of all the judges appointed by Presidents Johnson, Nixon, and Ford, over 98 percent were men and over 94 percent were non-Hispanic whites. Together, the three presidents appointed six women to the federal bench. Of 458 judicial appointments, Johnson, Nixon, and Ford appointed exactly three Asian Americans and six Latinos.[9]

Under Jimmy Carter, by contrast, women and minorities began to make progress in judicial appointments. Although Carter did not have the opportunity to appoint even one Supreme Court justice, he did appoint 202 district judges and 56 court of appeals judges. Carter's circuit court of appeals judges were chosen by a new system that emphasized merit selection and diversity; all were drawn from lists drawn up by Circuit Judge Nominating Commissions. At the district level, Carter encouraged individual senators to implement similar merit selection procedures.[10]

The results were impressive, at least in terms of diversity. Of Carter's fifty-six appellate appointees, eleven (19.6 percent) were women, nine (16.1 percent) were black, and three

(5.6 percent) were Hispanic or Asian American. Carter achieved somewhat less diversity at the district court level: 14.4 percent of his appointees were women, and 7.6 percent black, Hispanic, or Asian American. In all, Carter appointed more women and minorities to the federal bench than all his predecessors combined.[11]

Reagan, Bush, and Clinton   President Reagan dissolved the Circuit Judge Nominating Commissions in 1981. His judicial appointments emphasized ideology over diversity; Reagan, as the legal scholar Sheldon Goldman put it, was arguably engaged in "the most systematic judicial philosophical screening of judicial candidates ever seen." George Bush, who succeeded Reagan in 1989, continued in much the same way. When Bill Clinton was elected president in 1992, the federal bench was still 89 percent male and 90 percent non-Hispanic white.[12]

President Clinton, however, made the appointment of nontraditional judges a major priority. Nearly one-third of his first-term judicial appointments were women; almost 30 percent were nonwhite. Only one-third of his appointments, in fact, were white males. All told, Clinton increased women on the bench to 17.4 percent and racial minorities to 13.5 percent.

Despite Clinton's emphasis on affirmative action for women and racial minorities, the federal judiciary hardly resembles the population as a whole. In fact, except with respect to gender and race, Clinton's appointments were not very different from those of his predecessors:

- Because they are drawn from the ranks of successful lawyers, federal judges are far wealthier than the population as a whole. Less than one-fifth of all judicial appointments since Carter have had net worths of under $200,000; more than one-fifth have been millionaires.
- Presidents tend to appoint members of their own political party. Nearly 90 percent of Clinton's appointees were Democrats; over 90 percent of Bush and Reagan appointees were Republicans.
- Around half of all district court appointees are state or local judges—around 44 percent in Clinton's case, between 41 and 45 percent for his predecessors. Appointing sitting judges allows presidents to have a clear idea of the appointees' judicial philosophy and qualifications for the job.[13]

Helping the Judges: Law Clerks and Other Assistants   Although Justice Oliver Wendell Holmes bragged that Supreme Court justices "do our own work," today federal judges have a good deal of help in performing their duties. Most important are the law clerks—young men and women just out of law school who assist the judges with legal research and other duties. Any clerkship with a federal judge is extremely prestigious; clerkships at the Supreme Court are among the most coveted legal jobs in the country. Of the thirty-six Supreme Court clerks during 1988–1989, for example, sixteen graduated from Harvard or Yale Law School, and ten more from the University of Chicago, Stanford, and Columbia.

The exact role played by the clerks depends on the judge. Most judges rely on their law clerks to write the first draft of their opinions. Some judges use this first draft as the basis for writing an opinion in their own words; others simply edit the clerk's draft. Almost all Supreme Court clerks are responsible for screening the thousands of cases brought before the Court. Clerks typically write a one- or two-page summary of each case and recommend whether the justices should take the case. Final decisions are left to the judges themselves, of course, but most of the time the clerks' recommendations are accepted.[14]

Some critics argue that law clerks have become too powerful. The clerks' role is limited, however, for several reasons. First, law clerks work at the Court for only a year or two. Thus they never build up much experience with, or influence on, their justice. Second, clerks are selected not only for their legal talent but also because of their compatibility with their boss. Third, the justices themselves are strong-minded men and women who are rarely pushed around by anyone, much less by a young law clerk. As one former clerk put it, "In the course of my year, we never changed the Justice's mind on the result of any case. Our influence was close to nil. There was the fullest discussion, but he made the decisions. . . . The judge will listen if you say that some statement in his draft opinion is too broad or that a case is cited incorrectly. But if you tell him that such-and-such a constitutional amendment doesn't mean what he believes, you might as well stay in bed."[15]

SUPREME COURT

"That's right...five-ninths pepperoni and four-ninths sausage."

Other Judicial Assistants. Judges can hire a number of other assistants, including court reporters, stenographers, probation officers, and professional administrators. Federal district judges can also hire magistrates, whose duties differ greatly from those of the magistrates who work at the lower levels of the state judiciaries. U.S. magistrates are more or less assistant judges. They can preside over the preliminary stages of trials, issue arrest warrants, and set bail. With the consent of all parties, the magistrate can even hear civil and minor criminal cases.

How the Supreme Court Works

How Cases Get to the Supreme Court   Cases reach the Supreme Court of the United States by one of two routes. Under its **appellate jurisdiction,** the Court hears appeals from the federal, state, and territorial courts. Appeals from the state and territorial courts require that the litigants have exhausted all avenues of appeal within the state or territorial judicial system. On rare occasions, the Court may also hear cases directly, under its **original jurisdiction.** Usually these cases involve disputes between two states—as, for example, when New Jersey sued New York over the ownership of historic Ellis Island.[16]

Most cases reach the Supreme Court by **writ of certiorari** ("on cert," as the lawyers say). In any case involving "a federal question of substance"—whether from the state or federal courts—the losing party has the right to ask the Supreme Court to review the decision. To do so, the losing party files a petition for a writ of certiorari ("cert petition"). Whether the Court accepts the petition depends on whether the justices can be convinced that "it is vital that the questions involved be decided finally by the Supreme Court." Cert petitions are circulated to all nine justices; under the so-called **rule of four,** if four justices want to take the case, it is placed on the Court's docket. Even so, the Court typically denies between 85 and 90 percent of all cert petitions, usually without explaining why. In general, the Court takes cases only when they are important for the "operation of our federal system," as Justice Felix Frankfurter once explained. "Importance of the outcome merely to the parties is not enough." The Court has never considered itself responsible for correcting every error made by every court in the nation.[17]

Many cases brought to the Court's attention are brought by citizens—mainly prison inmates—who cannot afford to pay court costs. Under federal law, such citizens are permitted to file *in forma pauperis* petitions without fee. *In forma pauperis* petitions are "often fantastic, surpassing credulity . . . [and] for the most part frivolous." Not surprisingly, the Court accepts only about 1 percent of *in forma pauperis* petitions, although so many are filed that they make up a significant percentage of the Court's docket. Typically, the *in forma pauperis* petitions accepted by the Court come from federal prisoners who raise an important question of law or from state prisoners who raise valid constitutional claims.[18]

Written Briefs and Oral Argument   Once the Supreme Court accepts a case, both sides must prepare **written briefs**—papers that set forth the factual background and legal arguments on each side. Under the Court's guidelines, briefs "must be compact, . . . concise, and

Figure 15.1 **The United States Court System**

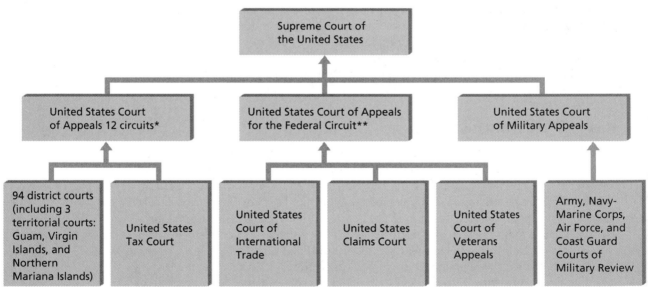

* Includes 11 regional courts of appeals and the Court of Appeals for the District of Columbia. These courts also review cases from a number of federal agencies.

** The Court of Appeals for the Federal Circuit also receives cases from the International Trade Commission, the Merit Systems Protection Board, the Patent and Trademark Office, and the Board of Contract Appeals.

free from burdensome, irrelevant matter." Briefs are generally limited to fifty pages. "Make your briefs clear, concise, honest, balanced, buttressed, convincing and interesting," Justice Wiley Rutledge once advised lawyers. "The last is not least. A dull brief may be good law. An interesting one will make the judges aware of this."[19]

The Supreme Court typically grants permission to individuals or organizations who are not parties to a case to file **amicus curiae** (or **"friend of the court"**) **briefs.** Such briefs are often filed by the United States government and by various interest groups; in especially controversial cases, such as those involving abortion, the number of groups filing amicus briefs may total sixty or more. Groups writing amicus briefs often coordinate their efforts with each other and with one of the parties to the case; thus amicus briefs may deal with critical issues not fully dealt with in the briefs written by the parties. The impact of amicus briefs in any particular case is difficult to judge, but occasionally one may be of decisive importance.[20]

The most dramatic stage in a Supreme Court case occurs when the lawyers appear before the justices to present their oral arguments. In most cases, each side is limited to thirty minutes. During **oral argument,** a lawyer does not make a speech to the Court; in fact, the justices frequently interrupt with questions or comments of their own and can easily faze an inexperienced advocate. "Though it is true that few cases have been won in oral argument," writes former solicitor general Charles Fried, who argued many cases before the Court, "many have been lost. Under what can be relentless and sometimes even sadistic questioning by the justices, a quite plausible case can fall apart entirely." A successful oral argument, Fried concludes, "is more like a compelling conversation than a lecture—this is aided by the fact that the lawyer's lectern in the Supreme Court is quite close to the bench, and the contact with the justices seems more intimate than in many other courts."[21]

Oral arguments also provide an opportunity for the public to see the Court in action, and can give court-watchers who follow the justices' questions and comments keen insights into how the Court is leaning in any particular case.

Deciding the Case   The justices discuss and debate the cases they have heard at conference, currently held all day Friday and Wednesday afternoon. The justices also use the conference to vote on certiorari petitions and to handle other routine Court business. Conference proceedings are strictly confidential, though some justices have kept notes for their own use or for later use by historians.

When deciding a case, it is customary for the chief justice to state his views first, followed by the other justices in order of seniority. By the time all nine justices have spoken, the outcome of the case is usually clear, and the chief justice announces the result; it takes five votes to make a majority. In the past, as Justice Lewis Powell once commented, the conference afforded "the principal opportunity for discussion, debate, and group deliberation. Justices may speak as frequently and as long as they wish . . . and not infrequently a conference has altered my

Oliver Wendell Holmes, "the Yankee from Olympus," shown here in a portrait commissioned in honor of his ninetieth birthday. Several of Holmes's dissenting opinions later became the law of the land.

original tentative view." Under Chief Justice William Rehnquist, however, the conference has become more businesslike and less deliberative. "The true purpose of the conference discussion of argued cases," he has written, "is not to persuade one's colleagues through impassioned advocacy to alter their views, but instead by hearing each justice express his own views to determine therefrom the view of the majority of the Court."[22]

After a case is discussed at conference, one justice is assigned to write the majority opinion, which is known as the **opinion of the court.** The chief justice, if in the majority, or the senior associate justice who is in the majority, makes the assignment. Opinions are drafted within the justice's chambers and circulated to all the other justices. Frequently negotiations are required to ensure that a majority of the Court is willing to sign the final opinion—otherwise, the opinion will not speak for the Court. Justices are also entitled to express their views individually, in the form of a **concurring opinion,** when they agree with the majority's resolution of the case but not with its reasoning, or a **dissenting opinion,** when they disagree with the majority result.

Opinions are announced from the bench, and the justices may read all or part of their opinions aloud. In their opinions, the justices lay out the legal principles and arguments that led them to their decision in the case. The opinions are closely scrutinized by lawyers and legal scholars—the former group to decide how to handle future cases, the latter to provide commentary, criticism, and analysis.

Concurring and dissenting opinions represent merely the opinions of individual judges. However, they can provide a focal point for legal discussion and commentary and a reference point for future justices. It is not uncommon for a dissenting opinion in one era to become the majority opinion in the next. Many of Justice Oliver Wendell Holmes's dissenting opinions, for example, were accepted years later by the full Court.[23]

The Supreme Court and Judicial Review

The Supreme Court's most distinctive role in the American system of government arises from its power to interpret and apply the provisions of the Constitution. Since the early days of the Republic, the Supreme Court and the lower federal courts have asserted and exercised their right to review the constitutionality of federal laws, and to nullify those that conflict with the Constitution. This power, known as **judicial review,** also extends to presidential and administrative actions that might conflict with the Constitution, as well as to the laws and actions of the states.

Use of the judicial review power to strike down acts of Congress is not common, but the mere existence of judicial review may have some effect on Congress's deliberations. Frequently, the courts have used the power of judicial review to *affirm* the constitutionality of congressional action.

Although judicial review is a power exercised by all federal courts (and even by the state courts), Supreme Court review of lower court decisions that nullify acts of Congress is virtually automatic. For that reason, this section focuses predominantly on the Supreme Court.

The Origins of Judicial Review

The Text and Meaning of the Constitution   The Constitution does not explicitly give the courts the power to declare acts of Congress unconstitutional. Article III does give the federal courts jurisdiction in any case "arising under" the Constitution, and Article VI declares the Constitution to be "the supreme Law of the Land; and the Judges in every State shall be bound thereby." It is difficult to ground judicial review on these two clauses, however. The first is vague, and the second implies at most the courts' power to review *state* laws that conflict with the federal Constitution.

In fact, the subject of judicial review over federal laws was hardly mentioned at the Philadelphia convention in 1787, and only six of the fifty-five delegates made statements endorsing the practice.[24] Most of the comments made about judicial review at the convention were made in passing and are difficult to put in context. There was considerable support for judicial review of state laws, but the most that can be said with regard to federal laws is that the convention did not reject the idea.

The question of judicial review came up during the ratification debates, in response to Antifederalist charges that the new federal judiciary would exercise despotic powers. The Antifederalists' arguments led Alexander Hamilton to respond, in the *Federalist* No. 78, with a defense of the federal judiciary. In the process, Hamilton endorsed the idea of judicial review.[25]

The Framers' ambiguous attitude toward judicial review perhaps explains why it took the Supreme Court fifteen years to adopt Hamilton's argument. It did so in the unlikely case of ***Marbury v. Madison,*** in 1803.[26]

James Otis, who argued in the Writs of Assistance Case *in 1761 that the courts should nullify unconstitutional acts of the British Parliament. The court rejected Otis's argument, but his rhetoric greatly advanced the revolutionary cause. In 1803, the idea of judicial review was accepted by the Supreme Court of the United States in* Marbury v. Madison.

Marbury v. Madison   The case that established the lofty principle of judicial review began in the trenches of Federalist-era politics. The election of 1800 was bitter and partisan, and resulted in a rout of the incumbent Federalist Party and a major victory for Thomas Jefferson and his "Democratic-Republicans" (or "Republicans," for short). The Federalists lost not only the presidency but control of Congress as well.

Under the law at that time, the new president and Congress did not take office until March 4, 1801. Meanwhile, the lame-duck Congress had three months to make trouble for the new administration. Among other things, it passed laws creating a number of new federal judgeships, thus giving outgoing President John Adams a last-minute opportunity to find jobs for loyal Federalists and to ensure continued Federalist control over the judicial branch.

Among these "midnight appointments" was that of William Marbury to be a justice of the peace for the District of Columbia. Marbury was a wealthy land speculator in Washington whose appointment was at least partly intended to annoy the Republicans. His nomination was properly made by the president and confirmed by the Senate, and his commission was signed by the president and sealed by the acting secretary of state, all according to law. Unfortunately for Marbury and the Federalists, the commission was never delivered, and Thomas Jefferson found it on the secretary of state's desk the next day. (Adams's acting secretary of state was none other than John Marshall, who was already chief justice and who would write the *Marbury* opinion. The blame for failing to deliver the commission probably belongs to Marshall's brother, who was trying to help out.)

Should the Supreme Court Follow the "Original Intent" of the Framers?

Virtually all Americans agree that the Supreme Court's authority to interpret the Constitution is necessary and appropriate. However, there is considerable disagreement over how the Court should approach its task of interpreting the constitutional text. In recent years, the debate among legal scholars has centered on whether or not the Court should follow the "original intent" of the Framers. In other words, should a provision of the Constitution mean what the Framers thought it meant? Or should the Court's interpretation allow the constitutional meaning to evolve and grow in light of modern realities and attitudes?

For original intent

Any approach other than original intent is inconsistent with constitutional democracy. To its proponents, the primary benefit of the original-intent approach is that it prevents judges from imposing their personal or political beliefs on the nation. "To allow the court to govern simply by what it views at the time as fair and decent, is a scheme of government no longer popular," declared Edwin Meese, who served as Ronald Reagan's attorney general. "A Court that makes rather than implements value choices," wrote Judge Robert Bork, "cannot be

squared with the presuppositions of a democratic society." Adds the legal scholar Richard S. Kay: "When honestly applied, original intentions adjudication seems to reduce the influence of the personal and idiosyncratic aspects of a judge's personality or ideology more than do alternative theories that rely on ill-defined standards of one kind or another." Only a theory of original intent, critics conclude, makes it clear that the Constitution applies to judges as much as to presidents and legislators.

Only the original-intent approach gives the Constitution the respect and deference it deserves. "A constitution that is viewed as only what the judges say it is, is no longer a constitution in the truest sense," said Meese. "Those who framed the Constitution chose their words carefully; they debated at great length the most minute points. It is incumbent upon the Court to determine what that meaning is." Advocates of original intention point out that even the Supreme Court "regularly insists that its results, and most particularly its controversial results, do not spring from the mere will of the Justices in the majority but are supported, indeed compelled, by a proper understanding of the Constitution of the United States. . . . The way an institution advertises tells you what it thinks its customers demand."

The original-intent approach provides stability and predictability, and demands that judicial decisions be principled. "Constitutional government exists to limit the sphere of appropriate governmental activity," writes Kay. Such limits are valuable, he argues, only if citizens can "'count on' government being constrained by certain procedures and within certain limits." A constitutional approach that allows the fundamental rules to change whenever the judges want them to undermines "the peculiar contribution of law to society." Adds Bork: "The Court's power is legitimate only if it has, and can demonstrate in reasoned opinions that it has, a valid theory, derived from the Constitution, of the respective spheres of majority and minority freedom."

Against original intent

Determining the Framers' intent is difficult, if not impossible. Critics of the original-intent approach counter that determining the Framers' intent is far more difficult than its supporters suggest. Even deciding who is a Framer is not a trivial task. "The most outspoken Framers disagreed with each other and did not necessarily reflect the opinions of the many who did not enter the debates," argues the historian Leonard W. Levy. "The Framers, who did not agree on their own constitutional issues, would not likely speak to us about ours with a single voice." Ironically, adds the legal scholar Paul Brest, the impossibility of accurately determining the original intent in most cases makes it impossible to predict future judicial decisions and thus undermines one of the originalists' strongest arguments.

The original-intent approach would "freeze" the Constitution's meaning in the distant past. "Time works changes, brings into existence new conditions and purposes," the Supreme Court declared a century ago. "Therefore, a principle to be vital must be capable of wider application than the mischief which gave it birth. This is particularly true of constitutions. They are not ephemeral enactments, designed to meet passing occasions. They are, to use the words of Chief Justice John Marshall, 'designed to approach immortality as nearly as human institutions can approach it.'" An insistence that the Constitution could not change with the times, opponents of original intent argue, was the fatal error behind such judicial disasters as the *Dred Scott* case.

Supporters of original intent merely seek to defend their own political and ideological preferences. "All that Ed Meese has done is to espouse what he thinks are 'conservative' interpretations of the Constitution and dubbed them 'original intent,'" writes the political theorist Harry Jaffa. Supporters of original intent "would radically change American constitutional law to make it conform to [their] idealized projection of it," agrees Levy. What the original-intent theory really does, writes the constitutional historian Alfred H. Kelly, is to supply "an apparent rationale for politically inspired activism that can be indulged in the name of constitutional continuity."

Only a "living constitution" approach can preserve the true intention of the Framers. The Constitution of the United States, declared Justice Brennan, "is a sparkling vision of the supremacy of the human dignity of every individual." To fulfill the ultimate purpose of the Constitution, "the precise rules by which we have protected human dignity" must be allowed to change, "in response to both transformations of social condition and evolution of our concepts of human dignity." Only through interpretation of the text, Brennan concludes, can judges account for and implement "the transformative purpose of the text."

SOURCES: Leonard W. Levy, *Original Intent and the Framers' Constitution* (New York: Macmillan, 1988); Edwin Meese III, "Address before the American Bar Association," Washington, D.C., July 9, 1985, and "The Law of the Constitution," Speech at Tulane Univ., October 21, 1986; Robert H. Bork, "Neutral Principles and Some First Amendment Problems," *Indiana Law Journal* 47 (1971), pp. 1–11; Paul Brest, "The Misconceived Quest for the Original Understanding," *Boston University Law Review* 60 (March 1980), pp. 204–238; Richard S. Kay, "Adherence to the Original Intentions in Constitutional Adjudication: Three Objections and Responses," *Northwestern University Law Review* 82 (Winter 1988), pp. 226–292.

Marbury asked the new president for the commission, or for a copy, but Jefferson refused. Thereupon Marbury brought suit, technically against the new secretary of state, James Madison, asking the Supreme Court to order the administration to hand over the commission. Without it, Marbury had no proof of his appointment and no authority to serve as a justice of the peace.

The legalities of the case were complex, but the political implications were clear. The Court, led by John Marshall and dominated by Federalists, seemed to have two choices. It could side with Marbury and order Madison (and Jefferson) to hand over the commission, or it could rule the other way and leave Marbury out in the cold. The problem with the first option was the likelihood that Jefferson would simply ignore the Court, thereby damaging its credibility. The Court, after all, did not enjoy the kind of prestige it has now, and there was no tradition of obedience to its decrees. Worse yet, an anti-Jefferson ruling would have been seen as a purely partisan act, dragging the Court down to the level of an ordinary political body. The other option was no more attractive: a ruling in favor of Jefferson would have amounted to abject surrender, clearly exposing the weakness of the Federalists in the face of the Republican juggernaut.

Remarkably, Marshall found a way out of the dilemma. In a long opinion, he first established that Marbury had a right to his commission, and that the administration's refusal to deliver it amounted to an illegal act. It was also appropriate, Marshall ruled, for Marbury to ask for a judicial order (or *writ of mandamus*) directing the secretary of state to hand over the commission. But Marshall did not issue such an order, holding instead that the Supreme Court of the United States could not legally issue the writ in this case.

Why not? Because, ruled Marshall, the Constitution prohibited the Court from issuing the kind of writ that Marbury sought, even though Congress had authorized such writs under the Judiciary Act of 1789. Marshall ruled that the relevant provision of this act was unconstitutional, and thus null and void.

Marshall's decision was a political masterstroke. His declaration that the administration had acted illegally pleased the Federalists. His refusal to order the delivery of the commission pleased the Republicans, and diffused their hostility toward the Court. In one motion he put the Court above politics, established its special tie to the Constitution, and laid the foundation for its extraordinary future in American politics.

Marshall's Argument for Judicial Review. The key decision in *Marbury* was that the Court had both the power and the duty to follow the commands of the Constitution, even if doing so meant overruling an act of Congress. From Marshall's point of view, the choice presented to him in *Marbury* was simple. He could follow the will of Congress, accept jurisdiction in the case, and grant the writ of mandamus. Or he could follow the Constitution, which barred the Court from granting such a writ. He could not do both.

Marshall offered three arguments in defense of his claim that "an act of the legislature, repugnant to the [C]onstitution, is void." The first relies on the basic principles of American government, the second on a close reading of the text of the Constitution, and the third on the nature of the judicial process.

- *Political theory.* Marshall first derived judicial review from the theoretical principles of American government. In doing so he closely followed Hamilton's argument in the *Federalist* No. 78. The Constitution not only established the federal government, Marshall wrote, but also set clear limits to the power of that government, particularly the legislative branch. If the legislature were free to transcend those limits at any time, the Constitution would cease to be "a superior, paramount law," and would be "on a level with ordinary legislative acts." Either an act contrary to the Constitution is void, Marshall wrote, or "written constitutions are absurd attempts, on the part of the people," to limit governmental power.

- *The constitutional text.* Marshall enlisted two specific provisions of the Constitution in defense of his position. First, he noted that judges are required to take an oath in support of the Constitution. That oath, as prescribed by Congress, requires a judge to administer justice "agreeably to *the constitution*, and laws of the United States." Second, he pointed to the Supremacy Clause, which declares the Constitution to be "the *Supreme law* of the land," along with all laws made "in pursuance thereof." By implication, Marshall wrote, laws *not* in pursuance of the Constitution are *not* the supreme law of the land, and are not binding on the judges.

- *The nature of the courts.* Marshall's final argument rested on the unique role of judges and courts in the governmental process. "It is emphatically the province and duty of the judicial department to say what the law is," he wrote in a famous passage. If both the Constitution and an act of Congress apply in a particular case, "the court must either decide that case conformably to the law, disregarding the constitution; or conformably to the constitution, disregarding the law; the court must determine which of these conflicting rules governs the case." Such judgments, he concluded are "of the very essence of judicial duty." Marshall's argument here strikes at the very heart of the issue. The courts, he suggested, are specially, if not uniquely, qualified to "say what the law is." Although the Constitution binds all three branches, it seems to bind the courts in a special relationship.

The Supreme Court and the States

Judicial Review of State Laws   The Federalists took it for granted that the Supreme Court would have the power to nullify state laws that conflicted with the national constitution. "In controversies relating to the boundary between the two jurisdictions [state and federal]," wrote James Madison, "the tribunal which is ultimately to decide, is to be established under the general government."[27] Opponents of the Constitution quickly realized the importance of this issue, which essentially left it to the federal government to decide the legitimate boundaries of state and national power. The Antifederalists had little doubt that the Court would use judicial review to increase the power of the national government, and they were right.

The Court did not officially claim the power to review state laws until 1810, seven years after *Marbury.* The case was *Fletcher* v. *Peck,* which arose out of a corruption scandal in the Georgia legislature in the 1790s.[28] Apparently the legislature, under the heavy influence of bribery, sold some 35 million acres to four land-grant companies, which in turn sold the land to unsuspecting buyers at a tidy profit. The corrupt legislators were thrown out of office, and the new legislature annulled all land purchases under the old act.

One of the new owners brought suit to challenge the constitutionality of the annulment, and the Supreme Court, led again by John Marshall, agreed that the repeal act violated the Contracts Clause, which bars the states from passing laws that "impair the Obligation of Contracts." The decision put Marshall in the uncomfortable position of siding with the corrupt land speculators over those who had cleaned up the mess, but the underlying constitutional principles survived. The Supreme Court's power to enforce the Constitution against the states became a critical weapon in the battle to establish national power.

Over the years, the Supreme Court has used its power of judicial review far more often against the states than against the national government. In a little under two hundred years, the Court has struck down 141 federal laws, in whole or in part, on average less than one a year. Only a handful of these nullifications interfered with or frustrated important federal policies. By contrast, the Court has struck down approximately 1,200 state laws since 1810, on average more than six a year.[29] Although in several recent cases the Supreme Court has protected the sovereignty of the states from infringement by the national government (see Chapter 3), most of the controversial Supreme Court decisions of the past fifty years have involved state rather than federal cases.

Review of State Court Decisions The Constitution clearly states that state judges, like federal judges, are bound to uphold its provisions. In an 1816 decision, the Marshall Court made it clear that state court decisions on matters of federal law (including the Constitution) were subject to review by the federal courts.

The case, known as *Martin* v. *Hunter's Lessee,* arose out of a dispute over land that the state of Virginia had confiscated from its British owners during the Revolutionary War.[30] One side claimed that the land was theirs, under the confiscation statute. The other argued that the confiscation statute violated two federal treaties protecting loyalist landholdings. The Virginia Supreme Court ruled against the loyalists, but the Supreme Court of the United States re-

"The courts ruled that we had to open it up to all stuffed animals."

versed. Next the Virginia Supreme Court refused to overturn its ruling, and the case went back to Washington. Because John Marshall had a financial interest in the case, the Supreme Court's decision was written down by his colleague Joseph Story of Massachusetts.

Story's opinion established the crucial principle that the national government—and not the states—would have the final say over matters of federal law, including the Constitution. That principle is easily taken for granted today, but at the time it was highly controversial, and without it a strong national government would have been impossible.

Today the Supreme Court's power to review state court decisions on matters of federal law provides an important mechanism for the enforcement of federal rights in state courts. Suppose a defendant in a state criminal case challenges the introduction of certain evidence on the ground that it was illegally obtained under federal law. If the state judge denies the claim, the matter can be appealed—eventually—to the United States Supreme Court. Under other circumstances state prisoners can be released, or at least have their claims heard, by the lower federal courts.

The threat of federal court review of state proceedings has undoubtedly made the state courts more sensitive to federal constitutional rights. Outright federal reversals in state cases, therefore, are uncommon. In recent years the Supreme Court has narrowed the rights of state prisoners to seek redress in the federal courts, especially in death penalty cases. Although the Court's goals of expediting justice and showing respect for the state courts are laudable, critics charge that the Court's new rules have greatly increased the odds that in some cases the innocent will be punished along with the guilty.

The Courts in American Government

The role of the courts in the American system of government extends beyond their power to judge state and federal laws unconstitutional. The federal courts also play key roles in interpreting the laws passed by Congress and in keeping watch over the activities of the federal bureaucracy. State courts play similar roles in interpreting state laws and in overseeing the state governments.

Statutory Interpretation

The federal courts' role in the legislative process includes the power to *interpret* acts of Congress. The legislative branch may write the laws, but in the end it is the judiciary that says what they mean.

Judicial interpretation of the laws passed by Congress is known as **statutory interpretation** (a statute is simply a written law passed by a legislative authority). Congress is often criticized for writing unclear and ambiguous laws, but in reality the need for judicial interpretation is almost impossible to avoid. The reason is clear: *laws are written to deal with general cases, but courts must deal with real-life situations.* A legislative body cannot foresee all the circumstances and conditions under which a particular statute will operate, and courts must be able to provide for extraordinary or unanticipated situations.

An interesting example of statutory interpretation occurred in 1994. A federal law provides for the appointment of a lawyer for any state death-row inmate "in any post-conviction proceeding." A Texas prisoner under sentence of death accordingly requested the appointment of a lawyer to assist him in appealing his conviction to the federal courts. The state of Texas argued that such an appointment was uncalled for, since until a federal court accepted the prisoner's case no "post-conviction proceeding" had actually begun. In oral arguments, Justice David Souter challenged the state's position. "Isn't it incumbent on us to construe a Federal statute so as not to turn it into a dead letter?" he asked. The state's interpretation of the law, he added, "turns it into farce." Ultimately the Court agreed that the prisoner had a right to the appointment of a lawyer.[31]

Over the years, the Supreme Court has evolved various rules and principles to guide it in interpreting congressional statutes. For example, the Court always tries to read statutes in such a way as to avoid a conflict with the Constitution. Also, the Court traditionally reads criminal statutes narrowly, so as to avoid imposing punishments for actions that do not fall clearly within the meaning of the law.

In interpreting acts of Congress, the Court looks to find the "congressional intent"—in other words, what Congress meant by the law at the time it was passed. Evidence of congressional intent includes language in committee reports, floor statements by senators and representatives, and language explicitly or implicitly rejected by Congress in passing the bill.

In reality, it is extremely difficult to discern Congress's intent on any particular provision of a statute. In fact, many legal scholars—including Justice Antonin Scalia—have suggested that the entire enterprise is artificial. The main problem is that Congress consists of 535 different people, each of whom may have his or her own idea of what a statutory provision means. To those critics, the process of reconstructing congressional intent is simply a way for the Court to rationalize its decisions.

Moreover, representatives and senators—and their staffs—know what the Court looks for in determining congressional intent, and go out of their way to create an artificial record that, they hope, will someday shape the Court's view of the law. For example, a senator might make a speech on the floor for the sole purpose of creating "evidence" of congressional intent. Especially at the committee and subcommittee levels, it is often possible to influence the Court by inserting language that would not be approved if voted on by Congress as a whole.

Despite the criticisms, the Court continues to use congressional intent in its efforts to discern the meaning of federal laws. Although the process is open to manipulation and error, no clear alternative exists. For example, reliance on the "plain language" of congressional statutes, as Justice Scalia has suggested, is deceptively difficult. Words have meaning only in context, and judicial efforts to interpret federal laws from the text alone would often amount to guesswork.[32]

Watchdog on the Bureaucracy

The federal courts provide an important check on the federal bureaucracy. As we saw in Chapter 14, the federal courts review administrative actions with regard to both procedure and substance. To be legally valid, agencies must comply with the procedural rules set out in the Constitution, the Administrative Procedures Act (APA), and any other relevant statutes. Agencies must also comply with rules they have voluntarily adopted. The substance of agency actions must be consistent with the expressed or implied will of Congress, though the courts give the agencies wide discretion when Congress's intent is unclear.

The Courts and the Democratic Process

The tension between majority rule and minority rights lies at the heart of American politics, and no institution more clearly reflects this tension than the Supreme Court. On the one hand, the Court has vigorously enforced individual rights and the rights of racial and ethnic minorities against the arbitrary or discriminatory actions of state and national majorities. On the other hand, the Court has dedicated itself to protecting the institutions of democracy and majority rule. At times these two roles reinforce each other, as when the Court enforces the voting rights of racial minorities. At other times, however, the roles are clearly in conflict.

The Courts and Minority Rights

Judged across the entire span of American history, the Supreme Court has as poor a record of defending minority rights as the legislative and executive branches. The Court, as we have seen, not only upheld the existence of slavery before the Civil War, but also sanctioned racial segregation afterward. Nor was the Court any more vigilant in defense of citizens who practiced unpopular religions or expressed unpopular viewpoints. (For a complete discussion of the Court's early approach to civil liberties and civil rights, see Chapters 4 and 5.)

Beginning in 1938, however, the Court signaled that it would play a more aggressive role in defense of minority rights. The turning point came in the case of *United States* v. *Carolene Products.* The case itself, which involved a federal law banning certain kinds of milk from interstate commerce, is of little interest. In upholding this law, however, the Court indicated its reluctance to interfere with Congress's decisions on economic regulation, essentially abandoning an area that had concerned it since the early 1800s. At the same time it indicated in a footnote its new concern with laws "directed at particular religious, or national, or racial minorities," and with situations where prejudice against such minorities interferes with the "political processes ordinarily to be relied upon" for their protection.[33] Although the Court was relatively silent during World War II, the "Carolene Products Footnote" became the manifesto of the post–World War II Court.

Thus it is no coincidence that many of the most important civil rights and civil liberties decisions in the Court's history have come in cases involving American society's least popular groups and individuals. The classic freedom-of-religion cases have involved Jews, Catholics, Jehovah's Witnesses, or atheists, all of whom have been the victims of bigotry and hatred. Major gains in freedom of speech and press were made on behalf of communists, civil rights protesters, anarchists, and Klansmen. Protection of the individual's rights to due process of law and to the security of his or her home has been advanced largely in cases dealing with convicted criminals.

Why has the burden of protecting minorities in our society fallen so frequently on the courts? It is precisely because the courts are *not* elected institutions, and can operate with at least some disregard for the mood swings of public opinion. Federal judges, as we have seen, serve for life, and can be removed from office only by impeachment for misconduct in office. They are trained to give a fair hearing to both sides in every case, and to ignore, or at least try to ignore, their own preconceptions and prejudices. Court proceedings are conducted in an atmosphere of dignity and reflection, with the public's role limited to observation only (except in jury trials; see the next section). Judicial decisions, at least at the level of appellate courts, are expressed in the form of written opinions, putting a premium on logical analysis. Finally, courts operate in a tradition of "equal justice under law," a tradition in which social and political hierarchies are deliberately ignored or suppressed.

Over the long term, of course, the federal courts reflect the views and mores of American society. Federal judges are not elected, but they are appointed and confirmed by the elected representatives of the people. Nothing about the judiciary prevented it from approving of segregation at a time when the other branches of the government, and for that matter most Americans, advocated the idea or at least were willing to tolerate it. Likewise, the modern Supreme Court reflects society's unwillingness to provide full legal protection to gays and lesbians, and has responded to the popular desire to "get tough on crime." In the long run, all that can be hoped is that the Court is on the leading edge of the larger society, willing and able to push it in the direction of ever-increasing tolerance and acceptance of minorities. Even that hope, however, is often frustrated.

The Courts and Majority Rule

The courts reflect the values of majoritarian democracy in more direct ways. The democratic nature of the courts should not be forgotten, although it is often overshadowed by dramatic decisions on minority rights. The courts' dedication to democratic principles is evident not only in their decisions but also in their structure.

Juries The most important democratic institution within the judicial system is the jury. The right to trial by jury is guaranteed by the Bill of Rights and extends to all federal criminal cases, to all state criminal cases in which the potential punishment exceeds six months' imprisonment,[34] and to all federal civil trials involving more than $20. Federal juries in criminal cases are composed of twelve persons chosen from the state and district in which the crime was allegedly committed, although the Supreme Court has permitted smaller juries (usually six persons) in federal civil cases and in all state cases. In federal criminal cases, the jury must reach a unanimous verdict; in civil cases and in state criminal cases, unanimity is not required. In criminal cases, juries can convict only on a finding that the defendant is guilty "beyond a reasonable doubt." The actual number of cases that go to jury trial is small, because most cases are settled by negotiation between the parties and because many litigants choose to waive their right to a jury trial and appear before only a judge.

Juries decide only questions of fact, leaving questions of law to the judge. In a murder case, for example, a judge would define the meaning of "premeditated" homicide, which is part of the definition of first-degree murder, in his or her *instructions* to the jury. The jury is then left to decide whether or not the actions of the defendant were in fact premeditated within the meaning of the judge's instruction. A jury acquittal in a criminal case cannot be appealed by the prosecution; but a verdict of guilty, and any verdict in a civil case, can be appealed, first to the trial judge and then to the higher courts. Except in cases of acquittal, judges have the authority to review, and overturn, a jury's decision—as was dramatically illustrated in 1997 in the case of British nanny Louise Woodward. Rejecting the jury's decision to convict Woodward of second-degree murder (which would have carried a life sentence), Massachusetts judge Hiller Zobel reduced the verdict to manslaughter, and released Woodward from prison.

Juries are democratic in two respects. First, they are drawn from a representative sample of the community at large. The Supreme Court has insisted that the pool from which the jury is drawn—although not necessarily any particular jury—fairly represent women and minority groups. Recently, the Court has banned either side from excluding individual jurors on the basis of race or gender in both civil and criminal cases.[35] Of course, there is no guarantee that a given jury will be representative, an issue of special importance when racial tensions run high. For example, the jury that acquitted the police officers charged with beating up a black motorist in the 1992 Rodney King case in Los Angeles contained no African Americans, largely because the trial had been moved to the nearly all-white suburbs due to pretrial publicity.

Second, juries have traditionally had the right to ignore the law altogether in order to acquit a defendant on political grounds (if they ignore the law to *convict* a defendant, of course, their decision can be overturned by the courts). Known as **jury nullification,** this is an old American practice, dating back to the 1735 trial of John Peter Zenger. Zenger, a colonial publisher, was charged with making libelous statements against the government. Although Zenger was clearly guilty under the law, the jury chose to express its dissatisfaction with the idea of government control of the press and returned an acquittal. The Supreme Court has held that juries have the right, and indeed the duty, to set aside a judge's instructions if they think them erroneous or unjust.

As the Rodney King case arguably demonstrates, jury nullification is a two-edged sword. Juries have often exercised their right to ignore the law in the name of justice and fundamental fairness. But they have also ignored the law simply to acquit a defendant whose victims were unpopular or powerless, or whose actions conformed to popular prejudices. In any event, juries in major cases can play an important role in the democratic process. Recently, for example, several juries have acquitted women of serious criminal charges on the grounds that the women were physically or psychologically abused. The most publicized example was the case of Lorena Bobbitt, who cut off her husband's penis with a knife. The jury accepted Bobbitt's argument that she had been abused, and found her not guilty by reason of temporary insanity. The Bobbitt decision, whether right or wrong, surely contributed to the national debate over the problem of spouse abuse.

Protecting the Democratic Process   Courts also promote democracy by ensuring that the nation's democratic institutions operate freely and fairly. Most important are the courts' efforts to protect voting rights and to ensure the fairness of representative institutions.

Voting Rights and Reapportionment. The Constitution bans any interference with the right to vote on the basis of race, sex, and age, for people over age eighteen. Before 1965, voting rights were enforced only weakly by the Court and Congress. In that year, however, Congress passed the Voting Rights Act, a sweeping piece of legislation that provided strong mechanisms for federal enforcement of voting rights, especially to prevent or remedy racial discrimination. The Supreme Court upheld the act in 1966 and has enforced it ever since, although controversial decisions in 1993 and 1995 limited the power of the states to create congressional districts designed to produce minority legislators.[36]

Since 1964, the Court has also insisted that voters be equally represented in the House of Representatives and in state and local legislatures. The Court has generally applied the rule of "one person, one vote" everywhere except the United States Senate. In effect, the one person, one vote rule means that legislative districts within the same state must be the same size, so that each member of a legislative chamber represents approximately the same number of constituents.* The state must have legitimate reasons for any variation from the one person, one vote standard.[37]

A full discussion of voting rights and reapportionment issues appears in Chapter 10.

Political Participation. Among the rights protected by the Bill of Rights and enforced by the courts are various rights of political participation. Especially in the past fifty years, the courts have been vigilant in protecting rights of free speech, free press, and freedom of assembly—especially when political issues are at stake. The Supreme Court has reiterated many times its basic position, which recognizes a "profound national commitment to the principle that debate on public issues should be uninhibited, robust, and wide-open."[38]

Thus the Court has weighed in with key decisions on the constitutionality of state and federal election laws and party procedures (see Chapters 9 and 10). In 1995, for example, the Court struck down an Ohio law banning the anonymous distribution of campaign literature, holding that the right to speak anonymously was protected by the First Amendment.[39]

Democracy and the Courts: An Assessment

With few exceptions, the Supreme Court's role in overseeing the democratic process is to ensure that minority groups are fairly represented and have an equal chance to participate. For the most part, the Court has interfered with the democratic process only when an entrenched majority has used its power to exclude a minority group from participation or to negate its influence.

Not surprisingly, the Court has intervened most often to protect the rights of racial minorities. But the Court has also moved in to protect other groups whose right to participate has been violated or limited. In 1986, for example, the Court held that a state legislature controlled by one political party could not use its power over the redistricting process to the detriment of the opposition party. In free speech cases, the Court has been particularly keen to protect the rights of those with unpopular views, such as communists and Klansmen.[40]

"The life of the law has not been logic, it has been experience."

—Oliver Wendell Holmes

For the most part, the Court's commitment to the protection of the democratic process has helped, not hindered, minority participation in politics.

The result is a political system that, at a minimum, guarantees that minorities will be allowed to make their voices heard by the governing majority. Beyond that, the Court can do little more than make sure that the civil rights and civil liberties of the minority are not infringed.

The power of the Supreme Court to protect minorities should not be overstated. Despite their political independence and their legal training, the judges can be counted on to reflect the broader values and principles of the larger society, at least in the long term. They are, after all, products of that society, and they are appointed and confirmed by the elected representatives of the American people.

---

* The constitutional requirements that House districts cannot cross state lines and that every state is entitled to at least one representative means that the "one person, one vote" rule applies only to voters within the same state.

The historical record bears out this expectation. Although the Supreme Court has at times been out of step with the governing majority in the White House and Congress, such episodes are rare and short-lived. Moreover, the Court has rarely tried to block the will of the other two branches on a subject of overriding importance, and has never succeeded in doing so.

Consider, for example, the New Deal crisis of the 1930s. Franklin Roosevelt, elected during the Great Depression with a strongly supportive Congress, embarked on the most ambitious legislative program in American history. Among the legislation passed during Roosevelt's first term were laws regulating the stock markets and the banks, and programs to aid farmers, miners, and manufacturers.

Over a two-year period, from 1935 to 1936, the Supreme Court struck down no fewer than a dozen new programs, effectively gutting the New Deal. The Court's opposition, however, did not last long. Roosevelt and the New Deal won a landslide election in 1936, and in 1937 the president proposed the infamous "Court-packing" plan, a program designed to create enough new vacancies on the Court to allow the appointment of a pro–New Deal majority. Whether influenced by the Court-packing plan or simply by the election returns, the Court capitulated quickly, approving federal regulation of labor unions in 1937 and of wages, hours, and working conditions in 1938. Never again did the Court interfere with Roosevelt's economic program.

Since 1937, the Court has rarely even tried to interfere with major federal laws and programs. Although it has invalidated a number of important federal laws, it has never prevented Congress and the president from acting on the key issues facing the nation. In both economic regulation and foreign affairs, the Court has given the other branches a virtual free hand.

Supreme Court decisions affecting *state* laws are another story. In the past forty years, the Court has rewritten state criminal procedure, outlawed school segregation, banned state-sponsored school prayer and other forms of state-supported religion, struck down state laws on abortion and contraception, and severely limited state power to deal with obscenity and other forms of indecent or unpopular speech. Most of the controversial Supreme Court decisions of the modern era have been directed primarily, or exclusively, at the powers of the states.

These developments continue a long historical trend. Throughout its history, the Court has generally taken a broad view of federal power and a narrower view of state power, and has consistently sided with the federal government when the states have challenged its authority (see the discussion in Chapter 3). The justices' preference for the national government arises directly from the nature of the appointments process, which favors men and women with national reputations and a national outlook.

The modern Supreme Court, like its predecessors, has mirrored the politics of the other branches. As the nation turned to more conservative presidents in the 1980s, the Court naturally turned to the right as well. Under the leadership of Chief Justice William Rehnquist, the Court has moved to limit the Warren and Burger Courts' restrictions on state power and has shown signs of trying to restrict the exercise of congressional power as well. Since 1981, for example, the Court has expanded the states' authority to regulate abortion, relaxed the rules governing search warrants and interrogation of prisoners, and permitted increased state support for religion. At the same time, the Court has refused to recognize new rights or expand old ones, and has followed the public mood in restricting death penalty appeals and fighting affirmative action.

The politics of the modern Court are complicated by divided government and by the decline of party strength. Because the executive branch plays the dominant role in the appointment of new justices and the Senate merely a supporting role, the justices have tended to mirror the political outlook of the executive rather than the legislative branch. At the same time, however, the Senate has been able to block the appointment of at least one conservative judge (Robert Bork, in 1987), and influenced the appointment of moderate, rather than extremist, judges in several other cases.

Summary

The judicial power of the United States government is vested in the federal courts, which include the United States Supreme Court and various lower courts established by Congress. The federal judiciary operates independently of the state and territorial judicial systems. Its jurisdiction is limited to specific types of cases, including federal criminal cases, cases to which the United States is a party, cases based on federal law, and certain civil cases, such as those involving citizens of different states.

Federal judges are appointed by the president, subject to confirmation by the Senate. Presidential appointments to the Supreme Court are among a president's most enduring legacy, and presidents typically take a personal interest in the appointments process. Supreme Court nominations fights have frequently been bitterly contested, especially in recent years, leading presidents to avoid divisive nominees and concentrate on men and women who can easily win Senate approval.

Overall, the federal judiciary does not mirror the nation as a whole. Although President Clinton has made a great effort to appoint women and minorities, on the whole the federal judiciary is overwhelmingly white, male, and well-to-do. Federal judges are assisted by law clerks, who are drawn from among the best law school graduates in the nation, as well as by magistrates and other assistants.

Cases arrive at the Supreme Court either directly or on appeal. Cases arising under the Court's original jurisdiction are rare, and usually involve disputes between two states. Most cases that reach the Supreme Court do so on appeal, from either the state or the federal courts, typically under a writ of certiorari. Under the rule of four, the Supreme Court takes a case only if four judges want to hear it. The majority of cases appealed to the Supreme Court are *in forma pauperis* petitions, typically made by state or federal prison inmates. Most are rejected out of hand, but now and then such cases create the occasion for a major decision.

Cases heard by the Supreme Court are accompanied by written briefs presented by each side. Usually, the justices also hear oral arguments. Finally the justices meet in conference to decide the case, after which they prepare formal written opinions and announce their ruling. Individual justices may file concurring or dissenting opinions.

The most important power exercised by the Supreme Court is that of judicial review, which allows the Court to examine federal and state laws and actions and to determine whether they violate the Constitution. The power of judicial review is not explicitly mentioned in the Constitution, but it was claimed by the Supreme Court in the 1803 case of *Marbury* v. *Madison* and has been exercised ever since.

The courts play two other key roles in American government. The first is statutory interpretation—deciding what the laws of Congress mean and how to apply them. The second is judicial supervision of the federal bureaucracy, to ensure that the agencies follow the laws and their own procedures.

Paradoxically, the courts play a key role in protecting not only minority rights but also majority rule. The courts protect minority rights by enforcing a range of civil rights and civil liberties decisions. The courts protect majority rule by ensuring that the democratic process is not compromised and through the jury system, which allows men and women drawn from a cross section of the population to participate directly in the governmental process.

Key Terms

Jurisdiction
Advisory opinions
Appellate jurisdiction
Original jurisdiction
Writ of certiorari
Rule of four
Written briefs

Amicus curiae (or "friend of the court") briefs
Oral argument
Opinion of the court
Concurring opinion
Dissenting opinion
Judicial review
Marbury v. *Madison*
Statutory interpretation
Jury nullification

Review Questions

1. How are federal judges selected? What are the predominant characteristics of those who make up the federal judiciary?

2. How do cases get to the United States Supreme Court? What are the roles of written briefs and oral argument?

3. What is judicial review? What arguments have been advanced to justify the Supreme Court's power of judicial review?

4. Discuss the political and constitutional implications of *Marbury* v. *Madison, Fletcher* v. *Peck,* and *Martin* v. *Hunter's Lessee.*

5. What is statutory interpretation? How does the Court go about trying to determine congressional intent?

6. How does the Supreme Court protect minority rights? How does it protect majority rule?

Suggested Readings

Abraham, Henry J. *The Judicial Process: An Introductory Analysis of the Courts of the United States, England, and France,* 6th ed. New York: Oxford University Press, 1993.

—— *Justices and Presidents: A Political History of Appointments to the Supreme Court,* 3d ed. New York: Oxford University Press, 1992.

Bickel, Alexander M. *The Least Dangerous Branch: The Supreme Court at the Bar of Politics.* Indianapolis: Bobbs-Merrill, 1962.

Hall, Kermit L., ed. *The Oxford Companion to the Supreme Court of the United States.* New York: Oxford University Press, 1992.

Lasser, William. *The Limits of Judicial Power: The Supreme Court in American Politics.* Chapel Hill: University of North Carolina Press, 1988.

McCloskey, Robert G. *The American Supreme Court,* 2d ed., rev. by Sanford Levinson. Chicago: University of Chicago Press, 1994.

O'Brien, David M. *Storm Center: The Supreme Court in American Politics,* 4th ed. New York: W. W. Norton, 1996.

Internet Resources

Legal links, including Supreme Court and lower court decisions, at:

http://www.findlaw.com

Full text of Supreme Court opinions since 1893 at:

http://www.findlaw.com/casecode/supreme.html

Supreme Court information, including texts of important historical cases, at:

http://supct.law.cornell.edu/supct

Supreme Court oral arguments available via RealAudios, at:

http://oyez.nwu.edu

★ 16 ★ Domestic Policy

The *New York Times* described it as "the fiscal equivalent of the fall of the Berlin Wall." On January 5, 1998, President Bill Clinton stood in the Cabinet Room of the White House and announced that his administration would submit a balanced budget for fiscal year 1999—three years ahead of the schedule he and Congress had negotiated two years earlier, and nearly three decades since a president had even proposed a balanced budget to Congress.

The politics of budget deficits dominated the fiscal debate throughout the 1980s and 1990s. The deficit, moderate throughout most of the 1970s, ballooned in the early 1980s—largely because the government cut taxes but did not cut spending. By the early 1990s, $200 billion deficits were routine, and there seemed little hope that the government would ever find its way back into the black. The enormous deficit put severe constraints on government spending, fueled the public's distrust of government, and helped bring Newt Gingrich and the congressional Republicans to power in 1994.

Bill Clinton was elected in 1993 despite, not because of, the public's increasing concern about the deficit. Clinton did propose modest tax increases, but he also called for increased spending to combat the nation's economic woes, and for massively expensive programs in health care, education, and social policy. In the wake of the 1994 Republican congressional sweep, however, Clinton changed his spots. Bending to the new realities, Clinton called on Congress to balance the budget, sparking an intense debate that obsessed Washington in 1995 and helped shape the contours of the 1996 presidential campaign.

By 1996, Clinton and the congressional Republicans found it in their common interest to agree on erasing the budget deficit by 2002. The disappearance of the deficit was due less to politics, however, than to economics.

Less than two years after the signing of the budget agreement, the rapidly expanding American economy had generated tax revenues beyond anyone's dreams; at the same time, low interest rates and low unemployment pushed federal spending down. While Clinton and the Republicans vied with each other to claim the credit, economists put the balanced budget down to extraordinary economic growth and a healthy dose of good luck.

Even as they announced the good news, Washington's power players made it clear that the new politics of balanced budgets and potential surpluses would not be tranquil. Hours before the president's announcement, Speaker Newt Gingrich proposed that any future surpluses be used in part to pay down accumulated debt and in part to fund tax cuts. Democrats called for "investment" in health care, education, and social programs. And some analysts—and even some politicians—suggested that this rare moment of opportunity be used to make meaningful reforms of social security and other long-term programs that

Budget director Franklin Raines (far right) joins President Bill Clinton and Vice President Al Gore to celebrate the disappearance of the federal budget deficit.

★★★

threaten the nation's fiscal balance decades down the road.[1]

In the end, much of politics is about what the government does with the money it takes in and with the money it spends. Although domestic policy involves more than dollars and cents, no area of policy can escape entirely from the constraints of budgetary politics.

Much of the political rhetoric of the 1980s and 1990s has concerned the question of larger versus smaller government. In 1993 and 1994, for example, Republicans and Democrats engaged in a highly spirited debate over whether the federal government's role in providing health care insurance should be expanded. Often, however, the debate over how to allocate the resources that the government takes in has been even more intense. Should more money be spent on defense and less on domestic programs? Should available dollars be spent on new prisons or on public schools? These issues may not always frame the domestic policy debate in America, but they make up the day-to-day issues with which both Congress and the White House must deal.

Previous chapters have laid the groundwork for understanding the process by which policy in the United States is made. This chapter looks more closely at some of the general concerns that policy makers must keep in mind as they make their decisions, and examines several key areas of domestic policy concern.

Questions to Keep in Mind

☑ *What arguments would liberals and conservatives make in favor of more or less government involvement with private economic or social relationships?*

☑ *Discuss the various types of government programs in economic and social policy. Give examples in the areas of economic and social policy.*

☑ *Who are the winners and losers in the domestic policy arena? Why do some groups succeed and others fail?*

Basic Concepts ★ ★ ★ ★ ★ ★ ★ ★ ★ ★ ★ ★ ★

If politics is the *process* by which the government makes key decisions, policy is the *result* of those decisions. Put another way, policy "is what the government says and does about perceived problems." Because the needs of modern societies are so diverse, government policy (or public policy) is concerned with a wide range of issue areas. These areas include the economy, health care, education, welfare, the environment, worker and consumer safety, and foreign affairs. This chapter deals with the policy-making process and with various aspects of social and economic policy; the next covers foreign and military policy.

The Constitution and Domestic Policy

Since the New Deal, the Supreme Court has given both the states and the national government broad latitude in the making of social and economic policy. In general, the Court has stepped in only to protect fundamental rights, such as freedom of speech and religion, and to prevent discrimination based on such classifications as race, gender, or religion. Otherwise, the modern Court has consistently subscribed to Justice Oliver Wendell Holmes's view that "a Constitution is not intended to embody a particular economic theory."[2] Classifications based on wealth or income need only be rationally related to legitimate government goals, while government regulation of business and of other economic activities is almost automatically upheld as constitutional. To avoid constitutional problems, the government need only ensure that the procedures it follows are fair and appropriate enough to satisfy the demands of the Due Process Clause.[3]

Thus, the areas of social and economic policy are relatively free from substantive constitutional constraints, and raise few relevant constitutional issues. Limitations on the power of the government come not from the Constitution or the courts but from the political process.

What Governments Do

In general, modern governments are involved with four types of activities: transfer of resources; subsidies and incentives; regulation; and development and administration.[4]

Transfer of Resources   Much of what a modern government does is to take money from some individuals and give it to others. This transfer of resources can be direct or indirect. Direct transfers include social security, in which workers are taxed to pay for retirees' pensions, and other forms of public assistance. Indirect transfers occur, for example, when the government buys goods or services from a private company, to the benefit of its employees or stockholders.

Because indirect transfers are merely the incidental results of policies chosen for other purposes, they need not concern us here. Direct transfers, however, are of more interest. Some government transfer payments are designed to reduce income inequalities among the citizenry or to provide a minimum level of services to the needy. Other transfers are essentially societywide insurance policies, under which all citizens pay a small amount in return for specific benefits. When the government provides relief to flood victims, for example, it effectively spreads the costs to all citizens rather than just to those directly affected.

Subsidies and Incentives Frequently the government seeks to achieve certain results by providing subsidies or incentives to particular industries, corporations, or citizens. These subsidies or incentives frequently have strings attached, meaning that the money is given only if certain conditions are met. To keep farm prices stable, for example, the government pays farmers to leave land unplanted. To encourage invention and artistic creativity, the government grants patents and enforces copyrights. The government also provides subsidies or incentives in the form of reductions in taxes. To encourage home ownership, for example, the government allows taxpayers to deduct mortgage interest from taxable income.

In recent years, the federal government has adopted many policies designed to influence the laws and policies of the states. Much education aid, for example, is given to state and local governments on condition that it be used for specific purposes, such as special education. Highway funds are given with the proviso that some percentage may be withheld if states do not adopt federal recommendations for speed limits and the minimum drinking age.

Regulation In its broadest sense, the term *regulation* can be applied to any governmental effort to restrict private behavior according to public rules. So defined, regulation would include a wide variety of government actions, including criminal laws banning murder, arson, or theft. In practice, however, the term is applied more narrowly, to government programs that impose rules or restrictions on the activities of individuals or corporations. Regulations may serve a variety of purposes, from protecting consumers to protecting the environment, from limiting competition in key industries to insisting on it. Usually, the government sets out specific rules mandating or prohibiting specific actions. A company that offers stock, for example, must comply with the rules set down by Congress and the Securities Exchange Commission. Failure to comply with government regulations may carry very serious penalties.

At the federal level, regulations are generally written and implemented by executive or independent agencies, acting under authority granted by Congress. Over the course of the twentieth century, the federal and state governments have dramatically expanded their regulatory role, leaving few areas of life untouched by government rules and regulations. In recent years, pressure has grown for a reduction in the scope and extent of government regulation.

Development and Administration For the most part the government carries out its policies directly. An obvious example is national defense; other examples include the management of the national parks, tax collection, and law enforcement. Some policies that the government carries out directly are more controversial, and in recent years there has been much pressure to transfer various government functions to the private sector. In many policy areas, the national government cooperates or coordinates its activities with state and local authorities, or relies on private contractors to carry out all or part of its programs.

Factors Influencing Policy

From the general to the specific, the many factors that influence what policies the government adopts and how they are carried out include the following:

- *Political culture.* A society's fundamental ideas on politics profoundly affect the way it deals with social and economic problems. American political culture, for example, with its emphasis on individual freedom and its distrust of government power, tends to emphasize a high degree of private sector involvement in solving society's problems. Thus American health policy, in sharp contrast to the policies pursued by most European countries, has refused to embrace a government-run medical system and has preserved an important role for private insurance companies. Likewise, Americans' traditional concerns about privacy and unchecked government power have led them to reject proposals to establish national identity cards, which are used in most other countries.[5]

> *"Politics is the art of the possible, the attainable . . . , the art of the next best."*
>
> —Otto von Bismarck, 1867

- *The constitutional framework.* The broad ground rules established in the Constitution have a clear impact on policy. For example, the federal system encourages local and state remedies to many problems (such as education) that in other nations would be handled by the central government. The separation of powers facilitates the representation of diverse interests, and thus forces the creation of public policies based on compromise rather than a strictly logical or systematic approach to problem solving.

- *The nature of individual government institutions.* As we have seen, the decentralized power structure in Congress and the executive branch has profound effects on public policy. Interest groups coalesce around particular subcommittees and agencies to form subgovernments, or "iron triangles," that control narrow realms of policy making. Similarly, the unique makeup of the federal courts strongly impacts the policies that emerge from the judicial branch.

- *The electoral and partisan context.* Electoral and partisan considerations can also affect policy making. During the Reagan and Bush administrations, for example, the federal government heeded demands by antiabortion groups and refused to support fetal tissue research. During the Clinton administration, the policy was reversed. Whether an election is close at hand or off in the distant future also plays a role. Voters may forget an unpopular vote made two years before election day, but they are unlikely to ignore a vote made just days before the election.

- *Ideas.* Many important government policies begin life as ideas, often expressed first by academics. The economic policies of the New Deal, for example, closely followed the economic theories of John Maynard Keynes. Similarly, America's post–World War II foreign policy of containment, which aimed to contain and thereby wear down Soviet communism, was articulated in *Foreign Affairs* magazine by George F. Kennan, counselor to the American embassy in Moscow.[6] Not all ideas are coined by academics, however. America's space program in the 1960s was driven by President John F. Kennedy's declaration that it was "time for this nation to take a clearly leading role in space achievement"; the civil rights laws of the 1960s were propelled, in large part, by a movement of African American citizens pursuing the simple idea of equality.[7]

- *Public opinion, the media, and interest groups.* The government does not operate in a vacuum, and must respond to the demands of both mobilized interest groups and the public at large. In this process, as we have seen, the media play a crucial part. Washington may ignore a policy for years until the media bring it to the public's attention, generating immediate demands for government action. Other matters receive little or no attention until interest groups bring their demands before government decision makers.

In general, public policy tilts toward satisfying organized interest groups, often at the expense of unorganized groups or the public at large. Powerful groups may also play a decisive role in blocking proposed changes, as President Bill Clinton learned when medical insurance and small business groups, among others, helped defeat his proposed health care reforms.

Hard Choices

Policy makers and political leaders must face hard choices in every area of government policy. These choices are typically influenced both by reasoned analysis and by politics, which do not always lead to the same conclusions. The most logical solution to a problem may be politically unpopular, or may upset influential interest groups. The government's approach to a particular problem may be so deeply entrenched in history and tradition that any meaningful deviation is difficult, if not impossible.

Which Level of Government? National policy makers must frequently decide whether to implement a national solution to a problem, leave the issue up to the state and local governments, or work out a cooperative arrangement in which more than one level of government participates. The decision depends on the constitutional distribution of powers between the states and the national government, on whether the problem in question lends itself to a uniform solution or to many local solutions, and on traditional practices. In the twentieth century, the national government has greatly expanded its role in policy areas that traditionally had been left to the states, including education, health care, and welfare, although recent years have seen something of a reversal of the trend.

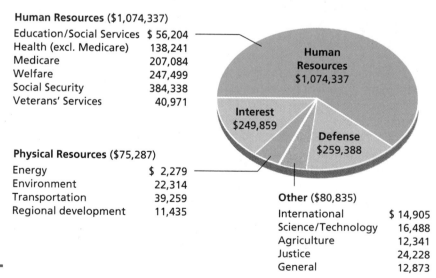

Human Resources ($1,074,337)

Education/Social Services	$ 56,204
Health (excl. Medicare)	138,241
Medicare	207,084
Welfare	247,499
Social Security	384,338
Veterans' Services	40,971

Physical Resources ($75,287)

Energy	$ 2,279
Environment	22,314
Transportation	39,259
Regional development	11,435

Other ($80,835)

International	$ 14,905
Science/Technology	16,488
Agriculture	12,341
Justice	24,228
General	12,873

Figure 16.1 **U.S. Budget by Function, 1997 (millions of dollars)***

*Estimated.
NOTE: Excludes commerce and housing credit and undistributed offsetting receipts.
SOURCE: *Budget of the United States Government,* Fiscal Year 1998, Historical Tables, p. 49.

Government or the Market?   Policy makers must often decide whether or not to interfere with the normal operations of economic markets, in which key decisions are left to private individuals and firms. In the United States, in sharp contrast to many other countries, there is a heavy presumption that markets should be left alone and that governments should intervene only to achieve overriding public goals or when the market fails to work effectively.

In any particular case, governments must decide both whether and how to intervene. One approach is to regulate private transactions directly. Another is to try to influence the market indirectly, by using economic incentives or disincentives to influence market choices. Government taxes on alcohol and tobacco, for example, may discourage consumption of those commodities. Government subsidies, on the other hand, may encourage individuals or firms to take certain actions that they would not take in the absence of government intervention.

There are several justifications for government interference with market-based decision making:

- *Protecting life, liberty, and property.* Some behavior is intolerable because it violates the rights of others, whether workers, consumers, or the public at large. Banning "nuisances" was the first form of regulation, and formed at least part of the rationale for the regulation of workplace safety, the environment, and the sale of stocks and bonds. To prevent fraud, for example, the government may require an honest exchange of information between buyer and seller; thus federal regulations require that sellers of automobiles disclose gas mileage estimates and other important information to prospective buyers.
- *Preventing recessions.* A capitalist system presumes that the forces of the marketplace will reach fair price and wage levels, but the market does not always work efficiently or effectively. During the Great Depression, for example, economists concluded that wage levels were so low that they were unable to sustain an economic recovery, putting workers at a permanent disadvantage in wage negotiations and underscoring the need for minimum wage laws.
- *Providing "public goods."* Overriding the market may be necessary in order to avoid the "free-rider" problem (see Chapter 8), in which individuals are able to avoid paying for goods (such as a clean environment or a strong national defense) that benefit everyone. Similarly, private transactions often hurt third parties or the public at large, creating social and economic costs that are not figured into the market price. Economists refer to such third-party costs as *externalities.* "If a train emits sparks that occasionally burn the crops of nearby farmers," explains the legal scholar (and now Supreme Court justice) Stephen Breyer, "the cost of destroyed crops is a spillover cost imposed upon the farmers by those who ship by train—so long as the shipper need not pay the farmer for the crop lost."[8] Similarly, the price of shipping goods by truck may not include the cost to society of cleaning up the resulting pollution. In such cases, it may be necessary to tax shippers or force them to take steps to minimize the damage.
- *Creating—or preventing—competition.* In the absence of competition, market forces are unlikely to work effectively. Government, therefore, may act to prevent one individual or firm from establishing a monopoly over a vital commodity or service. In the United

States, anticompetitive or monopolistic practices are banned under the antitrust laws. In 1995, for example, the United States government brought action against Microsoft Corporation for illegally restricting competition over operating system software for personal computers. On the other hand, the desire to guarantee specific services to the public or an overwhelming need for a single standard may create a rationale for government intervention. Such thinking lay behind past government policies forcing airlines to serve small markets and granting a single provider (the AT&T corporation) a monopoly on telephone service.

- *Reducing inequality.* Markets may favor those with greater resources, and may not provide for the needs of those with few resources. The market cannot guarantee that the poor have sufficient fuel to heat their homes, for example, since the price of fuel may be driven up by those willing and able to pay high prices.

Policy makers must also consider the costs of intervening in the market, including these:

- *Regulation hurts efficiency.* The advantages of market-based decision making, at least under normal conditions, are clear. Allowing buyers and sellers to set prices for various commodities is often the best way to ensure that goods and services are allocated efficiently to those who value them most. By contrast, government interference with the market cannot possibly take into account the varying needs and desires of all the people on an ongoing basis. As a result, consumers may pay higher prices, firms may make less money, and technological innovation may be slowed down. The result of deregulation in the airline and telephone industries illustrates the validity of this concern; when the government opened up these industries to competition, fares and phone bills dropped sharply.[9]

- *Government intervention may serve the interests of particular industries or private parties, rather than the public interest.* The historian Gabriel Kolko, for example, argues that the main beneficiaries of railroad regulation in the late 1800s and early 1900s were the railroads themselves; likewise, the demise or decline of long-established airline carriers (Eastern and Pan American to name just two) testifies to how much those airlines were helped by government regulatory policies. As the economist George Stigler put it, in such cases "regulation is acquired by the industry and is designed and operated primarily for its benefit."[10] The economic point is backed by an argument drawn from interest group politics—namely, that "firms seeking political protection find it easier to organize to wield political influence," because the per-person gains to them are great while the costs to unorganized individual consumers are low.

Similarly, some government subsidies benefit only a small number of firms or individuals while the cost is spread out among all taxpayers. In this case as well, well-organized groups with much to gain or lose may exert a disproportionate influence on government policy, both through direct lobbying efforts and through strategic use of campaign contributions. By contrast, the general public is poorly organized and has little incentive to unite to oppose highly focused government spending. To make matters worse, many government subsidies are so deeply buried in the fine print of government programs or so little publicized that the general public does not even know of their existence.

Incrementalism Versus Radical Change   Governments must often decide whether to make gradual changes in policy or undertake major changes all at once. The former, known as **incrementalism,** is far more common; but the latter, known as **radicalism,** may lead to more far-reaching results.

Backers of incrementalism point out that the full impact of a government policy may be difficult to foresee, and that a particular policy may have unintended, and potentially dangerous, consequences. Much of the criticism of President Bill Clinton's proposed health care reforms in 1993–1994, for example, centered on the danger of making sweeping changes in an area that comprises nearly 15 percent of the nation's economy. Incrementalism, by contrast, allows policy makers to build on past successes and avoid past mistakes.

In many cases, incrementalism is the result not of conscious choice but of the dynamics of politics. Interest groups and government agencies already involved in a particular policy area will often seek to expand their power and influence, and resist efforts to diminish or eliminate their roles. Moreover, government policies typically foster expectations among those affected, creating their own constituency for continuation or expansion. The federal government's encouragement of employer-based health coverage through private insurance companies after World War II, for example, created a set of powerful interests— among both consumers and the insurance industry—which were then in a position to oppose the sweeping changes proposed by Bill Clinton in the 1990s.

Supporters of a more radical approach to policy making point out that an incremental approach may prove more expensive in the long run than a quicker, more coherent approach. Thus it might be more efficient to buy up all the land for a state park at once at low prices, rather than announce a ten-year purchasing plan that causes prices to rise and costs more in the long run.[11] Moreover, supporters of a more radical approach argue that governments must seize opportunities for meaningful change in public policy and exploit them to the fullest. Often such opportunities are provided by moments of real or perceived crisis. The depression of the 1930s, for example, provided the opportunity for the radical expansion of the national government; the budget crisis of the 1990s provided the opportunity for fundamental change in the opposite direction.

Fairness Versus Efficiency   A final set of policy choices involves trade-offs between fairness and **efficiency.** A policy can be defined as efficient if it provides the greatest benefit to society at the least cost. The most efficient policy, however, may not be the fairest. For example, a government policy may benefit society at large but may greatly harm a few individuals. Government policies that banned the building of houses on beachfront property, for example, aimed to benefit all of society by preventing erosion and by protecting coastal ecosystems. In the process, however, a small number of property owners lost a fortune when the value of their property dropped to almost nothing.[12]

Sometimes the government may decide that fairness requires that society as a whole absorb the cost of providing benefits to a few. Thus all consumers might pay slightly higher prices for produce to protect farmers from ruinous swings in crop prices.

Determining whether or not to proceed with a given government policy often requires that policy makers weigh the costs and benefits of a proposed action. Such **cost-benefit analysis** is a useful tool, but it suffers from two key drawbacks. First, weighing the costs and benefits of a given policy is often difficult, especially when estimating noneconomic factors.

How much weight, for example, should be given to the happiness that nature lovers feel when they walk along a pristine beach? How much to the preservation of a particular animal species? How much to a human life? Long-term economic forecasts may also be difficult to estimate.

Second, cost-benefit analysis is heavily weighted toward the goal of efficiency over other goals, including fairness. A strict cost-benefit analysis aims to maximize economic efficiency, and does not concern itself with how costs and benefits are distributed across society. Thus many argue that cost-benefit analyses are no substitute for human judgments about whether efficiency is outweighed in any given case by other considerations.

Economic Policy

A central purpose of the Constitution was to "provide for the general Welfare," and the Constitution gives a central, although not exclusive, role to the national government in economic affairs. The national government has the power to tax and spend; borrow money; regulate commerce "with foreign Nations, and among the several States, and with the Indian tribes"; establish laws concerning bankruptcy; and coin money. States are prohibited from making "any Thing but gold and silver Coin a Tender in Payment of Debts."[13] Together, government programs and actions designed to manage or regulate the economy are known as economic policy.

The president's top economist, Janet Yellan, head of the Council of Economic Advisors.

The history of American economic policy has revolved around two key questions. First, how active a role should the government play in regulating or encouraging economic activity? Should it follow a policy of **laissez-faire**, essentially leaving private individuals and firms alone except in cases of theft or fraud? Or should it intervene aggressively in the economic arena, following policies designed, for example, to encourage innovation, reduce the economic power of big business, guarantee minimum wages to workers, or redistribute income from rich to poor? Second, how should the national and state governments divide their powers and responsibilities in economic policy? Should the primary role be played by Washington or by the states?

For the most part, these questions involve controversy over means rather than ends. In general, most Americans agree on the goals of economic policy. The ideal economy, most agree, would provide jobs to all who seek them, a high standard of living, expanded opportunities for all citizens, and a high rate of economic growth. The problem is how to bring about these results, and how to trade off these factors one against another. Here there is very little agreement; some economists go so far as to suggest that the best way for the government to accomplish these objectives is to stay out of the way and let the economy take care of itself.

Three factors complicate any analysis of economic policy, past or present. First, economists often disagree about how to interpret economic data, how best to achieve desired goals, and how to balance the various goals of economic policy against one another. Second, economic policy cannot be easily separated from more general developments in the political arena. The technical arguments of economists are complicated by the passionate views of politicians and ordinary citizens, whose jobs, investments, and spending power are at stake. Finally, American economic policy cannot be understood except in relation to the larger world economy.

Monetary Policy

The government's power to influence interest rates is vitally important to maintaining economic growth, limiting inflation, and avoiding economic downturns. Because interest rates directly influence the supply and demand for money, the government's efforts in this area are known as **monetary policy**.

In the United States, the government agency that exercises control over monetary policy is known as the **Federal Reserve Board (or "Fed")**. The Fed meets on a regular basis to review the state of the economy and to make adjustments in interest rates. In the simplest terms, a decrease in interest rates can help jump-start a depressed economy but risks increasing the inflation rate; an increase in interest rates can help control inflation but risks slowing down the economy. The Fed's decisions on monetary policy involve a complex balancing-act among competing interests, including the financial markets, the White House, and ordinary Americans.

Fiscal Policy

Before the 1930s, economists believed that the government was largely powerless in the face of an economic depression or recession. The laws of the business cycle seemed fixed and unchangeable: periods of economic boom would be followed by periods of economic bust, in an endlessly repeating pattern. Traditional economists could suggest nothing better than that government keep the money supply stable (usually by pegging it to the amount of available gold), balance its budget, and encourage thrift and savings in preparation for the inevitable rainy day.

The rainy day that began with the stock market crash of 1929 turned into a deluge that changed economics forever. Leading the way was the British economist John Maynard Keynes. Overturning the conventional wisdom, Keynes argued that the economic crisis was driven by depressed demand for goods and services. Thus the only way for the government to stimulate demand was by providing the unemployed with public jobs at good wages—even if that meant running a deficit in the government's budget. In fact, Keynes and his followers argued that during a recession the government should deliberately run a budget deficit to stimulate demand and bring the economy out of the doldrums. By contrast, government budget surpluses would be appropriate during times of economic expansion, to cool off excess demand and thus combat inflation.[14]

The strategic use of government budget deficits and surpluses to smooth out the ups and downs of the business cycle is known as **fis-**

Pepper . . . and Salt

THE WALL STREET JOURNAL

"Time we started gearing up for it. What comes after a trillion?"

cal policy. Keynesian fiscal policy dominated the federal government's economic approach from the 1930s until the 1980s, when an increasing number of economists began to challenge both its theoretical assumptions and its practical usefulness. Many economists now argue that public works projects simply take too long to get under way; by the time they do, the crisis has already passed and the supposed remedy may actually be harmful. For this and other reasons, these economists argued that the government should abandon efforts to influence the economy by way of fiscal policy.

From the late 1970s until the late 1990s, the federal government ran huge budget deficits. In time, government attempts to use surpluses and deficits as strategic tools gave way to efforts to bring the federal budget into balance or even produce a small surplus. For many years, the goal of a balanced budget seemed unattainable, but a combination of budget cuts, tax increases, and a steadily growing economy effectively wiped out the deficit by the late 1990s. Both Congress and the executive branch claimed credit for bringing about this result, and began lengthy debates over how to spend any future surpluses, and whether to return some or all of the surplus to the American people in the form of tax reductions.

Figure 16.2   **The Disappearing Deficit: Federal Receipts, Outlays, and Deficit/Surplus, 1970–2002***

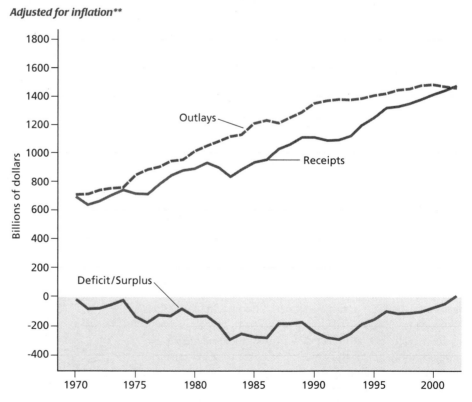

Adjusted for inflation**

*1997–2002 estimated
**1992 constant dollars
SOURCES: *The Budget of the United States, Fiscal Year 1999,* Historical Tables, Table 1.3.

According to many economists, the disappearance of the federal budget deficit may be a short-term phenomenon. Rising interest rates or an economic recession could bring back the deficit in the short term; the increasing costs of federal programs like Medicare and social security could bring it back in the long term. In any event, the elimination of the deficit has transformed the landscape of American politics, and has changed fundamentally the terms of the political debate.

Taxation

The amount of money the federal government raises in taxes now exceeds $1.5 trillion (thousand billion) a year. Around 45 percent of this money comes from individual income taxes; another 35 percent comes from payroll taxes to support social security and Medicare. The rest is divided almost evenly between corporate income taxes and a variety of special taxes, including customs duties, estate and gift taxes, and excises on alcohol and tobacco. The state and local governments raise another $400 billion in tax revenue.[15]

The federal income tax is a **progressive tax**: as income rises, income tax as a percentage of income rises as well. Other federal taxes—such as payroll taxes to support social security and Medicare—are regressive, which means that the wealthy pay a lower percentage of their income to support such programs than do the less well-off. Overall, the federal tax system is much less progressive than it was before the major changes in the tax code in the 1980s and 1990s.

Governments use taxation not only to raise money but also as a tool of social and economic policy. Taxation can be used to encourage or discourage specific behaviors; to redistribute wealth; or to achieve specific policy goals.

Regulation of Business

Modern regulation of industry began in the nineteenth century, with state and national efforts to regulate railroads, grain elevators, and other businesses affecting the public interest. Pressure to regulate came from interest groups representing workers and consumers, but also from industry, which often used government regulation to keep out competitors. Both state and federal regulation expanded in the twentieth century, especially during and after the New Deal. By 1940, areas regulated by the federal government included the public utility industry, stocks and bonds, food and drugs, radio broadcasting, and air transportation. Washington had also imposed a variety of general restrictions on businesses, particularly with respect to employee wages, hours, and working conditions. Increasingly, states imposed licensing and other requirements on a wide range of businesses and professions, including law and medicine, restaurants, barber shops and cosmetologists, and optometrists.

Federal regulation expanded even further in the 1960s and 1970s. New regulations stressed environmental protection, worker safety, and consumer protection. These regulations accomplished a great deal, from cleaning up the air and water to reducing workplace deaths and injuries. (In the ten years before the creation of the Occupational Safety and Health Administration in 1970, for example, the rate of workers killed on the job declined slowly, from 21 to 18 per 100,000 workers. Over the next twelve years, workplace deaths declined dramatically, to only 7 per 100,000 workers).[16] Nevertheless, by the mid-1970s, programs regulating business came under increasing attack. "Rules and regulations churned out by federal agencies were having a damaging effect on almost every aspect of American life," argued President Gerald Ford in his memoirs. "Red tape surrounded and almost smothered us; we as a nation were about to suffocate." The first steps toward the new goal of **deregulation** followed quickly, during the presidency of Jimmy Carter.[17] Finding the appropriate balance between regulation and deregulation remains a significant controversy in American politics; many consumer and environmental groups argue that deregulation threatens vital public interests and that regulation needs to be expanded rather than repealed.

Corporate Welfare

A number of studies in recent years have pointed out the enormous benefits that corporations receive from various government programs. Both liberal and conservative groups have engaged in a kind of can-you-top-this effort to detail what has come to be known as **corporate welfare.** Estimates of corporate subsidies range from $50 billion to $200 billion a year.[18]

Some subsidies take the form of direct spending. Consider agriculture, for example. Northwestern farmers typically pay only 10 percent of the cost of irrigation water provided by the federal Bureau of Reclamation. Businesses selling abroad may be eligible for low-interest loans from the Export-Import Bank. Peanut farmers receive $91 million in price support payments. The Department of Agriculture also spends $110 million a year advertising U.S. food products abroad—including $1.2 million for mink coats and $2.5 million for pineapples.

Other government subsidies for business take the form of guaranteed loans and government insurance programs. The Small Business Administration, for example, guarantees about $10 billion in loans that corporations otherwise could not obtain. If a company fails to pay back the loan, the government picks up the tab, at a cost of some $250 million a year. Government insurance of savings and loans, banks, and pension plans also carries a high price tag, although here individuals benefit as well as corporations.[19]

Corporations also benefit from a variety of tax subsidies. The industries that gain the most from the tax code include finance, agribusiness, timber, energy, and construction. Because corporations are ultimately owned (in the form of stocks and other securities) by human beings, this government subsidy ends up getting passed along to individuals, both at home and abroad. Such subsidies, of course, accrue disproportionately to the wealthy.

Other government assistance to corporations is less direct and thus more difficult to track. Government road-building programs, for example, benefit corporations in two ways: first by providing construction contracts for the private firms that help build the roads, then by subsidizing the transportation of goods. Of course, such programs also benefit workers and consumers, by creating jobs and lowering prices. Similarly, defense contractors make all or most of their money by selling airplanes, tanks, ships, uniforms, and countless other goods to the government. The disruptions in the defense industry following government cutbacks in defense spending attest to the enormous importance of government spending. Local businesses benefit enormously from government military bases, by providing goods and services to military and civilian workers. Corporations also profit from government programs designed to promote home ownership, in the form of construction contracts and higher real estate prices. The subsidies to corporations are offset, at least to some extent, by special taxes and user fees paid by those who benefit.

Some forms of corporate welfare are easily justified, but sorting out the worthwhile from the insupportable is a complex and difficult task. At a minimum, people who argue against government interference in private economic decisions need to take into account the government's role in subsidizing, as well as regulating, business.

Social Welfare and Health Policy

Millions of Americans receive money, food, or other necessities from the government. Together, these various social welfare programs (excluding health care) account for more than one-third of the federal budget—nearly $500 billion. States spend another $40 billion of their own money for the same purpose.

Goals of American Social Welfare Policy

Social welfare policy in the United States does not aim simply at reducing or eliminating poverty. Theodore R. Marmor, Jerry L. Mashaw, and Philip L. Harvey, for example, have identified four conceptions of purpose that lie behind the complex and often contradictory web of American social welfare policies:[20]

- *Providing social insurance.* Much of American welfare policy has been directed at preventing poverty rather than treating its effects. This approach requires individuals to contribute to various insurance funds while they are able to do so and then allows them to collect benefits when they need them. These programs include social security and Medicare. Social insurance programs, like private insurance programs, allow risks to be broadly shared among a large group, even the entire society.
- *Providing a safety net.* One goal of American welfare policy is to provide a minimum level of subsistence for people who have fallen through the cracks of the capitalist system. The outlines of a social policy inspired by the safety net are clear: "the net is close to the ground and the benefits are accordingly modest. . . . The clientele are the down and out; the eligibility criteria are designed to sort out the truly needy from the rest."[21] Many supporters of a safety-net approach argue that the federal government should play only a backup role; the first line of defense comprises families, churches, and other local charitable organizations; the second, state and local government agencies.
- *Changing behavior.* A persistent goal of welfare policy has been to induce the poor "to behave in a more socially acceptable manner." This approach, which dates to the English poor laws and poor houses of centuries past, assumes that the poor are poor because of the way they behave. "The most basic sense of humaneness" requires that the sufferings of the poor "be partially relieved," comment Marmor, Mashaw, and Harvey. "But generous assistance would reinforce the very behavior patterns that cause the suffering in the first place." This view of welfare policy lies behind arguments for "workfare"—the idea that the able-bodied poor should work for their benefits—and for limiting welfare benefits to a prescribed period—say, two years.
- *Redistributing wealth and power.* One purpose of welfare policy—somewhat out of vogue in recent years—is the idea that government should deliberately transfer income

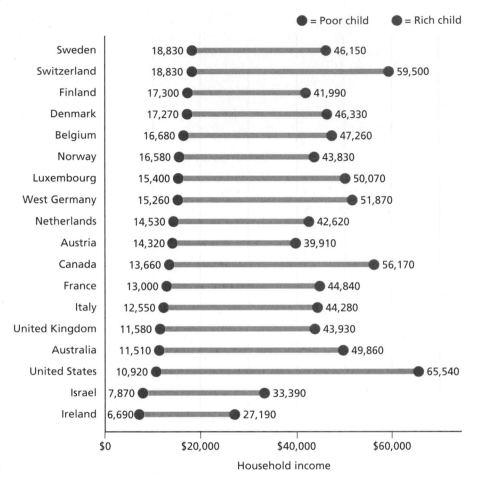

= Poor child   = Rich child

Sweden	18,830	46,150
Switzerland	18,830	59,500
Finland	17,300	41,990
Denmark	17,270	46,330
Belgium	16,680	47,260
Norway	16,580	43,830
Luxembourg	15,400	50,070
West Germany	15,260	51,870
Netherlands	14,530	42,620
Austria	14,320	39,910
Canada	13,660	56,170
France	13,000	44,840
Italy	12,550	44,280
United Kingdom	11,580	43,930
Australia	11,510	49,860
United States	10,920	65,540
Israel	7,870	33,390
Ireland	6,690	27,190

$0 $20,000 $40,000 $60,000

Household income

Figure 16.3 **Gap Between Rich and Poor Children**

SOURCE: Chart adapted from The *New York Times*, 14 August 1995, citing Luxembourg Income Study data. All figures are in 1991 dollars, with other currencies converted using adjustments for national differences in purchasing power.

from the rich to the poor in order to lessen inequality. This approach aims not merely at short-term income redistribution but at long-term social change. Proponents of this approach reject punitive or harsh approaches to welfare, stressing that the poor are not at fault but are the victims of economic and social forces over which they have little control. The redistributionist approach has hardly dominated the American approach to welfare, but it did find expression in some of the antipoverty programs of the 1960s.

The American welfare system has not drawn completely from any one of these four approaches. Instead, social welfare policy as a whole has drawn from all four, in various amounts at different times. Social security in particular was created and developed as a form of social insurance, whereas other forms of public assistance have been focused on the other goals.

Social Security

Social security was created in 1935, one of the major initiatives of Franklin D. Roosevelt's New Deal. The program established a system of retirement annuities payable at age sixty-five, to be financed from payroll taxes on workers and employers alike. The amount received by individual workers depends on how much they have contributed over the course of a lifetime, with special provisions for those who were unemployed, unable to work, or already retired. Because the government provides automatic cost-of-living adjustments for social security recipients every year, the amount retirees receive over time may exceed the amount they paid in.

Roosevelt's decision to pay for social security by a special payroll tax instead of through the income tax was controversial and was based primarily on political considerations. By arguing that retirees were only collecting money that they themselves had contributed, Roosevelt was able to deflect conservative charges that the act tended toward socialism, and also made it easier for proud Americans to accept a government check. But there was another reason for Roosevelt's decision. "I guess you're right on the economics," Roosevelt admitted in 1941, "but those taxes were never a problem of economics. They are politics all the way through. We put those payroll contributions there so as to give the contributors a legal, moral, and political right to collect their pensions and their unemployment benefits. With those taxes in there, no damn politician can ever scrap my social security program."[22]

Roosevelt's prediction has come true with a vengeance. Social security has become one of the most popular and untouchable of federal programs. In the early 1970s the Republican President Richard Nixon competed with House Ways and Means Chairman Wilbur Mills to offer social security recipients guaranteed cost-of-living adjustments (COLAs) to keep pace with inflation—which meant that social security checks were no longer based even nominally on the amounts contributed. Moreover, social security benefits were treated as nontaxable income, even for the very wealthy.[23]

Primarily as a result of COLAs, social security nearly went bankrupt in 1977 and 1983. With neither political party willing to take the risk of corralling this most sacred of sacred cows, the two parties acted together to establish a high-level commission to study the subject. The commission presented Congress with a compromise: raise social security taxes and raise the retirement age for future retirees. In addition, one-half of social security benefits were made taxable for individuals with incomes above a certain threshold. Beginning in tax year 1993, eighty-five percent of some taxpayers' social security benefits was subjected to taxation.

For the moment, social security is in no danger of bankruptcy. When the large baby-boom generation retires, however, its social security benefits will have to be paid by the significantly smaller post-baby-boom generation, potentially leading to another crisis.

Why has social security become so difficult to reform? Besides the reason given by Franklin Roosevelt, social security recipients form a strong interest group, represented most visibly by the American Association of Retired Persons (AARP). In general, social security recipients vote in high percentages and have a far greater incentive to oppose cuts in social security than the general public has in promoting them. For another, many of those who are not currently receiving social security benefits have been paying social security taxes for a long time; they realize that any cuts in social security will ultimately hurt them as much as or more than current beneficiaries.

Programs for the Needy

Governments recognized their obligation to aid those in need as early as the nineteenth century. Early relief programs, typically involving food and shelter rather than cash, were provided by local governments as a last resort for the truly desperate. In the 1920s, however, nearly half the states joined a growing movement to provide cash assistance to citizens who were physically unable to support themselves, a category that included the blind and the elderly. Public opinion and public policy still frowned on government support for the able-bodied.

The mass unemployment of the Great Depression changed American attitudes toward welfare. Nineteen million Americans—nearly one-sixth of the population—were on state relief rolls by early 1933. Given the almost complete absence of work, most Americans believed that the poor could not be blamed for their plight and were deserving of some help. The United States government came to the assistance of the states in 1932, making loans available for what was then called "relief." The money was never repaid, and was soon supplemented by larger and more elaborate programs, most of which were funded by Washington and administered by the states.

Aid to Families with Dependent Children and other federally funded social welfare programs help millions of Americans—mostly children—who live in poverty.

The welfare programs enacted during the New Deal were greatly expanded during the 1960s. The major programs included Aid to Families with Dependent Children (AFDC), Medicaid, food stamps, public housing and housing supplements, energy assistance, and the Earned Income Tax Credit. All of these programs came under great scrutiny in the 1990s, as a variety of politicians and social policy experts argued that federal welfare policy had created a culture of dependence, making it difficult or impossible for the poor to break the cycle of poverty and stand on their own. When President Bill Clinton announced his support for a major welfare overhaul, the stage was set for sweeping action. In 1996, Congress passed, and Clinton signed, legislation that turned welfare from a federally guaranteed entitlement to the poor into block grants to the states. The new law put a five-year limit on welfare benefits and requires many welfare recipients to work for their monthly benefits. The new law is partly responsible for reducing the total number of welfare recipients by some 26 percent since its height in 1994—including a drop of 14 percent in the first ten months after the law went into effect. Still, policy analysts warn that the long-term impact of the reforms is difficult to predict.[24]

"Welfare for the Rich"

For the most part, the wealthy do not enjoy special benefits; they simply take advantage of programs designed to help everyone. Still, many critics question whether the government should restrict government benefits to people who need them. For example, the government pays some $400 million a year on unemployment benefits for people with incomes over $120,000 a year. Similarly, it costs the government over $4 billion a year to provide tax breaks to Americans with home mortgages over $300,000. At least $100 billion of the government's annual interest payments on the national debt is paid to the 1 percent of families with the highest incomes.[25]

Finally, the wealthy gain from social security and Medicare—both of which provide benefits to all Americans of retirement age, regardless of income. The wealthy do pay taxes on part of their social security income, but still the richest 5 percent of retirees (those with annual incomes over $200,000 for married couples and $120,000 for individuals) receive nearly $10 billion a year from these programs.

Health Policy

Before 1965, the federal government's role in health policy was extremely limited. It provided medical care to current and former members of the armed forces through military and veterans' hospitals; encouraged the construction of hospitals and other health facilities through direct subsidies and favorable tax treatment; and encouraged employers to provide medical insurance, also by tax incentives. Medical insurance was provided entirely by private insurance companies, such as Blue Cross and Blue Shield, and care for the poor was provided by charitable organizations, state and local governments, and individual hospitals and doctors.[26]

The passage of the Medicare and Medicaid legislation in 1965 transformed the federal government's role in American medicine. Exactly what role the federal government should play in this area remains a matter of intense debate, especially in light of the failure of the Clinton administration in 1994 to persuade Congress to pass health care reform.

Medicare   Established in 1965 as part of President Lyndon B. Johnson's Great Society programs, **Medicare** provides health insurance for the elderly. Medicare is a highly popular program, but it suffers from one overwhelming problem: cost. A major goal of policy makers is to ensure that Medicare, along with other federal health programs, remains financially solvent while providing for the health-care needs of America's aging population.

Medicaid   Adopted in the same legislation as Medicare, **Medicaid** provides medical assistance to low-income individuals and families. As enacted, Medicaid was jointly funded by the federal and state governments. Although Washington set broad national guidelines, each state was free to set its own eligibility standards, determine the scope of services provided, and set the rate of payment for services. Like other federal welfare programs, Medicaid is currently under intense scrutiny by federal policy makers.

Veterans' Benefits   The federal government provides a network of Veterans' Hospitals, which provide treatment for certain categories of military veterans, including those disabled because of an injury or disease stemming from military duty, former prisoners of war, and those eligible for Medicaid.[27]

Reform Efforts   Health care reform was a major focus of the 1992 presidential campaign, and Bill Clinton took office with grand plans to reform the nation's health care system. Clinton and other critics identified two major problems with American health care: high cost and limited access.

Cost. Total spending on health care in the United States has skyrocketed in the past three decades. In 1960 the entire nation—government, business, and individual citizens together—spent just over $27 billion on health care. In 1993, the nation spent thirty-six times as much—a whopping $884 billion. Even after adjusting for the general increase in prices over this period, health spending still increased nearly six times. In 1960, Americans spent 5.3 percent of gross domestic product (GDP) on health care; in 1993, 13.9 percent.[28]

These massive increases in health care spending can be attributed to two forces besides economy-wide inflation: price increases beyond the general inflation level, and increased use (or consumption) of health care services. This increased consumption, in turn, is due to several factors, two of which are most important: the increasing life span of the average American, and advances in medical technology. The two forces work together, since

Figure 16.4   ***Who Lacks Health Coverage?***

Percentage of all persons not covered by health insurance at any time during the year, by selected characteristics, 1995

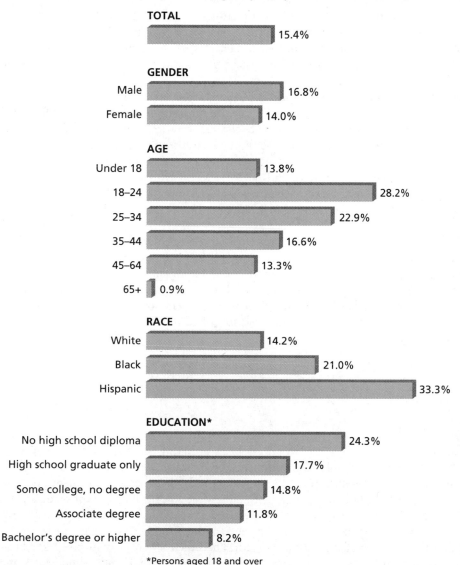

Percentage of all persons not covered by health insurance at any time during the year, by selected characteristics, 1995

TOTAL
15.4%

GENDER
Male   16.8%
Female   14.0%

AGE
Under 18   13.8%
18–24   28.2%
25–34   22.9%
35–44   16.6%
45–64   13.3%
65+   0.9%

RACE
White   14.2%
Black   21.0%
Hispanic   33.3%

EDUCATION*
No high school diploma   24.3%
High school graduate only   17.7%
Some college, no degree   14.8%
Associate degree   11.8%
Bachelor's degree or higher   8.2%

*Persons aged 18 and over

SOURCE: United States Bureau of the Census, Health Insurance Coverage, 1995, Table B, http://www.census.gov/hhes/hlthins/cover95/c95tabb.html.

technological change allows individuals to live longer and consume more—and more expensive—health care services. But new treatments can also lower health care costs. The use of antibiotics to treat peptic ulcers, for example, greatly lowers treatment costs compared with earlier approaches such as surgery.

The rate of increase of medical spending has slowed somewhat in recent years, due largely to aggressive cost containment measures by the government and private insurance companies.[29] But the long-term trend is unsettling. By one estimate, total spending on Medicare alone is projected to grow from 2.40 percent of GDP in 1993 to 9.35 percent of GDP by the year 2068. Measured in today's dollars, that would amount to a jump from about $153 billion to about $600 billion—making Medicare by far the largest item in the federal budget.[30]

Access. With average health care expenses of about $3,000 a person, quality health care is available only to those with large incomes, medical insurance, or government-subsidized care. Altogether, 85 percent of Americans are covered one way or another, either by private insurance, Medicare or Medicaid, or the military health care system. Fifteen percent of Americans (nearly 40 million people) are without any type of coverage. For many more, health care coverage is precarious, and may be cut off with the loss of a job or other change in status. The lowest insurance rates are found among the working poor, who have too much income to qualify for Medicaid but do not have employer-based health coverage.[31]

Clinton's health reform proposals quickly became bogged down under intense political pressure, and were ultimately rejected by Congress in 1994. Since then, Congress and the Clinton administration have been content to make minor changes in national health care policy. In 1996, for example, Congress passed legislation guaranteeing that workers who change jobs are immediately covered under their new employer's health insurance. The 1996 law also required insurance companies to extend their hospitalization coverage for new mothers.

Education Policy

Education in the United States has always been primarily the responsibility of private groups and of the state and local governments. Historically, the federal government's role has been small and sporadic. In the 1860s, for example, the federal government provided grants of land for the building of state universities (the so-called land-grant schools), and established a variety of schools for freed slaves. In the twentieth century, the federal government has played a key role in forcing the desegregation of southern schools.

Since the 1960s, the federal government has become more heavily involved in education. First, it has become a major player in funding education, by providing grants and loans both to individuals and schools. Second, it has directly or indirectly funded much of the scientific research that goes on at American universities, primarily through the Department of Defense.

One of the most successful federally funded education programs is Head Start, so named because it aims to give disadvantaged preschoolers a "head start" in school.

The federal education budget now tops $50 billion a year, some $30 billion of which is administered by the cabinet-level Department of Education. The remainder is funneled through the Department of Labor, largely for vocational education and training, and the Department of Health and Human Services, for early education and welfare-related programs.

Finally, the federal government has become heavily involved in setting educational goals and in coordinating and encouraging education reform efforts in the states. The National Education Goals, adopted in 1989 under a joint effort by the National Governors' Association and the federal government, established six goals to be achieved by the year 2000. These goals, which were renamed Goals 2000 by the Clinton administration and incorporated into federal law in 1993, declared that by the year 2000:

- all children in America will start school ready to learn;
- the high school graduation rate will be at least 90 percent;
- American students will "leave grades 4, 8, and 12 having demonstrated competency" in English, mathematics, science, history, and geography;
- U.S. students will be "first in the world" in science and mathematics;
- every adult in America will be literate;
- every school in America will be free of drugs and violence and will offer a disciplined environment conducive to learning.[32]

The Goals 2000 program came under fierce attack from conservatives, who were concerned about the increasing federal presence in education, the growth of "new

School Choice

American public education has traditionally provided little choice in school assignments. School districts simply assign students to particular schools on the basis of residency or other relevant criteria; students can attend the school to which they are assigned or pay to attend private school. Concern over the much publicized failures in American education, combined with conservative support for market-based alternatives to government provision of services, has fueled an intense debate over whether a new approach, based on student and parent choice, should be implemented.

There are many variants of the school choice approach. Some, for example, would allow students and parents to choose among all schools, public and private; others would be limited only to public schools. Central to all school choice proposals is the idea that schools would no longer count on a steady supply of students, but would have to compete with one another to attract them.

For school choice

School choice would replace monopolies with markets, encouraging competition and improving education. "In a free market economy, those who produce goods and services are ultimately answerable to the consumer: if the quality is shoddy, the customer will buy someone else's product," writes the former education secretary William Bennett. "It doesn't work that way in education, though. Even when armed with adequate information about school quality (which they rarely have), parents in most places around the country are not permitted to transfer their children from a bad school to a good one." The key to the choice proposal, ac-

cording to Bennett and others, "is that we need to break the monopoly currently exercised by the state-run schools and allow all schools—including private and religious schools—to compete for public dollars." Under Bennett's plan, students would receive government vouchers, redeemable at any school. To attract students, schools would have to offer what students and parents want—quality education.

School choice would advance the cause of social justice. In most states today, children in low-income neighborhoods are forced to go to a run-down, poorly funded school. Their well-off counterparts, by contrast, can attend a well-funded public school or can afford the private school of their choice. High-income families can even move to allow their children to attend a particular school. Supporters of school choice argue that a voucher system would extend this flexibility to all parents and students, regardless of income.

Choice would improve educational outcomes. "The three fundamental premises underlying the choice idea," writes one researcher, are that "(1) there is no one best school for everyone, (2) it is necessary to provide diversity in school structure and programs in order to accommodate all students and to enable them to succeed, and (3) students will perform better and accomplish more in learning environments they have freely chosen than in those to which they are simply assigned." Supporters of school choice point with pride to various studies, including one by John Chubb and Terry Moe that concluded that "private control means less bureaucratic influence; less bureaucratic influence leads to better school organization; and better school organization leads to higher student achievement."

School choice energizes and empowers parents and children. "If we invite parents to choose their schools," writes Bennett, "it can be a good first step in the critical effort of reenfranchising them. Choice among schools is a first involvement in the schools, a critical investment, and it may lead to further involvement, which is something teachers long for." A nationwide study based on sixty-six schools backs up Bennett's claim: "Choice parents spent more time talking to their child about high school plans," the researchers reported, and felt more positive about their children's educational experiences than their nonchoice counterparts.

Against school choice

School choice is a simplistic, quick fix that won't address the real problems of America's schools. The real crisis of American education is in its inner cities, critics argue, and despite all of its promises, school choice will not address that crisis. "Inner-city schools and children, who have been consistent losers in the competition for America's resources, will lose even more in the next round of school choice," writes one opponent of the school choice concept. In a study of school choice in St. Louis, for example, researchers found that minority and low-income students "have to be pushed out of their neighborhood schools and onto a bus heading for the suburbs by an assertive parent who is convinced that going to a suburban school is important." Unfortunately, such parents are relatively hard to find. Inner-city parents were "on average, more shy, self-conscious, and withdrawn. They . . . have a deep distrust of educators and an inability to act on their child's behalf in the world of the school." For many inner-city students and parents, school choice is an illusion, and a false promise.

School choice degrades community. By removing the geographic element from school assignments, critics argue, school choice plans weaken neighborhoods and communities. "A strong, local community is essential to psychological well-being, personal growth, social order, and a sense of political efficacy," concludes one study. Communities that are already strong (and have good schools) get stronger under a choice plan; but weaker communities (with their poorer schools) get weaker. Parents of children in noncommunity schools volunteer less, hold fewer parent-teacher conferences, and are less involved in parent-teacher associations.

Choice would undermine learning. Critics question the assertion that competition in education would improve educational outcomes. Results of research studies on the impact of school choice on learning have been mixed at best. Moreover, a freedom of choice approach would weaken schools' accountability to the public at large, and encourage citizens to ignore problems outside their own children's classrooms. "Our schools have problems," writes a California state legislator. "They need serious reforms: higher standards, safer classrooms, more job-related training. We need parents, teachers, and school administrators to forget the turf battles that have stymied fundamental change—and get down to the real business of reform."

Sources: K. L. Billingsley, ed., *Voices on Choice: The Education Reform Debate* (San Francisco: Pacific Research Institute for Public Policy, 1994); Mary Anne Raywid, *The Case for Public Schools of Choice* (Bloomington, Ind.: Phi Delta Kappa Educational Foundation, 1989); Edith Rasell and Richard Rothstein, eds., *School Choice: Examining the Evidence* (Washington, D.C.: Economic Policy Institute, 1993); Judith Pearson, *Myths of Educational Choice* (Westport, Conn.: Praeger, 1993).

bureaucracy," and the absence of public school choice (see box), which would give parents control over which schools their children would attend. Others criticized Goals 2000 for promising more than it could deliver, especially given the severe constraints on federal spending.[33]

Public Policy and the Public Interest

Does American public policy truly reflect the public interest? Not surprisingly, the answer to this question depends at least partly on how one defines the public interest.

Most political scientists would agree that American public policy rarely reflects the public interest in the Madisonian sense. That is, policies do not generally arise out of a dispassionate and disinterested analysis of the interests of the whole community over the long term. Instead, American public policy is developed and implemented piecemeal, and in response to the (often short-term) demands of large and small interest groups. For the most part, the Madisonian model comes into play only when a foreign or domestic crisis focuses the nation's attention on a particular problem and overrides politics as usual.

Nor does American policy making typically reflect the pure democracy model's view of the public interest. At the federal level, the ability of the people to influence public policy directly is severely limited. At the state and local levels, however, where more direct participation is permitted, the people's direct influence can be greater.

The pluralist model, which defines the public interest as the policies that arise out of the clash of interest groups, may come closer to the mark. To a great extent, American public policy is determined by the activities of various interest groups. Corporate welfare, for example, reflects the influence of interest groups; Medicare reflects the power of senior citizens. That interest groups do not play on a level field, however, seems clear. Many groups—the inner-city poor, gays and lesbians, and children, to take just three examples—have little political power, and see few of the benefits of public policy.

It does not follow, however, that American public policy is controlled by elite interests. Although many government programs do favor the well-connected and well-to-do, many more do not. Social security and other government welfare programs, for example, provide benefits mainly to the poor and the middle class. And while the tax system does contain many loopholes that allow the wealthy to reduce their obligations, overall those with the highest incomes do pay a higher share.

Although generalizations about American public policy are hazardous at best, it is possible to draw at least a few observations:

- *American public policy rewards organized groups, especially those with financial or political clout.* Interest groups with sufficient resources can exert a dominant influence over public policy. Likewise, groups whose members vote in large numbers and as a bloc can have a major effect. That the government provides more comprehensive health coverage for senior citizens than for children, for example, at least partly reflects the fact that senior citizens, in contrast to children, are well-organized and well-funded, and vote.

- *Policies often favor the middle class over both the rich and the poor.* Many government programs are aimed squarely at the middle class, although the wealthy may benefit as well. The popularity of social security and the home mortgage deduction, for example, is a result of these programs' broad base of support. Other government programs (education funding, for instance) may provide substantial benefits to the middle class while short-changing the poor; thus inner-city schools may crumble while suburban schools flourish.

- *Narrow interest groups can exert the most influence over programs that are specialized and invisible to the public.* Many of the programs that benefit special interest groups are little known to and poorly understood by the public. Thus a business group might succeed at getting the government to underwrite loans to foreign companies that buy American products. Such interest groups are particularly effect within the subgovernments, or iron triangles, that influence everyday policy making.

- *The government may give with one hand and take away with the other.* Because American policy making is decentralized and haphazard, government policies may overlap, or even work at cross-purposes. Thus the government both taxes the profits of corporations and provides billions in corporate subsidies. From an overall perspective, many such policies make no sense. But each individual policy can be justified and explained within its own political context.

American public policy does not always serve the public interest. But, for better or worse, it does generally reflect the underlying dynamics of American politics.

Summary

Public policy is "what the government says and does about perceived problems." In general, governments pursue four types of policies: transferring resources from one group of citizens to another; providing subsidies and incentives to encourage or discourage specific actions by firms or individuals; regulating individuals and firms through creation and enforcement of specific rules governing private activities; and developing and administering a variety of programs. Disagreements over public policy may involve controversy over the ends to be pursued as well as over the means to be used.

Many factors influence what policies the government adopts and how they are carried out. These include the nation's political culture and constitutional framework; the nature of individual government institutions; the electoral and partisan context of political decision making; ideas; and public opinion, the media, and interest groups. Public policy is the result of all of these forces working with and against each other; it is the *interconnection* of all of them that truly shapes public policy.

In determining public policies, government decision makers must frequently make difficult choices. These include which level of government should address a given problem, and whether cooperation between levels of government is necessary; whether the government should rely on the private market to solve a problem or interfere with the market; whether to approach a problem incrementally or all at once; and how to weigh the often competing interests of fairness and efficiency.

The United States government is involved in a wide variety of domestic policies. Economic policy involves government programs and actions designed to promote economic growth, maintain low inflation, and stabilize the value of the dollar overseas. There is general agreement on the goals of economic policy, at least in the broadest sense, but little agreement on how to achieve those goals. Some economists and politicians favor a hands-off, or laissez-faire, approach; others favor a high level of government involvement.

Another key area of government policy is regulation and deregulation. The government may intervene in the activities of private individuals and firms for a number of reasons—including to protect life, liberty, and property; to correct "market failures," in which the private economic marketplace does not function fairly or efficiently; and to create or prevent competition. Many economists and politicians today favor deregulation, arguing that too much regulation interferes with economic efficiency and often serves only the interests of narrow groups.

Although critics of government regulation focus on government actions that hinder private economic actors, in fact the government provides a high level of subsidies to various individuals and firms. It also provides many programs that are available to everyone but disproportionately benefit the wealthy.

Another key area of government policy is social welfare. Social welfare policy aims to provide social insurance, to create a safety net, to change the behavior of certain individuals, and to redistribute wealth and power. The largest social welfare program in the United States is social security, which provides pensions to retirees. Other government programs, including Supplemental Security Income and Aid to Families with Dependent Children, provide income assistance to the needy.

The federal government also plays a major role in health and education policy. In health policy, the government provides Medicare for the elderly and Medicaid for the poor; a more comprehensive federal health policy was proposed by the Clinton administration in 1993–1994 but was rejected by Congress. In education policy, it funds special programs and plays a "cheerleading" role, encouraging educational progress in the states and national educational improvement. The centerpiece of current federal education policy is Goals 2000, which aims to improve American education by the end of the century.

Key Terms

Incrementalism
Radicalism
Efficiency
Cost-benefit analysis
Laissez-faire
Monetary policy
Federal Reserve Board (or "Fed")
Fiscal policy
Progressive tax
Deregulation
Corporate welfare
Social security
Medicare
Medicaid

Review Questions

1. What are the four general types of government policy?

2. What factors influence government policy?

3. Describe some of the "hard choices" faced by politicians and policy makers.

4. What are the federal government's most important functions in the area of economic policy?

5. What purposes does regulation serve? Why do many politicians and economists currently favor deregulation?

6. What are examples of government subsidies to corporations and well-off individuals?

7. Briefly describe the federal government's roles in social welfare policy, education policy, and health policy.

Suggested Readings

Breyer, Stephen. *Regulation and Its Reform.* Cambridge, Mass.: Harvard University Press, 1982.

Galbraith, James K., and William Darity, Jr. *Macroeconomics.* Boston: Houghton Mifflin, 1994.

Jennings, John F., ed. *National Issues in Education: The Past Is Prologue.* Bloomington, Ind.: Phi Delta Kappa International. Washington, D.C.: Institute for Educational Leadership, 1993.

Mann, Thomas E., and Norman J. Orstein. *Intensive Care: How Congress Shapes Health Policy.* Washington, D. C.: American Enterprise Institute and The Brookings Institution, 1995.

Marmor, Theodore R., Jerry L. Mashaw, and Philip L. Harvey. *America's Misunderstood Welfare State: Persistent Myths, Enduring Realities.* New York: Basic Books, 1990.

Shively, W. Phillips. *Power and Choice: An Introduction to Political Science,* 5th ed. New York: McGraw-Hill, 1997.

Wilson, James Q. *The Politics of Regulation.* New York: Basic Books, 1980.

Internet Resources

Office of Management and Budget web site, including comprehensive documents on the Federal budget, at:

http://www.whitehouse.gov/WH/EOP/OMB/html/ ombhome.html

The University of Wisconsin's Health Policy Information web site, with updates and links on health policy issues, at:

http://www.uwex.edu/ces/flp/health

The National Center for Policy Analysis, with news, links and analysis on a variety of policy issues, including social security, welfare reform, crime, and education, at:

http://www.public-policy.org/~ncpa

★ 17 ★

Foreign and Military Policy

In early August of 1964, the White House released the news that the American destroyer *Maddox* had been fired on by North Vietnamese torpedo boats in the Gulf of Tonkin, between China and Vietnam. Two days later, the White House announced the news of a second attack, this time on the *Maddox* and another ship, the *C. Turner Joy*. That night, President Lyndon Baines Johnson ordered a retaliatory raid on North Vietnamese torpedo boats and their bases, and went on national television to tell the American people that, despite this "open aggression on the high seas against the United States of America . . . , [w]e still seek no wider war."

American involvement in Vietnam in August 1964 was very limited. For the most part, the United States was content to allow the South Vietnamese army to fight its own war, aided by some twenty-one thousand American military advisers, considerable American economic and military assistance, and the behind-the-scenes efforts of the Central Intelligence Agency.

Johnson's response to the incidents in the Gulf of Tonkin were grounded partly in foreign policy, and partly in the 1964 presidential campaign. The Republican challenger, Barry Goldwater, had charged Johnson with being "soft" on communism, and had advocated using all necessary force, including nuclear weapons, to defeat the North Vietnamese. As one of Johnson's biographers put it, "Johnson was running for President as a man of peace, but he had not the slightest intention of permitting Barry Goldwater to appear as the spokesman for the land of the free and the home of the brave."[1]

But Johnson also wanted to guard against Vietnam becoming "Johnson's war." Thus he sought congressional authorization to use "all necessary measures" to "repel any armed attack" against American forces and to "prevent further aggression." The Senate debated the measure, which became known as the Tonkin Gulf Resolution, for eight hours on August 6 and 7 before adopting it by a vote of 88 to 2. The House debated the resolution for forty minutes on August 7 before adopting it by a vote of 416 to 0. President Johnson signed the resolution into law the same day.

The Tonkin Gulf Resolution became the de facto declaration of the Vietnam War. Early in 1965, Johnson responded to a North Vietnamese attack on the U.S. Army advisers' barracks at Pleiku with a bombing campaign against North Vietnam. In June 1965, Johnson authorized American troops to search out the enemy and engage in combat. By July 1965 there were 125,000 American troops in Vietnam, a number that would eventually reach over 500,000. Before the war ended it would become the longest and most unsuccessful war in American history, with more than 58,000 Americans killed in a losing cause. The war also took its toll at home, as public support eroded both for the military effort and for the politicians in Washington.

Years after the Tonkin Gulf incidents, it seems clear that there never was a North

The last Americans are evacuated from the roof of the American embassy in Saigon in April 1975. The United States reestablished diplomatic relations with Vietnam—and once again took possession of the embassy building—in 1995.

Vietnamese attack on the *C. Turner Joy*. There may not even have been an attack on the *Maddox*. The Tonkin Gulf incidents were manufactured or misinterpreted out of mistakes and misunderstandings in the Gulf of Tonkin and in Washington, and out of the exigencies of presidential campaign politics.

In many ways, the democratic form of government is ill suited to the conduct of foreign policy. In the view of Alexis de Tocqueville, "Foreign policy does not require the use of any of the good qualities peculiar to democracy but does demand the cultivation of almost all those which it lacks." In particular, Tocqueville wrote, the great mass of the people

- find it difficult to coordinate the details of a great undertaking;
- have trouble fixing on a plan and carrying it through with determination;
- are uncomfortable with secrecy, and lack the specialized knowledge essential to the conduct of foreign policy;
- are impatient for results; and
- tend to base foreign policy on passions and emotion rather than calculation and reason.[2]

The Framers were well aware of these limitations, and so took steps to remove the day-to-day conduct of foreign policy from the normal channels of democratic politics.[3] Most important, they gave preeminence to the Senate and the president, both elected indirectly and for long terms of office. At the same time, the Framers made sure that the people had ample power to keep the president and the Senate in check: they gave the House of Representatives the power to initiate all spending bills, including expenditures for military and foreign affairs, and gave the House an equal role with the Senate in deciding whether or not to declare war.

The Framers' system was designed to serve an isolated nation whose interest in the rest of the world was largely confined to peaceful commerce. Europe was weeks away by sea; the United States had no army to speak of and a navy whose purpose and function were mainly defensive. In the twentieth century, as America grew into a military superpower and as technology brought the world closer to our doorstep, change was inevitable. The balance of power between the two branches tilted increasingly toward the White House, and by the end of World War II, the president was far and away the paramount force in both making and carrying out American foreign policy.

However it evolved, the American foreign-policy apparatus seems to have served the nation remarkably well. The Allied victory in World War II proved that the United States can plan and coordinate vast military operations. The successful conclusion of the fifty-year "cold war" against communism suggests that the nation is capable of great determination and consistency in foreign policy. From Korea to the Persian Gulf and in countless arenas in between, the United States has demonstrated that it can act coolly and deliberately, and, when necessary, with secrecy and dispatch.

America's success in foreign policy, however, has hardly been complete, and even its victories have often come at great cost. The absence of free and open debate over the conduct of foreign affairs has led to massive errors in judgment by those in power, most tragically in the long, painful, and unsuccessful war in Vietnam. The extraordinary system of secrecy surrounding all aspects of foreign policy has enabled political leaders to deceive and mislead the American people, even to the point of carrying out "secret" wars in Cambodia and Nicaragua. The need to secure popular support for foreign operations, especially in wartime, has led numerous presidents to appeal to public emotion rather than reason, creating wartime hysteria and encouraging military rather than diplomatic solutions. And all of this has meant a dreadful assault on civil liberties, from the internment of Japanese Americans during World War II and the persecution of communists and alleged communists during the cold war to the censorship of the press during the Persian Gulf War.

Clearly, a successful foreign policy does require some compromise of democratic principles. At least over the long haul, however, it is vitally necessary that the general purposes and methods of American foreign policy be decided by democratic means. Without a broad base of support, the nation cannot sustain either the human or the monetary costs that a successful foreign policy sometimes demands. Even more fundamentally, a nation whose foreign policy is given over to a chosen few, operating in secret and responsible to no one, ceases to be a democracy in any real sense.

The need to find a balance between short-term efficiency and long-term legitimacy forms the central challenge of American foreign policy. It is a problem that will become increasingly difficult in the ever more complex world of the twenty-first century.

Questions to Keep in Mind

How does the distribution of power under the Constitution reflect the Framers' concerns about the people's role in the making of foreign policy?

How should Americans decide whether or not to intervene in foreign conflicts? What interests—national, humanitarian, or strategic—might justify the expenditure of American money and American lives??

What is and what should be the relationship between Congress and the president in making and executing of foreign policy?

Basic Concepts ★ ★ ★ ★ ★ ★ ★ ★ ★ ★ ★ ★ ★

The Constitution is the starting point—but only the starting point—for understanding American foreign policy. Both the process and the substance of foreign policy owe more to history and practice than to constitutional law and theory. As America's role and position in the world have evolved, the constitutional text has been bent and stretched, so that if the Framers returned today they would hardly recognize the system they designed.

The Constitution and Foreign Policy

The Framers faced two central questions in distributing foreign policy power under the Constitution. The first was how to distribute power between the national and state governments. The second was how to divide power among the three branches of the national government, and particularly between Congress and the president.

Federalism   The Constitution gives the national government almost complete control in the areas of foreign and military policy. Even before the adoption of the Articles of Confederation, the states coordinated foreign policy through the Continental Congress; during the Revolutionary War, matters of strategy and tactics were left to Congress and to General Washington, and state militia units were placed under the authority of the central command.[4] The Articles of Confederation formalized this working arrangement, and the Constitution further consolidated and extended the national government's role in foreign and military policy.

Under the Constitution, the federal government was given the power to regulate "commerce with foreign nations . . . and with the Indian tribes"; to declare war, raise and support armies, provide and maintain a navy, and make rules and regulations for the government of the armed forces; and to punish piracies on the high seas and "offenses against the law of nations." The Constitution authorized the federal government to make treaties with foreign nations, and to send and receive ambassadors (and thus by implication to recognize or derecognize foreign governments). Following the Articles of Confederation, the Constitution barred the states from entering into treaties or alliances, imposing duties on imports or exports, or engaging in military action without the consent of Congress, except in cases of actual invasion.[5]

Over the years, the Supreme Court has read the federal government's foreign affairs power as broadly as possible. In 1958, for example, the Court declared that the federal government's power to regulate foreign affairs extends beyond the specific grants of power in the Constitution. A broad interpretation of the foreign affairs power, the Court said, was "indispensable to [the government's] functioning effectively in the company of sovereign nations."[6]

Separation of Powers   As the historian Leonard Levy has pointed out, there is no real controversy over how the Framers intended to divide power among the three branches. "The Framers intended the Senate to be the principal architect of foreign policy," he writes. "They meant . . . that the President should be the Senate's agent and, in matters involving war powers, the agent of Congress, in the sense of being the branch of government empowered to carry out or conduct policies formulated by the legislative branch."[7]

The Framers gave the Senate a major role in foreign policy largely because they feared the unchecked exercise of presidential power. However, they were not blind to the need for swift and sure action in cases of real emergency. South Carolina's Charles Pinckney, for example, objected to the proposal that Congress be authorized to "make war" on the grounds that legislative deliberations were too slow and that the House of Representatives was too big and met too infrequently to ensure safety. James Madison and Elbridge Gerry of Massachusetts then proposed that Congress be authorized to "declare war," explaining that this language would recognize the president's duty to "repel sudden attacks" against the United States. An energetic executive, Alexander Hamilton explained in *The Federalist Papers*, is "essential to the protection of the community against foreign attacks."[8]

Even so, the Framers expected the president's independent military authority to be strictly limited. The "command of armies" requires "secrecy, dispatch, and decision," which "can only be expected from one person," explained Pennsylvania's James Iredell. But the president's powers would be quite different from those of the British monarch:

The king of Great Britain is not only the commander-in-chief of the land and naval forces, but has power, in time of war, to raise fleets and armies. He also has the power to declare war. The President has not the power of declaring war by his own authority, nor that of raising fleets and armies. The power of declaring war is expressly given to Congress. . . . They have also . . . the powers of raising and supporting armies, and of providing and maintaining a navy.

Certainly the model the Constitutional Convention had in mind was General George Washington, who served as commander in chief during the Revolutionary War. "The instructions of the Congress," as one historian put it, "kept Washington on a short leash. . . . Congress did not hesitate to instruct the commander in chief on military or policy matters."9

Caught between the conflicting demands of liberty and efficiency, the Framers opted to divide foreign policy between the president and Congress. The House of Representatives, which was closest to the people, was given a share of the power of the purse and the power to declare war. In addition to being made the commander in chief, the president was given the role of receiving ambassadors from other nations. The central functions of appointing ambassadors and making treaties were divided between the president and the Senate, which would complement and check one another. Still it was the Senate, and not the president, that was expected to be the senior partner in formulating and guiding American foreign policy.

The Evolution of the Foreign Policy Power

The idea that the president would be subordinate to the Senate in the making of foreign policy did not survive the Washington presidency. By 1796, it was clear that the president would play a leading role in foreign affairs. Washington, for example, insisted on the sole authority to communicate with foreign nations, denied the House access to documents concerning treaty negotiations, and insisted on the right to negotiate treaties without prior Senate consultation. Other presidents also took a broad view of their powers under the Constitution. John Adams led a small, undeclared war with France, and Thomas Jefferson annexed Louisiana on his own authority. Congress basically acceded to this flow of power to the executive branch, although it continued to play a vital role in setting broad policies and in approving presidential actions after the fact.10

Over the next century, the pendulum of power in foreign policy swung back and forth between Congress and the White House. For nearly thirty years after the Civil War, Congress had the upper hand; for example, the Senate refused to ratify a single treaty during this period outside the area of immigration.11 Between 1900 and 1920, by contrast, Presidents Teddy Roosevelt and Woodrow Wilson took the lead. Roosevelt led American forces into Cuba and Santo Domingo, and built the Panama Canal. Wilson led America into World War I. Wilson especially took the position that in foreign policy the president "must utter every initial judgment, take every first step of action, supply the information upon which [the nation] . . . is to act, suggest and in large measure control its conduct." But Wilson's expansion of presidential authority provoked a strong congressional counterreaction, which culminated in the Senate's refusal to approve the Treaty of Versailles at the end of World World War I. For the next two decades no president dared to pursue bold initiatives in foreign affairs, and Congress regained some of its lost authority.

The Emergence of the Imperial Presidency   The third and fourth terms of the presidency of Franklin Roosevelt marked another swing in the pendulum. Relying on bold assertions of constitutional authority, Roosevelt steered America toward intervention in World War II despite strong congressional opposition. In 1940, without congressional approval, Roosevelt traded ships to England in return for military bases. In 1941, as one scholar explains, Roosevelt sent "American troops to Greenland and Iceland, declared a state of unlimited national emergency, and ordered the navy to convoy American ships and to shoot Nazi U-boats on sight, all without express congressional consent."[12] In subsequent years America's long-running fight against communism led American presidents to bolster presidential power, fighting undeclared wars in Korea and Vietnam and building up vast intelligence networks around the world (this fifty-year struggle against the Soviet Union and communist China, which ended with the break-up of the Soviet Union in the early 1990s, is known as the **Cold War**). From Roosevelt to Nixon, the "imperial presidents" engaged in widespread personal diplomacy and took on a preeminent role in world affairs (for further discussion of the imperial presidency, see Chapter 13).

The Reassertion of Congressional Authority   The pinnacle of the imperial presidency came with the Vietnam War in the 1960s and 1970s. Presidents Kennedy, Johnson, and Nixon ordered some five hundred thousand American soldiers to Vietnam with only the barest congressional authority. After twelve years of inconclusive fighting and fifty-eight thousand American deaths, Congress at last took steps to reclaim at least some degree of control over the foreign policy process.

The War Powers Resolution. Congress's first attempt in decades to insist on a systematic role in foreign affairs came in 1973, with the passage of the **War Powers Resolution**

President Franklin D. Roosevelt, on a 1942 cross-country "inspection tour" of U.S. arms manufacturers. The first "imperial president," Roosevelt dominated American foreign policy after 1940, leaving Congress to play a secondary and mostly supportive role.

(also known as the War Powers Act). The resolution, which was passed over Richard Nixon's veto, recognizes the president's primary responsibility to *initiate* military operations in response to crisis conditions. However, it requires the president to consult with Congress before doing so, and to report to Congress within forty-eight hours after American troops are introduced into hostilities or into situations where hostile action is imminent. The resolution requires that such troops be withdrawn from hostilities within sixty days, unless Congress has declared war or enacted specific authorization for the operation. Furthermore, it requires the president to withdraw such troops even before the end of the sixty-day period if Congress so directs.

The War Powers Resolution is difficult to enforce. Moreover, every president since Nixon has expressed concerns over the constitutionality of the resolution. Instead of following the literal requirements of the War Powers Resolution, therefore, Congress and the president have usually worked out a substitute mechanism to provide congressional input into the decision to deploy troops overseas. Typically, the president has simply asked Congress to pass a special resolution authorizing the military operation in question, thereby satisfying the spirit if not the letter of the War Powers Resolution. Presidents Reagan and Bush, for example, sought and received congressional approval of operations in Lebanon (1983), Panama (1989), and the Persian Gulf (1991). It may actually be in the president's interest to get Congress on board in such circumstances: when things go well, as in the Persian Gulf, it is the president rather than Congress who gets the credit; when things go badly, as when more than two hundred soldiers were killed in a terrorist attack in Lebanon in 1983, Congress shares the responsibility.

Bringing Legislative Power to Bear on Foreign Policy. Congress has learned in recent decades to use its broad legislative powers in the foreign policy context, particularly its power to approve all federal spending and to regulate interstate and foreign commerce.

Congress's power to control spending has tremendous impact on foreign policy. For example, Congress has the final word on the research, development, and deployment of weapons systems; on the size and makeup of the armed forces; and on spending for foreign aid. In recent times Congress has clashed with the White House on all of these matters. One of the most publicized conflicts was over research into the so-called Star Wars antimissile defense system, a highly controversial and very expensive proposal to design and implement a shield against missiles launched against the United States. Congress has also acted by law to limit the president's power to sell arms to foreign countries. In 1986, for example, Congress reduced a proposed multibillion-dollar arms sale to Saudi Arabia to just $354 million, and excluded Stinger missiles from the package.[13]

More controversial are Congress's attempts to use its spending power as leverage to make the White House carry out foreign policy in a certain way. In the 1980s, for example, Congress enacted a series of laws banning the expenditure of funds for covert operations to support the contra rebels in Nicaragua. The Reagan administration went to great lengths to evade this ban, including an attempt by at least some administration officials to trade arms to Iran in return for Iranian support for the contras. The result was the Iran-contra scandal, which proved greatly embarrassing to the administration.

Congress's power to regulate foreign commerce can also be a powerful weapon in the struggle for control of foreign policy. In the 1970s, for example, Congress banned trade

DEBATING THE CONSTITUTION

Does the President Have the Authority to Make War Without Congressional Approval?

The Framers of the Constitution gave Congress the power to declare war, made the president commander in chief of the armed forces, and gave him the leading role in foreign affairs. Throughout the centuries, the two branches have fought repeatedly over whether these powers give the president the authority to make war without congressional approval. Presidential war-making power reached a high point in the Korea and Vietnam conflicts, both of which were fought without a congressional declaration of war.

In 1973, in an effort to rein in the president's power, Congress passed the War Powers Resolution. Since then, presidents have generally proclaimed their independent authority to make war and declared the War Powers Resolution unconstitutional, while at the same time frequently asking Congress to approve specific military operations.

Consider the following thoughts and comments as well as the material in the text as you debate the president's power to make war without congressional approval.

For the President

"When the President acts in absence of either a congressional grant or denial of authority, he can rely only upon his own independent powers, but there is a zone of twilight in which he and Congress may have concurrent authority, or in which its distribution is uncertain. Therefore, congressional inertia, indifference, or quiescence may sometimes, at least as a practical matter, enable, if not invite, presidential responsibility."

—Supreme Court Justice Robert Jackson in The Steel Seizure Case, 1952

"[In the realm of foreign affairs,] with its important, complicated, delicate, and manifold problems, the President alone has the power to speak or listen as a representative of the nation. . . . [The President is] the sole organ of the federal government in the field of international relations. . . . He, not Congress, has the better opportunity of knowing the conditions which prevail in foreign countries, and especially is this true in time of war. He has his confidential sources of information. . . . Secrecy in respect of information gathered by them may be highly necessary. . . ."

—United States v. Curtiss-Wright, 1936

"I believe the Constitution gives the president not only the power, but the obligation to protect American lives, to enforce valid treaties and to defend other vital American interests. . . . When Congress steps beyond its capacities, it takes traits that can be helpful to collective deliberation and turns them into a harmful blend of vacillation, credit-claiming, blame avoidance, and indecision."

—Representative (later Defense Secretary) Dick Cheney, 1989

"We cannot take the time to have 535 secretaries of state or secretaries of defense."

—Former President Gerald R. Ford, 1986

"Guerrilla warfare blurred several distinctions: What constitutes war rather than some other form of violence? What is the political and legal status of war that is not quite civil war and not tidily war between sovereign states. . . . *The difficulty of fashioning America's responses to violence in a context of such blurring [as in Vietnam], and the fact that an obliterating war has been, potentially, just minutes away, led President Johnson's undersecretary of state, Nicholas Katzenbach, to tell Congress in August 1967 that 'the expression of declaring war is one that has been outmoded in the international arena.'"*

—George F. Will, during the 1991
debate over the Persian Gulf War

For Congress

"The President is to be Commander-in-Chief of the army and navy of the United States. In this respect his authority would be nominally the same with that of the king of Great Britain, but in substance much inferior to it. It would amount to nothing more than the supreme command and direction of the military and naval forces, as first general and first admiral . . . ; while that of the British king extends to the declaring of war and to the raising and regulating of fleets and armies—all of which, by the Constitution . . . would appertain to the legislature."

—Alexander Hamilton, Federalist No. 70

"It is 60 days since President Bush sent forces to confront Iraq in a context where war could have broken out at any minute, and can still. . . . President Bush [has asked] for broad congressional support for what he has done so far and [has solicited] support for what is to come by consulting key legislators informally. That way he avoids being drawn into the magnetic field of the War Powers Resolution, maximizes the support he has got and minimizes the chances for resistance to his policy to develop. This makes sense for a president in a crisis, but, of course, War Powers [Resolution] or no, it leaves Congress pliable and passive and out in the policy cold."

—Washington Post, October 9, 1990

"If the President can deal with the Arabs, and he can deal with the Soviets, then he ought to be able to deal with the U.S. Congress."

—House Majority Leader
Thomas P. "Tip" O'Neill, Jr., 1973

"Under the American Constitution, the president has no legal authority—none whatsoever—to commit the United States to war. Only Congress can make that decision."

—Senate Majority Leader George J. Mitchell, 1990

"It is the purpose of this joint resolution to fulfill the intent of the Constitution of the United States and insure that the collective judgment of both the Congress and the President will apply to the introduction of United States Armed Forces into hostilities, or into situations where imminent involvement in hostilities is clearly indicated by the circumstances, and to the continued use of such forces in hostilities or in such situations."

—The War Powers Resolution, 1973

"Every real war the United States has ever engaged in was declared or authorized by Congress up through and including World War II. . . . Whatever the [F]ramers meant by war it included half a million troops facing each other across a battle line. . . . If the declaration of war clause does not apply [to the Persian Gulf] . . . it will have been stripped out of the Constitution."

—Constitutional scholar Walter Dellinger, 1990

Sources: *Youngstown Sheet & Tube Co.* v. *Sawyer*, 343 U.S. 579 (1952), at 637; 299 U.S. 304 (1936), at 319–320; Quoted in the *Washington Post*, March 14, 1989, p. A4; Gerald R. Ford, "Congress, the Presidency, and National Security Policy," *Presidential Studies Quarterly* 16 (Spring 1986), p. 203; George F. Will, "Better 60-40 Than No Vote at All," *Washington Post*, January 9, 1991, p. A19; The 60-Day Clock," *Washington Post*, October 9, 1990, p. A20; *Congressional Quarterly Almanac*, 1973, p. 906; Mitchell interview on NBC's *Meet the Press*, October 21, 1990, quoted in *Congressional Quarterly Weekly Report*, October 27, 1990, p. 736; 87 Stat. 555 (1973); *Washington Post*, December 14, 1990, p. A46.

concessions to the Soviet Union in protest of the persecution of Soviet Jews. In the 1980s and 1990s Congress repeatedly threatened to impose trade sanctions on the People's Republic of China if that nation did not stop exploiting and abusing prisoners.

An Uneasy Truce   Congress's efforts to assert itself in the field of foreign policy have shown clear results over the past twenty-five years. Perhaps most important, Congress has changed its own attitude toward presidential power over foreign affairs. Over and over again the modern Congress has demonstrated that it is no longer willing to sit back and allow the executive branch to run foreign policy. It has demanded involvement in every aspect of foreign policy, and has repeatedly reasserted its claim to have the final say on how American power is used abroad.

Over the years a succession of presidents have sought to hammer out an arrangement that will keep Congress satisfied and yet not sacrifice the constitutional prerogatives of the presidency or the national interest as seen from the White House. As Secretary of State Henry Kissinger put it in 1975, "The decade-long struggle in this country over executive dominance in foreign policy is over. The recognition that Congress is a coequal branch of government is the dominant fact of national politics today. The executive accepts that Congress must have both the sense and the reality of participation: foreign policy must be a shared enterprise."[14]

Conflicts between the legislative and executive branches over foreign policy are probably inevitable, however. As Justice Jackson suggested in 1952, most important foreign policy decisions fall in the "zone of twilight" in which both branches have at least some authority. For either branch to dominate the other would upset the balance of the Constitution; for the two branches to engage in continual battles of their own is simply an expression of the constitutional separation of powers.

Nevertheless, Congress and the White House could improve their working relationship if each branch put aside all illusions of supremacy and admitted the legitimate roles and responsibilities of the other. However, the deep mistrust between the two branches over foreign policy—evident even when the same party controls both Congress and the White House—means that a thaw in relations could take place only gradually, with each side giving and taking a little at a time.

Managing Foreign Affairs in the Modern Era

As the United States has grown into a major world power, it has become necessary to expand the nation's foreign policy-making apparatus. Responsibility for foreign policy now extends into dozens of agencies, including those dealing with military operations, economic relations, environmental regulation, and law enforcement. In turn, this expansion has taxed the president's ability to manage foreign policy, and has led to a corresponding increase in the number of foreign affairs specialists on the White House staff and in the Executive Office of the President.

The legislative branch has also expanded its capacity to oversee and manage foreign policy, largely through the creation of specialized committees and subcommittees. Even the judiciary has not escaped the necessity of dealing with foreign nations and nationals. Here is a brief overview of who's who and what's what in American foreign policy.

Executive Branch Key foreign policy decisions are made in the White House, often by the president personally. In making these decisions, the president can turn to numerous sources of advice and information, including personal aides and confidants; the national security adviser and the National Security Agency staff; top officials and experts in various cabinet departments, including State, Defense, Treasury; the Central Intelligence Agency and other intelligence organizations; and outside experts, including academics and other specialists.

Routine matters and the day-to-day conduct of foreign policy are handled by the State Department, which has a large staff in Washington and ambassadors and consular officials around the globe. Many ambassadorial positions are held by career state department officials (known as foreign service offi-

President Bill Clinton meets with his key foreign policy advisers—including Vice President Al Gore, Secretary of Defense William Cohen, Secretary of State Madeleine Albright, and members of the Joint Chiefs of Staff.

cers), although the most glamorous posts are held by political appointees, who are often friends or financial supporters of the president.

In recent years the National Security Agency (headed by the national security adviser) has come to play a major role in making and coordinating foreign policy. During the Nixon administration, the national security adviser, Henry Kissinger, became the president's personal representative in foreign policy, displacing the secretary of state from his historic role as the chief foreign policy figure. Succeeding presidents have generally relegated the national security adviser to an advisory role.

Top military officers also play a key role in advising the president on foreign policy matters. In theory, the president has two distinct lines of communication with the Defense Department. Matters of general policy and operational orders go through the secretary of defense. Discussions about technical matters, including strategy and tactics, are handled by the Chairman of the Joint Chiefs of Staff. These distinctions are rarely followed in any strict sense. The president also has access to a variety of military and civilian intelligence experts.

Congress Although the White House and Congress often fight over the conduct of foreign policy, especially under conditions of divided government, key members of Congress can be important sources of advice for the president and the White House team. The House and Senate have primary responsibility for setting the foreign aid budget; ratifying treaties; passing legislation to implement treaties and executive agreements; and conducting oversight of foreign policy activities. Congress has also established intelligence oversight committees, which attempt to keep an eye on the activities of the CIA and related agencies.

Congress also plays an important role in the area of military policy, largely through the House and Senate Armed Services Committees, although operational control of the military is left to the commander in chief. Congress's power over the budget gives it a major say over long-range military planning, especially in the area of weapons acquisition and development. Congressional committees have conducted important after-the-fact investigations into the conduct of military operations—for example, after the 1983 invasion of Grenada. Congress is also responsible for the rules and regulations governing the armed forces. President Clinton's proposal to lift the ban on gay soldiers, for example, was subject to congressional review, forcing a compromise between the two branches. Likewise, the decision to allow women to participate in combat was made by Congress, not the executive branch.[15]

The chairmen of the House and Senate Armed Services Committees are typically seasoned veterans, with great knowledge of the substance and politics of foreign policy. They often become major players in the foreign policy process in their own right.

The Courts and Foreign Policy   Traditionally, the judiciary has stayed out of the foreign policy arena. Over the years, the courts have generally regarded foreign policy decisions as "political questions" outside the preview of the judicial branch. When the courts have made decisions affecting foreign policy, they have generally deferred to decisions already made by the legislative and executive branches. When the legislative and executive branches have clashed over foreign policy decisions, the judiciary has largely stayed out of the fight.

During the Vietnam War, for example, the Supreme Court refused to hear challenges to the constitutionality of undeclared wars. In 1981 the Court upheld the agreement between President Jimmy Carter and Iran that ended the year-long hostage crisis, even though Congress had had no role in the process. In particular, the Court held that the agreement could transfer all claims against Iran currently pending in American courts to a special international tribunal.[16]

The Substance of American Foreign Policy

For most of its history, the United States has had the luxury of being able to choose when and where to get involved in the affairs of other nations. Geographically separated from Europe, surrounded by friendly or powerless neighbors, and essentially self-sufficient, the United States could afford to worry far less about foreign policy than any other nation in the Western world.

Isolationism and Intervention

The Roots of Isolationism   America's geographical isolation was reinforced by a cultural tendency to withdraw from the endless fights between European nations and a decided lack of interest in colonial expansion outside North America. The new nation could not completely detach itself from the rest of the world, however. It still had to resolve a number of nagging issues left over from the Revolutionary War with Great Britain. It faced the constant need to protect its naval and commercial vessels on the high seas, and to assert its right to trade with all nations even when Europe was at war. Finally, it had to clear the way for westward expansion by persuading the European nations to abandon their colonial settlements and by pushing the Native American tribes (which were regarded as foreign nations) out of the way.

The essential **isolationism** of American foreign policy was eloquently summed up by George Washington in his famous *Farewell Address* in 1796. "Europe has a set of primary interests, which to us have none, or a very remote relation," he declared. "'Tis our true policy to steer clear of permanent alliances, with any portion of the foreign world. . . .Taking care always to keep ourselves . . . on a respectable defensive posture, we may safely trust in temporary alliances for extraordinary emergencies."[17]

> *"DIPLOMACY, n. The patriotic art of lying for one's country."*
>
> —Ambrose Bierce,
> *The Devil's Dictionary*

Americans in the early Republic combined this desire for isolation with a strong distrust of military power. Eighteenth-century Americans viewed a large, permanent military establishment as a constant threat to liberty—especially if the army was controlled by the national government. The colonists' discomfort with military power is easy to understand, for when they thought of a standing army they thought of the British Redcoats who had occupied Boston, enforced the evil decrees of Parliament, and fought the American patriots. Although the possibility of a military coup in the United States seems absurd today, the record of military regimes in other nations should convince us that these fears were solidly grounded.

The Roots of Intervention: The Monroe Doctrine

Americans might have wanted isolation from Europe, but the problems of the Old World kept intruding. In the first twenty-five years after the signing of the Constitution, the United States fought a major war with Great Britain and had minor skirmishes with France and the bashaw (or ruler) of Tripoli (the shores of which have been immortalized in *The Marines' Hymn)*. None of these encounters challenged the overriding policy of isolation, however, since they were all fought for defensive purposes or to establish the basic conditions of American neutrality.

The emergence of a number of new and independent nations in Central and South America after 1815 brought about a new American response. When fears rose of a French and Spanish attempt to retake parts of South America in 1823, President James Monroe at last decided to take a stand. In his annual message to Congress, Monroe made it clear that the United States was prepared to resist any European attempts to intervene militarily in the Western Hemisphere. "The American continents, by the free and independent condition which they have assumed and maintain, are henceforth not to be considered for future colonization by any European powers," he said. "We should consider any attempt on their part to extend their system to any portion of this hemisphere as dangerous to our peace and safety."[18]

The **Monroe Doctrine,** as this declaration is known, was primarily defensive in character. For the first time, however, the United States had adopted the view that American interests were not limited to North America. Moreover, the United States was prepared to protect those interests by military force. Although Monroe took no action in support of these words, the precedent he established for **interventionism** continues to influence American foreign policy even today.

Isolationism and Intervention in the Modern Era

The tension between isolation and intervention in foreign policy has continued throughout American history. For three years after World War I broke out in Europe, for example, the American public resisted U.S. involvement; President Woodrow Wilson had won reelection on the grounds that "he kept us out of war." At last the United States entered the war in 1917, sending nearly 5 million soldiers to Europe over the next two years. Although the public embraced the war effort, Americans readopted their isolationist attitudes with a vengeance once the war ended. Congress rejected American membership in the League of Nations (the precursor to the United Nations), and except for demanding high reparations payments from its former enemies, the United States largely turned away from foreign engagements for the next two decades.

As late as 1941, the majority of Americans opposed American entry into World War II on the grounds that the United States had no overriding interest in European politics. In mid-1940, the entire American military numbered under five hundred thousand—compared with more than 12 million by the end of World War II.[19] The famous World War II General George S. Patton, then head of the U.S. Army Tank Corps, used to joke that his entire command consisted of two tanks, only one of which was operational.

The Japanese attack on Pearl Harbor in December 1941 ended American isolationism for good. Once in the war, the United States mounted the most powerful military force in world history, overcoming both Japan and Nazi Germany within four years. At that point, unlike after World War I, the United States took decisive steps to ensure that it remained a major player—at times *the* major player—on the world stage.

America's willingness to take a leadership role in foreign policy after World War II was reinforced by the widespread view that the threat of Soviet-inspired communism constituted a vital threat to world peace and to American security. The years after 1945 saw the extraordinary effort to rebuild Europe (the Marshall Plan) and Japan, the creation of the United Nations with American sponsorship, and U.S. membership in the North Atlantic Treaty Organization and other "permanent alliances," in a direct rejection of Washington's principle. It also witnessed a dramatic buildup of U.S. defenses as compared with the prewar era, with peacetime forces reaching nearly 3 million soldiers and sailors by 1955 (peak strength during the Vietnam War a decade later was only about 20 percent higher). Since 1945 the United States has fought major wars in Korea, Vietnam, and the Persian Gulf, and stationed huge fighting forces in Europe and around the world.

Isolationists called on the United States to "put America first" and avoid involvement in World War II. Only the Japanese attack on Pearl Harbor in December 1941 put American public opinion solidly behind American involvement in the war.

Foreign Policy and the "New World Order"

The goals and challenges facing American foreign policy have been transformed in just the past decade. Long-term trends in economic and technological development have combined with short-term changes of nearly unprecedented proportions to force a fundamental rethinking of America's relationship to the rest of the world. Among the changes are the following:

- *The end of the Cold War.* From 1945 until 1989, American foreign policy was dominated by the political and military conflict between the United States and the Soviet Union. Typically depicted as a struggle between democracy and communism, this superpower conflict influenced American interests and involvements in every part of the world. The existence of the Cold War made the United States both more and less aggressive in foreign affairs: more aggressive, because of the perceived need to contain the spread of Soviet-sponsored communism; less so, because even the smallest of conflicts threatened to explode into a nuclear Armageddon.

- *The emergence of economic competition and integration.* After World War II, the United States stood alone as a first-rate economic power. Since the 1970s, however, both Europe and Asia have emerged as major players in the world economy. On the one hand, the globalization of the economy has meant increased competition for American manufacturers. On the other hand, American producers and consumers are now highly dependent on the economies of other nations. American companies routinely buy component parts abroad; rely on assembly plants in other countries; and, increasingly, look to the rest of the world's consumers as potential buyers of American products. The integration of the world economy has led the United States and its economic allies to act swiftly and dramatically to bail out other nations in economic difficulties. Thus the United States loaned billions to Mexico in 1995, while a group of countries loaned South Korea some $50 billion in 1997.

Figure 17.1 **World Military Expenditures**

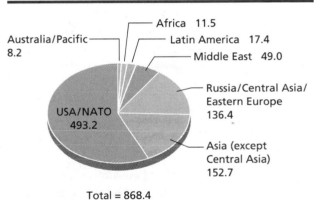

Total = 868.4

SOURCE: U. S. Arms Control and Disarmament Agency, *World Military Expenditures and Arms Transfers,* 1993–1994.

- *The information revolution.* Once, agents smuggled handwritten texts out of Russia. Today, messages are routinely traded by modem and fax machine, and via the Internet. The invention of the personal computer and the other technological wonders of the modern world has made international boundaries less relevant than ever before. Along with vast opportunities, the information revolution has created difficult problems, ranging from international copyright issues to international crime.

The economic and political transformation of the world in the late 1980s was symbolized by the dismantling of the Berlin Wall in 1989. A year later, in the midst of the buildup to the Persian Gulf War, President George Bush proclaimed the existence of a "New World

Order." Although many agree with Bush's assessment, there is little agreement on exactly what the new world order will look like or what it will mean for the United States. Many suggest that the new world order will hardly be orderly at all.

American Foreign Policy: To What Ends?

During the Cold War the ends of American foreign policy were clear, if at times controversial. America's primary goals were fourfold:

- to defend the United States from attack by the Soviet Union and its allies;
- to maintain the nuclear balance of power with the Soviet Union and China;
- to defend Western Europe from Soviet attack, in coordination with the North Atlantic Treaty Organization (NATO); and
- to resist the expansion of Soviet communism across the globe but especially in areas central to American interests, including the East Asian perimeter, the Western Hemisphere, and the Middle East.

No decision on foreign policy, no matter how apparently removed from the superpower conflict, could be made without consideration of these basic concerns. A civil war in Africa, a border dispute in Asia, terrorism in the Middle East—all were approached by American policy makers as aspects of a single, overarching conflict between democracy and communism.

Ironically, the war against communism comprised a wide range of American policies and approaches to foreign policy, some of which were mutually contradictory. In some instances, for example, the United States would take strong steps to protect human rights; in others, human rights violations would be overlooked in order to strengthen the hand of an anticommunist dictator. The Cold War also took a large share of American economic resources, which were diverted from civilian research and development to defense. Although the costs of the Cold War were only a minor problem in the boom years of the 1950s and 1960s, they took their toll on the American economy in the long term.[20]

Setting Priorities After the Cold War   The absence of the Soviet lodestar makes it extremely difficult for American policy makers to set the nation's priorities in foreign affairs. The various goals of U.S. policy are complex and require a difficult balancing act. Moreover, the United States no longer has the financial resources or worldwide preeminence to make key decisions alone. Instead it must constantly coordinate its actions with, and sometimes subordinate its policies to, those of its European and Asian allies, as well as of various regional and local powers and potentates. Furthermore, the absence of the communist threat has made it more difficult for Americans to agree on what our foreign policy goals should be or how we should go about pursuing them.

If America's foreign policy goals cannot be neatly rank-ordered, they can at least be broadly sketched:

Defense.   The importance of protecting the nation against foreign attack is obvious. While the threat of actual invasion is small, the United States remains highly vulnerable to terrorism, both at home and abroad. American installations overseas, both military and diplomatic, are particularly at risk, as are American commercial aircraft. For the most part the United States has been successful in keeping foreign terrorism off American soil, although the 1993 bombing at the World Trade Center in New York stands as a reminder of the devastation that terrorism can produce.

Protection of American Strategic Interests. Beginning with the Monroe Doctrine, the United States has identified areas of the world as impinging directly on America's strategic, or geopolitical, interests. The Cold War, with its emphasis on maintaining a balance of power between the United States and the Soviet Union, caused a great expansion in the number of these areas. The United States made it clear through policy statements, strategic alliances, and the deployment of troops that it would consider attacks against Western Europe, South and Central America, Israel, the Persian Gulf, South Korea, South Vietnam, and the Philippines as direct violations of American security interests. The fall of the Soviet Union and other developments have lessened, but not eliminated, America's strategic interest in most of these areas.

Protection of American Economic and Social Interests. A major goal of American foreign policy is to promote the nation's economic and social well-being. A wide range of policies come under this heading.

Probably the major justification for the Persian Gulf War, for example, was to prevent a major interruption in the flow of oil from the Gulf States to the United States. A disruption in the flow of oil would have increased the cost of gasoline and other petroleum products, President Bush argued, and would have greatly worsened a recession that was just getting under way. At one point, Secretary of State James Baker put the economic justification for the war in clear focus: "If you want to sum it up in one word," he said, "it's jobs."[21]

The protection of American economic interests has not always had a benign or beneficial effect on foreign peoples. On many occasions the United States has sanctioned or promoted the exploitation of foreign lands in order to magnify domestic profits and provide cheap commodities for American consumers. The list of foreign rulers who abused the rights of their people using American money and weapons is long and distressing, and includes the Shah of Iran, the Somoza regime in Nicaragua, and, at one time, Saddam Hussein of Iraq.

Promotion of Human Rights and Democracy. Since at least World War I, the United States has sought to promote the spread of peace, democracy, and freedom (Wilson himself declared that the purpose of World War I was to make the world "safe for democracy").[22] In a sense, of course, the promotion of democracy is in America's own interest: the collapse of communism, for example, is of obvious benefit to Americans, who can spend less on defense and sleep more soundly at night. Proponents of a **human rights policy,** however, typically argue that such a policy is justified in its own right.

Unfortunately, altruistic goals are the luxuries of foreign policy and typically take a backseat to economic or strategic concerns. All too often, human rights has become a rallying cry only to justify policies that have been implemented for other reasons. Even more often, human suffering has been ignored because action to prevent or alleviate it has not served America's economic or strategic interests. For example, American presidents since Nixon have been reluctant to allow human rights issues to interfere with the nation's political and economic relationship with the People's Republic of China.

Nuclear Nonproliferation. Another important goal is to prevent the spread of nuclear weapons, especially to countries with unstable or unreliable regimes. In recent years, the

United States has pursued this goal with both carrots and sticks. Carrots were used in 1994, when the United States agreed to subsidize North Korea's civilian nuclear power program in return for that country's acceptance of United Nations safeguards against the spread of nuclear weapons. Sticks were used in 1991, when as part of its Gulf War strategy the United States attempted to destroy Iraq's real or potential capacity to make nuclear weapons. In 1998, however, the United States was powerless to stop India and Pakistan from conducting tests of nuclear weapons.

Environmental protection. In recent decades, it has become clear that the protection of the environment is a matter of worldwide concern. Increasingly, therefore, the United States has turned to international agreements in this area. In 1997, for example, the Clinton administration negotiated an international agreement to reduce worldwide emissions of gases thought to produce global warming.[23]

Deciding How to Intervene

Once the United States has decided to intervene abroad, it must decide how best to achieve its goals. Two of the most important questions for Americans to decide are whether to rely on military or economic power, and whether to act alone or in coordination with its allies in the world community.

Economic and Conventional Warfare   More often than not, American foreign policy aims to force or persuade another nation to do something (or refrain from doing something). The war in the Persian Gulf provides a classic illustration, with the goal being the withdrawal of the Iraqi occupation force from Kuwait. Ironically, such situations are not limited to dealing with enemy nations. Recently, the United States has engaged in bitter disputes with both Japan and major European states over trade issues.

Once policy makers have fixed on a goal, they must then decide how much they are willing to pay to acheive it. The costs are figured not only in terms of money but also in terms of military and civilian casualties, on both sides. Political leaders must also factor in the impact of a foreign venture on their own support at home, the possibility that a foreign conflict will distract from other policy goals, and the threat of losing support among foreign allies.

In the modern era, the questions facing policy makers typically boil down to a choice between military and economic warfare. Both comprise a wide array of weapons and strategies, and can take total or limited forms. It is also possible to combine the two, using military force to reinforce economic sanctions.

Military Options. For decades, American policy makers have struggled to devise effective military strategies that do not involve the costs and risks of all-out war. Such strategies not only conserve lives and resources but may actually be more effective or create fewer problems than total wars. In Iraq, for example, a traditional total war strategy (as in World War II) would have required a continuation of the conflict until the Hussein regime surrendered or was toppled—leaving the United States with a host of new problems, including how to keep Iran from taking advantage of the power vacuum in Baghdad.

After Vietnam, military leaders made it clear that they, and not the White House, should determine what resources are necessary to achieve specific military results. The generation of military leaders who led America's victory in the Persian Gulf did not want a repeat of their Vietnam experience, in which policy makers set goals but then imposed such severe restrictions on military actors that they were unable to achieve them. In practice, the determination of goals and methods must be made together, with civilian leaders weighing the military requirements for any proposed course of action.

Military strategists have many options to consider under the rubric of limited war. For example, they can order air strikes, provide military advisers to other nations, block enemy communications, create "no fly" zones in which military aircraft are not allowed to get off the ground, or employ special forces or intelligence operatives to achieve specific objectives.

Economic Options. The alternative to military force is typically economic pressure. Depending on the situation, the United States can use a variety of methods to impose economic costs on another nation until or unless it complies with American demands.

With friendly nations, economic pressure generally takes the form of "trade wars," in which the United States imposes high taxes on imported goods to persuade the other side to conduct an economic policy friendlier to the United States. In recent years, the United States has engaged in trade wars with China, Japan, and the European Community, imposing punitive tariffs on such items as cellular phones, luxury cars, and white wine. All-out trade wars are rare, and disputes are marked more by symbolic rebukes than by real punishments.

Against enemy states, the United States can engage in all-out economic warfare. Sometimes, the United States freezes all economic activity with the nation in question, trying to inflict a high degree of economic damage, destabilize the enemy regime, and thus achieve compliance with American demands. Economic sanctions can be backed by a military blockade, and can even include air strikes to damage the enemy's productive capacity, power grid, and transportation infrastructure.

Unfortunately, economic sanctions have proved relatively unsuccessful. First, the American people are generally unwilling to apply economic sanctions in their most severe form. Exceptions for medical and other humanitarian supplies are usually made even when all other imports and exports are blocked, and such exceptions are notoriously difficult to police. Second, the effective application of economic sanctions requires the complete cooperation of other nations, a level of cooperation that is almost impossible to achieve. Despite worldwide support for sanctions against Iraq in the early 1900s, for example, Russia, France, and other powers balked at the continued imposition of sanctions in the late 1990s—even in the wake of Saddam Hussein's refusal in 1997 to permit unlimited United Nations inspections of alleged weapon sites. Third, the United States has consistently underestimated the ability of other nations to adapt to economic conditions that Americans would not accept, and it has also underestimated the willingness of despotic foreign leaders to allow their own people to suffer. Finally, economic sanctions can work well only where the enemy is a nation state with clearly defined borders. Trying to isolate one side in a civil war, for example, is virtually impossible.

This is not to say that the military option is always preferable. Economic sanctions may work sometimes, and in every case they allow more time for the peaceful resolution of the underlying conflict. Economic sanctions may not replace a war, but they may delay it, sometimes long enough to prevent it.

The Role of the United Nations. In many cases, international cooperation in carrying out foreign policy operations is either essential or desirable. Economic sanctions, for example, rarely work unless other nations cooperate with the United States in withholding trade or economic assistance. And although international cooperation can complicate purely military operations, such cooperation is often invaluable diplomatically. During the Persian Gulf War, President Bush was careful to avoid the appearance that the United States was acting alone, at least partly because unilateral American action would have made it more difficult for many Arab nations to support the effort. International cooperation can also be useful in spreading the burdens of war, so that the United States does not have to bear the full cost, in either dollars or casualties.

International cooperation is particularly important in complex and difficult situations, such as the civil war in the former Yugoslavia. Without such cooperation, American efforts to foster long-range solutions would probably be doomed to failure. Any hope of success requires the full participation of regional powers and neighboring states.

The United Nations was established after World War II to provide an arena for international cooperation in resolving conflicts around the world. For many years the United Nations was unable to play such a role, largely because it became merely another arena for the superpower conflict between the United States and the Soviet Union. With the collapse of the Soviet Union, the United Nations began to take on a more constructive role. The Persian Gulf War, for example, was fought entirely under its auspices.

The major problem for American policy makers is to retain control of U.S. troops and resources without compromising the cooperative efforts of the United Nations. When the United Nations effort is led by the United States anyway (as in the Persian Gulf), there is no difficulty. Some critics, however, including former Senator Robert Dole (R-Kans.), argue that any American president who allows U.S. troops to be placed under the control of the United Nations has abdicated the constitutional and moral responsibilities of the office. Other nations face the same problem on a routine basis, but America's position as the only remaining superpower allows it the luxury of demanding full control over its own soldiers.

Democracy and Foreign Policy

The Framers' belief that foreign policy was too dangerous and too difficult to be trusted to the people—a view confirmed by Alexis de Tocqueville's observations some forty years later—deserves reconsideration in the light of modern conditions.

In general, a case can always be made for allowing more or less democratic control of the policy-making process. The advantages of giving more power to political leaders are clear: they are experienced at making decisions, have access to a full range of information and intelligence, and are expected to act on reason and for the public interest rather than on passion and in their own interest. The advantages of democratic control are also obvious: when decisions are delegated to an elite group, the danger always exists that the decision makers will act in their own, rather than in the people's, interest.

The Framers (and Tocqueville) clearly thought that the disadvantages of democratic control outweighed the advantages. Their reasoning can be summarized as follows:

- *Mistakes in domestic policy may cause problems, but in foreign policy they can lead to disaster.* A wrongheaded economic policy may slow economic growth, or even lead to a depression. But a wrongheaded foreign policy can lead to defeat and surrender to a hostile power. With the nation's life and death at stake, decisions must be left in the hands of experts rather than the people.

- *Foreign policy decisions are inherently more difficult than domestic policy decisions, and depend on information that the average citizen simply does not have.* The Framers assumed that the people would be well acquainted with the day-to-day issues that affect their lives. By contrast, they would have little training or experience to deal with disputes between nations, and no access at all to secret intelligence.
- *Foreign policy requires determination, perseverance, and the ability to "coordinate the details of a great undertaking"—all qualities the people do not have.* In the Framers' time, the minimalist nature of domestic policy, especially at the federal level, required no such commitment.

All of these arguments were far more compelling in the Framers' time than in our own, partly because of changes in America's position in the world, and partly because of changes in the government's role in domestic affairs. Barring a nuclear disaster, for example, American foreign policy is no longer a matter of life and death for the nation. Mistakes in foreign policy can be tragic—as the families of thousands of dead soldiers would attest—but they no longer involve the nation's very existence. And although foreign policy is certainly more complicated today than it was in the Framers' time, it is hardly more complex than domestic policy. If democracy is not good enough for foreign policy, it may not be good enough for domestic policy either.

Of course, no one would suggest invoking the time-consuming and public process of democratic debate under conditions of true emergency. Some foreign policy situations, moreover, inherently call for secrecy or discretion. An analysis of the Framers' reasons for removing foreign policy from the arena of democratic politics does suggest, however, that fundamental questions in foreign policy can be settled through the democratic process. If the democratic process does not work under such circumstances, it may be because of flaws in the American system of government as a whole and not because of anything inherent to foreign policy.

Summary

The Framers viewed foreign affairs as both more dangerous and more difficult than domestic affairs, and took steps to remove the making of foreign policy from the direct influence of the people. In general they divided foreign policy power between the president and the Senate, with the Senate having the predominant role. The House had the vital power of the purse, but its direct role in foreign policy making was limited.

Presidents beginning with Washington quickly asserted their power in foreign affairs. Throughout the nineteenth century power ebbed and flowed between the executive and legislative branches. In the twentieth century, power gradually flowed to the White House, culminating in the rise of the "imperial presidency" between the 1930s and 1970s. Since the 1970s, however, Congress has tried to reassert its role in foreign policy, most significantly with the War Powers Resolution of 1973.

Today the White House and Congress share foreign policy power in an uneasy truce. At times the two branches work well together; at other times they clash strongly. Both the cooperation and the tensions between the two branches reflect the fact that neither branch can completely dominate the other, that much of the foreign policy power under the Constitution exists in what Supreme Court Justice Robert Jackson called the "zone of twilight," in which each branch can assert its legitimate authority.

The substance of American foreign policy reflects a continuing tension between isolationism and intervention. The roots of isolationism lie in the foreign policy of the Washington administration, which stressed the avoidance of "entangling alliances" with Europe. The roots of intervention lie in the Monroe Doctrine, which asserted America's interest in keeping the European powers out of the Western Hemisphere. Over the past fifty years, the United States has been more inclined toward intervention than isolationism, although a strong isolationist tendency remains in American politics.

In deciding whether to intervene in foreign affairs, policy

makers need to consider both the ends of American foreign policy and the means available to achieve those ends. The ends include defending the United States and its citizens, protecting American economic and strategic interests, and protecting human rights. The means include conventional warfare and various forms of economic warfare.

Despite the Framers' efforts to insulate foreign policy making from the people, modern American foreign policy makers must take into account public opinion. In the modern era, moreover, the Framers' arguments for removing foreign policy from the democratic process seem less compelling. Foreign policy no longer involves the very existence of the nation, nor is foreign policy any more complex than domestic policy. In the end, the role of the people in foreign policy should be essentially on a par with their role in domestic policy.

Key Terms

Cold War
War Powers Resolution
Isolationism
Monroe Doctrine
Interventionism
Human rights policy

Review Questions

1. How did the Framers distribute foreign policy power under the Constitution? Why?

2. How did the imperial presidency manifest itself in the area of foreign affairs?

3. What are the essential components of the War Powers Resolution? On what theory was it based?

4. Describe the current balance of foreign policy power between the president and Congress.

5. What is meant by the terms *isolationism* and *intervention* in foreign policy?

6. What are the various ends of American foreign policy? By what means can the United States seek to achieve those ends?

7. What role does public opinion play in the making of foreign policy? What are the broad outlines of American attitudes on foreign policy?

Suggested Readings

Ambrose, Stephen E. *Rise to Globalism: American Foreign Policy Since 1938*, 7th rev. ed. New York: Penguin Books, 1993.

Fisher, Louis. *The Politics of Shared Power: Congress and the Executive*, 3d ed. Washington, D.C.: CQ Press, 1993.

Henkin, Louis. *Foreign Affairs and the Constitution.* New York: W. W. Norton, 1972.

Karnow, Stanley. *Vietnam, a History*, rev. and updated ed. New York: Viking, 1991.

Kennedy, Paul M. *The Rise and Fall of the Great Powers: Economic Change and Military Conflict from 1500 to 2000.* New York: Random House, 1987.

Koh, Harold Hongju. *The National Security Constitution: Sharing Power After the Iran-Contra Affair.* New Haven: Yale University Press, 1990.

Ripley, Randall B., and James M. Lindsay, eds. *Congress Resurgent: Foreign and Defense Policy on Capitol Hill.* Ann Arbor: University of Michigan Press, 1993.

Internet Resources

State Department electronic reading room at:

http://foia.state.gov

Central Intelligence Agency web site, with information about the agency and a variety of reference information, at:

http://www.odci.gov/cia

Jane's Information Group, British publisher of magazines, yearbooks, and reports on defense related issues, at:

http://www.janes.com

The United Nations home page at:

http://www.un.org

Appendix

The Declaration of Independence

In Congress, July 4, 1776

The Unanimous Declaration of the Thirteen United States of America

When, in the course of human events, it becomes necessary for one people to dissolve the political bands which have connected them with another, and to assume, among the powers of the earth, the separate and equal station to which the laws of nature and of nature's God entitle them, a decent respect to the opinions of mankind requires that they should declare the causes which impel them to the separation.

We hold these truths to be self-evident: That all men are created equal; that they are endowed by their Creator with certain unalienable rights; that among these are life, liberty, and the pursuit of happiness; that, to secure these rights, governments are instituted among men, deriving their just powers from the consent of the governed; that whenever any form of government becomes destructive of these ends, it is the right of the people to alter or to abolish it, and to institute new government, laying its foundation on such principles, and organizing its powers in such form, as to them shall seem most likely to effect their safety and happiness. Prudence, indeed, will dictate that governments long established should not be changed for light and transient causes; and accordingly all experience hath shown that mankind are more disposed to suffer, while evils are sufferable, than to right themselves by abolishing the forms to which they are accustomed. But when a long train of abuses and usurpations, pursuing invariably the same object, evinces a design to reduce them under absolute despotism, it is their right, it is their duty, to throw off such government, and to provide new guards for their future security. Such has been the patient sufferance of these colonies; and such is now the necessity which constrains them to alter their former systems of government. The history of the present King of Great Britain is a history of repeated injuries and usurpations, all having in direct object the establishment of an absolute tyranny over these states. To prove this, let facts be submitted to a candid world.

He has refused to assent to laws, the most wholesome and necessary for the public good.

He has forbidden his governors to pass laws of immediate and pressing importance, unless suspended in their operation till his assent should be obtained; and, when so suspended, he has utterly neglected to attend to them.

He has refused to pass other laws for the accommodation of large districts of people, unless those people would relinquish the right of representation in the legislature, a right inestimable to them, and formidable to tyrants only.

He has called together legislative bodies at places unusual, uncomfortable, and distant from the depository of their public records, for the sole purpose of fatiguing them into compliance with his measures.

He has dissolved representative houses repeatedly, for opposing, with manly firmness, his invasions on the rights of the people

He has refused for a long time, after such dissolutions, to cause others to be elected; whereby the legislative powers, incapable of annihilation, have returned to the people at large for their exercise; the state remaining, in the mean time, exposed to all dangers of invasions from without and convulsions within.

He has endeavored to prevent the population of these states; for that purpose obstructing the laws for naturalization of foreigners; refusing to pass others to encourage their migration hither, and raising the conditions of new appropriations of lands.

He has obstructed the administration of justice, by refusing his assent to laws for establishing judiciary powers.

He has made judges dependent on his will alone, for the tenure of their offices, and the amount and payment of their salaries.

He has erected a multitude of new offices, and sent hither swarms of officers to harass our people and eat out their substance.

He has kept among us, in times of peace, standing armies, without the consent of our legislatures.

He has affected to render the military independent of, and superior to, the civil power.

He has combined with others to subject us to a jurisdiction foreign to our constitution, and unacknowledged by our laws, giving his assent to their acts of pretended legislation:

For quartering large bodies of armed troops among us:

For protecting them, by a mock trial, from punishment for any murders which they should commit on the inhabitants of these states;

For cutting off our trade with all parts of the world;

For imposing taxes on us without our consent;

For depriving us, in many cases, of the benefits of trial by jury;

For transporting us beyond seas, to be tried for pretended offenses;

For abolishing the free system of English laws in a neighboring province, establishing therein an arbitrary government, and enlarging its boundaries, so as to render it at once an example and fit instrument for introducing the same absolute rule into these colonies;

For taking away our charters, abolishing our more valuable laws, and altering fundamentally the forms of our governments;

For suspending our own legislatures, and declaring themselves invested with power to legislate for us in all cases whatsoever.

He has abdicated government here, by declaring us out of his protection and waging war against us.

He has plundered our seas, ravaged our coasts, burned our towns, and destroyed the lives of our people.

He is at this time transporting large armies of foreign mercenaries to complete the works of death, desolation, and tyranny already begun with circumstances of cruelty and perfidy scarcely paralleled in the most barbarous ages, and totally unworthy the head of a civilized nation.

He has constrained our fellow-citizens, taken captive on the high seas, to bear arms against their country, to become the executioners of their friends and brethren, or to fall themselves by their hands.

He has excited domestic insurrections among us, and has endeavored to bring on the inhabitants of our frontiers the merciless Indian savages, whose known rule of warfare is an undistinguished destruction of all ages, sexes, and conditions.

In every stage of these oppressions we have petitioned for redress in the most humble terms; our repeated petitions have been answered only by repeated injury. A prince, whose character is thus marked by every act which may define a tyrant, is unfit to be the ruler of a free people.

Nor have we been wanting in our attentions to our British brethren. We have warned them, from time to time, of attempts by their legislature to extend an unwarrantable jurisdiction over us. We have reminded them of the circumstances of our emigration and settlement here. We have appealed to their native justice and magnanimity; and we have conjured them, by the ties of our common kindred, to disavow these usurpations, which would inevitably interrupt our connections and correspondence. They, too, have been deaf to the voice of justice and of consanguinity. We must, therefore, acquiesce in the necessity which denounces our separation, and hold them, as we hold the rest of mankind, enemies in war, in peace friends.

We, therefore, the representatives of the United States of America, in General Congress assembled, appealing to the Supreme Judge of the world for the rectitude of our intentions, do, in the name and by the authority of the good people of these colonies, solemnly publish and declare, that these United Colonies are, and of right ought to be, FREE AND INDEPENDENT STATES; that they are absolved from all allegiance to the British crown, and that all political connection between them and the state of Great Britain is, and ought to be, totally dissolved; and that, as free and independent states, they have full power to levy war, conclude peace, contract alliances, establish commerce, and do all other acts and things which independent states may of right do. And for the support of this declaration, with a firm reliance on the protection of Divine Providence, we mutually pledge to each other our lives, our fortunes, and our sacred honor.

JOHN HANCOCK [President]
[and fifty-five others]

The Constitution of the United States

We the People of the United States, in Order to form a more perfect Union, establish Justice, insure domestic Tranquility, provide for the common defence, promote the general Welfare, and secure the Blessings of Liberty to ourselves and our Posterity, do ordain and establish this Constitution for the United States of America.

ARTICLE I.

Bicameral Congress — *Section 1.* All legislative Powers herein granted shall be vested in a Congress of the United States, which shall consist of a Senate and House of Representatives.

Membership of the House — *Section 2.* The House of Representatives shall be composed of Members chosen every second Year by the People of the several States, and the Electors in each State shall have the Qualifications requisite for Electors of the most numerous Branch of the State Legislature.

No person shall be a Representative who shall not have attained to the age of twenty five Years, and been seven Years a Citizen of the United States, and who shall not, when elected, be an Inhabitant of that State in which he shall be chosen.

Representatives and direct Taxes shall be apportioned among the several States which may be included within this Union, according to their respective Numbers, which shall be determined by adding to the whole Number of free Persons, including those bound to Service for a Term of Years, and excluding Indians not taxed, three fifths of all other Persons.[1] The actual Enumeration shall be made within three Years after the first Meeting of the Congress of the United States, and within every subsequent Term of ten Years, in such Manner as they shall by Law direct. The Number of Representatives shall not exceed one for every thirty Thousand, but each State shall have at Least one Representative; and until such enumeration shall be made, the State of New Hampshire shall be entitled to chuse three, Massachusetts eight, Rhode-Island and Providence Plantations one, Connecticut five, New-York six, New Jersey four, Pennsylvania eight, Delaware one, Maryland six, Virginia ten, North Carolina five, South Carolina five, and Georgia three.

When vacancies happen in the Representation from any State, the Executive Authority thereof shall issue Writs of Election to fill such Vacancies.

Power to impeach — The House of Representatives shall chuse their Speaker and other Officers; and shall have the sole Power of Impeachment.

Membership of the Senate — *Section 3.* The Senate of the United States shall be composed of two Senators from each State, *chosen by the Legislature thereof,*[2] for six Years; and each Senator shall have one Vote.

Immediately after they shall be assembled in Consequence of the first Election, they shall be divided as equally as may be into three Classes. The Seats of the Senators of the first class shall be vacated at the Expiration of the second Year, of the second Class at the Expiration of the fourth Year, and of the third Class at the Expiration of the sixth Year, so that one third may be chosen every second Year; *and if Vacancies happen by Resignation, or otherwise, during the Recess of the Legislature of any State, the Executive thereof may make temporary Appointments until the next Meeting of the Legislature, which shall then fill such Vacancies.*[3]

No Person shall be a Senator who shall not have attained to the Age of thirty Years, and been nine Years a Citizen of the United States, and who shall not, when elected, be an Inhabitant of that State for which he shall be chosen.

The Vice President of the United States shall be President of the Senate, but shall have no Vote, unless they be equally divided.

The Senate shall chuse their other Officers, and also a President pro tempore, in the Absence of the Vice President, or when he shall exercise the Office of President of the United States.

Power to try impeachments — The Senate shall have the sole Power to try all Impeachments. When sitting for that Purpose, they shall be on Oath or Affirmation.

NOTE: The topical headings are not part of the original Constitution. Excluding the Preamble and Closing, those portions set in italic type have been superseded or changed by later amendments.
1. Changed by the Fourteenth Amendment, section 2.
2. Changed by the Seventeenth Amendment.
3. Changed by the Seventeenth Amendment.

When the President of the United States is tried the Chief Justice shall preside: And no Person shall be convicted without the Concurrence of two thirds of the Members present.

Judgment in Cases of Impeachment shall not exceed further than to removal from Office, and disqualification to hold and enjoy any Office of honor, Trust or Profit under the United States: but the Party convicted shall nevertheless be liable and subject to Indictment, Trial, Judgment and Punishment, according to Law.

Laws governing elections
Section 4. The Times, Places and Manner of holding Elections for Senators and Representatives, shall be prescribed in each State by the Legislature thereof; but the Congress may at any time by Law make or alter such Regulations, except as to the Places of chusing Senators.

The Congress shall assemble at least once in every Year, and such Meeting shall be on the *first Monday in December, unless they shall by Law appoint a different Day.*[4]

Rules of Congress
Section 5. Each House shall be the Judge of the Elections, Returns and Qualifications of its own Members, and a Majority of each shall constitute a Quorum to do Business; but a smaller number may adjourn from day to day, and may be authorized to compel the Attendance of absent Members, in such Manner, and under such Penalties as each House may provide.

Each House may determine the Rules of its Proceedings, punish its Members for disorderly Behaviour, and, with the Concurrence of two thirds, expel a Member.

Each House shall keep a Journal of its Proceedings, and from time to time publish the same, excepting such Parts as may in their Judgment require Secrecy; and the Yeas and Nays of the Members of either House on any question shall, at the Desire of one fifth of those Present, be entered on the Journal.

Neither House, during the Session of Congress, shall, without the Consent of the other, adjourn for more than three days, nor to any other Place than that in which the two Houses shall be sitting.

Salaries and immunities of members
Section 6. The Senators and Representatives shall receive a Compensation for their Services, to be ascertained by Law, and paid

4. Changed by the Twentieth Amendment, section 2.

out of the Treasury of the United States. They shall in all Cases, except Treason, Felony and Breach of the Peace, be privileged from Arrest during their Attendance at the Session of their respective Houses, and in going to and returning from the same; and for any Speech or Debate in either House, they shall not be questioned in any other Place.

Bar on members of Congress holding federal appointive office
No Senator or Representative shall, during the Time for which he was elected, be appointed to any civil Office under the Authority of the United States, which shall have been created, or the Emoluments whereof shall have been encreased during such time; and no Person holding any Office under the United States, shall be a Member of either House during his Continuance in Office.

Money bills originate in House
Section 7. All Bills for raising Revenue shall originate in the House of Representatives; but the Senate may propose or concur with Amendments as on other Bills.

Procedure for enacting laws; veto power
Every Bill which shall have passed the House of Representatives and the Senate, shall, before it become a Law, be presented to the President of the United States; If he approve he shall sign it, but if not he shall return it, with his Objections to that House in which it shall have originated, who shall enter the Objections at large on their Journal, and proceed to reconsider it. If after such Reconsideration two thirds of that House shall agree to pass the Bill, it shall be sent, together with the Objections, to the other House, by which it shall likewise be reconsidered, and if approved by two thirds of that House, it shall become a Law. But in all such Cases the Votes of both Houses shall be determined by yeas and Nays, and the Names of the Persons voting for and against the Bill shall be entered on the Journal of each House respectively. If any Bill shall not be returned by the President within ten Days (Sundays excepted) after it shall have been presented to him, the Same shall be a Law, in like Manner, as if he had signed it, unless the Congress by their Adjournment prevent its Return, in which Case it shall not be a Law.

Every Order, Resolution, or Vote to which the Concurrence of the Senate and House of Representatives may be necessary (except on a question of Adjournment) shall be presented to the President of the United States; and before the Same shall take Effect, shall be approved by him, or being disapproved by him, shall be repassed by two thirds of the Senate and House of Representatives, according to the Rules and Limitations prescribed in the Case of a Bill.

Powers of Congress –taxes

Section 8. The Congress shall have Power To lay and Collect Taxes, Duties, Imposts and Excises, to pay the Debts and provide for the common Defence and general Welfare of the United States; but all Duties, Imposts and Excises shall be uniform throughout the United States.

–borrowing

To borrow Money on the credit of the United States;

–regulation of commerce

To regulate Commerce with foreign Nations, and among the several States, and with the Indian Tribes;

–naturalization and bankruptcy

To establish an uniform Rule of Naturalization, and uniform Laws on the subject of Bankruptcies throughout the United States;

–money

To coin Money, regulate the Value thereof, and of foreign Coin, and fix the Standard of Weights and Measures;

–counterfeiting

To provide for the Punishment of counterfeiting the Securities and current Coin of the United States;

–post office

To establish Post Offices and post Roads;

–patents and copyrights

To promote the Progress of Science and useful Arts, by securing for limited Times to Authors and Inventors the exclusive Right to their respective Writings and Discoveries;

–create courts

To constitute Tribunals inferior to the Supreme Court;

–punish piracies

To define and punish Piracies and Felonies committed on the high Seas, and Offences against the Law of Nations;

–declare war

To declare War, grant Letters of Marque and Reprisal, and make Rules concerning Captures on Land and Water;

–create army and navy

To raise and support Armies, but no Appropriation of Money to that Use shall be for a longer Term than two Years;

To provide and maintain a Navy;

To make Rules for the Government and Regulation of the land and naval Forces;

–call the militia

To provide for calling forth the Militia to execute the Laws of the Union, suppress Insurrections and repel Invasions;

To provide for organizing, arming, and disciplining, the Militia, and for governing such Part of them as may be employed in the Service of the United States, reserving to the States respectively, the Appointment of the Officers, and the Authority of training the Militia according to the discipline prescribed by Congress;

–govern District of Columbia

To exercise exclusive Legislation in all Cases whatsoever, over such District (not exceeding ten Miles square) as may, by Cession of Particular States, and the Acceptance of Congress, become the Seat of the Government of the United States, and to exercise like Authority over all Places purchased by the Consent of the Legislature of the State in which the Same shall be, for the Erection of Forts, Magazines, Arsenals, dock-Yards and other needful Buildings;—And

–"necessary-and-proper" clause

To make all Laws which shall be necessary and proper for carrying into Execution the foregoing Powers, and all other Powers vested by this Constitution in the Government of the United States, or in any Department or Officer thereof.

Restrictions on powers of Congress –slave trade

Section 9. The Migration or Importation of such Persons as any of the States now existing shall think proper to admit, shall not be prohibited by the Congress prior to the Year one thousand eight hundred and eight, but a Tax or duty may be imposed on such Importation, not exceeding ten dollars for each Person.

–habeas corpus

The Privilege of the Writ of Habeas Corpus shall not be suspended, unless when in Cases of Rebellion or Invasion the public Safety may require it.

–no bill of attainder or ex post facto law

No bill of Attainder or ex post facto Law shall be passed.

No Capitation, or other direct, Tax shall be laid, *unless in Proportion to the Census or Enumeration herein before directed to be taken.*[5]

–no interstate tariffs

No Tax or Duty shall be laid on Articles exported from any State.

–no preferential treatment for some states

No Preference shall be given by any Regulation of Commerce or Revenue to the Ports of one State over those of another; nor shall Vessels bound to, or from, one State, be obliged to enter, clear or pay Duties in another.

5. Changed by the Sixteenth Amendment.

–appropriations No Money shall be drawn from the Treasury, but in Consequence of Appropriations made by Law; and a regular Statement and Account of the Receipts and Expenditures of all public Money shall be published from time to time.

–no titles of nobility No Title of Nobility shall be granted by the United States: And no Person holding any Office of Profit or Trust under them, shall, without the Consent of the Congress, accept of any present, Emolument, Office, or Title, of any kind whatever, from any King, Prince, or foreign State.

Restrictions on powers of states Section 10.   No State shall enter into any Treaty, Alliance, or Confederation; grant Letters of Marque and Reprisal; coin Money; emit Bills of Credit; make any Thing but gold and silver Coin a Tender in Payment of Debts; pass any Bill of Attainder, ex post facto Law, or Law impairing the Obligation of Contracts, or grant any Title of Nobility.

No State shall, without the Consent of the Congress, lay any Imposts or Duties on Imports or Exports, except what may be absolutely necessary for executing its inspection Laws; and the net Produce of all Duties and Imposts, laid by any State on Imports or Exports, shall be for the Use of the Treasury of the United States; and all such Laws shall be subject to the Revision and Controul of the Congress.

No State shall, without the Consent of Congress, lay any Duty of Tonnage, keep Troops, or Ships of War in time of Peace, enter into any Agreement or Compact with another State, or with a foreign Power, or engage in War, unless actually invaded, or in such imminent Danger as will not admit of delay.

ARTICLE II.

Office of president Section 1.   The executive Power shall be vested in a President of the United States of America. He shall hold his Office during the Term of four Years, and, together with the Vice President, chosen for the same Term, be elected, as follows

Election of president Each State shall appoint, in such Manner as the Legislature thereof may direct, a Number of Electors, equal to the whole Number of Senators and Representatives to which the State may be entitled in the Congress: but no Senator or Representative, or Person holding an Office of Trust or Profit under the United States, shall be appointed an Elector.

The Electors shall meet in their respective States, and vote by Ballot for two Persons, of whom one at least shall not be an Inhabitant of the same State with themselves. And they shall make a List of all the Persons voted for, and of the Number of Votes for each; which List they shall sign and certify, and transmit sealed to the Seat of the Government of the United States, directed to the President of the Senate. The President of the Senate shall, in the Presence of the Senate and House of Representatives, open all the Certificates, and the Votes shall then be counted. The Person having the greatest Number of Votes shall be the President, if such Number be a Majority of the whole Number of Electors appointed; and if there be more than one who have such Majority, and have an equal Number of Votes, then the House of Representatives shall immediately chuse by Ballot one of them for President; and if no Person have a Majority, then from the five highest on the List the said House shall in like Manner chuse the President. But in chusing the President, the Votes shall be taken by States, the Representation from each State having one Vote; a quorum for this Purpose shall consist of a Member or Members from two thirds of the States, and a Majority of all the States shall be necessary to a Choice. In every Case, after the Choice of the President, the Person having the greatest Number of Votes of the Electors shall be the Vice President. But if there should remain two or more who have equal Votes, the Senate shall chuse from them by Ballot the Vice President.[6]

Requirements to be president The Congress may determine the Time of chusing the Electors, and the Day on which they shall give their Votes, which Day shall be the same throughout the United States.

No Person except a natural born Citizen, or a Citizen of the United States, at the time of the Adoption of this Constitution, shall be eligible to the Office of President; neither shall any person be eligible to that Office who shall not have attained to the Age of thirty five Years, and been fourteen Years a Resident within the United States.

In Case of the Removal of the President from Office, or of his Death, Resignation, or Inability to discharge the Powers and Duties of the said Office, the Same shall devolve on the Vice President, and the Congress may by Law provide for the Case of Removal, Death, Resignation or Inability, both of the President and Vice President, declaring what Officer shall then

6. Superseded by the Twelfth Amendment.

act as President, and such Officer shall act accordingly, until the Disability be removed, or a President shall be elected.[7]

Pay of president The President shall, at stated Times, receive for his Services, a Compensation, which shall neither be encreased nor diminished during the Period for which he shall have been elected, and he shall not receive within that Period any other Emolument from the United States, or any of them.

Before he enter on the Execution of his Office, he shall take the following Oath or Affirmation:—"I do solemnly swear (or affirm) that I will faithfully execute the Office of President of the United States, and will to the best of my Ability, preserve, protect and defend the Constitution of the United States."

Powers of president —commander in chief Section 2. The President shall be Commander in Chief of the Army and Navy of the United States, and of the Militia of the several States, when called into the actual Service of the United States; he may require the Opinion, in writing, of the principal Officer in each of the executive Departments, upon any Subject relating to the Duties of their respective Offices, and **—pardons** he shall have Power to grant Reprieves and Pardons for Offences against the United States, except in Cases of Impeachment.

—treaties and appointments He shall have Power, by and with the Advice and Consent of the Senate, to make Treaties, provided two thirds of the Senators present concur; and he shall nominate, and by and with the Advice and Consent of the Senate, shall appoint Ambassadors, other public Ministers and Consuls, Judges of the supreme Court, and all other Officers of the United States, whose Appointments are not herein otherwise provided for, and which shall be established by Law: but the Congress may by Law vest the Appointment of such inferior Officers, as they think proper, in the President alone, in the Courts of Law, or in the Heads of Departments.

The President shall have Power to fill up all Vacancies that may happen during the Recess of the Senate, by granting Commissions which shall expire at the End of their next Session.

Relations of president with Congress Section 3. He shall from time to time give to the Congress Information

of the State of the Union, and recommend to their Consideration such Measures as he shall judge necessary and expedient; he may, on extraordinary Occasions, convene both Houses, or either of them, and in Case of Disagreement between them, with Respect to the Time of Adjournment, he may adjourn them to such Time as he shall think proper; he shall receive Ambassadors and other public Ministers; he shall take Care that the Laws be faithfully executed, and shall Commission all the Officers of the United States.

Impeachment Section 4. The President, Vice President and all civil Officers of the United States, shall be removed from Office on Impeachment for, and Conviction of, Treason, Bribery, or other high Crimes and Misdemeanors.

ARTICLE III.

Federal courts Section 1. The judicial Power of the United States, shall be vested in one supreme Court, and in such inferior Courts as the Congress may from time to time ordain and establish. The Judges, both of the supreme and inferior Courts, shall hold their Offices during good Behaviour, and shall, at stated Times, receive for their Services, a Compensation, which shall not be diminished during their Continuance in Office.

Jurisdiction of courts Section 2. The judicial Power shall extend to all Cases, in Law and Equity, arising under this Constitution, the Laws of the United States, and Treaties made, or which shall be made, under their Authority;—to all Cases affecting Ambassadors, other public Ministers and Consuls;—to all Cases of admiralty and maritime Jurisdiction;—to Controversies to which the United States shall be a Party;—to Controversies between two or more States;—*between a State and Citizens of another State;*[8]—between Citizens of different States;—between Citizens of the same State claiming Lands under Grants of different States, and between a State, or the Citizens thereof, and foreign States, Citizens or Subjects.

—original In all Cases affecting Ambassadors, other public Ministers and Consuls, and those in which a State shall be Party, the supreme Court shall have original Jurisdiction. In all the other Cases before **—appellate** mentioned, the supreme Court shall have appellate Jurisdiction, both as to

---

7. Modified by the Twenty-fifth Amendment.

8. Modified by the Eleventh Amendment.

Law and Fact, with such Exceptions, and under such Regulations as the Congress shall make.

The Trial of all Crimes, except in Cases of Impeachment, shall be by Jury; and such Trial shall be held in the State where the said Crimes shall have been committed; but when not committed within any State, the Trial shall be at such Place or Places as the Congress may by Law have directed.

Treason   *Section 3.* Treason against the United States, shall consist only in levying War against them, or in adhering to their Enemies, giving them Aid and Comfort. No Person shall be convicted of Treason unless on the Testimony of two Witnesses to the same overt Act, or on Confession in open Court.

The Congress shall have Power to declare the Punishment of Treason, but no Attainder of Treason shall work Corruption of Blood, or Forfeiture except during the Life of the Person attainted.

ARTICLE IV.

Full faith and credit   *Section 1.* Full Faith and Credit shall be given in each State to the public Acts, Records, and judicial Proceedings of every other State. And the Congress may by general Laws prescribe the Manner in which such Acts, Records and Proceedings shall be proved, and the Effect thereof.

Privileges and immunities   *Section 2.* The Citizens of each State shall be entitled to all Privileges and Immunities of Citizens in the several States.

Extradition   A person charged in any State with Treason, Felony, or other Crime, who shall flee from Justice, and be found in another State, shall on Demand of the executive Authority of the State from which he fled, be delivered up, to be removed to the State having Jurisdiction of the Crime.

No Person held to Service or Labour in one State, under the Laws thereof, escaping into another, shall, in Consequence of any Law or Regulation therein, be discharged from such Service or Labour, but shall be delivered up on Claim of the Party to whom such Service or Labour may be due.[9]

Creation of new states   *Section 3.* New States may be admitted by the Congress into this Union; but no new State shall be formed or erected within the Jurisdiction of any other State; nor any State be formed by the

9. Changed by the Thirteenth Amendment.

Junction of two or more States, or Parts of States, without the Consent of the Legislatures of the States concerned as well as of the Congress.

Governing territories   The Congress shall have Power to dispose of and make all needful Rules and Regulations respecting the Territory or other Property belonging to the United States; and nothing in this Constitution shall be so construed as to Prejudice any Claims of the United States, or of any particular State.

Protection of states   *Section 4.* The United States shall guarantee to every State in this Union a Republican Form of Government, and shall protect each of them against Invasion; and on Application of the Legislature, or of the Executive (when the Legislature cannot be convened) against domestic Violence.

ARTICLE V.

Amending the Constitution   The Congress, whenever two thirds of both Houses shall deem it necessary, shall propose Amendments to this Constitution, or, on the Application of the Legislatures of two thirds of the several States, shall call a Convention for proposing Amendments, which, in either Case, shall be valid to all Intents and Purposes, as Part of this Constitution, when ratified by the Legislatures of three fourths of the several States, or by Conventions in three fourths thereof, as the one or the other Mode of Ratification may be proposed by the Congress; Provided that no Amendment which may be made prior to the Year One thousand eight hundred and eight shall in any Manner after the first and fourth Clauses in the Ninth Section of the first Article; and that no State, without its Consent, shall be deprived of its equal Suffrage in the Senate.

ARTICLE VI.

Assumption of debts of Confederation   All Debts contracted and Engagements entered into, before the Adoption of this Constitution, shall be as valid against the United States under this Constitution, as under the Confederation.

Supremacy of federal laws and treaties   This Constitution, and the Laws of the United States which shall be made in Pursuance thereof; and all Treaties made, or which shall be made, under the Authority of the United States, shall be the Supreme Law of the Land; and the Judges in every State shall be bound thereby, any Thing in the Constitution or Laws of any State to the Contrary notwithstanding.

No religious test   The Senators and Representatives before mentioned, and the Members of the several State Legislatures, and all executive and judicial Officers, both of the United States and of the several States, shall be bound by Oath or Affirmation, to support this Constitution; but no religious Test shall ever be required as a Qualification to any Office or public Trust under the United States.

ARTICLE VII.

Ratification procedure   The Ratification of the Conventions of nine States, shall be sufficient for the Establishment of this Constitution between the States so ratifying the Same.

Done in Convention by the Unanimous Consent of the States present the Seventeenth Day of September in the Year of our Lord one thousand seven hundred and Eighty seven and of the Independence of the United States of America the Twelfth In witness whereof We have hereunto subscribed our Names,

G̱ᵒ WASHINGTON—*Presidt*
and deputy from Virginia

New Hampshire	JOHN LANGDON
	NICHOLAS GILMAN
Massachusetts	NATHANIEL GORHAM
	RUFUS KING
New Jersey	WIL: LIVINGSTON
	DAVID BREARLEY
	Wᴹ PATERSON
	JONA: DAYTON
Pennsylvania	B FRANKLIN
	THOMAS MIFFLIN
	ROBᵀ MORRIS
	GEO. CLYMER
	THOˢ FITZSIMONS
	JARED INGERSOLL
	JAMES WILSON
	GOUV MORRIS
Delaware	GEO: READ
	GUNNING BEDFORD JUN
	JOHN DICKINSON
	RICHARD BASSETT
	JACO: BROOM
Connecticut	Wᴹ SAMᴸ JOHNSON
	ROGER SHERMAN

New York	ALEXANDER HAMILTON
Maryland	JAMES MᶜHENRY
	DAN OF Sᵀ THOˢ JENIFER
	DANᴸ CARROLL
Virginia	JOHN BLAIR—
	JAMES MADISON JR.
North Carolina	Wᴹ BLOUNT
	RICHᴰ DOBBS SPAIGHT
	HU WILLIAMSON
South Carolina	J. RUTLEDGE
	CHARLES COTESWORTH PINCKNEY
	CHARLES PINCKNEY
	PIERCE BUTLER
Georgia	WILLIAM FEW
	ABR BALDWIN .

[The first ten amendments, known as the "Bill of Rights," were ratified in 1791.]

AMENDMENT I.

Freedom of religion, speech, press, assembly   Congress shall make no law respecting an establishment of religion, or prohibiting the free exercise thereof, or abridging the freedom of speech, or of the press; or the right of the people peaceably to assemble, and to petition the Government for a redress of grievances.

AMENDMENT II.

Right to bear arms   A well regulated Militia, being necessary to the security of a free State, the right of the people to keep and bear Arms, shall not be infringed.

AMENDMENT III.

Quartering troops in private homes   No Soldier shall, in time of peace be quartered in any house, without the consent of the Owner, nor in time of war, but in a manner prescribed by law.

AMENDMENT IV.

Prohibition against unreasonable searches and seizures   The right of the people to be secure in their persons, houses, papers, and effects, against unreasonable searches and seizures, shall not be violated, and no Warrants shall issue, but upon probable cause, supported by Oath or affirmation, and particularly describing the place to be searched, and the persons or things to be seized.

AMENDMENT V.

Rights when accused; "due-process" clause No person shall be held to answer for a capital, or otherwise infamous crime, unless on a presentment or indictment of a Grand Jury, except in cases arising in the land or naval forces, or in the Militia, when in actual service in time of War or public danger; nor shall any person be subject for the same offence to be twice put in jeopardy of life or limb; nor shall be compelled in any criminal case to be a witness against himself, nor be deprived of life, liberty, or property, without due process of law, nor shall private property be taken for public use, without just compensation.

AMENDMENT VI.

Rights when on trial In all criminal prosecutions, the accused shall enjoy the right to a speedy and public trial, by an impartial jury of the State and district wherein the crime shall have been committed, which district shall have been previously ascertained by law, and to be informed of the nature and cause of the accusation; to be confronted with the witnesses against him; to have compulsory process for obtaining witnesses in his favor, and to have Assistance of Counsel for his defence.

AMENDMENT VII.

Common-law suits In Suits at common law, where the value in controversy shall exceed twenty dollars, the right of trial by jury shall be preserved, and no fact tried by a jury, shall be otherwise reexamined in any Court of the United States, than according to the rules of the common law.

AMENDMENT VIII.

Bail; no "cruel and unusual" punishments Excessive bail shall not be required, nor excessive fines imposed, nor cruel and unusual punishments inflicted.

AMENDMENT IX.

Unenumerated rights protected The enumeration in the Constitution, of certain rights, shall not be construed to deny or disparage others retained by the people.

AMENDMENT X.

Powers reserved for states The powers not delegated to the United States by the Constitution, nor prohibited by it to the States, are reserved to the States respectively, or to the people.

AMENDMENT XI.

[*Ratified in 1795.*]

Limits on suits against states The Judicial power of the United States shall not be construed to extend to any suit in law or equity, commenced or prosecuted against one of the United States by Citizens of another State, or by Citizens or Subjects of any Foreign State.

AMENDMENT XII.

[*Ratified in 1804.*]

Revision of electoral-college procedure The Electors shall meet in their respective states and vote by ballot for President and Vice President, one of whom, at least, shall not be an inhabitant of the same state with themselves; they shall name in their ballots the person voted for as President, and in distinct ballots the person voted for as Vice President, and they shall make distinct lists of all persons voted for as President, and of all persons voted for as Vice President, and of the number of votes for each, which lists they shall sign and certify, and transmit sealed to the seat of the government of the United States, directed to the President of the Senate;—The President of the Senate shall, in the presence of the Senate and House of Representatives, open all the certificates and the votes shall then be counted;—The person having the greatest number of votes for President, shall be the President, if such number be a majority of the whole number of Electors appointed; and if no person have such majority, then from the persons having the highest numbers not exceeding three on the list of those voted for as President, the House of Representatives shall choose immediately, by ballot, the President. But in choosing the President, the votes shall be taken by states, the representation from each state having one vote; a quorum for this purpose shall consist of a member or members from two-thirds of the states, and a majority of all the states shall be necessary to a choice. *And if the House of Representatives shall not choose a President whenever the right of choice shall devolve upon them, before the fourth day of March next following, then the Vice President shall act as President, as in the case of the death or other constitutional disability of the President.*—[10] The person having the greatest number of votes as Vice President, shall be the Vice President, if such number be a majority of the whole number of Electors appointed, and if no person have a majority, then from the two highest numbers

---

10. Changed by the Twentieth Amendment, section 3.

on the list, the Senate shall choose the Vice President; a quorum for the purpose shall consist of two-thirds of the whole number of Senators, and a majority of the whole number shall be necessary to a choice. But no person constitutionally ineligible to the office of President shall be eligible to that of Vice President of the United States.

AMENDMENT XIII.

[*Ratified in 1865.*]

Slavery prohibited   *Section 1.* Neither slavery nor involuntary servitude, except as a punishment for crime whereof the party shall have been duly convicted, shall exist within the United States, or any place subject to their jurisdiction.

Section 2. Congress shall have power to enforce this article by appropriate legislation.

AMENDMENT XIV.

[*Ratified in 1868.*]

Ex-slaves made citizens   *Section 1.* All persons born or naturalized in the United States and subject to the jurisdiction thereof, are citizens of the United States and of the State wherein they reside. No State shall make or enforce any law which shall abridge the privileges or immunities of citizens of the United States; nor shall any **"Due-process" clause applied to states "Equal-protection" clause** State deprive any person of life, liberty, or property, without due process of law; nor deny to any person within its jurisdiction the equal protection of the laws.

Reduction in congressional representation for states denying adult males the right to vote   *Section 2.* Representatives shall be apportioned among the several States according to their respective numbers, counting the whole number of persons in each State, excluding Indians not taxed. But when the right to vote at any election for the choice of electors for President and Vice President of the United States, Representatives in Congress, the Executive and Judicial officers of a State, or the members of the Legislature thereof, is denied to any of the male inhabitants of such State, being *twenty-one*[11] years of age, and citizens of the United States, or in any way abridged, except for participation in rebellion, or other crime, the basis of representation therein shall be reduced in the proportion which the number of such male citizens shall bear to the whole number of male citizens twenty-one years of age in such State.

Southern rebels denied federal office   *Section 3.* No person shall be a Senator or Representative in Congress, or elector of President and Vice President, or hold any office, civil or military, under the United States, or under any State, who, having previously taken an oath, as a member of Congress, or as an officer of the United States, or as a member of any State legislature, or as an executive or judicial officer of any State, to support the Constitution of the United States, shall have engaged in insurrection or rebellion against the same, or given aid or comfort to the enemies thereof. But Congress may by a vote of two-thirds of each House, remove such disability.

Rebel debts repudiated   *Section 4.* The validity of the public debt of the United States, authorized by law, including debts incurred for payment of pensions and bounties for services in suppressing insurrection or rebellion, shall not be questioned. But neither the United States nor any State shall assume or pay any debt or obligation incurred in aid of insurrection or rebellion against the United States, or any claim for the loss or emancipation of any slave; but all such debts, obligations and claims shall be held illegal and void.

Section 5. The Congress shall have power to enforce, by appropriate legislation, the provisions of this article.

AMENDMENT XV.

[*Ratified in 1870.*]

Blacks given right to vote   *Section 1.* The right of citizens of the United States to vote shall not be denied or abridged by the United States or by any State on account of race, color, or previous condition of servitude.

Section 2. The Congress shall have power to enforce this article by appropriate legislation.

AMENDMENT XVI.

[*Ratified in 1913.*]

Authorizes federal income tax   The Congress shall have power to lay and collect taxes on incomes, from whatever source derived, without apportionment among the several States, and without regard to any census or enumeration.

---

11. Changed by the Twenty-sixth Amendment.

AMENDMENT XVII.

[*Ratified in 1913.*]

Requires popular election of senators

The Senate of the United States shall be composed of two Senators from each State, elected by the people thereof, for six years; and each Senator shall have one vote. The electors in each State shall have the qualifications requisite for electors of the most numerous branch of the State legislatures.

When vacancies happen in the representation of any State in the Senate, the executive authority of such State shall issue writs of election to fill such vacancies: Provided, That the legislature of any State may empower the executive thereof to make temporary appointments until the people fill the vacancies by election as the legislature may direct.

This amendment shall not be so construed as to affect the election or term of any Senator chosen before it becomes valid as part of the Constitution.

AMENDMENT XVIII.

[*Ratified in 1919.*]

Prohibits manufacture and sale of liquor

Section 1.   After one year from the ratification of this article the manufacture, sale, or transportation of intoxicating liquors within, the importation thereof into, or the exportation thereof from the United States and all territory subject to the jurisdiction thereof for beverage purposes is hereby prohibited.

Section 2.   The Congress and the several States shall have concurrent power to enforce this article by appropriate legislation.

Section 3.   This article shall be inoperative unless it shall have been ratified as an amendment to the Constitution by the legislatures of the several States, as provided in the Constitution, within seven years from the date of the submission hereof to the States by the Congress.[12]

AMENDMENT XIX.

[*Ratified in 1920.*]

Right to vote for women

The right of citizens of the United States to vote shall not be denied or abridged by the United States or by any State on account of sex.

Congress shall have power to enforce this article by appropriate legislation.

12. Repealed by the Twenty-first Amendment.

AMENDMENT XX.

[*Ratified in 1933.*]

Federal terms of office to begin in January

Section 1.   The terms of the President and Vice President shall end at noon on the 20th day of January, and the terms of Senators and Representatives at noon on the 3d day of January, of the years in which such terms would have ended if this article had not been ratified; and the terms of their successors shall then begin.

Section 2.   The Congress shall assemble at least once in every year, and such meeting shall begin at noon on the 3d day of January, unless they shall by law appoint a different day.

Emergency presidential succession

Section 3.   If, at the time fixed for the beginning of the term of the President, the President elect shall have died, the Vice President elect shall become President. If a President shall not have been chosen before the time fixed for the beginning of his term, or if the President elect shall have failed to qualify, then the Vice President elect shall act as President until a President shall have qualified; and the Congress may by law provide for the case wherein neither a President elect nor a Vice President elect shall have qualified, declaring who shall then act as President, or the manner in which one who is to act shall be selected, and such person shall act accordingly until a President or Vice President shall have qualified.

Section 4.   The Congress may by law provide for the case of the death of any of the persons from whom the House of Representatives may choose a President whenever the right of choice shall have developed upon them, and for the case of the death of any of the persons from whom the Senate may choose a Vice President whenever the right of choice shall have devolved upon them.

Section 5.   Sections 1 and 2 shall take effect on the 15th day of October following the ratification of this article.

Section 6.   This article shall be inoperative unless it shall have been ratified as an amendment to the Constitution by the legislatures of three-fourths of the several States within seven years from the date of its submission.

AMENDMENT XXI.

[*Ratified in 1933.*]

Repeals Prohibition

Section 1.   The eighteenth article of amendment to the Constitution of the United States is hereby repealed.

Section 2. The transportation or importation into any State, Territory, or possession of the United States for delivery or use therein of intoxicating liquors, in violation of the laws thereof, is hereby prohibited.

Section 3. This article shall be inoperative unless it shall have been ratified as an amendment to the Constitution by conventions in the several States, as provided in the Constitution, within seven years from the date of the submission hereof to the States by the Congress.

AMENDMENT XXII.

[*Ratified in 1951.*]

Two-term limit for president

Section 1. No person shall be elected to the office of the President more than twice, and no person who has held the office of President, or acted as President, for more than two years of a term to which some other person was elected President shall be elected to the office of the President more than once. But this Article shall not apply to any person holding the office of President when this Article was proposed by the Congress, and shall not prevent any person who may be holding the office of President, or acting as President, during the term within which this Article becomes operative from holding the office of President or acting as President during the remainder of such term.

Section 2. This Article shall be inoperative unless it shall have been ratified as an amendment to the Constitution by the legislatures of three-fourths of the several States within seven years from the date of its submission to the States by the Congress.

AMENDMENT XXIII.

[*Ratified in 1961.*]

Right to vote for president in District of Columbia

Section 1. The District constituting the seat of Government of the United States shall appoint in such manner as the Congress may direct:

A number of electors of President and Vice President equal to the whole number of Senators and Representatives in Congress to which the District would be entitled if it were a State, but in no event more than the least populous State; they shall be in addition to those appointed by the States, but they shall be considered, for the purposes of the election of President and Vice President, to be electors appointed by a State; and they shall meet in the District and perform such duties as provided by the twelfth article of amendment.

Section 2. The Congress shall have power to enforce this article by appropriate legislation.

AMENDMENT XXIV.

[*Ratified in 1964.*]

Prohibits poll taxes in federal elections

Section 1. The right of citizens of the United States to vote in any primary or other election for President or Vice President, for electors for President or Vice President, or for Senator or Representative in Congress, shall not be denied or abridged by the United States or any State by reason of failure to pay any poll tax or other tax.

Section 2. The Congress shall have power to enforce this article by appropriate legislation.

AMENDMENT XXV.

[*Ratified in 1967.*]

Presidential disability and succession

Section 1. In case of the removal of the President from office or of his death or resignation, the Vice President shall become President.

Section 2. Whenever there is a vacancy in the office of the Vice President, the President shall nominate a Vice President who shall take office upon confirmation by a majority vote of both Houses of Congress.

Section 3. Whenever the President transmits to the President pro tempore of the Senate and the Speaker of the House of Representatives his written declaration that he is unable to discharge the powers and duties of his office, and until he transmits to them a written declaration to the contrary, such powers and duties shall be discharged by the Vice President as Acting President.

Section 4. Whenever the Vice President and a majority of either the principal officers of the executive departments or of such other body as Congress may by law provide, transmit to the President pro tempore of the Senate and the Speaker of the House of Representatives their written declaration that the President is unable to discharge the powers and duties of his office, the Vice President shall immediately assume the powers and duties of the office as Acting President.

Thereafter, when the President transmits to the President pro tempore of the Senate and the Speaker of the House of Representatives his written declaration that no inability exists, he shall resume the powers and duties of his office unless the Vice President and a majority of either the principal officers of the executive department[s] or of such other body as Congress may by law provide, transmit within four days to the President pro tempore of the Senate and the Speaker of the House of Representatives their written declaration that the President is unable to discharge the powers and duties of his office. Thereupon Congress shall decide the issue, assembling within forty-eight hours for that purpose if not in session. If the Congress, within twenty-one days after receipt of the latter written declaration, or, if Congress is not in session, within twenty-one days after Congress is required to assemble, determines by two-thirds vote of both Houses that the President is unable to discharge the powers and duties of his office, the Vice President shall continue to discharge the same as Acting President; otherwise, the President shall resume the powers and duties of his office.

AMENDMENT XXVI.

[*Ratified in 1971.*]

Voting age lowered to eighteen

Section 1. The right of citizens of the United States, who are eighteen years of age or older, to vote shall not be denied or abridged by the United States or by any State on account of age.

Section 2. The Congress shall have power to enforce this article by appropriate legislation.

AMENDMENT XXVII.

[*Ratified in 1992.*]

Congressional pay raises

No law varying the compensation for the services of the Senators and Representatives shall take effect, until an election of Representatives shall have intervened.

The Federalist No. 10

November 22, 1787

James Madison

TO THE PEOPLE OF THE STATE OF NEW YORK.

Among the numerous advantages promised by a well constructed Union, none deserves to be more accurately developed than its tendency to break and control the violence of faction. The friend of popular governments, never finds himself so much alarmed for their character and fate, as when he contemplates their propensity to this dangerous vice. He will not fail therefore to set a due value on any plan which, without violating the principles to which he is attached, provides a proper cure for it. The instability, injustice and confusion introduced into the public councils, have in truth been the mortal diseases under which popular governments have every where perished; as they continue to be the favorite and fruitful topics from which the adversaries to liberty derive their most specious declamations. The valuable improvements made by the American Constitutions on the popular models, both ancient and modern, cannot certainly be too much admired; but it would be an unwarrantable partiality, to contend that they have as effectually obviated the danger on this side as was wished and expected. Complaints are every where heard from our most considerate and virtuous citizens, equally the friends of public and private faith, and of public and personal liberty; that our governments are too unstable; that the public good is disregarded in the conflicts of rival parties; and that measures are too often decided, not according to the rules of justice, and the rights of the minor party; but by the superior force of an interested and over-bearing majority. However anxiously we may wish that these complaints had no foundation, the evidence of known facts will not permit us to deny that they are in some degree true. It will be found indeed, on a candid review of our situation, that some of the distresses under which we labor, have been erroneously charged on the operation of our governments; but it will be found, at the same time, that other causes will not alone account for many of our heaviest misfortunes; and particularly, for that prevailing and increasing distrust of public engagements, and alarm for private rights, which are echoed from one end of the continent to the other. These must be chiefly, if not wholly, effects of the unsteadiness and injustice, with which a factious spirit has tainted our public administrations.

By a faction I understand a number of citizens, whether amounting to a majority or minority of the whole, who are united and actuated by some common impulse of passion, or of interest, adverse to the rights of other citizens, or to the permanent and aggregate interests of the community.

There are two methods of curing the mischiefs of faction: the one, by removing its causes; the other, by controlling its effects.

There are again two methods of removing the causes of faction: the one by destroying the liberty which is essential to its existence; the other, by giving to every citizen the same opinions, the same passions, and the same interests.

It could never be more truly said than of the first remedy, that it is worse than the disease. Liberty is to faction, what air is to fire, an aliment without which it instantly expires. But it could not be a less folly to abolish liberty, which is essential to political life, because it nourishes faction, than it would be to wish the annihilation of air, which is essential to animal life, because it imparts to fire its destructive agency.

The second expedient is as impracticable, as the first would be unwise. As long as the reason of man continues fallible, and he is at liberty to exercise it, different opinions will be formed. As long as the connection subsists between his reason and his self-love, his opinions and his passions will have a reciprocal influence on each other; and the former will be objects to which the latter will attach themselves. The diversity in the faculties of men from which the rights of property originate, is not less an insuperable obstacle to a uniformity of interests. The protection of these faculties is the first object of Government. From the protection of different and unequal faculties of acquiring property, the possession of different degrees and kinds of property immediately results: and from the influence of these on the sentiments and views of the respective proprietors, ensues a division of the society into different interests and parties.

The latent causes of faction are thus sown in the nature of man; and we see them every where brought into different degrees of activity, according to the different circumstances of civil society. A zeal for different opinions concerning religion, concerning Government and many other points, as well of speculation as of practice; an attachment to different leaders ambitiously contending for pre-eminence and power; or to persons of other descriptions whose fortunes have been interesting to the human passions, have in turn divided mankind into parties, inflamed them with mutual animosity, and rendered them much more disposed to vex and oppress each other, than to cooperate for their common good. So strong is this propensity of mankind to fall into mutual animosities, that where no substantial occasion presents itself, the most frivolous and fanciful distinctions have been sufficient to kindle their unfriendly passions, and excite their most violent conflicts. But the most common and durable source of factions, has been the various and unequal distribution of property. Those who hold, and those who are without property, have ever formed distinct interests in society. Those who are creditors, and those who are debtors, fall under a like discrimination. A landed interest, a manufacturing interest, a mercantile interest, a monied interest, with many lesser interests, grow up of necessity in civilized nations, and divide them into different classes, actuated by different sentiments and views. The regulation of these various and interfering interests forms the principal task of modern Legislation, and involves the spirit of party and faction in the necessary and ordinary operations of Government.

No man is allowed to be a judge in his own cause; because his interest would certainly bias his judgment, and, not improbably, corrupt his integrity. With equal, nay with greater reason, a body of men, are unfit to be both judges and parties, at the same time; yet, what are many of the most important acts of legislation, but so many judicial determinations, not indeed concerning the rights of single persons, but concerning the rights of large bodies of citizens, and what are the different classes of legislators, but advocates and parties to the causes which they determine? Is a law proposed concerning private debts? It is a question to which the creditors are parties on one side, and the debtors on the other. Justice ought to hold the balance between them. Yet the parties are and must be themselves the judges; and the most numerous party, or, in other words, the most powerful faction must be expected to prevail. Shall domestic manufactures be encouraged, and in what degree, by restrictions on foreign manufactures? are questions which would be differently decided by the landed and the manufacturing classes; and probably by neither, with a sole regard to justice and the public good. The apportionment of taxes on the various descriptions of property, is an act which seems to require the most exact impartiality; yet, there is perhaps no legislative act in which greater opportunity and temptation are given to a predominant party, to trample on the rules of justice. Every shilling with which they over-burden the inferior number, is a shilling saved to their own pockets.

It is in vain to say, that enlightened statesmen will be able to adjust these clashing interests, and render them all subservient to the public good. Enlightened statesmen will not always be at the helm: Nor, in many cases, can such an adjustment be made at all, without taking into view indirect and remote considerations, which will rarely prevail over the immediate interest which one party may find in disregarding the rights of another, or the good of the whole.

The inference to which we are brought, is, that the *causes* of faction cannot be removed; and that relief is only to be sought in the means of controlling its *effects*.

If a faction consists of less than a majority, relief is supplied by the republican principle, which enables the majority to defeat its sinister views by regular vote: It may clog the administration, it may convulse the society; but it will be unable to execute and mask its violence under the forms of the Constitution. When a majority is included in a faction, the form of popular government on the other hand enables it to sacrifice to its ruling passion or interest, both the public good and the rights of other citizens. To secure the public good, and private rights, against the danger of such a faction, and at the same time to preserve the spirit and the form of popular government, is then the great object to which our enquiries are directed: Let me add that it is the great desideratum, by which alone this form of government can be rescued from the opprobrium under which it has so long labored, and be recommended to the esteem and adoption of mankind.

By what means is this object attainable? Evidently by one of two only. Either the existence of the same passion or interest in a majority at the same time, must be prevented; or the majority, having such co-existent passion or interest, must be rendered, by their number and local situation, unable to concert and carry into effect schemes of oppression. If the impulse and the opportunity be suffered to coincide, we well know that neither moral nor religious motives can be relied on as an adequate control. They are not found to be such on the injustice and violence of individuals, and lose their efficacy in proportion to the number combined together; that is, in proportion as their efficacy becomes needful.

From this view of the subject, it may be concluded, that a pure Democracy, by which I mean, a Society, consisting of a small number of citizens, who assemble and administer the Government in person, can admit of no cure for the mischiefs of faction. A common passion or interest will, in almost every case, be felt by a majority of the whole; a communication and concert results from the form of Government itself; and there is nothing to check the inducements to sacrifice the weaker party, or an obnoxious individual. Hence it is, that such Democracies have ever been spectacles of turbulence and contention; have ever been found incompatible with personal security, or the rights of property; and have in general been as short in their lives, as they have been violent in their deaths. Theoretic politicians, who have patronized this species of Government, have erroneously supposed, that by reducing mankind to a perfect equality in their political rights, they would, at the same time, be perfectly equalized and assimilated in their possessions, their opinions, and their passions.

A republic, by which I mean a government in which the scheme of representation takes place, opens a different prospect, and promises the cure for which we are seeking. Let us examine the points in which it varies from pure democracy, and we shall comprehend both the nature of the cure and the efficacy which it must derive from the union.

The two great points of difference, between a democracy and a republic, are, first, the delegation of the government, in the latter, to a small number of citizens, elected by the rest; secondly, the greater number of citizens, and greater sphere of country, over which the latter may be extended.

The effect of the first difference is, on the one hand, to refine and enlarge the public views, by passing them through the medium of a chosen body of citizens, whose wisdom may best discern the true interest of their country, and whose patriotism and love of justice, will be least likely to sacrifice it to temporary or partial considerations. Under such a regulation, it may well happen, that the public voice, pronounced by the representatives of the people, will be more consonant to the public good, than if pronounced by the people themselves, convened for the purpose. On the other hand the effect may be inverted. Men of factious tempers, of local prejudices, or of sinister designs, may by intrigue, by corruption, or by other means, first obtain the suffrages, and then betray the interest of the people. The question resulting is, whether small or extensive republics are most favorable to the election of proper guardians of the public weal, and it is clearly decided in favor of the latter by two obvious considerations.

In the first place, it is to be remarked that, however small the republic may be, the representatives must be raised to a certain number, in order to guard against the cabals of a few; and that however large it may be, they must be limited to a certain number, in order to guard against the confusion of a multitude. Hence, the number of representatives in the two cases not being in proportion to that of the constituents, and being proportionally greatest in the small republic, it follows, that if the proportion of fit characters be not less in the large than in the small republic, the former will present a greater option, and consequently a greater probability of a fit choice.

In the next place, as each Representative will be chosen by a greater number of citizens in the large than in the small Republic, it will be more difficult for unworthy candidates to practise with success the vicious arts, by which elections are too often carried; and the suffrages of the people being more free, will be more likely to center on men who possess the most attractive merit, and the most diffusive and established characters.

It must be confessed, that in this, as in most other cases, there is a mean, on both sides of which inconveniences will be found to lie. By enlarging too much the number of electors, you render the representatives too little acquainted with all their local circumstances and lesser interests; as by reducing it too much, you render him unduly attached to these, and too little fit to comprehend and pursue great and national objects. The Federal Constitution forms a happy combination in this respect; the great and aggregate interests being referred to the national, the local and particular, to the state legislatures.

The other point of difference is, the greater number of citizens and extent of territory which may be brought within the compass of Republican, than of Democratic Government; and it is this circumstance principally which renders factious combinations less to be dreaded in the former, than in the latter. The smaller the society, the fewer probably will be the distinct parties and interests composing it; the fewer the distinct parties and interests, the more frequently will a majority be found of the same party; and the smaller the number of individuals composing a majority, and the smaller the compass within which they are placed, the more easily will they concert and execute their plans of oppression. Extend the sphere, and you take in a greater variety of parties and interests; you make it less probable that a majority of the whole will have a common motive to invade the rights of other citizens; or if such a common motive exists, it will be more difficult for all who feel it to discover their own strength, and to act in unison with each other. Besides other impediments, it may be remarked, that where there is a consciousness of unjust or dishonorable purposes, communication is always checked by distrust, in proportion to the number whose concurrence is necessary.

Hence it clearly appears, that the same advantage, which a Republic has over a Democracy, in controlling the effects of factions, is enjoyed by a large over a small Republic—is enjoyed by the Union over the States composing it. Does this advantage consist in the substitution of Representatives, whose enlightened views and virtuous sentiments render them superior to local prejudices, and to schemes of injustice? It will not be denied, that the Representation of the Union will be most likely to possess these requisite endowments. Does it consist in the greater security afforded by a greater variety of parties, against the event of any one party being able to outnumber and oppress the rest? In an equal degree does the increased variety of parties, comprised within the Union, increase this security? Does it, in fine, consist in the greater obstacles opposed to the concert and accomplishment of the secret wishes of an unjust and interested majority? Here, again, the extent of the Union gives it the most palpable advantage.

The influence of factious leaders may kindle a flame within their particular States, but will be unable to spread a general conflagration through the other States: a religious sect, may degenerate into a political faction in a part of the Confederacy but the variety of sects dispersed over the entire face of it, must secure the national Councils against any danger from that source: a rage for paper money, for an abolition of debts, for an equal division of property, or for any other improper or wicked project, will be less apt to pervade the whole body of the Union, than a particular member of it; in the same proportion as such a malady is more likely to taint a particular county or district, than an entire State.

In the extent and proper structure of the Union, therefore, we behold a Republican remedy for the diseases most incident to Republican Government. And according to the degree of pleasure and pride, we feel in being Republicans, ought to be our zeal in cherishing the spirit, and supporting the character of Federalists.

PUBLIUS

The Federalist No. 51

November 22, 1787

James Madison

TO THE PEOPLE OF THE STATE OF NEW YORK.

To what expedient then shall we finally resort for maintaining in practice the necessary partition of power among the several departments, as laid down in the constitution? The only answer that can be given is, that as all these exterior provisions are found to be inadequate, the defect must be supplied, by so contriving the interior structure of the government, as that its several constituent parts may, by their mutual relations, be the means of keeping each other in their proper places. Without presuming to undertake a full development of this important idea, I will hazard a few general observations, which may perhaps place it in a clearer light, and enable us to form a more correct judgment of the principles and structure of the government planned by the convention.

In order to lay a due foundation for that separate and distinct exercise of the different powers of government, which to a certain extent, is admitted on all hands to be essential to the preservation of liberty, it is evident that each department should have a will of its own; and consequently should be so constituted, that the members of each should have as little agency as possible in the appointment of the members of the others. Were this principle rigorously adhered to, it would require that all the appointments for the supreme executive, legislative, and judiciary magistracies, should be drawn from the same fountain of authority, the people, through channels, having no communication whatever with one another. Perhaps such a plan of constructing the several departments would be less difficult in practice than it may in contemplation appear. Some difficulties however, and some additional expense, would attend the execution of it. Some deviations therefore from the principle must be admitted. In the constitution of the judiciary department in particular, it might be inexpedient to insist rigorously on the principle; first, because peculiar qualifications being essential in the members, the primary consideration ought to be to select that mode of choice, which best secures these qualifications; secondly, because

the permanent tenure by which the appointments are held in that department, must soon destroy all sense of dependence on the authority conferring them.

It is equally evident that the members of each department should be as little dependent as possible on those of the others, for the emoluments annexed to their offices. Were the executive magistrate, or the judges, not independent of the legislature in this particular, their independence in every other would be merely nominal.

But the great security against a gradual concentration of the several powers in the same department, consists in giving to those who administer each department, the necessary constitutional means, and personal motives, to resist encroachments of the others. The provision for defense must in this, as in all other cases, be made commensurate to the danger of attack. Ambition must be made to counteract ambition. The interest of the man must be connected with the constitutional right of the place. It may be a reflection on human nature, that such devices should be necessary to control the abuses of government. But what is government itself but the greatest of all reflections on human nature? If men were angels, no government would be necessary. If angels were to govern men, neither external nor internal controls on government would be necessary. In framing a government which is to be administered by men over men, the great difficulty lies in this: You must first enable the government to control the governed; and in the next place, oblige it to control itself. A dependence on the people is no doubt the primary control on the government; but experience has taught mankind the necessity of auxiliary precautions.

This policy of supplying by opposite and rival interests, the defect of better motives, might be traced through the whole system of human affairs, private as well as public. We see it particularly displayed in all the subordinate distributions of power; where the constant aim is to divide and arrange the several offices in such a manner as that each may be a check on the other; that the private interest of every individual, may be a sentinel over the public rights. These inventions of prudence cannot be less requisite in the distribution of the supreme powers of the state.

But it is not possible to give each department an equal power of self defense. In republican government the legislative authority, necessarily, predominates. The remedy for this inconveniency is, to divide the legislature into different branches; and to render them by different modes of election, and different principles of action, as little connected with each other, as the nature of their common functions, and their common dependence on the society, will admit. It may even be necessary to guard against dangerous encroachments by still further precautions. As the weight of the legislative authority requires that it should be thus divided, the weakness of the executive may require, on the other hand, that it should be fortified. An absolute negative, on the legislature, appears at first view to be the natural defense with which the executive magistrate should be armed. But perhaps it would be neither altogether safe, nor alone sufficient. On ordinary occasions, it might not be exerted with the requisite firmness; and on extraordinary occasions, it might be perfidiously abused. May not this defect of an absolute negative be supplied, by some qualified connection between this weaker department, and the weaker branch of the stronger department, by which the latter may be led to support the constitutional rights of the former, without being too much detached from the rights of its own department?

If the principles on which these observations are founded be just, as I persuade myself they are, and they be applied as a criterion, to the several state constitutions, and to the federal constitution, it will be found, that if the latter does not perfectly correspond with them, the former are infinitely less able to bear such a test.

There are moreover two considerations particularly applicable to the federal system of America, which place that system in a very interesting point of view.

First. In a single republic, all the power surrendered by the people, is submitted to the administration of a single government; and usurpations are guarded against by a division of the government into distinct and separate departments. In the compound republic of America, the power surrendered by the people, is first divided between two distinct governments, and then the portion allotted to each, subdivided among distinct and separate departments. Hence a double security arises to the rights of the people.

The different governments will control each other; at the same time that each will be controlled by itself.

Second. It is of great importance in a republic, not only to guard the society against the oppression of its rulers; but to guard one part of the society against the injustice of the other part. Different interests necessarily exist in different classes of citizens. If a majority be united by a common interest, the rights of the minority will be insecure. There are but two methods of providing against this evil: The one by creating a will in the community independent of the majority, that is, of the society itself, the other by comprehending in the society so many separate descriptions of citizens, as will render an unjust combination of a majority of the whole, very improbable, if not impracticable. The first method prevails in all governments possessing an hereditary or self appointed authority. This at best is but a precarious security; because a power independent of the society may as well espouse the unjust views of the major, as the rightful interests, of the minor party, and may possibly be turned against both parties. The second method will be exemplified in the federal republic of the United States. While all authority in it will be derived from and dependent on the society, the society itself will be broken into so many parts, interests and classes of citizens, that the rights of individuals or of the minority, will be in little danger from interested combinations of the majority. In a free government, the security for civil rights must be the same as for religious rights. It consists in the one case in the multiplicity of interests, and in the other, in the multiplicity of sects. The degree of security in both cases will depend on the number of interests and sects; and this may be presumed to depend on the extent of country and number of people comprehended under the same government. This view of the subject must particularly recommend a proper federal system to all the sincere and considerate friends of republican government: Since it shows that in exact proportion as the territory of the union may be formed into more circumscribed confederacies or states, oppressive combinations of a majority will be facilitated, the best security under the republican form, for the rights of every class of citizens, will be diminished; and consequently, the stability and independence of some member of the government, the only other security, must be proportionally increased. Justice is the end of government. It is the end of civil society. It ever has been, and ever will be pursued, until it be obtained, or until liberty be lost in the pursuit. In a society under the forms of which the stronger faction can readily unite and oppress the weaker, anarchy may as truly be said to reign, as in a state of nature where the weaker individual is not secured against the violence of the stronger: And as in the latter state even the stronger individuals are prompted by the uncertainty of their condition, to submit to a government which may protect the weak as well as themselves: So in the former state, will the more powerful factions or parties be gradually induced by a like motive, to wish for a government which will protect all parties, the weaker as well as the more powerful. It can be little doubted, that if the state of Rhode Island was separated from the confederacy, and left to itself, the insecurity of rights under the popular form of government within such narrow limits, would be displayed by such reiterated oppressions of factious majorities, that some power altogether independent of the people would soon be called for by the voice of the very factions whose misrule had proved the necessity of it. In the extended republic of the United States, and among the great variety of interests, parties and sects which it embraces, a coalition of a majority of the whole society could seldom take place on any other principles than those of justice and the general good; and there being thus less danger to a minor from the will of the major party, there must be less pretext also, to provide for the security of the former, by introducing into the government a will not dependent on the latter; or in other words, a will independent of the society itself. It is no less certain than it is important, notwithstanding the contrary opinions which have been entertained, that the larger the society, provided it lie within a practicable sphere, the more duly capable will be of self government. And happily for the *republican cause,* the practicable sphere may be carried to a very great extent, by a judicious modification and mixture of the *federal principle.*

PUBLIUS

Presidents of the United States, 1789–1999

Name	*Party*	*Term*
1. George Washington (1732–1799)	Federalist	1789–1797
2. John Adams (1735–1826)	Federalist	1797–1801
3. Thomas Jefferson (1743–1826)	Democratic-Republican	1801–1809
4. James Madison (1751–1836)	Democratic-Republican	1809–1817
5. James Monroe (1758–1831)	Democratic-Republican	1817–1825
6. John Quincy Adams (1767–1848)	Democratic-Republican	1825–1829
7. Andrew Jackson (1767–1845)	Democratic	1829–1837
8. Martin Van Buren (1782–1862)	Democratic	1837–1841
9. William Henry Harrison (1773–1841)	Whig	1841
10. John Tyler (1790–1862)	Whig	1841–1845
11. James K. Polk (1795–1849)	Democratic	1845–1849
12. Zachary Taylor (1784–1850)	Whig	1849–1850
13. Millard Fillmore (1800–1874)	Whig	1850–1853
14. Franklin Pierce (1804–1869)	Democratic	1853–1857
15. James Buchanan (1791–1868)	Democratic	1857–1861
16. Abraham Lincoln (1809–1865)	Republican	1861–1865
17. Andrew Johnson (1808–1875)	Union	1865–1869
18. Ulysses S. Grant (1822–1885)	Republican	1869–1877
19. Rutherford B. Hayes (1822–1893)	Republican	1877–1881
20. James A. Garfield (1831–1881)	Republican	1881
21. Chester A. Arthur (1830–1886)	Republican	1881–1885
22. Grover Cleveland (1837–1908)	Democratic	1881–1889
23. Benjamin Harrison (1833–1901)	Republican	1889–1893
24. Grover Cleveland (1837–1908)	Democratic	1893–1897
25. William McKinley (1843–1901)	Republican	1897–1901
26. Theodore Roosevelt (1858–1919)	Republican	1901–1909
27. William Howard Taft (1857–1930)	Republican	1909–1913
28. Woodrow Wilson (1856–1924)	Democratic	1913–1921
29. Warren G. Harding (1865–1923)	Republican	1921–1923
30. Calvin Coolidge (1871–1933)	Republican	1923–1929
31. Herbert Hoover (1874–1964)	Republican	1929–1933
32. Franklin Delano Roosevelt (1882–1945)	Democratic	1933–1945
33. Harry S Truman (1884–1972)	Democratic	1945–1953
34. Dwight D. Eisenhower (1890–1969)	Republican	1953–1961
35. John F. Kennedy (1917–1963)	Democratic	1961–1963
36. Lyndon B. Johnson (1908–1973)	Democratic	1963–1969
37. Richard M. Nixon (1913–1994)	Republican	1969–1974
38. Gerald R. Ford (b. 1913)	Republican	1974–1977
39. Jimmy Carter (b. 1924)	Democratic	1977–1981
40. Ronald Reagan (b. 1911)	Republican	1981–1989
41. George Bush (b. 1924)	Republican	1989–1993
42. Bill Clinton (b. 1946)	Democratic	1993–

Glossary ★

Adjudication. Administrative hearings conducted to resolve conflicts over the application of agency rules and regulations to specific cases.

Administrative Procedures Act (APA). A 1946 law that established procedures for government agencies when creating and applying rules and policies.

Advisory Opinions. Legal opinions on issues that do not arise in the context of particular cases. The federal courts do not have the power to issue advisory opinions.

Affirmative Action. Any program that attempts to promote equality by making distinctions and, at times, granting preferences to individuals based on characteristics such as race or gender.

American Creed. The core tenets of U.S. political culture, including such values as self-reliance, individual liberties and rights, political equality, property rights, rule of law, community, and religious belief.

American Exceptionalism. The widely accepted notion that the United States has a unique political culture that sets it apart from other nations.

***Amicus Curiae*, or "Friend of the Court" Briefs.** Written legal arguments filed in the Supreme Court by third parties—often interest groups—not directly involved in the case.

Antifederalists. Opponents and critics of the proposed ratification of the Constitution of the United States in the 1780s. They were particularly opposed to the Constitution's provisions expanding the power of the national government.

Appellate Jurisdiction. The legal authority of a court to hear cases appealed as the result of a lower court decision. Under the Constitution, the Supreme Court has broad appellate jurisdiction, but limited jurisdiction to hear newly filed cases.

Appropriation. Congressional approval of funds necessary to finance a previously authorized program or agency.

Aristocracy. Government by an elite ruling class.

Articles of Confederation. The first framework of national government in the U.S., adopted by Congress in 1777. The Articles provided for limited national power, treating each state as independent and equal.

Authorization. Congressional approval of a government program (or agency) that includes the rules governing the expenditure of program funds. The funds themselves usually must be approved through a separate appropriations process.

Bandwagon Effect. The tendency for individuals to adopt the views of the majority, particularly as expressed in a public opinion poll.

Bicameralism. A system which has two separate legislative chambers, or houses, such as the United States Senate and House of Representatives.

Bill of Rights. The first ten amendments to the Constitution, ratified in 1791, which recognize and protect the rights of the people, including the freedoms of speech, press, assembly, and religion; freedom from unreasonable searches and seizures; due process of law; and privacy.

Block Grants. Financial grants from the U.S. government to states and localities for broad, general purposes (such as law enforcement or education), with little national control over how the funds are to be spent.

***Brown* v. *Board of Education*.** A United States Supreme Court decision (1954) that overruled the earlier case of *Plessy* v. *Ferguson* and held that racial segregation of public schools was unconstitutional under the Equal Protection Clause of the Fourteenth Amendment.

***Buckley* v. *Valeo* (1976).** A United States Supreme Court decision that invalidated several provisions of the Federal Election Campaign Act, including limitations on independent campaign expenditures by individuals and groups.

Bureaucracy. Complex organizations in which tasks are specialized and power is exercised hierarchically, from the top down; also, the executive departments and independent agencies responsible for administering governmental programs.

Busing. A method of achieving racial integration of public schools by transporting students of one race into schools populated predominantly by students of another race.

Cabinet. The heads of the major executive departments, including, among others, the attorney general and the secretaries of state, defense, and the treasury.

Casework (Constituent Service). Assistance with the federal bureaucracy provided by members of Congress and their staffs to individuals within their respective districts or states.

Categorical Grants. Financial grants from the U.S. government to states and localities for narrowly defined purposes (such as prison and school construction), generally with specific national guidelines on how the funds are to be spent.

Checks and Balances. The principle by which the different branches of government share some of the powers of the other branches. Checks and balances allow the branches to regulate and oversee potential abuses of authority and promote negotiation and compromise.

Citizens' Groups. Interest groups that are open to all concerned individuals, regardless of their occupational or business association.

Civil Liberties. Individual rights guaranteed by the Bill of Rights, including freedoms of speech, press, assembly, and religion; protection against unreasonable search and seizure; the right to privacy; and various rights guaranteed by the Due Process clause.

Civil Rights. Rights of individuals to equality under the law, regardless of race, gender, ethnicity, or other group status.

Civil Rights Act of 1964. National legislation that prohibited most forms of discrimination and segregation based upon race, color, religion, national origin, or sex, in public accommodations, public education, and employment, and in programs receiving federal assistance.

Clear and Present Danger Test. A legal standard developed in 1918 by the Supreme Court that permits the government to regulate certain forms of speech only when there is a "clear and present danger" that they will cause some harm—such as a threat to the public safety—that the government can constitutionally prevent.

Cold War. Post-World War II period of intense competition between the United States and the Soviet Union for global supremacy, ending with the downfall of the Soviet Union in 1989.

Commander-in-Chief Clause. Constitutional provision (Article II) establishing the president as commander-in-chief of American military forces.

Concurring Opinion. An opinion written by a judge who agrees with the majority as to the outcome of a case, but who disagrees with the legal reasoning underlying the majority's decision or who wishes to add or extend the reasoning of the majority.

Confederation. A political system that establishes a central government for purposes of convenience but in which all power ultimately resides within each independent state or province.

Conference Committee. A special committee made up of members of both houses of the United States Congress created to resolve differences between the House and Senate versions of a bill.

Congressional Oversight. Congress's ability to review the activities of the executive branch, through both formal and informal mechanisms.

Conservatism. Historically, a political ideology that stressed order, tradition, and the preservation of established institutions; in modern usage, an ideology stressing the importance of limited government intervention in the economy.

Cooperative Federalism. A political arrangement in which the national, state, and local governments combine their efforts to address problems of mutual concern (such as law enforcement).

Corporate Welfare. Benefits that corporations receive from the government, including direct cash payments, loan guarantees, tax exemptions, and indirect subsidies.

Cost-Benefit Analysis. The determination of the costs and benefits of a policy, making possible the evaluation of its efficiency.

Creative Federalism. A particular form of cooperative federalism, characteristic of the 1960s antipoverty programs of the Great Society, in which the national government increased its power over state and local government activity by increasing its financial and regulatory control.

Critical Elections. Watershed elections (e.g., 1860) that signal a critical realignment. Critical elections are characterized by high voter interest and participation; heightened ideological differences between the parties, especially around a single critical issue; changes in the relative strength and coalition bases of the major political parties, and changes in party control of Congress and the presidency.

Declaration of Independence. Formal written expression of and justification for the American colonies' break from Great Britain, written in 1776 in large part by Thomas Jefferson and approved unanimously by representatives of the thirteen colonies.

Delegation Doctrine. Constitutional limits on the delegation of legislative power by Congress to the executive branch, the judiciary, or the private sector. Last enforced by the Supreme Court in the 1930s.

Democracy. Government by the people, either in person (direct democracy) or through representation (representative democracy).

Deregulation. The repeal of previously existing government regulations, especially of particular economic sectors or industries.

Desegregation. The elimination of laws requiring racial segregation in education, housing, restaurants, hotels, and other areas.

Deviating Elections. Elections that do not follow established voting patterns due to short-term factors (such as war or scandal), but that do not lead to long-term changes in voters' party loyalty or in the balance between the two parties.

Discretionary Spending. Appropriations for programs (or agencies) that can be increased or decreased by Congress each year without changing the programs' underlying legal authority.

Dissenting Opinion. An opinion written by a judge who disagrees with the decision of the majority in a case.

Divided Government. Control of the presidency and the congress by different parties, as in much of the modern era.

Dred Scott v. *Sandford*. A United States Supreme Court decision (1857) that denied to Congress the power to regulate slavery in the territories and to black Americans the basic rights of citizenship, and that thus helped precipitate the Civil War.

Dual Federalism. A form of federalism in which the national and state governments are sovereign within their respective spheres of authority.

Due Process of Law. The constitutional guarantee, contained in both the Fifth and the Fourteenth Amendments, which prohibits the government from denying to any person "life, liberty, or property" unless it follows the appropriate legal procedures. The clause has also been held to protect certain liberties, such as a woman's right to obtain an abortion.

Efficiency. The ratio of total benefits to total costs in a policy.

Elastic Clause. A constitutional provision (Article I, Section 8), also known as the "Necessary and Proper" Clause, which gives Congress a broad choice of means to use in carrying out its delegated powers.

Electoral College. A group of delegates chosen from each state (and, since 1964, the District of Columbia) that casts the actual ballots that elect the president and vice president of the United States. Each delegation (equal to the size of its House and Senate membership, three for D.C.) is now generally expected to cast all of their votes (winner-take-all) for the presidential candidate who secured the most popular votes in their state, with a majority (270) needed for election.

Elite Model. A model of government that suggests that representative processes such as elections merely create the illusion of democracy, while real political power rests with economic, professional, and cultural elites rather than with the common people.

Emancipation Proclamation. Statement issued in 1862 by President Abraham Lincoln freeing all slaves in the rebellious Confederate states. Having neither immediate means of enforcement nor applying to slaves in the border states, this proclamation nevertheless signaled the Union's intention to abolish slavery after the Civil War.

Entitlements. Government programs (for example, social security) that provide services or benefits to any individual who meets specified eligibility requirements.

Equal Rights Amendment (ERA). A proposed constitutional amendment (approved by Congress in 1972) intended to guarantee equality of rights under the law to all citizens regardless of gender. The ERA failed to be ratified by the required vote of three-fourths of the state legislatures.

Equal Time Rule. An FCC regulation stipulating that if a broadcaster provides air time to a particular candidate or to one of the major political parties, the broadcaster must also provide equal time to opposing candidates or the opposing major party.

Establishment Clause. First Amendment provision stating that "Congress shall make no law respecting an establishment of religion."

Ex Post Facto Laws. Laws that retroactively define as crimes acts that were not illegal when they were committed. Prohibited by the Constitution.

Exclusionary Rule. A court-imposed rule that, under most circumstances, makes it impossible for the government to introduce in a criminal trial evidence collected in violation of the defendant's constitutional rights, including those secured by the Fourth and Fifth Amendments.

Executive Agreements. Agreements with other nations negotiated by the president and similar to treaties, yet not subject to Senate ratification.

Executive Office of the President (EOP). A group of agencies and officials who advise and assist the president.

Executive Power Clause. A provision in Article II of the Constitution vesting the "executive power" in the president of the United States.

Faction. According to James Madison, a group of citizens—whether amounting to a majority or a minority of the whole—motivated by a common interest or passion adverse to the rights of other citizens or to the long-term interests of the community as a whole.

Federal Election Campaign Act (FECA). Congressional legislation, approved in 1971 and amended in 1974, requiring disclosure of contributions to federal campaigns; setting limits on campaign spending, contributions, and independent expenditures; and providing for partial public funding of presidential campaigns. Parts of FECA were invalidated by the Supreme Court in the 1976 case of *Buckley* v. *Valeo*.

Federal Reserve Board (or "Fed"). An independent government agency largely responsible for setting U.S. monetary policy through its control over interest rates.

Federalism. A political arrangement in which power is allocated independently to both national and state or regional governments.

Federalists. Supporters of the ratification of the Constitution, particularly its provisions for a stronger national government. Leading Federalists included James Madison and Alexander Hamilton.

Fifteenth Amendment. Constitutional provision, ratified in 1870, prohibiting the denial of voting rights to any citizen on the basis of race, color, or previous condition of servitude.

Filibuster. Unlimited floor debate by any senator, allowed by the Senate's procedural rules, intended to prevent the passage of legislation otherwise preferred by a majority of members. Filibusters can only be ended by a vote of sixty senators (cloture).

Fiscal Policy. The use of governmental budgetary decisions in an effort to control or stimulate national economic growth.

Fourteenth Amendment. Constitutional provision, ratified in 1868, granting U.S. citizenship to all persons "born or naturalized in the United States," including the former slaves, and guaranteeing to all persons the equal protection of the laws and due process of law.

Free Exercise Clause. First Amendment provision guaranteeing each individual's right to exercise his or her religious beliefs without interference from the government.

Free-Rider Problem. The difficulty interest groups face in obtaining the active membership of otherwise supportive individuals who perceive that they will benefit from the policies promoted by the group even if they do not actively work to promote them.

Freedom of Assembly. First Amendment provision allowing individuals to gather together peacefully to protest government policies or otherwise to exercise their rights.

Freedom of Association. First Amendment right of individuals to gather together to pursue a common purpose, such as political activities or religious worship. Derived from the First Amendment guarantees of speech, religion, and assembly.

Freedom of Information Act (FOIA). A federal law requiring federal agencies to make information about their operations available to any citizen who requests it. FOIA makes exceptions for certain categories of information, such as material that is properly classified or that would compromise an individual's right to privacy.

Gender Gap. The difference between the attitudes, beliefs, and political behavior of men and women.

General Elections. Elections in which candidates from different parties (and sometimes independent candidates) compete for government office (such as the presidency or state legislative office).

Gibbons v. *Ogden.* A United States Supreme Court case (1824) that broadly interpreted Congress's commerce power (Article I, Section 8) to include all trade and navigation not completely confined within a state's boundaries.

Government. A group of individuals (or an institution) with the authority to make and enforce decisions regulating and protecting a community. Two characteristics set the government apart from other decision-making groups: (1) the government has authority over an entire community; and (2) the government has a monopoly over the legitimate use of force.

Great Compromise. The constitutional arrangement adopted by the Constitutional Convention of 1787 that created two house of Congress, one to be apportioned by population, and the other to consist of equal representation for each state.

Great Society. The collective term for the antipoverty and civil rights programs proposed by President Lyndon Johnson and adopted by Congress in the mid-1960s.

Habeas Corpus. Constitutional provision permitting prisoners to petition the courts to inquire into the reasons for their detention and to order the government to release those who are being detained illegally. Most frequently used to allow federal court review of state criminal cases.

House Majority Leader. Next to the Speaker, the second most important official in the majority party of the House, generally responsible for maneuvering legislation through the final floor vote.

Human Rights Policy. Foreign policy that seeks to advance U.S. political ideals, such as democracy and freedom, and to alleviate injustice and human suffering.

Imperial Presidency. The presidency between 1932 and 1974, marked by greatly expanded powers, especially in foreign affairs, and heightened public expectations.

Incorporation. A legal doctrine developed in Supreme Court decisions, beginning in 1897, that has resulted in the application of virtually the entire Bill of Rights to the states.

Incrementalism. Gradual policy change made in "increments," rather than all at once.

Independent Agencies. Agencies created by Congress that operate outside of the standard executive branch chain of command. Typically, the president lacks the formal power to control directly the policy decisions of independent agencies.

Initiative. A proposed law (or state constitutional amendment) placed on an election ballot by way of a popular petition and then voted on directly by the people. Not allowed in all states or at the national level.

Insider Lobbying. The attempt by interest group representatives to influence government officials through personal contacts rather than through public pressure.

Integration. Governmental action designed to combat segregation by actively promoting mixed-race schools, housing, and other facilities.

Interest Group. An association of individuals who try to influence government policy on an issue or set of issues.

Interventionism. A foreign policy that seeks to advance American interest and ideals through international alliances and the projection of U.S. military and economic power abroad.

Isolationism. A foreign policy that stresses separation from international alliances and conflicts.

Jim Crow Laws. Laws enacted in the southern states between 1890 and 1910 requiring the separation of blacks and whites in educational institutions, hotel and transportation facilities, and most other areas of public life.

Judicial Review. The power of the United States Supreme Court to review the constitutionality of acts of Congress, as well as executive actions and state laws, and, if unconstitutional, to declare them null and void.

Jurisdiction. The scope (or breadth) of legal power and authority, especially of a court.

Jury Nullification. The traditional right of juries to ignore the law in order to acquit criminal defendants on political or other non-legal grounds.

King, Martin Luther, Jr. The leader of the civil rights movement in the 1950s and 1960s. An advocate of nonviolent civil disobedience, King is best known for his 1963 "I Have a Dream" speech. He was assassinated in 1968.

Laissez-faire. An economic policy in which the government deliberately declines to regulate businesses, workers, or other private sector activities.

Libel. Published, written falsehoods that injure a person's reputation.

Liberalism. A political philosophy rooted in a belief in individual liberty and equality. Classical liberalism stressed minimal governmental interference in all areas of private life; modern liberalism opposes governmental regulations of private social conduct, but favors governmental actions regulating business and promoting social welfare and equality.

Libertarianism. A political philosophy that rejects all but the most essential forms of governmental interference in the lives of citizens.

Locke, John. Seventeenth-century English social philosopher whose ideas on natural rights, natural law, and the social contract profoundly influenced Thomas Jefferson and his contemporaries in the 1700s.

Magna Carta. An agreement signed by King John (1215) of England guaranteeing some measure of individual liberty and rights to some of his subjects. This charter provided the colonists with an early example of a written expression of basic governing principles.

Majority Rule. A decision-making rule in which the position of the voting majority determines what shall be done.

Marbury **v.** *Madison.* An 1803 decision of the United States Supreme Court that established the Court's power of judicial review of acts of Congress.

Marshall, John. Chief Justice of the United States Supreme Court (1801–1835) who promoted decisions increasing the power of the Court and of the national government in general.

McCulloch **v.** *Maryland.* An 1819 decision of the United States Supreme Court that established the principles that Congress's delegated powers should be interpreted broadly; that Congress should have broad discretion in deciding how to carry out its constitutional powers; and that valid national laws take precedence over conflicting state laws and actions.

Medicaid. A federal program providing medical care to those with low incomes.

Medicare. A federal program providing medical care to senior citizens.

Melting Pot. A metaphor conventionally used to characterize the tendency of immigrant groups and other racial, ethnic, and religious minorities to blend into the American cultural mainstream.

Mill, John Stuart. Nineteenth-century English political theorist and influential advocate of classical liberalism.

Minority Rights. Limitations on majority rule established to prevent tyranny against minorities and the denial to minorities of fundamental rights.

Miranda Rights. Summary of constitutional rights required to be read to criminal suspects at times of arrest under the Supreme Court's decision in *Miranda* v. *Arizona* (1966).

Mixed Sector Groups. That small proportion of all U.S. interest groups that include members from both the profit and nonprofit sectors of the economy.

Monetary Policy. Governmental efforts to control the supply and demand of money in the economy, primarily through the control of interest rates.

Monroe Doctrine. Warning issued by President James Monroe in 1823 declaring that the United States would oppose, if necessary by force, European attempts to extend power in the Western Hemisphere.

Montesquieu, Charles Secondat, Baron de. Influential eighteenth-century French philosopher who promoted the notion of separation of powers as a means of preserving liberty.

Multiculturalism. The belief that American culture is best appreciated as a community of racial, ethnic, and religious subcultures, rather than as a single, homogeneous culture.

New Deal. The collective term for the economic and social programs enacted under President Franklin Roosevelt in the 1930s to deal with the effects of the Great Depression and to prevent a future economic collapse.

New Federalism. A form of cooperative federalism in which the states are given greater responsibility for making and carrying out various social policies.

New Media. Communications media that utilize new technologies or the innovative use of existing technologies. Includes talk radio and the Internet.

Nonprofit and Public Sector Groups. Interest groups that represent the concerns of individuals within the not-for-profit sector, or who work within government.

Nullification. A doctrine, supported by John C. Calhoun and others in the early to mid-1800s, that held that individual states could declare acts of Congress to be unconstitutional, and prevent their enforcement.

Office of Management and Budget (OMB). The office responsible for preparing and overseeing the implementation of the president's annual budget proposal, and for helping the president coordinate and manage the executive agencies.

Opinion of the Court. The written explanation of a Supreme Court decision, expressing the views of the majority of the justices and thus of the court.

Oral Argument. The oral presentation of a legal case by an attorney before the Supreme Court.

Original Jurisdiction. The legal authority of the Supreme Court to hear cases that have not been previously heard in a lower court. Very few cases are heard under the Court's original jurisdiction.

Outsider Lobbying. The attempt by interest groups to influence governmental officials by generating public support for their position and communicating those views, either directly or through the media to those officials.

Pack Journalism. The tendency of media organizations to cover the very same stories that other media organizations cover, and in the same way, moving together in a "pack."

Party Identification. A voter's tendency to identify with a particular political party. When held strongly, party identification conditions potential voters' perceptions of issues and events, and determines their voting behavior.

Party System. The relationship between and among political parties in a given country at a given time, defined by the number of parties; the scope and nature of competition between or among the parties; the degree to which each party articulates a clear and different philosophy; and the ability of each party to control the behavior of voters, candidates, and officeholders who identify with that party.

Party Unity Votes. Those congressional votes in which a majority of one party votes in opposition to a majority of the opposition party.

Pendleton Act. An 1883 federal law that replaced the "spoils system" of government appointments based on political loyalty, with the civil service system of appointments based on merit.

Plessy v. *Ferguson*. An 1896 decision of the United States Supreme Court case that upheld the legal segregation of the races under the doctrine that "separate but equal" facilities were not unconstitutional. *Plessy* was overturned by the Supreme Court in *Brown* v. *Board of Education* (1954).

Pluralism. A system of representation in which individuals join interest groups that then compete with each other to achieve their respective public policy goals.

Pluralist Model. A model of government that explains government decision making in terms of competition and compromise between interest groups.

Political Action Committees (PACs). Organized groups whose main purpose is to collect money and then spend it directly on behalf of particular causes or candidates, or contribute it to candidates or parties.

Political Culture. Widely prevalent beliefs, values, and attitudes that structure political behavior in a society.

Political Party. An organization of officeholders, activists, and voters collectively working to secure broad-based public policy goals by winning elective office and controlling government institutions.

Political Socialization. The process of assimilation into a political culture, most commonly involving the transfer of political beliefs, values, and attitudes from one generation to the next. This transmission starts with the family, and is reinforced or weakened by schools, peer groups, and the media.

Politics. The process by which societies are governed. Politics determine who governs, how the government makes decisions, and "who gets what" as a result.

Populism. A political ideology based on a belief in the political virtue and wisdom of ordinary people, coupled with suspicion of political and economic elites.

Postmodern Presidency. The presidency since 1974. The postmodern presidency is an office caught between unreasonably high public expectations for the office and newly emerging constraints on the exercise of presidential power.

Primary Elections (Primaries). Elections in which voters choose the nominees of the respective parties, who then compete in the general election.

Prior Restraints. A court order obtained by the government to prevent the publication or broadcast of a particular document or news story.

Profit Sector Groups. Groups representing the concerns of individuals within agricultural, labor, business, and professional interests operating within the fee-for-service or profit sector of the economy.

Progressive Tax. A tax levied at a rate that increases as a person's income increases.

Proportional Representation. An electoral system in which each party receives legislative representation in proportion to the number of votes it receives.

Public Interest. The interest of the people as a whole. Political theorists debate what constitutes the public interest and whether it is advanced effectively through democratic processes.

Public Interest Groups. Interest groups that work to secure policies that benefit society at large, or that do not directly or disproportionately benefit members of the group, but instead benefit others—often those who cannot effectively work on their own behalf.

Public Opinions. Views and beliefs held by all members of society, often measured by some form of survey. Often used to refer to the collective opinion of a public at a given time, thereby defining a nation's current political beliefs.

Public Opinion Poll. A survey of a representative sample of a given population, used to measure that population's views on a particular subject or subjects.

Pure (or Direct) Democracy. A form of government in which every citizen participates equally and directly in decision making.

Radicalism. Fundamental policy change undertaken all at once, rather than gradually.

Realignments. Periods of transition between party systems in which the debate between the parties and the attachments of voters to each party are dramatically altered. Realignments can also bring changes in which party controls the institutions of government, and can result in dramatic changes in public policy.

Reapportionment. The redistribution of the number of House seats allocated to each state to reflect population changes, as measured by the decennial census; or the redrawing of House (as well as state and local) legislative districts in order to equalize each district's population in light of population changes.

Reconstruction. The period immediately following the Civil War (1865–1876), marked by the military occupation of the South by federal troops and by the passage of laws and constitutional amendments designed to abolish slavery in the South and protect the rights of the newly freed slaves.

Referendum. A proposed law (or state constitutional amendment) placed on an election ballot by a state's legislature to be voted on directly by the public. Not allowed in all states or at the national level.

Representative Democracy. Indirect democracy in which citizens select leaders and hold them accountable through elections.

Reserved Powers. Powers retained by the states, being neither delegated to the national government by the Constitution nor expressly denied to the states.

Response Bias. A problem with certain public opinion polls, generally caused by respondents' inability or unwillingness to answer questions accurately or honestly, or by a disproportionate response to a survey by a certain unrepresentative subset of a population.

Revenue Sharing. Financial grants from the U.S. government to states to be used as the states see fit, with little if any national guidance.

Revolving Door. The back-and-forth movement of influential individuals between positions in the legislative or executive branches of government and firms or associations that lobby those branches.

Right to Privacy. A constitutional right recognized by the Supreme Court and including the right to use contraception and a woman's right to obtain an abortion.

Roe v. Wade. Historic, highly controversial Supreme Court ruling (1973) that established abortion as a constitutionally protected privacy right.

Rule of Four. The rule whereby the Supreme Court agrees to hear a case if at least four of the nine justices agree to do so.

Rules. Formal directives (or orders) issued by administrative agencies under the authorization of a congressional statute. Rules have the force of law and may be enforceable with criminal or civil penalties.

Rules Committee. A standing committee of the House of Representatives that is responsible for scheduling the order and terms of debate of legislation on the House floor, including whether amendments can be offered to proposed legislation.

Salad Bowl (or Mosaic). A metaphor created to compete with the conventional "melting pot" metaphor for racial, ethnic, and religious diversity in the United States. Advocates of the "salad bowl" metaphor take pride in their distinct racial, ethnic, and religious identities, and want to foster cultural diversity.

Sample Bias. A problem with certain public opinion polls caused by the selection (sampling) of an unrepresentative subset of a population.

Sampling. The selection of a subset of a given population that will be polled or measured in order to estimate the opinions of that entire population.

Senate Majority Leader. The most important official in the Senate, chosen by the Senate majority party membership.

Separation of Powers. Principle by which governmental power is functionally dispersed among the executive, legislative, and judicial branches of government.

Shared Powers. Powers that can be constitutionally exercised by both the national and state governments.

Shays's Rebellion. An armed uprising of western Massachusetts farmers in 1786 demanding relief from their indebtedness. Although unsuccessful, this rebellion helped prompt Congress to call for a national convention to alter the Articles of Confederation.

Social Security. A federal retirement program that also provides benefits to certain other categories of individuals.

Socialism. A political philosophy that establishes economic and political equality as the overriding objectives of government policy.

Sound Bites. Brief and attention-grabbing statements by a candidate or official meant to accommodate the limited exposure offered by the broadcast media, particularly TV news.

Speaker of the House. The presiding official of the House of Representatives, selected by the majority party.

Split-Ticket Voting. The practice of voting for candidates of different parties for different offices.

Spoils System. A system of appointments in which an elected official, such as the president, rewards political supporters with government jobs or other benefits, so that "to the victor belong the spoils."

States' Rights. A general philosophy that argues against increasing the authority of the national government over the states generally or that attempts to maintain exclusive state sovereignty over certain public policy areas.

Statutory Interpretation. The judicial interpretation of laws written by Congress.

Strict Scrutiny. The high standard applied by the courts in reviewing the necessity of categorizing individuals into suspect classifications or limiting an individual's fundamental rights.

Subgovernments. Combinations of individuals drawn from particular executive agencies, legislative subcommittee, and interest groups, all concerned about a particular area of policy and often sharing similar viewpoints.

Supremacy Clause. Constitutional provision (Article IV) that declares the Constitution to be "the supreme law of the land."

Suspect Classification. Categorization of individuals by characteristics (such as race) viewed by the courts as raising the suspicion that the classification is designed to discriminate against members of a particular group or groups. Laws or actions based on suspect classifications must satisfy the strict scrutiny test.

Take Care Clause. Constitutional provision (Article II) that requires the president to "take care that the laws be faithfully executed"; often cited as a source of presidential power.

Thirteenth Amendment. Constitutional amendment, ratified in 1865, that abolished slavery and "involuntary servitude."

Traditional Presidency. The presidency prior to 1932. The traditional presidency was a modest office of little power or prestige, secondary to Congress in the national government except under extraordinary circumstances.

Treaties. Formal agreements with other nations; they are negotiated by the president but must be ratified by two-thirds of the Senate.

Unitary System. A political system in which all power ultimately resides within a central government, but in which, for purposes of convenience, local governments may be granted limited authority.

Unreasonable Searches and Seizures. Constitutionally banned attempts to collect evidence using procedures or methods that fail to respect privacy, decency, or the presumption of innocence, thereby violating the Fourth Amendment.

Veto. The power of the president to deny approval of a bill enacted by Congress by refusing to sign the bill into law.

Visuals. Highlighted images of campaigns and official activities that show well on TV, often intentionally manufactured to strengthen the appeal of a candidate, an official, or message.

Voter Turnout. The percentage of eligible voters who actually vote in a given election.

Voting Rights Act of 1965. National legislation that prohibited virtually all racial discrimination in elections (such as the use of literacy tests) and that provided the federal government with the means to enforce that prohibition in states that had a clear voting discrimination history.

Wall of Separation. An interpretation of the First Amendment "Establishment Clause," favored by Thomas Jefferson and many modern civil libertarians, which calls for a strict separation of church and state.

War Powers Resolution. Congressional resolution, enacted in 1973, which was intended to make the president more fully accountable to the Congress in the conduct of military operations.

Warren Court. Period (1953–1969) in which an activist Supreme Court, under Chief Justice Earl Warren, promoted civil rights and greatly expanded the scope of civil liberties.

Winner-Take-All System. An electoral system in which only one candidate can be chosen by voters to represent a well-defined geographic district.

Writ of Certiorari. A legal order used by the Supreme Court to take up cases appealed from the lower courts.

Written Briefs. Written papers explaining the factual background and legal arguments pertaining to cases heard by the Supreme Court.

References

CHAPTER 1 *Introduction*

1. *Federalist No. 1.*
2. Sidney Hillman, *Political Primer for All Americans*, 1944, p. 1. See also Harold Lasswell, *Politics: Who Gets What, When, How* (New York: McGraw-Hill, 1936).
3. *Federalist No. 10.*
4. For the Antifederalist position on direct democracy, see Wood, *Creation of the American Republic;* for a modern view, see Robert Paul Wolff, *In Defense of Anarchism* (New York: Harper, 1970), pp. 21–67.
5. On representative democracy, see Alexander Hamilton, John Jay, and James Madison, *The Federalist Papers*, especially *No. 10.* For a detailed commentary on the Federalists' views on democracy, see Gordon S. Wood, *The Creation of the American Republic* (Chapel Hill: University of North Carolina Press, 1969).
6. On pluralism, see Robert A. Dahl, *A Preface to Democratic Theory* (Chicago: University of Chicago Press, 1956) and Robert A. Dahl and Charles E. Lindblom, *Politics, Economics and Welfare* (New York: Harper, 1953).
7. For a classic elitism argument, see C. Wright Mills, *The Power Elite* (New York: Oxford University Press, 1956). For an interesting view of "circulating elites," see Robert A. Dahl, *A Preface to Democratic Theory* (Chicago: University of Chicago Press, 1956).

CHAPTER 2 *The Constitution*

1. Quoted in Gordon S. Wood, *The Creation of the American Republic, 1776–1787* (New York: W. W. Norton, 1972), p. 267 (capitalization modernized).
2. James Madison, *Federalist No. 10.*
3. Quoted in Wood, *Creation of the American Republic*, p. 525.
4. *Federalist No. 54.*
5. George J. Graham Jr., "Pennsylvania: Representation and the Meaning of Republicanism," in Michael Allen Gillespie and Michael Lienesch, eds., *Ratifying the Constitution* (Lawrence: University Press of Kansas, 1989).
6. 17 U.S. (4 Wheat.) 316 (1819).
7. *Federalist No. 43.*
8. Michael Kammen, *A Machine That Would Go of Itself* (New York: Vintage Books, 1986), p. 11.
9. *McCulloch* v. *Maryland*, 4 Wheaton 316 (1819) [italics omitted].
10. See *United States* v. *Belmont*, 301 U.S. 324 (1937).
11. Wood, *Creation of the American Republic*, pp. 497, 495, 490.

12. Ibid., p. 484.
13. Donald G. Nieman, *Promises to Keep: African-Americans and the Constitutional Order, 1776 to the Present* (New York: Oxford University Press, 1991), p. 9.
14. Wood, *Creation of the American Republic*, p. 486.
15. *Federalist No. 10.*
16. Ibid.
17. Quoted in Wood, *Creation of the American Republic*, p. 548.
18. *Federalist No. 47.*
19. Adam Smith, *An Inquiry into the Nature and Causes of the Wealth of Nations*, Edwin Cannen, ed. (New York: Modern Library, 1937), p. 14.
20. *Federalist No. 51.*
21. Quoted in Herbert Storing, *What the Antifederalists Were For* (Chicago: University of Chicago Press, 1981), p. 72.
22. Ibid.

CHAPTER 3 *Federalism*

1. *Printz* v. *United States,* 117 S. Ct. 2365 (1997).
2. Gordon S. Wood, *The Creation of the American Republic* (New York: Norton, 1972), pp. 524–532.
3. Drawn from David C. Nice, *Federalism: The Politics of Intergovernmental Relations* (New York: St. Martin's Press, 1987), pp. 4–9.
4. The classic statement of the dual federalism principle appears in *Cooley* v. *Board of Wardens of Philadelphia*, 12 Howard 299 (1851).
5. See, for example, *Southern Pacific* v. *Arizona*, 325 U.S. 761 (1945), and *South Carolina State Highway Department* v. *Barnwell Brothers*, 303 U.S. 177 (1938).
6. 1 Cranch (5 U.S.) 137 (1803).
7. 6 Cranch (10 U.S.) 87 (1810).
8. 1 Wheat. (14 U.S.) 304 (1816).
9. *McCulloch* v. *Maryland*, 17 U.S. (4 Wheat.) 316 (1819), at 421.
10. Ibid., at 431, 433.
11. 9 Wheat. (22 U.S.) 1 (1824).
12. See generally David B. Walker, *Toward a Functioning Federalism* (Cambridge, Mass.: Winthrop Publishing, 1981), pp. 51–54.
13. Ibid., p. 61.
14. Ibid., p. 63.
15. See, for example, *United States* v. *E. C. Knight*, 156 U.S. 1 (1895); *Houston E. W. Texas Ry. Co.* v. *United States [The Shreveport Rate Case]*, 234 U.S. 342 (1914); and *Hammer* v. *Dagenhart*, 247 U.S. 251 (1918); see also *Lochner* v. *New*

York, 198 U.S. 45 (1905) and *Adkins* v. *Children's Hospital,* 261 U.S. 525 (1923). But compare *Muller* v. *Oregon,* 208 U.S. 412 (1908).

16. Peter Fearon, *War, Prosperity and Depression: The U.S. Economy 1917–1945* (Lawrence: University Press of Kansas, 1987), pp. 110, 120, 207.

17. Among the New Deal laws invalidated by the Court were the National Labor Relations Act, *Schechter Poultry* v. *United States,* 295 U.S. 495 (1935), and the Bituminous Coal Conservation Act of 1935, *Carter* v. *Carter Coal Co.,* 298 U.S. 238 (1936). The Supreme Court's "switch" occurred in *National Labor Relations Board* v. *Jones & Laughlin Steel Corp.,* 301 U.S. 1 (1937), upholding the National Labor Relations Act.

18. *United States* v. *Lopez,* 514 U.S. 549 (1995).

19. *National League of Cities* v. *Usery,* 426 U.S. 833 (1976); *Garcia* v. *San Antonio Metropolitan Transit Authority,* 469 U.S. 528 (1985).

20. *New York* v. *United States,* 505 U.S. 144 (1992), at 161.

21. *Printz* v. *United States,* 117 S. Ct. 2365 (1997).

22. Morton Grodzins, "The American Federal System," in Robert A. Goldwin, *A Nation of States: Essays on the American Federal System* (Chicago: Rand McNally, 1963), p. 3.

23. *Miranda* v. *Arizona,* 384 U.S. 436 (1966).

24. *Philiadelphia* v. *New Jersey,* 437 U.S. 617 (1978).

25. "Money to Burn," *The Economist,* August 14, 1993, p. 23.

26. Martin Feldstein and Marian Vaillant, "Can State Taxes Redistribute Income?" Working Paper No. 4785 (Cambridge, Mass.: National Bureau of Economic Research, Inc., 1994).

CHAPTER 4 *Civil Liberties*

1. *Texas* v. *Johnson,* 491 U.S. 397 (1989).

2. John Locke, *Second Treatise on Civil Government* (Buffalo, N.Y.: Prometheus Books, 1986), p. 70.

3. Ibid., p. 69.

4. John Stuart Mill, *On Liberty,* ed. David Spitz (New York: W. W. Norton, 1975), pp. 18, 62–63.

5. Holmes quote from *Abrams* v. *United States,* 250 U.S. 616 (1919), Holmes, dissenting. Brandeis quote from *Whitney* v. *California,* 274 U.S. 357 (1927), Brandeis, concurring.

6. *New York Times* v. *Sullivan,* 376 U.S. 255 (1964).

7. *Federalist* No. 84.

8. Abraham Lincoln, "Message to Congress in Special Session, July 4, 1861, in John G. Nicolay and John Hay, *Abraham Lincoln: Complete Works* (New York: The Century Co., 1894), VI: 297–325.

9. *Barron* v. *Baltimore,* 7 Pet. 420 (1833).

10. *Chicago, Burlington, & Quincy Railroad Company* v. *Chicago,* 166 U.S. 226 (1897); *Gitlow* v. *New York,* 268 U.S. 652 (1925).

11. On grand juries, see *Hurtado* v. *California,* 110 U.S. 516 (1884); on unanimous jury verdicts, see *Johnson* v. *Louisiana,* 406 U.S. 356 (1972) and *Apodaca* v. *Oregon,* 406 U.S. 400 (1972).

12. *Board of Education* v. *Pico,* 457 U.S. 853 (1982).

13. Thomas Jefferson, letter to W. S. Smith, November 13, 1787, in *The Papers of Thomas Jefferson,* vol. 12, 1787–1788 (Princeton, NJ: Princeton University Press, 1955), p. 356.

14. *Zurcher* v. *Stanford Daily,* 436 U.S. 547 (1978).

15. Louis Fisher, *Constitutional Dialogues: Interpretation as Political Process* (Princeton, NJ: Princeton University Press, 1988).

16. *Cooper* v. *Aaron,* 358 U.S. 1 (1958).

17. *Martin* v. *Hunter's Lessee,* 14 U.S. (1 Wheat.) 304 (1816), at 347.

18. *Schenck* v. *United States,* 249 U.S. 47 (1919), at 52.

19. *Yates* v. *United States,* 354 U.S. 298 (1957).

20. *Hess* v. *Indiana,* 414 U.S. 105 (1973), at 106.

21. *Chaplinsky* v. *New Hampshire,* 315 U.S. 568 (1942).

22. *Terminiello* v. *Chicago,* 337 U.S. 1 (1949), at 4.

23. *Miller* v. *California,* 413 U.S. 15 (1973).

24. *Jenkins* v. *Georgia,* 418 U.S. 152 (1974); *Pope* v. *Illinois,* 481 U.S. 497 (1977); *Jacobellis* v. *Ohio,* 378 U.S. 184, at 197.

25. *Forsythe County* v. *The Nationalist Movement,* 505 U.S. 123 (1992); *Tinker* v. *Des Moines,* 393 U.S. 503 (1969); *Collin* v. *Village of Skokie,* 578 F.2d. 1197 (1978).

26. *Texas* v. *Johnson,* 491 U.S. 397 (1989); *R. A. V.* v. *St. Paul,* 112 U.S. 377 (1992); *West Virginia* v. *Barnette,* 319 U.S. 624 (1943).

27. *Barnes* v. *Glen Theatre, Inc.,* 501 U.S. 560 (1991).

28. For an early case, see *Near* v. *Minnesota,* 283 U.S. 697 (1931).

29. *New York Times* v. *United States,* 403 U.S. 713 (1971); *United States* v. *Progressive, Inc.,* 467 F. Supp. 990 (W.D.Wis. 1979).

30. *New York Times* v. *Sullivan,* 376 U.S. 225 (1964); *Curtis Publishing Co.* v. *Butts* and *Associated Press* v. *Walker,* 388 U.S. 130 (1967); *Gertz* v. *Robert Welch, Inc.,* 418 U.S. 323 (1974); *Time* v. *Firestone,* 424 U.S. 448 (1976), at 453.

31. *Hustler Magazine* v. *Falwell,* 485 U.S. 46 (1988).

32. *FCC* v. *Pacifica Foundation,* 438 U.S. 726 (1978); *Reno* v. *ACLU,* No. 96-511 (1997).

33. *McDaniel* v. *Paty,* 435 U.S. 618 (1978).

34. *Reynolds* v. *United States,* 98 U.S. 145 (1879); *Wisconsin* v. *Yoder,* 406 U.S. 205 (1972).

35. *Employment Division* v. *Smith,* 494 U.S. 872 (1990).

36. *Church of the Lukumi Babalu Aye* v. *City of Hialeah,* 508 U.S. 520 (1993), at 4588, 4594.

37. *Board of Education of the Westside Community Schools* v. *Mergens,* 496 U.S. 226 (1990) [unsponsored prayer]; *Marsh* v. *Chambers,* 463 U.S. 783 (1983) [prayer in legislative chamber]; *Lynch* v. *Donnelly,* 465 U.S. 688 (1984) and

Allegheny County v. *American Civil Liberties Union, Greater Pittsburgh Chapter,* 492 U.S. 573 (1989) [holiday displays]; *Mueller* v. *Allen,* 463 U.S. 388 (1983) [incentives]; and *Lee* v. *Weisman,* 505 U.S. 577 (1992) [graduation prayer].

38. *Walz* v. *Tax Commission,* 397 U.S. 664 (1971), at 669.
39. *Edwards* v. *South Carolina,* 372 U.S. 229 (1963); *Cox* v. *Louisiana,* 379 U.S. 559 (1965); *Madsen* v. *Women's Health Center,* 512 US. 753 (1994).
40. *NAACP* v. *Alabama* ex. rel. *Patterson,* 357 U.S. 449 (1958); *Hurley* v. *Irish-American Gay, Lesbian, and Bisexual Group of Boston,* 115 S.Ct. 2338 (1995); *New York State Club Association* v. *City of New York,* 487 U.S. 1 (1988); *Roberts* v. *United States Jaycees,* 468 U.S. 609 (1984).
41. *Mapp* v. *Ohio,* 367 U.S. 643 (1961).
42. *United States* v. *Leon,* 468 U.S. 897 (1984).
43. *Miranda* v. *Arizona,* 384 U.S. 436 (1966).
44. *Fulminante* v. *Arizona,* 499 U.S. 279 (1991).
45. George F. Cole, *Criminal Justice: Law and Politics,* 4th ed. (Monterey, Calif.: Brooks/Cole, 1984), p. 139. By one estimate, 4.1 percent of criminal cases are lost due to the *Miranda* warnings. This relatively high estimate takes into account the decreased confession rate after *Miranda* was implemented. Paul G. Cassell, "How Many Criminals Has *Miranda* Set Free?" *Wall Street Journal,* March 1, 1995, p. A15.
46. *Furman* v. *Georgia,* 408 U.S. 238 (1972); *Gregg* v. *Georgia,* 428 U.S. 153 (1976); *Woodsen* v. *North Carolina,* 428 U.S. 280 (1976).
47. Linda Greenhouse, "Supreme Court Puts Sharp Curbs on Death Row Appeals," *The New York Times,* April 17, 1991, p. A1.
48. *Penry* v. *Lynaugh,* 492 U.S. 302 (1989); Stanford v. Kentucky, 492 U.S. 361 (1991).
49. *McCleskey* v. *Kemp,* 481 U.S. 279 (1987); *Gideon* v. *Wainwright,* 372 U.S. 335 (1963); *Smith* v. *Texas,* 311 U.S. 128 (1940); *Batson* v. *Kentucky,* 476 U.S. 79 (1986); *J. E. B.* v. *Alabama,* 511 U.S. 127 (1994).
50. *Hutto* v. *Finney,* 437 U.S. 679 (1978); see also *Wilson* v. *Seiter,* 501 U.S. 294 (1991).
51. Quoted in Samuel D. Warren and Louis D. Brandeis, "The Right to Privacy," *Harvard Law Review* 4 (December 15, 1890), 195; *Olmstead* v. *United States,* 277 U.S. 438 (1928), at 478.
52. *Rochin* v. *California,* 342 U.S. 165 (1951), at 166, 172.
53. *Griswold* v. *Connecticut,* 381 U.S. 479 (1965), at 485.
54. *Meyer* v. *Nebraska,* 262 U.S. 390 (1923), at 399.
55. *Pierce* v. *Society of Sisters,* 268 U.S. 510 (1925), at 534.
56. *Roe* v. *Wade,* 410 U.S. 113 (1973).
57. *Harris* v. *McRae,* 448 U.S. 297 (1980), at 316; *Planned Parenthood* v. *Danforth,* 428 U.S. 52 (1976); *Ohio* v. *Akron Center for Reproductive Health,* 497 U.S. 502 (1990); *Thornburgh* v. *American College of Obstetricians and Gynecologists,* 476 U.S. 747 (1986).
58. *Webster* v. *Reproductive Health Services,* 492 U.S. 490 (1989).
59. *Planned Parenthood of Southeastern Pennsylvania* v. *Casey,* 505 U.S. 833 (1992).
60. *Rust* v. *Sullivan,* 500 U.S. 173 (1991).
61. *Loving* v. *Virginia,* 388 U.S. 1 (1967).
62. *Bowers* v. *Hardwick,* 478 U.S. 186 (1986); *Romer* v. *Evans,* No. 94–1039 (1996).

CHAPTER 5 *Civil Rights*

1. *Korematsu* v. *United States,* 323 U.S. 214 (1944), at 243.
2. Ibid., at 239.
3. William O. Douglas, *The Court Years, 1939–1975: The Autobiography of William O. Douglas* (New York: Random House, 1980), p. 280.
4. *San Antonio Independent School District* v. *Rodriguez,* 411 U.S. 1 (1973); *Bowers* v. *Hardwick,* 478 U.S. 186 (1986).
5. Peter Kolchin, "Slavery: I: The Institution of Slavery," in Eric Foner and John A. Garraty, eds., *The Reader's Companion to American History* (Boston: Houghton-Mifflin, 1991), p. 991.
6. Wendell Phillips Garrison and Francis Jackson Garrison, *William Lloyd Garrison, 1805–1879* (New York: Arno Press, 1969), III: 52.
7. 19 Howard (60 U.S.) 393 (1857).
8. Lincoln to Horace Greeley, August 22, 1862, in John G. Nicolay and John Hay, *Abraham Lincoln: Complete Works* (New York: Century, 1894), II: 227–228.
9. *Slaughterhouse Cases,* 16 Wall. (83 U.S.) 36 (1873); *Civil Rights Cases,* 109 U.S. 3 (1883).
10. Samuel Eliot Morrison, *The Oxford History of the American People* (New York: Oxford University Press, 1965), p. 793.
11. Donald G. Nieman, *Promises to Keep: African-Americans and the Constitutional Order, 1776 to the Present* (New York: Oxford University Press, 1991), p. 107.
12. *Missouri ex rel. Gaines* v. *Canada,* 305 U.S. 337 (1938).
13. *Sweatt* v. *Painter,* 339 U.S. 629 (1950).
14. *McClaurin* v. *Oklahoma State Regents,* 339 U.S. 637 (1950).
15. *Brown* v. *Board of Education,* 347 U.S. 483 (1954), at 495; *Bolling* v. *Sharpe,* 347 U.S. 497 (1954), at 500.
16. *Brown* v. *Board of Education,* 349 U.S. 294 (1955), at 301.
17. Donald G. Nieman, *Promises to Keep* (New York: Oxford, 1991), p. 177.
18. Nieman, *Promises to Keep,* p. 150.
19. *Heart of Atlanta Motel* v. *United States,* 379 U.S. 241 (1964); *Katzenbach* v. *McClung,* 379 U.S. 294 (1964); *South Carolina* v. *Katzenbach,* 383 U.S. 301 (1966).

20. *Allen v. State Board of Elections,* 393 U.S. 544 (1969); *Georgia v. United States,* 411 U.S. 526 (1973).

21. *The Report of the National Advisory Commission on Civil Disorders,* 1968, p. 1.

22. See, for example, *Pasadena Board of Education v. Spangler,* 427 U.S. 424 (1976); *Milliken v. Bradley,* 418 U.S. 717 (1979).

23. Quoted in "40 Years After Brown, Segregation Persists," *New York Times,* May 18, 1954, p. B7.

24. *Goesart v. Cleary,* 335 U.S. 464 (1948).

25. *Hoyt v. Florida,* 368 U.S. 57 (1961), at 62.

26. *Reed v. Reed,* 404 U.S. 71 (1971); *Frontiero v. Richardson,* 411 U.S. 677 (1973).

27. *Mississippi University for Women v. Hogan,* 458 U.S. 718 (1982), at 726.

28. *Craig v. Boren,* 429 U.S. 190 (1976); *Mississippi v. Hogan,* 458 U.S. 718 (1982); *Orr v. Orr,* 440 U.S. 268 (1979); *United States v. Virginia,* No. 94–1941 (1996); *Meritor Savings Bank v. Vinson,* 477 U.S. 57 (1986); *Rostker v. Goldberg,* 453 U.S. 57 (1981).

29. "Women in Elective Office 1997," Center for the American Woman and Politics, National Information Bank on Women in Public Office, Eagleton Institute of Politics, Rutgers University.

30. Russell Thornton, "Population," in Mary B. Davis, ed., *Native America in the Twentieth Century: An Encyclopedia* (New York: Garland Publishing, 1994), pp. 461–463.

31. Ward Churchill, "American Indian Movement," in Davis, *Native America,* pp. 35–38.

32. *Statistical Abstract of the United States,* 1993, tables 733, 734, 741, pp. 468, 471; "This Land Is Their Land," *Time,* January 14, 1991, p. 18.

33. "Experiment in Tribal Justice: 2 Youths Are Banished," *New York Times,* September 3, 1994, p. 6.

34. *Statistical Abstract of the United States,* 1992, table 14, p. 16; Frank L. Schick and Renee Schick, *Statistical Handbook of U.S. Hispanics* (Phoenix: Oryx Press, 1991), p. 26.

35. See generally Tatcho Mindiola, "Population Growth and Distribution," in Nicolás Kanellos, ed., *The Hispanic-American Almanac* (Detroit: Gale Research, 1993), pp. 199–207.

36. *Statistical Abstract of the United States,* 1992, table 698, p. 447; Mindiola, "Population Growth," pp. 205–207.

37. Guadalupe San Miguel, Jr., "Education," in Kannellos, *Hispanic-American Almanac,* pp. 302–307; Schick and Schick, *Statistical Handbook,* p. 99; Cary Davis, Carl Haub, and JoAnne L. Willette, "U.S. Hispanics: Changing the Face of America," in Edna Acosta-Belén and Barbara R. Sjostrom, eds., *The Hispanic Experience in the United States: Contemporary Issues and Perspectives* (New York: Praeger, 1988), pp. 38–42.

38. This section draws heavily from Ronald Takaki, *Strangers from a Different Shore: A History of Asian Americans* (New York: Penguin Books, 1989).

39. *Bowers v. Hardwick,* 478 U.S. 186 (1986).

40. *Bakke v. Regents of the University of California,* 438 U.S. 265 (1978).

41. *Fullilove v. Klutznick,* 448 U.S. 448 (1980); *Firefighters Local Union No. 1794 v. Stotts,* 467 U.S. 561 (1984).

42. *Adarand Constructors, Inc. v. Pena,* 115 S.Ct. 2097 (1995); *Miller v. Johnson,* 115 S.Ct. 2475 (1995).

43. *Haywood v. State of Texas,* No. 94-50569 (5th CCA).

CHAPTER 6 *Political Culture*

1. Arthur Asa Berger, *Political Culture and Public Opinion* (New Brunswick, New Jersey: Transaction Publishers, 1989), p. 2.

2. See, for example, Aaron Wildavsky, "Choosing Preferences by Constructing Institutions: A Cultural Theory of Preference Formation," in Berger, *Political Culture,* pp. 21–46.

3. George H. Gallup, *The Gallup Poll: Public Opinion 1935–1948* (New York: Random House, 1972), I: 259, 534. In a 1992 survey, over 70 percent of those who responded disagreed with the statement "This country would be better off if we just stayed at home and did not concern ourselves with problems in other parts of the world" (1992 National Election Study).

4. See, for example, Richard Hofstadter, *The American Political Tradition* (New York: Vintage Books, 1972), p. xxxviii.

5. See, among many examples, Alexis de Tocqueville, *Democracy in America,* ed. J. P. Mayer (Garden City, N.Y.: Anchor Books, 1969); Louis Hartz, *The Liberal Tradition in America* (New York: Harcourt, Brace, 1955); Richard Rose, "How Exceptional Is American Government?" *Studies in Public Policy* 150 (Glasgow: Center for the Study of Public Policy, University of Strathclyde, 1985); and Seymour Martin Lipset, "American Exceptionalism Reaffirmed," in Byron E. Shafer, ed., *Is America Different?* (Oxford: Clarendon Press, 1991), pp. 1–45.

6. Tocqueville, *Democracy in America,* pp. 9, 509, 290.

7. Hartz, *Liberal Tradition,* pp. 1–9; Lipset, "American Exceptionalism Reaffirmed," pp. 6–8.

8. Clinton Rossiter, *Conservatism in America* (New York: Vintage Books, 1962), p. 72.

9. Quoted in Herbert McClosky and John Zeller, *The American Ethos: Public Attitudes Toward Capitalism and Democracy* (Cambridge, Mass.: Harvard University Press, 1984), pp. 112–113.

10. Ibid., p. 108.

11. Gerald F. Seib, "Washington Wire," *The Wall Street Journal,* December 16, 1994, p. A1.

12. Tocqueville, *Democracy in America,* p. 270.

13. Lipset, "American Exceptionalism Reaffirmed," p. 33.

14. For an excellent discussion of Americans' historic commitment to the rule of law and of judges, see Robert G. McCloskey, *The American Supreme Court,* rev. ed. (Chicago: University of Chicago Press, 1994), pp. 6–10.

15. David M. Potter, *The Impending Crisis, 1848–1861* (New York: Harper and Row, 1976), pp. 47–48.

16. Tocqueville, *Democracy in America,* pp. 294–301.

17. National Election Study, 1992; William G. Mayer, *The Changing American Mind: How and Why American Public Opinion Changed Between 1960 and 1988* (Ann Arbor: University of Michigan Press, 1992), p. 379; McCloskey, *American Ethos,* p. 26; Mayer, *Changing American Mind,* p. 381.

18. Charles W. Dunn, *Religion in American Politics* (Washington, D.C.: CQ Press, 1989), p. xx.

19. Linda L. M. Bennett and Stephen Earl Bennett, *Living With Leviathan: Americans Coming to Terms with Big Government* (Lawrence, Kansas: The University Press of Kansas, 1990), p. 51; Lewis Carroll, *Through the Looking Glass,* ch. 6.

20. Arthur Sanders, *Making Sense of Politics* (Ames: Iowa State University Press, 1990), p. 19.

21. According to the 1994 National Election Study, for example, 47.8 percent of Americans described themselves as "moderate," "slightly liberal," or "slightly conservative." Another 26.6 percent did not know where to classify themselves or hadn't thought much about it.

22. See generally Hartz, *Liberal Tradition,* pp. 7–8.

23. Bernard Bailyn, *The Ideological Origins of the American Revolution* (Cambridge, Mass.: Harvard University Press, 1967), pp. 18–20; Gordon S. Wood, *The Creation of the American Republic, 1776–1787* (New York: W. W. Norton, 1972), pp. 44–45.

24. William H. Flanigan and Nancy H. Zingale, *Political Behavior of the American Electorate,* 8th ed. (Washington, D.C.: CQ Press, 1994), p. 138.

25. National Election Study, 1996

26. See Sanders, *Making Sense,* pp. 23–26.

27. Barbara Ritter Dailey, "Anne Hutchinson," in Eric Foner and John A. Garraty, eds., *The Reader's Companion to American History* (Boston: Houghton Mifflin, 1991), pp. 529–531.

28. Tocqueville, *Democracy in America,* p. 255.

29. Herbert McClosky and Alida Brill, *Dimensions of Tolerance: What Americans Believe About Civil Liberties* (New York: Russell Sage Foundation, 1983), pp. 53–54.

30. First two statistics from National Election Study, 1996; last from Mayer, *Changing American Mind,* p. 79.

31. Paul R. Abramson, *Political Attitudes in America* (San Francisco: W. H. Freeman, 1983), pp. 11–14.

32. Bailyn, *Ideological Origins of the American Revolution,* pp. 123–127.

33. Richard Hofstadter, "The Paranoid Style in American Politics," in *"The Paranoid Style in American Politics" and Other Essays* (New York: Knopf, 1965), pp. 3–40.

34. Quoted in Arthur Schlesinger, Jr., *The Disuniting of America* (New York: W. W. Norton, 1972), p. 26.

35. Ibid, p. 26.

36. Ibid., p. 138.

CHAPTER 7 *Public Opinion*

1. See Michael Barone, *Our Country: The Shaping of America from Roosevelt to Reagan* (New York: Free Press, 1990), pp. 431–432. On the Tet Offensive, see Peter Braestrup, *Big Story* (Boulder, CO: Westview Press, 1977).

2. M. Kent Jennings and Richard G. Niemi, *The Political Character of Adolescents: The Influence of Families and Schools* (Princeton: Princeton University Press, 1974), p. 231.

3. Timothy E. Cook, "Democracy and Community in American Children's Literature," in Ernest J. Yanarella and Lee Sigelman, eds., *Political Mythology and Political Fiction* (New York: Greenwood Press, 1988), p. 41.

4. Jennings and Niemi, *Political Character of Adolescence,* pp. 38–39, 87.

5. Russell J. Dalton, "The Pathways of Parental Socialization," *American Politics Quarterly* 10 (April 1982): pp. 142–148.

6. Ibid., pp. 140–141.

7. Richard E. Dawson and Kenneth Prewitt, *Political Socialization* (Boston: Little, Brown, 1969), pp. 143–175. Dawson and Prewitt divide the influence of schools into "classroom" and "nonclassroom" forms.

8. Ellen Condliffe Lagemann, "Education: to 1877," in Eric Foner and John A. Garraty, eds., *The Reader's Companion to American History* (Boston: Houghton Mifflin, 1991), p. 314.

9. Quoted in Dawson and Prewitt, *Political Socialization,* p. 163; Jennings and Niemi, *Political Character of Adolescence,* pp. 205–206.

10. Paul R. Abramson, *Political Attitudes in America: Formation and Change* (San Francisco: W. H. Freeman, 1983), pp. 177–182, 243.

11. V. O. Key, *Public Opinion and American Democracy* (New York: Knopf, 1964), pp. 341–343.

12. For information in this section, see generally Walter A. Rosenbaum, *Political Culture* (New York: Praeger, 1975), pp. 13–16; and M. Margaret Conway, *Political Participation in the United States* (Washington, D.C.: CQ Press, 1991), pp. 55–58, 175–177.

13. Jennings and Niemi, *Political Character of Adolescence,* p. 241.

14. Dawson and Prewitt, *Political Socialization,* p. 184.
15. Ibid., pp. 191–194.
16. Doris A. Graber, *Mass Media and American Politics,* 4th ed. (Washington, D.C.: CQ Press, 1993), pp. 206–208.
17. Ibid., p. 208.
18. Robert S. Erikson, Norman R. Luttbeg, and Kent L. Tedin, *American Public Opinion: Its Origins, Content, and Impact,* 4th ed. (New York: Macmillan, 1991), pp. 53–54.
19. As of March 1975, Americans favored the Equal Rights Amendment by 58 to 24 percent (*The Gallup Poll: Public Opinion 1972–1977* [Wilmington, Del.: Scholarly Resources], I:447).
20. Key, *Public Opinion,* pp. 413–422.
21. John Leo, "Lessons from a Sanitized War," *U.S. News & World Report,* March 18, 1991, p. 26; Helio Fred Garcia, "On Strategy and War: Public Relations Lessons from the Gulf," *Public Relations Quarterly* 36 (Summer 1991): 29–32.
22. Quoted in William Safire, *Safire's Political Dictionary* (New York: Random House, 1978), p. 577.
23. Michael X. Delli Carpini and Scott Keeter, "Stability and Change in the U.S. Public's Knowledge of Politics," *Public Opinion Quarterly* 55 (1991), 591–593.
24. Ibid.
25. National Election Study, 1992.
26. Ibid.
27. See, for example, V. O. Key, *The Responsible Electorate* (Cambridge, Mass.: Harvard University Press, 1966); and Norman H. Nie, Sidney Verba, and John R. Petrocik, *The Changing American Voter* (Cambridge, Mass.: Harvard University Press, 1976).
28. Graber, *Mass Media and American Politics,* p. 225.
29. See, for example, Scott Keeter and Cliff Zukin, *Uninformed Choice: The Failure of the New Presidential Nominating System* (New York: Praeger, 1983).
30. National Election Study, 1992.
31. Ibid.
32. Ibid.
33. Ibid.
34. Ibid.
35. Ibid.
36. Lee Sigelman and Susan Welch, *Black Americans' Views of Racial Inequality: The Dream Deferred* (New York: Cambridge University Press, 1991), p. 43.
37. Sigelman and Welch, *Black Americans' Views,* pp. 135–139.
38. Susan Welch and Lee Sigelman, "The Politics of Hispanic Americans: Insights from National Surveys, 1980–1988," *Social Science Quarterly* 74 (March 1993): pp. 76–94.
39. Richard G. Niemi, John Mueller, and Tom W. Smith, *Trends in Public Opinion: A Compendium of Survey Data* (New York: Greenwood Press, 1989), pp. 180, 185.
40. Sigelman and Welch, *Black Americans' Views,* p. 53; National Election Study, 1992.
41. National Election Study, 1992.
42. Ibid.
43. Ibid.
44. David Maraniss, "Duke and the Hidden Vote," *Washington Post,* September 15, 1991.
45. Tom W. Smith, "That Which We Call Welfare by Any Other Name Would Smell Sweeter: An Analysis of the Impact of Question Wording on Response Patterns," *Public Opinion Quarterly* 51 (Spring 1987): p. 77.

CHAPTER 8 *Interest Groups*
1. *Taxman* v. *Board of Education of the Township of Piscataway;* Marcia Coyle, "Race Tops the Docket." *National Law Journal,* October 6, 1997; Joan Biskupic, "Rights Groups Pay to Settle Bias Case." *Washington Post,* November 22, 1997, p. A1.
2. Jeffrey M. Berry, *The Interest Group Society,* 3rd ed. (New York: Longman, 1997), p. 5.
3. *Federalist No. 10 (emphasis added).*
4. Classifications by issue area or political purpose are commonplace. For example, James Q. Wilson, *Political Organizations* (New York: Basic Books, 1973), devotes chapters to labor unions, business associations, and civil rights organizations.
5. For an example of such a classifications scheme—and the one drawn on most heavily in this section—see Jack L. Walker, Jr., *Mobilizing Interest Groups in America* (Ann Arbor: University of Michigan Press, 1991).
6. Walker, *Mobilizing Interests,* p. 59.
7. Michael Weisskopf, "Businesses Desert Key Health Bills," *Washington Post,* August 10, 1994, p. A1.
8. Walker, *Mobilizing Interest Groups,* p. 59.
9. Ibid.
10. Ibid.
11. *Evans* v. *Romer,* Supreme Court of Colorado, 94 SA 48 (1994).
12. Philip A. Mundo, *Interest Groups: Cases and Characteristics* (Chicago: Nelson-Hall Publishers, 1992), p. 176.
13. Wilson, *Political Organizations,* p. 323.
14. On religious interest groups, see generally James L. Gouth, John C. Green, Lyman A. Kellstedt, and Corwin E. Smidt, "Onward Christian Soldiers: Religious Activist Groups in American Politics," in Cigler and Loomis, *Interest Group Politics,* 4th ed., pp. 55–76.
15. Berry, *Lobbying for the People,* p. 6.
16. Ibid., pp. 7–9.
17. V. O. Key, *Politics, Parties, and Pressure Groups* (New York: Thomas Y. Crowell, 1964), p. 11.
18. Ibid.

19. Allen J. Cigler and Burdett A. Loomis, *Interest Group Politics,* 4th ed. (Washington, D.C.: CQ Press, 1995), p. 7.

20. The traditional view is summarized in Mancur Olson, Jr., *The Logic of Collective Action: Public Goods and the Theory of Groups* (Cambridge, Mass.: Harvard University Press, 1965), pp. 4–7.

21. Wilson, *Political Organizations,* pp. 39–44. Wilson uses the term *solidary* instead of *social* benefits.

22. Ibid., pp. 45–51. Again, Wilson's terminology differs; he uses the term *purposive* instead of *ideological* incentives.

23. Walker, *Mobilizing Interest Groups,* p. 49.

24. Wilson, *Political Organizations,* pp. 197–198.

25. Olson, *The Logic of Collective Action,* pp. 9–16.

26. Walker, *Mobilizing Interest Groups,* pp. 85–94.

27. Sidney Verba, Kay Lehman Schlozman and Henry E. Brady, *Voice and Equality: Civic Volunteerism in American Politics* (Cambridge: Harvard University Press, 1995), pp. 190, 291–5, 319.

28. Hedrick Smith, *The Power Game: How Washington Works* (New York: Ballantine Books, 1988), pp. 230–235.

29. Ibid., pp. 235–238.

30. Alan Rosenthal, *The Third House: Lobbyists and Lobbying in the States* (Washington, D.C.: CQ Press, 1993), pp. 152–153.

31. Richard Rose, *The Postmodern Presidency,* p. 70.

32. Hugh Heclo, "Issue Networks and the Executive Establishment," in Anthony King, ed., *The New American Political System* (Washington, D.C.: American Enterprise Institute, 1978), pp. 102–103.

33. *Bowers* v. *Hardwick,* 478 U.S. 186 (1986).

34. *Geduldig* v. *Aiello,* 417 U.S. 484 (1974), reversed by the Pregnancy Discrimination Act of 1978.

35. P.L. 102–166, November 7, 1991.

36. Walker, *Mobilizing Interest Groups,* p. 182.

37. Ibid., pp. 162–164, 166.

38. Paul Rauber, "Under the Influence," *Sierra* (September/October 1994), p. 28.

39. This discussion borrows heavily from Burdett A. Loomis and Allan J. Cigler, "Introduction: The Changing Nature of Interest Group Politics," in Allan J. Cigler and Burdett A. Loomis, eds., *Interest Group Politics,* 4th ed. (Washington, D.C.: CQ Press, 1995), pp. 1–2.

40. Advertisement in the *New York Times,* April 6, 1993, p. A17.

41. Phillip Longman, "Catastrophic Follies," *The New Republic* (August 1989): 16–18.

42. *Congressional Ethics: History, Facts, Controversy* (Washington, D.C.: CQ Press, 1992), pp. 117–144.

43. "The Man Who Tried to Buy Washington," *Congressional Quarterly Weekly Report,* November 27, 1989, pp. 18–24.

44. Richard J. Hrebenar, *Interest Group Politics in America* (Armonk, NY: M.E. Sharpe, 1997), p. 201; "Study Documents How Money Followed Power Shift on Capitol Hill," Press Release, Center for Responsive Politics, November 25, 1997.

45. Center for Responsive Politics, "Beyond the Limits," February 1997.

46. Quoted in Elizabeth Drew, *Politics and Money: The New Road to Corruption* (New York: Macmillan, 1983), p. 146.

47. 18 U.S.C. 207; Executive Order No. 1 (January 21, 1993).

48. Dean Baquet, "Ex-Aide Is Now Lobbyist with White House Ties," *New York Times,* May 12, 1994, pp. A1, B10.

CHAPTER 9 *Political Parties*

1. *The Patriot Party of Pennsylvania* v. *Mitchell,* 826 F. Supp. 926 (1993).

2. E. E. Schattschneider, *The Semisovereign People: A Realist's View of Democracy in America* (1960; Hinsdale, Ill.: Dryden Press, 1975), pp. 46–59.

3. Gerald M. Pomper, *Passions and Interests: Political Party Concepts of American Democracy* (Lawrence: University Press of Kansas, 1992), pp. 2–4.

4. William Nisbet Chambers, "Party Development in the American Mainstream," in William Nisbet Chambers and Walter Dean Burnham, eds., *The American Party Systems: Stages of Political Development,* 2nd ed. (New York: Oxford University Press, 1975), p. 6.

5. V. O. Key, *Politics, Parties, and Pressure Groups,* pp. 200–201; Walter Dean Burnham, "Party Systems in the Political Process," in Chambers and Burnham, *The American Party Systems,* p. 281.

6. Henry Fairlie, *The Parties: Republicans and Democrats in This Century* (New York: St. Martin's Press, 1978), p. 12.

7. 1997 Statistical Abstract, Table 461, p. 287.

8. CNN Exit Poll <http://allpolitics.com/1996/elections/natl.exit.poll/index1.html>; *New York Times,* Nov. 11, 1994, p. 84.

9. Warren E. Miller and Santa A. Traugett, *American Election Studies Data Sourcebook, 1952–1982* (Cambridge, Mass.: Harvard University Press, 1909), p. 81; 1997 Statistical Abstract, Table 461, p. 287; National Election Studies, 1992, 1996.

10. Federal Election Commission; L. Sandy Maisel, ed. *Political Parties and Elections in the United States* (New York: Garland Publishing, 1991): I:251–258, II:943–950.

11. Richard Rose, *The Postmodern Presidency: George Bush Meets the World,* 2d ed. (Chatham, N.J.: Chatham House, 1991), pp. 118–124; "Presidential Success History," *Congressional Quarterly Weekly Report,* December 31, 1994, p. 3620.

12. CQ Almanac, 1997, pp. 6–8.

13. Janet Hook, "Republicans Vote in Lock Step, But Unity May Not Last Long," *Congressional Quarterly Weekly Report,* February 18, 1995, p. 495.

14. David S. Cloud, "GOP's Balancing Act Gets Tricky As Budget Amendment Stalls," *Congressional Quarterly Weekly Report,* March 4, 1995, pp. 671–676.

15. Sheldon Goldman and Elliot Slotnick, "Clinton's First-Term Judiciary: Many Bridges to Cross," *Judicature* 80 (May-June), 1997, p. 261.

16. Walter Dean Burnham, *Critical Elections and the Mainsprings of American Politics* (New York: W. W. Norton, 1970), p. 4.

17. For a variety of viewpoints on these questions, see Byron Shafer, ed., *The End of Realignment? Interpreting American Electoral Eras* (Madison: University of Wisconsin Press, 1991).

18. On the concept of realignment, see, in addition to the works cited above, James L. Sundquist, *Dynamics of the Party System: Alignment and Realignment of Political Parties in the United States,* rev. ed. (Washington, D.C.: Brookings Institution, 1983) and William H. Flanigan and Nancy H. Zingale, *The Political Behavior of the American Electorate,* 8th ed. (Washington, D.C.: CQ Press, 1994).

19. William Nisbet Chambers, "From National Faction to National Party," in William Nisbet Chambers, *The First Party System: Federalists and Republicans* (New York: John Wiley & Sons, 1972), pp. 48–49; and Morton Grodzins, "Political Parties and Issues to 1800," in ibid., pp. 57–66.

20. Paul Goodman, "The First American Party System," in Chambers and Burnham, *The American Party Systems,* pp. 85–89.

21. Daniel Walker Howe, *The Political Culture of the American Whigs* (Chicago: University of Chicago Press, 1979) and Arthur M. Schlesinger, *The Age of Jackson* (Boston, Little, Brown, 1945).

22. Walter Dean Burnham, "Party Systems and the Political Process," in Chambers and Burnham, *American Party Systems,* p. 300.

23. On GOPAC, see Jonathan D. Salant, "Ethics Spotlight Puts Heat on Speaker Gingrich," *Congressional Quarterly Weekly Report,* March 4, 1995, pp. 657–661.

24. Thomas B. Edsall, "Will the GOP Go the Way of All Democrats?" *Washington Post National Weekly Edition,* February 27–March 5, 1995, pp. 23–24.

25. Rhodes Cook, "Clinton's Danger Zone: The Geographic 'L,'" *Congressional Quarterly Weekly Report,* November 19, 1994, p. 3382. 1996 data supplied by author.

CHAPTER 10 *Campaigns and Elections*

1. *Federalist No. 52.*

2. *Federalist No. 10.*

3. Quoted in *Federalist No. 53.*

4. Marc W. Kruman, "Suffrage," in Eric Foner and John A. Garraty, eds., *The Reader's Companion to American History* (Boston: Houghton Mifflin, 1991), pp. 1043–1047.

5. *Oregon v. Mitchell,* 400 U.S. 112 (1970).

6. See *Guinn and Beal v. United States,* 238 U.S. 347 (1915); *Myers v. Anderson,* 238 U.S. 368 (1915); *Lassiter v. Northampton Election Board,* 360 U.S. 45 (1959); *Breedlove v. Suttles,* 302 U.S. 277 (1967); and *Butler v. Thompson,* 341 U.S. 937 (1951) (per curiam).

7. *Smith v. Allwright,* 321 U.S. 649 (1944).

8. *Katzenbach v. Morgan,* 384 U.S. 641 (1966).

9. See *Colegrave v. Green,* 328 U.S. 549 (1946).

10. *Baker v. Carr,* 369 U.S. 186 (1962; *Reynolds v. Sims*), 377 U.S. 533 (1964).

11. *Sailors v. Board of Education,* 387 U.S. 195 (1967); *Dusch v. Davis,* 387 U.S. 112 (1967); *Abate v. Mundt,* 403 U.S. 182 (1971).

12. *Davis v. Bandemer,* 478 U.S. 109 (1986).

13. *Miller v. Johnson,* 63 U.S.L.W. 476 (1995). See also *Shaw v. Reno,* 113 S. Ct. 2816 (1993).

14. Richard A. Watson, *The Presidential Contest,* 3d ed. (Washington, D.C.: CQ Press, 1988), p. 60.

15. In practice, state laws requiring the electors to vote for the candidates to whom they are pledged are unenforceable.

16. To ensure that New Hampshire would remain the first primary state, its legislature passed a law setting its primary one week before the first primary held in any other state (New Hampshire Revised Statutes Annotated 653:9 [1993]).

17. Quoted in David Frum, "Righter Than Newt," *Atlantic Monthly* (March 1995), p. 94; Ronald D. Elving, "Gramm Launches Campaign Stressing Familiar Themes," *Congressional Quarterly Weekly Report,* February 25, 1995, p. 630.

18. Stephen J. Wayne, *The Road to the White House 1992: The Politics of Presidential Elections* (New York: St. Martin's Press, 1992), p. 91.

19. Jack W. Germond and Jules Witcover, "Presidential Debates: An Overview," in Austin Ranney, ed., *The Past and Future of Presidential Debates* (Washington, D.C.: The American Enterprise Institute, 1979), pp. 196, 192.

20. F. Christopher Arterton, "Campaign '92: Strategies and Tactics of the Candidates," in Gerald M. Pomper, ed., *The Election of 1992: Reports and Interpretations* (Chatham, N.J.: Chatham House Publishers, 1993), p. 96.

21. Germond and Witcover, "Presidential Debates," p. 192.

22. *Vital Statistics on American Politics,* p. 209. Excludes third party candidates.

23. Clyde Wilcox, *The Latest American Revolution: The 1994 Elections and Their Implications for Governance* (New York: St. Martin's Press, 1995), p. 23; Juliana Gruenwald and Deborah Kalb, "Despite Push, Democrats Fail to Topple GOP." *CQ Weekly Report,* November 9, 1996, 3225–3229.

24. In 1992, for example, the total spent on all elections was $3.2 billion; the amount spent on the presidential election was $550 million. See Herbert E. Alexander, *Financing Politics: Money, Elections, and Political Reform,* 4th ed. (Washington, D.C.: CQ Press, 1992), pp. 79–81.

25. *New York Times,* November 9, 1994, p. B1.

26. Jefferson to Samuel Harrison Smith, September 21, 1814, in Saul K. Padover, ed., *A Jefferson Profile As Revealed in His Letters* (New York: John Day, 1956), p. 245.

27. Alexander, *Financing Politics,* p. 12.

28. *Buckley* v. *Valeo,* 424 U.S. 1 (1976), at 20, 21.

29. Frank J. Sorauf, *Inside Campaign Finance: Myths and Realities* (New Haven: Yale University Press, 1992), pp. 49–50.

30. Ibid., pp. 49–50.

31. *Federal Election Commission v. National Conservative Political Action Committee,* 470 U.S. 480 (1985); Gabriel Kahn, "Foley, North Top Two Targets of Independent Expenditures," *Roll Call,* November 7, 1994.

32. Common Cause, "The Money Trail," <http://www.commoncause.org/soft_money/quanda.htm>.

33. *New York Times,* November 9, 1994, p. 88.

34. Lydia Saad, "Americans Not Holding Their Breath on Campaign Finance Reform," *The Gallup Poll,* October 11, 1997 <http://www.gallup.com/poll.news/9710//.htm>.

35. Ken Auletta, "On and Off the Bus: Lessons from Campaign '92," in *1-800-President* (New York: Twentieth Century Fund, 1993), pp. 64–65.

36. Doris A. Graber, *Mass Media in American Politics,* 4th ed. (Washington: CQ Press, 1993), pp. 251–252.

37. Gwen Ifill, "The Clinton Team's 'Utility Infielder' Is Becoming a Major-League Hitter," *New York Times,* September 1, 1992, p. A15.

38. Kathleen Hall Jamieson, *Packaging the Presidency: A History and Criticism of Presidential Campaign Advertising* (New York: Oxford, 1984), p. 452.

39. For a discussion of this problem, see Robert J. Samuelson, "Overworked Americans," *Newsweek,* March 16, 1992, p. 50, and "Breaking Point," *Newsweek,* March 6, 1995, pp. 56, 92.

40. *Congressional Quarterly Weekly Report,* February 6, 1993, p. 264.

41. Studies show, for example, that young voters score lower on an index of citizen duty than older voters. See Warren E. Miller and Santa A. Traugott, *American National Election Studies Data Sourcebook, 1952–1986* (Cambridge, Mass.: Harvard University Press, 1989), p. 285.

42. Paul R. Abramson, *Political Attitudes in America: Formation and Change* (San Francisco: W. H. Freeman, 1983), pp. 292–294.

43. Abramson, *Political Attitudes,* p. 294; Miller and Traugott, *American National Election Studies Data Sourcebook,*

p. 367; 1992 National Election Study; Ruy A. Teixeira, *The Disappearing American Voter* (Washington, D.C.: The Brookings Institution, 1992), p. 32.

44. William H. Flanigan and Nancy H. Zingale, *Political Behavior of the American Electorate,* 8th ed. (Washington, D.C.: CQ Press, 1994), pp. 51–55.

45. *New York Times,* November 9, 1994, p. B8.

CHAPTER 11 *The Media*

1. Beth Snyder and Anne Marie Kerwin, "Clintern' Story Raises Issues for Cyberjournalism," *Advertising Age,* February 2, 1998, p. 32.

2. "*Newsweek's* Decision," *Newsweek,* February 2, 1998, p. 45.

3. For two viewpoints, see Zecharia Chafee, Jr., *Free Speech in the United States* (Cambridge, Mass.: Harvard University Press, 1941), and Leonard W. Levy, *Freedom of Speech and Press in Early American History: Legacy of Suppression* (New York: Harper and Row, 1963).

4. *New York Times Co.* v. *United States,* 376 U.S. 254 (1971); *United States* v. *Progressive, Inc.,* 467 F Supp. 990 (W.D. Wis. 1979).

5. *Miami Herald Publishing Co.* v. *Tornillo,* 418 U.S. 241 (1974).

6. *New York Times* v. *United States,* 376 U.S. 225 (1964); see also *Curtis Publishing* v. *Butts* and *Associated Press* v. *Walker,* 388 U.S. 130 (1967).

7. *Houchins* v. *KQED,* 438 U.S. 1 (1978); *Branzburg* v. *Hayes,* 408 U.S. 665 (1972); *Zurcher* v. *Stanford Daily,* 436 U.S. 547 (1978).

8. See *Red Lion Broadcasting Co.* v. *FCC,* 395 U.S. 367 (1969).

9. Graber, *Mass Media and American Politics,* pp. 68–70; Ansolabehere et al., *The Media Game,* pp. 31–32; *FCC* v. *Pacifica,* 438 U.S. 726 (1978); *Red Lion Broadcasting Co.* v. *FCC,* 395 U.S. 367 (1969). Cf. *Miami Herald Publishing Co.* v. *Tornillo,* 418 U.S. 241 (1974).

10. Stephen Ansolabehere, Roy Behr, and Shanto Iyengar, *The Media Game: American Politics in the Television Age* (New York: Macmillan, 1993), pp. 42–49; Roper Organization, *America's Watching: Public Attitudes Toward Television, 1991* (New York: Author, 1991).

11. George Gerbner, Larry Gross, Michael Morgan, and Nancy Signorielli, "Charting the Mainstream: Television's Contributions to Political Orientations," *Journal of Communication* 32 (1982): 111.

12. Shanto Iyengar, "Television News and Citizens' Explanations of National Affairs," *American Political Science Review* 81:3 (September 1987), pp. 815–831.

13. Stanley Rothman and S. Robert Lichter, "The Nuclear Energy Debate: Scientists, the Media, and the Public," *Public Opinion* 5 (1982), pp. 47–52.

14. Doris A. Graber, *Mass Media and American Politics,* 4th ed. (Washington, D.C.: CQ Press, 1993), p. 15.

15. Ibid., pp. 310–311; Ansolabehere et al., *The Media Game,* pp. 52–53.

16. Graber, *Mass Media and American Politics,* pp. 126, 289–291; 298–301; 310–312.

17. Doris A. Graber, *Mass Media and American Politics,* 5th ed. (Washington: CQ Press, 1997), p. 115.

18. William Glaberson, "Some News Coverage by the Networks Exceeds that of Newspapers," *The New York Times,* April 6, 1995, p. A26.

19. Michael R. Hawthorne, "The Media, Economic Development, and Agenda-Setting," in Robert J. Spitzer, ed., *Media and Public Policy* (Westport, Conn.: Praeger, 1993), p. 84.

20. Virginia Bill of Rights, June 12, 1776; *New York Times Co. v. United States,* 403 U.S. 713 (1971) at 171.

21. Alfred McClung Lee, *The Daily Newspaper in America* (New York: Macmillan, 1937), p. 183.

22. Arthur M. Schlesinger, *A Thousand Days: John F. Kennedy in the White House* (Boston: Houghton Mifflin, 1965), p. 674.

23. "Nixon Denounces Press as Biased," *The New York Times,* November 8, 1962, pp. 1, 7; Arthur M. Schlesinger, *The Imperial Presidency* (Boston:Houghton Mifflin, 1973), p. 229; quoted in Daniel D. Baker, *Political Quotations* (Detroit: Gale Research, 1990), p. 64.

24. Carl Bernstein and Bob Woodward, *All the President's Men* (New York: Simon and Schuster, 1974).

25. Frank Newport, "Small Business and the Military Generate Most Confidence in Americans," *The Gallup Poll,* August 15, 1997 http://www.gallup.com/poll/news/970815.html.

26. George Gallup, Jr., *The Gallup Poll: Public Opinion 1991.* (Wilmington, DE: Scholarly Resources, 1992), p. 33.

27. Graber, *Mass Media and American Politics,* p. 259.

28. Robert Lichter, Stanley Rothman, and Linda S. Lichter, *The Media Elite* (Bethesda, MD: Adler Publishers, 1986), pp. 20–44, 294–296.

29. Herbert J. Gans, "Are U.S. Journalists Dangerously Liberal?" *Columbia Journalism Review* (November/December 1985), pp. 29–33.

30. Ansolabehere et al., *The Media Game,* pp. 216–217.

CHAPTER 12 *Congress*

1. Carroll J. Doherty, "Weld Fires a Broadside At Immovable Helms," *CQ Weekly Report,* July 19, 1997, p. 1723; Carroll J. Doherty, "Weld, Crusading for Confirmation, May Have Eyes on Another Prize," *CQ Weekly Report,* August 7, 1997, pp. 1877–1878; Donna Cassata, "Helms Lashes Back at Critics, Holds Firm on Blocking Weld," *CQ Weekly Report,* September 13, 1997, p. 2159; Donna Cassata "Weld Blows Bitter Kisses As Curtain Comes Down," *CQ Weekly Report,* September 20, 1997, p. 2240.

2. *Federalist No. 51.*

3. *Youngstown Sheet and Tube* v. *Sawyer,* 343 U.S. 579 (1952), at 587.

4. *Statistical Abstract of the United States,* 1994, Table 34, p. 33.

5. *Powell* v. *McCormick,* 395 U.S. 486 (1969); *U.S. Term Limits* v. *Thornton,* Supreme Court of the United States, No. 93–1828 (decided May 22, 1995).

6. *The Federalist No. 62.*

7. Ibid.

8. Roger H. Davidson and Walter J. Oleszek, *Congress and Its Members,* 4th ed. (Washington, D.C.: CQ Press, 1994), p. 396.

9. Ibid., p. 346.

10. Ibid., p. 328.

11. Ibid, pp. 224–225; *Congressional Quarterly Weekly Report,* January 20, 1990, p. 151.

12. David Hosansky, "Portman Forged Compromise," *Congressional Quarterly Weekly Report,* March 18, 1995, p. 806.

13. Davidson and Oleszek, *Congress and Its Members,* p. 351.

14. Ibid., p. 247.

15. In his Budget Message for Fiscal Year 1999, President Bill Clinton projected a $9.5 billion surplus, the first in three decades. *Budget of the United States Government, 1999,* p. 345.

16. On the Balanced Budget Amendment, see Andrew Tyler, "Amendment Remains a Gamble Despite Its Popularity," *Congressional Quarterly Weekly Report,* January 14, 1995, pp. 141–147. The House passed a balanced budget amendment on January 26, 1995; the Senate rejected the amendment by two votes on March 2, 1995.

17. Morris P. Fiorina, *Congress: Keystone of the Washington Establishment,* 2d ed. (New Haven: Yale University Press, 1989), p. 76.

18. Allan Freedman, "Lawyers Take a Back Seat In the 105th Congress," *CQ Weekly Report,* January 4, 1997, pp. 27–29. These numbers are correct as of the beginning of the 105th Congress.

19. Glenn R. Parker, *Studies of Congress* (Washington, D.C.: Congressional Quarterly, 1985), p. 389.

20. Hedrick Smith, *The Power Game: How Washington Works* (New York: Ballantine Books, 1988), p. 152.

21. Lawrence C. Dodd and Richard L. Schott, *Congress and the Administrative State* (New York: Wiley, 1979), pp. 269–271.

22. David M. Olson, *Democratic Legislative Institutions: A Comparative View* (New York: St. Martin's Press, 1994), p. 49.

23. Richard Rose, *The Postmodern Presidency: George Bush Meets the World,* 2d ed. (Chatham, N.J.: Chatham House, 1991), p. 133.

24. Janet Hook, "Republicans Vote in Lock Step, But Unity May Not Last Long," *Congressional Quarterly Weekly Report,* February 18, 1995, pp. 495–496.

25. Adapted from Lawrence C. Dodd and Bruce I. Oppenheimer, *Congress Reconsidered,* 4th ed. (Washington, D.C.: Congressional Quarterly, 1989), pp. 443–446.

26. "Rules Changes Open the Process . . . But Strengthen the Reins of Power," *Congressional Quarterly Weekly Report,* January 7, 1995, pp. 14–15.

27. Richard F. Fenno, *Congressmen in Committees* (Boston: Little Brown, 1973), p. 1.

28. Tip O'Neill, *All Politics is Local, and Other Rules of the Game* (New York: Times Books, 1994).

29. Allan Friedman, "Expanded Waste Flow Bill Heads to Senate Floor," *Congressional Quarterly Weekly Report,* March 25, 1995, p. 868.

30. Jon Healey, "Sen. Byrd Steers $90 Million to West Virginia Highway," *Congressional Quarterly Weekly Report,* September 24, 1994, p. 2681.

31. See generally Michael J. Malbin, "Delegation, Deliberation and the New Role of Congressional Staff," in Thomas E. Mann and Norman J. Ornstein, eds., *The New Congress* (Washington, D.C.: AEI, 1981), pp. 134–177.

32. Ibid., p. 170.

33. Joseph P. Harris, *Congressional Control of Administration,* quoted in Joel D. Aberbach, *Keeping a Watchful Eye: The Politics of Congressional Oversight* (Washington, D.C.: Brookings Institution, 1990), p. 217.

34. Dodd and Schott, *Congress and the Administrative State,* pp. 243–244.

35. Aberbach, *Keeping a Watchful Eye,* p. 167.

36. See generally Catherine E. Rudder, "Can Congress Govern?" in Dodd and Oppenheimer, *Congress Reconsidered,* pp. 365–374.

37. David R. Mayhew, *Divided We Govern: Party Control, Lawmaking, and Investigations, 1946–1990* (New Haven: Yale University Press, 1991).

38. See the sources cited in Rudder, "Can Congress Govern?" p. 372.

CHAPTER 13   *The Presidency*

1. *Youngstown Sheet and Tube* v. *Sawyer,* 343 U.S. 579, at 653 (Jackson, concurring).

2. Quoted in *Clinton* v. *Jones,* No. 95-1853 [slip opinion], decided May 27, 1997, p. 14.

3. *Clinton* v. *Jones,* No. 95-1853 (1997).

4. *Federalist No. 68.*

5. Ann Devroy, "Clinton Cancels Abortion Restrictions of Reagan-Bush Era; 'Gag Rule' on Clinics, Federal Ban on Fetal Tissue Research Are Lifted," *Washington Post,* January 23, 1993, p. A1.

6. Calvin Mackenzie, *The Politics of Presidential Appointments* (New York: Free Press, 1981), pp. 3–4.

7. See, for example, *United States* v. *Humphrey's Executor,* 295 U.S. 602 (1935).

8. United States Constitution, Article I, §7; Article II, § 3.

9. P.L. 88-408, 78 Stat. 384 (August 10, 1964).

10. The War Powers Resolution, 87 Stat. 555 (1973); J. Woodruff Howard, Jr., "War Powers Act of 1973," in Kermit L. Hall, ed., *The Oxford Companion to the Supreme Court of the United States* (New York: Oxford University Press, 1992), pp. 911–912.

11. *Guaranty Trust Co.* v. *United States,* 304 U.S. 126 (1938), at 137–138.

12. *Dames & Moore* v. *Regan,* 453 U.S. 654 (1981); *United States* v. *Belmont,* 301 U.S. 324 (1937). See generally J. Woodruff Howard, Jr., "Executive Agreements," in Hall, *Oxford Companion,* pp. 266–267.

13. *United States* v. *Curtiss-Wright Export Corp.,* 299 U.S. 304 (1936).

14. Neustadt, *Presidential Leadership,* pp. 33–57.

15. Ibid., p. 179.

16. Paul C. Light, *The President's Agenda: Domestic Policy Choice from Kennedy to Reagan,* rev. ed. (Baltimore: Johns Hopkins University Press, 1991), pp. 26–34.

17. Sam Kernell, *Going Public: New Strategies of Presidential Leadership* (Washington, D.C.: CQ Press, 1986).

18. William Safire, *Safire's New Political Dictionary* (New York: Random House, 1993), pp. 89–90.

19. R. W. Apple, Jr., "7 Nations' Leaders Open Tokyo Talks; Expectations Low; Tariff Accord is Reached; Pact is Called a Breakthrough, But Many Are Skeptical," *New York Times,* July 8, 1993, p. A1.

20. Bill Clinton, press conference, April 20, 1995.

21. James David Barber, *The Presidential Character: Predicting Performance in the White House* (Englewood Cliffs, N.J.: Prentice-Hall, 1972).

22. Ibid., pp. 9–10.

23. For a discussion of Barber and his critics, see Michael Nelson, "James David Barber and the Psychological Presidency," in David Pederson, *The "Barberian" Presidency: Theoretical and Empirical Readings* (New York: Peter Lang, 1989), pp. 93–110.

24. John P. Burke, *The Institutional Presidency* (Baltimore: Johns Hopkins University Press, 1992), p. 6.

25. Arthur M. Schlesinger, Jr., *The Imperial Presidency* (Boston: Houghton Mifflin, 1973).

26. Stephen L. Carter, *The Confirmation Mess: Cleaning Up the Federal Appointments Process* (New York: Basic Books, 1994).

27. *Time,* June 21, 1993, pp. 14–16.

28. See, for example, Roger Ebert, "Stranger Than Fiction," *Chicago Sun-Times,* January 23, 1998, p. B8.

29. Richard Rose, *The Postmodern Presidency: George Bush Meets the World,* 2d ed. (Chatham, N.J.: Chatham House, 1988), p. 25.

30. Arthur M. Schlesinger, *The Coming of the New Deal* (Boston: Houghton Mifflin, 1959), pp. 514–516.

31. President's Commission on Administrative Management, *Administrative Management in the Government of the United States* (Washington, D.C.: United States Government Printing Office, 1937).

32. John P. Burke, *The Institutional Presidency* (Baltimore: Johns Hopkins University Press, 1992), pp. 14–15.

33. *Federal Civilian Workforce Statistics: Employment and Trends as of May 1994* (Washington, D.C.: United States Office of Personnel Management, 1994).

34. Burke, *The Institutional Presidency,* pp. xii–xiv.

35. W. Craig Bledsoe, "Cabinet," in *Cabinets and Counselors: The President and the Executive Branch* (Washington, D.C.: CQ Press, 1989), pp. 57–59.

36. Samuel L. Popkin, "The Art of Managing the White House," in Samuel Kernell and Samuel L. Popkin, eds., *Chief of Staff: Twenty-Five Years of Managing the Presidency* (Berkeley: University of California Press, 1986), p. 10.

37. Rose, *The Postmodern Presidency,* p. 180.

38. *Congressional Digest,* February 1993, p. 40.

39. "Legislative Line Item Veto Act: Report of the Committee on the Budget, U.S. Senate, on S. 14," February 27, 1995, pp. 6–7; *Clinton v. City of New York,* No. 97-1374, decided June 25, 1998.

40. Richard L. Berke, "Clinton Coattails Debated After Senate Loss in Texas," *New York Times,* June 7, 1993, p. A1.

41. *Federalist No. 73.*

42. Quoted in Arthur M. Schlesinger, Jr., *The Age of Jackson* (Boston: Little, Brown and Co., 1945), p. 43.

CHAPTER 14   *The Bureaucracy*

1. Matthew L. Wald, "A Consensus, but No Conclusions, on Flight 800, *New York Times,* December 13, 1997, p. A1; "The Largest Jigsaw in the World," *Newsday,* December 8, 1997, p. 19; "Aviation Officials Grilled at TWA Hearing," *CNN Interactive,* December 9, 1997.

2. James Q. Wilson, *Bureaucracy: What Government Agencies Do and Why They Do It* (New York: Basic Books, 1989), p. 114.

3. Ari Hoogenboom, "Civil Service Reform," in Eric Foner and John A. Garraty, eds., *The Reader's Companion to American History* (Boston: Houghton Mifflin, 1991), p. 183; James P. Pfiffner, *The Modern Presidency* (New York: St. Martin's Press, 1994), p. 128; "Spoils System," in Foner and Garraty, *Reader's Companion,* p. 1021.

4. Hoogenboom, "Civil Service Reform," pp. 181–182.

5. Walter Gellhorn, Clark Byse, Peter L. Strauss, Todd Rakoff, and Roy A. Schotland, *Administrative Law: Cases and Comments,* 8th ed. (Mineola, N.Y.: Foundation Press, 1987), pp. 226–227.

6. Excluding employees of the post office, which operates as an independent government corporation.

7. *Kent v. Dulles,* 357 U.S. 116 (1958); *Regan v. Wald,* 468 U.S. 222 (1984).

8. *United States v. Humphrey's Executor,* 295 U.S. 602 (1935); *Wiener v. United States,* 357 U.S. 349 (1958).

9. *Bowsher v. Synar,* 478 U.S. 714 (1986).

10. *Field v. Clark,* 143 U.S. 649 (1892); *United States v. Grimaud,* 220 U.S. 506 (1911), at 517; *Panama Refining Co. v. Ryan,* 293 U.S. 388 (1935), at 415. See also *Schechter Poultry v. United States,* 295 U.S. 495 (1935), and *Carter v. Carter Coal Co.,* 298 U.S. 238 (1936).

11. *Yakus v. United States,* 321 U.S. 414 (1944), at 426.

12. See, for example, *Motor Vehicles Manufacturers Assn. of U.S., Inc. v. State Farm Mutual Insurance Co.,* 463 U.S. 29 (1983).

13. P.L. 95-203, P.L. 96-273, 21 U.S.C. 348 (1994).

14. *Packard Motor Co. v. National Labor Relations Board,* 330 U.S. 485 (1947).

15. Quoted in Richard Neustadt, *Presidential Power: The Politics of Leadership from FDR to Carter* (New York: Macmillan, 1980), p. 9.

16. *Marshall v. Barlow's, Inc.,* 436 U.S. 307 (1978).

17. *Rust v. Sullivan,* 500 U.S. 173 (1991).

18. Cass R. Sunstein, "Constitutionalism After the New Deal," *Harvard Law Review* 101 (1987), pp. 486–487.

CHAPTER 15   *The Courts*

1. *City of Boerne v. Flores,* No. 95-2074 (1997).

2. Alexis de Tocqueville, *Democracy in America,* ed. J. P. Mayer (Garden City, N.Y.: Anchor Books, 1969), p. 270.

3. The Court refused to issue advisory opinions as early as 1793. See Joan R. Gunderson, "Advisory Opinions," in Kermit L. Hall, ed., *The Oxford Companion to the Supreme Court of the United States* (New York: Oxford University Press, 1992), p. 18.

4. Sheldon Goldman and Eliot Slotnick, "Clinton's First-Term Judiciary: Many Bridges to Cross," *Judicature* 80 (May–June 1997), pp. 254–255.

5. Roger E. Hartley and Lisa M. Holmes, "Increasing Senate Scrutiny of Lower Federal Court Nominees," *Judicature* 80 (May–June 1997), p. 278.

6. Ibid.

7. Abraham, *Judicial Process,* pp. 75–85; David O'Brien, *Storm Center: The Supreme Court in American Politics,* 2d ed. (New York: W. W. Norton, 1990), pp. 69–76; John R.

Schmidhauser, "Appointment and Removal Power," in Hall, *Oxford Companion to the Supreme Court,* pp. 40–42.

8. Quoted in O'Brien, *Storm Center,* p. 70.

9. Data drawn from tables in Sheldon Goldman, "Reagan's Judicial Legacy: Completing the Puzzle and Summing Up," *Judicature* 72 (April–May 1989), pp. 321–325. To Goldman's data were added two Supreme Court nominations by Johnson, four by Nixon, and one by Ford, of whom only one—Thurgood Marshall—was black and none was a woman.

10. Abraham, *Judicial Process,* pp. 29–30.

11. Goldman, "Reagan's Judicial Legacy," pp. 321–325; Abraham, *Judicial Process,* p. 30n.

12. Goldman, "Reagan's Judicial Legacy," p. 319; Sheldon Goldman, "The Bush Imprint on the Judiciary: Carry on a Tradition," *Judicature* 74 (April–May 1991), pp. 294–306; Sheldon Goldman and Matthew D. Saronson, "Clinton's Nontraditional Judges: Creating a More Representative Bench," *Judicature* 78 (September–October 1994), p. 69.

13. Goldman and Slotnick, "Clinton's First-Term Judiciary," pp. 261, 267, 270.

14. O'Brien, *Storm Center,* pp. 159–170; Bob Woodward and Scott Armstrong, *The Brethren: Inside the Supreme Court* (New York: Simon and Schuster, 1979), which touched off a major controversy by asserting that the law clerks have undue influence on the Court's decisions. For a rebuttal, see Abraham, *Judicial Process,* pp. 239–244.

15. Quoted in Abraham, *Judicial Process,* p. 243.

16. *New Jersey* v. *New York,* 120 orig. (1998).

17. Chief Justice Fred Vinson, quoted in Abraham, *Judicial Process,* pp. 175–177.

18. Abraham, *Judicial Process,* pp. 181–182; Karen J. Maschke, "In Forma Pauperis," in Levy, *Oxford Companion,* p. 428.

19. Bryan A. Garner, "Briefs," in Levy, *Oxford Companion,* p. 91.

20. For further discussion, see Stephen L. Wasby, "Amicus Briefs," in Hall, *Oxford Companion to the Supreme Court,* pp. 31–32. For a discussion of the role of amicus briefs in *Roe* v. *Wade,* see Lee Epstein and Joseph F. Kobylka, *The Supreme Court and Legal Change* (Chapel Hill: University of North Carolina Press, 1992), pp. 167–178.

21. Charles Fried, "Oral Argument," in Hall, *Oxford Companion to the Supreme Court,* p. 612.

22. Robert J. Janosik, "The Conference," in Hall, *Oxford Companion to the Supreme Court,* pp. 174–175; Abraham, *Judicial Process,* p. 195.

23. Two of Holmes's most famous dissents came in *Lochner* v. *New York,* 198 U.S. 45 (1905) and *Abrams* v. *United States,* 250 U.S. 616 (1919). In *Lochner,* Holmes disagreed with the majority's decision that the Due Process Clause of the Fourteenth Amendment guaranteed an individual's "right to contract." He asserted that "a constitution is not intended to embody a particular economic theory" and accused the court of improperly substituting its own judgment for that of the legislature. In *Abrams,* Holmes argued that Congress could punish subversive speech only if there existed a "clear and present danger" of serious harm. Holmes's position in both cases was eventually adopted by the majority of the Court.

24. Leonard W. Levy, *Original Intent and the Framers' Constitution* (New York: Macmillan, 1988), p. 102.

25. Ibid., pp. 104–105.

26. *Marbury* v. *Madison,* 1 Cranch (5 U.S.) 137 (1803).

27. *Federalist No. 39.*

28. *Fletcher* v. *Peck,* 6 Cranch (10 U.S.) 87 (1810).

29. Figures from Henry Abraham, *Judicial Process,* pp. 272–273.

30. *Martin* v. *Hunter's Lessee,* 1 Wheat. (14 U.S.) 304 (1816).

31. *McFarland* v. *Collins* (sub. nom. *McFarland* v. *Scott*), No. 93-6497, 62 U.S.L.W. 4718 (1994); oral argument quoted in the *New York Times,* March 30, 1994, p. A10.

32. For an interesting discussion of this point in the constitutional context, see Sanford Levinson, "Law as Literature," 60 Tex. L. Rev. 373 (1982).

33. 304 U.S. 144 (1938), at 152 n. 4.

34. *Duncan* v. *Louisiana,* 391 U.S. 145 (1968); *McKeiver* v. *Pennsylvania,* 403 U.S. 528 (1971).

35. *Batson* v. *Kentucky,* 476 U.S. 79 (1986); *Edmonson* v. *Leesville Concrete,* 500 U.S. 614 (1991).

36. *South Carolina* v. *Katzenbach,* 383 U.S. 301 (1966); *Katzenbach* v. *Morgan,* 384 U.S. 641 (1966). See also *Shaw* v. *Reno,* 113 S. Ct. 2816 (1993) and *Miller* v. *Johnson,* 115 S.Ct. 2475 (1995).

37. *Wesberry* v. *Sanders,* 376 U.S. 1 (1964); *Reynolds* v. *Sims,* 377 U.S. 533 (1964); *Karcher* v. *Daggett,* 462 U.S. 725 (1983).

38. *New York Times* v. *Sullivan,* 376 U.S. 255 (1964), at 270.

39. *McIntyre* v. *Ohio Elections Commission,* 63 U.S.L.W. 4279 (1995).

40. See, for example, *Brandenburg* v. *Ohio,* 395 U.S. 444; *Scales* v. *United States,* 367 U.S. 203 (1961); and *Noto* v. *United States,* 367 U.S. 290 (1961).

CHAPTER 16 *Domestic Policy*

1. James Bennet, "Clinton Will Seek Balanced Budget Years in Advance," *New York Times,* January 6, 1998, p. A1; Richard W. Stevenson, "Free-for-All, Driven by Ideology and Special Interests, *New York Times,* January 6, 1998; p. A12.

2. *Lochner* v. *New York,* 198 U.S. 45, 75 (1905).

3. See, for example, *Goldberg* v. *Kelly,* 397 U.S. 254 (1970).

4. This typology is adapted from W. Phillips Shively, *Power and Choice: An Introduction to Political Science,* 3d ed. (New York: McGraw-Hill, 1993), pp. 70–73.

5. For an extended treatment of these themes in an international context, see Anthony King, "Ideas, Institutions and the Policies of Governments: A Comparative Analysis: Parts I and II," *British Journal of Political Science* 3 (1973), pp. 291–313 and Anthony King, "Ideas, Institutions and the Policies of Governments: A Comparative Analysis: Part III," *British Journal of Political Science* 3 (1973), pp. 409–423.

6. George F. Kennan, "The Sources of Soviet Conduct," *Foreign Affairs* XXV (July 1947), pp. 566–582. The original article was signed "X."

7. John F. Kennedy, "Special Message to Congress," May 25, 1961, *Public Papers of the Presidents of the United States— John F. Kennedy* (Washington, D.C.: National Archives and Record Service, 1961), p. 404.

8. Stephen Breyer, *Regulation and Its Reform* (Cambridge, Mass.: Harvard University Press, 1982.

9. Ibid., pp. 1–2.

10. Quoted in James Q. Wilson, ed., *The Politics of Regulation* (New York: Basic Books, 1980), p. 358.

11. Shively, *Power and Choice,* p. 97.

12. Ibid., p. 95. In *Lucas* v. *South Carolina Coastal Commission,* 112 S. Ct. 2886 (1992), the Supreme Court ruled that government regulations that deprive land of all its economic value may violate the Fifth Amendment guarantee that private property not be taken for public use "without just compensation."

13. U.S. Constitution, Preamble; Article I, §§8, 10.

14. Galbraith and Darity, *Macroeconomics,* pp. 6–8, 341.

15. *Statistical Abstract of the United States,* 1997, table 516, p. 323; p. 295.

16. *Statistical Abstract of the United States,* 1994, table 676, p. 436.

17. Quoted in martha Derthick and Paul J. Quirk, *The Politics of Deregulation* (Washington, D.C.: Brookings Institution, 1985), p. 30.

18. Steve Tidrick, "The Budget Inferno," *The New Republic,* May 29, 1995, p. 19; Daniel D. Huff, "Upside-Down Welfare," *Public Welfare* (Winter 1992), p. 38.

19. "The President's Proposals, Listed by Category," *Congressional Quarterly Weekly Report,* February 11, 1995, p. 416; Tidrick, "Budget Inferno," p. 21.

20. Theodore R. Marmor, Jerry L. Mashaw, and Philip L. Harvey, *America's Misunderstood Welfare State: Persistent Myths, Enduring Realities* (New York: Basic Books, 1990), pp. 23–31. I have changed the order in which Marmor et al. present their four conceptions of purpose and altered the labels they affix to each conception.

21. Ibid., p. 26.

22. Quoted in Arthur M. Schlesinger, Jr., *The Coming of the New Deal* (Boston: Houghton Mifflin, 1959), pp. 308–309.

23. Michael Barone, *Our Country: The Shaping of America from Roosevelt to Reagan* (New York: Free Press, 1990), pp. 486, 511.

24. Jeffrey L. Katz, "Long-Term Challenges Temper Cheers for Welfare Successes," *CQ Weekly Report,* October 25, 1997, pp. 260–261.

25. Tidrick, "Budget Inferno," pp. 18–19.

26. See Marmor, Mashaw, and Harvey, *America's Misunderstood Welfare State,* p. 178.

27. "Social Security Programs in the United States, 1993," *Social Security Bulletin* 56 (Winter 1993), p. 57.

28. Katherine R. Levit, et al., "National Health Spending Trends, 1960–1993," *Health Affairs* 13 (Winter 1994), p. 15. The consumer price index increased by a factor of 4.88 between 1960 and 1993 (*Statistical Abstract of the United States,* 1994), table 747, p. 488.

29. Ibid., pp. 17–18.

30. Guy King, "Health Care Reform and the Medicare Program," *Health Affairs* 13 (winter 1994), p. 41.

31. "Health Insurance Coverage—1993," Bureau of the Census Statistical Brief, October 1994.

32. John F. Jennings, ed., *National Issues in Education: The Past Is Prologue* (Bloomington, Ind.: Phi Delta Kappa International; Washington, D.C.: Institute for Educational Leadership, 1993), pp. 11–12.

33. Jennings, *National Issues in Education,* pp. 45–47; see also "Should the House Pass the 'Goals 2000: Educate America' Act?" *Congressional Digest,* January 1994, pp. 16–XX.

CHAPTER 17   *Foreign and Military Policy*

1. Eric F. Goldman, *The Tragedy of Lyndon Johnson* (New York: Knopf, 1969), p. 176.

2. Alexis de Tocqueville, *Democracy in America,* ed. J. P. Mayer (Garden City, N.Y.: Anchor Books, 1969), pp. 228–229.

3. See, for example, *Federalist No. 64.*

4. David Gray Adler, "The President's War-Making Power," in Thomas E. Cronin, ed., *Inventing the American Presidency* (Lawrence, Kans.: University Press of Kansas, 1989), p. 127.

5. Article I, section 10.

6. *Perez* v. *Brownell,* 356 U.S. 44 (1958).

7. Leonard Levy, *Original Intent and the Framers' Constitution* (New York: Macmillan, 1988), p. 30.

8. Ibid., p. 37; *Federalist No. 70.* See also Louis Fisher, *Constitutional Conflicts Between Congress and the President,* 3d

ed., rev. (Lawrence: University Press of Kansas, 1991), pp. 244–246.

9. Quoted in Adler, "The President's War-Making Power," p. 127.

10. Harold Hongju Koh, *The National Security Constitution: Sharing Power After the Iran-Contra Affair* (New Haven: Yale University Press, 1990), pp. 74–84.

11. Koh, *National Security Constitution,* p. 86.

12. Ibid., p. 96.

13. Steven V. Robers, "Senate Upholds Arms for Saudis, Backing Reagan," *New York Times,* June 6, 1986, p. A1.

14. Quoted in ibid., p. 277.

15. Bill Clinton, Speech at the National Defense University, July 19, 1993; P.L. 103–160 (November 30, 1993).

16. *Dames & Moore* v. *Regan,* 453 U.S. 654 (1981).

17. Washington, "Farewell Address" (September 17, 1796) in James D. Richardson, *Messages and Papers of the Presidents* (New York: Bureau of National Literature, 1897), 1: 205–216.

18. James Monroe, Seventh Annual Message (December 2, 1823), in Richardson, *Messages and Papers,* 2: 776–789.

19. U.S. Bureau of the Census, *Historical Statistics of the United States:* Colonial Times to 1970s, Bicentennial Edition, Part 2 (Washington, D.C.: 1975), p. 1141.

20. See Paul Kennedy, *The Rise and Fall of the Great Powers: Economic Change and Military Conflict from 1500 to 2000* (New York: Random House, 1987).

21. Tony Kornheiser, "The Shifting Job Line," *Washington Post,* November 18, 1990, p. G1.

22. Quoted in Daniel D. Baker, *Political Quotations* (Detroit: Gale Research, 1990), p. 25.

23. Kevin Sullivan and Joby Warrick, "Weary delegates Set Emissions Cuts for Developed Nations," *Washington Post,* December 11, 1997, p. A1.

Index to References ★★★★★★★★★★★★★★★★★★★★★★★★★★

Index ★★★★★★★★★★★★★★★★★★★★★★★★★★★

Illustration Credits ★★★★★★★★★★★★★★★★★★★★★★★★★★★★

(continued from copyright page)

CHAPTER 2

p. 21, Nixon saluting: Richard Nixon Materials Project/National Archives; **p. 23,** Constitutional Convention: Virginia Museum of Fine Arts, Richmond, VA. Gift of Colonel and Mrs. Edgar W. Garbisch ©1993 Virginia Museum of Fine Arts; **p. 27,** James Madison: Library of Congress; **p. 29,** Slaves ensnarled: Musee de l'Homme; **p. 34,** Prohibition: Archive Photos; **p. 41,** cartoon "Founding Fathers": Dana Fradon. ©1972 The New Yorker Magazine, Inc.

CHAPTER 3

p. 49, Handgun: Markel/Gamma Liason; **p. 53,** McVeigh: David Longstreath/Wide World Photos; **p. 55,** John Marshall: Duke University Archives; **p. 59,** child labor: Corbis-Bettmann; **p. 61,** LBJ: Culver Pictures; **p. 70,** cartoon "Look the American people": Bob Mankoff from The Cartoon Bank, Inc.

CHAPTER 4

p. 75, Gregory Johnson: People Weekly ©1989 Mimi Cotter; **p. 80,** Student Prayer: Bob Crandall/Stock Boston; **p. 83,** Gun Poster: Gamma Liason; **p. 85,** Earl Warren: Paul Conklin; **p. 90,** Students with poster: Michael J. Kienitz Imaging; **p. 92,** Judge from Nanny case: Gamma Liason; **p. 95,** cartoon "Where are you going": Mike Keefe ©1994; **p. 103,** Norma McCorvey: Wide World Photos; **p. 104,** Pro choice: Diana Walker/Time Magazine.

CHAPTER 5

p. 109, Japanese/America: Myron H. Davis/ Life Magazine ©1997 Time, Inc.; **p. 112,** cartoon "I hate": Peter Arno ©1952, 1980 The New Yorker Magazine, Inc.; **p. 115,** Lynching: Gilman Paper Company Collection; **p. 116,** 1992 protest: UPI Bettmann; **p. 120,** Brown v. Board of Education: Library of Congress; **p. 122,** MLK: Bob Adelman/Magnum; **p. 123,** Fireman: Charles Moore/Black Star; **p. 125,** Initiative on Race: W. McNamee/Sygma; **p. 127,** Local 34: Virginia Blaisdell; **p.129,** Russell Means: Dirck Halstead/Time, Inc.; **p. 132,** cartoon "It's time": Steve Kelly/Copley News Service.

CHAPTER 6

p. 143, Cammermeyer: Chris Bennoin/Gamma Liason; **p. 145** (L), Rosie the Riveter: Ellen Kaiper collection; **p. 145** (R), Steinem: Mary Ellen Mark; **p. 146,** Pledge of allegiance: Bob Daemmrich; **p. 153,** Community event: Bob Daemmrich; **p. 161,** McCarthy: UPI Bettmann; **p. 165,** cartoon "office party": Reprinted by permission of Tribune Media Service.

CHAPTER 7

p. 169, Troops in Somalia: Peterson/Gamma Liason; **p. 172,** Pollster: Billy Barnes/Stock Boston; **p. 176,** Rush Limbaugh: Jacques

Chenet/Gamma Liason; **p. 179,** cartoon "Participating democrat": SIGNE/Cartoonists and Writers Syndicate; **p. 184,** Lee: Gamma Liaison; **p. 187,** Promisekeepers: Gamma Liaison; **p. 193,** cartoon "This is so insulting": Steve Kelly/Copley News Service; **p. 195,** Dewey defeats Truman: UPI/Bettmann.

CHAPTER 8

p. 199, Sharon Taxman: Associated Press/ Wide World Photos; **p. 205,** Union: Reuters/Mark Wilson/Archive Photos; **p. 206,** Global warming: Associated Press/Wide World Photos; **p. 207,** AARP: Spencer Grant/Picture Cube; **p. 208,** CDF poster: Children's Defense Fund; **p. 216,** Courtesy of Gamma Liaison Network ©Steve Liss.

CHAPTER 9

p. 229, Perot supporters: Reuters/Lee Celano/Archive Photos; **p. 238,** Goldwater button; **p. 240,** Presidential Candidate: Jim Bourg/Gamma Liason; **p. 247,** Richard Aldy: AP Photo/Wide World Photos; **p. 248,** Jimmy Stewart: Museum of Modern Art Film Still Archive; **p. 253,** cartoon: ©Mark Stevens from the Cartoon Bank, Inc.; **p. 255,** Watts: AP Photo/Wide World Photos/Chuck Burton.

CHAPTER 10

p. 259, Perot: ©1993 CNN, Inc. All rights reserved.; **p. 261,** election for judge: Bob Daemmrich; **p. 263,** Gerry mandering: The Bettmann Archive; **p. 270,** Democratic Convention: Tom Sobolik/Black Star; **p. 271,** Dole and Kemp: AP Photo/Wide World Photos; **p. 276,** Gore/Buddhist Temple: AP Photo/Wide World Photos/Joe Marquette; **p. 280,** cartoon: ©1995 Mick Stevens from The Cartoon Bank, Inc.; **p. 282,** Bus tour: Ira Wyman/Sygma; **p. 283,** Carville and Matalin: Gamma Liason; **p. 284,** cartoon: Drawing by C. Barscotti ©1992 The New Yorker Magazine, Inc.; **p. 286,** cartoon "Cleveland": Library of Congress; **p. 291,** cartoon: Reprinted by permission of John Trevor, Albuquerque Journal.

CHAPTER 11

p. 299, Lewinsky: Courtesy of Newsweek; **p. 303,** cartoon "Jury in deliberation": By permission of Mike Luckovich and Creative Syndicate; **p. 307,** Press conference: Larry Downing/Sygma; **p. 309,** cartoon "tabloid": Reprinted by permission of United Feature Syndicate, Inc.; **p. 313,** Viet Nam prisoner: AP Photo/Wide World Photos; **p. 314,** All the President's Men: Museum of Modern Art Film Stills Archive; **p. 321,** cartoon "Media bias": Joe Heller ©1990 Green Bay Press Gazette.

CHAPTER 12

p. 327, Helms and Weld: Ken Lambert/Gamma Liaison; **p. 331,** Moseley-Braun: James Colburn/Photoreporters, Inc.; **p. 333,** cartoon: Mike Thompson/Copley News Service; **p. 345,** Waters/Black

Caucus: Bob Crandall/Stock Boston; **p. 347,** cartoon "Let's never forget": ©1995 Bob Mankoff from The Cartoon Bank, Inc.; **p. 354,** Lott: J. Ficara/Sygma.

CHAPTER 13

p. 363, Paula Jones: Markel/Gamma Liaison; **p. 369,** FDR: Franklin D. Roosevelt Library; **p. 370,** cartoon "Gatorade state": Jim Borgman/Cincinnati Enquirer; **p. 375,** cartoon "Optimist": ©1995 Mick Stevens from The Cartoon Bank, Inc.; **p. 376,** Calvin Coolidge: Library of Congress; **p. 379,** JFK: Photo No. ST-A26-11-62 in the John F. Kennedy Library; **p. 380,** Bush: Ken Hawkins/Sygma; **p. 386,** cartoon "If reelected": ©1995 Mick Stevens from The Cartoon Bank, Inc.; **p. 387,** Hillary Clinton: Cynthia Johnson/Time, Inc.

CHAPTER 14

p. 397, TWA: Reuters/Luc Novovitch/Archive Photos; **p. 403,** Cabinet: Gamma Liaison ©Markel; **p. 404,** cable: Clifford/Gamma Liaison; **p. 411,** CFO Bulletin; **p. 415,** Challenger.

CHAPTER 15

p. 421, Bourne: Bob Daemmrich; **p. 423,** Supreme Court: Robert Trippett/SIPA; **p. 424,** Susan Webber: AP Photo/Danny Johnston; **p. 425,** Rodney King: SIPA Press; **p. 429,** cartoon "Supreme Court": ©1995 Reprinted courtesy of Bunny Hoest and Parade Magazine; **p. 431,** Oliver Wendell Holmes: Courtesy of Harvard Law Art Collection; **p. 433,** James Otis: Massachusetts Historical Society; **p. 438,** cartoon "Teddy Bear picnic": Drawing by M. Tuohy ©1993 The New Yorker Magazine, Inc.

CHAPTER 16

p. 449, Clinton celebrating budget: AP Photo/J. Scott Applewhite; **p. 458,** Janet Yellen: Diana Walker/Gamma Liaison; **p. 459,** cartoon "Salt & Pepper"; **p. 466,** Welfare: Bob Daemmrich; **p. 468,** cartoon "Don't touch": Reprinted by permission of Tribune Media Service; **p. 471,** Head Start Program: Lauren Greenfield/Sygma.

CHAPTER 17

p. 479, Evacuation: UPI Bettmann; **p. 484,** FDR: UPI/Corbis Bettmann; **p. 489,** foreign policy meeting: DoD/CNP/Archive Photos; **p. 492,** first war poster: Herbert Hoover Library.